W9-BVT-764

Theory & Practice of Group Counseling

EIGHTH EDITION

GERALD COREY

California State University, Fullerton
Diplomate in Counseling Psychology,
American Board of Professional Psychology

BROOKS/COLE
CENGAGE Learning

AUSTRALIA · BRAZIL · JAPAN · KOREA · MEXICO · SINGAPORE · SPAIN · UNITED KINGDOM · UNITED STATES

BROOKS/COLE
CENGAGE Learning

Theory and Practice of Group
Counseling, Eighth Edition

Gerald Corey

Acquisitions Editor: Seth Dobin

Assistant Editor: Arwen Petty

Editorial Assistant: Suzanna Kincaid

Media Editor: Elizabeth Momb

Senior Marketing Manager: Trent
Whatcott

Marketing Assistant: Darlene
Macanan

Marketing Communications Manager:
Tami Strang

Content Project Manager: Rita
Jaramillo

Design Director: Rob Hugel

Art Director: Caryl Gorska

Print Buyer: Rebecca Cross

Rights Acquisitions Specialist:
Roberta Broyer

Production Service: Ben Kolstad,
Glyph International

Text Design: Kim Ciabattari, Ingalls
Design

Text Researcher: Isabel Alves

Copy Editor: Kay Mikel

Cover Designer: Ingalls Design

Cover Image: African White Pelicans
by Keren Su

Compositor: Glyph International

For product information and technology assistance, contact us at
Cengage Learning Customer & Sales Support, 1-800-354-9706

For permission to use material from this text or product,
submit all requests online at www.cengage.com/permissions
Further permissions questions can be e-mailed to
permissionrequest@cengage.com

Library of Congress Control Number: 2010928556

Student Edition:
ISBN-13: 978-0-8400-3386-4
ISBN-10: 0-8400-3386-9

Loose-leaf Edition:
ISBN-13: 978-1-111-51956-8
ISBN-10: 1-111-51956-0

Brooks/Cole
20 Davis Drive
Belmont, CA 94002-3098
USA

Cengage Learning is a leading provider of customized learning solutions with office locations around the globe, including Singapore, the United Kingdom, Australia, Mexico, Brazil, and Japan. Locate your local office at **www.cengage.com/global.**

Cengage Learning products are represented in Canada by Nelson Education, Ltd.

To learn more about Brooks/Cole, visit **www.cengage.com/brookscole**

Purchase any of our products at your local college store or at our preferred online store **www.cengagebrain.com.**

Printed in the United States of America
1 2 3 4 5 6 7 14 13 12 11 10

To Marianne Schneider Corey—my wife of 47 years,
best friend, valued colleague, and coauthor—who
has contributed immensely to
the quality of my life and my work.

 **GERALD COREY** is Professor Emeritus of Human Services and Counseling at California State University at Fullerton. He received his doctorate in counseling from the University of Southern California. He is a Diplomate in Counseling Psychology, American Board of Professional Psychology; a licensed psychologist; a National Certified Counselor; a Fellow of the American Psychological Association (Counseling Psychology); a Fellow of the American Counseling Association; and a Fellow of the Association for Specialists in Group Work. Along with his wife, Marianne Schneider Corey, Jerry received the Eminent Career Award from ASGW in 2001. He also received the Outstanding Professor of the Year Award from California State University at Fullerton in 1991. He regularly teaches both undergraduate and graduate courses in group counseling and ethics in counseling. He is the author or coauthor of 16 textbooks in counseling currently in print, along with numerous journal articles. His book, *Theory and Practice of Counseling and Psychotherapy*, has been translated into Arabic, Indonesian, Portuguese, Turkish, Korean, and Chinese. *Theory and Practice of Group Counseling* has been translated into Korean, Chinese, Spanish, and Russian. *Issues and Ethics in the Helping Professions* has been translated into Korean, Japanese, and Chinese.

Jerry and Marianne Schneider Corey often present workshops in group counseling. In the past 30 years the Coreys have conducted group counseling training workshops for mental health professionals at many universities in the United States as well as in Canada, Mexico, China, Hong Kong, Korea, Germany, Belgium, Scotland, England, and Ireland. In his leisure time, Jerry likes to travel, hike and bicycle in the mountains, and drive his 1931 Model A Ford. The Coreys have been married since 1964; they have two adult daughters and three grandchildren.

He holds memberships in the American Counseling Association; the American Psychological Association; the Association for Specialists in Group Work; the American Group Psychotherapy Association; the Association for Spiritual, Ethical, and Religious Values in Counseling; the Association for Counselor

Education and Supervision; and the Western Association for Counselor Education and Supervision.

Recent publications by Jerry Corey, all with Brooks/Cole, Cengage Learning, include:

- *Becoming a Helper*, Sixth Edition (2011, with Marianne Schneider Corey)
- *Issues in Ethics in the Helping Professions*, Eighth Edition (2011, with Marianne Schneider Corey and Patrick Callanan)
- *Groups: Process and Practice*, Eighth Edition (2010, with Marianne Schneider Corey and Cindy Corey)
- *I Never Knew I Had a Choice*, Ninth Edition (2010, with Marianne Schneider Corey)
- *Theory and Practice of Counseling and Psychotherapy*, Eighth Edition (and *Student Manual*) (2009)
- *Case Approach to Counseling and Psychotherapy*, Seventh Edition (2009)
- *The Art of Integrative Counseling*, Second Edition (2009)
- *Group Techniques*, Third Edition (2004, with Marianne Schneider Corey, Patrick Callanan, and J. Michael Russell)

Jerry is the coauthor (with Barbara Herlihy) of *Boundary Issues in Counseling: Multiple Roles and Responsibilities,* Second Edition (2006), and *ACA Ethical Standards Casebook*, Sixth Edition (2006); he is the coauthor (with Robert Haynes, Patrice Moulton, and Michelle Muratori) of *Clinical Supervision in the Helping Professions: A Practical Guide,* Second Edition (2010); he is the author of *Creating Your Professional Path: Lessons From My Journey* (2010). All four of these books are published by the American Counseling Association.

He has also made several educational video programs on various aspects of counseling practice: (1) *Gerald Corey's Perspectives on Theory and Practice of Group Counseling—DVD and Online Program* (2012); (2) *Theory in Practice: The Case of Stan—DVD and Online Program* (2009); (3) *Groups in Action: Evolution and Challenges—DVD and Workbook* (2006, with Marianne Schneider Corey and Robert Haynes); (4) *CD-ROM for Integrative Counseling* (2005, with Robert Haynes); and (5) *Ethics in Action*: *CD-ROM* (2003, with Marianne Schneider Corey and Robert Haynes). All of these programs are available through Brooks/Cole, Cengage Learning.

BRIEF CONTENTS

CONTENTS

EIGHT **Psychodrama in Groups** 190

NINE **The Existential Approach to Groups** 222

TEN **The Person-Centered Approach to Groups** 253

PART 3   INTEGRATION AND APPLICATION   453

Group counseling is an increasingly utilized therapeutic intervention in a variety of settings. Although many textbooks deal with groups, very few present an overview of various theoretical models and describe how these models apply to group counseling. This book outlines the basic elements of group process, deals with ethical and professional issues special to group work, and presents an overview of the key concepts and techniques of 11 approaches to group counseling. The book also attempts an integration of these approaches and encourages students to develop a framework that leads to their own synthesis.

Theory and Practice of Group Counseling is written in a clear and simple style, so that you will have no difficulty understanding the theoretical concepts and their relationship to group practice. Many of you may have taken a course in counseling theories before your group counseling course, and that background will certainly be useful in understanding and applying the material in this book.

This book is for graduate or undergraduate students in any field involving human services. It is especially suitable for students enrolled in any of the courses under the general designation of "Theory and Practice of Group Counseling." The book is also for practitioners who are involved in group work or for students and trainees who are interested in leading various types of groups. This book is also useful for psychiatric nurses, ministers, social workers, psychologists, marriage and family therapists, addiction counselors, rehabilitation counselors, community agency counselors, school counselors, licensed professional counselors, and mental health professionals who lead groups as a part of their work.

Overview of the Book

The eighth edition emphasizes the practical applications of the theoretical models to group work. The central purpose is to help you to develop your own synthesis of various aspects of these approaches. The book also includes two detailed chapters on the stages of a group's development, providing a guide for leaders in the practice of counseling.

Part One (Chapters 1 through 5) treats the basic elements of group process and practice that you'll need to know regardless of the types of groups you may lead or the theoretical orientation you may hold. Chapter 1 presents an overview of the various types of groups and discusses some general principles that can be applied in working with the reality of cultural diversity in groups. Chapter 2 deals with basic concerns of group leadership, such as the personal characteristics of effective leaders, the problems they face, the different styles of leadership, the range of specific skills required for effective leading, and the components of an effective multicultural group counselor. A new section on the role of research in group counseling addresses the issues of combining research with the practice of group work, evidence-based practice in group work, and the advantages of practice-based evidence as an alternative to evidence-based practice. Chapter 3 addresses important ethical issues that you will inevitably encounter as you lead groups. The emphasis is on the rights of group members and the responsibilities of group leaders. Both the "Best Practice Guidelines," developed by the Association for Specialists in Group Work (2008), and the "Ethical Guidelines for Group Therapists," developed by the American Group Psychotherapy Association (2002), are presented in the *Student Manual* that accompanies this book. In Chapters 4 and 5 you are introduced to the major developmental tasks confronting a group as it goes through its various stages from the formation of a group to its termination, including evaluation and follow-up. The central characteristics of the stages that make up the life history of a group are examined, with special attention paid to the major functions of the group leader at each stage. These chapters also focus on the functions of the members of a group and the possible problems that are associated with each stage in the group's evolution. There are many new references and suggested readings for Part One.

Part Two (Chapters 6 through 16) examines eleven theoretical approaches to group counseling. Most of the revisions for this edition are found in Part Two. These chapters are designed to provide you with a good overview of a variety of theoretical models underlying group counseling, so that you can see the connection between theory and practice. Each of these theoretical orientations has something valid to offer you as a future group leader.

To provide a framework that will help you integrate the theoretical models, these 11 chapters have a common structure. Each chapter begins by describing the key concepts of the theory and their implications for group practice. This is followed by a discussion of the role and functions of the group leader according to the particular theory and, when applicable, the stages of development of that particular group process. Next are discussions of how each theory is applied to group practice; the major techniques employed within the framework of each theory; concepts and techniques that have applicability to group work in the school; and how the approach can be applied with diverse client populations. Illustrative examples make the use of these techniques more concrete. Each chapter contains my evaluation of the approach under discussion—an evaluation based on what I consider to be its major strengths and limitations.

The necessity for flexibility and a willingness to adapt techniques to fit the group member's cultural background is emphasized in each chapter. You are given recommendations regarding where to look for further training in each of the theoretical approaches. Updated annotated lists of reading suggestions and extensive references at the end of these chapters are offered to stimulate you to expand on the material and broaden your learning through further reading.

Part Three (Chapters 17 and 18) focuses on the practical application of the theories and principles covered in Parts One and Two, making these applications more vivid and concrete. Chapter 17 is designed to help you pull together the various methods and approaches, realizing commonalities and differences among them. The chapter concludes with a description of an "integrative model of group counseling," which combines concepts and techniques from all the approaches that have been examined and which should help students attempt their own personal integration. The model I present integrates *thinking, feeling,* and *doing* perspectives, with varying emphases at each stage of a group's development. My rationale is to show which aspects of each theory I draw on at the various stages of the group, as well as to offer a basis for blending what may look like diverse approaches to the practice of group work. I strive to give you some guidance in thinking about ways to develop your own synthesis of the various group approaches.

Chapter 18 follows a group in action and applies an integrative perspective, demonstrating how my coleader (Marianne Schneider Corey) and I draw from various approaches as we work with a group. This final chapter consists of our version of an integrative approach in working with certain typical themes that might emerge in a group, emphasizing the theoretical and therapeutic rationale behind our interventions with specific members. This is a case of the unfolding of a group in action, an actual 3-day residential group coled by Marianne and Jerry Corey.

To get a general overview of the basic issues and for comparisons among the 11 theories, I recommend that you read Part Three (Chapters 17 and 18) early in the course (after reading Chapters 1 through 5). Of course, these two chapters will be most important as tools for integrating and synthesizing concepts after you have studied the contemporary approaches in Part Two.

New to the Eighth Edition

In this eighth edition several chapters in Part Two have been significantly rewritten to reflect recent trends; minor revisions were made in the chapters in Part One and Part Three.

Revisions to Part One (Basic Elements of Group Process) include updated research on the beneficial aspects of group work; a new and expanded discussion of the role of research in group work; a new section on evidence-based practices in group work and a discussion of practice-based evidence as an alternative; a new discussion of bridging the gap between research and clinical practice; an expanded discussion on integrating research into the practice of group work; group counseling for college students; current discussion of ethical issues in group work (such as informed consent, confidentiality, diversity issues, and competence of group leaders); stages of a group; various perspectives on the role of cohesion in a group; and therapeutic factors in a group.

The revisions found in Part Two (Theoretical Approaches to Group Counseling) are based on the recommendations of expert reviewers of each of the separate theories, who provided suggestions for updating the various approaches with regard to current trends, new studies, and recent developments in the practice of the approach. Each of the theory chapters has been revised to reflect contemporary practice and to include the most current references available. More specifically, below are some of the changes in each of the theory chapters.

Chapter 6 (The Psychoanalytic Approach to Groups): There is an expansion on the discussion of the following topics: transference and countertransference, the role of the group therapist, interpretation, the working-through process, and the advantages of a group format in working with older adults. There is a new section on attachment theory and group psychotherapy. More emphasis has been given to how the past, present, and future are related to the practice of group therapy. The discussion of brief psychodynamic group therapy has been expanded as well.

Chapter 7 (Adlerian Group Counseling): This chapter contains relatively minor revisions of the discussion on the stages of the Adlerian group, the importance of the therapeutic relationship, and the role of encouragement in all phases of a group. There is new material on techniques and revised material on applying this approach to group counseling with children in schools.

Chapter 8 (Psychodrama): This chapter has undergone some major revisions. Aspects that have been reconsidered and revised include differentiating classical psychodrama from using psychodrama in an integrative way; the facilitation of spontaneity among members; the importance of working in the present moment; the meaning of encounter; tele as a therapeutic factor; more on the use of the empty chair technique; revised discussion of some techniques commonly used in psychodrama; and an expanded discussion of how to integrate psychodrama with other approaches.

Chapter 9 (Existential Approach to Groups): Minor changes includes revisions to the implications of the meaning of death as applied to group therapy; the value of an existential group for older persons to assist them in dealing with losses associated with aging; new material on the aims of an existential group and the role of the group leader; the increased international interest in the existential approach; and new literature on the approach.

Chapter 10 (The Person-Centered Approach to Groups): Some revisions of this chapter include continued development of the approach; different styles of person-centered group facilitation; and revision of the core conditions as applied to group work.

Chapter 11 (Gestalt Therapy in Groups): This chapter has an updated discussion of diversity perspectives. There is increased coverage of the differences between techniques and experiments. More attention has been given to the evolution of Gestalt therapy and to the current emphasis on relational factors, including the relationships between the leader and members. There is a revised discussion of the balance of safety and risk in the Gestalt group.

Chapter 12 (Transactional Analysis in Groups): Substantive changes in many sections in this chapter pertain to clarification of existing material or expansion of concepts. Some of these revisions of key points include the ego states; the role of strokes; parental injunctions; games; rackets; basic life positions; the stages of a TA group; guidelines for establishing a therapeutic contract; and evaluation of the approach. There is new material on life scripts, basic life positions, and the role of contracts in a TA group.

Chapter 13 (Cognitive Behavioral Approaches to Groups): Some of the salient revisions include more attention to the third-generation behavior therapies; reworking the material in the stages of a CBT group; new material on the informed consent process in CBT groups; new material on cognitive therapy; expansion of the problem-solving process; and the contributions of the CBT approach.

Chapter 14 (Rational Emotive Behavior Therapy in Groups): This chapter has been streamlined by condensing some material. Many of the changes are relatively minor but are aimed at increased accuracy and current practices. A few of these changes are in the sections on the role of the group leader; cognitive, behavioral, and emotive techniques used in REBT groups; and more on the international interest in REBT.

Chapter 15 (Reality Therapy in Groups): This chapter contains some new areas of emphasis: differentiating between choice theory and reality therapy; creating a safe environment in a group; and an updated discussion of the WDEP model applied to group work.

Chapter 16 (Solution-Focused Brief Therapy in Groups): This chapter has undergone major revision and expansion of the concepts, techniques, and current practices. More emphasis is given to creating a therapeutic alliance. A substantial section on *motivational interviewing* has been added to this chapter. Motivational interviewing offers some unique ways to consider ambivalence regarding change, strategies to minimize reluctance and resistance, and how to create a context for increasing the motivation to change. Research supporting the efficacy of motivational interviewing is included, as are some applications to different clinical populations. The commonalities between solution-focused brief therapy and motivational interviewing are delineated as well. New material is provided on applying solution-focused counseling in the schools and also on multicultural applications of brief therapy. Other topics that have been revised and expanded include establishing member goals; termination issues; and an expanded discussion of techniques.

Supplements to the Book

The CourseMate website includes a series of audio lectures that I present for each chapter of *Theory and Practice of Group Counseling*. New to this eighth edition is an online video presentation of lectures that I give for each chapter, which are different from the audio lectures. These video lectures, titled *Gerald Corey's Perspectives on Theory and Practice of Group Counseling*, are available as an online program and also as a DVD. Visit the Theory and Practice of Group Counseling CourseMate website at www.cengagebrain.com/shop/ISBN/0840033869 to watch Gerald Corey presenting lectures for each chapter of this book.

A DVD program titled *Groups in Action: Evolution and Challenges* is an integral supplement to this book. Part One of this DVD program (*Evolution of a*

Group) depicts central features that illustrate the development of the group process and how coleaders facilitate a process as the group moves through the various stages: initial, transition, working, and ending. Chapters 4 and 5 of this textbook deal with all of the stages of a group. Chapter 18 provides illustrative examples and vignettes from the DVD program, *Evolution of a Group,* as a way of demonstrating how to integrate many of the theories. Central themes for each of the stages of a group are addressed in this chapter and demonstrated in the DVD. These samples of group work are intended to make the theoretical perspectives come alive, to provide some flavor of the differences and similarities among the approaches, and to show some ways of drawing on the diverse approaches in working with material that emerges from a group. The DVD also emphasizes the application of techniques in working with the material that unfolds in the here-and-now context of the group.

An eighth edition of the *Student Manual for Theory and Practice of Group Counseling* is available to help you gain maximum benefit from this book and actually experience group process and techniques. The manual includes questions for reflection and discussion, suggested activities for the whole class and for small groups, ideas for supervised training groups, summary charts, self-inventories, study guides, comprehension checks and quizzes, self-tests, group techniques, examples of cases with open-ended alternatives for group counseling practice, and a glossary of key terms. An ideal learning package is *Theory and Practice of Group Counseling; Student Manual for Theory and Practice of Group Counseling;* and *Groups in Action: Evolution and Challenges, DVD and Workbook* (Corey, Corey, & Haynes, 2006).

An *Instructor's Resource Manual* is also available in electronic form. It has been revised to reflect the changes in both the textbook and the student manual. The IRM contains chapter outlines, suggestions for teaching a group counseling course, test items, additional exercises and activities, online resources, a glossary of key terms for each chapter, a study guide for each chapter, and PowerPoint presentations for each chapter.

Acknowledgments

Many of the revisions that have become a part of this textbook since its original edition in 1981 have come about in the context of discussions with students, colleagues, and professors who use the book. Those students and professionals whom I teach continue to teach me in return, and most of my ideas are stimulated by interactions with them. The supportive challenge of my friends and colleagues (with whom I offer classes and workshops and with whom I colead groups) continues to keep my learning fresh and provides me with encouragement to keep practicing, teaching, and writing. I especially want to recognize the influence on my life and my books of my wife and colleague, Marianne Schneider Corey, with whom I regularly work professionally. Her critique and feedback have been especially valuable in preparing these revisions, and many of the ideas in the book are the product of our many hours of discussions about group work.

The comments of those who provided reviews either before or after the manuscript was revised have been most helpful in shaping the final product.

Those who reviewed the entire manuscript of the eighth edition and offered useful feedback are: Patrick Callanan, California State University at Fullerton; Lon Helton, Cleveland State University; Larry Lewis, East Los Angeles College; Charles Merrill, Sonoma State University; and Mary Kate Reese, Argosy University, Atlanta. I especially value input from student reviewers, as they study this book closely. For this edition I received useful commentaries from three students: Julie Tomlinson, MSW program, University of Southern California; and Rebecca Cunningham and Hollis Paegel, both graduates from California State University at Fullerton.

For the eighth edition, I thank the following people for their assistance in updating specific chapters:

Chapter 6 (Psychoanalytic Approach): William Blau, Copper Mountain College, Joshua Tree, California; and J. Michael Russell, California State University, Fullerton

Chapter 7 (Adlerian Group Counseling): James Bitter, East Tennessee State University, who has played a key role in the development of this chapter over the course of each revision and who coauthored this chapter; and Richard Watts, Sam Houston State University

Chapter 8 (Psychodrama): Adam Blatner, Private Practice, Sun City/Georgetown, Texas, who has had a significant role in the evolution of this chapter since its earliest edition; and thanks to other psychodrama practitioners, authors, and teachers who reviewed this latest chapter: Jacob Gershoni, who has a private practice in Manhattan, and is also Co-Director of the Psychodrama Training Institute in New York City; Eva Leveton, author, teacher, and trainer in psychodrama; Zerka T. Moreno, co-creator of psychodrama, Charlottesville, VA; Catherine Nugent, Private Practice, Laurel, MD, and Edward Schreiber, of the Zerka T. Moreno Foundation for Training, Research & Education, Amherst, MA.

Chapter 9 (Existential Approach to Groups): Emmy van Deurzen, New School of Psychotherapy and Counselling, London, England; and Bryan Farha, Oklahoma City University

Chapter 10 (Person-Centered Approach to Groups): Martin Adams, New School of Psychotherapy and Counselling, London, England; Colin Lago, Director of the Counselling Center, University of Sheffield, UK; and Natalie Rogers, Person-Centered Expressive Arts Program, Saybrook University, CA

Chapter 11 (Gestalt Therapy in Groups): Jon Frew, Private Practice, Vancouver, Washington and Pacific University, Oregon

Chapter 12 (Transactional Analysis): Ray Quiett; and Tim Schnabel

Chapter 13 (Cognitive Behavioral Approach to Groups): Sherry Cormier, West Virginia University; and Frank M. Dattilio, Harvard Medical School and the University of Pennsylvania School of Medicine.

Chapter 14 (Rational Emotive Behavior Therapy in Groups): Sherry Cormier, West Virginia University; and Windy Dryden, Professor of Psychotherapeutic Studies at Goldsmiths College, London

Chapter 15 (Reality Therapy in Groups): Robert Wubbolding, Center for Reality Therapy, Cincinnati, Ohio

Chapter 16 (Solution-Focused Brief Therapy in Groups): Linda Metcalf, Texas Women's University and the Solution Focused Institute for Education and Training; John Murphy, University of Central Arkansas; Sherry Cormier, West Virginia University; and Cynthia J. Osborn, Kent State University.

I appreciate the members of the Brooks/Cole, Cengage Learning team who continue to offer support for our projects. These people include Seth Dobrin, editor of counseling, social work, and human services; Julie Martinez, consulting editor, who monitored the review process; Caryl Gorska, for her work on the interior design and cover of this book; Arwen Petty, supplemental materials for the book; Michelle Muratori, Johns Hopkins University, for her work on updating the Instructor's Resource Manual and assisting in the revision of the *Student Manual*; and Rita Jaramillo, project manager. We thank Ben Kolstad of Glyph International, who coordinated the production of this book. Special recognition goes to Kay Mikel, the manuscript editor of this edition, whose exceptional editorial talents continue to keep this book reader friendly. We appreciate Susan Cunningham's work in preparing the index. The efforts and dedication of all of these people certainly contribute to the high quality of this edition.

—Gerald Corey

PART 1

BASIC ELEMENTS OF GROUP PROCESS: AN OVERVIEW

CHAPTER ONE

Introduction to Group Work

Today, more than ever, mental health practitioners are being challenged to develop new strategies for both preventing and treating psychological problems. Although there is still a place in community agencies for individual counseling, limiting the delivery of services to this model is no longer practical. Group counseling offers real promise in meeting today's challenges. Group counseling enables practitioners to work with more clients—a decided advantage in these managed care times—in addition, the group process has unique learning advantages. Group counseling may well be the treatment of choice for many populations. If group work is to be effective, however, practitioners need a theoretical grounding along with the skill to use this knowledge creatively in practice.

The Increasing Use of Groups

In conducting workshops around the United States, and in other countries as well, I have found a surge of interest in group work. Professional counselors are creating an increasing variety of groups to fit the special needs of a diverse clientele in many different settings. In fact, the types of groups that can be designed are limited only by one's imagination. This expanded interest underscores the need for broad education and training in both the theory and the practice of group counseling. This book provides a fundamental knowledge base applicable to the many kinds of groups you will be leading.

Groups can be used for therapeutic or educational purposes or for a combination of the two. Some groups focus primarily on helping people make fundamental changes in their ways of thinking, feeling, and behaving. Groups with an educational focus help members learn specific coping skills. This chapter provides a brief overview of various types of groups and the differences among them.

In the human services field, you will be expected to be able to use group approaches with a variety of clients for a variety of purposes. In a psychiatric hospital, for example, you may be asked to design and lead groups for patients with various problems, for patients who are about to leave the hospital and reenter the community, or for patients' families. Insight groups, remotivation groups, social skills training groups, bereavement groups, and recreational/vocational therapy groups are commonly found in these hospitals.

If you work in a community mental health center, a college counseling center, or a day-treatment clinic, you will be expected to provide therapeutic services in a wide range of group settings. Your client population will most likely be diverse with respect to age, ability/disability, problems, socioeconomic status, level of education, race or ethnicity, sexual identity, and cultural background. Community agencies are making increased use of groups, and it is not uncommon to find groups for women's issues, men's issues, consciousness-raising groups for men, groups for children of alcoholics, support groups, parent education groups, groups for cancer patients, groups for individuals with eating disorders, groups for people who have experienced trauma and crisis, groups for senior citizens, HIV/AIDS support groups, and groups aimed at reducing substance abuse.

Your theoretical approach may be based primarily on a single system. Increasingly, however, group practitioners are becoming more integrative as they draw on techniques from various theoretical approaches (see Norcross & Goldfried, 2005). Although there are numerous pathways toward integration, all of these routes are characterized by the desire to increase therapeutic effectiveness and applicability by looking beyond the confines of single theories and the techniques associated with them (Norcross, 2005a).

Groups have particular advantages for school counseling. Special groups in schools are designed to deal with students' educational, vocational, personal, or social problems. If you work in a school, you may be asked to form a career exploration group, a self-esteem group, a group for children of divorce, a group for acting-out children, a group aimed at teaching interpersonal skills, or a personal growth group. Elementary school counselors are now designing therapeutic groups as well as psychoeducational groups. On the high school level, groups are aimed at helping students who are in drug rehabilitation, who have been victims of crime, or who are going through a crisis or recovering from a trauma.

Counseling groups in schools include a wide array of topics and formats. These groups are a mainstay of the psychological services offered by schools. Groups for children and adolescents occupy a major place in a comprehensive, developmental school counseling program because of their efficacy in delivering information and treatment. Considerable empirical support has been gathered for the effectiveness of groups aimed at both prevention and remediation (Goodnough & Lee, 2004; Riva & Haub, 2004). Riva and Haub (2004) maintain that "the real benefit of school-based treatment is that it can potentially reach many students before they need remedial counseling for more serious mental health problems" (p. 318). Goodnough and Lee (2004) conclude that "providing effective group counseling experiences to students requires leadership, specialized knowledge and skills, and the ability to advocate effectively for the inclusion of a program of group counseling within schools" (pp. 179–180).

Reviews of the group psychotherapy literature have indicated that group work is a beneficial and cost-effective approach to treatment (Burlingame, MacKenzie, & Strauss, 2004). Barlow (2008) contends that groups can be effectively used for both prevention and education purposes: "Through ever-growing research and continuing improvements in clinical application, groups remain a powerful intervention tool across the life span, positively impacting childhood, adult, and geriatric disorders" (p. 244). In sum, a group approach can help people meet almost any need.

One reason the group approach has become so popular is that it is frequently more effective than the individual approach. This effectiveness stems from the fact that group members not only gain insight but practice new skills both within the group and in their everyday interactions outside the group. In addition, members of the group benefit from the feedback and insights of other group members as well as those of the practitioner. Groups offer many opportunities for modeling, and members can learn how to cope with their problems by observing others with similar concerns.

Even practitioners with advanced degrees in one or another of the helping professions often have very little exposure to the theory and techniques of group work. Many of these professionals find themselves thrust into the role of group leader without adequate preparation, training, or supervision. It is not surprising that some of them become anxious when faced with this challenge. Although this book is not intended to be an exclusive means of preparing competent group leaders, it is aimed at providing practitioners with the knowledge and skills necessary for coping with the demands of effective group leadership.

Overview of the Counseling Group

Group counseling has preventive as well as remedial aims. Generally, the counseling group has a specific focus, which may be educational, career, social, or personal. Group work emphasizes interpersonal communication of conscious thoughts, feelings, and behavior within a here-and-now time frame. Counseling groups are often problem oriented, and the members largely determine their content and aims. Group members typically do not require extensive personality reconstruction, and their concerns generally relate to the developmental tasks of the life span. Group counseling tends to be growth oriented in that the emphasis is on discovering internal resources of strength. The participants may be facing situational crises and temporary conflicts, struggling with personal or interpersonal problems of living, experiencing difficulties with life transitions, or trying to change self-defeating behaviors. The group provides the empathy and support necessary to create the atmosphere of trust that leads to sharing and exploring these concerns. Group members are assisted in developing their existing skills in dealing with interpersonal problems so that they will be better able to handle future problems of a similar nature.

The group counselor uses verbal and nonverbal techniques as well as structured exercises. Basically, the role of the group counselor is to facilitate interaction among the members, help them learn from one another, assist them in establishing personal goals, and encourage them to translate their insights into concrete plans that involve taking action outside of the group. Chapter 2 describes the skills competent group leaders use to accomplish these tasks. Group counselors perform their role largely by teaching members to focus on the here-and-now and to identify the concerns they wish to explore in the group.

GOALS

Ideally, members will decide the specific goals of the group experience for themselves. Here are some possible goals for members of counseling groups:

- To increase awareness and self-knowledge; to develop a sense of one's unique identity
- To recognize the commonality of members' needs and problems and to develop a sense of connectedness
- To help members learn how to establish meaningful and intimate relationships
- To assist members in discovering resources within their extended family and community as ways of addressing their concerns
- To increase self-acceptance, self-confidence, self-respect, and to achieve a new view of oneself and others
- To learn how to express one's emotions in a healthy way
- To develop concern and compassion for the needs and feelings of others
- To find alternative ways of dealing with normal developmental issues and of resolving certain conflicts
- To increase self-direction, interdependence, and responsibility toward oneself and others
- To become aware of one's choices and to make choices wisely
- To make specific plans for changing certain behaviors
- To learn more effective social skills
- To learn how to challenge others with care, concern, honesty, and directness
- To clarify one's values and decide whether and how to modify them

ADVANTAGES

In addition to the member advantages of achieving the goals just listed, group counseling provides a re-creation of the participants' everyday world, especially if the membership is diverse with respect to age, interests, background, socioeconomic status, and type of problem. As a microcosm of society, the group provides a sample of reality—members' struggles and conflicts in the group are similar to those they experience outside of it—and the diversity that characterizes most groups also results in unusually rich feedback for and from the participants, who can see themselves through the eyes of a wide range of people.

The group offers understanding and support, which foster the members' willingness to explore problems they have brought with them to the group. The participants achieve a sense of belonging, and through the cohesion that develops, group members learn ways of being intimate, of caring, and of challenging. In this supportive atmosphere, members can experiment with new behaviors. As they practice these behaviors in the group, members receive encouragement and learn how to bring their new insights into their life outside the group experience.

Ultimately, it is up to the members themselves to decide what changes they want to make. They can compare the perceptions they have of themselves with the perceptions others have of them and then decide what to do with this

information. Group members are able to get a picture of the kind of person they would like to become, and they come to understand what is preventing them from becoming that person.

VALUE FOR SPECIFIC POPULATIONS

Group counseling can be designed to meet the needs of specific populations such as children, adolescents, college students, or older persons. Examples of these counseling groups are described in *Groups: Process and Practice* (M. Corey, Corey, & Corey, 2010), which offers suggestions on how to set up these groups and the techniques to use for dealing with the unique problems of each of them. Following is a brief discussion of the value of counseling groups for several specific populations.

Counseling Groups for Children Counseling groups for children can serve preventive or remedial purposes. In schools, group counseling is often suggested for children who display behaviors or attributes such as excessive fighting, inability to get along with peers, violent outbursts, poor social skills, and lack of supervision at home. Small groups can provide children with the opportunity to express their feelings about these and related problems. Identifying children who are developing serious emotional and behavioral problems is extremely important. If these children can receive psychological assistance at an early age, they stand a better chance of coping effectively with the developmental tasks they must face later in life.

Counseling Groups for Adolescents Group counseling is especially suited for adolescents because it gives them a place to express conflicting feelings, to explore self-doubts, and to come to the realization that they share these concerns with their peers. A group allows adolescents to openly question their values and to modify those that need to be changed. In the group, adolescents learn to communicate with their peers, benefit from the modeling provided by the leader, and can safely experiment with reality and test their limits. Because of the opportunities for interaction available in the group situation, the participants can express their concerns and be heard, and they can help one another on the road toward self-understanding and self-acceptance.

Counseling Groups for College Students Students encounter a range of developmental tasks during their undergraduate and graduate years. They experiment with defining themselves, and they seek to discover who they are in relationships with others (Johnson, 2009). Counseling groups are a valuable vehicle for meeting the developmental needs of both traditional and nontraditional students. Today's college students have had a variety of significant life experiences, including some who are veterans returning from Iraq and Afghanistan. Those who seek services at college counseling centers are increasingly older and more diverse in their life experiences, making group work more challenging (McCeneaney & Gross, 2009).

Many college counseling centers offer groups designed for relatively healthy students who are experiencing personal and interpersonal relationship problems. The main purpose of these groups is to provide participants with an opportunity for growth and a situation in which they can deal with career decisions, intimate relationships, identity problems, educational plans, and feelings of isolation on an impersonal campus. Theme or issue groups, which are time-limited and focus on a developmental issue or address a specific problem that the participants have in common, are popular in university counseling centers. These groups promote well-being by assisting people in dealing effectively with developmental tasks (Drum & Knott, 2009).

Counseling Groups for Older People Counseling groups can be valuable for older persons in many of the same ways they are of value to adolescents. As people grow older, they often experience isolation. Like adolescents, older people often feel unproductive, unneeded, and unwanted. Many older people accept myths about aging, which then become self-fulfilling prophecies. An example is the misconception that older people cannot change or that once they retire they will most likely be depressed. Counseling groups can do a lot to help older people challenge these myths and deal with the developmental tasks that they, like any other age group, must face in such a way that they can retain their integrity and self-respect. The group situation can assist people in breaking out of their isolation and offer older people the encouragement necessary to find meaning in their lives so that they can live fully and not merely exist.

Other Types of Groups

Although the focus of this book is on counseling groups, the practice of group work has broadened to encompass psychotherapy groups, psychoeducational groups, and task groups as well as counseling groups. Many of these groups share some of the procedures, techniques, and processes of counseling groups. They differ, however, with respect to specific aims, the role of the leader, the kind of people in the group, and the emphasis given to issues such as prevention, remediation, treatment, and development. Let's take a brief look at how psychotherapy groups, psychoeducational (structured) groups, and task groups differ from counseling groups.

GROUP PSYCHOTHERAPY

A major difference between group *therapy* and group *counseling* lies in the group's goals. Counseling groups focus on growth, development, enhancement, prevention, self-awareness, and releasing blocks to growth, whereas therapy groups focus on issues such as remediation, treatment, and personality reconstruction. **Group psychotherapy** is a process of reeducation that includes both conscious and unconscious awareness and both the present and the past. Some therapy groups are primarily designed to correct emotional and behavioral disorders that impede one's functioning or to remediate in-depth psychological problems. The goal may be either a minor or a major transformation of personality structure, depending on the theoretical orientation of the group therapist. Because of this goal, therapy groups tend to be more long term than other kinds of groups. The people who make up the group may be suffering from severe emotional problems, deep personal conflicts, effects of trauma, or psychotic states. Many of these individuals are in need of remedial treatment rather than developmental and preventive work.

Group therapists are typically clinical or counseling psychologists, licensed professional counselors, and clinical social workers. They use a wide range of verbal modalities (which group counselors also use), and some employ techniques to induce regression to earlier experiences, to tap unconscious dynamics, and to help members reexperience traumatic situations so that catharsis can occur. As these experiences are relived in the group, members become aware of and gain insight into past decisions that interfere with current functioning. The group therapist assists members in developing a corrective emotional experience and in making new decisions about the world, others, and themselves.

PSYCHOEDUCATIONAL GROUPS

Psychoeducational groups, or groups structured by some central theme, are gaining in popularity. These groups feature the presentation and discussion of factual information and skill building through the use of planned skill-building exercises. Psychoeducational groups serve a number of purposes: imparting information, sharing common experiences, teaching people how to solve problems, offering support, and helping people learn how to create their own support systems outside of the group setting. These groups can be thought of as educational and therapeutic groups in that they are structured along the lines of certain content themes. It is clear that psychoeducational groups are finding a place in many settings, and they appear to be increasingly used in community agencies and in schools.

Psychoeducational groups are designed to help people develop specific skills, understand certain themes, or progress through difficult life transitions. Although the topics do vary according to the interests of the group leader and the clientele, such groups have a common denominator of providing members with increased awareness of some life problems and tools to better cope with them. The goal is to prevent an array of educational and psychological disturbances.

Many psychoeducational groups are based on a learning theory model and use behavioral procedures. Chapter 13 provides detailed descriptions of such groups, including social skills training groups, stress management groups, and cognitive therapy groups.

Psychoeducation groups are well suited to populations of all ages. Here are a few examples of such groups for various developmental levels; they are described in detail in *Groups: Process and Practice* (M. Corey, Corey, & Corey, 2010):

- A group for elementary school children of divorce and an anger management group for children
- An HIV/AIDS support group
- A women's group and a men's group
- A domestic violence group
- A women's support group for survivors of incest
- A successful aging group
- A bereavement group for older persons

All of these groups are psychoeducational in that they contain certain content themes to provide structure for the sessions, encourage sharing and feedback among the members, are designed to increase self-awareness, and are aimed at facilitating change in members' daily lives. These groups can be designed for just about every client group and can be tailored to the specific needs of the individuals represented.

TASK FACILITATION GROUPS

Task facilitation groups are designed to assist task forces, committees, planning groups, community organizations, discussion groups, study circles, learning groups, team building, program development consultation, and other similar groups to correct or develop their functioning. These groups address the application of principles and processes of group dynamics that can foster accomplishment of identified work goals. Increasingly, human services workers are being asked to help improve program planning and evaluation within organizations. Whether task groups are created for organizational purposes or to meet certain needs of clients, the tasks of these groups center around decision making and problem solving (Conyne, Wilson, & Ward, 1997).

Oftentimes, those involved in task groups want to get down to business quickly, yet focusing exclusively on the task at hand (content) can create problems for the group. A leader's failure to attend to here-and-now factors is likely to result in a group that becomes overly focused on content concerns, with process issues relegated to a minor role. If interpersonal issues within the group are ignored, cooperation and collaboration will not develop, and it is likely that group goals will not be met. It is essential that group leaders recognize that process and relationships are central to achieving the goals of a task group.

It is the leader's role to assist task group participants in understanding how attention to this interpersonal climate directly relates to achieving the purpose and goals of the group (Hulse-Killacky, Killacky, & Donigan, 2001). The balance between content and process in task groups is best achieved by attending to the guiding principles of warm-up, action, and closure. When this is done effectively, task groups are likely to be more successful and productive.

Task groups are commonly used by school counselors who assemble a group of school personnel to develop a plan to assist students. A team works together to determine how services can best be implemented. Rather than focusing on individual growth, task groups in school settings are concerned with accomplishing common goals to assist a range of students (Falls & Furr, 2009).

Professionals who work in the community are often called on to apply their group work expertise to meet the needs of the community. Task groups have many uses in community intervention. Many of the problems people face are the result of being disenfranchised as individuals or as members of the community. One of the tasks of professionals engaged in community work is to assist individuals and the community in acquiring access to valued resources in moving toward a greater degree of empowerment. Group workers need to understand how sociopolitical influences impinge on the experiences of individuals from diverse racial and ethnic groups.

Working with the community usually means working with a specific group or in a situation in which competing or collaborating groups are dealing with an issue or set of issues in a community. Most of the work in community change is done in a small group context, and skills in organizing task groups are essential.

BRIEF GROUP WORK

Strictly speaking, brief groups are not a type of group. Many of the groups already described are characterized by a time-limited format. In the era of managed care, brief interventions and short-term groups have become a necessity. Economic pressures and a shortage of resources have resulted in major changes in the way mental health services are delivered, and these pressures are reshaping group therapy practices (MacKenzie, 1994). Managed care also has influenced the trend toward developing all forms of briefer treatment, including group treatment. A variety of approaches to brief group treatment have been developed, and there is evidence that these treatments are both effective and economical (Rosenberg & Wright, 1997).

In their review of research on brief, time-limited *outpatient* group therapy, Rosenberg and Zimet (1995) found clear evidence for the effectiveness of time-limited group therapy. Their review also showed that behavioral and cognitive behavioral approaches were particularly well suited to brief group therapy. In addition, they found that when modifications were made, long-term psychodynamic approaches also could be useful. Klein, Brabender, and Fallon (1994) report positive results with short-term *inpatient* therapy groups with a variety of client populations and a broad range of problems. Brief interventions and time limitations are especially relevant for a variety of counseling groups, structured groups, and psychoeducational groups. The realistic time constraints in most settings demand that practitioners employ briefer approaches with demonstrated effectiveness. However, it is essential that those who lead these groups have had training and supervision in brief group interventions.

Rosenberg and Wright (1997) maintain that brief group therapy is well suited to the needs of both clients and managed care. Brief group therapy and managed care both require the group therapist to set clear and realistic treatment goals with members, to establish a clear focus within the group structure, to maintain an active therapist role, and to work within a limited time frame. Rosenberg and Wright conclude, "In an era of increasingly limited resources, brief group treatment remains underutilized despite clear evidence of its efficacy and efficiency. There is little doubt that group psychotherapy can make important contributions to the provision of mental health services within managed care settings" (p. 116).

Group Counseling in a Multicultural Context

In a pluralistic society, the reality of cultural diversity is recognized, respected, and encouraged. Within groups, the worldviews of both the group leader and the members also vary, and this is a natural place to acknowledge and promote pluralism. Multicultural group work involves attitudes and strategies that cultivate understanding and appreciation of diversity in such areas as culture, ethnicity, race, gender, class, ability/disability, language, religion, sexual identity, and age. We each have a unique multicultural identity, but as members of a group, we share a common goal—the success of the group. To that end, we want to learn more about ourselves as individuals and as members of diverse cultural groups.

DeLucia-Waack (1996) states that the multicultural context of group work requires attention to two tasks: (1) the application and modification of theories and techniques of group work to different cultures in ways that are congruent with cultural beliefs and behaviors, and (2) the development of the theory and practice of group work that makes full use of the diversity among members as a way to facilitate change and growth. Multiculturalism is inherent in all group work, and our uniqueness as individuals is a key factor in how groups operate.

In addition to understanding the range of clients' cultural similarities and differences, group counselors must be willing and able to challenge the culturally encapsulated view of a group's structure, goals, techniques, and practices. A fundamental step for group counselors is reexamining the underlying culturally learned assumptions of all the major theories in light of their appropriateness in a multicultural context. Comas-Diaz (2011) believes that effective psychotherapy recognizes the crucial role of awareness, respect, acceptance, and appreciation of cultural diversity. However, most traditional therapy models are grounded in a monocultural framework wherein mainstream cultural values overshadow the multicultural worldviews that may be present among group members. Eason (2009) contends that all major theories of group psychotherapy should address the Eurocentric assumptions associated with each theory. Acknowledging specific Eurocentric biases can provide an opening for a conversation regarding cultural perspectives in relation to the theory.

In their discussion of *multicultural intentionality* in group counseling, Ivey, Pedersen, and Ivey (2008) state that it is no longer adequate to mainly look to internal dynamics within the individual as a source of problems. Instead, it is essential that we examine ourselves as contextual/cultural beings. We must expand our awareness of issues pertaining to gender, sexual orientation, degree of physical and emotional ability, spirituality, and socioeconomic status. It is not necessary to discard traditional theories and techniques of counseling, but we must conceptualize them in ways that recognize the environmental influences on individual distress.

PERSPECTIVES ON MULTICULTURAL GROUP COUNSELING

The term *multicultural* refers to the complexity of culture as it pertains to delivery of services. From a broad perspective, **multicultural counseling** focuses on understanding not only racial and ethnic minority groups (African Americans, Asian Americans, Latinos, Native Americans, and White ethnics) but also people with physical disabilities, older people, women, gay and bisexual men, lesbian and bisexual women, transgendered individuals, and a variety of special needs populations. The changing demographics of American society makes it imperative that multicultural counseling address differences between counselor and client in areas such as gender, social class, language, sexual identity, ability/disability, and race and ethnicity (Lee & Ramsey, 2006).

Multicultural counseling challenges the notion that problems are found exclusively within the person. Going beyond this stance of "blaming the victim," the multicultural approach emphasizes the social and cultural context of human behavior and deals with the self-in-relation. It is essential that group workers recognize that many problems reside outside the person. For example, prejudice and discrimination are realities in the social environment whose effects go far beyond working with individuals. If group workers hope to make culturally effective interventions, they will, at times, need to assume nontraditional roles that may include advocate, change agent, consultant, adviser, and facilitator of indigenous support or healing systems (Atkinson, 2004).

According to Pedersen (1991, 1997), the multicultural perspective seeks to provide a conceptual framework that both recognizes the complex diversity of a pluralistic society and suggests bridges of shared concern that link all people, regardless of their differences. This enables group counselors to look both at the unique dimensions of a person and at how this person shares themes with those who are different. Such a perspective respects the needs and strengths of diverse client populations, and it recognizes the experiences of these clients. Mere knowledge of certain cultural groups is not enough; it is important to understand the variability within groups. Each individual must be seen in the context of his or her cultural identities, the degree to which he or she has become acculturated, and the level of multicultural self-awareness.

Pedersen (1997, 2000) emphasizes the importance of understanding both group and individual differences in making accurate interpretations of behavior. Whether practitioners pay attention to cultural variables or ignore them, culture will continue to influence both group members' and group leaders' behavior as well as the group process. Group counselors who ignore culture will provide less effective services. For group counselors to successfully lead multicultural groups, it is essential that they be invested in becoming *culturally competent*. Group workers must become aware of their worldview, value diversity, learn about different worldviews, acquire and incorporate cultural knowledge as a part of their interventions, increase their multicultural skills, and adapt to diversity and to the cultural context of clients (Comas-Diaz, 2011). Leaders also need to have a good understanding of the diversity of cultural worldviews and the potential impact of differing worldviews on relationships, behaviors, and the willingness of members to actively participate in group work (DeLucia-Waack & Donigian, 2004).

Pedersen (2000) claims that culture is complicated, not simple; it is dynamic, not static. Nevertheless, the tapestry of culture that is woven into the fabric of all helping relationships need not be viewed as a barrier through which you must break. In his workshops, Pedersen typically says that multiculturalism can make your job as a counselor easier and more fun; it can also improve the quality of your life if you adopt a perspective that cultural differences are positive attributes that add richness to relationships.

SOME GUIDELINES FOR SERVING MULTICULTURAL POPULATIONS

Adequate preparation is one of the best ways to increase the chances of a successful group experience for all members. Reflecting on these guidelines may increase your effectiveness in serving diverse client populations:

- Learn more about how your own cultural background influences your thinking and behaving. Become familiar with some of the ways that you may be culturally encapsulated. What specific steps can you take to broaden your base of understanding both of your own culture and of other cultures?

- Identify your basic assumptions—especially as they apply to diversity in culture, ethnicity, race, gender, class, religion, and sexual identity—and think about how your assumptions are likely to affect your practice as a group counselor.

- Recognize that all encounters are multicultural.

- Move beyond the perspective of looking within the individual for the sources of his or her problems, and strive to adopt a self-in-relation perspective. Take into account the environmental and systemic factors that often contribute to an individual's struggles.

- Respect individual differences and recognize that diversity enhances a group.

- Learn to pay attention to the common ground that exists among people of diverse backgrounds. What are some of the ways that we all share universal concerns?

- Realize that it is not necessary to learn everything about the cultural background of your clients before you begin working with them. Allow them to teach you how you can best serve them.

- Spend time preparing clients for a successful group experience, especially if some of their values differ from the values that form the foundation of group work. Teach clients how to adapt their group experience to meet the challenges they face in their everyday lives.

- Recognize the importance of being flexible in applying the methods you use with clients. Don't be wedded to a specific technique if it is not appropriate for a given group member.

- Remember that practicing from a multicultural perspective can make your job easier and can be rewarding for both you and your clients.

In your journey toward becoming a culturally skilled group counselor, you will probably need to think about ways of adapting theoretical approach and techniques to better serve individuals from diverse cultural backgrounds. Chapter 2 deals with what it takes to become a diversity-competent group counselor, and Chapter 3 introduces you to ethical issues that may arise in multicultural group counseling. The remaining chapters in Part One describe the various stages of groups and group work.

Part Two addresses some of the major strengths and limitations of 11 major theories from a multicultural perspective. The general principles of effective multicultural group counseling discussed here provide some background for understanding that more detailed discussion later in the book. As you study the 11 theories explored later in this book, give careful consideration to the underlying value issues that are likely to have a clear impact on your practice. The direct application of many contemporary models of therapy may be inappropriate for some clients. However, many concepts and techniques drawn from the various therapeutic schools do have cultural relevance. As a group practitioner, you will use a range of key concepts and techniques associated with the various theoretical systems. It is important to develop selection criteria that will enable you to systematically integrate those tools that best meet the needs of diverse client populations.

At this point, I suggest that you take time to read the two chapters in Part Three. Chapter 17 deals with comparisons, contrasts, and integration of the various theoretical models of group counseling. Many students have said they found it helpful at various points during the course to read the illustration of the evolution of a group provided in Chapter 18 because it provides a framework for applying the different perspectives to an actual group. Chapter 18 is based on a video titled *Evolution of a Group*, which is part of the DVD program *Groups in Action: Evolution and Challenges* (Corey, Corey, & Haynes, 2006).

AUTHOR LECTURES

Watch *Gerald Corey's Perspectives on Theory and Practice of Group Counseling* DVD or visit the *Theory and Practice of Group Counseling* CourseMate website at www.cengagebrain.com/shop/ISBN/0840033869 to watch videos of Dr. Gerald Corey presenting lectures for each chapter. Also available are unique eAudio lectures for each chapter and quiz questions for self-study.

CHAPTER TWO

Group Leadership

This chapter focuses on the influence of the group leader—as a person and as a professional—on the group process. After discussing the personal characteristics of effective leaders, I analyze the skills and techniques that are necessary for successful leadership and the specific functions and roles of group leaders. This chapter will give you enough information about these crucial topics to allow you to benefit fully from the discussion in the next three chapters, which deal with the ethics of group practice and the stages in a group's development. The topics covered here also represent an important prelude to the theory chapters in Part Two.

The Group Leader as a Person

Group leaders can acquire extensive theoretical and practical knowledge of group dynamics and be skilled in diagnostic and technical procedures, yet still be ineffective in stimulating growth and change in the members of their groups. Leaders bring to every group their personal qualities, values, and life experiences and their assumptions and biases. To promote growth in the members' lives, leaders need to live growth-oriented lives themselves. To inspire others to break away from deadening ways of being, leaders need to be willing to seek new experiences themselves. In short, group leaders become an influential force in a group when they are able to model effective behavior rather than merely describe it.

I am not implying that group leaders must be problem-free. The issue is not whether leaders have personal problems but whether they are willing to make a serious attempt to live the way they encourage members to live. More important than being a finished product is the willingness to continually examine whether one's life reflects life-giving values. The key to success as a group leader is a commitment to the never-ending journey toward becoming a more effective human being.

PERSONALITY AND CHARACTER

Group counseling techniques cannot be divorced from the leader's personal characteristics and behaviors. Some personal characteristics are vitally related to effective group leadership; their presence or absence can facilitate or inhibit the group process. As you read about these characteristics, evaluate your own strengths and areas for improvement.

Presence Being emotionally present means being moved by the joy and pain that others experience. If leaders recognize and give expression to their own emotions, they can become more emotionally involved with others. The ability of leaders to draw on these experiences makes it easier for them to empathize with and be compassionate toward group members. Presence also has to do with "being there" for the members, which involves genuine caring and a willingness to enter their psychological world. Being present means that leaders are not fragmented when they come to a group session, that they are not preoccupied with other matters, and that they are open to their reactions in the group.

Personal Power Personal power involves self-confidence and an awareness of one's influence on others. If group leaders do not feel a sense of power in their own lives (or if they do not feel in control of their destiny), it is difficult for them to facilitate members' movement toward empowerment. In short, it is not possible to give to others what you do not possess. It should be stressed that power does not mean domination and exploitation of others; these are abuses of power. Truly powerful leaders use the effect they have on group participants to encourage members to get in contact with their own unused power, not to foster their dependency. Group leaders promote a sense of empowerment by encouraging group members to become *client colleagues*. If members risk change, the bulk of the credit belongs to them.

Courage Effective group leaders show courage in their interactions with group members and do not hide behind their special role as counselors. They show courage by taking risks in the group and admitting mistakes, by being vulnerable, by being willing to challenge members in respectful ways, by acting on intuitions and beliefs, by discussing with the group their thoughts and feelings about the group process, and by being willing to share their power with group members. Leaders can model important lessons to members by taking a stance toward life and acting in spite of the fact that they are imperfect. When members push themselves to leave familiar and secure patterns, they often report being anxious and scared. Group leaders can demonstrate, through their own behavior, their willingness to move ahead in spite of sometimes being fearful.

Willingness to Confront Oneself One of the leader's central tasks is to promote self-investigation in clients. Self-awareness entails the willingness to take an honest look at oneself, and group leaders must show that they are willing to question themselves. This essential characteristic includes awareness not only of one's needs and motivations but also of personal conflicts and problems, of defenses and weak spots, of areas of unfinished business, and of the potential influence of all of these on the group process. Leaders who are self-aware are able to work therapeutically with the transferences that emerge within the group setting, both toward themselves and toward other members. Furthermore, group leaders are aware of their own vulnerabilities, especially their potential counter-transferences, and take responsibility for their own reactions.

Sincerity and Authenticity One of the leader's most important qualities is a sincere interest in the well-being and growth of others. Because sincerity involves being direct, it can also involve telling members what may be difficult for them to hear. For a group leader, caring means challenging the members to look at parts of their lives that they are denying and discouraging any form of dishonest behavior in the group. Giving members useful feedback requires sincerity and respect in the sense that the client's best interest is paramount.

Authenticity is a form of sincerity. Authentic group leaders do not live by pretenses and do not hide behind defenses or facades. Authenticity entails the willingness to appropriately disclose oneself and share feelings and reactions to what is going on in the group. Authenticity does not imply indiscriminately sharing every fleeting thought, perception, feeling, fantasy, and reaction, however. For instance, even though a leader might initially be attracted to a member, it would not be wise to disclose this reality at the initial session. Such "holding back" does not imply inauthenticity; rather, it shows respect and consideration for members at this early stage of the group.

Sense of Identity If group leaders are to help others discover who they are, leaders need to have a clear sense of their own identity. This means knowing what you value and living by these standards, not by what others expect. It means being aware of your own strengths, limitations, needs, fears, motivations, and goals. It means knowing what you are capable of becoming, what you want from life, and how you are going to get what you want. Being aware of your cultural heritage, your ethnicity, and your sexual and gender identities are vital components of this sense of identity.

Belief in the Group Process and Enthusiasm The leader's deep belief in the value of the group process is essential to the success of the group. Practitioners who lead groups simply because they are expected to, without being convinced that group interventions make a difference, are unlikely to inspire group members. Why should members believe the group experience will be of value to them if the leader is without enthusiasm for it? The enthusiasm group leaders bring to their groups can have an infectious quality. If leaders radiate life, the chances are slim that they will be consistently leading "stale groups." Leaders need to show that they enjoy their work and like being with their groups. A leader's lack of enthusiasm is generally reflected in members' lack of excitement about coming to group sessions and in members' inability to do significant work.

Inventiveness and Creativity Leaders should avoid getting trapped in ritualized techniques and programmed presentations. It may not be easy to approach each group with new ideas. Inventive and creative leaders are open to new experiences and to worldviews that differ from their own. One of the main advantages of group work is that it offers many opportunities for being inventive.

Portrait of Highly Effective Therapists In *Master Therapists,* Skovholt and Jennings (2004) describe their qualitative research project on the personality characteristics of 10 master therapists—those considered the "best of the best" among mental health professionals. Skovholt and Jennings's investigation yielded a portrait of highly effective therapists that includes the following dimensions:

- A drive to master, yet a sense of never arriving
- An ability to deeply enter the world of another without losing a sense of self
- The ability to provide an emotionally safe environment for clients while challenging them
- The ability to draw on their therapeutic power to help others while maintaining a sense of humility
- Integration of their personal and professional selves with clear boundaries between each dimension
- The ability to give of self to others while being able to nurture and take care of themselves
- The ability to accept feedback about themselves without becoming destabilized by this feedback

Other specific one-word characteristics associated with this portrait of the master therapist include being alive, congruent, committed, determined, intense, open, curious, tolerant, vital, reflective, self-aware, generous, mature, optimistic, analytic, fun, discerning, energetic, robust, inspiring, and passionate (pp. 133–134). Certainly, these 10 master therapists did not possess all of these traits all of the time, but this research project shed light on the personal characteristics of therapists considered outstanding by their professional colleagues, and, as well, indicated how such characteristics are manifested in a therapist's professional work.

A CONCLUDING COMMENT

As you review the characteristics of effective group leaders, consider these personal qualities on a continuum. As you examine your own courage, self-awareness, and clear sense of identity, be aware that it will be easier for you to facilitate members' self-exploration as your self-awareness increases. The challenge is for you to take an honest look at your personal qualities and make an assessment of your ability as a person to inspire others. Your own commitment to living up to your potential is a key tool. The best way to lead others is to demonstrate what you believe in through your own life. Experiencing your own therapy (either individually or in groups) is one way to remain open to looking at the direction of your life. It is certainly not a matter of being the perfectly integrated group leader who has "arrived." After all, once you have arrived, there is no place to go!

The personal dimensions described in the preceding pages are essential, but they are not sufficient for successful leadership. Specialized knowledge and skills, as identified by the Association for Specialists in Group Work in "Professional Standards for the Training of Group Workers" (ASGW, 2000) and described in Chapter 3, are central to effective group leadership. These leadership skills are examined in greater detail later in the chapter.

Special Problems and Issues for Beginning Group Leaders

Through my work in training and supervising group leaders and providing in-service workshops, I have come across a number of topics that have special relevance for beginning leaders. These issues must be faced by all group leaders regardless of their experience, but they are especially significant for those who are relatively inexperienced.

You may wonder whether you have what it takes to be an effective leader. My advice is to be patient with yourself and not to demand that you immediately become the "perfect group leader." Most practitioners I know (including myself) struggled over their competence when they began leading groups and still have difficult times. Such self-doubts are less of a problem if you are willing to continue to seek training and to work under supervision.

INITIAL ANXIETY

Before you lead your first group, you will no doubt be anxious about getting the group started and about keeping it moving. In other words, you will probably be asking yourself questions like these with a certain degree of trepidation:

- What do the participants really expect of me?
- Will I be able to get the group started? How?
- Will I run out of things to say or do before the end of the session?
- What if members of my group perceive my inexperience as incompetence?
- Should I take an active role, or should I wait for the group to start on its own?
- Should I have an agenda, or should I let the group members decide what they want to talk about?
- Do I possess the cultural competence to lead this group?
- What techniques shall I use during the early stages of the group?
- What if nobody wants to participate? And what if too many people want to participate? How will I be able to take care of those who want to get involved?
- Will the group members want to come back?

It is essential for group counselors to identify and examine their internal dialogue. Even the most effective group leaders may find themselves slipping into distorted ways of thinking and engaging in negative thinking. It is not easy to erase self-defeating thought patterns, yet it is possible to question the assumptions we make and the conclusions we form. As cognitive therapy teaches us, by being willing to continually challenge our core beliefs, we can avoid being controlled by negative internal dialogues.

Beginning leaders are encouraged to recognize that their doubts and concerns are normal. Moderate anxiety is beneficial because it can lead to honest self-appraisal. Anxiety can be counterproductive, however, if it begins to feed on itself and is allowed to freeze us into inactivity. It is a good practice for beginning leaders to voice their questions and concerns and to explore them in the course of the training sessions. Their very willingness to do this can allay some unnecessary anxiety, for the trainees discover that their peers share their concerns. Students frequently say that their peers appear to be so much more knowledgeable, skilled, talented, and self-confident than they themselves are. When they hear their peers express anxieties and feelings of inadequacy, these students realize that those who appear to be extremely self-confident are also struggling with self-doubts. Exploring their concerns with peers and a supervisor can help beginning leaders distinguish between realistic and unrealistic anxiety and thus defuse unwarranted and counterproductive anxiety.

SELF-DISCLOSURE

Regardless of their years of experience, group leaders can struggle with the problem of self-disclosure. For beginning leaders, the issue is of even greater concern. Although *what* to reveal and *when* are factors in determining the appropriateness of self-disclosure, the issue centers on *how much* to reveal. It is not uncommon to err on either extreme, disclosing too little or disclosing too much.

Too Little Self-Disclosure If you try very hard to maintain stereotyped role expectations and keep yourself mysterious by hiding behind your professional facade, you can lose your personal identity in the group and allow very little of yourself to be known. The reasons for functioning in a role (rather than as a person who has certain functions to perform) are many. One may be the fear of appearing unprofessional or of losing the respect of the members. Another may be the need to keep a distance or to maintain a "doctor–patient" relationship.

In addition to being unwilling to share your personal life, you may also be hesitant to disclose how you feel in the group or how you are affected by certain members. As a way of avoiding sharing your own reactions to what is occurring within the group, you might limit your interventions to detached observations. Such "professional" aloofness may be expressed by making interpretations and suggestions, asking questions rather than making personal statements, acting as a mere coordinator, providing one structured exercise after another to keep the group going, and clarifying issues.

In my opinion, the most productive form of sharing is disclosure that is related to what is going on in the group. For instance, if you have a persistent feeling that most members are not very motivated and are not investing themselves in the session, you are likely to feel burdened by the constant need to keep the meetings alive all by yourself, with little or no support from the participants. Disclosing how you are affected by this lack of motivation is generally very useful and appropriate.

Too Much Self-Disclosure At the other end of the continuum are the problems associated with excessive self-disclosure. Most beginning group leaders (and many experienced ones) have a strong need to be approved of and accepted by group members. It is easy to make the mistake of "paying membership dues" by sharing intimate details to prove that you are just as human as the members. There is a fine line between appropriate and inappropriate self-disclosure. It is a mistake to assume that "the more disclosure, the better." Considering the reasons for your disclosures, the readiness of the members, the impact your sharing of intimate details is likely to have on them, and the degree to which your disclosures are relevant to the here-and-now process of the group should go hand-in-hand with self-disclosure.

You may be tempted to submit to group pressure to share more of yourself. Members often say to leaders: "We don't know much about you. Why don't you say more about yourself? We talked about ourselves, and now we'd like to see you open up too!" The members can exert more subtle, but no less strong, pressures for you to "become a member" of the group you are leading. In an attempt to avoid getting lost in a professionally aloof role, you may try too hard to be perceived as a friend and a fellow group member. If you decide to share personal concerns, it should be for the benefit of your clients. The place to explore these concerns (and thus serve your own needs) is in a group in which you are a participant yourself. Group leading is demanding work, and you can make this work even more difficult by confusing your role and functions with those of the participants.

Appropriate and Facilitative Self-Disclosure Appropriate, facilitative self-disclosure is an essential aspect of the art of group leading. It is *not* necessary to disclose details of your past or of your personal life to make yourself known as a person or to empathize with the participants. A few words can convey a great deal, and nonverbal messages—a touch, a look, a gesture—can express feelings of identification and understanding. Appropriate disclosure does not take the focus away from the client and is never a contrived technique to get group members to open up. Your sensitivity to how people respond can teach you a lot about the timeliness and value of your disclosures. Timeliness is a truly critical factor: something that is inappropriate to disclose during the early stages of a group could be very useful when disclosed at a later stage. Beginning group leaders are advised to err on the side of caution rather than on the side of uninhibited and unexamined self-disclosure.

Yalom (2005) stresses that a leader's self-disclosure must be instrumental in helping the members attain their goals. He cautions against indiscriminate leader disclosures and calls for selective disclosure that provides members with acceptance, support, and encouragement. Yalom believes that group leaders who disclose here-and-now reactions rather than detailed personal events from their past tend to facilitate the movement of the group. The main rationale for the group leader's personal disclosures is the assumption that such sharing will facilitate the work of the group. At times, a group therapist's self-disclosure involves communicating his or her observations and personal reactions to an individual member or to what is happening in the group at a given point in time. When done in a sensitive and caring manner, this can be a powerful way to model giving interpersonal feedback in the group, and it can have a therapeutic impact.

Hill and Knox (2002) emphasize that it is critical that therapists understand how their disclosures are affecting their clients and that they use self-disclosures appropriately. Based on a review of the empirical evidence about the effectiveness of therapist self-disclosure, Hill and Knox present the following guidelines for using disclosure in practice:

- It is well for therapists to disclosure infrequently.
- Therapists might consider disclosing for the purpose of normalizing experiences, modeling, strengthening the therapeutic alliance, validating reality, or offering alternative ways to think or act.
- Therapists should avoid self-disclosure that is used to meet their own needs, takes the focus off the client's experiencing, interferes with the flow of the session, burdens the client, blurs the boundaries in the relationship, or contaminates the transference.
- It is important for therapists to observe how clients react to the disclosures, to ask clients how they react to sharing personal material, and to decide how to intervene next.
- Different clients react differently to therapist disclosure, so it is important to determine what clients need from the therapist.

THE CHALLENGES OF DEALING WITH A SYSTEM

Most of the groups you lead will be under the auspices of some type of institution—a school system, a community mental health organization, a state mental hospital, a clinic, or a local or state rehabilitation agency. When conducting groups in an institutional setting, one quickly discovers that mastering group leadership theory and practice doesn't guarantee successful groups. Being able to deal effectively with institutional demands and policies may at times be as important as being professionally competent.

A common problem among those who regularly do group work in an institutional setting is the constant struggle to retain dignity and integrity in a system in which administrators are more concerned with cost cutting and less with the pursuit of genuine group therapy or counseling. Another common problem besetting counselors in an institution relates to demands that they function as leaders of groups that they are unequipped or ill-equipped to handle. This problem is intensified by the fact that few institutions provide the training group leaders need.

These problems exist, and it is up to you to deal with them and to work within the system while, at the same time, maintaining your professional standards and integrity. Ultimately, the responsibility for conducting successful groups is yours. It does not help to blame external factors for failures in your group counseling programs. I know from personal experience how taxing and draining any battle with a bureaucracy can be. There are times when the hassle of merely trying to get a group started is overwhelming to the point of questioning whether the effort is worth it. My point is that whatever the external obstacles, it is our responsibility to face them and not allow them to render us powerless. It is important that we learn how to advocate for ourselves within a system.

Professional impotency of any kind is a condition that feeds on itself. When counselors abdicate their own power, they assume the role of victims, or they develop the cynical attitude that all their proposals and efforts are doomed—that nothing they do matters or makes any difference. When we surrender our power by placing all the responsibility for the failure of our programs outside of ourselves, we are in jeopardy of having our work devitalize us when it should be having the opposite effect.

Group Leadership Skills

It is a mistake to assume that anyone with certain personal qualities and a desire to help will be an effective group leader. Successful leadership requires specific group leadership skills and the appropriate performance of certain functions. Like most skills, leadership skills need to be learned and practiced. Think about your own skill level as you read about these essential group leadership skills.

Active Listening Active listening involves paying total attention to the speaker and being sensitive to what is being communicated at both the verbal and nonverbal levels. Your ability to hear what is being communicated improves as your expertise improves. Many leaders make the mistake of focusing too intently on the content and, in doing so, don't pay enough attention to the way in which group members express themselves. Being a skilled group leader entails picking up the subtle cues provided by members through their style of speech, body posture, gestures, voice quality, and mannerisms. Not only do group leaders need to listen well to members, it is important that leaders teach members how to listen actively to one another. (Active listening is dealt with in greater detail in Chapter 10; attending and listening are key concepts of the person-centered approach to group work.)

Restating In a sense, restating (or paraphrasing) is an extension of listening. It means recasting what someone said into different words so that the meaning is clearer to both the speaker and the group. Effective restating zeroes in on the core of a person's message, bringing it into sharper focus and eliminating ambiguity. By capturing the essence of a member's message and reflecting it back, the leader helps the person continue the self-exploration process at a deeper level.

Restating is not an easy skill to master. Some group leaders, for example, confine themselves to simply repeating what was said, adding little new meaning and not really clarifying the message. Others overuse the technique and sound mechanical and repetitive. The value of accurate and concise restating is twofold: it tells the participants that they are being listened to, and it helps them see more clearly the issues they are struggling with and their own feelings and thoughts about these issues. (This skill is explored in detail in Chapter 10.)

Clarifying Clarifying, too, is an extension of active listening. It involves responding to confusing and unclear aspects of a message by focusing on underlying issues and helping the person sort out conflicting feelings. Members often say that they have ambivalent feelings or are feeling many things at once; clarification can help sort out these feelings so that members can focus more sharply on what they are actually experiencing. The same procedure applies to thinking. In clarifying, the group leader stays within the individual's frame of reference while at the same time helping the group member put things into perspective; this, in turn, may lead to a deeper level of self-exploration on the part of the member. (This skill is explored in detail in Chapter 10.)

Summarizing The skill of pulling together the important elements of a group interaction or part of a session is known as summarizing. This ability is particularly useful when making a transition from one topic to another. Rather than merely proceeding from issue to issue, identifying common elements can increase learning and maintain continuity.

Summarizing is especially needed at the end of a session. It is a mistake for a group leader to end a session abruptly, with little attempt to pull the session together. One of the leader's functions is to help members reflect on and make sense of what has occurred in their group. Summarizing encourages participants to think about what they have learned and experienced in a session and about ways of applying it to their everyday lives. At the end of the session, group leaders may offer their own brief summary or ask each member in turn to summarize what has taken place, what the highlights of the session were, and how each member responded to the interaction.

Questioning Questioning is probably the technique that inexperienced group leaders tend to overuse most. Asking members question after question can have a negative impact on the group interaction. There are several problems with the ineffective use of questioning. Members feel as if they have been subjected to the "third degree." The questioner probes for personal information while remaining safe and anonymous behind the interrogation. Also, a low-level questioning style on the leader's part provides a poor model for the members, who soon begin to imitate the leader's ineffective questioning style when they deal with one another.

Not all questioning is inappropriate, but closed questions—those that require a mere "yes" or "no" response—are generally not helpful. "Why" questions usually lead to intellectual ruminating or put members on the defensive, neither of which is helpful. Instead, use open-ended questions that elicit alternatives and new areas of self-investigation. These questions can be of real value. For example, "What are you experiencing right now?" "What is happening with you at this moment?" and "How are you dealing with your fear in this group?" are questions that can help participants become more focused and feel their emotions more deeply. It is important that leaders ask questions that explore issues in greater depth.

Group leaders need to develop skills in raising questions at the group level as well as asking individual members questions. Examples of group process questions that can be productively addressed to the group as a whole include the following: "How are others being affected by Simone's work right now?" "Where is the group with this topic now?" "I'm noticing that many of you are silent. I wonder what is not being said." "How much energy is in the group at this time?" Questions at the group level can assist members in reflecting on what is happening in the group at different points. (The topic of questioning is dealt with in greater detail in Chapters 15 and 16 as special procedures used in reality therapy and solution-focused brief therapy.)

Interpreting The leader interprets when he or she offers possible explanations for a participant's thoughts, feelings, or behavior. By offering tentative hypotheses concerning certain patterns of behavior, interpreting helps the individual see new perspectives and alternatives. Interpreting requires a great deal of skill. Interpreting too soon, presenting an interpretation in a dogmatic way, or encouraging the members to become dependent on the leader to provide meanings and answers are common mistakes. One way of interpreting is for leaders to share their hunches with members, asking them to reflect on how accurate these hunches are. It is best to offer interpretations after a leader has had enough experience with members so that these interpretations are based on knowledge gathered about the members. Timing is especially important. Interpretations not only have to be made at a time when the person is likely to be willing to consider them, but also need to be expressed in a tentative way that gives the person a chance to assess their validity. Although an interpretation may be technically correct, it may be rejected if the leader is not sensitive to the client's willingness or unwillingness to accept it.

In addition to making interpretations for individuals, group leaders need to be skilled at making whole-group interpretations. An example of this is a leader pointing out how many members may be invested in attempting to draw a particular member out. At times, a group may be characterized by members who probe others for information. A leader could interpret such behavior as an avoidance pattern on the part of the group as a whole. (We return to the topic of interpreting in Chapters 6, 7, and 11.)

Confronting Confrontation can be a powerful way of challenging members to take an honest look at themselves. However, when handled poorly, confrontation also has the potential of being detrimental both to the person being confronted and to the group process. Many leaders shy away from confrontation because they fear its possible repercussions: blocking the group interaction, hurting someone, or becoming the target of retaliation. Confrontation can easily be seen as an uncaring attack. Skilled group counselors confront behavior inconsistencies in a way that gives the person ample opportunity to consider what is being said. Skillful confrontation specifies the behavior or the discrepancies between verbal and nonverbal messages that are being challenged so that no labeling can possibly occur.

As is true of most of these skills, confronting is a skill leaders need to learn in challenging individual members and the group as a whole. For example, if the group seems to be low in energy and characterized by superficial discussions, the leader might challenge the members to assess what they see going on in their group and determine whether they want to change what they notice about their functioning as a group. (Confrontation is discussed in more detail in Chapters 5, 11, 14, and 15.)

Reflecting Feelings Reflecting feelings is the skill of responding to the essence of what a person has communicated. The purpose is to let members know that they are being heard and understood. Although reflection entails mirroring certain feelings that the person has expressed, it is not merely a bouncing-back process. Reflection is dependent on attention, interest, understanding, and respect for the person. When reflection is done well, it fosters further contact and involvement; feeling understood and achieving a clearer grasp of one's feelings are very reinforcing and stimulate the person to seek greater self-awareness. (This skill is explored in detail in Chapter 10.)

Supporting Supporting means providing group members with encouragement and reinforcement, especially when they are disclosing personal information, exploring painful feelings, or taking risks. A leader can provide support by being fully present at the appropriate time. This full presence requires a combination of skills: listening actively to what is being said and what is being conveyed nonverbally, being psychologically present with the client, and responding in a way that encourages the client to continue working and to move forward.

The essence of this skill is in knowing when it will be facilitative and when it will be counterproductive. Some group leaders make the mistake of being overly supportive, or of supporting too soon. If leaders limit themselves to a style that is almost exclusively supportive, they deprive the members of potentially valuable challenges. Leaders who offer support too quickly when someone is exploring painful material tend to defuse the intensity of the experience and pull group members away from their feelings. (We return to this topic in Chapter 10.)

Empathizing The core of the skill of empathy lies in the leader's ability to sensitively grasp the subjective world of the participant and yet retain his or her own separateness. To empathize effectively, a leader needs to care for the group members. One form of empathizing is for leaders to demonstrate cultural empathy, which is the ability to assume the worldview of others (Comas-Diaz, 2011). A background that includes a wide range of experiences can help the leader identify with others. (Empathy, too, is discussed in more detail in Chapter 10.)

Facilitating Facilitating is aimed at enhancing the group experience and enabling the members to reach their goals. Facilitation skills involve opening up clear and direct communication among the participants and helping them assume increasing responsibility for the direction of the group. Facilitating is a vital tool in the person-centered approach, and it will be explored in more depth in Chapter 10.

Initiating Good initiating skills on the leader's part keep the group from floundering. These skills include using catalysts to get members to focus on meaningful work, knowing how to employ various techniques that promote deeper self-exploration, and providing links for various themes being explored in the group. Whereas appropriate leader direction can give the group a focus and keep it moving, too much direction can lead to passivity on the part of members. Initiating is a key skill in structuring a group session and in working with the group as a whole.

Setting Goals Productive goal setting is at the core of group counseling. Note that group leaders do not set goals for members; they help group members select and clarify their own specific goals. Although goal setting is especially important during the initial stages of a group, throughout the group's life leaders need to encourage participants to take another look at their goals, to modify them if necessary, and to determine how effectively they are accomplishing them. Leaders who don't develop the intervention skills of challenging members to formulate concrete goals often find that their groups are characterized by aimless and unproductive sessions. (This topic is dealt with in most of the theory chapters, but especially in Chapters 13 and 15.)

Evaluating Evaluating is an ongoing process that continues for the duration of a group. After each session, the leader assesses what is happening in the group as a whole and within individual members. Leaders teach participants how to evaluate themselves and how to appraise the movement and direction of their group. For example, if at the end of a session most participants agree that the session was superficial, they can be challenged to find the reasons for the unsatisfactory outcome and to decide what they are willing to do to change the situation. Members also need to be taught how to evaluate what they have learned at the end of their group experience. (This topic is also explored in more depth in Chapters 13 and 15.)

Giving Feedback A skilled group leader gives specific and honest feedback based on his or her observation of and reaction to the members' behaviors and encourages the members to give feedback to one another. One of the great advantages of groups is that participants can tell each other their reactions to what they observe. The purpose of feedback is to provide a realistic assessment of how a person appears to others. The skill involved in productive feedback relates to the ability to present the feedback so that it is acceptable and worthy of serious consideration. Feedback that is specific and descriptive rather than global and judgmental is the most helpful. (This skill is explored in detail in Chapter 5.)

Suggesting Suggestion is a form of intervention designed to help participants develop an alternative course of thinking or action. It can take many forms, a few of which are giving information and advice, giving "homework assignments," asking members to think of experiments they might try inside and outside of the group, and encouraging members to look at a situation from a different perspective. Giving information and providing appropriate suggestions for alternative plans of action can hasten the progress members make in a group. Suggestions need not always come from the leader; members can make suggestions for others to consider, especially at a later stage of the group.

The overuse of persuasion, suggestions, and advice entails some dangers. One is that members can be led to believe that simple solutions exist for complex problems. Another is that members may remain dependent on other people to suggest what they should do in the face of future problems instead of learning how to solve their own problems. There is a fine line between suggesting and prescribing, and the skill consists in using suggestions to enhance an individual's movement toward independence.

Protecting Without assuming a parental attitude toward the group, leaders need to be able to safeguard members from unnecessary psychological or physical risks associated with being in a group. Although the very fact of participating in a group does entail certain risks, leaders can step in when they sense that psychological harm may result from a series of group interactions. For example, intervention is called for when a member is being treated unfairly or when an avalanche of feelings from the group is directed toward one person.

Disclosing Oneself When leaders reveal personal information, they usually have an impact on the group. The skill consists of knowing what, when, how, and how much to reveal. If the leader shares appropriately, the effects on the group are likely to be positive. If the leader shares too much too soon, the effects are likely to be adverse because the members may not be able yet to handle such disclosure. The most productive disclosure is related to what is taking place within the group. (Self-disclosure is more fully addressed in Chapter 5.)

Modeling Group members learn by observing the leader's behavior. If leaders value honesty, respect, openness, risk taking, and assertiveness, they can foster these qualities in the members by demonstrating them in the group. From a leader who shows respect by really listening and empathizing, members learn a direct and powerful lesson in how respect is shown behaviorally. In short, one of the best ways to teach more effective skills of interpersonal relating is by direct example. Leaders can also teach members how to model for one another. (Modeling is discussed more fully in Chapter 13.)

Linking One way of promoting interaction among the members is to look for themes that emerge in a group and then to connect the work that members do to these themes. This is a most important skill to teach in a group and to foster involvement on the part of many members. Group leaders with an interactional bias—that is, those who develop the norm of member-to-member rather than leader-to-member communication—rely a great deal on linking. They encourage members to address others in the group directly rather than looking at the leader and talking about others who are present. Members often have shared concerns, and through effective linking they can be helped to work through their problems. By being alert for common concerns, the leader can promote interaction and increase the level of group cohesion. Through linking several members together, the leader is also teaching members how to take responsibility for involving themselves in the work of others. When members learn how to bring themselves into group interactions, they become more independent of the leader and are also likely to feel a greater sense of belongingness by being connected to others.

Blocking Sometimes a leader must intervene to stop counterproductive behaviors within the group. Blocking is a skill that requires sensitivity, directness, and the ability to stop the activity without attacking the person. The attention should be on the specific behavior and not on the character of the person, and labeling should be avoided. For example, if a member is invading another member's privacy by asking probing and highly personal questions, the leader will point to this behavior as being unhelpful, without referring to the person as a "peeping tom" or an "interrogator." When members judge or criticize others, pressure others to take a specific course of action or to express feelings in a group, or habitually ask questions of others, the group leader may need to block this behavior. Other behaviors that group leaders need to watch for and block when necessary include making excuses to justify failure to make changes, breaking confidences, invading a member's privacy, perpetually giving advice, storytelling, gossiping, offering support inappropriately, and making inaccurate or inappropriate interpretations. Whatever the behavior, blocking must be carried out firmly, but sensitively.

Terminating Group leaders need to learn when and how to terminate their work with individuals as well as groups. The skills required in closing a group session or ending a group successfully include providing members with suggestions for applying what they've learned in the group to their daily lives, preparing the participants to deal with the problems they may encounter outside of the group, providing for some type of evaluation and follow-up, suggesting sources of further help, and being available for individual consultation should the need arise. (This topic is explored in detail in Chapter 5.)

DON'T OVERWHELM YOURSELF!

It is not unusual for beginning group counselors to feel somewhat overwhelmed when they consider all these skills. My hope is that you will be patient with yourself and not expect mastery all at once. By systematically learning certain principles and practicing certain skills, you can expect to gradually refine your leadership style and gain the confidence you need to use these skills effectively. Participating in a group as a member is the optimal way of developing these skills, for you can learn a lot by observing experienced people. Of course, you also need to practice these skills by leading groups under supervision. Feedback from group members, your coleader, and your supervisor is essential to the refinement of your leadership skills. Seeing yourself in action on videotape can be a great source of feedback to help you identify the specific areas you most need to strengthen.

Like all skills, group leadership skills exist in degrees, not on an all-or-nothing basis. They may be developed only minimally, or they may be highly refined and used appropriately. Through training and supervised experience, you can continue to improve your leadership skills. The *Student Manual for Theory and Practice of Group Counseling* (Corey, 2012) has a checklist and self-evaluation of the 22 skills discussed here. This inventory is useful for rating yourself on your leadership skills and can be used in rating your coleader. Of course, your coleader can rate you on each of the skills, too. This instrument can provide topics for you and your coleader to discuss in your meetings.

Table 2.1 presents an overview of the group leadership skills discussed in the preceding pages.

TABLE 2.1 OVERVIEW OF GROUP LEADERSHIP SKILLS

SKILL	DESCRIPTION	AIMS AND DESIRED OUTCOMES
ACTIVE LISTENING	Attending to verbal and nonverbal aspects of communication without judging or evaluating	To encourage trust and client self-disclosure and exploration
RESTATING	Paraphrasing what a participant has said to clarify its meaning	To determine if the leader has understood correctly the client's statement; to provide support and clarification
CLARIFYING	Grasping the essence of a message at both the feeling and thinking levels; simplifying client statements by focusing on the core of the message	To help clients sort out conflicting and confused feelings and thoughts; to arrive at a meaningful understanding of what is being communicated
SUMMARIZING	Pulling together the important elements of an interaction or session	To avoid fragmentation and give direction to a session; to provide for continuity and meaning
QUESTIONING	Asking open-ended questions that lead to self-exploration of the "what" and "how" of behavior	To elicit further discussion; to get information; to stimulate thinking; to increase clarity and focus; to provide for further self-exploration

(contd.)

TABLE 2.1 (contd.)

SKILL	DESCRIPTION	AIMS AND DESIRED OUTCOMES
INTERPRETING	Offering possible explanations for certain thoughts, feelings, and behaviors	To encourage deeper self-exploration; to promote full use of potentials; to bring about awareness of self-contradictions
CONFRONTING	Challenging members to look at discrepancies between their words and actions or their bodily and verbal messages; pointing to conflicting information or messages	To encourage honest self-investigation; to promote full use of potentials; to bring about awareness of self-contradictions
REFLECTING FEELINGS	Communicating understanding of the content of feelings	To let members know that they are being heard and understood beyond the level of words
SUPPORTING	Providing encouragement and reinforcement	To create an atmosphere that encourages members to continue desired behaviors; to provide help when clients are facing difficult struggles; to create trust
EMPATHIZING	Identifying with clients by assuming their frames of reference	To foster trust in the therapeutic relationship; to communicate understanding; to encourage deeper levels of self-exploration
FACILITATING	Opening up clear and direct communication within the group; helping members assume increasing responsibility for the group's direction	To promote effective communication among members; to help members reach their own goals in the group
INITIATING	Promoting participation and introducing new directions in the group	To prevent needless group floundering; to increase the pace of the group process
SETTING GOALS	Planning specific goals for the group process and helping participants define concrete and meaningful goals	To give direction to the group's activities; to help members select and clarify their goals
EVALUATING	Appraising the ongoing group process and the individual and group dynamics	To promote better self-awareness and understanding of group movement and direction
GIVING FEEDBACK	Expression of concrete and honest reactions based on observation of members' behaviors	To offer an external view of how the person appears to others; to increase the client's self-awareness
SUGGESTING	Offering advice and information, direction, and ideas for new behavior	To help members develop alternative courses of thinking and action
PROTECTING	Safeguarding members from unnecessary psychological risks in the group	To warn members of possible risks in group participation; to reduce these risks
DISCLOSING ONESELF	Revealing one's reactions to here-and-now events in the group	To facilitate deeper levels of group interaction; to create trust; to model ways of revealing oneself to others
MODELING	Demonstrating desired behavior through actions	To provide examples of desirable behavior; to inspire members to fully develop their potential

LINKING	Connecting the work that members do to common themes in the group	To promote member-to-member interactions; to encourage the development of cohesion
BLOCKING	Intervening to stop counterproductive group behavior	To protect members; to enhance the flow of group process
TERMINATING	Preparing the group to close a session or end its existence	To help members assimilate, integrate, and apply in-group learning to everyday life

Source: The format of this chart is based on Edwin J. Nolan, "Leadership Interventions for Promoting Personal Mastery," *Journal for Specialists in Group Work*, 1978, 3(3), 132–138.

Special Skills for Opening and Closing Group Sessions

Opening a group session effectively sets the tone for the rest of the session. Unfortunately, many leaders lack the skills necessary to effectively open or close a group session. For example, some leaders simply select one member and focus on that person while the other group members wait their turn. When a group session begins poorly, it may be difficult to accomplish any sustained work during the rest of the meeting.

The way each session is closed is as important as the way it is initiated. I have observed group leaders who simply allowed the time to elapse and then abruptly announced, "Our time is up; we'll see you all next week." Because of the leader's failure to summarize and offer some evaluation of the session, much of the potential value of the meeting was lost. Effectively opening and closing each session ensures continuity from meeting to meeting. Continuity makes it more likely that participants will think about what occurred in the group when they are outside of it, and they will be more likely to try to apply what they have learned to their everyday lives. Together with encouragement and direction from the leader, effective summarizing and evaluation facilitate the members' task of assessing their own level of participation at each session.

PROCEDURES FOR OPENING A GROUP SESSION

With groups that meet on a weekly or regular basis, group leaders have a variety of options for opening the session.

1. Participants can be asked to briefly state what they want to get from the session. My preference is for a quick "go-around" in which each group member identifies issues or concerns that could be explored during the session. Before focusing on one person, it is good to give all members a chance to at least say what they want to bring up during the meeting. In this way a tentative agenda can be developed, and if a number of people are concerned with similar themes, the agenda can incorporate the involvement of several members.

2. Members can be given a chance to express any thoughts they may have had about the previous session or to bring up for consideration any unresolved issues from an earlier meeting. Unresolved issues among members themselves or between members and the leader can make progressing with the current agenda most difficult. The hidden agenda will interfere with productive work until it has surfaced and been dealt with effectively.

3. Participants can be asked to report on the progress or difficulties they experienced during the week. Ideally, they have been experimenting with other ways of behaving outside of the group, they are getting involved in carrying out "homework assignments," and they are working on concrete, action-oriented plans. If these desirable activities have not yet taken place, time can be profitably used at the beginning of a session to share successes or to bring up specific problems.

4. In an open group (one where membership changes somewhat from week to week), it is a good idea to encourage those members who have been part of the group for a while to share with newcomers what the group has meant to them. Those who are just joining the group can say something about what they hope to get from the experience and perhaps share any of their anxieties pertaining to coming to the group.

5. In addition to facilitating member involvement in opening a session, group leaders may want to make some observations about the previous meeting or relate some thoughts that have occurred to them since the group last met.

One way to open a group session is through the use of a structured exercise that assists members in identifying the concerns they want to explore. Depending on how, when, and why they are used, structured exercises can enhance interaction and provide a focus for work, or they can promote member dependence on the leader for continuing to provide direction. In their eagerness to get a group moving and keep it moving, some leaders rely too much on exercises and structured activities. Exercises that relate to the overall plan of the group and are appropriately applied in a timely manner can be useful tools for promoting change. However, lacking proper application, such exercises can be counterproductive to the group process and to an individual's growth.

Structured exercises can be very useful during the initial and the final stages of a group or as a way to open a meeting. At the beginning of a group, it may help to use certain exercises designed to assist members in clarifying their personal goals, in dealing with their expectations and fears, and in building trust. These exercises could consist of asking members to work in pairs on some selected topic—for example, what they hope to get from a group session.

PROCEDURES FOR CLOSING A GROUP SESSION

Before closing a session, it is essential to allow time for integrating what has occurred, for reflecting on what has been experienced, for talking about what the participants may do between now and the next session, and for summarizing. The leader may also find it useful to check with the group around the midpoint of the session and say something like this: "I'm aware that we still have an hour left before we close today. I want to see if there are any matters you want to bring up before we close"; or this: "I'd like each of you to give me an idea of how you feel about this session. So far, have you gotten what you wanted from it?" Although these assessments in the middle of a session don't have to be made routinely, doing so from time to time can encourage members to evaluate their progress. If members are not satisfied with either their own participation or what is going on in the session, there is still time to change the course of the group before it ends.

Generally, members do not automatically evaluate the degree of their investment in the group or the extent of the gains they have made. The leader can do a great deal to guide participants into reflecting on the time limitations of their group and on whether they are satisfied with their participation. Members also need guidance in appraising how fully their goals are being achieved and how effectively the group is operating. If this periodic appraisal is done well, members have a chance to formulate plans for changes in the group's direction before it is too late. Consequently, it is less likely they will leave the group feeling that they didn't get what they had hoped for when they joined.

In sum, the leader's closing skills bring unity to the group experience and consolidate the learning that has occurred during a session. Here are some steps group leaders can take toward the end of each weekly session to help members evaluate their participation and bridge the gap between the group and their daily existence.

1. Group leaders should strive to close the session without closing the issues raised during the session. It may not be therapeutic to wrap up a concern or solve a problem too quickly. Many leaders make the mistake of forcing resolution of problems prematurely. Being task-oriented, they feel uncomfortable allowing members the time they need to explore and struggle with personal problems. In such instances, the leader's intervention has the effect of resolving quite superficially what may be complex matters that need to be fully explored. It is good for people to leave a session with unanswered questions, as this can motivate them to think more about their concerns and to come up with some tentative solutions on their own. Leaders need to learn the delicate balance between bringing temporary closure to a topic at the end of a session and closing the exploration of an area of personal concern completely.

2. Summarizing can be effective at the end of each session. It is helpful to ask members to summarize both the group process and their own progress toward their goals. Comments can be made about common themes and issues that have emerged. The group leader can add summary comments, especially as they pertain to group process, but it is even better to teach members how to integrate what they have learned for themselves.

3. Participants can be asked to tell the group how they perceived the session, to offer comments and feedback to other members, and to make a statement about their level of investment in the session. By doing this regularly, members share in the responsibility of deciding what they will do to change the group's direction if they are not satisfied with it.

4. It is helpful to focus on positive feedback, too. Individuals who get involved should be recognized and supported for their efforts by both the leader and other participants.

5. Members can report on their homework assignments, in which they tried to put into practice some of their new insights, and they can make plans for applying what they have learned to problem situations outside the group.

6. Participants can be asked whether there are any topics or problems they would like to put on the agenda for the next session. Doing this can add to a sense of ownership and responsibility for and to the group and to the members' own change process. Besides linking sessions, asking members to participate in setting an agenda prompts them to think about ways of exploring these concerns in the next meeting—that is, to work between sessions.

7. Group leaders may want to express their own reactions to the session and make some observations. These reactions and comments about the direction of the group can be very useful in stimulating thought and action on the part of the members.

8. In a group with changing membership, it is good to remind members a week before that certain members will be leaving the group. Those who are terminating need to talk about what they have gotten from the group and what it is like for them to be leaving. Other members will most likely want to give feedback to the terminating member.

In summary, the leader interventions I have described illustrate that careful attention to opening and closing group sessions facilitates learning. It has the effect of challenging members to recognize their role in determining the direction a group is moving as well as determining the outcomes of the group.

Becoming a Diversity-Competent Group Counselor

Special knowledge and skills are required for dealing with culturally diverse groups. If you are open to the values inherent in a diversity perspective, you will find ways to avoid getting trapped in provincialism, and you will be able to challenge the degree to which you may be culturally encapsulated (Wrenn, 1985). Take an inventory of your current level of awareness, knowledge, and skills that have a bearing on your ability to function effectively in multicultural situations by reflecting on these questions:

• Are you aware of how your own culture influences the way you think, feel, and act?

• What could you do to broaden your understanding of both your own culture and other cultures?

• Are you able to identify your basic assumptions, especially as they apply to diversity in culture, ethnicity, race, gender, class, religion, language, and sexual identity?

• How are your assumptions likely to affect the manner in which you function as a group counselor?

• Can you be flexible in applying the techniques you use in your groups, depending on the specific makeup of the membership?

- How prepared are you to understand and work with individuals from different cultural backgrounds in a group?
- Is your academic program preparing you to work with diverse client populations in different kinds of groups?
- What life experiences have you had that will help you to understand and make contact with group members who have a different worldview from yours?
- Can you identify any areas of cultural bias or any of your assumptions that could inhibit your ability to work effectively with people who are different from you? If so, what steps might you take to challenge your biases and assumptions?

Cultural competence refers to the knowledge and skills required to work effectively in any cross-cultural encounter (Comas-Diaz, 2011). However, knowledge and skills alone are not enough for effective group work. Becoming a diversity-competent group counselor demands self-awareness and an open stance on your part. You need to be willing to modify strategies to fit the needs and situations of the individuals within your group. It is clear that no one "right" technique can be utilized with all group members, irrespective of their cultural background. It is important to realize that it takes time, study, and experience to become an effective multicultural group counselor. Acquiring multicultural competence is an ongoing process.

Developing cultural competence enables practitioners to appreciate and manage diverse worldviews (Comas-Diaz, 2011). It is your responsibility as a group counselor to have a general understanding of your members' cultural values. For example, an Afrocentric approach to group counseling involves understanding the worldview, set of social standards, and ethical values that reflect African American culture. Understanding the values associated with the spiritual and communal nature of African American people is basic to effective group work with African Americans, and this perspective may be helpful with many other cultural groups as well (Pack-Brown, Whittington-Clark, & Parker, 1998). Effective multicultural practice in group work with diverse populations requires cultural awareness and sensitivity, a body of knowledge, and a specific set of skills.

D. W. Sue, Arredondo, and McDavis (1992) and Arredondo and her colleagues (1996) have developed a conceptual framework for multicultural counseling competencies in three areas: (1) awareness of beliefs and attitudes, (2) knowledge, and (3) skills. What follows is a modified and brief version of the multicultural competencies identified by D. W. Sue and Sue (2008), Sue and his colleagues (1992, 1998), Arredondo and her colleagues (1996), and the ASGW's (1999) "Principles for Diversity Competent Group Workers."

Beliefs and Attitudes Diversity-competent group leaders recognize and understand their own values, biases, ethnocentric attitudes, and assumptions about human behavior. They do not allow their personal values or problems to interfere with their work with clients who are culturally different from them. They are aware of their negative and positive emotional reactions toward other racial and ethnic groups that may prove detrimental to establishing collaborative relationships within the group. They seek to understand the world from the vantage point of their clients. Rather than maintaining that their cultural heritage is superior, they are able to accept and value cultural diversity.

They welcome diverse value orientations and diverse assumptions about human behavior, and thus, they have a basis for sharing the worldview of their clients as opposed to being culturally encapsulated. They respect clients' religious and spiritual beliefs and values and are comfortable with differences between themselves and others in gender, race, ethnicity, culture, sexual orientation, abilities, age, and beliefs. They value bilingualism and do not view another language as an impediment to counseling.

Effective multicultural group workers monitor their functioning through consultation, supervision, and continuing education. They realize that group counseling may not be appropriate for all clients or for all problems. If necessary, they are willing to refer a client if it becomes evident that group counseling is not an appropriate form of treatment for the client or if, for example, a more homogeneous support group seems warranted.

Knowledge Diversity-competent group practitioners understand their own racial and cultural heritage and know how it affects them personally and professionally. Because they understand the dynamics of oppression, racism, discrimination, and stereotyping, they are aware of the institutional barriers that prevent minorities from accessing the mental health services available in their community. They acknowledge their own biases and prejudices. They do not impose their values and expectations on their clients from differing cultural backgrounds, and they avoid stereotyping clients. They strive to understand the worldview of their clients. They possess knowledge about the historical background, traditions, and values of the groups with whom they are working. They have knowledge of minority family structures, hierarchies, values, and beliefs. They are knowledgeable about communication style differences and how their style may clash with or foster the group process. Because they understand the basic values underlying the therapeutic group process, they know how these values may differ from the cultural and family values of various minority groups. Furthermore, these practitioners are knowledgeable about community characteristics and resources. They know how to help clients make use of indigenous support systems. In areas where they are lacking in knowledge, they seek resources to assist them. The greater their depth and breadth of knowledge of culturally diverse groups, the more likely they are to be effective group workers.

Skills and Intervention Strategies Effective group counselors have acquired certain skills in working with culturally diverse populations. Multicultural counseling is enhanced when practitioners use methods and strategies and define goals that are consistent with the life experiences and cultural values of their clients. Such practitioners modify and adapt their interventions in a group to accommodate cultural differences. They are able to exercise institutional intervention skills on behalf of their clients. They become actively involved with minority individuals outside of the group setting (community events, celebrations, and neighborhood groups) as this is called for and to the extent possible. They are not limited to one approach in helping and recognize that helping strategies may be culture-bound. They do not force their clients to fit within one counseling approach. They are able to send and receive both verbal and nonverbal messages accurately and appropriately. They are willing to seek out educational, consultative, and training experiences to enhance their ability to work with diverse client populations. They consult regularly with other professionals regarding matters of culture to determine whether or where referral may be necessary. Diversity-competent group counselors take responsibility in educating the members of their groups about the way the group process works, including matters such as goals, expectations, legal rights, and alternative resources for continued growth.

Recognize Your Limitations Although it is unrealistic to expect that you will have an in-depth knowledge of all cultural backgrounds, it is feasible for you to have a comprehensive grasp of general principles for working successfully amid cultural diversity. You do yourself an injustice if you overwhelm yourself with all that you do not know or if you feel guilty over your limitations or parochial views. You will not become more effective by expecting that you must be completely knowledgeable about the cultural backgrounds of all the members of your groups, by thinking that you should have a complete repertoire of skills, or by demanding perfection as a multicultural group worker. Instead, recognize and appreciate your efforts toward becoming a more effective person and professional. The first step is to become more comfortable in accepting diversity as a positive value and in taking actions to increase your ability to work with a range of clients. In developing models for counseling culturally diverse clients, Vontress (1996) emphasizes that we need to recognize simultaneously the commonalities and the differences of human beings. He writes, "Cross-cultural counseling, in short, does not intend to teach specific interventions for each culture, but to infuse the counselor with a cultural sensitivity and tolerant philosophical outlook that will befit all cultures" (p. 161).

Ivey, Pedersen, and Ivey (2008) write about the notion of multicultural intentionality, or the ability of a group leader to work effectively with many types of individuals with diverse cultural backgrounds. To the key components of awareness, knowledge, and skills, they add the characteristics of humility, confidence, and recovery skills as critical to becoming a diversity-competent group counselor. These attributes mean that group counselors do not have to possess all the answers, that they can learn from their mistakes, and that they can develop confidence in their ability to become flexible with challenging situations. The ability to recover from mistakes gracefully is more important than not making any mistakes.

The ability to express empathy on both cognitive and affective levels is an important skill for all counseling professionals, but to practice competently and effectively with diverse group members, it is also essential to strive for **cultural empathy**—the ability to place yourself in the other's culture (Comas-Diaz, 2011). You can develop cultural empathy by engaging in self-reflection, exploring your own worldview, challenging ethnocentrism, developing openness toward cultural differences, and recognizing power dynamics. If you truly respect the members in your group, you will patiently attempt to enter their world as much as possible. It is not necessary that you have the same experiences as your clients, but it is important that you attempt to be open to a similar set of feelings and struggles. If this kind of cultural empathy exists, all of the members will benefit from the cultural diversity within the group.

Group members can inform and teach you and other group members about relevant aspects of their culture. It is a good practice to ask members to provide you and the others in the group with the information they will need to effectively interact with them. It is helpful to assess a client's degree of acculturation and identity development. This is especially true for individuals who have the experience of living in several cultures. Although they often have allegiance to their own home culture, they may also find certain characteristics of their new culture attractive and experience conflicts in integrating the two cultures. These core struggles can be productively explored in a group context if you and the other members respect this cultural conflict.

As you study the contemporary theories and apply them to group counseling, strive to think about the cultural implications of the techniques that grow out of them. Consider which techniques may be more appropriate with specific client populations and in specific contexts. Even more important, think about ways to adapt the techniques you will be learning to a group member's cultural background. Perhaps most important of all, consider how you might acquire the personal characteristics required to become a diversity-competent group counselor.

If your groups are composed of individuals from a variety of ethnic and cultural backgrounds that differ from your own, you can benefit from reading articles that address diversity perspectives. I recommend the following sources for educating yourself about issues of multicultural competence: Atkinson (2004); Atkinson and Hackett (2004); Pedersen (1997, 2000); D. W. Sue and D. Sue (2008); Sue, Ivey, and Pedersen (1996); and D. W. Sue and his colleagues (1998).

In the *Student Manual for Theory and Practice of Group Counseling* (Corey, 2012) you will find a checklist for becoming a diversity-competent group counselor. Use this checklist to assess your current level of skill development in the multicultural competencies. The ASGW's (1999) "Principles for Diversity Competent Group Workers" can be retrieved online at www.asgw.org/diversity.htm. I recommend that you download this document and take some time to think about how these principles might apply to your group work.

Developing Your Group Leadership Style

There are as many styles of group counseling as there are leaders, and even leaders who subscribe to a primary therapeutic model, such as behavior therapy or transactional analysis, show considerable variation in the way they lead groups. As a group leader, you bring your background of experiences and your personality, worldview, biases, and unique talents and skills to the group you lead. You also bring to it your theoretical preferences.

One determinant of your leadership style is whether you lead short- or long-term groups. As you will see in Chapter 6, psychoanalytic groups tend to be long term, with the major aim of bringing about change in character structure. However, such a broad goal is not possible in short-term groups, such as in solution-focused brief group therapy (see Chapter 16). As a group leader, your role in short-term groups is quite different from the leadership role in long-term therapy groups.

Most likely you will be expected to set up and conduct a variety of short-term groups, which means you will need to be active, directive, conscious of time limitations, and concerned with assisting members in identifying specific problem areas dealing with their current life situation. Brief groups require a more structured style so that members can attain specific goals. For example, you will be more concerned with present issues than with exploring the members' past. In conducting short-term groups the leader needs to pay particular attention to pregroup screening and preparation of potential members prior to the group; maintain a focus on a particular set of themes during the sessions; strive to develop group cohesion quickly; remind members of the time limits on the group's duration; and do follow-up work once the group ends. Leaders need to be more active in brief group work than in long-term groups, both in setting up the group and in conducting group sessions, because of the necessity of attending to the foregoing tasks within a relatively short time duration (Rosenberg & Wright, 1997).

Whether you work mostly with short- or long-term groups, it is important that you know yourself and develop a style that fits your personality. I hope you will develop a leadership style that is your own and that expresses your uniqueness as a person. If you attempt to copy someone else's style, you can lose much of your potential effectiveness as a group leader. You will be influenced, of course, by supervisors, coleaders, and the leaders of groups and workshops you attend as a participant. But it is one thing to be influenced by others and another to deny your own uniqueness by copying others' therapeutic styles, which may work well for them but may not be suited to you.

The theoretical stance that you are challenged to develop must be closely related to your values, beliefs, and personal characteristics. You may advocate an approach that emphasizes thinking, or one that stresses experiencing and expressing feelings, or one that focuses on action-oriented methods. Or your approach may integrate the thinking, feeling, and acting dimensions. Regardless of the approach you favor, your theoretical preferences will no doubt influence your style, especially with regard to the aspects of the group interaction on which you choose to focus.

One way to build a foundation for a personal leadership style is to know the diverse range of theories of group counseling and their implications for styles of leading. Leading a group without an explicit theoretical rationale is somewhat like flying an airplane without a map and instruments. Theory can be viewed as a set of general guidelines that you can use in your practice. A theory is a map that provides direction and guidance in examining your basic assumptions about human beings, in determining your goals for the group, in clarifying your role and functions as a leader, in explaining the group interactions, and in evaluating the outcomes of the group.

Developing a theoretical stance involves more than merely accepting the tenets of any one theory. It is an ongoing process in which group leaders keep questioning the "what," "how," and "why" of their practice. It is wise to take a critical look at the key concepts of the various theories and also to consider the theorists behind them because a theory is generally a personal expression of the person who developed it. It is important to remain open and to seriously consider the unique contributions as well as the limitations of different approaches. If you settle on one theory and don't recognize its limitations, you are likely to misuse it and to assume that it is an axiom and a set of proven facts rather than a tool for inquiry. If your theoretical perspective causes you to ignore all others, you may force your clients to fit its confines instead of using it to understand them. If you embrace a theory in its entirety, the theory may not serve the diverse needs of your group.

Many group workers align their practice with one particular theoretical orientation on the grounds that their theory of choice provides a good explanation of human behavior and provides them with a unified and consistent basis for intervening in their groups. I have no quarrel with practitioners who have carefully evaluated a theory and identify with a particular orientation. However, some adopt a theory without knowing why they prefer the approach, and these practitioners rarely have an open stance toward incorporating alternative perspectives.

As you study the 11 theoretical models of group counseling presented in Part Two, the commonalities and differences among these models and the ways in which the various perspectives can shape your style as a group leader will become clear. As you study each theory, reflect on the applications for developing short-term groups. Given the managed care emphasis on being both efficient and effective, today's group leaders need to learn as much as possible about short-term groups. Among all of the theories described, the psychoanalytic approach is most geared to long-term therapy groups, although short-term psychodynamic groups are being developed today. Most of the other theoretical approaches covered in Part Two lend themselves well to brief interventions and to time-limited groups.

The Role of Research in the Practice of Group Work

Effective group workers appreciate the role research can play in enhancing practice. Ideally, theory informs your practice, and practice refines your approach. Research can help you come to a better understanding of the specific factors that contribute to successful outcomes of groups. Applied research can help you identify factors that interfere with group effectiveness as well as confirm the efficacy of your interventions. Clinical work can be greatly aided by research findings and can inform research (Stockton & Morran, 2010). Even if practitioners do not have the time or the expertise required to conduct their own research, they can work with researchers to integrate research findings into their group practice.

Many group workers are either unwilling or unable to devote time to devising evaluative instruments as part of their clinical practice, and too often research findings are not integrated into clinical practice. Some practical considerations that can limit practitioners' active participation in research include the constant pressure to meet clinical demands, a lack of time, a lack of financial remuneration for doing research, and a lack of the skills and knowledge required to conduct research (Lau, Ogrodniczuk, Joyce, & Sochting, 2010). Yalom (2005) admits that few group practitioners will ever have the time, funding, and institutional backing to engage in large-scale research, yet he contends that "many can engage in intensive single-patient or single-group research, and all clinicians must evaluate published clinical research" (p. 562).

Familiarity with research in the group work field is becoming an essential part of practice in the era of managed care. You will likely be expected to gather evaluation data that will support the value of your group services. Accountability is now being stressed in all settings. Many schools and agencies are requiring some form of evaluation of the effectiveness of a group. As a practitioner, it is essential that what you do in your groups be informed by research on the process and outcomes of groups. Part of your development as a group practitioner involves thinking of ways to make evaluation a basic part of your group practice.

Collaboration between practitioners and researchers can benefit both parties as well as the field of group work (Kalodner & Riva, 1997; Lau et al, 2010). To develop genuinely collaborative relationships, it is critical that researchers invite contributions from group practitioners regarding meaningful research questions and study design. The researcher's focus on evaluating treatment will benefit from complementary input by the clinician who has experience in actual group work. Lau, Ogrodniczuk, Joyce, and Sochting (2010) suggest replacing classical empirical research aimed at systematically evaluating treatments under controlled conditions with qualitative research methods and case studies. This "effectiveness research" would emphasize clinical aspects of group work done in real-world situations. Increasing cooperation between clinicians and researchers will likely result in more useful and relevant research results (Lau et al., 2010).

THE HISTORY OF GROUP WORK RESEARCH

Both consumers and funding agencies have increasingly demanded that practitioners demonstrate the value of their therapeutic strategies. Based on empirical investigations of more than four decades of group work, Dies (1992) finds that there is relatively little difference in outcome between individual and group treatments. With the pressures to justify the expense of psychotherapy, Dies suggests that clinicians are likely to face increased pressure to explain why the treatment of choice for most clients is not group therapy.

Over the past two decades, the focus of group studies has shifted from an emphasis on process research to an examination of outcome studies. There are many unanswered questions related to group process variables, such as matching certain individuals to specific groups, member selection and group composition, style of group leadership, and interventions at various stages of a group (Riva & Smith, 1997). Although research on group counseling has improved over the past two decades, many research studies of group work suffer from serious methodological problems. Future group research needs to inform practice, and, at the same time, research needs to be guided by the expertise of clinicians who conduct groups. Lau and colleagues (2010) propose a community-based research paradigm that involves clinicians as full partners with researchers. In this context, clinicians define research priorities, determine the type of evidence that will have an impact of their practice, and develop strategies for translating and implementing research findings into group practice.

A survey of more than 45 years of research provides an abundance of evidence that group approaches are associated with clients' improvement in a variety of settings and situations (Bednar & Kaul, 1994). But the general consensus among experts is that the current knowledge of the effects of specific group treatments is modest at best. Researchers know little about how group processes mediate change in participants, how members influence group processes, and what dimensions of psychological functioning are most amenable to change in small groups. Quite simply, although researchers know that group treatments can be effective, they don't know much about why this is so.

In their description of the history of research on group work, Horne and Rosenthal (1997) indicate that we have learned much about the complex nature of group work. They state that the efficacy of group treatment appears to have less to do with a specific theoretical orientation than with finding an optimum combination of pregroup training, client characteristics, therapeutic factors, group structure, and stages of group development.

GROUP PRACTITIONERS' PERCEPTIONS OF RESEARCH IN GROUP WORK

A Canadian survey of group psychotherapists was conducted by Ogrodniczuk, Piper, Joyce, Lau, and Sochting (2010) to evaluate practitioners' perceptions of the role of research in group therapy. Contrary to popular belief, this survey reveals that difficulties integrating research findings into the practice of group work are not due to a lack of interest or unfamiliarity with research. A substantial number of group therapists have a high level of appreciation for research, and a large proportion of respondents to this survey indicated past and current participation in research.

The findings of this survey suggest that group therapists do indeed have an interest in research:

- 25% of respondents were currently involved with a research project.
- 69% expressed a desire to participate in a research project in the future.
- 71% were interested in participating in a research network with other group therapists and researchers.
- 51% reported being at least moderately familiar with the psychotherapy research literature.
- 73% indicated that the way they practice psychotherapy has been influenced by psychotherapy research.
- 79% wished they were more familiar with the research literature.
- 100% believed that a therapist's effectiveness can be enhanced by being informed by the research literature.
- 90% believed a priority research topic should be linking group process with outcomes.
- 90% identified the study of group leader issues as a priority topic, including the role of supervision, job satisfaction, group leader self-disclosure, group leader training, practitioners' motivation for providing group therapy, therapeutic orientation, and traits of the group therapist.
- 83% were interested in research on the cost-effectiveness of group therapy.
- 95% indicated that researchers do not give enough attention to qualitative studies of group therapy.
- 84% believed that researchers tend to minimize the study of relationship variables in favor of studying specific treatment techniques.
- 77% believed that research findings are not communicated to group practitioners in a clear and relevant way.

Survey respondents stated that without effective communication the results from even the best of studies will have only a slight impact on practice. They suggested that research findings be communicated in a brief manner and that findings emphasize the practical implications for those who conduct groups in the real world. Practitioners' dissatisfaction with reports of research findings seems to be a significant factor in the poor integration of research and clinical practice.

Respondents indicated that current research tends to ignore the complexities that are a part of group psychotherapy. They were critical of the lack of emphasis on qualitative research and the heightened emphasis of empirical studies evaluating the different brands of therapy used in a group. Clinicians in this survey want to see more qualitative research and case studies in the professional journals. Stockton and Morran (2010) note that a key reason research findings are often not integrated into clinical practice is due to the constraints of experimental research that limit the applicability of findings to a real-world context. Although experimental studies may have internal validity, they may have little practical value to group workers. Ogrodniczuk and colleagues (2010) conclude, "By increasing dialogue with clinicians about research that has relevance to them, by engaging clinicians in the process of generating new knowledge, and by utilizing communication methods that would fit with the needs of clinicians, it would appear possible to achieve a meaningful synthesis of science and practice in the group therapy field" (p. 174).

EVIDENCE-BASED PRACTICE IN GROUP WORK

In recent years a shift has occurred toward promoting the use of specific interventions for specific problems or diagnoses based on empirically supported treatments (APA Presidential Task Force on Evidence-Based Practice, 2006). Increasingly, clinicians who practice in a behavioral health care system are encountering the concept of evidence-based practice (Norcross, Hogan, & Koocher, 2008). **Evidence-based practice** (EBP) is "the integration of the best available research with clinical expertise in the context of patient characteristics, culture, and preferences" (APA Presidential Task Force on Evidence-Based Practice, 2006, p. 273). This idea encompasses more than simply basing interventions on research. Group therapists are being asked to provide convincing evidence that the particular forms of group therapy they practice actually work with the particular types of members in their groups (Klein, 2008).

The *Practice Guidelines for Group Psychotherapy of the American Group Psychotherapy Association* (2007) identify the factors of the group therapist's expertise, cultural variables, and group member values as playing a crucial role in thinking of ways to address accountability issues. The AGPA's practice guidelines are more descriptive rather than a prescriptive set of standards.

Norcross, Hogan, and Koocher (2008) advocate for inclusive evidence-based practices that incorporate these three pillars: best available evidence, clinician expertise, and client characteristics. The APA Presidential Task Force on Evidence-Based Practice (2006) makes it clear that psychotherapy is a collaborative venture in which clients and clinicians develop ways of working together that are likely to result in positive outcomes. The APA Task Force (2006) has broadened the concept of evidence-based practice to consider the best research evidence in light of therapist and client factors. The involvement of an active, informed client is crucial to the success of therapy services. Based on their clinical expertise, therapists make the ultimate judgment regarding particular interventions, and they make these decisions in the context of considering the client's values, needs, and preferences. For group leaders to base their practices exclusively on interventions that have been empirically validated may seem to be the ethical and competent path to take, yet some view this as being overly restrictive.

Critique of the Evidence-Based Practice Model Many group practitioners believe that relying on evidence-based practice is mechanistic and does not take into full consideration the relational dimensions of the therapeutic process. These clinicians do not think matching techniques that have been empirically tested with specific problems is a meaningful way of working. Practitioners with a relationship-oriented approach (such as person-centered therapy and existential therapy) emphasize understanding the world of the client and healing through the therapeutic relationship. Norcross, Beutler, and Levant (2006) remind us that many aspects of treatment—the therapy relationship, the therapist's personality and therapeutic style, the client, and environmental factors—contribute to the success of psychotherapy and must be taken into account in the treatment process. Evidence-based practices tend to emphasize only one of these aspects—interventions based on the best available research.

The therapist's clinical expertise is a critical element in forming a collaborative relationship with clients. In addition, client characteristics, culture, personal values, and preferences are critical aspects in the therapeutic relationship. There is substantial research to support this position that the *client* actually accounts for more of the treatment outcome than either the relationship or the therapist's method employed (Duncan, Miller, Wampold, & Hubble, 2010).

Currently, there is pressure by insurance companies to deliver services that are brief, standardized, and operationalized by reliance on a treatment manual. Indeed, relying exclusively on standardized treatments for specific problems may raise a host of practical and theoretical issues. One of these issues is the reliability and validity of these empirically based techniques. Human change is complex and difficult to measure unless researchers operationalize the notion of change at such a simplistic level that the change may be meaningless. Although the goal of EBP is to enhance the effectiveness of delivering services, Norcross and his colleagues (2006) warn that the move toward evidence-based practices has the potential for misuse and abuse by third-party payers who could selectively use research findings as cost-containment measures rather than to improve the quality of services delivered. Norcross and his colleagues show that there is a great deal of controversy and discord when it comes to EBP. They stress the value of informed dialogue and respectful debate as a way to gain clarity and to make progress.

For further reading on the topic of evidence-based practices, I recommend the APA Presidential Task Force on Evidence-Based Practice (2006), Norcross, Beutler, and Levant (2006), and Norcross, Hogan, and Koocher (2008).

Another Approach: Practice-Based Evidence Duncan, Miller, and Sparks (2004) have suggested a different way to incorporate data to improve treatment decisions. They argue that the most useful focus is on using data generated during treatment to inform the process and outcome of treatment. Significant improvements in client retention and outcome have been shown where therapists regularly and purposefully collect data on the client's experience of the alliance and progress in treatment. As an alternative to evidence-based practice, they propose the approach of *practice-based* evidence.

Miller, Hubble, Duncan, and Wampold (2010) emphasize the importance of enlisting the client's active participation in the therapeutic venture. They argue that you do not need to know ahead of time what approach to use for a given diagnosis. What is most important is to systematically gather and use formal client feedback to inform, guide, and evaluate treatment. Applied to group counseling, monitoring the progress of each group member through systematic data collection on how each member is experiencing the group can help leaders make adjustments to their interventions and enhance the group process. Members could complete a very brief form at the end of each group session, and their ratings on specific items can be tallied as a way to get a sense of the progress of the group as a whole.

For a more complete discussion of practice-based evidence as an alternative to evidence-based practice, see Duncan, Miller, and Sparks (2004).

DEVELOPING A RESEARCH ORIENTATION

Yalom (2005) claims that group trainees need to know more than how to implement techniques in a group—they also need to know how to learn. Faculty should teach and model a basic research orientation characterized by an open, self-critical, inquiring attitude toward clinical and research evidence. He writes that students need to critically evaluate their own work and maintain sufficient flexibility to be responsive to their own observations. Stockton and Morran (2010) believe that promoting students' positive attitudes toward research can motivate them to be good research consumers as well as clinician members of research teams. Stockton and Morran note that most students enrolled in master's programs receive only basic research training and thus may not feel adequately prepared to understand the research literature, or to apply research findings to their clinical practice, or to become involved in research projects. Stockton and Morran recommend including more research course work and research team participation as a part of master's degree programs.

According to Yalom (2005), a research orientation enables group therapists, throughout their career, to remain flexible and responsive to new evidence. Practitioners who lack a research orientation will have no basis to critically evaluate new developments in the field of group work. Without a consistent framework to evaluate evidence of the efficacy of innovations in the field, practitioners run the risk of being unreasonably unreceptive to new approaches. Or, in contrast, they uncritically embrace one fad after another. Whether you conduct research with your groups is less important than your willingness to keep informed about the practical applications of research on group work. At the very least, you need to be up to date with the research implications for practice.

In learning how to become a group practitioner, it is necessary to progress from a beginner to a skilled clinician in stages. Likewise, a developmental approach can be useful for teaching students about group research. Rex Stockton (Stockton & Toth, 1997) advocates an apprenticeship model in which students improve their clinical skills through practice, consultation, supervision, and discussion with mentors and peers. Likewise, they can learn about group research techniques through the same kind of exposure, practice, consultation, and collaboration with those who are doing research.

Make systematic observation and assessment basic parts of your practice of group work. Instead of thinking exclusively in terms of rigorous empirical research, practitioners can begin to consider alternatives to traditional scientific methods. One such alternative is evaluative research, which is aimed at gathering and assessing data that can be of value in making decisions about programs and in improving the quality of professional services (Dies, 1983a).

In group work, pure research should not be seen as the only type of inquiry that has value. Practitioners and researchers can choose to do good field research as well (Morran & Stockton, 1985).

AUTHOR LECTURES

Watch *Gerald Corey's Perspectives on Theory and Practice of Group Counseling* DVD or visit the *Theory and Practice of Group Counseling* CourseMate website at www.cengagebrain.com/shop/ISBN/0840033869 to watch videos of Dr. Gerald Corey presenting lectures for each chapter. Also available are unique eAudio lectures for each chapter and quiz questions for self-study.

CHAPTER THREE

Ethical and Professional Issues in Group Practice

Those who seek to be professional group leaders must be willing to examine both their ethical standards and their level of competence. Among the ethical issues treated in this chapter are the rights of group members, including informed consent and confidentiality; the psychological risks of groups; personal relationships with clients; socializing among members; the impact of the group leader's values; working effectively and ethically with diverse clients; and the uses and misuses of group techniques. In my opinion, a central ethical issue in group work pertains to the group leader's competence. Special attention is given to ways of determining competence, professional training standards, and adjuncts to academic preparation of group counselors. Also highlighted are ethical issues involved in training group workers. The final section outlines issues of legal liability and malpractice.

As a responsible group practitioner, you are challenged to clarify your thinking about the ethical and professional issues discussed in this chapter. Although you are obligated to be familiar with, and bound by, the ethics codes of your professional organization, many of these codes offer only general guidelines. You will need to learn how to make ethical decisions in practical situations. The ethics codes provide a general framework from which to operate, but you must apply these principles to concrete cases. The Association for Specialists in Group Work (2008) "Best Practice Guidelines" is reproduced in the *Student Manual* that accompanies this textbook. You may want to refer to these guidelines often, especially as you study Chapters 1 through 5.

The Rights of Group Participants

My experience has taught me that those who enter groups are frequently unaware both of their basic rights as participants and of their responsibilities. As a group leader, you are responsible for helping prospective members understand what their rights and responsibilities are. This section offers a detailed discussion of these issues.

A BASIC RIGHT: INFORMED CONSENT

If basic information about the group is discussed at the initial session, the participants are likely to be far more cooperative and active. A leader who does this as a matter of policy demonstrates honesty and respect for group members and fosters the trust necessary for members to be open and active. Such a leader has obtained the *informed consent* of the participants. **Informed consent** is a process that begins with presenting basic information about group treatment to potential group members to enable them to make better decisions about whether or not to enter and how to participate in a group (Fallon, 2006). Members have a right to receive basic information *before* joining a group, and they have a right to expect certain other information *during* the course of the group. Informed consent is not a one-time event, and clients should be informed at the outset that informed consent is an ongoing process (Pomerantz, 2005).

It is a good policy to provide a professional disclosure statement to group members that includes written information on a variety of topics pertaining to the nature of the group, including therapists' qualifications, techniques often used in the group, the rights and obligations of group members, and the risks and benefits of participating in the group. Other information that potential members should have includes alternatives to group treatment; policies regarding appointments, fees, and insurance; and the nature and limitations of confidentiality in a group. Group leaders should not overwhelm members with too much information at one time because an overly lengthy informed consent process may replace a collaborative working relationship with a legalistic framework, which is not in the best interests of group members (Fallon, 2006).

Pregroup Disclosures Here is a list of what group participants have a right to expect before they make the decision to join a group:

- A clear statement regarding the purpose of the group
- A description of the group format, procedures, and ground rules
- An initial interview to determine whether this particular group with this particular leader is at this time appropriate to their needs
- An opportunity to seek information about the group, to pose questions, and to explore concerns
- A discussion of ways the group process may or may not be congruent with the cultural beliefs and values of group members
- A statement describing the education, training, and qualifications of the group leader
- Information concerning fees and expenses including fees for a follow-up session, should there be one; also, information about length of group, frequency and duration of meetings, group goals, and techniques being employed
- Information about the psychological risks involved in group participation
- Knowledge of the circumstances in which confidentiality must be broken because of legal, ethical, or professional reasons
- Clarification of what services can and cannot be provided within the group
- Help from the group leader in developing personal goals

- A clear understanding of the division of responsibility between leader and participants
- A discussion of the rights and responsibilities of group members

Clients' Rights During the Group Here is a list of what members have a right to expect during the course of the group:

- Guidance concerning what is expected of them
- Notice of any research involving the group and of any audio- or videotaping of group sessions
- Assistance from the group leader in translating group learning into action in everyday life
- Opportunities to discuss what one has learned in the group and to bring some closure to the group experience so participants are not left with unnecessary unfinished business
- A consultation with the group leader should a crisis arise as a direct result of participation in the group, or a referral to other sources of help if further help is not available from the group leader
- The exercise of reasonable safeguards on the leader's part to minimize the potential risks of the group; respect for member privacy with regard to what the person will reveal as well as to the degree of disclosure
- Observance of confidentiality on the part of the leader and other group members
- Freedom from having values imposed by the leader or other members
- The right to be treated as an individual and accorded dignity and respect

It is critical that group leaders stress that participation in groups carries certain responsibilities as well as rights. These responsibilities include attending regularly, being prompt, taking risks, being willing to talk about oneself, giving others feedback, maintaining confidentiality, and defining one's personal goals for group participation. Some of these group norms may pose problems for certain members because of their cultural background. It is essential that the expectations for group members be clear from the outset and that members be in agreement with such expectations. Of course, part of the group process involves the participation of members in developing norms that will influence their behavior in a group situation.

ISSUES IN INVOLUNTARY GROUPS

When participation is mandatory, informed consent is as important as it is when working with voluntary groups. Much effort needs to be directed toward fully informing involuntary members of the nature and goals of the group, the procedures to be used, their rights and responsibilities, the limits of confidentiality, and what effect their level of participation in the group will have on critical decisions about them outside of the group. When groups are involuntary, every attempt should be made to enlist the cooperation of the members and encourage them to continue attending voluntarily. One way of doing this is to spend some time with involuntary clients helping them reframe the notion "I have to come to this group." They do have some choice whether they will attend group or deal with the consequences of not being in the group. If "involuntary" members choose not to participate in the group, they will need to be prepared to deal with consequences such as being expelled from school, doing jail time, or being in juvenile detention.

Another alternative would be for the group leader to accept involuntary group members only for an initial limited period. There is something to be said for giving reluctant members a chance to see for themselves what a group is about and then eventually (say, after three sessions) letting them decide whether they will return. Group leaders can inform members that it is their choice of how they will use the time in the group. The members can be encouraged to explore their fears and reluctance to fully participate in the group, as well as the consequences of not participating in the group. Ethical practice would seem to require that group leaders fully explore these issues with clients who are sent to them.

THE FREEDOM TO LEAVE A GROUP

Leaders should be clear about their policies pertaining to attendance, commitment to remaining in a group for a predetermined number of sessions, and leaving a particular session if they do not like what is going on in the group. If members simply drop out of the group, it is extremely difficult to develop a working level of trust or to establish group cohesion. The topic of leaving the group should be discussed during the initial session, and the leader's attitudes and policies need to be clear from the outset.

In my view, group members have a responsibility to the leaders and other members to explain why they want to leave. There are a number of reasons for such a policy. For one thing, it can be deleterious to members to leave without having been able to discuss what they considered threatening or negative in the experience. If they leave without discussing their intended departure, they are likely to be left with unfinished business, and so are the remaining members. A member's dropping out may damage the cohesion and trust in a group; the remaining members may think that they in some way "caused" the departure. It is a good practice to tell members that if they are even thinking of withdrawing they should bring the matter up for exploration in a session. It is critical that members be encouraged to discuss their departure, at least with the group leader.

If a group is counterproductive for an individual, that person has a right to leave the group. Ideally, both the group leader and the members will work cooperatively to determine the degree to which a group experience is productive or counterproductive. If, at a mutually agreed-upon time, members still choose not to participate in a group, I believe they should be allowed to drop out without being subjected to pressure by the leader and other members to remain.

FREEDOM FROM COERCION AND UNDUE PRESSURE

Members can reasonably expect to be respected by the group and not to be subjected to coercion and undue group pressure. However, some degree of group pressure is inevitable, and it is even therapeutic in many instances. People in a group are challenged to examine their self-defeating beliefs and behaviors and are encouraged to recognize what they are doing and determine whether they want to remain the way they are. Further, in a counseling group, there is pressure in sessions to speak up, to make personal disclosures, to take certain risks, to share one's reactions to the here-and-now events within the group, and to be honest with the group. All of these expectations should be explained to potential group members during the screening and orientation session. Some individuals may not want to join a group if they will be expected to participate in personal ways. It is essential for group leaders to differentiate between destructive pressure and therapeutic pressure. People often need a certain degree of pressure to challenge them to take the risks involved in becoming fully invested in the group.

It is well to keep in mind that the purpose of a group is to help participants find their own answers, not to coerce them into doing what the group thinks is the appropriate course. Members can easily be subjected to needless anxiety if they are badgered to behave in a certain way. Members may also be pressured to take part in structured exercises or nonverbal exercises designed to promote interaction. It is essential that leaders be sensitive to the values of members who decline to participate in certain group exercises. Leaders must make it genuinely acceptable for members to abstain by mentioning this option periodically, when appropriate. Furthermore, it is a good practice for group leaders to teach all members how to resist undue group pressure and how to decline gracefully from participating in activities if they so choose.

THE RIGHT TO CONFIDENTIALITY

Confidentiality is a central ethical issue in group counseling, and it is an essential condition for effective group work. The legal concept of privileged communication is not recognized in a group setting unless there is a statutory exception. However, protecting the confidentiality of group members is an ethical mandate, and it is the responsibility of the counselor to address this at the outset of a group (Wheeler & Bertram, 2008). The American Counseling Association's (2005) *ACA Code of Ethics* makes this statement concerning confidentiality in groups: "In group work, counselors clearly explain the importance and parameters of confidentiality for the specific group being entered"(B.4.a.). The ASGW (2008) addresses the added complexity entailed in coming to a mutual understanding of confidentiality in diverse groups: "Group Workers maintain awareness and sensitivity regarding the cultural meaning of confidentiality and privacy. Group Workers respect differing views toward disclosure of information" (A.6.). As a leader, you are required to keep the confidences of group members, but you have the added responsibility of impressing on the members the necessity of maintaining the confidential nature of whatever is revealed in the group. This matter bears reinforcement along the way, from the initial screening interview to the final group session.

Although group leaders are themselves ethically and legally bound to maintain confidentiality, a group member who violates another member's confidences faces no legal consequences (Lasky & Riva, 2006). If the rationale for confidentiality is clearly presented to each individual during the preliminary interview and again to the group as a whole at the initial session, there is less chance that members will treat this matter lightly. Confidentiality is often on the minds of people when they join a group, so it is timely to fully explore this issue. A good practice is to remind participants from time to time of the danger of inadvertently revealing confidences. My experience continues to teach me that members rarely gossip maliciously about others in their group. However, people do tend to talk more than they should outside the group and can unwittingly offer information about fellow members that should not be revealed. If the maintenance of confidentiality seems to be a matter of concern, the subject should be discussed fully in a group session.

In groups in institutions, agencies, and schools, where members know and have frequent contact with one another outside of the group, confidentiality becomes especially important and is more difficult to maintain. Clearly, there is no way to ensure that group members will respect the confidences of others. As a group leader, you cannot guarantee confidentiality in a group setting because you cannot control absolutely what the members do or do not keep private. Members have a right to know that absolute confidentiality in groups is difficult and at times even unrealistic (Lasky & Riva, 2006). However, you can discuss the matter, express your convictions about the importance of maintaining confidentiality, have members sign contracts agreeing to it, and even impose some form of sanction on those who break it. Your own modeling and the importance that you place on maintaining confidentiality will be crucial in setting norms for members to follow. Ultimately, it is up to the members to respect the need for confidentiality and to maintain it.

Members have the right to know of any audio- or videotape recordings that might be made of group sessions, and the purpose for which they will be used. Written permission should be secured before recording any session. If the tapes will be used for research purposes or will be critiqued by a supervisor or other students in a group supervision session, the members have the right to deny permission.

Exceptions to Confidentiality Group leaders have the ethical responsibility of informing members of the limits of confidentiality within the group setting. For instance, leaders can explain to members when they are legally required to break confidentiality. Leaders can add that they can assure confidentiality on their own part but not on the part of other members. It is important to encourage members to bring up matters pertaining to confidentiality whenever they are concerned about them. The *ACA Code of Ethics* (ACA, 2005) identifies exceptions to confidentiality that members should understand:

> The general requirement that counselors keep information confidential does not apply when disclosure is required to protect clients or identified others from serious and foreseeable harm or when legal requirements demand that confidential information must be revealed. Counselors consult with other professionals when in doubt as to the validity of an exception. Additional considerations apply when addressing end-of-life issues. (B.2.a.)

It is a good policy for group workers to give a written statement to each member setting forth the limitations of confidentiality and spelling out specific situations that would require the breaching of confidences. Such straightforwardness with members from the outset does a great deal to create trust because members then know where they stand.

Of course, it is imperative that those who lead groups become familiar with the state laws that have an impact on their practice. Group leaders do well to let members know that legal privilege does not apply to group treatment, unless provided by state statute (ASGW, 2008). The American Group Psychotherapy Association (AGPA, 2002) states: "The group therapist is knowledgeable about the limits of privileged communication as they apply to group therapy and

informs group members of those limits" (2.2). Counselors are legally required to report clients' threats to harm themselves or others. This requirement also covers cases of child abuse or neglect, incest, or child molestation, elder abuse, and dependent-adult abuse. Taking an extreme case, if one of your group members convincingly threatens to seriously injure another person, you may have to consult your supervisor or other colleagues, warn the intended victim, and even notify the appropriate authorities. The threat need not involve others; clients may exhibit bizarre behavior that requires you to take steps to have them evaluated and possibly hospitalized.

If you lead a group at a correctional institution or a psychiatric hospital, you may be required to act as more than a counselor; for instance, you will probably have to record in a member's file certain behaviors that he or she exhibits in the group. At the same time, your responsibility to your clients requires you to inform them that you are recording and passing on certain information. Generally speaking, you will find that you have a better chance of gaining the cooperation of group members if you are candid about a situation rather than hiding your disclosures and thereby putting yourself in the position of violating their confidences.

Confidentiality With Minors In a group for children in a school setting, care needs to be exerted to ensure that what goes on within the group is not a subject for discussion in class or on the playground. If children begin to talk about other members outside of the group, this will certainly block progress and damage the cohesion of the group. As is the case for adults and adolescents, children require the safety of knowing they will be treated respectfully. Group leaders must also be careful in how they talk about the children to teachers and administrators. Those who do groups with children need to explain what will be kept confidential and what may need to be shared with school personnel.

Do parents have a right to information that is disclosed by their children in a group? The answer to that question depends on whether you are looking at it from a legal, ethical, or professional viewpoint. It is a good practice to require written permission from parents before allowing a minor to enter a group. It is useful to have this permission include a brief statement concerning the purpose of the group, along with comments regarding the importance of confidentiality as a prerequisite to accomplishing such purposes, and your intention not to violate any confidences. It may sometimes be useful to provide parents with information about their child if this can be done without violating confidences. One useful practice to protect the privacy of what goes on in the group is to provide feedback to parents in a session with the child and one or both parents. In this way the child will have less cause to doubt the group leader's integrity in keeping his or her disclosures private.

Group leaders have a responsibility in groups that involve children and adolescents to take measures to increase the chances that confidentiality will be kept. It is important to work cooperatively with parents and guardians as well as to enlist the trust of the young people. It is also useful to teach minors, in terms that they are capable of understanding, about the nature, purposes, and limitations of confidentiality. In summary, group leaders would do well to continue to remind members to bring up their concerns about confidentiality for discussion whenever the issue is on their minds.

The Issue of Psychological Risks in Groups

Groups can be powerful catalysts for personal change, and they can also pose definite risks for group members. The nature of these risks—which include life changes that cause disruption, hostile and destructive confrontations, scapegoating, and harmful socializing among members—and what the leader can do about them are the subject of this section. It is unrealistic to expect that a group will not involve risk, for all meaningful learning in life involves taking some kind of risk. Therefore, what needs to be guarded against are the potential negative outcomes that can occur by participating in a group. It is the ethical responsibility of the group leader to ensure that prospective group members are aware of the potential negative outcomes that are associated with various risks and to take every precaution against them.

The *ACA Code of Ethics* (ACA, 2005) specifies that "In a group setting, counselors take reasonable precautions to protect clients from physical, emotional, or psychological trauma" (A.8.b.). This includes discussing the impact of potential life changes and helping group members explore their readiness to deal with such changes. A minimal expectation is that group leaders discuss with members the advantages and disadvantages of a given group, that they prepare the members to deal with any problems that might grow out of the group experience, and that they be alert to the fears and reservations that members might have.

It is also incumbent on group leaders to have a broad and deep understanding of the forces that operate in groups and how to mobilize those forces for ethical ends. Unless leaders exert caution, members not only may miss the benefits of a group but also could be harmed by it psychologically. Fallon (2006) suggests that leaders have a responsibility to explain both the potential benefits and risks of group therapy as part of the informed consent process. However, merely informing participants does not absolve leaders of their responsibility. From an ethical perspective, group leaders must take precautionary measures to reduce unnecessary psychological risks. Ways of reducing these risks include knowing members' limits, respecting their requests, developing an invitational style as opposed to an aggressive or dictatorial style, avoiding abrasive confrontations, describing behavior rather than making judgments, and presenting hunches in a tentative way.

Here are a few of the problems group leaders can warn members about and work toward minimizing:

1. Members should be made aware of the possibility that participating in a group (or any other therapeutic endeavor) may disrupt their lives. As members become increasingly self-aware, they may make changes in their lives that, although constructive in the long run, can create turmoil along the way. For example, changes that a woman makes as a result of what she gains in a group may evoke resistance, even hostility, in her partner, with a resulting strain on their relationship. Furthermore, others with whom she is close may not appreciate her changes and may prefer the person she was before getting involved in counseling.

2. Occasionally an individual member may be singled out as the scapegoat of the group. Other group members may "gang up" on this person, blaming him or her for problems of the group. Clearly, the group leader must take

firm steps to deal with such occurrences. For more on the topic of scapegoating in group therapy, see Moreno (2007).

3. Confrontation, a valuable and powerful tool in any group, can be misused, especially when it is employed to destructively attack another. Intrusive interventions, overly confrontive leader tactics, and pushing members beyond their limits often produce negative outcomes. Here, again, leaders (and members as well) must be on guard against behavior that can pose a serious psychological risk for group participants. To lessen the risks of destructive confrontation, leaders can model the type of confrontation that focuses on specific behaviors and can avoid making judgments about members. They can teach members how to talk about themselves and the reactions they are having to a certain behavior pattern of a given member.

One way to minimize psychological risks in groups is to use a contract in which the leader specifies his or her responsibilities and the members specify their commitment by stating what they are willing to explore and do in the group. Such a contract reduces the chances that members will be exploited or will leave the group feeling that they have had a negative experience.

Another safeguard against unnecessary risk is the ability of leaders to recognize the boundaries of their competence and to restrict themselves to working only with those groups for which their training and experience have properly prepared them. Ultimately, the group leader is responsible for minimizing the inevitable psychological risks associated with group activity. To best assume this responsibility, the leader will undergo the supervised practice and course work described later in this chapter.

The Ethics of Group Leaders' Actions

Being a group practitioner demands sensitivity to the needs of the members of your group and to the impact your values and techniques can have on them. It also demands an awareness of community standards of practice, the policies of the agency where you work, and the state laws that govern group counseling. In the mental health professions in general, there is a trend toward accountability and responsible practice. Graduate programs in counseling and social work are increasingly requiring course work in ethics and the law.

Almost all of the professional organizations have gone on record as affirming that their members should be aware of prevailing community standards and of the impact that conformity to or deviation from these standards will have on their practice. These organizations state explicitly that professionals will avoid exploitation of the therapeutic relationship, will not damage the trust that is necessary for a relationship to be therapeutic, and will avoid dual relationships if they interfere with the primary therapeutic aims. Typically, the ethics codes caution against attempting to blend social or personal relationships with professional ones and stress the importance of maintaining appropriate boundaries.

Group counselors need to be mindful about misusing their role and power to meet their personal needs at the expense of clients. When group leaders meet their personal needs for power and prestige at the expense of what is best for the members, they commit an ethical violation. The role of leaders is to help members meet their goals, not to become friends with their clients. Of course, leaders who develop sexual relationships with current group members are acting unethically. They not only jeopardize their license and their professional career, but they also degrade the profession at large. For a more complete discussion of these topics, see Herlihy and Corey (2006a, 2006b).

Socializing Among Group Members

An issue to consider is whether socializing among group members hinders or facilitates the group process. This concern can become an ethical issue if members are forming cliques and gossiping about others in the group or if they are banding together and talking about matters that are best explored in the group sessions. If hidden agendas develop through various subgroups within the group, it is likely that the progress of the group will come to an abrupt halt. Unless the hidden agenda is brought to the surface and dealt with, it seems very likely that many members will not be able to use the group therapeutically or meet their personal goals.

Yalom (2005) maintains that a therapy group teaches people how to form intimate relationships but is not designed to provide these relationships. He also points out that members meeting outside of the group have a responsibility to bring information about their meeting into the group. Any type of out-of-group socialization that interferes with the functioning of the group is counterproductive and should be discouraged. This is especially true in those situations in which participants discuss issues relevant to the group, but avoid bringing up the same issues in the group itself. As Yalom (2005) explains, "It is not the subgrouping per se that is destructive to the group, but the conspiracy of silence that generally surrounds it" (p. 352).

In some cases, out-of-group contact and socialization can be beneficial. From the perspective of feminist group therapy, out-of-group socialization is not viewed as harmful. This is especially true if members are selected carefully and are able to manage out-of-group contact so that it works to their own best interests and to the good of the group as a whole. During out-of-group contact, members often have the opportunity to expand on their goals outside of the group.

One of the best ways for the group leader to prevent inappropriate and counterproductive socialization among group members is to bring this issue up for discussion. It is especially timely to explore the negative impact of forming cliques when the group seems to be stuck and is getting nowhere or when it appears that members are not talking about their reactions to one another. The members can be taught that what they do not say in the group itself might very well prevent their group from attaining any level of cohesion or achieving its goals.

The Impact of the Leader's Values on the Group

In all controversial issues related to the group process, the leader's values play a central role. Your awareness of how your values influence your leadership style is in itself a central ethical issue. Although it is not your proper function to persuade clients to accept a certain value system, it is appropriate that you be clear about your own values and how your values influence the interventions you make in a group.

Value-laden issues are often brought to a group—religion, spirituality, abortion, divorce, gender roles in relationships, and family struggles, to name just a few. The purpose of the group is to help members clarify their beliefs and examine options that are most congruent with their own value system. Group counseling is not a forum in which leaders impose their worldview on the members; it is a way to assist members in exploring their own cultural values and beliefs.

You need to be clear about your own values and remain objective when working with values that are different from your own. Doing this may necessitate that you seek consultation or supervision, especially if you become aware of a value conflict that interferes with your ability to respect a particular value of a member. It is critical that group counselors increase their awareness of how their personal reactions to members may inhibit the group process. They must monitor their countertransference and recognize the danger of stereotyping individuals on the basis of race, ethnicity, gender, age, or sexual identity.

Members are best served if they learn to evaluate their own behavior to determine how it is working for them. If they come to the realization that what they are doing is not serving them well, it is appropriate for you to challenge them to develop alternative ways of behaving that will enable them to reach their goals. A group is an ideal place for members to assess the degree to which their behavior is consistent with their own values. They can get feedback from others, yet it will be their responsibility to make their own decisions.

Ethical Issues in Multicultural Group Counseling

BECOMING AWARE OF YOUR CULTURAL VALUES

If group leaders ignore some basic differences in people, they can hardly be doing what is in the best interests of these clients, which is an ethical matter. Regardless of your ethnic, cultural, and racial background, if you hope to build bridges of understanding between yourself and group members who are different from you, it is essential that you guard against stereotyped generalizations about social and cultural groups.

Johnson, Santos Torres, Coleman, and Smith (1995) write about issues that group counselors are likely to encounter as they attempt to facilitate culturally diverse counseling groups. These authors point out that group members typically bring with them their values, beliefs, and prejudices, which quickly become evident in a group situation. For Johnson and her colleagues, one goal of multicultural group counseling is to provide new levels of communication among members. This can be instrumental in assisting members in challenging their stereotypes by providing accurate information about individuals. Another goal of a diverse group is to promote understanding, acceptance, and trust among members of various cultural groups. For group leaders to facilitate this understanding and acceptance in a diverse group, it is essential that they are aware of their biases and that they have challenged their stereotypes.

Social justice issue often surface when working with people from culturally diverse backgrounds (MacNair-Semands, 2007). In these instances, group leaders have an opportunity to transform the group experience and work toward healing rather than perpetuating harmful interactions marked by sexism, racism, and heterosexism. Leaders can do this by assisting members in evaluating their attitudes about a range of diversity issues. The ASGW (2008) "Best Practice Guidelines" offers this guidance on recognizing the role of diversity in the practice of group work:

> Group workers practice with broad sensitivity to client differences including but not limited to ethnic, gender, religious, sexual, psychological maturity, economic class, family history, physical characteristics or limitations, and geographic location. Group workers continuously seek information regarding the cultural issues of the diverse population with whom they are working both by interaction with participants and from using outside resources. (B.8.)

An essential aspect of training for group leaders is promoting sensitivity and competence in addressing diversity in all forms of group work. Ethical practice requires that multicultural issues be incorporated in the training of group counselors (Debiak, 2007). There is increased recognition that all group work is multicultural; thus effective training of group counselors must address multicultural dimensions (DeLucia-Waack & Donigian, 2004; Ivey, Pedersen, & Ivey, 2008). Addressing diversity is an ethical mandate, but this practice is also a route to more effective group work.

TRANSCENDING CULTURAL ENCAPSULATION

Cultural encapsulation is a potential trap that all group counselors are vulnerable to falling into. If you accept the idea that certain cultural values are supreme, you limit yourself by refusing to consider alternatives. If you possess cultural tunnel vision, you are likely to misinterpret patterns of behavior displayed by group members who are culturally different from you. Unless you understand the values of other cultures, you are likely to misunderstand these clients. If you are able to appreciate cultural differences and do not associate such differences with superiority or inferiority, you can increase your psychological resourcefulness.

Cultural encapsulation, or provincialism, can afflict both group members and the group leader. As group counselors, we have to confront our own distortions as well as those of the members. Culture-specific knowledge about a client's background should not lead counselors to stereotype the client. Culturally competent group leaders recognize both differences among groups and differences within groups. It is essential that you avoid perceiving individuals as simply belonging to a group. Indeed, the differences between individuals within a group are often greater than the differences among the various groups (Pedersen, 2000). Not all Native Americans have the same experiences, nor do all African Americans, Asians, women, older people, or people with disabilities. It is important to explore individual differences among members of the same cultural group and not to make general assumptions based on an individual's group. Regardless of your cultural background, you must be prepared to deal with the complex differences among individuals from a variety of groups. You need to be prepared to deal with differences in areas such as race, culture, ethnicity, sexual orientation, disability status, religion, socioeconomic status, gender, and age (Lee & Ramsey, 2006).

Certain practitioners may encounter resistance from some people of color because they are using traditional White, middle-class values to interpret these clients' experiences. Such culturally encapsulated practitioners are not able to view the world through the eyes of all of their clients. Wrenn (1985) defines the **culturally encapsulated counselor** as one who has substituted stereotypes for the real world, who disregards cultural variations among clients, and who dogmatizes technique-oriented definitions of counseling and therapy. Such individuals, who operate within a monocultural framework, maintain a cocoon by evading reality and depending entirely on their own internalized value assumptions about what is good for society and the individual. These encapsulated people tend to be trapped in one way of thinking, believing their way is the universal way. They cling to an inflexible structure that resists adaptation to alternative ways of thinking.

Western models need to be adapted to serve the members of certain ethnic groups, especially those clients who live by a different value system. Many clients from non-Western cultures, members of ethnic minorities, and women from nearly all cultural groups tend to value interdependence more than independence, social consciousness more than individual freedom, and the welfare of the group more than their own welfare. Western psychological thought emphasizes self-sufficiency, individualism, directness of communication, assertiveness, independence from family, and self-growth. However, many Asian Americans come from collectivistic cultures that value interconnectedness with family and community (Chung, 2004). In Asian cultures, moreover, family roles tend to be highly structured, and "filial piety" exerts a powerful influence; that is, obligations to parents are respected throughout one's life, especially among the male children. The roles of family members are highly interdependent, and family structure is arranged so that conflicts are minimized while harmony is maximized. Traditional Asian values emphasize reserve and formality in most social situations, restraint and inhibition of intense feelings, obedience to authority, and high academic and occupational achievement. The family structure is traditionally patriarchal in that communication and authority flow vertically from top to bottom. The inculcation of guilt and shame are the main techniques used to control the behavior of individuals within a family (D. Sue & Sue, 1993).

These traditional values are shared by other cultural groups. For instance, Latinos emphasize *familismo*, which stresses interdependence over independence, affiliation over confrontation, and cooperation over competition. Parents are afforded a great deal of respect, and this respect governs all interpersonal relationships. The role of fate is often a pervasive force governing behavior. Latinos typically place a high value on spiritual matters and religion (Comas-Diaz, 1990). Torres-Rivera (2004) describes research that suggests that the common topics of discussion among Latino group members include relationships, friendship, intimacy, sexuality, time, money, parenting, commitment and responsibility, decision making, power, rules, and morality.

The central point is that if the group experience is largely the product of values that are alien to certain group members, it is easy to see that such members will not embrace the group. Group counselors who practice exclusively with a Western perspective are likely to meet with a considerable amount of resistance from clients with a non-Western worldview. Culturally sensitive group practice can occur only when leaders are willing to reveal the underlying values of the group process and determine whether these values are congruent with the cultural values of the members. Group members can also be encouraged to express their values and needs. The major challenge for group leaders is to determine what techniques are culturally appropriate for which individuals.

Religious and spiritual beliefs are part of the cultural background of clients and can be considered as an aspect of multiculturalism. Group workers need education on how to effectively incorporate exploration of members' spiritual and religious values as a part of a group experience. It is essential that group counselors also understand their own spiritual beliefs and values. Being sensitive to how cultural and spiritual values influence their own thinking and behavior will help group leaders work ethically and effectively with members who are culturally different from themselves. It is clear that ethical practice demands that group counselors possess the self-awareness, knowledge, and skills that are basic components of diversity-competent practitioners.

Uses and Misuses of Group Techniques

In leading groups, it is essential that you have a clear rationale for each technique you use. This is an area in which theory is a useful guide for practice. As you will see, the 11 theories at the core of this book give rise to many therapeutic strategies and techniques. Such techniques are a means to increase awareness, to accomplish change, or to promote exploration and interaction. They can certainly be used ethically and therapeutically, yet they also can be misused.

Some of the ways in which leaders can practice unprofessionally are using techniques with which they are unfamiliar, using techniques in a mechanical way, using techniques to serve their own hidden agendas or to enhance their power, or using specific techniques to pressure members. Many techniques that are used in a group do facilitate an intense expression of emotion. For example, guided fantasies into times of loneliness as a child can lead to deep psychological memories. Such techniques should be congruent with the overall purpose of the group. If leaders use such techniques, they must be ready to deal with any emotional release.

Leaders should avoid pushing members to "get into their emotions." Some group leaders measure the efficacy of their group by the level of catharsis, and group leaders who need to see members experience intense emotions can exploit the group members. This expression of emotion can sometimes reveal the leader's needs rather than the needs of the members.

Techniques have a better chance of being used appropriately when there is a rationale underlying their use. Techniques are aimed at fostering the client's self-exploration and self-understanding. At their best, they are invented in each unique client situation, and they are a collaborative effort between the leader and members. Techniques assist the group member in experimenting with some form of new behavior. It is critical that techniques be introduced in a timely and sensitive manner, with respect for the client, and that they be abandoned if they are not working.

In working with culturally diverse client populations, leaders may need to modify some of their interventions to suit the client's cultural and ethnic background. For example, if a client has been taught not to express his feelings in public, it may be inappropriate to quickly introduce techniques aimed at bringing out his feelings. It would be useful first to find out if this member is interested in exploring what he has learned from his culture about expressing his feelings. In another situation, perhaps a woman has been socialized to obey her parents without question. It could be inappropriate to introduce a role-playing technique that would have her confronting her parents directly. Leaders can respect the cultural values of members and at the same time encourage them to think about how these values and their upbringing have a continuing effect on their behavior. In some cases members will decide to modify certain behaviors because the personal price of retaining a value is too high. In other cases they will decide that they are not interested in changing certain cultural values or behaviors. The techniques used by leaders can help such members examine the pros and cons of making these changes. For a more detailed discussion of ethical considerations in using group techniques, see Corey, Corey, Callanan, and Russell (2004).

Group Leader Competence

DETERMINING ONE'S OWN LEVEL OF COMPETENCE

How can leaders determine whether they have the competence to use a certain technique? Although some leaders who have received training in the use of a technique may hesitate to use it (out of fear of making a mistake), other overly confident leaders without training may not have any reservations about trying out new methods. It is a good policy for leaders to have a clear theoretical and therapeutic rationale for any technique they use. Further, it is useful if leaders have experienced these techniques as members of a group. The issue of whether one is competent to lead a specific group or type of group is an ongoing question that faces all professional group leaders. You will need to remain open to struggling with questions such as these:

- Am I qualified through education and training to lead this specific group?
- What criteria can I use to determine my degree of competence?
- How can I recognize the boundaries of my competence?
- If I am not as competent as I'd like to be as a group worker, what specifically can I do?
- How can I continue to upgrade my leadership knowledge and skills?
- What techniques can I effectively employ?
- With what kinds of clients do I work best?
- With whom do I work least well, and why?
- When and how should I refer clients?
- When do I need to consult with other professionals?

There are no simple answers to these questions. Different groups require different leader qualities. For example, you may be fully competent to lead a group of relatively well-adjusted adults or of adults in crisis situations yet not be competent to lead a group of seriously disturbed people. You may be well trained for, and work well with, adolescent groups, yet you may not have the skills or training to do group work with younger children. You may be successful leading groups dealing with domestic violence yet find yourself ill-prepared to work successfully with children's groups. In short, you need supervised experience to understand the challenges you are likely to face in working with different types of groups.

Most practitioners have had their formal training in one of the branches of the mental health field, which include counseling psychology, clinical psychology, clinical social work, community counseling, educational psychology, school counseling, couples and family counseling, nursing, pastoral psychology, rehabilitation counseling, mental health counseling, and psychiatry. Generally, however, those who seek to become group practitioners find that formal education, even at the master's or doctoral level, does not give them the practical grounding they require to effectively lead groups. Practitioners often find it necessary to take a variety of specialized group therapy training workshops to gain experience.

The American Group Psychotherapy Association (AGPA) and the Association for Specialists in Group Work (ASGW) both address competence in group work. For example, "The group psychotherapist must be aware of his/her own individual competencies, and when the needs of the patient/client are beyond the competencies of the psychotherapist, consultation must be sought from other qualified professionals or other appropriate sources" (AGPA, 2002, 3.1). Professional competence is not arrived at once and for all; it is an ongoing developmental process for the duration of your career.

The "Best Practice Guidelines"(ASGW, 2008, section A), which are reproduced in the *Student Manual for Theory and Practice of Group Counseling*, provide some general suggestions for enhancing your level of competence as a group worker:

- Remain current and increase your knowledge and skill competencies through activities such as continuing education, professional supervision, and participation in personal and professional development activities.

- Utilize consultation and/or supervision to ensure effective practice regarding ethical concerns that interfere with effective functioning as a group leader.

- Be open to getting professional assistance for personal problems or conflicts of your own that may impair your professional judgment or work performance.

Part of being a competent group counselor involves being able to explain to group members the theory behind your practice, telling members in clear language the goals of the group and how you conceptualize the group process, and relating what you do in a group to this model. As you acquire competence, you will be able to continually refine your techniques in light of your model. Competent group counselors possess the knowledge and skills that are described in the following section.

PROFESSIONAL TRAINING STANDARDS FOR GROUP COUNSELORS

Effective group leadership programs are not developed by legislative mandates and professional codes alone. For proficient leaders to emerge, a training program must make group work a priority. Unfortunately, most master's programs in counseling require only one group course, and it is typical for this single course to cover both the didactic and experiential aspects of group process. This course often deals with both theories of group counseling and group process as well as providing students with opportunities to experience a group as a member. It is a major challenge to train group counselors adequately in a single course!

The ASGW (2000) "Professional Standards for the Training of Group Workers" specify two levels of competencies and related training. First is a set of *core knowledge* and *skill competencies* that provides the foundation on which *specialized* training is built. At a minimum, one group course should be included in a training program, and it should be structured to help students acquire the basic knowledge and skills needed to facilitate a group.

The ASGW (2000) training standards state that group leadership skills (which were described in Chapter 2) are best mastered through supervised practice that involves observation and participation in a group experience. Although a minimum of 10 hours of supervised practice is required, 20 hours is recommended as part of the core training. Furthermore, these training standards require that all counselor trainees complete core training in group work during their entry-level education.

Once counselor trainees have mastered the core knowledge and skill domains, they have the platform to develop a group work specialization in one or more of four areas, which were described in Chapter 1: (1) task groups, (2) psychoeducational groups, (3) group counseling, or (4) group psychotherapy. The standards outline specific knowledge and skill competencies for these specialties and also specify the recommended number of hours of supervised training for each.

The current trend in training group workers focuses on learning group process by becoming involved in supervised experiences. Certainly, the mere completion of one graduate course in group theory and practice does not equip one to effectively lead groups. Both direct participation in planned and supervised small groups and clinical experience in leading various groups under careful supervision are needed to provide leaders with the skills to meet the challenges of group work.

Ieva, Ohrt, Swank, and Young (2009) investigated the impact on master's students who participated in experiential personal growth groups. The students' perceptions of their experience supported the following assumptions:

- Group process is a beneficial aspect of training.
- Experience in a personal growth group increases knowledge about groups and leadership skills.
- Experience in a personal growth group enhances students' ability to give and receive feedback.

All study participants reported some personal or professional progress as a result of their experience in a group. Areas of benefit included interpersonal learning, knowledge about group process, self-awareness, empathy for future clients, and opportunities to learn by observing group process in action. The participants' confidence in facilitating a group increased after having experience as a group member, and they believed their participation assisted them in developing their own personal leadership style. Not only did the counselors-in-training report benefiting both personally and professionally from participating in personal growth groups, but they thought this should be a requirement for all students in a master's level counseling program. Ieva and colleagues (2009) conclude that this study provides counselor educators with valuable information that can help them design and facilitate training experiences that are positive, beneficial, and ethically responsible.

THREE IMPORTANT ADJUNCTS TO THE TRAINING OF GROUP COUNSELORS

If you expect to lead groups, you will want to be prepared for this work, both personally and academically. If your program has not provided this preparation, it will be necessary for you to seek in-service workshops in group processes. It is not likely that you will learn how to lead groups merely through reading about them and listening to lectures.

I recommend at least three experiences as adjuncts to a training program for students learning about group work: (1) participation in personal counseling, (2) participation in group counseling or a personal growth group, and (3) participation in a training and supervision group. Following is a discussion of these three adjuncts to the professional preparation of group counselors.

Personal Counseling for Group Leaders I believe that extensive self-exploration is necessary for trainees to identify countertransference feelings, to recognize blind spots and biases, and to use their personal attributes effectively in their group work. Group trainees can benefit greatly from the experience of being a client at some time. To me it makes sense that group leaders need to demonstrate the courage and willingness to do for themselves what they expect members in their groups to do—expand their awareness of self and the effect of that self on others.

What does research reveal on this subject? More than 90% of mental health professionals report positive outcomes from their own counseling experiences (Geller, Norcross, & Orlinsky, 2005). In his synthesis of 25 years of research on the personal therapy of mental health professionals, Norcross (2005b) states: "The cumulative results indicate that personal therapy is an emotionally vital, interpersonally dense, and professionally formative experience that should be central to the development of health care psychologists" (p. 840). Norcross points out that most mental health care practitioners strongly value experiential over didactic learning.

Increasing self-awareness is a major reason to seek out personal counseling. In leading a group, you will encounter many instances of transferences, both among members and toward you. **Transference** refers to the unconscious process whereby members project onto you, the group leader, past feelings or attitudes that they had toward significant people in their lives. Of course, you can easily become entangled in your own feelings of **countertransference**, which often involves both conscious and unconscious emotional responses to group members. You may have unresolved personal problems, which you can project onto the members of your group. Through personal counseling, you can become increasingly aware of personal triggers and can also work through some of your unfinished business that could easily interfere with your effectiveness in facilitating groups. If you are not actively involved in the pursuit of healing your own psychological wounds, you will probably have considerable difficulty entering the world of a client. Through being a client yourself, you can gain an experiential frame of reference to view yourself as you are. This experience will increase your compassion for your clients and help you learn ways of intervening that you can use in the groups you facilitate. For further reading on this topic, I highly recommend *The Psychotherapist's Own Psychotherapy* (Geller, Norcross, & Orlinsky, 2005).

Self-Exploration Groups for Group Leaders Being a member of a variety of groups can prove to be an indispensable part of your training as a group leader. By experiencing your own cautiousness, resistances, fears, and uncomfortable moments in a group, by being confronted, and by struggling with your problems in a group context, you can experience what is needed to build a trusting and cohesive group.

In addition to helping you recognize and explore personal conflicts and increase self-understanding, a personal growth group can be a powerful teaching tool. One of the best ways to learn how to assist group members in their struggles is to participate yourself as a member of a group.

Yalom (2005) states that a substantial number of training programs require both personal therapy and a group experience for trainees. Some of the benefits of participating in a therapeutic group that he suggests are experiencing the power of a group, learning what self-disclosure is about, coming to appreciate the difficulties involved in self-sharing, learning on an emotional level what one knows intellectually, and becoming aware of one's dependency on the leader's power and knowledge.

Participation in Experiential Training Workshops I have found training workshops most useful in helping group counselors develop the skills necessary for effective intervention. The trainees can also learn a great deal about their response to feedback, their competitiveness, their need for approval, their concerns over being competent, and their power struggles. In working with both university students learning about group approaches and with professionals who want to upgrade their group skills, I have found an intensive weekend or weeklong workshop to be an effective format. In these workshops the participants all have ample opportunity to lead their small group for a designated period with the benefit of direct supervision. After a segment in which a participant leads the group, my colleagues and I who are supervising their group offer feedback to those who led the group, a commentary of the process, and facilitate discussion of what happened in the group by the entire group.

MY JOURNEY TOWARD BECOMING A GROUP WORK SPECIALIST

I want to share some highlights of what I found helpful in becoming a teacher and practitioner of group counseling. In my doctoral studies in the mid-1960s, I had no formal course work in group counseling. It was my experiences as a participant in many different kinds of groups after getting my doctorate that perked my interest in becoming a group practitioner, in teaching group courses, in training and supervising group workers, and in writing textbooks on group counseling.

During my 30s and 40s I availed myself to a wide range of different groups, a few of which included overnight marathon groups, traditional weekly therapy groups, and various residential workshops done in a group format. I participated in many personal growth workshops and encounter groups, which lasted in length from a weekend to 10 days. My early experiences as a group member provided insights and were instrumental in leading me to make significant changes in my personal life. This encouraged me to continue seeking out various groups aimed at personal and professional development. Although my main motivation for participating in these group workshops was not to learn techniques or to acquire skills in conducting groups, I received indirect benefits that I was able to apply to my professional work. This led to finding ways to incorporate group work into my teaching and professional practice. I learned significant lessons about organizing and facilitating groups from my experience as a group member even though I had concerns about the way some of the groups I attended were set up or conducted. These experiences were important in my learning how to design different kinds of therapeutic groups, and they helped me to think about ethics in group practice. Many of the specific dimensions of group facilitation that I address in this book came about as a result of the experiential learning and training I acquired beyond my doctoral program.

My own journey into group work has convinced me of how crucial it is for those who want to facilitate groups to open themselves to the experience of being in groups as a member. Certainly course work in group counseling is crucial, as is supervision when we are beginning to lead groups; in addition, what we can learn about ourselves personally by being a member of a group can pay dividends in our professional work. For a more detailed description of my journey into group work, both from a personal and professional perspective, see *Creating Your Professional Path: Lessons From My Journey* (Corey, 2010).

ETHICAL ISSUES IN TRAINING GROUP COUNSELORS

Training programs differ on whether participating in a group is optional or required. My own bias is clear on the importance of doing our own work in a group as a prerequisite to becoming group counselors. To be sure, requiring participation in a therapeutic group as part of a training program can present some practical and ethical problems of its own. A controversial ethical issue in the preparation of group workers involves combining experiential and didactic training methods.

I consider an experiential component to be essential when teaching group counseling courses. Admittedly, there are inherent problems in teaching students how groups function by involving them on an experiential level. Such an arrangement entails their willingness to engage in self-disclosure, to become active participants in an interpersonal laboratory, and to engage themselves on an emotional level as well as a cognitive one. Time and again, however, my colleagues and I hear both students and professionals who participate in our group training workshops comment on the value of supervised experience in which they have both leadership and membership roles. Through this format, group process concepts come alive. Trainees experience firsthand what it takes to create trust and what resistance feels like. They often say that they have gained a new appreciation of the group experience from a member's perspective.

In talking with many other counselor educators throughout the country who teach group courses, I find that it is common practice to combine the experiential and didactic domains. Sometimes students colead a small group with a peer and are supervised by the instructor. Of course, this arrangement is not without problems, especially if the instructor also functions in the roles of facilitator and supervisor. Students may fear that their grade will be influenced by their participation (or lack of it) in the experiential part of the class.

In grading and evaluating students in group courses, the professionalism of the instructor is crucial. Ethical practice requires instructors to spell out their grading criteria clearly. The criteria may include the results of written reports, oral presentations, essay tests, and objective examinations. Most group counselor educators agree that students' performance in the experiential group should not be graded, but they can be expected to attend regularly and to participate. Clear guidelines need to be established so that students know what their rights and responsibilities are at the beginning of the group course.

There is potential for abuse when using experiential approaches in training group leaders, but this does not warrant the conclusion that all such experiences are inappropriate or unethical. I view it as a mistake to conclude that group work educators should be restricted to the singular role of providing didactic information. The challenge of educators is to provide the best training available. I am convinced that teaching group process by involving students in personal ways is the best way for them to learn how to eventually set up and facilitate groups. I am in agreement with Stockton, Morran, and Krieger (2004) who indicate that there is a fine line between offering experiential activities and safeguarding against gaining information that could be used in evaluating students. Faculty who use experiential approaches are often involved in balancing multiple roles, which requires consistent monitoring of boundaries. Stockton and colleagues emphasize that group work educators need to exert caution so that they offer training that is both ethical and effective.

Liability and Malpractice

Although the topics of professional liability and malpractice are not strictly a part of ethical practice, these are legal dimensions with implications for group practitioners. Group leaders are expected to practice within the code of ethics of their particular profession and also to abide by legal standards. Practitioners are subject to civil penalties if they fail to do right or if they actively do wrong to another. If group members can prove that personal injury or psychological harm was caused by a leader's failure to render proper service, either through negligence or ignorance, the leader is open to a malpractice suit. **Negligence** consists of departing from the standard and commonly accepted practices of others in the profession. Practitioners involved in a malpractice action may need to justify the techniques they use. If their therapeutic interventions are consistent with those of other members of their profession in their community, they are on much firmer ground than if they employ uncommon techniques.

Group leaders need to keep up to date with the laws of their state as they affect their professional practice. Ignorance is not a sufficient excuse. Those leaders who work with groups of children and adolescents, especially, must know the law as it pertains to matters of confidentiality, parental consent, the right to treatment or to refuse treatment, informed consent, and other legal rights of clients. Such awareness not only protects the group members but also protects group leaders from malpractice suits arising from negligence or ignorance.

The best way to protect yourself from getting involved in a malpractice suit is to take preventive measures, which means not practicing outside the boundaries of your competence. Following the spirit of the ethics codes of your professional organization is also important. The key to avoiding a malpractice suit is maintaining reasonable, ordinary, and prudent practices. Here are some prudent guidelines for ethical and professional standards of practice:

- Be willing to devote the time it takes to adequately screen, select, and prepare the members of your group.
- Develop written informed consent procedures at the outset of a group. Give the potential members of your groups enough information to make informed choices about group participation. Do not mystify the group process.
- Provide an atmosphere of respect for diversity within the group.
- Become aware of local and state laws that limit your practice, as well as the policies of the agency for which you work. Inform members about these policies and about legal limitations (such as exemptions to confidentiality, mandatory reporting, and the like).
- Emphasize the importance of maintaining confidentiality before the group begins and at various times during the life of a group.
- Restrict your practice to client populations for which you are prepared by virtue of your education, training, and experience.
- Be alert for symptoms of psychological debilitation in group members, which may indicate that their participation should be discontinued. Be able to put such clients in contact with appropriate referral resources.
- Do not promise the members of your group anything that you cannot deliver. Help them realize that their degree of effort and commitment will be key factors in determining the outcomes of the group experience.
- In working with minors, secure the written permission of their parents, even if this is not required by state law.
- Always consult with colleagues or supervisors whenever there is an ethical or legal concern. Document the nature of these consultations.
- Make it a practice to assess the general progress of a group, and teach members how to evaluate their progress toward their personal goals; keep adequate clinical records on this progress.
- Learn how to assess and intervene in cases in which clients pose a threat to themselves or others.
- Avoid blending professional relationships with social ones. Avoid engaging in sexual relationships with either current or former group members.
- Remain alert to ways in which your personal reactions might inhibit the group process, and monitor your countertransference. Avoid using the group you are leading as a place where you work on personal problems.
- Continue to read the research, and use group interventions and techniques that are supported by research as well as by community practice.
- Have a theoretical orientation that serves as a guide to your practice. Be able to describe the purpose of the techniques you use in your groups.

As you read about the stages of group development in Chapters 4 and 5, reflect on the issues raised in this chapter as they apply to the tasks and challenges you will face as a group leader during various group phases. Realize that there are few simple answers to the ethical aspects of group work. Learn how to think through the ethical considerations that you will face as a group practitioner. Being willing to raise questions and think about an ethical course to follow is the beginning of becoming an ethical group counselor. The *Student Manual for Theory and Practice of Group Counseling* (8th edition) contains a number of resources that will help you develop your awareness of ethical group practice. I urge you to consult these resources frequently as you begin to formulate your own ideas about ethical practice in group work. For a more comprehensive discussion of ethical issues in group work, see Corey, Corey, and Callanan (2011, chap. 12) and for more on malpractice and risk management, see Corey, Corey, and Callanan (2011, chap. 5).

AUTHOR LECTURES

Watch *Gerald Corey's Perspectives on Theory and Practice of Group Counseling* DVD or visit the *Theory and Practice of Group Counseling* CourseMate website at www.cengagebrain.com/shop/ISBN/0840033869 to watch videos of Dr. Gerald Corey presenting lectures for each chapter. Also available are unique eAudio lectures for each chapter and quiz questions for self-study.

CHAPTER FOUR

Early Stages in the Development of a Group

Chapters 4 and 5 provide a road map of the stages through which a group progresses. This map is based on my own experience, as well as my study of the literature and research in group work, and describes the essential issues that characterize the development of a group.

The stages described in this chapter don't correspond to discrete and neatly separated phases in the life of a real group. There is considerable overlap between the stages, and groups don't conform precisely to some preordained time sequence that theoretically separates one phase from the next. Also, the content of the group process varies from group to group, and different aspects of the process may be stressed depending on the theoretical orientation of the leader, the purpose of the group, and the population that makes up the group. In spite of these differences, however, there does seem to be a general pattern to the evolution of a group.

A clear grasp of the stages of group development, including an awareness of the factors that facilitate group process and of those that interfere with it, will maximize your ability to help the members of your groups reach their goals. By learning about the problems and potential crises of each stage, you learn when and how to intervene. As you gain a picture of the systematic evolution of groups, you become aware of the developmental tasks that must be successfully met if a group is to move forward, and you can predict problems and intervene therapeutically. Finally, knowledge of the developmental sequence of groups will give you the perspective you need to lead group members in constructive directions by reducing unnecessary confusion and anxiety.

This chapter begins with an examination of the leader's concerns in forming a group. Stage 1, the *formation stage,* includes getting prepared, announcing the group, screening and selecting the members, and preparing them for a successful experience. Stage 2, the *orientation phase,* is a time of exploration during the initial sessions. Stage 3, the *transition stage,* is characterized by dealing with conflict, defensiveness, and resistance.

Chapter 5 continues with Stage 4, the *working stage.* This stage is marked by action—dealing with significant personal issues and translating insight into action both in the group and outside of it. In Stage 5, the *consolidation stage,* the focus is on applying what has been learned in the group and putting it to use in everyday life. I conclude with an examination of postgroup concerns in Stage 6, which includes *evaluation* and *follow-up* issues. The description of these stages is based largely on my colleagues and my observations of the way in which groups typically evolve.

Stage 1: Pregroup Issues—Formation of the Group

For a group to be successful, you need to devote considerable time to planning. In my view planning should begin with drafting a written proposal containing the basic purposes of the group, the population to be served, a clear rationale for the group—namely, the need for and justification of that particular group—ways to announce the group and recruit members, the screening and selection process for members, the size and duration of the group, the frequency and time of meetings, the group structure and format, the methods of preparing members, whether the group will be open or closed, whether membership will be voluntary or involuntary, and the follow-up and evaluation procedures.

It cannot be overstressed that leader preparation in this formative phase is crucial to the outcome of a group. Thus it is time well spent to think about the kind of group you want and to prepare yourself psychologically. If your expectations are unclear, and if the purposes and structure of the group are vague, the members will surely flounder needlessly. However, at times students may be thrust into an internship at a community mental health center and find they are leading groups that are not well planned. Because of their role as interns in the agency, students may find it difficult to speak up about their concerns. If you find yourself in this kind of situation, I suggest that you address your concerns to both your supervisor at your university and to your field supervisor at your agency. Even if the situation does not change, at least you have made your concerns known.

ANNOUNCING A GROUP AND RECRUITING MEMBERS

How a group is announced influences the way it will be received by potential members and the kind of people who will be attracted to it. It is imperative that you say enough to give prospective members a clear idea about the group's rationale and goals.

When recruiting potential members for a group, I am in favor of making direct contact with the population that is most likely to benefit from the group. For example, if you are planning a group at a school, make personal visits to several classes to introduce yourself and to tell the students about the group. You could also distribute a brief application form to anyone who wanted to find out more about the group.

SCREENING AND SELECTING GROUP MEMBERS

The ACA's (2005) ethical standard pertaining to screening group members reads as follows:

> Counselors screen prospective group counseling/therapy participants. To the extent possible, counselors select members whose needs and goals are compatible with goals of the group, who will not impede the group process, and whose well-being will not be jeopardized by the group experience. (A.8.a.)

As you screen and select group members, ask yourself these two questions: "How can I decide who is most likely to benefit from this group?" "Who is likely to be disturbed by group participation or be a negative influence for the other members?" If you have an open group, you would want to ask this question as well: "How might this potential member fit with members already in the group?"

The setting in which leaders work may make it difficult to screen members individually, but there are other ways of accomplishing this. For example, in agency settings, clients are often court-ordered to a group, which makes screening impractical. Even in these instances, however, the group leader can still attempt to meet with each client for a pregroup interview rather than a formal screening session. If screening is not possible, the initial group meeting can be structured as an information and screening session.

Once potential members have been recruited, the leader must determine who (if anyone) should be excluded. Careful screening will lessen the psychological risks of inappropriate participation in a group. During the screening session, the leader can spend some time exploring with potential members any fears or concerns they have about participating in a group.

The leader can help members make an assessment of their readiness for a group and discuss the potential life changes that might come about. Members can benefit from knowing that there is a price for remaining the same as well as for making substantive changes. If individuals go into a group unaware of the potential impact of their personal changes on others in their lives, their motivation for continuing is likely to decrease if they encounter problems with their family.

Screening should be a two-way process, and potential members should have an opportunity at the private screening interview to ask questions to determine whether the group and the leader are right for them. Group leaders should encourage prospective members to be involved in the decision concerning the appropriateness of their participation in the group. It is sometimes difficult to determine which candidates will benefit from a group. During the private interview, individuals may be vague about what they hope to get from the group. They may be frightened, tense, and defensive, and they may approach the personal interview as they would a job interview, especially if they are anxious about being admitted to the group.

Of course, there is always the possibility that the leader may have real reservations about including some people who are quite determined to join the group. Some people can quite literally drain the energy of the group so that little is left for productive work. Also, the presence of certain people can make group cohesion difficult to attain. This is especially true of individuals who have a need to monopolize and dominate, of hostile or aggressive clients with a need to act out, and of people who are extremely self-centered and who seek a group as an audience.

The purpose of screening is to prevent potential harm to group members, not to make the leader's job more pleasant. Some leaders screen out people based on their own personal dislike or countertransference issues, even though these individuals might benefit from a group experience. Although some individuals may appear somewhat reluctant or defensive, this alone is not a sufficient reason to rule them out of participating in a group. The basic question for the selection of a group member is this: "Will the group be productive or counterproductive for this individual?" If the answer is "counterproductive," he or she should not be placed in a group because doing so is likely to result in a negative experience.

According to Burlingame, Fuhriman, and Johnson (2002), people who should probably be excluded from a group include those who are actively psychotic or organically impaired, those severely limited in interpersonal skills and impervious to feedback, and those who are unable or unwilling to abide by a contract. Others who should generally be excluded from most groups are people who are in a state of extreme crisis, who are suicidal, who have sociopathic personalities, who are highly suspicious, or who are lacking in ego strength and are prone to fragmented and bizarre behavior.

It is difficult to say categorically that a certain kind of person should be excluded from all groups; the type of group will determine who may benefit from the group experience. For example, an alcoholic might be excluded from a personal growth group but be an appropriate candidate for a homogeneous group of individuals who suffer from addiction problems, be it addiction to alcohol, to other drugs, or to food. As to those who are good candidates to include in a group, Burlingame, Fuhriman, and Johnson (2002) list individuals who define problems as interpersonal, are able to give and receive feedback, have a capacity for empathy, and are highly motivated.

The screening session is an opportunity for the leader to evaluate candidates and to determine what they want from the group experience. It is also a chance for prospective members to get to know the leader and to develop a feeling of confidence. The manner in which this initial interview is conducted has a lot to do with establishing the trust level of the group. During this interview, I stress the two-way exchange, hoping that members will feel free to ask the questions that will help them determine whether they want to join this group at this particular time. Here are some questions I consider in screening:

- Does this person appear to want to do what is necessary to be a productive group member?
- Has the decision to join the group been made by the person?
- Will this person be able to attend to the group tasks?
- Does the candidate have a sense of what he or she would want to accomplish by being in a group?
- Is the individual open and willing to share something personal?
- How is a prospective member likely to fit with other members so that the group can work?

The selection of members to ensure optimum group balance often seems very challenging, if not an impossible task. In the context of group psychotherapy, Yalom (2005) argues that unless careful selection criteria are employed clients may end up discouraged and not helped. He maintains that it is easier to identify those who should be excluded from a therapy group than it is to identify those who should be included. Citing clinical studies, Yalom lists the following as poor candidates for a heterogeneous, outpatient, intensive-therapy group: brain-damaged people, paranoid clients, hypochondrial individuals, those who are addicted to drugs or alcohol, acutely psychotic individuals, and sociopathic personalities. In terms of criteria for inclusion, Yalom contends that the client's level of motivation to work is the most important variable. From his perspective, groups are useful for people who have interpersonal problems such as loneliness, an inability to make or maintain intimate contacts, feelings of being unlovable, fears of being assertive, and dependency. Individuals who lack meaning in life, who suffer from diffuse anxiety, who are searching for an identity, who fear success, and who are compulsive workers might also profit from a group experience.

Whether a person is to be included or excluded has much to do with the purposes of the group. You have a responsibility to determine whether a prospective member is suitable for a given group; this decision will protect both the prospective member and the group itself. Perhaps the most important thing is to choose people who are likely to work well together, even though the group may be a heterogeneous one. At times, you may have to inform prospective members that a particular group could be harmful to them. If you decide that certain members are not appropriate for your group, provide these individuals with the reasons for your decision and make appropriate referrals.

PRACTICAL CONCERNS IN THE FORMATION OF A GROUP

Open Versus Closed Groups As a result of managed care, many groups tend to be short term, solution oriented, and characterized by changing membership. Whether the group will be open or closed may be determined, in part, by the population and the setting. But the issue needs to be discussed and decided before the group meets, or at the initial session. There are some distinct advantages to both kinds of groups. In a closed group, no new members are added for the predetermined duration of its life. This practice offers a stability that makes continuity possible and fosters cohesion among group members. If too many members drop out of a closed group, however, the group process is drastically affected.

In an open group, new members replace those who are leaving, and this can provide new stimulation. A disadvantage of the open group is that new members may have a difficult time becoming part of the group because they are not aware of what has been discussed before they joined. Another disadvantage is that changing group membership can have adverse effects on the cohesion of the group. Therefore, if the flow of the group is to be maintained, the leader needs to devote time and attention to preparing new members and helping them become integrated.

Voluntary Versus Involuntary Membership Should groups be composed only of members who are there by their own choice, or can groups function even when they include involuntary members? Obviously, there are a number of advantages to working with a group of clients who are willing to invest themselves in the group process. Attending a group because one has been "sent" there by someone often minimizes the chance of success. However, many of the negative attitudes that involuntary candidates have about groups can be changed by adequately preparing members for a group.

I have found that many involuntary members learn that a group counseling experience can help them make some of the changes they want. In many agencies and institutions, practitioners are expected to lead groups with an involuntary clientele. It is important for these counselors to learn how to work within such a structure rather than hold to the position that they can be effective only with a voluntary population. By presenting the group experience in a favorable light, the leader can help involuntary members see the potential benefits of the experience and the chance of productive work taking place will be increased. However, it probably will take more time and work to achieve a level of trust in an involuntary group. The key to successful participation lies in thorough member orientation and preparation and in the leader's belief that the group process has something to offer to these prospective members.

Homogeneous Versus Heterogeneous Groups Group leaders need to decide the basis for the homogeneity of their groups. By homogeneous I mean composed of people who, for example, are similar in ages, such as a group for children, for adolescents, or for older persons. Other homogeneous groups may be based on a common interest or problem. Short-term groups are usually characterized by homogeneous membership. The unitary focus in a homogeneous group tends to foster group cohesion, and common problem areas of group members promote sharing experiences and learning from one another.

Although homogeneous membership can be more appropriate for certain target populations with definite needs or with short-term groups, heterogeneous membership has some definite advantages for many personal growth groups, whether short or long term. A heterogeneous group represents a microcosm of the social structure that exists in the everyday world and offers participants the opportunity to experiment with new behaviors, develop social skills, and get feedback from many diverse sources. If a simulation of everyday life is desired, it is well to have a range of ages, races, cultural and ethnic backgrounds, gender and sexual identity, and a variety of concerns.

Meeting Place Another pregroup concern is the setting. Privacy, a certain degree of attractiveness, and a place that allows for face-to-face interaction are crucial. A poor setting can set a negative tone that will adversely affect the cohesion of the group, so every effort should be made to secure a meeting place that will facilitate in-depth work.

Group Size The desirable size for a group depends on factors such as the age of the clients, the type of group, the experience of the group counselors, and the type of problems explored. Another element to be taken into consideration is whether the group has one leader or more. For ongoing groups with adults, about eight members with one leader seems to be a good size. Groups with children may be as small as three or four. In general, the group should have enough people to afford ample interaction so that it doesn't drag and yet be small enough to give everyone a chance to participate frequently without, however, losing the sense of "group."

Frequency and Length of Meetings How often should groups meet and for how long? These issues, too, depend on the type of group and, to some extent, on the experience of the leader. Once a week is a typical format for most counseling groups. With children and adolescents, it is usually better to meet more frequently for shorter sessions. For adults who are functioning relatively well, a 2-hour group each week is long enough to allow for some intensive work. Outpatient groups often meet for a 90-minute session, whereas inpatient groups may have shorter sessions. Groups do not necessarily have to meet weekly, even though this is typical.

Short-Term Versus Long-Term Groups It is wise to set a termination date at the outset of a closed group so members have a clear idea of their commitment. The duration varies from group to group, depending on the type of group, the population, and the requirements of the agency. Many community agencies have policies that limit groups to a relatively short duration. For brief group therapy, length of treatment is a defining characteristic. Time-limited groups have a specific focus, and interventions have the aim of being as efficient as possible.

Some closed groups have long-term goals that require long-term commitments of members. This is particularly true of psychodynamic groups that aim for deeper work. In private practice, groups can be either short or long term. Some of these groups last for 12 to 20 weeks, some for 30 to 50 weeks, and some for more than a year. Many college and high school groups typically run for the length of a semester (about 15 weeks). The group should meet long enough to allow for cohesion and productive work, yet not so long that it seems to drag on interminably.

THE USES OF A PREGROUP MEETING OR THE INITIAL SESSION

Once group membership has been established, the leader can turn his or her attention to this question: "What is the group leader's responsibility in preparing members to get the maximum benefit from their group experience?" My bias is that systematic preparation is essential and that it begins at the private screening interview and continues during the first few sessions. Preparation consists essentially of exploring with members their expectations, fears, goals, and misconceptions; the basics of group process; the psychological risks associated with group membership and ways of minimizing them; the values and limitations of groups; guidelines for getting the most from the group experience; and the necessity of confidentiality. This preparation can be done through a preliminary meeting of all those who will be joining the group.

In addition to the private interview with each person before the group is formed, I use the initial session as a group screening device. The initial session is a good place to talk about the purposes of the group, to let members know how they will be using group time, to explore many of the possible issues that might be considered in the group, to discuss the ground rules and policies, and to begin the getting-acquainted process. Because I prefer to have people decide early if they are ready for a group and willing to become active members, I encourage participants to consider the first session as an opportunity to help them make such a decision.

Structuring the group, including the specification of norms and procedures, should be accomplished early in the group's history. Although structuring begins at the private intake session, it will be necessary to continue this process the first time the group actually meets. In fact, structuring is an ongoing process that is a vital part of the early phases of your group. Some group members expect a low degree of structure, and others prefer a group that is highly structured with clearly defined tasks.

MULTICULTURAL CONSIDERATIONS IN PREPARING MEMBERS FOR A GROUP EXPERIENCE

Screening, selecting, and orienting members to group procedures are especially critical in working with individuals from diverse cultural groups. Many group members hold values and expectations that make it difficult for them to participate fully in a group experience. For example, the free participation and exchange of views in therapy groups may conflict with Asian values of humility and modesty. Asian clients can experiencing difficulty in a group, especially if they are expected to make deeply personal disclosures too quickly. Therefore, screening and adequate preparation are essential for Asian American clients who have had no prior therapeutic experience in a group setting. In working with Asian members, Chen and Han (2001) state that preparation is critical because many of the behaviors expected in a group may be foreign to what people do in their everyday lives. For example, some cultures (such as Latino and Asian) value indirect communication; however, group members are told to be direct as they speak to one another.

In daily life, people are often encouraged to mask their real feelings so that they will not offend others. In some cultures, individuals are not encouraged to express their feelings openly, to talk about their personal problems with people whom they do not know well, or to tell others what they think about them. For individuals of other ethnic groups, preparation is no less important. Group workers need to be aware that reluctance or hesitation to participate fully in a group may be more the result of cultural background than of an uncooperative attitude.

Many group members, regardless of their cultural background, may hesitate to reveal personal matters for fear of being judged and of being rejected. In a group situation, members are generally expected to abide by the norms of openness, honesty, and directness, and they are expected to make themselves emotionally vulnerable. Depending on one's cultural background, some group norms may be very demanding and may go against the grain of a member's personal and cultural value system.

Members need to know the purpose of the group, how the group experience can be of personal value to them, and how they can get the most from a group experience. Adequate preparation of members is one of the best ways to increase the chances of a successful group experience for all clients. It is essential that the goals and the purposes of the group be appropriate for the cultural context of clients with diverse cultural backgrounds. This is why a discussion of the aims of a group and the importance of members' establishing their own goals is so important.

GUIDELINES FOR ORIENTATION AND PREPARATION OF MEMBERS

Although I believe strongly in the value of systematic and complete preparation of group members, I also do see the danger of overpreparation. For example, I typically ask members to talk early in the group about any fears or reservations they might have. I also explore a few common risks of participating in a group. In this particular area, however, if the leader becomes too specific, some members may end up developing concerns or even fears that they never had before and that may become self-fulfilling prophecies. In addition, too much structure imposed by the leader can stifle any initiative on the part of the members. The risks inherent in overpreparation should be balanced against those that accompany insufficient preparation. Excessive floundering and useless conflict during the group's later stages are often the result of a failure to acquire basic skills and a lack of understanding of the group process.

I begin my preparation program at the time of screening each potential member, and I devote most of the first group meeting (what I call the pregroup meeting) to orientation about group process. This orientation continues during the initial phase of the group. Group process issues emerge naturally while the group is taking shape, and these concerns are dealt with as they arise.

I start by discussing with the participants the importance of their own preparation for group work. I stress that what they get from their group will depend largely on their level of investment. During the pregroup meeting and continuing into the initial group sessions, I view my role as helping members examine and decide on their level of commitment. We focus on what they want to get from participating in a group, and I assist them in defining clear, specific, and meaningful personal goals. After they have decided on some personal goals that will guide their work in the group, they are asked to refine these goals by developing a contract. (For details on ways to help members define personal goals and formulate contracts, see the discussions of transactional analysis, behavioral group therapy, rational emotive behavior therapy, reality therapy, and solution-focused brief therapy in Chapters 12 through 16.)

At the pregroup meeting I ask members to raise any questions they have about the group and encourage members to talk about their expectations, their reasons for being in the group, their fears or concerns about participating, and their hopes. I also provide some guidelines on what members can do to maximize the benefit of the group in enabling them to make the changes they desire in their lives. Especially important is a discussion regarding the rationale for appropriate self-disclosure. Members are told that it is their decision to select the personal themes they want to explore in the group. They also hear that it is critical that they be willing to share persistent reactions they are having to here-and-now group interactions. My purpose is to teach them that the group will function only if they are willing to express what they are thinking and feeling about being in the group. In fact, their reactions provide the direction in which we typically proceed during the first few sessions. I also encourage them to bring up any questions or concerns they have about group process.

Members are asked to give some thought before they come to each session about personal issues they are willing to bring up for exploration. Although they may have a specific agenda when they come to a group meeting, I encourage them to remain flexible by being willing to work on other concerns that may emerge spontaneously as others are interacting in the group.

Group members are typically asked to keep a journal and to spontaneously write about the range of reactions they have while they are in the group as well as reactions to what they experience between the sessions. They are encouraged to bring into the group a summary of what they have been writing in their journals. In this way they are taught about the value of continuing work that was begun during a session. Group members uniformly comment about the value of the writing they do throughout the life of a group. Their journaling not only keeps them focused on their goals but also provides them with a basis for identifying ways that they have changed. Journal entries also provide a mechanism for self-assessment of their involvement in the group.

Members frequently hear about the importance of using the group to practice new behaviors. They learn that the group is not an end in itself but only a means to help them acquire new ways of thinking, feeling, and behaving. They are continually invited to try out new styles of behavior during the sessions to see if they might want to make certain changes. I suggest that members write in their journals about their reactions to behavior they have experimented with during the group sessions and also about new behaviors they have implemented in everyday life.

Chapter 1 of the *Student Manual* that accompanies this book contains a set of suggestions entitled "Ways of Getting the Most From Your Group Experience." These guidelines serve as one method of teaching members how to become active participants.

SUMMARY OF PREGROUP ISSUES

Member Functions and Possible Problems Before joining a group, individuals need to have the knowledge necessary for making an informed decision concerning their participation. Members should be active in the process of deciding whether a group is right for them. Here are some issues that pertain to the role of members at this stage:

- Members should have adequate knowledge about the nature of the group and understand the impact the group may have on them.
- Members need to determine if a particular group is appropriate for them at this time.
- Members can profit by preparing themselves for the upcoming group by thinking about what they want from the experience and identifying personal themes that will guide their work in a group.

Problems can arise if members are coerced into a group, do not have adequate information about the nature of the group, or are passive and give no thought to what they want or expect from the group.

Leader Functions These are the main tasks of group leaders during the formation of a group:

- Identify the general goals and specific purposes of the group.
- Develop a clearly written proposal for the formation of a group.
- Announce the group in a way that provides adequate information to prospective participants.
- Conduct pregroup interviews for screening and orientation purposes.
- Make decisions concerning the selection of members.
- Organize the practical details necessary to launch a successful group.
- Get parental permission (if appropriate).
- Prepare psychologically for leadership tasks and meet with a coleader (if appropriate).
- Arrange for a preliminary group session to get acquainted, present ground rules, and prepare members for a successful group experience.
- Make provisions for informed consent and explore with participants the potential risks involved in a group experience.

Final Comments Many groups that flounder at an early developmental stage do so because the foundations were poorly laid at the outset. What is labeled "resistance" on the part of group members is often the result of the leader's failure to give members adequate orientation. The nature and scope of pregroup preparation are determined largely by the type of group, yet common elements can be addressed in most groups, such as member and leader expectations, basic procedures of the group, misconceptions about groups, and the advantages and limitations of group participation. This preparation can begin at the individual screening and can be continued during the initial session. Although building pregroup preparation into the design of a group takes considerable effort, the time involved pays dividends as the group evolves. Many potential barriers to a group's progress can be avoided by careful planning and preparation.

Stage 2: Initial Stage—Orientation and Exploration

CHARACTERISTICS OF THE INITIAL STAGE

The initial stage of a group is a time of orientation and exploration: determining the structure of the group, getting acquainted, and exploring the members' expectations. During this phase, members learn how the group functions, define their own goals, clarify their expectations, and look for their place in the group. At the initial sessions members tend to keep a "public image"; that is, they present the dimensions of themselves they consider socially acceptable. This phase is generally characterized by a certain degree of anxiety and insecurity about the structure of the group. Members are tentative because they are discovering and testing limits and are wondering whether they will be accepted.

Typically, members bring to the group certain expectations, concerns, and anxieties, and it is vital that they be allowed to express them openly. At this time the leader needs to clear up any misconceptions and, if necessary, demystify groups.

PRIMARY TASKS OF THE INITIAL STAGE: INCLUSION AND IDENTITY

Finding an identity in the group and determining the degree to which one will become an active group member are the major tasks of the initial stage. Members often ask themselves these questions at the initial sessions:

- Will I be accepted or rejected by this group?
- How much do I want to reveal of myself?
- How much do I want to risk?
- How safe is it to take risks?
- Can I really trust these people?
- Do I fit and belong in here?
- Whom am I drawn to, and whom do I feel distant from?
- Can I be myself and, at the same time, be a part of the group?

THE FOUNDATION OF THE GROUP: TRUST

Establishing trust is vital to the continued development of the group. Without trust, group interaction will be superficial, little self-exploration will take place, constructive challenging of one another will not occur, and the group will operate under the handicap of hidden feelings.

It is a mistake to assume that people will "naturally" trust one another as soon as they enter a group—and why should they trust without question? How do they know that the group will offer a more accepting and safer climate than society at large? My view is that people make a decision whether to trust a group. Such a decision depends in part on the leader's ability to demonstrate that the group is a safe place where members can reveal themselves. By encouraging members to talk about any factors that inhibit their trust, the leader supports the therapeutic atmosphere necessary for openness and risk-taking on the part of the members.

Ways of Establishing Trust The leader's success in establishing a basic sense of trust and security depends in large part on how well he or she has prepared for the group. Careful selection of members and efforts to make sure that the group is appropriate for them are very important, and so is the way in which the leader presents the ground rules of the group. Leaders who show that they are interested in the welfare of individual members and of the group as a whole engender trust. Talking about matters such as the rights of participants, the necessity of confidentiality, the diversity that exists within the group, and the need for respecting others demonstrates that the leader has a serious attitude toward the group and values the rights of the individual. If the leader cares, chances are that the members will also care enough to invest themselves in the group to make it successful.

Trust building is not the exclusive province of group leaders, however. True, leaders can engender trust by their attitudes and actions, but the level of trust also depends in large part on the members—individually and collectively. Members usually bring to the group some fears as well as their hopes. Participants will trust the group more if they are encouraged to expose their fears, because talking about them is likely to reveal that others share their fears. If one member, for example, is concerned about not being able to express herself effectively, and someone else expresses the same concern, almost invariably a bond is established between the two members.

Silences and awkwardness are characteristically part of the beginning session. The more unstructured the group, the greater the anxiety and ambiguity about how one is to behave in a group. The members are floundering somewhat as they seek to discover how to participate. More often than not, in these initial sessions, the issues raised tend to be safe ones, and there is some talking about other people and there-and-then material. This is one way that members go about testing the waters. It is as though they are saying, "I'll show a part of myself—not a deep and sensitive one—and I'll see how others treat me." As the sessions progress, members generally find it easier to raise issues and participate in the discussion.

Ways of Maintaining Trust Another characteristic of this initial phase is the tendency for some participants to jump in and try to give helpful advice as problems are brought up. It is the leader's task to make sure that these "problem-solving interventions" do not become a pattern; they may cause enough irritation in other members to precipitate a confrontation with those who are quick to offer remedies for everyone's troubles.

The group's atmosphere of trust is also affected by the negative feelings members often experience at the initial stage toward certain other members or toward the leader and over the fact that the group is not proceeding the way they would like to see it proceed. This is an important turning point in a group, and trust can be lost or enhanced depending on the manner in which conflict is dealt with. If conflict is brought out into the open and negative feelings are listened to nondefensively, there's a good chance that the situation producing these feelings can be changed. Members need to know that it is acceptable to have and express a range of feelings. Only then can the group move ahead to a deeper level of work.

As members reveal more of themselves, the group becomes cohesive; in turn, this emerging cohesion strengthens the trust that exists in the group and creates the right atmosphere for members to try new ways of being in the group. When the members trust one another, they also trust the feedback they receive, which they can use as they try to implement these newly acquired behaviors in their daily lives.

ROLE OF THE GROUP LEADER AT THE INITIAL STAGE

Modeling When you lead a group, you set the tone and shape the norms by the attitudes and behaviors you model in the group. It is important to state your own expectations for the group openly during the first session and to model interpersonal honesty, respect, and spontaneity. You need to be aware of your own behavior and of the impact you have on the group and to practice the skills that create a therapeutic milieu. To be effective as a leader, you must be psychologically present in the group and be genuine. How can you expect the participants to get involved and believe in the potential of your group if you don't believe in what you are doing or if you are apathetic?

With regard to empathy—both cognitive and affective—you can create a therapeutic situation by being able to see and understand the world from the internal vantage point of the members. Another key characteristic is your sensitivity in attending and responding not only to what is said but also to the subtle messages conveyed beyond words. This applies to individual members as well as to the group as a whole. Finally, the people who make up your group need to sense that you have respect and positive regard for them.

Helping Identify Goals Another of your main tasks as a group leader is to help the participants get involved. You can do a lot to motivate and inspire people to want to get the most from their group. It is during the initial phase that this process needs to take place if the members are to derive the maximum benefit from the group. At this stage you do it mostly by helping members identify, clarify, and develop meaningful goals. There are general group goals, which vary depending on the purpose of the group, and there are group process goals, which apply to most groups. Some examples of process goals are staying in the here-and-now, making oneself known to others, challenging oneself and others, taking risks both in the group and in daily life, giving and receiving feedback, listening to others, responding to others honestly and concretely, dealing with conflict, dealing with feelings that arise in the group, expressing one's feelings and thoughts, deciding what to work on, acting on new insights, and applying new behavior in and out of the group.

In addition to establishing these group process goals, members may need help in establishing their own personal goals. It is important for you to help members see the relationship between group process goals and their individual goals so that they can invest in both. Typically, people in the early stages of a group have vague ideas about what they want. These vague ideas need to be translated into specific, concrete goals with regard to the desired changes and to the efforts the person is actually willing to make to bring about changes. It is clear that cultural factors need to be considered in helping members identify their personal goals. It is important for you to help members clearly identify why they are in a group. You can provide this assistance by focusing members on where they are now and where they want to go. It is important that members fully realize that group counseling involves change. They should be made aware of the possible consequences of change, not only for themselves but also for others in their lives.

One of the leader's basic tasks, and a most challenging one, is to bring hidden agendas out into the open. For example, some members may have hidden goals that are at cross-purposes with group goals. They may have a need to be the center of attention, or they may sabotage intimacy in a group because of their discomfort with getting close to others. If the leader allows these personal goals to remain hidden, rather than making them explicit, they are bound to undermine the effectiveness of the group.

The Division of Responsibility A basic issue that group leaders must consider is responsibility for the direction and outcome of the group. Is a nonproductive group the result of the leader's lack of skill, or does the responsibility rest with the group members?

One way of conceptualizing the issue of leader responsibility is to think of it in terms of a continuum. At one end are leaders who assume a large share of the responsibility for the direction and outcomes of the group. Such leaders tend to function in active and directive ways. They see their role as that of the expert, and they actively intervene to keep the group moving in ways that they deem productive. At the other end of the responsibility continuum are leaders who place the bulk of the responsibility on the members for both individual outcomes and the outcomes of the group as a whole.

Both styles of leadership have certain advantages, but they have disadvantages as well. A disadvantage of an active leadership style is that it does not encourage members to assume the responsibility that is rightfully theirs. A disadvantage of a passive leadership style is that it does not foster a collaborative relationship between the leader and the members. Ideally, you will discover a balanced style, accepting a rightful share of the responsibility but not usurping the members' responsibility. Consider your own personality in the determining how much responsibility to assume and what, specifically, this responsibility will include. How you deal with the balance of responsibility has implications for other group process matters as well.

Structuring Like responsibility, structuring exists on a continuum. The leader's theoretical orientation, the type of group, and the membership population are some factors that determine the amount and type of structuring employed. Providing therapeutic structuring is particularly important during the initial stage when members are typically confused about what behavior is expected in the group and are therefore anxious. Structure can be either useful or inhibiting in a group's development. Too little structure results in members' becoming unduly anxious, which inhibits their spontaneity. Too much structuring and direction can foster dependent attitudes and behavior. The members may wait for the leader to "make something happen" instead of taking responsibility for finding their own direction.

In my own groups, the type of structure provided in the initial stage is aimed at assisting members to identify and express their fears, expectations, and personal goals. For example, members participate in dyads, go-arounds, and structured questions as ways of making it easier for them to talk to one another about their life issues. After talking to several people on a one-to-one basis, they feel more comfortable talking openly to the entire group. From the outset I try to help them become aware of what they are thinking and feeling in the here-and-now and encourage them to express their reactions. My interventions are aimed at promoting a high degree of interaction within the group, as opposed to creating the norm of having a few individuals do prolonged work while other members merely observe. This type of structuring is designed to let members assume increased responsibility for getting the most out of the group. As they learn basic norms, they tend to take the initiative rather than waiting for my direction.

Yalom (2005) believes that both too much and too little leader activity or leader management are detrimental to the members' growth as well as to the autonomy of the group. Too much leader direction tends to limit the growth of members, and too little results in aimless groups. Yalom sees the basic task of the group leader as providing enough structure to give a general direction to the members while avoiding the pitfall of fostering dependency on the leader. His message to leaders is to structure the group in a way that promotes each member's autonomous functioning. Instead of inviting or calling on members to speak, for example, leaders can show them how to bring themselves into the interactions without being called on.

Research has shown the value of an initial structure that builds supportive group norms and highlights positive interactions among members. The leader must carefully monitor and assess this therapeutic structure throughout the life of a group rather than waiting to evaluate it during the final stage. Structuring that offers a coherent framework for understanding the experiences of individuals and the group process will be of the most value. When therapeutic goals are clear, when appropriate member behaviors are identified, and when the therapeutic process is structured to provide a framework for change, members tend to engage in therapeutic work more quickly (Dies, 1983b). Leader direction during the early phases of a group tends to foster cohesion and the willingness of members to take risks by making themselves known to others and by giving others feedback (Stockton & Morran, 1982).

Another leader task during the early stage of a group involves being aware of the nature of members' concerns about self-disclosure. Leaders can intervene by helping members identify and process their concerns early in the life of a group. Robison, Stockton, and Morran (1990) cite research indicating that early structure provided by the leader tends to increase the frequency of therapeutically meaningful self-disclosure, feedback, and confrontation. It appears that this structuring can also reduce negative attitudes about self-disclosure.

In summary, although many variables are related to creating norms and trust during the early phase of development, the optimum balance between too much and too little leader direction is one of the most important. The art is to provide structuring that is not so tight that it robs group members of the responsibility of finding their own structure. Involving group members in a continual process of evaluating their own progress and that of the group as a whole is one effective way of checking for the appropriate degree of structure. Members need to be taught specific skills of monitoring group process if they are to assume this responsibility.

SUMMARY OF THE INITIAL STAGE

Stage Characteristics The early phase of a group is a time for orientation and determining the structure of the group. These are some of the distinguishing events of this stage:

- Participants test the atmosphere and get acquainted.
- Members learn what is expected, how the group functions, and how to participate in a group.
- Members display socially acceptable behavior; risk-taking is relatively low and exploration is tentative.
- Group cohesion and trust are gradually established if members are willing to express what they are thinking and feeling.
- Members are concerned with whether they are included or excluded, and they are beginning to define their place in the group.
- A central issue is trust versus mistrust.
- There are periods of silence and awkwardness; members may look for direction and wonder what the group is about.
- Members are deciding whom they can trust, how much they will disclose, how safe the group is, whom they like and dislike, and how much to get involved.
- Members are learning the basic attitudes of respect, empathy, acceptance, caring, and responding—all attitudes that facilitate trust building.

Member Functions and Possible Problems Early in the course of the group, these specific member roles and tasks are critical to shaping the group:

- Taking active steps to create a trusting climate
- Learning to express one's feelings and thoughts, especially as they pertain to interactions in the group
- Being willing to express fears, hopes, concerns, reservations, and expectations concerning the group
- Being willing to make oneself known to others in the group
- Being involved in the creation of group norms
- Establishing personal and specific goals that will govern group participation
- Learning the basics of group process, especially how to be involved in group interactions

Some of the problems that can arise are these:

- Members may wait passively for "something to happen."
- Members may keep to themselves feelings of distrust or fears pertaining to the group and thus entrench their own resistance.
- Members may keep themselves vague and unknown, making meaningful interaction difficult.
- Members may slip into a problem-solving and advice-giving stance with other members.

Leader Functions The major tasks of group leaders during the orientation and exploration phase of a group are these:

- Teaching participants some general guidelines and ways to participate actively that will increase their chances of having a productive group
- Developing ground rules and setting norms
- Teaching the basics of group process
- Assisting members in expressing their fears and expectations and working toward the development of trust
- Modeling the facilitative dimensions of therapeutic behavior
- Being open with members and being psychologically present for them
- Clarifying the division of responsibility
- Helping members establish concrete personal goals
- Dealing openly with members' concerns and questions
- Providing a degree of structuring that will neither increase member dependence nor promote excessive floundering
- Assisting members to share what they are thinking and feeling about what is occurring within the here-and-now group context
- Teaching members basic interpersonal skills such as active listening and responding
- Assessing the needs of the group and facilitating in such a way that these needs are met

Exercises and activities designed to develop leadership skills for each of the stages of a group are included in the *Student Manual* accompanying this book.

Stage 3: Transition Stage—Dealing With Resistance

Before a group can begin doing a deeper level of work, it typically goes through a somewhat challenging transition phase. During this stage, members deal with their anxiety, defensiveness, conflict, and ambivalence about participating in the group. If a level of trust has been established during the initial stage, members are usually willing to express certain feelings, thoughts, and reactions that they may not have been willing to verbalize during earlier sessions. The leader helps the members learn how to begin working on the concerns that brought them to the group.

CHARACTERISTICS OF THE TRANSITION STAGE

Anxiety The transition stage is generally characterized by increased anxiety and defensiveness. These feelings normally give way to genuine openness and trust in the stages that follow. Participants may articulate their anxieties in the form of statements or questions such as these, directed to themselves or to the group:

- I wonder whether these people really understand me and whether they care.
- I don't know how much I have in common with people in here. I'm not sure that I will be understood.
- What good will it do to open up in here? Even if it works, what will it be like when I attempt to do the same outside of this group?
- What if I lose control? What if I cry?
- I see myself standing before a door but afraid to open it for fear of what I'll find behind it. I'm afraid to open the door because once I open it I'm not sure I'll be able to shut it again.
- How close can I get to others in this group? How much can I trust these people with my inner feelings?

Anxiety grows out of the fear of letting others see oneself on a level beyond the public image. Anxiety also results from the fear of being judged and misunderstood, from the need for more structure, and from a lack of clarity about goals, norms, and expected behavior in the group situation. As the participants come to trust more fully the other members and the leader, they become increasingly able to share of themselves, and this openness lessens their anxiety about letting others see them as they are.

Recognizing and Dealing With Conflict Before conflict can be dealt with and constructively worked through, it must be recognized. Too often both the members and the leader want to bypass conflict out of the mistaken assumption that it is something to be feared and avoided at all costs. If conflict exists and is ignored in a group, what originally produced the conflict festers and destroys the chance for genuine contact. When conflict is recognized and dealt with in such a way that those who are involved can retain integrity, the foundations of trust between the parties are established. Recognizing that conflict is often inevitable and that it can strengthen trust is likely to reduce the probability that members and the leader will try to dodge the conflicts that are a natural part of a group's development.

Ignoring conflicts and negative reactions requires energy, and that energy can be better employed to develop an honest style of facing and working through inevitable conflicts. As a group evolves, members continue to discover whether the group is a safe place to disagree, to have and express the full range of feelings, and to experience interpersonal conflict. They are testing the degree to which they can be accepted when they are not living up to social expectations. The way conflict is recognized, accepted, and worked with has critical effects on the progress of the group. If it is poorly handled, the group will probably never reach a productive stage of development. If it is dealt with openly and with concern, the members discover that their relationships are strong enough to withstand an honest level of challenge.

Certain group behaviors tend to elicit negative reactions that reflect conflict:

- Remaining aloof and being more of an observer
- Talking too much and actively interfering with the group process through questioning, giving abundant advice, or in other ways distracting people from their work
- Dominating the group, using sarcasm, belittling the efforts that are being made, and demanding attention

Intermember conflict is often the result of transference. Members may have intense reactions to one another; by exploring these reactions to specific individuals in a group, members can discover some important connections to the ways in which they transfer feelings from significant people in their lives to others. Here are some statements that can represent transference reactions:

- You seem self-righteous. Every time you begin to talk, I want to leave the room.
- You bother me because you look like a well-functioning computer. I don't sense any feeling from you.
- Your attempts to take care of everyone in here really bother me. You rarely ask anything for yourself, but you're always ready to offer something. I don't trust that.

Challenging the Group Leader Conflicts also often involve the group leader. You may be challenged on professional as well as personal grounds. You may be criticized for being "too standoffish" and not revealing enough of yourself, or members may take issue with you for being "one of the group" and revealing too much of your private life. Here are some of the comments you may hear from your group members:

- You're judgmental, cold, and stern.
- No matter what I do, I have the feeling that it'll never be enough to please you.
- You really don't care about us personally. I sense that you're just doing a job and that we don't count.
- You don't give us enough freedom. You control everything.
- You push people too much. I feel you aren't willing to accept a "no."

It is helpful to distinguish between a challenge and an attack. An attack can take the form of "dumping" or "hit-and-run" behavior. Members who attack group leaders with "This is how you are" statements don't give leaders much chance to respond. The leader has already been judged, categorized, and dismissed. However, it is critical that the leader deals with this. It is quite another matter to openly confront a leader with how the members perceive and experience that person. A member leaves room for dialogue when she says: "I'm aware that I'm not opening up in here. One reason is that if I do I feel that you'll push me beyond where I want to go." This member openly states her fears, but leaves enough room for the leader to respond and to explore the issue further. This is a challenge, not an attack.

Confronting the leader is often a participant's first significant step toward self-direction. Most members experience the struggle of dependence versus independence. If members are to become free of their dependency on the leader that is characteristic of the initial group stage, the leader must deal directly with these revealing challenges to his or her authority. It is well for leaders to be aware that some members, because of their cultural values and socialization, will be very hesitant to confront a leader. In these cases, it is not generally facilitative for leaders to expect or to push members to express everything they are feeling.

The way in which you accept and deal with challenges to you personally and to your leadership style greatly determines your effectiveness in leading the group into more advanced levels of development. If you can learn to appreciate the opportunities that challenges from group members offer, you have a better chance of dealing with these interactions directly, nondefensively, and honestly. You are also in a better position to share how you are affected by the confrontation and to ask members to check out their assumptions.

Resistance Resistance is behavior that keeps members from exploring personal issues or painful feelings in depth. Taken in context, resistance generally makes sense and serves a protective purpose. It is an inevitable phenomenon in groups, and unless it is recognized and explored, it can seriously interfere with the group process. Resistance is an integral part of one's typical defensive approach to life, and it serves to reduce anxiety. For group leaders not to respect members' resistances is akin to not respecting the members themselves. An effective way of dealing with resistances is to treat them as an inevitable aspect of the group process; that is, the leader acknowledges that resistance is a member's natural response to getting personally involved in a risk-taking experience. An open atmosphere that encourages people to acknowledge and work through whatever hesitations and anxieties they may be experiencing is essential. The participants must be willing to recognize their resistance and to talk about what might be keeping them from full participation.

Before proceeding with this discussion, several points need to be made. One is that the members' unwillingness to cooperate is not always a form of resistance in the proper sense of the term. There are times when member "resistance" is the result of factors such as an unqualified leader, conflict between coleaders, a dogmatic or authoritarian leadership style, a leader's failure to prepare the participants for the group experience, or a lack of trust engendered by the leader. In other words, group members may be unwilling to share their feelings because they don't trust the group leader or because the group is simply not a safe place in which to open up. It is imperative that those who lead groups look honestly at the sources of resistance, keeping in mind that not all resistance stems from the members' lack of willingness to face unconscious and threatening sides of themselves.

Cultural factors need to be considered in addressing what may appear to be resistance. Racial and ethnic minority clients may display behavior that group leaders interpret as resistance. It is important to make a distinction between uncooperative behavior as a manifestation of resistance and as a hesitation to participate fully in the group process. Often, these clients are not so much resistant as they are reluctant or, in some cases, simply politely respectful. Such clients are not helped to participate more actively by leaders or other members who demonstrate little understanding or appreciation of these clients' underlying cultural values. For example, silence in a group should not always be interpreted as a refusal to participate. In some cultures, silence is a customary sign of respect for others; talking too much or interrupting others is considered impolite. Quiet clients may think that being silent is better than talking frequently or verbalizing without careful thought. Their quietness could reflect their fear of being perceived as seeking attention. They may be waiting to be called on by the group leader, whom they view with respect. Some clients may be hesitant to talk about members of their family. This hesitation should not necessarily be interpreted as a stubborn refusal to be open and transparent. Instead, such clients may be influenced by taboos against openly discussing family matters.

Beutler, Moleiro, and Talebi (2002) view resistance through the lens of **reactance theory**, which holds that we experience psychological reactance at those times when we believe free behaviors are being threatened with elimination. Reactance theory conceptualizes resistance as a normal process aimed at protecting our sense of personal freedom rather than as a pathological process. Beutler and colleagues state that by viewing resistive behaviors (noncompliance, rigidity, uncooperativeness, and oppositional behavior) as a struggle against loss of freedom, therapists might consider being less directive and quit striving to get clients to change. By reducing the level of therapist directiveness, difficult clients may be assisted in developing a greater sense of self-responsibility.

Decreasing resistive behavior in a group is rarely accomplished by labeling participants as "resistant group members." There are many problems involved in categorizing people and reducing them to labels such as "the monopolist," "the intellectualizer," "the dependent one," or "the quiet seducer." Although it is understandable that prospective leaders will be interested in learning how to handle "problem members" and the disruption of the group that they can cause, the emphasis should be on *actual behaviors* rather than on labels. Regardless of the type of behavior a member exhibits as a characteristic style, he or she is more than that particular behavior. The manner in which you conceptualize resistance contributes a great deal to either melting or entrenching what appears to be uncooperative or counterproductive behavior. To categorize someone as a "resistant" and "difficult" member often leads to blaming the person, which tends to reinforce the member's uncooperative behavior. If you see and treat a person just as a "monopolizer" or an "advice giver" or a "help-rejecting complainer," you contribute to cementing that particular behavior instead of helping the person work on the problems behind the behavior. By using more descriptive and nonjudgmental terminology, it is likely that leaders will change their attitude toward members who appear to be "difficult" (Corey, Corey, & Haynes, 2006). For example, if Maria is treated as a "monopolizer" and is not encouraged to explore the impact she has on the group, she will continue to see herself as others see her and respond to her. You can help Maria, as well as the entire group, by investigating the reasons for her need to keep the spotlight on herself and the effects of her behavior on the group. People need to become aware of the defenses that may prevent them from getting involved in the group and of the effects of these defenses on the other members. However, they should be confronted with care and in such a way that they are *invited* to recognize their defensive behaviors and encouraged to go beyond them.

Another limitation of identifying "problem members" rather than problem behaviors is that most of those who participate in groups exhibit, at one time or another, some form of resistance. Occasional advice giving, questioning, or intellectualizing is not in itself a problem behavior. As a matter of fact, the group leader needs to be aware of the danger of letting participants become overly self-conscious of how they behave in the group. If clients become too concerned about being identified as "problem group members," they will not be able to behave spontaneously and openly.

DIFFICULT GROUP MEMBER, OR DIFFICULT GROUP LEADER?

Many students in group counseling classes want to talk about the "difficult" members in the groups they are leading. At times certain members may display behaviors that are problematic such as monopolizing the group's time, storytelling, asking many questions, making interpretations for others, being overly intellectual and detached, being overly silent, or giving advice or reassurance when it is not appropriate. Such behavior often gets in the way of those members who want to work on their concerns.

Members exhibit problematic or defensive behaviors at times because of problematic behaviors on the part of group leaders. Even in effective groups, certain members may manifest problematic behaviors that are a source of difficulty to themselves, other members, and the leader. Learning how to deal therapeutically with resistance and the many forms it takes is a central challenge for group leaders. When beginning counselors encounter members who are highly resistant, they often take the matter personally. They seem to view themselves as not being competent enough to cope with certain problematic members. If they were able to "break through" the layers of defenses of some of these difficult members, they believe that they would then feel competent.

The best way to deal therapeutically with difficult member behaviors is to simply describe what we are observing and let members know how we are affected by what we see and hear. This approach is an invitation for members to determine whether what they are doing is working for them. A shift in your attitude can allow you to understand certain behaviors as the result of a member's fear, confusion, and cautiousness. As you change the lens by which you perceive members' behaviors, it will be easier to adopt an understanding attitude and to encourage members to explore ways they are reluctant, cautious, and self-protective.

Some common denominators characterize appropriate group leader interventions when dealing with difficult behaviors of group members. Here are some guidelines for effectively dealing with members who sometimes can be challenging:

- Express annoyance with a member without denigrating the character of the person.
- Avoid responding to a sarcastic remark with sarcasm.
- Educate the member about how the group works to demystify the process.
- Encourage a member to explore his or her fears or any form of resistance rather than ignore them.
- Avoid labeling and judging any member and instead describe the behavior of the member.
- State observations and hunches in a tentative way rather than being dogmatic.

- Demonstrate sensitivity to a member's culture and avoid stereotyping the individual.
- Let members who are difficult for you know how they are affecting you in a nonblaming way.
- Avoid using the role and power of the leader to intimidate members.
- Monitor your own countertransference reactions.
- Challenge members in a caring and respectful way to do things that may be painful and difficult.
- Avoid retreating when conflict arises.
- Provide a balance between support and challenge.
- Refrain from taking member reactions in an overly personal way.
- Facilitate a more focused exploration of a problem rather than give simple solutions.
- Meet the member's needs, not your own.
- Invite group members to state how they are personally affected by problematic behaviors of other members, but block judgments, evaluations, and criticisms.

When working with a group member who exhibits difficult behaviors, put these behavioral patterns into the context of the meaning and purpose of this behavior for the individual. People in a group are likely doing the best they know how, even if they become aware that what they are doing is not working well for them. It is always useful to remind ourselves that the very reason people seek a group is to assist them in finding more effective ways of expressing themselves and dealing with others.

DEALING WITH YOUR OWN REACTIONS TO MEMBER RESISTANCE

Look at how you are being personally affected by the wide variety of problem behaviors you encounter. Many of us would display a variety of avoidance strategies if we were in a group. As old patterns are confronted and as we experience the anxiety that accompanies personal change, we are likely to be very creative in devising a pattern of defensive or protective strategies. Remember, resistance does make sense and emerges from members for a purpose.

When group members exhibit what you consider to be problematic behavior, examine your own desire to respond with strong feelings. You may feel threatened by those members who dominate and attempt to control the group; you may be angered by members who display resistive behavior; you may blame certain clients or the group as a whole for the slow pace or lack of productivity of the group; and you may take any signs of resistance personally. If you ignore your own reactions, you are in essence leaving yourself out of the interactions that occur in the group. Your own responses—be they feelings, thoughts, or observations—are often the most powerful resource at your disposal in effectively handling resistant behaviors.

One rationale for group leaders to experience their own group therapy is that this kind of self-exploration increases the chances that they will gain awareness of their own blind spots and potential vulnerabilities. Frequently, members we perceive as being "difficult" and who affect us the most are those who remind us of aspects of ourselves, or of significant people in our lives.

In dealing with countertransference, supervision is most helpful. As a trainee, you have the opportunity to explore with your supervisor and fellow group leaders your feelings of attraction or dislike toward certain members and to learn a lot about yourself in the process. If you are leading a group alone and no longer have supervision, it is important that you be willing to consult with a qualified professional to work through unresolved problems that may lie behind your feelings of countertransference. One of the advantages of working with a coleader is that your partner can offer valuable feedback from an objective point of view and thus help you see things that may be blocked from your awareness. Handling countertransference is discussed further in Chapter 6.

SUMMARY OF THE TRANSITION STAGE

Stage Characteristics The transitional phase of a group's development is marked by feelings of anxiety and defenses to allay this anxiety. Members experience a variety of feelings and may once again question their involvement with the group process and test it in some of these ways:

- Wonder what they will think of themselves if they increase their self-awareness, and wonder about others' acceptance or rejection of them
- Test the leader and other members to determine how safe the environment is
- Experience some struggle for control and power and some conflict with other members or the leader
- Learn how to work through conflict and confrontation
- Feel reluctant to get fully involved in working on their personal concerns because they are not sure others in the group will care about them
- Observe the leader to determine if he or she is trustworthy and learn from this person how to resolve conflict
- Learn how to express themselves so that others will listen to them

Member Functions and Possible Problems A central role of members at this time is to recognize and deal with the many forms of defensiveness. These tasks include the following:

- Recognizing and expressing the range of feelings and thoughts
- Respecting their own struggles yet continuing to explore them in group
- Moving from dependence to independence
- Taking increased responsibility for what they are doing in the group
- Learning how to confront others in a constructive manner
- Being willing to face and deal with reactions toward what is occurring in the group
- Being willing to work through conflicts rather than avoiding them

   Some problems can arise with members at this time:

- Members can be categorized as a "problem type," or they can limit themselves with a self-imposed label.
- Members may refuse to express persistent negative reactions, thus contributing to the climate of distrust.

- If confrontations are poorly handled, members may retreat into defensive postures and issues will remain hidden.
- Members may identify a scapegoat to project their own feelings on.
- Members may collude by forming subgroups and cliques, expressing negative reactions outside of the group but remaining silent in the group.

Leader Functions Perhaps the central challenge that leaders face during the transition phase is the need to intervene in the group in a sensitive manner and at the right time. The basic task is to provide both the encouragement and the challenge necessary for the members to face and resolve the conflicts that exist within the group and their own defenses against anxiety. As I indicated earlier, the genuine cohesion that allows for productive exploration and interaction to develop demands that this difficult phase of defensiveness and conflict be experienced and dealt with successfully.

Here are some of the major tasks you need to perform during this critical period in a group's development:

- Teach group members the importance of recognizing and expressing their anxieties, reluctances, and here-and-now reactions to what is happening in the sessions.
- Help participants recognize the ways in which they react defensively and create a climate in which they can deal with their resistances openly.
- Teach the members the value of recognizing and dealing openly with conflicts that occur in the group.
- Point out behavior that is a manifestation of the struggle for control, and teach members how to accept their share of responsibility for the direction of the group.
- Assist group members in dealing with any matters that will influence their ability to become both independent and interdependent.
- Encourage members to keep in mind what they want from the group and to ask for it.
- Provide a model for the members by dealing directly and honestly with any challenges to you as a person or as a professional.
- Continue to monitor your own reactions to members who display problematic behavior. Explore your potential countertransference through supervision or personal therapy.

Leaders need to be especially active during the first and second stages of a group. During the transition stage, active intervention and structuring are important because generally the participants have not yet learned to work effectively on their own. If a conflict arises, for example, some members may attempt to move on to more pleasant topics or in some other way ignore the conflict. Group leaders need to teach members constructive ways to deal with conflict and the value of expressing their feelings, thoughts, and reactions to such conflicts.

Destructive confrontations, with an attacking quality, can lead to entrenchment of resistance and breed hostility and mistrust. Confrontation is appropriate even during the early stages of a group if it is done with sensitivity and respect. In fact, trust is often facilitated by caring confrontations on the leader's part. How leaders deal with conflict, resistance, anxiety, and defensiveness does much to set the tone of the group. In my view, members have a tendency to follow the leader's manner of confronting.

Concluding Comments

This chapter has addressed various issues of group membership and group process that are central to your effectiveness as a group leader. I have focused on key concerns as the group is being formed, at its initial phase, and at the transitional period in a group's history. I have emphasized the central characteristics of the group at each phase, the member functions and possible problems, group process concepts, and the leader's key tasks. Your approach to leadership functions and skills hinges on your understanding of the roles that members play at the various stages in the group. Only if you are clear in your own mind about the various aspects of productive and unproductive member behaviors can you help group participants acquire the skills necessary for a successful group experience and correct behaviors that hinder self-exploration and involvement in the group. Chapter 5 continues this account of the unfolding of a group.

AUTHOR LECTURES

Watch *Gerald Corey's Perspectives on Theory and Practice of Group Counseling* DVD or visit the *Theory and Practice of Group Counseling* CourseMate website at www.cengagebrain.com/shop/ISBN/0840033869 to watch videos of Dr. Gerald Corey presenting lectures for each chapter. Also available are unique eAudio lectures for each chapter and quiz questions for self-study.

CHAPTER FIVE

Later Stages in the Development of a Group

Continuing the discussion of the evolutionary process of a group in action, this chapter focuses on the working stage, the final stage, and the postgroup issues of evaluation and follow-up. The major characteristics of the group at each phase, the member functions and possible problems that are likely to occur, and the group leader's key functions are discussed.

Stage 4: Working Stage—Cohesion and Productivity

There are no arbitrary dividing lines between the phases of a group, and considerable overlapping of stages is common in all groups. This is especially true of movement from the transition stage to the working stage, which is characterized by a more in-depth exploration of significant problems and by effective action to bring about the desired behavioral changes. The working stage is characterized by the commitment of members to explore significant problems they bring to the sessions and by their attention to the dynamics within the group. At this time in a group's evolution, I find that my degree of structuring and intervention is much less than during the initial and transition stages. By now the participants have learned how to involve themselves in group interactions in more spontaneous ways.

To be sure, work and learning also occur during the initial and transition stages. However, a higher degree of cohesion, a clearer notion of what members want from their group, and a more intensive level of interaction among the members are characteristic of the working stage. This is the time when participants tend to realize that they are responsible for their lives. Thus they must be encouraged to decide what concerns to explore in the group and to learn how to become an integral part of the group and yet retain their individuality. Group members must filter the feedback they receive and decide what they will do about it. Consequently, it is very important at this stage that neither the group leader nor other members attempt to decide on a course of action or make prescriptions for another member.

DEVELOPMENT OF GROUP COHESION

Nature of Group Cohesion Group cohesion involves a sense of belonging, inclusion, solidarity, and an attractiveness of a group for its members. Cohesiveness is the result of all the forces acting on the members that make them want to remain in the group. Members experience a sense of belonging and of having a connection with one another. In a group, the therapeutic alliance that develops from this feeling of being accepted involves multiple relationships: member-to-group, member-to-member, member-to-leader, and leader-to-members.

Although cohesion may begin to develop in the early stages of a group, at the working stage it becomes a key facilitative element of the group process. Establishing cohesion in the early stages may be related to the ability of members to deal with conflict that often comes during the working stage (Burlingame et al., 2002). The group becomes a cohesive unit once trust has been established and conflict and negative feelings have been expressed and worked through. Groups do not have to experience conflict to become cohesive, but if conflict is present in the group and is smoothed over or somehow ignored, it will get in the way of building cohesion. If the group has successfully navigated a testing period, members will conclude, "If it's OK to express negative reactions and conflict, then maybe it's OK to get close." Cohesion is not fixed, however; it fluctuates throughout the life of the group in response to the interactions of group members.

When cohesion occurs, people open up on a deeper level and are willing to reveal painful experiences and take other risks. Often, the route to this increased level of interaction within the group is due to a willingness of members to stay in the here-and-now, especially their willingness to express persistent reactions they are having to one another. The honest sharing of deeply significant personal experiences and struggles binds the group together because the process of sharing allows members to identify with others by seeing themselves in others. Cohesion provides the group with the impetus to move forward. Groups do not become cohesive automatically. Cohesion is the result of a commitment by the participants and the leader to take the steps that lead to a group-as-a-whole feeling. Group leaders play a critical role in the development of cohesion; they should establish clarity about how the group works in early sessions because higher levels of structure often lead to higher levels of self-disclosure and cohesion in later sessions (Burlingame et al., 2002).

Yalom (2005) believes that cohesion is a strong determinant of a positive group outcome. He contends that group cohesion by itself is not a sufficient condition for effective group work, but cohesiveness is necessary for other group therapeutic factors to operate. Cohesion fosters action-oriented behaviors such as immediacy, mutuality, confrontation, risk-taking, and translation of insight into action. Also, without group cohesion the participants will not feel secure enough to maintain a high level of trust and engage in meaningful self-disclosure. If members experience little sense of belonging or attraction to the group, there is little likelihood that they will benefit, and they may well experience negative outcomes. According to Yalom, groups with a here-and-now focus are almost invariably vital and cohesive. In contrast, groups in which members merely talk about issues with a "there-and-then" focus rarely develop much cohesiveness.

Another Perspective on Cohesion Although cohesiveness helps build relationships that provide the groundwork for effective group work, it can potentially hinder the group's development. When cohesiveness is not accompanied by a challenge to move forward by both the members and the leader, the group may reach a plateau. Group members may settle for feeling secure and comfortable rather than being open to taking the risks necessary for growth. Furthermore, to the extent that cohesiveness is associated with the pressure to conform and to the degree that unity may overshadow individual expression, cohesiveness might have negative implications for the members of a therapy group (Hornsey, Dwyer, Oei, & Dingle, 2009).

Some researchers suggest that linking cohesiveness to positive outcomes in a therapy group is not supported by empirical evidence. Joyce, Piper, and Ogrodniczuk (2007) examined whether therapeutic alliance and group cohesion predict positive outcomes for members in short-term group psychotherapy. Although they found evidence that the quality of the therapeutic alliance predicted positive outcomes, the benefits of cohesion were not clearly established. Hornsey, Dwyer, Oei, and Dingle (2009) add that "social psychological theory and research cast doubt over the extent to which cohesiveness necessarily leads to positive outcomes" (p. 276). They believe the term *cohesiveness* is too amorphous to serve as an adequate organizing principle for theory and research in group psychotherapy and that the concept should be replaced with more cogent and specific alternatives.

Cohesion as a Unifying Force Despite recent challenges from researchers, my experience in facilitating groups continues to convince me that cohesion is a valuable concept and that it can be a unifying force for group members. In many of the adult groups that I lead, common human themes arise that most of the members can relate to personally, regardless of their age, sociocultural background, or occupation. In the earlier stages of the group, members are likely to be aware of the differences that separate them, but as the group reaches a level of cohesion, it is quite common for members to comment on how alike they are in the feelings that connect them. These commonalties can be expressed in a variety of ways:

- I'm not alone in my pain and with my problems.
- I'm more lovable than I thought I was.
- I used to think I was too old to change and that I'd just have to settle for what I have in life. Now I see that what I feel is no different from what the younger people in here feel.
- I'm hopeful about my future, even though I know I have a long way to go and that the road will be rough.
- There are a lot of people in here I feel close to, and I see that we earned this closeness by letting others know who we are.
- I learned that the loneliness I felt was shared by most of the people in this group.

As a group becomes cohesive, it is not uncommon for a woman in her early 20s to discover that she shares many struggles with a man in his late 50s. Both of them may still be searching for parental approval, and they may both be learning how futile it is to look outside of themselves for confirmation of their worth. A woman learns that her struggles with femininity have much in common with a man's struggles with his masculinity. A man learns that he is not alone when he discovers that he feels resentment over the many demands his family makes on him. An older man sees in a younger male member "his son" and allows himself to feel tenderness and compassion that he did not let himself experience earlier.

Other common themes evolving in this stage lead to an increase of cohesion: remembering painful experiences of childhood and adolescence, becoming aware of the need for and fear of love, learning to express feelings that have been repressed, struggling to find a meaning in life, recognizing commonalties that link us together as humans, coming to an increased appreciation of our differences and the ways we are unique, feeling guilt over what we have done or failed to do, longing for meaningful connections with significant people, and beginning a process of finding our identity. The leader can foster the development of cohesion by pointing out the common themes that link members of the group.

CHARACTERISTICS OF AN EFFECTIVE WORKING GROUP

Stage 4 is characterized by productiveness that builds on the effective work done in the initial and transition stages. Now that members have truly become a group and have developed relationship skills that allow them a greater degree of autonomy, they are less dependent on the leader. Mutuality and self-exploration increase, and the group is focused on producing lasting results. Although the specific characteristics of a cohesive and productive group vary somewhat with the type of group, here are some general trends that identify a group in its working stage:

- There is a here-and-now focus. People have learned to talk directly about what they are feeling and doing in the group sessions, and they are generally willing to have meaningful interactions. They talk to one another, not about one another. They pay more attention to what is going on in the group than on stories about people outside of the group. When outside issues are brought up, they are often related to what is going on within the group.

- Members more readily identify their goals and concerns, and they take responsibility for them. They are clear about what the group and the leader expect of them.

- Members are willing to work and practice outside the group to achieve behavioral changes. They are carrying out "homework assignments," and they bring into the sessions any difficulties they have had in practicing new ways of thinking, feeling, and behaving. They are willing to try to integrate thoughts, emotions, and behaviors in their everyday situations. They are better able to catch themselves when they are thinking and acting in old patterns.

- Most of the members feel included in the group. A few members may be on the periphery and may feel distant from those members who are doing intensive work. Members who are having a difficult time feeling a sense of connection or belonging are likely to mention this in the sessions.

- The group has almost become an orchestra in that individuals listen to one another and do productive work together. Although the participants may still look to the leader for direction, as musicians look to the conductor for cues, they also tend to initiate a direction in which they want to move.

- Members continually assess their level of satisfaction with the group, and they take active steps to change matters if they see that the sessions need changing. In a productive group, members realize that they have a part in the outcome. If they are not getting what they want, they generally say so.

THERAPEUTIC FACTORS OF A GROUP

The following brief overview provides a summary of the specific factors that ensure that a group will move beyond the security of cohesiveness into productive work. The major aspects of the working stage are addressed in detail.

Trust and Acceptance Group members at the working stage trust one another and the leader, or at least they openly express a lack of trust. Trust is manifested in the participants' attitudes of acceptance and in their willingness to take risks by sharing meaningful here-and-now reactions. Feeling that they are accepted, the members recognize that in the group they can be who they are without risking rejection. At the working stage trust is generally high because members have been willing to deal with any barriers to its establishment and maintenance. As is the case with other interpersonal relations, however, trust is not a static entity. Trust may ebb and flow, and members may need to talk about how safe they feel even during the advanced stages of a group.

Empathy and Caring Empathy involves a deep capacity to recall, relive, and tap one's feelings through the intense experiences of others. By understanding the feelings of others—such as the need for love and acceptance, hurt about past experiences, loneliness, joy, and enthusiasm—members come to see themselves more clearly. Empathy means caring, and caring is expressed in a group by genuine and active involvement with the other members. It is also expressed by compassion, support, tenderness, and even confrontation. As people open themselves to others by showing their pain, struggles, joy, excitement, and fears, they make it possible for others to care for them, and even to love them. It is empathy that bridges the gap between people of different ethnic and cultural groups and allows them to share in universal human themes. Although clients' specific life circumstances may differ depending on their cultural background, groups allow a diverse range of people to come to realize what they have in common.

Intimacy Genuine intimacy develops in a group when people have revealed enough of themselves for others to identify with them. I have found that intimacy increases as people work through their struggles together. Members see that, regardless of their differences, they all share certain needs, wants, anxieties, and problems. When members learn that others have similar problems, they no longer feel isolated; identification with others eventually brings about closeness, which enables the members to help one another work through fears related to intimacy. The group setting provides an ideal arena for members to discover their fears of getting close to others. The ultimate goal is to understand how one has avoided intimacy outside of the group and how one can accept intimacy in life without fear.

During the working phase, members ideally not only recognize their concerns about interpersonal intimacy but also demonstrate a willingness to work through the fears associated with getting close to others. Members may fear that if they allow themselves to care, they may suffer abandonment again; if they allow intimacy, they may be anxious about opening themselves up to being emotionally wounded.

A productive group offers many opportunities for members to face and deal with these fears. They are able to use the here-and-now group experience as a way of working through past hurts and early decisions that block intimacy. Old and unfinished issues are relived in the group context, and new decisions are made possible. Members are able to see connections between ways in which they are avoiding interpersonal intimacy both in the group and with significant others. Ormont (1988) describes what occurs within a group as the members develop mature forms of intimacy: members make emotional space for one another; talk is simple and direct; there are no hidden agendas in the group; members are openly taking risks with one another; powerful feelings are present; members regard one another with a freshness that they have not shown before; and they are able to live in the moment, for the lingering remnants of their past hurts have been worked through successfully.

Bemak and Epp (1996) have written about the healing power of love in a group and contend that love has traditionally been ignored by group counselors. Bemak and Epp believe "love is a powerful therapeutic tool that can aid in the transition of group clients from a pattern of failed or unhealthy love relationships to a greater understanding of love's reality" (p. 125). The authentic experience of empathy, acceptance, caring, and intimacy that develop within a group certainly can be a manifestation of love in the best sense. The intimacy and love that develop among members is often the outcome of the commitment of members to let themselves be known in significant ways, which makes it possible to genuinely love others. Group counselors have the significant role of harnessing the healing power of love and assisting members in appreciating the dynamics of love in the group situation.

Hope If change is to occur, members must believe that change is possible, that they need not remain trapped in their past, and that they can take active steps to make their lives more authentic. Hope is therapeutic in itself because it gives members the incentive to commit themselves to the demanding work that change requires. Perhaps the greatest builder of hope occurs when the members see what they have created in the group by challenging their fears and speaking of their problems honestly. As Yalom (2005) has indicated, instilling and maintaining hope are crucial in group therapy so that members will remain in the group and other therapeutic factors can take effect. The therapist's belief in the group process is critical to motivating clients. Yalom cites research demonstrating that clients' high expectations that therapy will help them are significantly correlated with positive outcomes.

Freedom to Experiment Experimentation with different modes of behavior is a significant aspect of the working stage. The group is now a safe place in which to try out novel behavior. After such experiments members can decide what behaviors they want to change. In everyday transactions people often behave in rigid and unimaginative ways, not daring to deviate from familiar and predictable patterns. With group support, participants can practice more functional ways of being. Role playing is often an effective way to practice new skills in interpersonal situations; then these skills can be applied to out-of-group situations. This topic is explored more fully in the discussions of psychodrama (Chapter 8) and Gestalt groups (Chapter 11).

Catharsis The expression of pent-up feelings can be therapeutic because it releases energy that has been tied up in withholding certain threatening feelings. This emotional release, which sometimes occurs in an explosive way, leaves the person feeling freer. The individual discovers that keeping a lid on anger, pain, frustration, hatred, and fear prevents spontaneous feelings such as joy, affection, delight, and enthusiasm from emerging. This emotional release plays an important part in many kinds of groups, but both group leaders and members sometimes make the mistake of concluding that mere catharsis implies "real work." Some members who do not have emotional releases are disappointed and may think that they are not really working. They may be convinced that they are not getting as much from the group as those who have had more catharses than they have. Although it is often healing, catharsis *by itself* is limited in producing long-lasting changes.

Yalom (2005) notes that catharsis is an interpersonal process. People do not get enduring benefits from ventilating feelings in an empty closet. Although catharsis is related to a positive outcome and is often necessary for change, Yalom stresses that it is certainly not sufficient to produce change by itself. He puts the impact of catharsis into perspective: "The open expression of affect is without question vital to the group therapeutic process; in its absence a group would degenerate into a sterile academic exercise. Yet it is only a part of the process and must be complemented by other factors" (p. 91). Some form of awareness, insight, or learning is essential for change to occur.

My experience has taught me that catharsis may be a vital part of a person's work in a group, especially if the client has a reservoir of unrecognized and unexpressed feelings. I have also learned that it is a mistake to assume that no real work occurs without a strong ventilation of feelings. Many people appear to benefit from the catharses of others. Dealing with the feelings that emerge for members who are affected by a group member's cathartic expression is extremely important. Members can benefit from trying to gain understanding of the meaning of a cathartic experience. Some kind of cognitive work is often necessary to help members make new decisions based on what they have experienced emotionally. From my perspective, it is also essential to understand catharsis within a cultural context. Certain cultures may prescribe or prohibit catharsis. A culturally competent group leader will not push for cathartic releases without being aware of the cultural background of members and considering how their socialization is likely to affect their ability and willingness to express intense emotions. The topic of catharsis is explored in greater detail in Chapters 8 and 11.

Cognitive Restructuring A central part of the work done in a group consists of challenging and exploring beliefs about situations. As indicated above, understanding the meaning of intense emotional experiences is essential to further self-exploration. This cognitive component includes explaining, clarifying, interpreting, providing the cognitive framework needed for change, formulating ideas, and making new decisions. Groups offer members many opportunities to evaluate their thinking and to adopt constructive beliefs in place of self-limiting ones. For example, a member might believe it is not worth it to get close to people because then they can take advantage of him. He can explore the degree to which this belief has been true of his experience in the group. He may discover that there are benefits to letting himself be known in this group, and this can prompt him to replace some of his negative thinking with more realistic beliefs. The process of cognitive restructuring forms a central role in several therapeutic approaches, including Adlerian groups (Chapter 7), transactional analysis (Chapter 12), cognitive behavioral groups (Chapter 13), and rational emotive behavior therapy (Chapter 14).

Commitment to Change For change to occur, a person must believe that change is possible, but hoping for change is not enough. Constructive change requires a firm resolve to actually do whatever is necessary in order to change. Members must decide what to change as well as how to change it. Participants need to formulate a plan of action, commit themselves to it, and use the tools offered by the group process to explore ways of carrying it out. The support offered by the group is invaluable in encouraging the members to stick with their commitments even when they experience temporary setbacks. An inherent advantage of groups is that members can use one another to help themselves maintain their commitments. They can agree to call another member when they encounter difficulties in carrying out their plans, or they can call when they have made a successful breakthrough. A "buddy system" can be instrumental in teaching members how to ask for help and how to give this help to others. The topic of commitment in group counseling is examined in more detail in the discussion of reality therapy (Chapter 15).

Self-Disclosure Disclosure is not an end in itself; it is the means by which open communication can occur within a group. If disclosure is limited to safe topics or if it is equated with exposing secrets, the group cannot move beyond a superficial level. There are many barriers within us that keep us from self-disclosure—for example, fear of the intimacy that accompanies self-revelation, avoidance of responsibility and change, feelings of guilt and shame, fear of rejection, and cultural taboos. The willingness to overcome these barriers and make oneself known to others is a basic requirement at every stage of a group. During the working stage, most members have developed enough trust to risk disclosing threatening material.

Self-disclosure is the principal vehicle of group interaction, and it is critical that group participants have a clear understanding of what self-disclosure is—and what it is not. One level of self-disclosure involves sharing one's persistent reactions to what is happening in the group. Another level entails revealing current struggles, unresolved personal issues, goals and aspirations, joys and hurts, and strengths and weaknesses. If people are unwilling to share of themselves, they make it very hard for others to care for them. In the process of talking about concerns that occurred outside of the group or in the past, it is important for members to relate these issues to the here-and-now. By focusing on the here-and-now, participants make direct contact with one another and generally express quite accurately what they are experiencing in the present. The interactions become increasingly honest and spontaneous as members become more willing to risk revealing their reactions to one another.

Self-disclosure does not mean revealing one's innermost secrets and digging into one's past. Nor does it mean "letting everything hang out" or expressing every fleeting reaction to others. Self-disclosure should not be confused with telling stories about oneself or with letting group pressure dictate the limits of one's privacy. At times, in striving to be "open and honest" or in perceiving pressure from others in the group, some members say more than is necessary for others to understand them. They disclose so much that nothing remains private, and as a result they may feel deprived of their dignity and their privacy. Oftentimes members will psychologically withdraw after engaging in too much self-disclosure.

Self-disclosure is highly valued in most of the traditional counseling approaches covered in this book, but keep in mind the fact that self-disclosure is foreign to the values of some cultural groups. Pushing for early disclosure of highly personal material or expecting members to be completely open can entrench resistance in group members. Some individuals may take longer to develop trust and to participate in the disclosure that is based on this trust. Group leaders who understand the worldview of their clients are better able to be patient in helping these clients begin to speak. If such clients feel that they are respected, there is a greater chance that they will begin to challenge their hesitation. Chen and Han (2001) note that if cultural conflicts have not been sensitively acknowledged during the initial and transition stage, an Asian member may have difficulty during the working stage in engaging in a deeper level of self-disclosure. The premium that is placed on self-disclosure by most therapeutic approaches is often in conflict with the values of some European ethnic groups that stress that problems should be kept "in the family." Generally, group members may be slow to self-disclose until they are fairly certain that it is safe to do so, which usually involves some testing of the leader and others in the group. This slowness to trust should not necessarily be seen as resistance (Chung, 2004).

Unless clients challenge the obstacles to disclosure, their participation in a group will be very limited. As a group leader, you can recognize that individuals from some ethnic and cultural backgrounds will have difficulties in readily sharing their feelings and reactions, let alone revealing their deeper struggles. You can help these individuals by demonstrating respect for their cultural values and at the same time encouraging them to express what they want from you and from the group. With your support and the understanding of other members, they are in a position to clarify their values pertaining to self-disclosure and can decide the degree to which they are willing to make themselves known to others. A good starting point is for them to talk about their difficulty in revealing themselves in a group setting. The topic of self-disclosure is addressed more fully in later chapters as it applies to existential groups (Chapter 9) and person-centered groups (Chapter 10).

Confrontation Like self-disclosure, confrontation is a basic ingredient of the working stage; if it is absent, stagnation results. Constructive confrontation is an invitation to examine discrepancies between what one says and what one does, to become aware of unused potential, and to carry insights into action. When confrontation takes place in the supportive environment of a group, it can be a true act of caring.

In a successful group, confrontation occurs in such a way that the confronters share their reactions to the person being confronted rather than their judgments of the person. A negative style of confrontation—that is, confrontation done in a hostile, indirect, or attacking way—leaves people feeling judged and rejected. Done with care and sensitivity, confrontation by others ultimately helps members develop the capacity for the self-confrontation necessary to identify and work through the problems they need to resolve.

Confrontation is an issue that group members, as well as group leaders, frequently misunderstand; it is often feared, misused, and seen as a negative act to be avoided at all costs. In my opinion, although support and empathy are certainly essential to group process, they can become counterproductive if carried to excess. A group can cease to be effective if its members have colluded to interact only on a supportive level and agreed to focus almost exclusively on strengths and positive feedback. The unwillingness to challenge others to take a deeper look at themselves may result in overly polite and supportive exchanges that bear little resemblance to everyday interactions and that provide no incentive to extend oneself.

However, confrontation needs to be couched in a cultural context if it is to be therapeutic. Confrontation (or challenging) is therapeutic when it invites clients to more deeply explore a particular issue in their lives and when it is appropriate and well timed. However, confrontation that is harsh, attacking, hostile, and uncaring does not have a beneficial impact. Even therapeutic confrontation may not always be appropriate for clients from certain cultures, especially if it is done too soon. For example, Asian cultures place a high value on authority, and Asian clients may not be willing to confront the group leader, whom they view as an authority figure (DeLucia-Waack, 1996). Asian clients may perceive the directness associated with confrontation as a personal attack; they often view confrontation as a negative behavior and avoid it at all costs (Chen & Han, 2001; Leong, 1992). Individuals from many cultures may associate confrontation with a significant sense of shame, making it difficult for them to return to the group setting. Loss of face is a key dynamic for some clients, and leaders need to keep this in mind when doing group work (Chung, 2004). If such individuals feel insulted, chances are that they will also feel rejected or angry, and these feelings may deter them from becoming involved or remaining in a group.

Group leaders can productively devote time to helping the participants clear up their misconceptions regarding confrontation and learn what to challenge and how to do this in a constructive way. One of the most powerful ways of teaching constructive and caring confrontation is for leaders to model this behavior in their interactions in the group. By being direct, honest, sensitive, respectful, and timely in their confrontations, leaders provide members with valuable opportunities to learn these skills through observing the leader's behavior.

I typically emphasize the following points about effective confrontation:

- Remember that confrontation must be based on respect for others and that it is aimed at challenging others to look at unrecognized and unexplored aspects of themselves.

- Use confrontation only if you want to get closer to a client and only if you are willing to stay with the person after the confrontation.

- Learn to discriminate between what may be a judgmental attack and a caring challenge. For example, instead of saying, "All you do is take from the group; you never give anything of yourself," you may say, "I miss hearing from you. I'm wondering whether you'd like to be saying more. Are you aware of anything that's preventing you from expressing your feelings and thoughts?"

- When you confront a person, address his or her specific behaviors that affect others in the group.
- Take responsibility for your behaviors instead of blaming others for how you respond. Instead of saying, "You're boring," say, "I sometimes have a hard time staying with you when you speak, and I find that I'm getting lost."

In sum, confrontation should be done so as to preserve the dignity of the one being confronted, without prejudice to the client, and with the purpose of helping the person identify and see the consequences of his or her behavior. Effective positive confrontation should open up the channels of communication, not close them.

Benefiting From Feedback Although I treat the topics of self-disclosure, confrontation, and feedback separately for the purpose of discussion, these therapeutic factors have some degree of overlap in actual practice. The definitions of **feedback** tend to address information about a person, from an external source, about the individual's behavior and/or the effects of that behavior (Claiborn, Goodyear, & Horner, 2002). Most feedback entails self-disclosure, and sometimes feedback can be confrontational. For example, a group member may say this to another member: "I was very affected by the way you role-played talking to your father. It reminded me of my own father and the way I struggle with getting close to him." This is an example of both giving feedback and of self-disclosure. Now consider the group member who says this: "When you talked about your father, your fists were clenched, yet you were smiling. I don't know which to believe—your fists or your smile." This type of feedback involves a challenge and invites the member to explore the topic further.

The main role of the group leader with respect to feedback is to create a climate of safety within the group that will allow for an honest exchange of feedback and to establish norms that will help members give and receive feedback (Claiborn et al., 2002). The exchange of feedback among group members is widely considered to be a key element in promoting interpersonal learning and group development (Morran, Stockton, & Whittingham, 2004). For members to benefit from feedback, they need to be willing to listen to a range of reactions that others have to their behavior. It is important that there be a balance between "positive" feedback and corrective feedback (sometimes referred to as "negative" feedback). If members give one another their reactions and perceptions honestly and with care, participants are able to hear what impact they have had on others and can decide what, if anything, they want to change. Such feedback can be of great help to the person who is exploring a problem, attempting to resolve a difficult situation, or trying different ways of behaving. Here are some guidelines that can help members learn how to give and receive feedback:

- Global feedback is of little value. Reactions to specific behavior in the group, in contrast, provide clients with an immediate, independent assessment that they can compare with their own view.

- Concise feedback given in a clear and straightforward manner is more helpful than qualified statements and interpretive or mixed feedback (Stockton & Morran, 1980).

- Positive feedback is almost invariably rated as more desirable, more acceptable, more influential, and more conducive to change than corrective feedback. Such feedback focuses on the person's strengths as well as behaviors that might be a source of difficulty (Morran, Robison, & Stockton, 1985; Morran & Stockton, 1980; Morran, Stockton, & Harris, 1991; Riva, Wachtel, & Lasky, 2004).

- Group members tend to be more accepting of positive feedback than of difficult-to-hear feedback. Positive feedback is especially useful during the early stages of a group to establish trust and cohesion. Positive and corrective feedback should be balanced during the middle and later stages (Claiborn et al., 2002; Morran et al., 2004).

- It is good to offer positive feedback before giving corrective comments. Corrective feedback is more readily accepted when it follows the exchange of positive feedback (Morran et al., 2004; Morran, Stockton, Cline, & Teed, 1998; Riva et al., 2004).

- Positive feedback tends to be useful as a way to reinforce appropriate behaviors at any stage of a group (Morran et al., 2004).

- Difficult-to-hear feedback must be timed well and given in a nonjudgmental way, otherwise the person receiving it is likely to become defensive and reject it

- Group members are often more reluctant to deliver corrective feedback than positive feedback. This reluctance is due partly to fears of rejection by other members and partly to fears of causing harm to the feedback recipient (Morran, Stockton, & Bond, 1991). Thus it can be helpful for members to explore their fears about giving and receiving feedback. Members need to be taught the value of giving a range of feedback, as well as ways to deliver their reactions.

- Corrective feedback is more helpful when it is focused on observable behaviors, and it is easier to accept if the speaker says how he or she has been affected by these behaviors. This practice lessens the chances that members will be judged, for those who give feedback are focusing on themselves at the same time that they are talking to others about their behavior.

- Feedback with a quality of immediacy—that is, feedback given as a here-and-now reaction—is especially valuable and is far better than "stored up" reactions.

- Leader feedback is generally of higher quality than member feedback, but it is not more readily accepted (Morran et al., 1985).

- Leaders do well to model giving effective feedback and to encourage members to engage in thoughtful feedback exchange (Morran et al., 1998; Stockton et al., 2004).

- Feedback should not be imposed on others. There are times when members are not able to hear feedback because of emotional vulnerability, and this should be respected.

Members sometimes make a global declaration such as "I'd like feedback!" If such clients have said very little, it is difficult to give them feedback. Members need to learn how to ask for specific feedback and how to receive it. There is value in listening nondefensively to feedback, in really hearing what others want to say to us, and then in considering what we are willing to do with this information. As the group progresses to a working stage, members are typically more willing to freely give one another their reactions.

Commentary Not all groups reach the working stage described here. This does not necessarily mean that the leader or the group is ineffective. Changing membership in a group can block its progress. Some populations simply may not be ready for the level of intensity that is often part of a working phase, and that needs to be respected.

If the tasks of the initial and transition stages were never mastered, it can be expected that the group will get stuck. For instance, some groups don't get beyond the hidden agendas and unspoken conflicts that were typical of earlier sessions. Or the members may simply not be willing to give much of themselves beyond safe and superficial encounters. They may have made a decision to stop at a safe level characterized by mutual support rather than also challenging one another to move into unknown territory. Early interchanges between members and the leader or among members may have been abrasive, creating a climate of hesitancy and an unwillingness to trust others. The group may be oriented toward solving problems or patching up differences. This orientation can discourage self-exploration, for as soon as a member raises a problem, other members may be quick to offer advice on how to remedy the situation. For these reasons and others, some groups never progress beyond the initial stage or the transition stage.

When a group does get to the working stage, it doesn't necessarily progress as tidily as this characterization may suggest. Earlier themes of trust, unconstructive conflict, and the reluctance to participate surface time and again in a group's history. As the group faces new challenges, deeper levels of trust have to be earned. Also, considerable conflict may be resolved during the initial stage or transition stage, but new conflicts emerge in the advanced phases and must be faced and worked through. As is true with any intimate relationship, the relationships in the group are not static. Utopia is never reached, and the smooth waters may well turn into stormy seas for a time.

SUMMARY OF THE WORKING STAGE

Stage Characteristics When a group reaches the working stage, it has these central characteristics:

- The level of trust and cohesion is high, although variable and fluid.
- Communication within the group is open and involves an accurate expression of what is being experienced.
- Members interact with one another freely and directly.
- There is a willingness to risk threatening material and to make oneself known to others.
- Conflict among members is recognized and dealt with directly and effectively.

- Confrontation occurs in a way in which those doing the challenging avoid labeling others in judgmental ways.
- Participants feel supported in their attempts to change and are willing to risk new behavior.
- Members feel hopeful that they can change if they are willing to take action; they do not feel helpless.

Member Functions and Possible Problems The working stage is characterized by the exploration of personally meaningful material. To reach this stage, members must fulfill these tasks and roles:

- Bring into group sessions issues they are willing to discuss.
- Give others feedback and be open to receiving it.
- Share how they are affected by others' presence and work in the group.
- Practice new skills and behaviors in daily life and bring the results to the sessions.
- Continually assess their satisfaction with the group and actively take steps to change their level of involvement in the sessions if necessary.

Some problems may arise at this time:

- Members may gain insights in the sessions but not see the necessity of action outside of the group to bring about change.
- Members may withdraw after intense self-disclosure or because of anxiety over others' intensity.
- Members may take refuge through observing others' work.

Leader Functions The central leadership functions at this stage are these:

- Provide systematic reinforcement of desired group behaviors that foster cohesion and productive work.
- Look for common themes among members' work that provide for some universality.
- Continue to model appropriate behavior, especially caring confrontation, and disclose ongoing reactions and perceptions.
- Interpret the meaning of behavior patterns at appropriate times so that members will be able to reach a deeper level of self-exploration and consider alternative behaviors.
- Be aware of the therapeutic factors that operate to produce change and intervene in such a way as to help members make desired changes in thoughts, feelings, and actions.

Stage 5: Final Stage—Consolidation and Termination

One of the group leadership skills that is especially important as a group evolves and is moving toward a final stage is the capacity to assist members in transferring what they have learned in the group to their outside environments. During each stage of the group, participants are applying lessons learned in the sessions to their daily lives. The consolidation of this learning takes on special meaning as a group moves toward termination; this is a time for summarizing, pulling together loose ends, and integrating and interpreting the group experience. Joyce, Piper, Orgrodniczuk, and Klein (2007) identify the following as essential tasks to address during the termination phase of group therapy:

- Review and reinforce changes made by each of the members of the group.
- Assist members in reexamining their relationship with the group leader and other group members.
- Help participants learn how to face future challenges with the tools they acquired in the group.

I see the initial and final stages as the most decisive times in the group's life history. If the initial phase is effective, the participants get to know one another and establish their own identities in the group. An atmosphere of trust develops, and the groundwork is laid for later intensive work. Throughout the life of a group, the members are engaging in the cognitive work necessary to make decisions regarding what they are learning about themselves and others. As a group evolves into its final stage, cognitive work takes on particular importance, as well as exploring feelings associated with endings. To maximize the impact of the group experience, participants need to conceptualize what they learned, how they learned it, and what they will do about applying their insights to situations once the group ends. If the final phase is handled poorly by the group leader, the chances that the members will be able to use what they have learned are greatly reduced. Worse yet, members can be left with unresolved issues and without any direction for how to bring these issues to closure.

It is essential that termination issues be brought up early in the course of a group's history. In every beginning the end is always a reality, and members need periodic reminders that their group will eventually end. According to Mangione, Forti, and Iacuzzi (2007), endings in a therapeutic group are frequently emotionally charged and complex events. Rutan, Stone, and Shay (2007) state that termination often evokes emotional reactions pertaining to death and mortality, separation and abandonment, and hopes for a new beginning. Leaders have the task of facilitating a discussion of the emotional aspects associated with termination.

As a group leader, unless you recognize your own feelings about termination and are able to deal with them constructively, you are in no position to help members deal with their separation issues. Mangione and colleagues (2007) maintain that group workers need to be aware of their personal limitations pertaining to endings or loss if they expect to act ethically and effectively when assisting members at this stage of the group experience. It may be that you find endings difficult, for a variety of reasons, which will likely mean that you will not facilitate members' expressions of feelings about endings.

Avoiding acknowledging a group's completion may reflect an unconscious desire on the part of the leader or members not to deal with the role that endings play in their lives. I have found that many people have had negative experiences with endings in their personal relationships. Frequently, people leave us with the assurance they will keep in contact, yet many of them fade away in spite of our efforts to keep in touch. Some of us have friends and relatives who have ended a relationship with anger, leaving us with unfinished business. In our everyday lives, we often lack the modeling for dealing effectively with termination, which is the reason that doing so becomes especially important in group counseling. When termination is not dealt with, the group misses an opportunity to explore an area about which many members have profound feelings. Even more important, much of what clients take away from a group is likely to be lost and forgotten if they do not make a sustained effort to review and make sense of the specifics of work they have done. Dealing with termination is essential for all types of groups, whatever their duration.

There is a danger that as group members become aware that the end of the group is nearing they will isolate themselves so that they do not have to deal with the anxiety that accompanies separation. Work generally tapers off, and new issues are rarely raised. If members are allowed to distance themselves too much, they will fail to examine the possible effects of their group experience on their out-of-group behavior. It is crucial that the leader helps the participants put into meaningful perspective what has occurred in the group.

EFFECTIVE WAYS OF TERMINATING A GROUP

This section deals with ways of terminating the group experience by exploring questions such as these: How can members best complete any unfinished business? How can members be taught, as they leave the group, to carry what they have learned with them and to use it to deal more effectively with the demands of their daily existence? What are the relevant issues and activities in the closing phases of a group? Because of space limitations, most of my discussion focuses on the termination of a *closed group*, that is, a group that consists of the same members throughout its life and whose termination date has been decided in advance. Issues pertaining to termination are given brief coverage here; for a more comprehensive treatment of tasks associated with termination in psychotherapy, see Joyce, Piper, Orgrodniczuk, and Klein (2007).

Dealing With Feelings During the final stages of the group, it is a good practice for the leader to remind members that there are only a few sessions remaining. This allows members to prepare themselves for termination and to achieve successful closure of the group experience. Members need help in facing the reality that their group will soon end. Feelings about separation, which often take the form of avoidance or denial, need to be fully explored. It is the leader's job to facilitate an open discussion of the feelings of loss and sadness that accompany the eventual termination of an intense and highly meaningful experience. The members can be helped to face separation by the leader's disclosure of his or her own feelings about terminating the group.

During the initial phase, members are often asked to express their fears of *entering* fully into the group. Now, members should be encouraged to share their fears or concerns about *leaving* the group and having to face day-to-day realities without the group's support. It is not uncommon for members to say that they have developed genuine bonds of intimacy and have found a trusting and safe place where they can be themselves without fear of rejection. They may dread the prospect of being deprived of this intimacy and support. Also common are concerns of not being able to be so trusting and open with people outside the group. One of your leadership tasks is to remind the participants that if their group is special—close, caring, and supportive—it is because the members made the choice and did the work together. Therefore, they can make similar choices and commitments, and be equally successful, in their relationships outside the group. This "boost of confidence" is not intended to deny the sense of loss and the sadness that may accompany the ending of a group. On the contrary, mourning the separation can be an enriching experience if the members of the group are encouraged to fully express their feelings of loss and anxiety.

Examining the Effects of the Group on Oneself Toward the end of the group it is useful to give all members an opportunity to put into words what they have learned from the entire group experience and how they intend to apply their increased self-understanding. I routinely discuss the various ways in which participants can go further with what they have learned in the group. This is a time for making specific plans for ways members can continue to build on what they learned in their group. To be meaningful, this discussion must be concrete and specific. Global statements such as "This group has been great. I really grew a lot, and I learned a lot about people as well as myself" are so general that the person who made the comments will soon forget what specifically was meaningful about the group experience. When someone makes this kind of sweeping statement, you can help the person express his or her thoughts and feelings more concretely by asking these questions: "How has the group been good for you? In what sense have you grown a lot? What do you mean by 'great'? What are some of the things you actually learned about others and yourself?" Emphasizing the importance of being specific, helping members to conceptualize, and encouraging the open expression of feelings about endings and the meaning of the group can increase the chances that members will retain and use what they have learned. If members have kept up their writing about their group experience in their journal, they often have an excellent basis for assessing the impact of the group as a factor in bringing about significant change. During the final stage, I suggest that members of my groups write about most of the topics that are addressed in this section.

Giving and Receiving Feedback Giving and receiving feedback are crucial during the final phase. Although members of an effective group have been sharing their perceptions and feelings at each session, the opportunity to give and receive summary feedback has a value of its own. To help participants take advantage of this opportunity, during one of the last few sessions I generally ask members to give a brief summary of how they have perceived themselves in the group, what conflicts have become clearer, what the turning points were, what they expect to do with what they have learned, and what the group has meant to them. Then the others in the group say how they have perceived and felt about that person. I have found that concise and concrete feedback that also relates to the hopes and fears that the person has expressed is most valuable. Vague comments such as "I think you're a great person" are of little long-term value. It is useful to ask members to write down specific feedback in their journals. If they do not record some of the things that people say to them, they tend to forget quickly. If they make a record, months later they can look at what others told them to determine whether they are progressing toward their goals.

Completing Unfinished Business Addressing unfinished business should not be put off to the very last session. Time should be allotted in previous sessions to work through any unfinished business relating to transactions between members or to the group process and goals. Even if some matters cannot be resolved, members should be encouraged to talk about them. For example, a member who has been silent throughout most of the group may say that she never felt safe enough to talk about her real concerns. Although it may be too late to work through this member's comment to everyone's satisfaction, it is still important to look at this statement rather than completely ignoring it. In another case, two people who were in conflict may be ending the group without fully resolving their differences. If they come to understand what has blocked them from working through the conflict, both will have learned something about themselves in the process.

SUMMARY OF THE FINAL STAGE

Stage Characteristics During the final phase of a group, the following characteristics are typically evident:

- There may be some sadness and anxiety over the reality of separation.
- Members are likely to pull back and participate in less intense ways in anticipation of the ending of the group.
- Members are deciding what courses of action they are likely to take.
- Members may express their hopes and concerns for one another.
- There may be talk about follow-up meetings or some plan for accountability so that members will be encouraged to carry out their plans for change

Member Functions and Possible Problems The major task facing members during the final stage of a group is consolidating their learning and transferring what they have learned to their outside environment. Of course, they have probably been doing this to some extent between sessions if the group has been meeting on a weekly basis. This is the time for members to review the process and outcomes of the entire group and put into some cognitive framework the meaning of the group experience. After their group has ended, the members' main functions are to continue applying what they have learned to an action program in their daily lives and to attend a follow-up group session (if appropriate). Here are some of the tasks for members at this time:

- Deal with their feelings and thoughts about separation and termination.
- Complete any unfinished business, either issues they have brought into the group or issues that pertain to people in the group.
- Make decisions and plans concerning ways they can generalize what they have learned to everyday situations.
- Identify ways of reinforcing themselves so that they will continue to grow.
- Explore ways of constructively meeting any setbacks after termination of a group.
- Evaluate and express the impact of the group experience.

  Some problems can occur at this time:

- Members may avoid reviewing their experience and fail to put it into some cognitive framework, thus limiting the generalization of their learning.

- Due to separation anxiety, members may distance themselves.
- Members may dwell on conflicts that occurred in their group.
- Members may consider the group an end in itself and not use it as a way of continuing to grow.

Leader Functions The group leader's central tasks in the consolidation phase are to provide a structure that enables participants to clarify the meaning of their experiences in the group and to assist members in generalizing their learning from the group to everyday situations. The leader should focus on these tasks:

- Reinforce changes members have made and ensure that members have information about resources to enable them to make further changes.
- Assist members in determining how they will apply specific skills in a variety of situations in daily life, including helping them to develop specific contracts and action plans aimed at change.
- Help members to conceptualize what is taking place in the group and identify key turning points.
- Help members to summarize changes they made and to see commonalities with other members.
- Assist participants to develop a conceptual framework that will help them understand, integrate, consolidate, and remember what they have learned in the group.
- Create an aftercare plan for members to use at a later point.

Stage 6: Postgroup Issues—Evaluation and Follow-Up

Just as the formation of a group and the leader's preparatory activities greatly affect the group's progress through its various stages, the work of the leader once the group has come to an end is also highly important. The last session of the group is not a signal that the leader's job is finished, for there are important considerations after termination. Two issues are dynamically related to the successful completion of a group's development: evaluation and follow-up.

Part of effective practice entails developing strategies to ensure continuing assessment and designing follow-up procedures for a group. To aid this work, consider the following questions: What is the group leader's responsibility in evaluating the outcomes of a group? How can the leader help members evaluate the effectiveness of their group experience? What kind of follow-up should be provided after the termination of a group? What are the ethical considerations in evaluating a group and arranging for follow-up procedures?

EVALUATING THE PROCESS AND OUTCOMES OF A GROUP

Evaluation is a basic aspect of any group experience, and it can benefit both members and the leader. Ethical practice requires a realistic assessment of the learning that has occurred. Evaluation is not a procedure to use only at the termination of a group. It should be an ongoing process throughout the life of a group—or at least at important turning points in the group—that tracks the progress of individual members and the group as a whole.

In many agencies, group counselors are required to use objective measures as a means of demonstrating the effectiveness of a group. Standardized instruments can assess individual changes in attitudes and values. Some type of rating scale can also be devised to give the leader a good sense of how each member experienced and evaluated the group. Such practical evaluation instruments can help members make a personal assessment of the group and can also help the leader know what interventions were more, or less, helpful. A willingness to build evaluation into the structure of the group is bound to result in improving the design of future groups, and it increases the leader's professional credibility and accountability.

Writing done by members about the group experience is a very useful basis for subjectively evaluating the meaning of a group experience. Generally, I ask people before they enter a group to put down in writing what their concerns are and what they expect from the group. I strongly encourage members to keep an ongoing journal of their experiences in the group and in their everyday lives between sessions. This writing process helps participants focus on relevant trends and on the key things they are discovering about themselves and others through group interaction. Journal writing gives participants a chance to recall significant occurrences in the group and helps them identify what specifically they liked most and least about the group. The writing process is a useful tool for self-evaluation and is in itself therapeutic.

Finally, I often ask members to fill out a brief questionnaire or survey when we come together for the postgroup meeting. This procedure can also be used at various points throughout the group. Members are asked to evaluate the techniques used, the group leader, the impact of the group on them, and the degree to which they think they have changed because of their participation in the group. These questions are designed to get information on key matters:

- Did the group have any negative effects on you?
- How has the group influenced you in relation to others?
- Have your changes been lasting so far? Is so, how?

The questionnaire is a good way to get members focused before the exchange of reactions that occurs in the follow-up session. It also provides useful data for evaluating the group. If the group was coled, it is important that the coleaders make time to meet to discuss what they can learn from the members' evaluations and to make revisions and plans for future groups.

THE FOLLOW-UP GROUP SESSION

It is wise at the final session of a group to decide on a time for a follow-up session to discuss the group experience and put it in perspective. This session is valuable not only because it offers the group leader an opportunity to assess the outcomes of the group but also because it gives members the chance to gain a more realistic picture of the impact the group has had on them and their peers.

At the follow-up session members can discuss the efforts they have made since termination of the group to implement their learning in the real world. They can report on the difficulties they have encountered, share the joys and successes they have experienced in life, and recall some of the things that occurred in the group. A follow-up session also provides people with the opportunity to express and work through any afterthoughts or feelings connected with the group experience. At this time the mutual giving of feedback and support is extremely valuable. It is also a good time to assist members in locating specific referral resources for further growth once the group ends. All members can be encouraged to find some avenues of continued support and challenge so that the ending of the group can mark the beginning of a new search for self-understanding.

The element of accountability that a follow-up session encourages maximizes the chances of long-lasting benefits from the group experience. Many people have reported that simply knowing that they would be coming together as a group one or more months after the group's termination and that they would be giving a self-report provided the stimulus they needed to stick with their commitments. Finally, the follow-up session offers leaders another opportunity to remind participants that they are responsible for what they become, and that if they hope to change their situation they must take active steps to do so.

INDIVIDUAL FOLLOW-UP SESSIONS

In addition to the group follow-up session, I endorse the idea of leaders arranging for a one-to-one follow-up session with each member, if it is practical. If you administered any pretests to assess beliefs, values, attitudes, and levels of personal adjustment before the group sessions began, it is a good idea to administer some of these same instruments during one of the final sessions for comparison purposes. When you meet with members on an individual basis at the follow-up session to review how well they have accomplished their personal goals, these assessment devices can be of value in discussing specific changes in attitudes and behaviors.

These individual interviews after the termination of a group, which may last only 20 minutes, help the leader determine the degree to which members have accomplished their goals. Members may reveal reactions in the individual session that they would not share with the entire group. Also, this one-to-one contact tells the participants that the leader is concerned and does care. The individual interview provides an ideal opportunity to discuss referral sources and the possible need for further professional involvement—matters that are probably best handled individually. Although it is ideal to conduct individual follow-up sessions, this may not be practical in some settings.

Concluding Comments

I have mentioned more than once that the stages in the life of a group do not generally flow neatly and predictably in the order described in these two chapters. In actuality there is considerable overlap between stages, and once a group moves to an advanced stage of development there may be temporary regressions to earlier developmental stages.

However, knowledge of the major tasks that commonly confront participants and the leader during the different stages of the group's evolution enables you to intervene at the right time and with a clear purpose. Having a clear grasp of typical stages of group development gives you a conceptual map from which to operate. Knowledge of the group's critical turning points enables you to assist the members in mobilizing their resources to successfully meet the demands facing them as their group progresses. Knowledge of the typical pattern of groups gives you an overall perspective that enables you to determine which interventions might be more useful at a particular time. Also, this perspective allows you to predict and prepare for certain crises in the life of the group and to manage them more effectively.

Chapter 18 describes an actual group as it progresses from the initial through the final stages of development. I highly recommend that you read Chapter 18 now, prior to delving into the survey of theories contained in Part Two. Rereading Chapter 18 after you have completed Part Two will then provide a good way for you to pull all the theories together.

AUTHOR LECTURES

Watch *Gerald Corey's Perspectives on Theory and Practice of Group Counseling* DVD or visit the *Theory and Practice of Group Counseling* CourseMate website at www.cengagebrain.com/shop/ISBN/0840033869 to watch videos of Dr. Gerald Corey presenting lectures for each chapter. Also available are unique eAudio lectures for each chapter and quiz questions for self-study.

Alle-Corliss, L., & Alle-Corliss, R. (2009). *Group work: A practical guide to developing groups in agency settings.* Hoboken, NJ: Wiley.

American Counseling Association. (2005). *ACA code of ethics.* Alexandria, VA: Author.

American Group Psychotherapy Association (AGPA). (2002). *AGPA and NRCGP guidelines for ethics.* Retrieved May 14, 2009, from http://www.groupsinc.org/group/ethicalguide.html.

American Group Psychotherapy Association. (2007). *Practice guidelines for group psychotherapy.* New York : Author.

APA Presidential Task Force on Evidence-Based Practice. (2006). Evidence-based practice in psychology. *American Psychologist, 61*(4), 271–285.

Arredondo, P., Toporek, R., Brown, S., Jones, J., Locke, D., Sanchez, J., & Stadler, H. (1996). Operationalization of multicultural counseling competencies. *Journal of Multicultural Counseling and Development, 24*(1), 42–78.

Association for Specialists in Group Work. (1999). Principles for diversity competent group workers. *The Group Worker, 28*(3), 1–6.

Association for Specialists in Group Work. (2000). Professional standards for the training of group workers. *The Group Worker, 28*(3), 1–10.

Association for Specialists in Group Work. (2004, March). Special issue on teaching group work. *Journal for Specialists in Group Work, 29*(1).

Association for Specialists in Group Work. (2008). Best practice guidelines. *Journal for Specialists in Group Work, 33*(2), 111–117.

Atkinson, D. R. (2004). *Counseling American minorities* (6th ed.). Boston, MA: McGraw-Hill.

Atkinson, D. R., & Hackett, G. (2004). *Counseling diverse populations* (3rd ed.). Boston, MA: McGraw-Hill.

Barlow, S. H. (2008). Group psychotherapy specialty practice. *Professional Psychology: Research and Practice, 39*(2), 240–244.

Bednar, R. L., & Kaul, T. J. (1994). Experiential group research: Can the cannon fire? In A. E. Bergin & S. L. Garfield (Eds.), *Handbook of psychotherapy and behavior change* (pp. 631–663). New York: Wiley.

Bemak, F., & Chung, R. C-Y. (2004). Teaching multicultural group counseling: Perspectives for a new era. *Journal for Specialists in Group Work, 29*(1), 31–41.

Bemak, F., & Epp, L. R. (1996). The 12th curative factor: Love as an agent of healing in group psychotherapy. *Journal for Specialists in Group Work, 21*(2), 118–127.

Bernard, H., Burlingame, G., Flores, P., Greene, L., Joyce, A., Kobos, J. C., Leszcz, M., MacNair-Semands, R. R., Piper, W. E., Slocum McEneaney, A. M., & Feirman, D. (2008). Clinical practice guidelines for group psychotherapy. *International Journal of Group Psychotherapy, 58*(4), 455–542.

Beutler, L. E., Moleiro, C. M., & Talebi, H. (2002). Resistance. In J. C. Norcross (Ed.), *Psychotherapy relationships that work* (pp. 129–143). New York: Oxford University Press.

Bowman, V. E., & DeLucia, J. L. (1993). Preparation for group therapy: The effects of preparer and modality on group process and individual functioning. *Journal for Specialists in Group Work, 18*(2), 67–79.

Brabender, V. (2006). The ethical group psychotherapist. *International Journal of Group Psychotherapy, 56*(4), 395–414.

Brabender, V. (2007). The ethical group psychotherapist: A coda. *International Journal of Group Psychotherapy, 57*(1), 41–47.

Brabender, V. M., & Fallon, A. (2009). Ethical hot spots of combined individual and group therapy:

---

* Books and articles marked with an asterisk (*) are suggested for further study.

Applying four ethical systems. *International Journal of Group Psychotherapy, 59*(1), 127–147.

Budman, S. H., Simeone, P. G., Reilly, R., & Demby, A. (1994). Progress in short-term and time-limited group psychotherapy: Evidence and implications. In A. Fuhriman & G. Burlingame (Eds.), *Handbook of group psychotherapy: An empirical and clinical synthesis* (pp. 319–339). New York: Wiley.

Burlingame, G. M., Fuhriman, A., & Johnson, J. E. (2002). Cohesion in group psychotherapy. In J. C. Norcross (Ed.), *Psychotherapy relationships that work* (pp. 71–87). New York: Oxford University Press.

Burlingame, G. M., MacKenzie, K. R., & Strauss, B. (2004). Small group treatment: Evidence for effectiveness and mechanisms of change. In M. J. Lambert (Ed.), *Bergin & Garfield's handbook of psychotherapy and behavior change* (5th ed., pp. 647–696). New York: Wiley.

Chen, M., & Han, Y. S. (2001). Cross-cultural group counseling with Asians: A stage specific interactive approach. *Journal for Specialists in Group Work, 26*(2), 111–128.

Chung, R. C-Y. (2004). Group counseling with Asians. In J. L. DeLucia-Waack, D. Gerrity, C. R. Kalodner, & M. T. Riva (Eds.), *Handbook of group counseling and psychotherapy* (pp. 200–212). Thousand Oaks, CA: Sage.

Claiborn, C. D., Goodyear, R. K., & Horner, P. A. (2002). Feedback. In J. C. Norcross (Ed.), *Psychotherapy relationships that work* (pp. 217–233). New York: Oxford University Press.

Codes of ethics for the helping professions (4th ed.). (2011). Belmont, CA: Brooks/Cole, Cengage Learning.

Comas-Diaz, L. (1990). Hispanic/Latino communities: Psychological implications. *Journal of Training and Practice in Professional Psychology, 4*(1), 14–35.

Comas-Diaz, L. (2011). Multicultural theories of psychotherapy. In R. Corsini & D. Wedding (Eds.), *Current psychotherapies* (9th ed., pp. 536–567).

Belmont, CA: Brooks/Cole, Cengage Learning.

Conyne, R. K., Wilson, F. R., & Ward, D. E. (1997). *Comprehensive group work: What it means and how to teach it.* Alexandria, VA: American Counseling Association.

Corey, G. (2009a). *The art of integrative counseling* (2nd ed.). Belmont, CA: Brooks/Cole, Cengage Learning.

Corey, G. (2009b). *Case approach to counseling and psychotherapy* (7th ed.). Belmont, CA: Brooks/Cole, Cengage Learning.

Corey, G. (2009c). *Theory and practice of counseling and psychotherapy* (8th ed.). Belmont, CA: Brooks/Cole, Cengage Learning.

Corey, G. (2010). *Creating your professional path: Lessons from my journey.* Alexandria, VA: American Counseling Association.

Corey, G. (2012). *Student manual for theory and practice of group counseling* (8th ed.). Belmont, CA: Brooks/Cole, Cengage Learning.

Corey, G., & Corey, M. (2010). *I never knew I had a choice* (9th ed.). Belmont, CA: Brooks/Cole, Cengage Learning.

Corey, G., Corey, M., & Callanan, P. (2011). *Issues and ethics in the helping professions* (8th ed.). Belmont, CA: Brooks/Cole, Cengage Learning.

Corey, G., Corey, M., Callanan, P., & Russell, J. M. (2004). *Group techniques* (3rd ed.). Belmont, CA: Brooks/Cole, Cengage Learning.

Corey, G., Corey, M., & Haynes, R. (2003). *Ethics in action* (CD-ROM). Belmont, CA: Brooks/Cole, Cengage Learning.

Corey, G., Corey, M., & Haynes, R. (2006). *Groups in action: Evolution and challenges. DVD and workbook.* Belmont, CA: Brooks/Cole, Cengage Learning.

Corey, G., Ellis, A., & Cooker, P. (1998). Challenging the internal dialogue of group counselors. *Journal of the Mississippi Counseling Association, 6*(1), 36–44.

Corey, G., & Haynes, R. (2005). *CD-ROM for integrative counseling.* Belmont, CA: Brooks/Cole. Cengage Learning.

Corey, M., & Corey, G. (2004). Reframing resistance. *The Group Worker: Association for Specialists in Group Work, 32*(2), 5–8.

Corey, M., & Corey, G. (2011). *Becoming a helper* (6th ed.). Belmont, CA: Brooks/Cole, Cengage Learning.

Corey, M., Corey, G., & Corey, C. (2010). *Groups: Process and practice* (8th ed.). Belmont, CA: Brooks/Cole, Cengage Learning.

Debiak, D. (2007). Attending to diversity in group psychotherapy: An ethical imperative. *International Journal of Group Psychotherapy, 57*(1), 1–12.

DeLucia-Waack, J. L. (1996). Multiculturalism is inherent in all group work. *Journal for Specialists in Group Work, 21*(4), 218–223.

DeLucia-Waack, J. L., & Donigian, J. (2004). *The practice of multicultural group work: Visions and perspectives from the field.* Belmont, CA: Brooks/Cole, Cengage Learning.

Dies, R. R. (1983a). Bridging the gap between research and practice in group psychotherapy. In R. R. Dies & K. R. MacKenzie (Eds.), *Advances in group psychotherapy: Integrating research and practice* (pp. 1–16). New York: International Universities Press.

Dies, R. R. (1983b). Clinical implications of research on leadership in short-term group psychotherapy. In R. R. Dies & K. R. MacKenzie (Eds.), *Advances in group psychotherapy: Integrating research and practice* (pp. 27–78). New York: International Universities Press.

Dies, R. R. (1992). The future of group therapy. *Psychotherapy, 29*(1), 58–64.

Drum, D. J., & Knott, J. E. (2009). Theme groups at thirty. *International Journal of Group Psychotherapy, 57*(4), 491–510.

*Duncan, B. L., Miller, S. D., & Sparks, J. A. (2004). *The heroic client: A revolutionary way to improve effectiveness through client-directed, outcome-informed therapy* (Rev. ed.). San Francisco: Jossey-Bass.

*Duncan, B. L., Miller, S. D., Wampold, B. E., & Hubble, M. A. (Eds.). (2010). *The heart and soul of change: Delivering what works in therapy* (2nd ed.). Washington DC: American Psychological Association.

Eason, E. A. (2009). Diversity and group theory, practice, and research. *International Journal of Group Psychotherapy, 59*(4), 563–574.

Fallon, A. (2006). Informed consent in the practice of group psychotherapy. *International Journal of Group Psychotherapy, 56*(4), 431–453.

Falls, L., & Furr, S. (2009). Group work, types of. In American Counseling Association (Ed.), *The ACA encyclopedia of counseling* (pp. 251–254). Alexandria, VA: American Counseling Association.

Geller, J. D., Norcross, J. C., & Orlinsky, D. E. (Eds.). (2005). *The psychotherapist's own psychotherapy: Patient and clinician perspectives.* New York: Oxford University Press.

Goodnough, G. E., & Lee, V. V. (2004). Group counseling in schools. In B. T. Erford (Ed.), *Professional school counseling: A handbook of theories, programs & practices* (pp. 173–182). Austin, TX: CAPS Press.

Herlihy, B., & Corey, G. (2006a). *ACA ethical standards casebook* (6th ed.). Alexandria, VA: American Counseling Association.

Herlihy, B., & Corey, G. (2006b). *Boundary issues in counseling: Multiple roles and relationships* (2nd ed.). Alexandria, VA: American Counseling Association.

Hill, C. E., & Knox, S. (2002). Self-disclosure. In J. C. Norcross (Ed.), *Psychotherapy relationships that work* (pp. 255–265). New York: Oxford University Press.

Horne, A. M., & Rosenthal, R. (1997). Research in group work: How did we get where we are? *Journal for Specialists in Group Work, 22*(4), 228–240.

Hornsey, M. J., Dwyer, L., Oei, H.P.S., & Dingle, G. A. (2009). Group processes and outcomes in group psychotherapy: Is it time to let go of "cohesiveness"? *International Journal of Group Psychotherapy, 59*(2), 267–278.

*Hubble, M. A., Duncan, B. L., Miller, S. D., & Wampold, B. E. (2010). Introduction. In B. L. Duncan, S. D. Miller, B. E. Wampold, & M. A. Hubble (Eds.), *The heart and soul of change: Delivering what works in therapy* (2nd ed., pp. 23–46). Washington DC: American Psychological Association.

Hulse-Killacky, D., Killacky, J., & Donigan, J. (2001). *Making task groups work in your world.* Upper Saddle River, NJ: Merrill/Prentice-Hall.

Ieva, K. P., Ohrt, J. H., Swank, J. M., & Young, T. (2009). The impact of experiential groups on master's students counselor and personal development: A qualitative investigation. *Journal for Specialists in Group Work, 34*(4), 351–368.

Ivey, A. E., Pedersen, P. B., & Ivey, M. B. (2008). *Group microskills: Culture-centered group process and strategies.* Hanover, MA: Microtraining Associates.

Jacobs, E. E., Harvill, R. L., & Masson, R. L. (2009). *Group counseling: Strategies and skills* (6th ed.). Belmont, CA: Brooks/Cole, Cengage Learning.

Johnson, I. H., Santos Torres, J., Coleman, V. D., & Smith, M. C. (1995). Issues and strategies in leading culturally diverse counseling groups. *Journal for Specialists in Group Work, 20*(3), 143–150.

Johnson, C. V. (2009). A process-oriented group model for university students: A semi structured approach. *International Journal of Group Psychotherapy, 59*(4), 511–528.

Joyce, A. S., Piper, W. E., & Orgrodniczuk, J. S. (2007). Therapeutic alliance and cohesion variables as predictors of outcome of short-term group psychotherapy. *International Journal of Group Psychotherapy, 57,* 269–296.

Joyce, A. S., Piper, W. E., Orgrodniczuk, J. S., & Klein, R. H. (2007). *Termination in psychotherapy: A psychodynamic model of processes and outcomes.* Washington, DC: American Psychological Association Press.

Kalodner, C. R., & Riva, M. T. (1997). Group research: Encouraging a collaboration between practitioners and researchers—A conclusion. *Journal for Specialists in Group Work, 22*(4), 297.

Klein, R. H. (2008). Toward the establishment of evidence-based practices in group psychotherapy. *International Journal of Group Psychotherapy, 58*(4), 441–454.

Klein, R., Brabender, V., & Fallon, A. (1994). Inpatient group therapy. In A. Fuhriman & G. Burlingame (Eds.), *Handbook of group psychotherapy: An empirical and clinical synthesis* (pp. 370–415). New York: Wiley.

Knapp, S., & VandeCreek, L. (2007). When values of different cultures conflict: Ethical decision making in a multicultural context. *Professional Psychology: Research and Practice, 38*(6), 660–666.

Knauss, L. K. (2006). Ethical issues in recordkeeping in group psychotherapy. *International Journal of Group Psychotherapy, 56*(4), 415–430.

Lasky, G. B., & Riva, M. T. (2006). Confidentiality and privileged communication in group psychotherapy. *International Journal of Group Psychotherapy, 56*(4), 455–476.

Lau, M. A., Ogrodniczuk, J., Joyce, A. S., & Sochting, I. (2010). Bridging the practitioner-scientist gap in group psychotherapy research. *International Journal of Group Psychotherapy, 60*(2), 177–196.

Lee, C. C., & Ramsey, C. J. (2006). Multicultural counseling: A new paradigm for a new century. In C. C. Lee (Ed.), *Multicultural issues in counseling: New approaches to diversity* (3rd ed., pp. 3–11). Alexandria, VA: American Counseling Association.

Leong, F.T.L. (1992). Guidelines for minimizing premature termination among Asian American clients in group counseling. *Journal for Specialists in Group Work, 17*(4), 218–228.

Luke, M., & Hackney, H. (2007). Group coleadership: A critical review.

Counselor Education and Supervision, 46(4), 280–293.

MacKenzie, K. R. (1994). Where is here and when is now? The adaptational challenge of mental health reform for group psychotherapy. *International Journal of Group Psychotherapy, 44,* 407–428.

MacNair-Semands, R. R. (2007). Attending to the spirit of social justice as an ethical approach in group therapy. *International Journal of Group Psychotherapy, 57*(1), 61–66.

Mangione, L., Forti, R., & Iacuzzi, C. M. (2007). Ethics and endings in group psychotherapy: Saying good-bye and saying it well. *International Journal of Group Psychotherapy, 57*(1), 25–40.

McCeneaney, A.M.S., & Gross, J. M. (2009). Introduction to special issue: Group interventions in college counseling centers. *International Journal of Group Psychotherapy, 57*(4), 455–460.

*Miller, S. D., Hubble, M. A., Duncan, B. L., & Wampold, B. E. (2010). Delivering what works. In B. L. Duncan, S. D. Miller, B. E. Wampold, & M. A. Hubble (Eds.), *The heart and soul of change: Delivering what works in therapy* (2nd ed., pp. 421–429). Washington DC: American Psychological Association.

Moreno, J. K. (2007). Scapegoating in group psychotherapy. *International Journal of Group Psychotherapy, 57*(1), 93–104.

Morran, D. K., Robison, F. F., & Stockton, R. (1985). Feedback exchange in counseling groups: An analysis of message content and receiver acceptance as a function of leader versus member delivery, session, and valence. *Journal of Counseling Psychology, 32,* 57–67.

Morran, D. K., & Stockton, R. (1980). Effect of self-concept on group member reception of positive and negative feedback. *Journal of Counseling Psychology, 27,* 260–267.

Morran, D. K., & Stockton, R. (1985). Perspectives on group research programs. *Journal of Specialists for Group Work, 10*(4), 186–191.

Morran, D. K., Stockton, R., & Bond, L. (1991). Delivery of positive and corrective feedback in counseling groups. *Journal of Counseling Psychology, 38*(4), 410–414.

Morran, D. K., Stockton, R., Cline, R. J., & Teed, C. (1998). Facilitating feedback exchange in groups: Leader interventions. *Journal for Specialists in Group Work, 23*(3), 257–268.

Morran, D. K., Stockton, R., & Harris, M. (1991). Analysis of group leader and member feedback messages. *Journal of Group Psychotherapy, Psychodrama, and Sociometry, 43,* 126–135.

Morran, D. K., Stockton, R., & Whittingham, M. H. (2004). Effective leader interventions for counseling and psychotherapy groups. In J. L. DeLucia-Waack, D. Gerrity, C. R. Kalodner, & M. T. Riva (Eds.), *Handbook of group counseling and psychotherapy* (pp. 91–103). Thousand Oaks, CA: Sage.

Nolan, E. (1978). Leadership interventions for promoting personal mastery. *Journal for Specialists in Group Work, 3*(3), 132–138.

Norcross, J. C. (2005a). A primer on psychotherapy integration. In J. C. Norcross & M. R. Goldfried (Eds.), *Handbook of psychotherapy integration* (2nd ed., pp. 3–23). New York: Oxford University Press.

Norcross, J. C. (2005b). The psychotherapist's own psychotherapy: Educating and developing psychologists. *American Psychologist, 60*(8), 840–850.

Norcross, J. C. (2010). The therapeutic relationship. In B. L. Duncan, S. D. Miller, B. E. Wampold, & M. A. Hubble (Eds.), *The heart and soul of change: Delivering what works in therapy* (2nd ed., pp. 113–141). Washington DC: American Psychological Association.

*Norcross, J. C., Beutler, L. E., & Levant, R. F. (2006). *Evidence-based practices in mental health: Debate and dialogue on the fundamental questions.* Washington, DC: American Psychological Association.

Norcross, J. C., & Goldfried, M. R. (Eds.). (2005). *Handbook of psychotherapy integration* (2nd ed.). New York: Oxford University Press.

*Norcross, J. C., Hogan, T. P., & Koocher, G. P. (2008). *Clinician's guide to evidence-based practices*. New York: Oxford University Press.

Ogrodniczuk, J. S., Piper, W. E., Joyce, A. S., Lau, M. A., & Sochting, I. (2010). A survey of Canadian group psychotherapy association members' perceptions of psychotherapy research. *International Journal of Group Psychotherapy, 60*(2), 159–176.

Okech, J. E. A., & Kline, W. B. (2005). A qualitative exploration of group co-leader relationships. *Journal for Specialists in Group Work, 30*(2), 173–179.

Okech, J. E. A., & Kline, W. B. (2006). Competency concerns in group co-leader relationships. *Journal for Specialists in Group Work, 31*(2), 165–180.

Ormont, L. R. (1988). The leader's role in resolving resistances to intimacy in the group setting. *International Journal of Group Psychotherapy, 38*(1), 29–46.

Pack-Brown, S. P., Whittington Clark, L. F., & Parker, W. M. (1998). *Images of me: A guide to group work with African-American women*. Boston: Allyn & Bacon.

Pedersen, P. (1991). Multiculturalism as a generic approach to counseling. *Journal of Counseling and Development, 70*(1), 6–12.

Pedersen, P. (1997). *Culture-centered counseling interventions: Striving for accuracy*. Thousand Oaks, CA: Sage.

Pedersen, P. (2000). *A handbook for developing multicultural awareness* (3rd ed.). Alexandria, VA: American Counseling Association.

Pomerantz, A. M. (2005). Increasing informed consent: Discussing distinct aspects of psychotherapy at different points in time. *Ethics and Behavior, 15*(4), 351–360.

Riva, M. T., & Haub, A. L. (2004). Group counseling in the schools. In J. L. DeLucia-Waack, D. Gerrity, C. R. Kalodner, & M. T. Riva (Eds.), *Handbook of group counseling and psychotherapy* (pp. 309–321). Thousand Oaks, CA: Sage.

Riva, M. T., & Kalodner, C. R. (1997). Group research: Encouraging a collaboration between practitioners and researchers. *Journal for Specialists in Group Work, 22*(4), 226–227.

Riva, M. T., & Smith, R. D. (1997). Looking into the future of group research: Where do we go from here? *Journal for Specialists in Group Work, 22*(4), 266–276.

Riva, M. T., Wachtel, M., & Lasky, G. B. (2004). Effective leadership in group counseling and psychotherapy: Research and practice. In J. L. DeLucia-Waack, D. Gerrity, C. R. Kalodner, & M. T. Riva (Eds.), *Handbook of group counseling and psychotherapy* (pp. 37–48). Thousand Oaks, CA: Sage.

Robison, F. F., Stockton, R., & Morran, D. K. (1990). Anticipated consequences of self-disclosure during early therapeutic group development. *Journal of Group Psychotherapy, Psychodrama, and Sociometry, 43*(1), 3–18.

Rosenberg, S., & Wright, P. (1997). Brief group psychotherapy and managed mental health care. In R. M. Alperin & D. G. Phillips (Eds.), *The impact of managed care on the practice of psychotherapy: Innovation, implementation, and controversy* (pp. 105–119). New York: Brunner/Mazel.

Rosenberg, S., & Zimet, C. (1995). Brief group treatment and managed mental health care. *International Journal of Group Psychotherapy, 45*, 367–379.

*Rutan, J. S., Stone, W. N., & Shay, J. J. (2007). *Psychodynamic group psychotherapy* (4th ed.). New York: Guilford Press.

Skovholt, T. M., & Jennings, L. (2004). *Master therapists: Exploring expertise in therapy and counseling*. Boston: Pearson (Allyn & Bacon).

Stockton, R., & Morran, D. K. (1980). The use of verbal feedback in counseling groups: Toward an effective system. *Journal for Specialists in Group Work, 5*, 10–14.

Stockton, R., & Morran, D. K. (1982). Review and perspective of critical dimensions in therapeutic small group research. In G. M. Gazda (Ed.), *Basic approaches to group psychotherapy and group counseling* (3rd ed., pp. 37–85). Springfield, IL: Charles C Thomas.

Stockton, R., & Morran, D. K. (2010). Reflections on practitioner-researcher collaborative inquiry. *International Journal of Group Psychotherapy, 60*(2), 295–305.

Stockton, R., Morran, D. K., & Krieger, K. M. (2004). An overview of current research and best practices for training beginning group leaders. In J. L. DeLucia-Waack, D. Gerrity, C. R. Kalodner, & M. T. Riva (Eds.), *Handbook of group counseling and psychotherapy* (pp. 65–75). Thousand Oaks, CA: Sage.

Stockton, R., & Toth, P. L. (1997). Applying a general research training model to group work. *Journal for Specialists in Group Work, 22*(4), 241–252.

Sue, D., & Sue, D. W. (1993). Ethnic identity: Cultural factors in the psychological development of Asians in America. In D. R. Atkinson, G. Morten, & D. W. Sue (Eds.), *Counseling American minorities: A cross-cultural perspective* (pp. 199–210). Madison, WI: Brown & Benchmark.

Sue, D. W., Arredondo, P., & McDavis, R. J. (1992). Multicultural counseling competencies and standards: A call to the profession. *Journal of Counseling and Development, 70*(4), 477–486.

Sue, D. W., & colleagues. (1998). *Multicultural counseling competencies: Individual and organizational development.* Thousand Oaks, CA: Sage.

Sue, D. W., Ivey, A. E., & Pedersen, P. (1996). *A theory of multicultural counseling and therapy.* Pacific Grove, CA: Brooks/Cole.

Sue, D. W., & Sue, D. (2008). *Counseling the culturally diverse: Theory and practice* (5th ed.). New York: Wiley.

Torres-Rivera, E. (2004). Psychoeducational and counseling groups with Latinos. In J. L. DeLucia-Waack, D. Gerrity, C. R. Kalodner, & M. T. Riva (Eds.), *Handbook of group counseling and psychotherapy* (pp. 213–223). Thousand Oaks, CA: Sage.

Vontress, C. E. (1996). A personal retrospective on cross-cultural counseling. *Journal of Multicultural Counseling and Development, 24*(3), 156–166.

*Wampold, B. E. (2001). *The great psychotherapy debate: Models, methods, and findings.* Mahwah, NJ: Erlbaum.

*Wheeler, N., & Bertram, B. (2008). *The counselor and the law: A guide to legal and ethical practice* (5th ed.). Alexandria, VA: American Counseling Association.

Wrenn, C. G. (1985). Afterward: The culturally encapsulated counselor revisited. In P. Pedersen (Ed.), *Handbook of cross-cultural counseling and therapy* (pp. 323–329). Westport, CT: Greenwood Press.

Yalom, I. D. (with Leszcz, M). (2005). *The theory and practice of group psychotherapy* (5th ed.). New York: Basic Books.

PART 2

THEORETICAL APPROACHES TO GROUP COUNSELING

The Psychoanalytic Approach to Groups

Introduction

Psychoanalytic theory has influenced most of the other models of group work presented in this textbook. Some of these other approaches are extensions of the analytic model, some are modifications of analytic concepts and procedures, and some have emerged as a reaction against psychoanalysis. It is fair to say that most theories of group counseling have borrowed concepts and techniques from psychoanalysis. As a group counselor, you may have neither the training nor the motivation to conduct analytic groups. However, even if you do not use psychoanalytic *techniques,* some basic psychoanalytic *concepts* can become an integral part of your own theoretical approach.

This chapter includes an overview of the psychoanalytic and psychosocial perspectives, a brief introduction to contemporary trends in psychoanalytic thinking, and the stages of development in an individual's life. Sigmund Freud made significant contributions to our understanding of the individual's *psychosexual development* during early childhood. However, he wrote little about the *psychosocial* influences on human development beyond childhood. For this reason, I discuss Erik Erikson's (1963, 1982) psychosocial perspective, which provides a comprehensive framework for understanding the individual's basic concerns at each stage of life from infancy through old age. Erikson can be considered a psychoanalyst as well as an ego psychologist; he built on Freudian concepts by continuing the story of human development where Freud left off.

The person credited with first applying psychoanalytic principles and techniques to groups is Alexander Wolf, a psychiatrist and psychoanalyst. He began working with groups in 1938 because he did not want to turn away patients who needed but could not afford intensive individual therapy. His experiences increased his interest in this approach, and he made it his primary mode of therapy.

GOAL OF THE ANALYTIC GROUP

The goal of the analytic process is restructuring the client's character and personality system. This goal is achieved by making unconscious conflicts conscious and examining them. Specifically, psychoanalytic groups reenact the family of origin in a symbolic way via the group so that the historical past of each group member is repeated in the group's presence. Wolf (1963, 1975) developed group applications of basic psychoanalytic techniques such as working with transference, free association, dreams, and the historical determinants of present behavior. He stresses the re-creation of the original family, which allows members to work through their unresolved problems in the group. Their reactions to fellow members and to the leader are assumed to reveal symbolic clues to the dynamics of their relationships with significant figures from their family of origin. Although these reactions are taken from the here-and-now, there is a constant focus on tracing them back to the early history of the members (Tuttman, 1986).

Some psychoanalytic groups seek to duplicate the original family in many respects. The group leader applies understanding to the family-like connections that arise among the members and between the members and the therapist. Participants in a group often reexperience conflicts that originated in the family context. Because of the family-like atmosphere, the group provides opportunities to evoke associations to both family-of-origin and present life experiences (Rutan, Stone, & Shay, 2007).

Key Concepts

INFLUENCE OF THE PAST

Psychoanalytic work focuses on the influence of the past on current personality functioning. Experiences during the first 6 years of life are seen as the roots of one's conflicts in the present. Typical problems that bring many clients to therapy groups include the following: an inability to freely give and accept love; difficulty recognizing and dealing with feelings such as anger, resentment, and aggression; an inability to direct one's own life and resolve dependence and independence conflicts; difficulty in separating from one's parents and becoming a unique person; the approach and avoidance of intimacy; difficulty in accepting one's own sexual identity; and guilt over sexual feelings. According to the psychoanalytic view, these problems of adult living have their origin in early development. Early learning is not irreversible, but to change its effects one must become aware of how certain early experiences have contributed to one's present personality structure.

Although practitioners with a psychoanalytic orientation focus on the historical antecedents of current behavior, it is a mistake to assume that they dwell on the past to the exclusion of present concerns. Contemporary analytically oriented practitioners are interested in their clients' past, but they intertwine that understanding with the present and with the future. A common misconception about psychoanalytic work is that it resembles an archaeologist digging up relics from the past. The past is relevant only as it influences the present and the future, and in this sense all three have an essential place in group therapy (Rutan et al., 2007). Locke (1961) points out that psychoanalytic group work consists of "weaving back and forth between past and present, between present and past. . . . It is essential that the therapist move back and forth in time, trying always to recapture the past or to see the repetition in the present and to become aware of the early traumatic event which made for the neurotic pattern of the individual today" (pp. 30–31). Kernberg (1997) indicates that there is an increasing interest in contemporary psychoanalytic therapy to focus on the unconscious meanings in the here-and-now before attempting to reconstruct the past.

It is essential that participants understand and use historical data in their group work, but they also need to be aware of the pitfalls of getting lost in their past by recounting endless and irrelevant details of their early experiences. In the view of Wolf and Kutash (1986), the recital of yesterday's events can be uselessly time consuming and can inhibit progress. They see this use of history as essentially a form of resistance, and they suggest that talking about events in one's childhood is not as useful as dealing with the past in relation to here-and-now interactions within the group.

THE UNCONSCIOUS

The concept of the unconscious is one of Freud's most significant contributions and is the key to understanding his view of behavior and the problems of personality. The **unconscious** consists of those thoughts, feelings, motives, impulses, and events that are kept out of our awareness as a protection against anxiety. Freud believed that most of human behavior is motivated by forces outside conscious experience. What we do in everyday life is frequently determined by these unconscious motives and needs. Painful experiences during early childhood and the feelings associated with them are buried in the unconscious. These early traumas are such that conscious awareness would cause intolerable anxiety to the child. The child's repression of them does not automatically lift with time, and the client reacts to threats to the repression as if the anxiety associated with the early events would still be intolerable if these were recalled. Thus, the "shadow of the past" haunts the present. By bringing unconscious material to awareness within the group, the member realizes that the anxiety is not intolerable. The trauma was intolerable only to the child; with an adult perspective on the world, the client can handle the memory with relative ease.

Unconscious experiences have a powerful impact on our daily functioning. Indeed, Freud's theory holds that most of our "choices" are not freely made; rather, forces within us of which we are unaware guide our choices. Thus, we select mates to meet certain needs that may never have been satisfied; we select a job because of some unconscious motive; and we continually experience personal and interpersonal conflicts whose roots lie in unfinished experiences that are outside the realm of our awareness.

According to psychoanalytic theory, consciousness is only a small part of the human experience. Like the greater part of the iceberg that lies below the surface of the water, the larger part of human experience exists below the surface of awareness. The aim of psychoanalysis is to make the unconscious conscious, for it is only when we become aware of the motivations underlying our behavior that we can choose and become autonomous. The unconscious can be made more accessible to awareness by working with dreams, by using free-association methods, by learning about transference, by understanding the meaning of resistances, and by employing the process of interpretation—techniques discussed later in this chapter.

The concept of the unconscious has deep significance for analytic group therapy. Although it is true that exhaustive work with the unconscious determinants of behavior and personality reconstruction is beyond the scope of group counseling as it is generally practiced, group counselors should have an understanding of how unconscious processes operate. This understanding provides group practitioners with a conceptual framework that helps them make sense of interactions in a group, even if members do not deal with the unconscious directly.

ANXIETY

To appreciate the psychoanalytic model, one must understand the dynamics of anxiety. **Anxiety** is a feeling of dread and impending doom that results from repressed feelings, memories, desires, and experiences bubbling to the surface of awareness. It is triggered by something in the environment or within the individual. Anxiety stems from the threat of unconscious material breaking through the wall of repression. We experience anxiety when we sense that we are dealing with feelings that threaten to get out of our control. Anxiety is often "free-floating"; that is, it is vague and general, not yet having crystallized into specific form. The next section deals with the function of ego-defense mechanisms, which are an integral part of the individual's attempt to cope with anxiety.

EGO-DEFENSE MECHANISMS

Ego defense mechanisms were first formulated by psychoanalytic theorists as a way of explaining behavior. These defense mechanisms protect the ego from threatening thoughts and feelings. Conceptually, the **ego** is that part of the personality that performs various organizing functions, including keeping in contact with reality. The ego should not be equated with consciousness. Aspects of the ego are unconscious, including much of the functioning of defenses. The ego organizes and mediates between the impulses of the id, the demands of reality, and the imagined demands of parental figures and others. When there is a threat to the ego, anxiety is experienced. Although we may be interested in the growth that comes from facing reality directly, we attempt to protect ourselves from experiencing anxiety. The ego defenses enable us to soften the blows that come with emotional wounding, and they are one way of maintaining a sense of personal adequacy. Although the ego defenses do involve self-deception and distortion of reality, they are not considered essentially pathological. It is only when these defenses are rigidly used or when they impair a person's ability to deal effectively with the tasks of life that their use becomes problematic. Even though these mechanisms are learned and become a habitual mode of defense against anxiety, they typically operate outside one's consciousness.

There are many opportunities to observe a variety of defensive behaviors in a group. Defenses that we used in childhood, when we were threatened, often continue into adulthood and are activated when we feel threatened in the group. Through feedback from the group therapist and the other members, individuals can become increasingly aware of their defensive styles of interaction. With awareness, group members are able to be more flexible in the use of defenses, and they are eventually able to choose direct forms of dealing with anxiety-producing situations as they emerge in a group.

Several common ego defenses are typically manifested in the pattern of interactions in the therapeutic group:

- **Repression** involves excluding from consciousness threatening or painful thoughts and desires. By pushing distressing thoughts or feelings into the unconscious, people manage the anxiety that grows out of situations involving guilt and conflict. Repression underlies most of the other ego defenses. If adults were physically or emotionally abused in childhood, they might well have blocked out the pain and anxiety associated with these traumatic events by pushing the memories into the unconscious. For example, adults may have no recollection of the details of incestuous events that occurred in early childhood. However, as other members experience a catharsis and work through the pain associated with recalled incest, a member who has repressed an incestuous experience may be emotionally triggered, and unconscious material may surface to awareness.

- **Denial** plays a defensive role similar to that of repression, yet it generally operates at the preconscious or conscious level. In denial there is an effort to suppress unpleasant reality. It consists of coping with anxiety by "closing our eyes" to the existence of anxiety-producing reality. In a therapy group members sometimes refuse to accept that they have any problems. They may attempt to deceive both themselves and others by saying that they have "worked on" certain problems and that they therefore no longer have any concerns to deal with in the group.

- **Regression** involves returning to a less mature developmental level. In the face of severe stress or crisis, we sometimes revert to old patterns that worked for us earlier. For instance, a man in a therapy group may retreat to childlike behaviors and become extremely frightened and dependent as he faces a crisis precipitated by a loved one's decision to separate from him.

- **Projection** involves attributing our own unacceptable thoughts, feelings, behaviors, and motives to others. In a group setting, members may be very able to see the faults of others. They may also attribute to other members certain feelings and motives that would lead them to feel guilty if they owned these feelings and motives themselves. Of course, groups offer many opportunities to view projection in action. Members who have difficulty accepting their aggressive or sexual feelings may see other group members as hostile or seductive. Group leaders should be aware, however, that members who do make inappropriate hostile or seductive comments often defend themselves by labeling as "projection" any negative feedback they receive in the group.

- **Displacement** entails a redirection of some emotion (such as anger) from a real source to a substitute person or object. Group members who are frustrated are likely to feel angry. If the leader confronts members for pouting or employing some other attention-seeking behaviors, for example, they may lash out in a hostile way toward some member who is relatively nonthreatening. Although their anger may be a result of a group leader's confrontation, they pick a safer target on whom to vent their hostility.

- **Reaction formation** involves behaving in a manner that is opposite to one's real feelings. It serves as a defense against anxiety that would result from accepting feelings that one is striving to disown. This defense is exhibited in a group by the woman who is "sugary sweet" yet really harbors many hostile feelings that she dares not express. It is also displayed by the man who tries to convince himself and others that he does not care if others reject him, either in this group or at home, yet who underneath very much wants the acceptance of others. These behaviors cover up one's real feelings, for dealing with hostility or rejection would be painful. In these cases there is an exaggeration of being sweet or of being emotionally indifferent to rejection. The excessive quality of these behaviors is what makes them recognizable as a form of defense.

- **Rationalization** is a defense mechanism whereby we try to justify our behavior by assigning logical and admirable motives to it. Some people manufacture "good" reasons to explain away a bruised ego. This defense involves an attempt to minimize the severity of disappointment over losses or failures. In groups there are many opportunities to observe this behavioral pattern in action. Members may devote a great deal of energy to focusing on "others out there" as the source of their problems.

Everyone uses ego-defense mechanisms, and they have some adaptive value; nevertheless, their overuse can become problematic. It is true that self-deception can soften harsh reality, but the fact is that reality does not change through the process of distorting those aspects of it that produce anxiety. In the long run, when these defensive strategies do not work, the result is even greater anxiety. The group situation is ideal for enabling individuals to learn to recognize the indirect methods that they resort to when they feel emotionally threatened. To avoid judging such behavior, it is possible to work with members in therapeutic ways so that they can increase their tolerance for coping with anxiety and can learn direct ways of dealing with difficult interpersonal situations.

RESISTANCE

In psychoanalytic therapy, **resistance** is defined as the individual's reluctance to bring into conscious awareness threatening unconscious material that has been previously repressed or denied. It can also be viewed as anything that prevents members from dealing with unconscious material and thus keeps the group from making progress. Resistance is the unconscious attempt to defend the self against the high degree of anxiety that the client fears would result if the material in the unconscious were uncovered. Rutan, Stone, and Shay (2007) remind us that "resistance is not a process designed to resist treatment; it is a defensive process designed to resist emotional pain" (p. 206). As Locke (1961) puts it, group members need to protect themselves against the "flooding of the conscious by the forbidden feeling, fantasy, or memory" (p. 72). Resistance is the "fight to maintain the defense"; thus, it is "the defense of the defense." Durkin (1964) stresses that resistance is a basic part of the analytic group, and she warns group leaders not to be surprised by or impatient with it. She recommends that leaders not view resistance as a sign of their own ineptness.

There are many kinds of resistances, some relating to apprehension about joining a group, some to participation in the group process, and some to the desire to leave the group (Locke, 1961). Wolf (1963) lists various sources of resistance in group members: fear that one's privacy will be invaded; need to "own" the therapist exclusively; fear of "meeting" again one's original family in the group—namely, recognizing one's parents or siblings in some of the participants—and having to deal with the anxiety produced by these encounters; unconscious fear of giving up neurotic trends; and anxiety about the freedom that a group offers, including the freedom to discuss anxiety.

Wolf also identifies other forms of resistance that surface during the advanced stages of group analysis. Some members hide behind the analysis of other members, and some engage in lengthy recitations of their life histories, thus avoiding the challenge of facing the present. Additional manifestations of resistance include these behaviors:

- Typically arriving late or not showing up at all
- Maintaining an attitude of complacency or indifference
- Intellectualizing
- Exhibiting an exaggerated need to help others in the group
- Showing distrust
- Behaving uncooperatively
- Inappropriate or impulsive behavior, including comments or gestures offensive to any group members
- Using the group for mere socializing

These are by no means the only manifestations of resistive behavior; what they all have in common is the fear of recognizing and dealing with that part of oneself that is locked in the unconscious.

How do group therapists deal with resistance? Durkin (1964) maintains that to penetrate and work through resistances the therapist needs to enlist the cooperation of members. Therefore, he or she must start with the client's immediate problems as they are manifested through resistive behaviors, which should not be viewed as something to be overcome. Because resistances are valuable indications of the client's defenses against anxiety, they should be acknowledged and worked through by the therapist and client together, with the clear understanding that they are both working toward the same ends. Group therapists should take care not to label or censure group members; unacceptable criticism will only increase resistive behaviors. It can also be useful to bring other group members into the analysis of individual member's resistances.

TRANSFERENCE

Transference, a basic concept of the psychoanalytic group approach, involves the unconscious repetition of the past in the present. Transference refers to the member unconsciously shifting feelings, attitudes, and fantasies (both positive and negative) that stem from reactions to significant persons from the past onto the therapist (or other group members). Transference reflects the patterning of old experiences and earlier acquired distortions as they emerge in present relationships (Luborsky, O'Reilly-Landry, & Arlow, 2011). Groups offer many opportunities for the exploration of these transference reactions that have roots in prior relationships (Rutan et al., 2007).

In the analytic setting, unlike the original situation, the person may experience and express these feelings without punishment. A psychoanalytic group provides a safe, neutral environment in which members can express spontaneous thoughts and feelings. This allows the transference process to emerge in a group, which clearly contributes to the success of group therapy (Kauff, 2009). If a group member perceives the therapist as a stern and rejecting father, he or she does not receive from the therapist the expected negative responses. Instead, the therapist accepts the member's feelings and helps the person understand them. Analytically oriented group therapists consider the process of exploring and interpreting transference feelings as the core of the therapeutic process because this work helps the group member achieve increased awareness and personality change.

Group participants tend to compete for the attention of the leader—a situation reminiscent of earlier times when they had to vie for their parents' attention with their brothers and sisters. These attempts can be explored to discover whether they reflect the member's need for universal approval and how such a need governs the person's life. Members can gain increased awareness of how they dealt with competition as children and how their past success or lack of it affects their present interactions with others.

Group therapy also offers the possibility of multiple transferences. In individual therapy, the client's projections are directed toward the therapist alone; in group therapy, they are also directed toward other members. By combining individual and group psychotherapy, the transference process can be illuminated and explored; benefits of the group format include facilitating separation/individuation, providing transference objects through other members in addition to the therapist, and dealing with resistances (Kauff, 2009).

The group constellation lends itself to multiple transferences that provide for reenacting past unfinished events, especially when other members stimulate such intense feelings in an individual that he or she "sees" in them some significant figure such as a father, mother, sibling, life partner, spouse, ex-lover, or boss. The group is a conducive milieu in which to relive significant past events because "the group of today becomes the family of yesterday," says Locke (1961, p. 102). Wolf (1963) and Wolf and Schwartz (1962) observe that group members serve as transference figures for other members and that the main work of the analytic group consists of identifying, analyzing, and resolving these projections onto family surrogates in the group. The leader has the task of helping members discover the degree to which they respond to others in the group as if they were their parents or siblings.

Groups can provide a dynamic understanding of how people function in out-of-group situations. By reliving the past through the transference process, members gain increased awareness of the ways in which the past is obstructing present functioning. By interpreting and working through their transferences, participants become increasingly aware of their fixations and deprivations and of the ways in which past events interfere with their ability to appraise and deal with reality in everyday life.

COUNTERTRANSFERENCE

The therapist's own feelings may become entangled in the therapeutic relationship, obstructing or even destroying objectivity. According to psychoanalytic theory, **countertransference** consists of a therapist's unconscious emotional responses to a client, resulting in a distorted perception of the client's behavior. Rutan, Stone, and Shay (2007) describe countertransference as "the therapist experiencing feelings from the past that are reactivated by the patient in the present" (p. 249). In a broader sense, countertransference involves the therapist's total emotional response to a client. Hayes (2004) refers to countertransference as the therapist's reactions to clients that are based on his or her own unresolved conflicts. No analytic leader is totally free of involvement in transference or countertransference (Wolf, 1983).

Comas-Diaz (2011) points out that therapists and their clients respond to conscious and unconscious dimensions of their culture. She reminds us that therapists from dominant cultures may not be aware of the cultural, ethnic, and racial aspects of transference and countertransference: "Identifying the cultural parameters of transference and countertransference is central to multicultural psychotherapists. They recognize that ethnic, cultural, gender, and racial factors often lead to a more rapid unfolding of core problems in psychotherapy" (p. 553). Relationships between members and the leader and among the members provide fertile ground for exploring a wide range of projections, and a culturally competent group practitioner can invite conversations on cultural differences and similarities within the group. By identifying and addressing the various aspects of diversity in a group, members can explore how their experiences pertaining to their differences have influenced them and may be playing a role in their participation in the group.

To the degree that countertransference is present, group therapists react to members as if they were significant figures of their own original family. Group leaders need to be alert to signs of unresolved conflicts within themselves that could interfere with the effective functioning of a group and create a situation in which members are used to satisfy their own unfulfilled needs. If, for example, a group leader has an extreme need to be respected, valued, and confirmed, the leader can become overly dependent on the members' approval and reinforcement. The result is that much of what the leader does is designed to please the group members and ensure their continued support. It is important to differentiate between appropriate emotional reactions and countertransference. Following are some manifestations of countertransference that can arise in a therapeutic group:

- Seeing oneself in certain members and overidentifying with them to the point of becoming less able to work effectively with them
- Projecting onto members some traits that one despises in oneself and regarding such clients as not amenable to treatment or impossible to work with
- Engaging in seductive behavior and taking advantage of the leader's role to win the special affection of certain group members

Group therapists' unresolved conflicts and repressed needs can seriously interfere with the group process and can lead them to abuse their position of leadership. The difficulty in recognizing one's own countertransference and the necessity that such reactions be acknowledged and therapeutically dealt with provide a rationale for group leaders to experience their own therapy. The analytic approach requires that therapists undergo analytic psychotherapy to become conscious of their own dynamics and of the ways in which these dynamics can obstruct therapeutic tasks.

Brabender (1987) states that countertransference can be an avenue for understanding the dynamics of a group, but she reminds us that group therapists are not immune to feelings of hate, envy, guilt, admiration, and love. Her position is that "the full experience and tolerance of all of these therapist feelings within the inpatient group enables group members to realize the richness of their humanity in relation to one another" (p. 566).

It is essential that the therapist's feelings be conscious and self-acknowledged. Bemak and Epp (2001) identify five typical countertransference patterns that a group counselor may experience: (1) becoming emotionally withdrawn and remaining unavailable to the group; (2) passivity; (3) being overly controlling; (4) regressing to maladaptive behaviors based on one's own unresolved personal issues; and (5) being paternalistic and adopting a role as a rescuer. The resolution of countertransference is an essential skill that requires systematic reflection and exploration: "The group counselor's countertransference has the potential to be utilized as a powerful therapeutic force for the group and its leader, given good supervision and training" (Bemak & Epp, 2001, p. 310). Countertransference provides the group therapist with useful information about group members as well as about him- or herself.

Understanding countertransference is a form of self-therapy that is essential for the personal and professional development of group counselors. Based on their review of the literature on countertransference in group work and their experience training group counselors, Bemak and Epp identify some important aspects of this issue for both group leaders and students:

- Countertransference is a phenomenon that group counselors commonly experience.
- Given the number of participants in a group, there is an increased opportunity and likelihood that group leaders will encounter countertransference.
- If group leaders are unaware of their unresolved personal issues and their emotional responses, it will be difficult for them to effectively facilitate a group.
- Understanding one's own countertransference leads to enhanced effectiveness in facilitating groups and adds to the potential richness of the group experience.
- Countertransference is often associated with a range of emotionally charged responses such as withdrawal, anger, love, hate, annoyance, powerlessness, avoidance, collusion, overidentification, control, and sadness.
- It is essential that graduate programs create a context that facilitates a critical self-analysis of countertransference by student trainees.

It is critical that countertransference be managed and used for the benefit of working with the client. When therapists study their own internal reactions and use them to understand their clients, countertransference can greatly benefit the therapeutic work. Hayes (2004) reports that most research on countertransference has dealt with its deleterious effects and how to manage these reactions and suggests that it would be useful to undertake systematic study of the potential therapeutic benefits of countertransference as well. Gelso and Hayes (2002) contend that it is important to study and understand all of the therapist's emotional reactions to the client that fit under the broad umbrella of countertransference. Theory alone is not enough; according to Gelso and Hayes, "evidence suggests that theory in conjunction with personal awareness is a key to the therapeutic use of countertransference" (p. 280).

Role and Functions of the Group Leader

Leadership styles vary among psychoanalytically oriented group therapists, ranging from leaders characterized by objectivity, warm detachment, and relative anonymity to those who favor a role that is likely to result in a collaborative relationship with group members. If they remain more anonymous, some psychoanalytically oriented leaders believe members will project onto them more of their own images of what they expect leaders to be, images that are seen as expressions of the members' unconscious needs.

Strupp (1992) maintains that transference and countertransference remain the cornerstones of psychodynamic therapy. The group analyst welcomes manifestations of transference in the group as opportunities for fruitful work (Wolf, 1963). Exploring transference reactions should be done with care so as not to create resistance within the group participant. Kernberg (1997) issues this warning: "Transference is to be handled like radioactive material, very responsibly, and with an awareness of how easily it can be misused" (p. 22).

Although such analysis of transference is still viewed as a hallmark of psychodynamic therapy, in the minds of many practitioners today, the model of the impersonal therapist is far from ideal and "represents a serious and frequently noxious miscarriage of the therapeutic role" (Strupp, 1992, p. 23). Aviv (2010) contends that a neutral, nonparticipatory stance is unattainable and that striving toward it may bring the group therapist to an empty and irrelevant place.

Rutan and colleagues (2007) believe that "the therapist's role is essentially to react rather than to initiate. The dynamic therapist waits for the group process to occur and then comments on it" (p. 170). Therapist roles can be conceptualized on a continuum from active to nonactive, transparent to opaque, and gratifying to frustrating. Group therapists must remain flexible in their approach. As group interaction increases, the leader pursues participants' unconscious motivations and investigates the historical roots of these motivations through analysis and interpretation.

According to Strupp (1992), one of the most significant developments of psychoanalytically oriented therapy is the growing recognition of the central importance of the therapeutic relationship. In contrast to the classical model of the impersonal and detached analyst, the contemporary formulation places emphasis on the **therapeutic alliance**, a working relationship in which the therapist "communicates commitment, caring, interest, respect, and human concern for the patient" (p. 23). In addition, the group therapist also performs these functions:

- Gives support when support is therapeutic and the group is not providing it
- Helps members face and deal with resistances within themselves and in the group as a whole
- Assists members to gain an awareness of the subtle aspects of behavior through questions and interpretations

To carry out these many functions effectively, group leaders have the paramount obligation of understanding their own dynamics and countertransference throughout the therapeutic process. To do so, they may need consultation and supervision. Personal therapy is valuable in helping leaders to recognize signs of countertransference and in discovering how their own needs and motivations influence their group work.

Application: Therapeutic Techniques and Procedures

THE THERAPEUTIC PROCESS

The therapeutic process focuses on re-creating, analyzing, discussing, and interpreting past experiences and on working through defenses and resistances that operate at the unconscious level. The working-through process represents the final phase of the analytic group and results in increased consciousness and integration of the self. Insight and cognitive understanding are important, as are the feelings and memories associated with self-understanding. Because clients need to relive and reconstruct their past and work through repressed conflicts to understand how the unconscious affects them in the present, psychoanalytic group therapy tends to be a long-term and intensive process.

Self-disclosure and transparency have become more acceptable to contemporary psychodynamic group practitioners (Aviv, 2010; Rutan et al., 2007). Modern analytic practitioners are leaving behind the "detached-observer" model of classical psychoanalysis for a more intersubjective style called **relational analysis** (DeAngelis, 1996). Relational analysis places emphasis on both the therapist's and the client's reactions and experiences within the group situation.

A group format that uses psychoanalytic concepts and techniques has these specific advantages over individual analysis:

- Members are able to establish relationships similar to those that existed in their own families; this time, however, the relationships occur in a group setting that is safe and conducive to favorable outcomes.
- Group participants have many opportunities to experience transference feelings toward other members and the leader; they can identify and deal with these feelings to increase their self-understanding.
- Participants can gain a clear sense of how their defenses and resistances are manifested.
- Dependence on the authority of the therapist is not as great as in individual therapy because group members also get feedback from other members.
- From observing the work of others in a group, members learn that it is acceptable to have and to express intense feelings that they may have kept out of awareness.
- Members have many opportunities to learn about themselves and others, in fact and in fantasy, through interactions with peers as well as with the leader. The material for analysis is available not only in terms of historical recollection but also on the basis of interaction with fellow members.
- The group setting encourages members to examine their ego defenses. Resistance melts away in the atmosphere of mutual revelation and exploration in a group to a greater extent than is typically true of one-to-one therapy.
- Analysis in groups therapeutically challenges a member's idealistic expectation of having an exclusive relationship with the therapist. The experience

of supporting others and the discovery of universal struggles encourage a fuller range of responses than does individual therapy.

- Analytic group therapy provides a context for addressing contemporary social issues, including class, race, and cultural differences.

EXPLORING ANXIETY IN THE GROUP SITUATION

How the group leader recognizes and deals with anxiety, both within the individual and within the group as a whole, is a key technique in the psychoanalytic group. Anxiety is not something to overcome; it is essential to recognize, understand, and explore the function that the defenses against it serve. Anxiety is a necessary by-product of taking risks in the group, a process that eventually leads to constructive changes.

FREE ASSOCIATION

The basic tool for uncovering repressed or unconscious material is **free association**—communicating whatever comes to mind regardless of how painful, illogical, or irrelevant it may seem. Group members are expected to report feelings immediately, without trying to exercise censorship, and the group discussion is left open to whatever the participants may bring up rather than revolving around an established theme. Foulkes (1965) refers to this process as "free-floating discussion" or "free group association."

One adaptation of free association to groups is the "go-around technique," which uses free association to stimulate member interactions (Wolf, 1963). Once a good rapport has developed in the conducive atmosphere fostered by sharing dreams and fantasies, members are encouraged to free-associate about each person in the group. Each participant goes around to each of the other members and says the first thing that comes to mind about that person. According to Wolf, the go-around method makes all the members adjunct therapists; that is, instead of remaining passive recipients of the leader's insights, the participants actively contribute to the interpretation of key meanings. Wolf (1963) contends that if group members say whatever comes into their heads about another "they will intuitively penetrate a resistive facade and identify underlying attitudes" (p. 289). As a result, the participants reveal inner feelings, become less guarded, and often develop the ability to see underlying psychic conflicts. Also, all group members have an opportunity to know how the other participants view them.

Wolf and Kutash (1986) suggest that it is useful when a client reports a dream to ask other members to free-associate with it. In this way members are being active and do not feel excluded as they listen to the details of another member's dream. The group can explore both the dreamer's and the other members' associations.

In summary, free association encourages members to become more spontaneous and to uncover unconscious processes, which leads to the discovery of keener insights into their psychodynamics. This procedure also promotes unity and active participation in the group process.

INTERPRETATION

Interpretation is a therapeutic technique used in the analysis of free associations, dreams, resistances, and transference feelings. "An interpretation is designed to make unconscious phenomena conscious, to attach meaning to events, behaviors, and feelings" (Rutan et al., 2007, p. 94). Group therapists have shifted to a more collaborative stance in recent years, offering interpretations as tentative hypotheses to group members for their consideration. "In today's clinical practice, an interpretation is a proposal of meaning. It is not a truth but an effort to mutually gain understanding of an individual behavior or affect state" (Rutan et al., 2007, p. 93). Scheidlinger (1987) maintains that an interpretation is simply a hypothesis and that, no matter how elegantly conceived, it is still subject to confirmation or refutation. When group members reject a therapist's interpretation, it may mean the interpretation is inaccurate, not that members are being resistant.

Interpretation requires considerable skill. Well-timed and accurate interpretations help clients integrate new data that can lead to new insights. Correct timing of an interpretation in group therapy is critical. Group therapists need to understand and accept members' readiness to hear an interpretation. Premature interpretations are likely to promote undue anxiety and lead to considerable resistance. If clients are presented with an accurate interpretation at an inappropriate time, they may fight the therapeutic process and resist other interventions. According to Scheidlinger (1987), the way interpretations are phrased and their manner of presentation will certainly affect the degree to which members consider them. If therapists force their interpretations on clients in a dogmatic fashion, clients are likely to close off and become increasingly defensive.

Interpretations cast in the form of questions and presented as hypotheses and not as facts are more likely to be considered by group members. For example, Sam keeps making inappropriate interventions when other members express intense feelings and thus causes the others to lose contact with their feelings. The leader finally intervenes and says: "Sam, you seem to want to convince Julie that everything will work out for her. Is it possible that you become uncomfortable when you see a person in pain; so you rush in, trying to take that person's pain away? Could it be that you're trying to avoid painful experiences yourself?" This comment alerts Sam to a possible reason for his behavior in the group. If he thinks about the leader's interpretation, he may discover other meanings of which he is not now conscious. Whether he will respond nondefensively has a lot to do with the manner in which the interpretation is made. In this case, the leader's tentative approach doesn't pose a threat and doesn't push Sam into accepting something that he may not be ready to accept.

In making interpretations, a few other general rules are useful:

- Interpretation should deal with material that is close to the member's awareness so the member will be ready and able to incorporate it.
- Interpretation should begin from the surface and go as deep as the member can emotionally tolerate.
- It is best to point out a form of defense or resistance before interpreting the feeling or conflict that lies underneath it.

Some therapists direct interpretation to the group as a whole as well as to individual participants. For example, group members may be operating under the unspoken agreement that they will be polite and supportive and that they will not challenge one another. By observing the group process and sharing these observations with the group, the therapist can be instrumental in helping the members see their hidden motives and reach a deeper level of interaction. Here, too, *how* the leader presents the observations is crucial.

One of the advantages of the psychoanalytic method in groups is that members are encouraged to share their insights about other participants. This process can be very supportive and can accelerate progress. Even though the members may not systematically make interpretations, leaving that function to the therapist, they can have a significant effect on other members by being direct and unrehearsed. The disadvantages of peer interpretations are that they are sometimes ill-timed, too superficial or too deep, or inaccurate (Rutan et al., 2007). Because group members may be less defensive to hearing feedback from peers than from the group therapist, fellow members' reactions may elicit more consideration and thought than those coming from the group therapist. Rutan and colleagues contend that interpretations from peers can have unique power in groups. As members become more familiar with one another, they will increasingly be able to recognize defensive strategies and offer perceptive observations.

DREAM ANALYSIS

Freud (1955) saw dreams as "the royal road to the unconscious." Dreams express unconscious needs, conflicts, wishes, fears, and repressed experiences. When a dream is shared in a group and worked through, the participant gains new insight into the motivations and unresolved problems behind it. Some motivations are so unacceptable to the person that they can be expressed only in disguised or symbolic form. An advantage of working with dreams in a group is that it enables members to deal in a concrete way with feelings and motivations that they otherwise would not face. After exploring the various facets and possible meanings of a dream in a supportive group, members may be more willing to accept themselves and explore other unresolved problems that elicit feelings of guilt and shame.

It should be noted that dreams have both a manifest (or conscious) content and a latent (or hidden) content. The **manifest content** is the dream as it appears to the dreamer; the **latent content** consists of the disguised, unconscious motives that represent the hidden meaning of the dream. A psychoanalytic group works at both levels. Because dreams are viewed as the key that unlocks what is buried in the unconscious, the goal is to search for the latent beneath the manifest and to gradually uncover repressed conflicts.

In the first session, group members are told that sharing their dreams, fantasies, and free associations is essential to the analysis and understanding of the dynamics behind confused thinking, feeling, and behaving. Even though therapists may have insight into clients' dreams, they generally give little analysis during the early stages of a group. Instead, the members are encouraged to offer their own interpretations (Mullan & Rosenbaum, 1978). The dream experience itself, often without interpretation, taps unconscious mental activity in a manner unequaled by most other clinical experiences (Kolb, 1983).

According to Wolf (1963), the interpretation of dreams is an essential aspect of the analytic process and should continue throughout the various stages of a group. It is an essential technique because the unconscious material that dreams reveal has a liberating effect on the participants. Members are encouraged to interpret and to free-associate with one another's dreams to reach the deepest levels of interaction. Wolf reports that the entire group becomes "engrossed in dream analysis with its attendant associations, catharsis, sense of liberation and mutuality, all of which contribute toward the group unity which is so important in the first stages of treatment" (p. 287). He stresses the importance of a nonjudgmental attitude on the part of the leader toward the emerging unconscious material. The leader's tolerant approach encourages a similar attitude in the members, and the group may soon become a compassionate and supportive family.

Besides their value for unblocking unconscious material from the group member's past, dreams also contain a wealth of meaningful material concerning what is going on in the group. Members' dreams often reveal their reactions to the therapist and to other group members (Locke, 1961). The dreamer reports the dream and tells the group what meanings and associations it has for him or her. Then the group as a whole responds; other group members give their reactions to the dream and suggest cross-associations. The result is stimulation within the group.

Exploring dreams in a group has another valuable aspect. As members analyze the dreams of others and offer their own associations, they also project significant dimensions of themselves. In other words, the group members are both interpreting and projecting, a process that often leads to extremely valuable insights. Wishes, fears, and attitudes are revealed as members associate with one another's dreams. One person's dream becomes the dream of the whole group, a process that is the "true essence of dream work in group psychoanalysis" (Locke, 1961, p. 133).

INSIGHT AND WORKING THROUGH

Insight means awareness of the causes of one's present difficulties. In the psychoanalytic model, insight is a cognitive and emotional awareness of the connection of past experiences to present problems. As group members develop keener insight, they become increasingly able to recognize the many ways in which these core conflicts are manifested, both in the group and in their daily lives. New connections are formed, and dominant themes begin to emerge. For example, if in the course of group work some members discover that they need to please everyone at all costs, they come to see the effects of their need for approval on their lives.

The analytic process does not end at the insight level, however. The psychodynamic group "is an arena in which patients demonstrate their pathologies in great richness and subtlety" (Rutan et al., 2007, p. 106), and working through core problems and conflicts is an essential aspect of analytically oriented groups and individual therapy. **Working through** involves repeating interpretations and overcoming resistance, thereby enabling group members to resolve dysfunctional patterns that originated in childhood and to make choices based on new insights. If group members hope to change some aspect of their personality, they are challenged to work through resistances and old patterns—typically a long and difficult process. Working through is one of the most complex aspects of analysis, and it requires deep commitment. The working-through process involves reexperiencing the unfinished business in the context of transference (multiple transference, in group analysis). Group participants learn to accept their defenses, understand how they served a valid function in the past, and realize that they have become too burdensome in the present. Conflicts stemming from a member's early life experiences are rarely completely worked through. Most individuals will have to deal again with these deeply rooted issues from time to time. Thus it is a mistake to think of working through as a technique that completely frees the individual from any vestige of old patterns.

Developmental Stages and Their Implications for Group Work

This section describes a developmental model that has significant implications for group work. The model is based on Erikson's eight stages of human development and on the Freudian stages of psychosexual development. Such a combination provides group leaders with the conceptual framework required for understanding trends in development, major developmental tasks at each stage of life, critical needs and their satisfaction or frustration, potentials for choice at each stage of life, critical turning points or crises, and the origins of faulty personality development that can lead to later personality conflicts.

Erikson (1963, 1982) built on and extended Freud's ideas by stressing the psychosocial aspects of development. Although he was intellectually indebted to Freud, he did not accept all of Freud's views. Erikson's theory of development holds that psychosexual and psychosocial growth occur together and that at each stage of life we face the task of establishing an equilibrium between ourselves and our social world. **Psychosocial theory** stresses the integration of the biological, psychological, and social aspects of development. Erikson describes development in terms of the entire life span, which he divides into eight stages, each of which is characterized by a specific crisis to be resolved. According to Erikson, each crisis represents a *turning point* in life. At these turning points, we either achieve successful resolution of our conflicts and move forward or fail to resolve the conflicts and regress. To a large extent, our lives are the result of the choices we make at each stage.

This conceptual framework is useful for all group leaders, regardless of their theoretical orientation. Irrespective of the model underlying one's group practice, the following questions need to be raised as group work proceeds:

- What are some of the themes that give continuity to a person's life?
- What are the client's ongoing concerns and unresolved conflicts?
- What is the relationship between this individual's current problems and significant events in earlier years?
- What influential factors have shaped the person's character?
- What were the major turning points and crises in the client's life?
- What choices did the individual make at these critical periods, and how did he or she deal with these various crises?
- In what direction does the person seem to be moving now?

STAGE 1: INFANCY—TRUST VERSUS MISTRUST (BIRTH TO 12 MONTHS)

Freud labeled the first year of life the **oral stage;** sucking the mother's breast satisfies the infant's need for food and pleasure. According to the psychoanalytic view, the events of this period are extremely important for later development.

Later personality problems that stem from the oral stage include a mistrustful view of the world, a tendency to reject love, a fear of loving and trusting, and an inability to establish intimate relationships.

According to Erikson (1963), an infant's basic task is to develop a sense of trust in self, others, and the world. Infants need to count on others and to feel wanted and secure. If, however, parents are not responsive to infants' needs, they develop an attitude of mistrust toward the world, especially toward interpersonal relationships.

Implications for Group Work The connection between these ideas and the practice of group psychotherapy seems quite clear. A common theme explored in groups is the feeling of being unloved and uncared for and the concomitant acute need for someone who will deeply care and love. Time after time, group members recall early feelings of abandonment, fear, and rejection, and many of them have become fixated on the goal of finding a symbolic "parent" who will accept them. Thus, much of their energy is directed to seeking approval and acceptance. The problem is compounded by the fact that, being unable to trust themselves and others, they are afraid of loving and of forming close relationships.

Group leaders can assist these clients to express the pain they feel and to work through some of the barriers that are preventing them from trusting others and fully accepting themselves. Erikson (1968) observes that these clients tend to express their basic mistrust by withdrawing into themselves every time they are at odds with themselves, others, or the world. It should be noted that each stage builds on the psychological outcomes of the previous stage(s). In this regard, establishing a sense of basic trust is a foundation for later personality development.

Problems associated with each of these developmental stages may become manifest in an analytic group in which the family of origin is recapitulated. Some regression to behaviors associated with earlier developmental stages is common in this type of group. For example, in this first stage members may project hostile feelings onto the leader or other members. These individuals may feel justified in harboring unrealistic fears and may not have enough trust to check such projections for accuracy. It is essential that leaders do what is necessary to establish a group atmosphere that allows members to feel safe so they can explore possible projections. If a member does not develop this trust, he or she could easily become isolated in the group.

Analytic group therapists use their knowledge of developmental stages to understand patterns in which the members may be "stuck." The group leader's comments, questions, and interpretations can then be framed to help the participants resolve fixations and crises linked to specific developmental stages.

STAGE 2: EARLY CHILDHOOD—AUTONOMY VERSUS SHAME AND DOUBT (12 MONTHS TO 3 YEARS)

Freud called the next two years of life the **anal stage.** The main tasks that children must master during this stage include learning independence, accepting personal power, and learning how to express negative feelings such as jealousy, rage, aggression, and destructiveness. It is at this stage that children begin their journey toward autonomy. They play an increasingly active role in taking care of their own needs and begin to communicate what they want from others. This is also the time when they continually encounter parental demands: they are restricted from fully exploring their environment, and toilet training is being imposed on them. The Freudian view is that parental feelings and attitudes during this stage have significant consequences for later personality development.

From Erikson's viewpoint the years between ages 1 and 3 are a time for developing a sense of *autonomy.* Children who don't master the task of gaining some measure of self-control and the ability to cope with the world develop a sense of *shame* and *doubt* about themselves and their adequacy. At this age children need to explore the world, to experiment and test their limits, and to be allowed to learn from their mistakes. If parents do too much for their children, it can keep them dependent, and they are likely to inhibit the children's autonomy and hamper their capacity to feel competent in the world.

Implications for Group Work By understanding the dynamics of this stage of life, the group leader can gain access to a wealth of useful material. Many of those who seek help in a group have not learned to accept their anger and hatred toward those they love. They need to get in touch with the disowned parts of themselves that are at the bottom of these conflicting feelings. To do this, they may need to relive and reexperience situations in their distant past when they began to repress intense feelings. In the safe environment of the group, they can gradually learn ways of expressing their pent-up feelings, and work through the guilt associated with some of these emotions. Groups offer many opportunities for catharsis (expressing pent-up feelings) and for relearning.

STAGE 3: THE PRESCHOOL AGE—INITIATIVE VERSUS GUILT (3 TO 6 YEARS)

In Freud's **phallic stage** sexual activity becomes more intense. The focus of attention is on the genitals, and sexual identity takes form. Preschool children become curious about their bodies. They explore them and experience pleasure from genital stimulation. And they show increased interest in the differences between the sexes and ask questions about reproduction. The way in which parents respond, verbally and nonverbally, to their children's emerging sexuality and sexual interest is crucial in influencing the kinds of attitudes, sexual and otherwise, their children develop.

According to the Freudian view, the basic conflict of the phallic stage centers on the unconscious incestuous desires that children develop for the parent of the opposite sex. These feelings are highly threatening, so they are repressed; yet they remain as powerful determinants of later personality development. Along with the wish to possess the parent of the opposite sex comes the unconscious wish to displace the parent of the same sex, a wish epitomized by the slaying of the father in the Oedipus myth.

Erikson, in contrast, emphasizes that the basic task of the preschool years is to establish a sense of *competence* and *initiative.* This is the time for becoming psychologically ready to pursue activities of one's own choosing. If children are allowed the freedom to select meaningful activities, they tend to develop a positive outlook characterized by the ability to initiate and follow through. But if they are not allowed to make at least some of their own decisions or if their choices are criticized, they are likely to develop a sense of guilt over taking initiative. Typically, they will refrain from taking an active stance and will increasingly let others make decisions for them.

Implications for Group Work In most therapy and counseling groups, participants struggle with issues related to gender-role identity. Many individuals have incorporated stereotypical notions of what it means to be a woman or a man, and they have consequently repressed many of their feelings that don't fit these stereotypes. A group can be the place where individuals challenge such restricting views and become more whole.

Because concerns about sexual feelings, attitudes, values, and behavior are often kept private, people feel very much alone with their sexual concerns. Groups offer the chance to express these concerns openly, to correct faulty learning, to work through repressed feelings and events, and to begin to formulate a different view of oneself as a female or male sexual being. Perhaps the most important function of a group is that it gives clients permission to have feelings and to talk honestly about them.

STAGE 4: THE SCHOOL AGE—INDUSTRY VERSUS INFERIORITY (6 TO 12 YEARS)

Freudians call middle childhood the **latency stage.** After the torrent of sexual impulses of the preceding years, this period is relatively quiescent. There is a decline in sexual interests, which are replaced by interests in school, playmates, sports, and a whole range of new activities. Around age 6, children begin to reach out for new relationships.

Erikson stresses the active, rather than the latent, aspect of this stage and the unique psychosocial tasks that must be met at this time if healthy development is to take place. Children need to expand their understanding of the physical and social worlds and continue to develop appropriate gender-role identities. They must also form personal values, engage in social tasks, learn to accept people who are different from them, and acquire the basic skills needed for schooling. According to Erikson, the central task of middle childhood is the achievement of a sense of *industry,* and the failure to do so results in a sense of *inadequacy* and *inferiority.* Industry refers to setting and achieving goals that are personally meaningful. If children fail at this task, they are unlikely to feel adequate as adults, and the subsequent developmental stages will be negatively influenced.

Implications for Group Work Some problems originating at this stage that group leaders may expect to encounter include a negative self-concept, feelings of inadequacy relating to learning, feelings of inferiority in establishing social relationships, conflicts about values, a confused gender-role identity, unwillingness to face new challenges, dependency, and lack of initiative. It is crucial that members learn to recognize patterns that originated during childhood because those patterns will inevitably unfold in a group.

To see how the leader's knowledge of the problems and promises of this period of life can help the therapeutic process, let's look at a participant who suffers from feelings of inferiority. Rachel fears failure so much that she shies away from college because she is convinced she could never make it. In a group, she can be helped to see possible connections between her feelings of inadequacy and some events that occurred when she was in elementary school. Perhaps she had a series of negative learning experiences, such as being told, openly or not, by her teachers that she was stupid and couldn't learn. Before Rachel can overcome her feelings that she cannot meet the demands of college, she may have to go back to the traumatic events of her childhood, relive them, and express the pain she felt then. Through the support of the group she can experience many of these repressed feelings and begin to put the events of her past in a different perspective. Eventually, she may also come to realize that she doesn't have to give up an academic career now because of something that happened in grade school.

STAGE 5: ADOLESCENCE—IDENTITY VERSUS IDENTITY CONFUSION (12 TO 20 YEARS)

Adolescence is a stage of transition between childhood and adulthood. It is a time for continually testing limits, rejecting ties of dependency, and establishing a new identity. It is most of all a time of conflict, especially between the desire to break away from parental control and the fear of making independent decisions and living with the consequences. Adolescence is marked by a resurgence of Oedipal feelings. From the Freudian perspective, the **Oedipus complex** is the unconscious desire of the son for his mother, along with feelings of hostility and fear toward his father.

In Freudian theory adolescence initiates the final psychosexual stage of development, the **genital stage,** which is the longest stage and extends far beyond adolescence. It begins at the time of puberty and lasts until senility sets in, at which time the individual tends to regress to earlier stages. Erikson did not believe that personality development ended with puberty, and he separated Freud's genital stage into four stages of development, beginning with adolescence. He saw the crisis that characterizes adolescence—the identity crisis—as the most important of life.

What does Erikson mean by **identity crisis?** He means that most conflicts of the adolescent years are related to the development of a personal identity. Adolescents struggle to define who they are, where they are going, and how they will get there. Because all kinds of changes—physical as well as social—are taking place and because society applies diverse pressures, many adolescents have difficulty finding a stable identity. They often experience conflicting pressures and demands. In the midst of this turmoil, the adolescent has the task of ultimately deciding where he or she stands in the face of these varying expectations. If the adolescent fails, *identity confusion* results, and the person will lack purpose and direction in later years.

Implications for Group Work In many groups a good deal of time is devoted to the exploration and resolution of the dependence/independence conflicts that are so prevalent in adolescence. A central struggle involves the process of separation from one's parents and moving toward individuality or autonomy.

At times one or several members may manifest a rebellious attitude toward the leader. Although challenging the leader often signals a move toward independence, attacking a leader may well be a symptom of rebellion against parents or any other authority. It is essential that leaders be aware of their own dynamics and potential countertransferences, especially when confronted in this way by members. Leaders will be less likely to react defensively if they understand the transference nature of this behavior.

The unresolved problems of adolescence are manifest in many of the problems that adults bring to a group. Until adults recognize this unfinished issue from their earlier years, they cannot effectively meet the challenges presented by other stages of life.

STAGE 6: EARLY ADULTHOOD—INTIMACY VERSUS ISOLATION (20 TO 35 YEARS)

In Erikson's view we enter adulthood after we have mastered the conflicts of adolescence and established a firm personal identity. During the sixth stage, early adulthood, our sense of identity is tested again by the challenge of *intimacy* versus *isolation*.

An essential characteristic of the psychologically mature person is the ability to form intimate relationships. To achieve true intimacy with others, we need to have confidence in our own identity. Intimacy involves commitment and the ability to share and to give from our own centeredness; the failure to achieve intimacy leads to alienation and isolation. Early adulthood is also a time for focusing on one's interests, for becoming established in an occupation, and for carving out a satisfying lifestyle. It is a time for dreams and life plans but also a time for productivity.

Implications for Group Work In many adult groups considerable time is devoted to exploring the members' priorities. Participants struggle with concerns of interpersonal intimacy, talk about their unfulfilled dreams, question the meaningfulness of their work, wonder about the future, and reevaluate the patterns of their lives to determine what changes they need to make. Perhaps the greatest value of a group for people engaged in these struggles is the opportunity to take another look at their dreams and life plans and determine the degree to which their lives reflect these aspirations. If the gap is great, the participants are encouraged to find ways of changing the situation

Typically, young adults bring to a group the problems related to living with another person and establishing a family. The central struggle of this period is the intimacy crisis, a conflict between the need to maintain a sense of one's own separateness and the need to establish close relationships. The successful resolution of the intimacy crisis involves achieving a balance between taking care of oneself and actively caring for others. Those who fail to strike this balance either focus exclusively on the needs of others, thus neglecting their own needs, or are self-centered and have little room for concern about others. The quality of the young adult's ability to form interpersonal relationships is greatly influenced by what took place during early development.

How members deal with intimacy within the group reveals patterns they learned about getting close or keeping distant during their young adulthood. For many people in groups, forming close bonds with others is extremely difficult. This pattern of being uncomfortable and frightened of both receiving and giving love and compassion is likely to unfold in the group sessions. The group is an ideal place for members who are struggling with intimacy issues to recognize and challenge their fears.

STAGE 7: MIDDLE ADULTHOOD—GENERATIVITY VERSUS STAGNATION (35 TO 65 YEARS)

The seventh stage is characterized by a need to go beyond ourselves and our immediate family and to be actively involved with helping and guiding the next generation. This is a time when we are likely to engage in a philosophical reexamination of how we are living, which often leads to a reinvention of our way of being. The mature years can be one of the most productive periods of our lives, but they can also entail the painful experience of facing the discrepancy between what we set out to accomplish in early adulthood and what we have actually accomplished.

Erikson sees the stimulus for continued growth during this stage in the conflict between *generativity* and *stagnation.* Generativity is a broad concept that is manifested in the ability to love well, work well, and play well. If people fail to achieve a sense of personal competence, they begin to stagnate and to die psychologically. When we reach middle age, we become more sharply aware of the inevitability of our own eventual death. This awareness of mortality is one of the central features of the midlife crisis and colors our evaluations of what we are doing with our lives.

Implications for Group Work The changes that occur during this life stage and the crises and conflicts that accompany them represent valuable opportunities for group work. Participants are often challenged to make new assessments, adjustments, and choices to open up new possibilities and reach new levels of meaning. Knowledge of adult development allows the group leader to watch for the hopelessness that some people experience during middle age and to help them go beyond the destructive view that "that's all there is to life." It takes caring and skilled leadership to inspire people to look for new meanings and to "invent themselves" in novel ways.

STAGE 8: LATER LIFE—INTEGRITY VERSUS DESPAIR (ABOVE 65 YEARS)

The eighth, and last, stage of life confronts the individual with crucial developmental tasks, such as adjusting to the death of a spouse or friends, maintaining outside interests, adjusting to retirement, and accepting losses in physical and sensory capacities. But the central task of the final stage is reviewing the past and drawing conclusions.

According to Erikson, the successful resolution of the core crisis of this stage—the conflict between *integrity* and *despair*—depends on how the person looks back on the past. Ego integrity is achieved by those who feel few regrets. They see themselves as having lived productive and worthwhile lives, and they feel that they have coped with their failures as well as their successes. They are not obsessed with what might have been and are able to derive satisfaction from what has been. They see death as a part of the life process and can still find meaning and satisfaction in the time left. Failure to achieve ego integrity often leads to feelings of despair, hopelessness, guilt, resentment, and self-rejection.

Implications for Group Work Older adults are increasingly aware that they have a limited time left to live, and many of their issues can be productively addressed in a group. They realize that the joys associated with old age, such as wisdom and integrity, are limited in a way not recognized in earlier years (Henderson & Gladding, 2004). Themes prevalent with older adults include loss and grief; loneliness and social isolation; poverty; feelings of rejection; the struggle to find meaning in life; dependency; feelings of uselessness, hopelessness, and despair; the inevitability of death; sadness over physical and mental deterioration; and regrets over past events. Although these themes present major difficulties for many older people, they also have a range of life experiences and personal strengths that are often overlooked. Group work with older adults is one way to promote the positive aspects of aging as well as helping participants cope with the tasks associated with this stage of life. The interpersonal nature of groups can be therapeutic for older persons, especially those who are isolated and lonely (Henderson & Gladding, 2004).

The salient issues of this stage of life have implications not only for group leaders working with older adults but also for those who work with young or middle-aged adults. As people begin to see the years slip by, they feel increasing pressure to make something of their lives. Fears of being alone when they are old or of financial or physical dependency on others begin to surface. Group leaders can help these members prepare now for a satisfying life as they grow older. Asking "What would you like to be able to say about your life when you reach old age?" is a good way to start. What the members say in answer to this question (to themselves and in the group) can influence the decisions they need to make now and the specific steps they must take to achieve a sense of integrity at a later age.

Contemporary Trends in Psychoanalytic Group Theory

Psychoanalytic theory continues to evolve. Freud's ideas were based on an id psychology, characterized by conflicts over the gratification of basic needs. Later, writers in the social-psychological school moved away from Freud's orthodox position and contributed to the growth and expansion of the psychoanalytic movement by incorporating the cultural and social influences on personality. Then ego psychology, with its stress on psychosocial development throughout the life span, was developed by Erikson, among others. Anna Freud, with her identification of defense mechanisms, is a central figure in ego psychology although she is not particularly associated with the life-span interests of Erikson.

Psychoanalytic approaches are being applied to both family systems therapy and group therapy, and some contemporary psychoanalysts stress the interpersonal dimension more than the insight aspects of therapy. This is true of both object relations theory and attachment theory. According to Strupp (1992), the notion of unconscious conflict is still fundamental to psychodynamic thought. However, more attention is now being given to internal structures of personality that are significantly influenced by experiences with significant figures during one's infancy and early childhood. Strupp notes that the Oedipus complex is no longer considered a universal phenomenon. Instead, there is an increased focus on disturbances and arrests in infancy and early childhood that stem from deficiencies in the mother–child relationship.

OBJECT RELATIONS THEORY

Psychoanalytic theory expanded to include **object relations theory** in the 1970s and 1980s. Object relations are interpersonal relationships as they are represented intrapsychically. Although there is no single, generally accepted school or theory of object relations, this approach includes *self psychology* and *relational psychoanalysis.* Many theorists have contributed ideas to an evolving body of concepts that deal with object relations (St. Clair, 2004).

The term *object* was used by Freud to refer to that which satisfies a need, or to the significant person or thing that is the object or target of one's feelings or drives. It is used interchangeably with the term *other* to refer to an important person to whom the child and, later, the adult becomes attached. At birth, the infant has no sense of separateness; self and other are fused. The process of separation/individuation begins when the infant perceives that pleasure and discomfort are related to objects external to the self. The infant at this stage will typically make an attachment to the mother's breast before any recognition of her as a whole person.

Mahler (1968) believes the individual begins in a state of psychological fusion with the mother and progresses gradually to separation. The unfinished crises and residues of the earlier state of fusion, as well as the process of individuating, have a profound influence on later relationships. Object relations of later life build on the child's search for a reconnection with the mother (St. Clair, 2004). Psychoanalytic practitioners believe there is continuity in the development of self–other relations from their infantile origins to mature involvement with other persons. Thus, object relations are interpersonal relationships that shape the individual's current interactions with people (St. Clair, 2004).

The contemporary theoretical trend in psychoanalytic thinking centers on predictable developmental sequences in which the early experiences of the self shift in relation to an expanding awareness of others. Once self–other patterns are established, it is assumed, they influence later interpersonal relationships. This influence occurs through a process of searching for a type of experience that comes closest to the patterning established by the early experiences. These newer theories provide insight into how an individual's inner world can cause difficulties in living in the actual world of people and relationships (St. Clair, 2004). Psychological development can be thought of as the evolution of the way in which individuals differentiate themselves from others.

Object relations therapy is based on the premise that early in life the individual has drives that are satisfied through attachment to specific people, primarily parents. These early interactions lay the foundation for relationship patterns later in life (Marshall & Fitch, 2009). In group work, participants can experience how they are bringing very early patterns into their present interactions. For example, a group member who appears closely involved with others at one meeting may seem distant and removed at the next, leaving everyone wondering what happened to the level of work that seemed to have been achieved. This pattern might repeat what Mahler (1968) calls the "ambitendency" of an infant who goes back and forth between wanting to be held by its mother and wanting to be left free to roam and explore. In a therapy group, the participants work through self-destructive interactional patterns. The primary goals in a therapy group are to create a corrective emotional experience and change self-defeating relationship patterns (Marshall & Fitch, 2009).

ATTACHMENT THEORY AND GROUP PSYCHOTHERAPY

John Bowlby (1988) studied the importance of attachment, separation, and loss in human development and developed **attachment theory**, one of several extensions of psychoanalytic theory. **Attachment** involves an emotional bonding with another who is perceived as a source of security (Pistole & Arricale, 2003). According to Bowlby, the affectional bonds that the infant has with others, especially the mother (or another "attachment figure"), are essential for human survival. Infant attachment relationships can be broadly classified as secure or insecure. The quality of care an infant receives is related to the quality of that individual's relationships in later life (Peluso, Peluso, White, & Kern, 2004).

According to Marshall and Fitch (2009), a therapeutic group experience helps members meet their needs for being involved with others, for feeling attached, and for feeling appreciated. Attachment theory, which can be considered an offspring of object relations theory, is a part of the newer relational models within the psychodynamic approach. Flores (2008) believes that this theory synthesizes the best ideas of psychoanalysis, cognitive sciences, child development research, and neurobiology. He states: "Attachment is a primary motivational force with its own dynamics, and these dynamics have far-reaching and complex consequences, not just for development but also for the importance of the relationship and alliance in treatment" (p. 128).

BORDERLINE AND NARCISSISTIC PERSONALITY DISORDERS

Perhaps the most significant developments of recent psychoanalytic theory involve borderline and narcissistic personality disorders. The essential features of the **borderline personality** are an unstable view of one's self and instability in relating to others. With borderline individuals, relationships are dominated by the need to defend against the fear of abandonment or rejection. The essential features of **narcissistic personality disorder** are a pervasive pattern of grandiosity, hypersensitivity to the evaluations of others, and a lack of empathy. Every relationship with a narcissistic individual requires adulation and perfect responsiveness from the partner (Masterson, 1997). Both of these personality patterns begin by early adulthood. Among the most significant theorists in this area are Kernberg (1975, 1976) and Kohut (1971, 1977, 1984). Kohut maintains that people are their healthiest and best when they can feel both independence and attachment, taking joy in themselves and also being able to idealize others.

Object relations theory sheds new light on the understanding of personality disorders. According to St. Clair (2004), borderline and narcissistic disorders seem to result from traumas and developmental disturbances during separation/individuation. However, the full manifestations of the personality and behavioral symptoms tend to develop in adolescence or early adulthood. Narcissistic and borderline symptoms, such as omnipotence, grandiosity, and splitting (a defensive process of keeping incompatible feelings separate), are behavioral manifestations of developmental tasks that were disturbed or not completed earlier.

Borderline Personality A borderline personality disorder is characterized by bouts of irritability, self-destructive acts, impulsive anger, and extreme mood shifts. People with borderline dynamics typically experience extended periods of disillusionment punctuated by occasions of euphoria. Interpersonal relations are often intense and unstable, with marked changes of attitude over time. *Splitting* is a term often attributed to the tendency of people with borderline characteristics to think in "either-or" categories. For example, a formerly valued group member (or therapist) may suddenly be seen as worthless if he or she angers the member who exhibits borderline features. Impulsive and unpredictable behavior frequently can cause physical harm. A marked identity disturbance is generally manifested by uncertainty about life issues pertaining to self-image, sexual orientation, career choice, and long-term goals. Kernberg (1975) describes the syndrome as including a lack of clear identity, a lack of deep understanding of other people, poor impulse control, and the inability to tolerate anxiety. In recent years a great deal more clarity about individuals with borderline dynamics has emerged, especially due to the work of Kernberg and other theorists. They may be more disorganized than neurotics but more integrated than psychotic individuals. People who manifest borderline dynamics have not fully achieved separation/individuation and tend to have a chaotic, primitive personality structure.

William Blau (personal communication, March 1, 2009) points out that the diagnosis of a borderline personality is being applied rather broadly in clinical settings. Some authors describe individuals with borderline personality disorder as being characterized primarily by the inability to effectively manage emotional intensity, which is a less pathologizing view. Blau believes people with borderline characteristics are amenable to treatment, although their problems may be more difficult to resolve than simple neuroses because they are embedded in relatively permanent personality patterns. He also prefers to refer to borderline "dynamics" rather than borderline "personalities." Blau's view is consistent with that of Yalom (2005), who contends that borderline personality disorder does not represent a homogeneous diagnostic category. Yalom states that diagnosing whether a person has a borderline personality disorder depends on the characteristics of the individual being screened rather than on a broad diagnostic category.

Implications for Group Work According to Yalom (2005), the core problem of individuals with borderline features lies in the area of intimacy, and a group setting offers the therapeutic factors of cohesiveness and reality testing. He contends that if these individuals can accept feedback and observations provided by other members, and if their behavior is not highly disruptive, the group can offer them supportive refuge from daily stresses. Although individuals with borderline dynamics may express primitive, chaotic needs and fears, they are continually confronted with reality through the group process, which helps keep these feelings somewhat under control. Yalom writes that people with borderline disorders are referred to group therapy not because they work well or easily in a group but because they are so difficult to treat in individual therapy.

Clients with borderline personalities may be treated with a group format developed by Linehan (1993b), which is based on **dialectical behavior therapy (DBT).** DBT includes some psychodynamic concepts in a cognitive behavioral framework. DBT skills training groups should be used with borderline clients in conjunction with individual psychotherapy. DBT groups validate the client's behavior "as it is in the moment," confront resistance, and emphasize "the therapeutic relationship as essential to treatment" while teaching clients skills necessary to change (Linehan, 1993b, pp. 5–6). This topic is taken up in more detail in Chapter 13 on cognitive behavior therapy.

For those interested in learning more about treating individuals with borderline personality disorders from an object relations perspective, see Clarkin, Yeomans, and Kernberg (2006). There is a excellent discussion of working with people with borderline and narcissistic disorders in psychodynamic therapy groups in Rutan, Stone, and Shay (2007).

Narcissistic Personality Children who lack the opportunity either to differentiate or to idealize others while also taking pride in themselves may later suffer from narcissistic personality disorders. This syndrome is characterized by an exaggerated sense of self-importance and an exploitive attitude toward others, which serves the function of masking a frail self-concept. Such individuals tend to display exhibitionistic behavior. They seek attention and admiration from others, and they tend toward extreme self-absorption. Narcissism may also present itself as very low self-esteem and an overreadiness to idealize others (see Gabbard, 2000).

Kernberg (1975) characterizes people with narcissistic dynamics as focusing on themselves in their interactions with others, having a great need to be admired, possessing shallow affect, and being exploitive and at times establishing parasitic relationships with others. He writes that individuals who are narcissistically oriented have a shallow emotional life, enjoy little other than tributes received from others, and tend to depreciate those from whom they expect few narcissistic pleasures.

There is also a growing trend to see narcissism as a striking lack of self-esteem. Kohut (1971) characterizes narcissistically oriented people as being highly threatened in maintaining their self-esteem and as having feelings of emptiness and deadness. These individuals are typically searching for someone who will serve as an object to feed the famished self. Kohut uses the term *selfobject* to refer to a person who is used to foster the narcissist's self-esteem and sense of well-being. These clients look for people whom they can admire for their power because they see themselves as worthwhile only if they are associated with such selfobjects. Yet their inner void cannot be filled, so their search for confirmation by others is never-ending. Because of their impoverished sense of self and their unclear boundaries between self and others, they have difficulty differentiating between their own thoughts and feelings and those of the selfobject.

Implications for Group Work Yalom (2005) discusses the problems that arise when individuals with narcissistic dynamics enter group therapy. They typically have difficulty sharing group time, understanding and empathizing with others, and forming relationships with other members. These clients have a constant need for center stage. They often assess a group's usefulness to them in terms of how much time is devoted to them and how much attention they receive from the therapist. They are likely to be bored and impatient while other members are working, and they also tend to divert the discussion back to themselves. These individuals have unrealistic expectations of the other members. They feel that they are special and deserve the group's attention, yet they are not willing to give attention to others. According to Yalom, a major task of the therapist is to manage such highly vulnerable members in the group. The leader must focus on the way members who display narcissistic traits relate to others in the group.

In *Interactive Group Therapy,* Earley (2000) provides an informative discussion about the challenges of dealing with members who exhibit borderline and narcissistic tendencies. One of the main problems for group leaders is the potential countertransference reactions that are stirred up in them. The intense anger and splitting defenses that people with borderline disorders often display can result in a leader becoming intimidated by the client's anger or by becoming angry in return. The grandiosity, self-centeredness, and demeaning comments of a member displaying narcissistic tendencies can also elicit intense feelings of anger in both the leader and the members. Earley states that members with borderline and narcissistic disorders tend to provoke intense reactions in group therapists. This makes it particularly important for therapists to become aware of their reactions toward certain members, to avoid acting on their feelings as much as possible, and to seek supervision when needed.

According to J. Michael Russell (personal communication, January 16, 2010), countertransference reactions can be of value in understanding group members with borderline and narcissistic characteristics. Traits that initially might elicit negative reactions can be treated more therapeutically if the group leader's feelings are understood as resulting from members trying to communicate something about long-standing styles of interaction. For example, a member's moodiness might be seen as an attempt to communicate the moody nature of some early parental relationship.

The spirit of psychoanalysis requires taking the time to form a deep relationship with a minimum agenda in a carefully structured frame. Some of the most powerful tools for understanding borderline and narcissistic personality organization have emerged within this tradition. This way of working draws from the developmental models of Mahler and the competing visions of transference and countertransference put forward by Kernberg and Kohut.

THE FUTURE OF PSYCHOANALYTICALLY ORIENTED THERAPY

In 1992 Strupp wrote that the various modifications of psychoanalysis "have infused psychodynamic psychotherapy with renewed vitality and vigor" (p. 25). In his forecast, he suggested that this approach would undergo further revisions and that it would maintain its prominence in individual, group, marital, and family therapy. Although contemporary psychodynamic forms diverge considerably in many respects from the original Freudian emphasis on drives, the basic concepts of unconscious motivation, influence of early development, transference, countertransference, and resistance are still central to these newer psychodynamic therapies. Strupp also noted a decline in practices based on the classical analytic model, due to reasons such as time commitment, expense, limited applications to diverse client populations, and questionable benefits. He acknowledged that the realities stemming from managed care would place increasing emphasis on short-term treatments for specific disorders, limited goals, and containment of costs. Strupp identified the following trends and predicted some future directions that psychodynamic theory and practice would take:

- The emphasis on treatment has shifted from the "classical" interest in curing neurotic disorders to the problems of dealing therapeutically with chronic personality disorders, borderline conditions, and narcissistic personality disorders.

- There is increased attention on establishing a good therapeutic alliance early in the course of psychodynamic group therapy. A collaborative relationship is now viewed as a key factor related to a positive therapeutic outcome.

- Psychodynamic group therapy is becoming more popular and receiving widespread acceptance. This approach provides clients with opportunities to learn how they function in groups, and it offers a unique perspective on understanding problems.

- There is a renewed interest in development of briefer forms of psychodynamic group therapy, largely due to societal pressures for accountability and cost-effectiveness. The indications are that time-limited therapy will receive increasing attention in the future.

Strupp's assessment of the current scene and his predictions of what was to come were quite accurate.

Toward Integrative Approaches Some efforts have been made to develop integrative models in contemporary psychodynamic therapy. For example, it is possible to combine techniques of the cognitive behavioral therapies with the conceptual framework of contemporary psychoanalytic therapies. Morgan and MacMillan (1999) developed an integrated counseling model based on theoretical constructs of object relations and attachment theory that incorporates behavioral techniques. Morgan and MacMillan state that there is increasing support in the literature that integrating contemporary psychodynamic theory with cognitive behavioral techniques can lead to observable, constructive client changes. If treatment goals are well defined, it is possible to work through the various phases of therapy in a reasonable amount of time. Adapting the conceptual foundation of psychoanalytic thinking to relatively brief therapy makes this approach useful in time-limited therapy.

Brief Psychodynamic Therapy Brief therapy is one of the "future developments" Messer and Warren (2001) predicted for psychoanalytic practice. Brief psychodynamic therapy (BPT) applies the principles of psychoanalytic theory and therapy to treating selective disorders within a preestablished time limit of generally 10 to 25 sessions. BPT uses key psychoanalytic and psychodynamic concepts such as the enduring impact of psychosexual, psychosocial, and object relational stages of development; the existence of unconscious processes; reenactment of the client's past emotional issues in relationship to the therapist; the therapeutic alliance; and repetitive behavior.

Brief dynamic therapy tends to emphasize a client's strengths and resources in dealing with real-life issues. Levenson (2010) notes that a major modification of the psychoanalytic technique is the emphasis on the here-and-now of the client's life rather than exploring the there-and-then of childhood. Also, the brief dynamic therapist tends to think psychodynamically yet is open to using a variety of intervention strategies. Brief dynamic therapy "is an *integrative* short-term approach that interweaves major principles of time-sensitive clinical work" (p. 13).

To limit the duration of therapy, therapists actively maintain a circumscribed focus with limited goals (Levenson, 2010). A central theme, topic, or problem is needed to guide the work. The aim of brief psychodynamic therapy is not to bring about a cure but to foster changes in behavior, thinking, and feeling. Brief therapy is an opportunity to begin the process of change that will continue long after therapy is terminated.

Rutan and his colleagues (2007) point out that there has been increased emphasis on shorter, more cost-effective group treatments. They predict that there will be continuing pressure to provide group treatment as effectively and inexpensively as possible. BPT "has an important role in sustaining the values of psychoanalytic treatment, which is to understand and treat people's problems in the context of their current situation and earlier life experience" (Messer & Warren, 2001, p. 83). Levenson (2010) acknowledges that brief dynamic therapy is not suited for all clients and all therapists. For example, this approach is generally not suited for individuals with severe characterological disorders or for those with severe depression. Some therapists are not well suited to the interactive, directive, and self-disclosing strategies of brief dynamic therapy. Although time-limited groups are not the best choice for all people, these groups offer a viable treatment alternative for those who do not want to commit themselves to an open-ended, longer-term group.

For time-limited groups, members must formulate clear and precise treatment goals that are directly related to the organizing group theme. In these groups, the leader assumes a more active role and offers earlier interventions than would be typical in a long-term psychodynamic group. Here-and-now behaviors and interactions are given more attention, and in some very brief groups the therapist may focus exclusively on here-and-now interactions. The working-through process of past conflicts would be unlikely to be pursued in these groups. According to Rutan and his colleagues (2007), one advantage of such groups is knowing that a time limit exists; this keeps members focused on addressing specific personal problems. One disadvantage is that deeper conflicts or underlying problems remain untouched; members concentrate on more superficial levels of understanding.

Analytically oriented therapists tend to be skeptical of "quick fix" techniques and simplistic solutions to complex psychodynamic problems. However, many psychoanalytically oriented group therapists support the move to the use of briefer therapy, especially when this is indicated by the client's needs rather than arbitrarily set by third-party payers. Levenson (2010) believes brief therapy groups can be very rewarding, for "the work combines an optimistic, pragmatic, results-oriented attitude with the experience of deep emotional commitment" (p. 114). Having practiced brief dynamic therapy for 30 years, Levenson notes: "I have been phenomenally enriched, changed, and moved in countless small and dramatic ways by the power of being let into someone's life, albeit for a short stay" (p. 114). It has been found that most people, regardless of their cultural background, prefer brief approaches to therapy (Levenson, 2010).

If you are interested in a more comprehensive discussion of brief dynamic therapy, I highly recommend Levenson (2010).

Applying the Psychoanalytic Approach to Group Work in Schools

The developmental perspective addressed in considerable detail earlier in this chapter is useful for group counselors working in schools. Group work with children is enhanced by the counselor's understanding of the developmental needs and tasks related to themes of industry versus inferiority. Adolescent groups function better if the counselor understands core struggles around identity versus identity confusion. Groups can be structured to assist the members in learning age-appropriate skills to enhance daily living. The development of the ego functions can be facilitated by conceptualizing and structuring a remedial counseling group as a supportive surrogate family.

The analytic model provides a conceptual framework for understanding a child's or an adolescent's current problems. Although the use of psychoanalytic techniques is generally beyond the scope of group counseling in the school setting, group counselors can draw upon certain psychoanalytic concepts that have been elaborated in this chapter. Exploring the historical context of an elementary or high school student's problems is beyond the scope and limitations of school groups. However, understanding how past events may continue to have a present influence on the problems can reframe the group counselor's approach. A group leader can be aware of factors such as resistance, transference, anxiety, and the functioning of the ego-defense mechanisms. This awareness will add some depth to the interventions the group leader makes, even though he or she does not encourage excursions into past trauma or unconscious conflicts. Understanding these psychoanalytic concepts affords group counselors a way to develop empathy and to work compassionately with here-and-now problems of children and adolescents, as is demonstrated by Sheila Zaretsky's (2009) conversation group.

Zaretsky is a director and faculty member of the Academy of Clinical and Applied Psychoanalysis. She drew from psychoanalytic theory and applied psychoanalytic techniques in her work with a group of recently immigrated Chinese high school students who wished to improve their spoken English. The students in this group displayed a host of resistances to being emotionally available, which Zaretsky worked through using psychoanalytic group techniques. By the end of the school year, these students were able to discuss a wide range of meaningful concerns in English. Zaretsky (2009) concludes: "I am convinced that psychoanalytic theory and technique are an invaluable resource for teachers. It is my hope that universities and training institutes will create opportunities to offer those in the field of education our treasure. It is my mission to continue to do so" (p. 355).

Applying the Psychoanalytic Approach With Multicultural Populations

When considering whether a given theory is appropriate for working with diverse client populations in a group setting, one key criterion is the consistency between the concepts and techniques of a theory and the cultural values of the group members. Consider how well the underlying assumptions and key concepts mesh with the cultural values of diverse client groups. Although the basic concepts of psychoanalytic theory can be applied to understanding people from diverse cultures, the psychoanalytically oriented group therapist must also consider those instances when specific psychotherapeutic techniques may not fit with a client's cultural background.

Many cultural groups place a high priority on family history. A review of a client's past and of how this past is having an important bearing on current functioning may be appropriate as a conceptual framework. Working in symbolic ways can also be powerful, especially with clients who are reluctant to talk about their personal problems. For example, there is value in using pictures of the family at different periods of the client's childhood. The leader might say: "Select a picture that has particular meaning for you. Tell me what you remember during these times. As you look at the picture, what thoughts and feelings come to you?" Once group members begin talking to one another about their memories based on these pictures, they are likely to be more open in dealing with emotional material.

As we have seen, group therapists need to be aware of the ways in which the interpretations they make are influenced by their cultural background and their theoretical assumptions. Although practitioners can still conceptualize the struggles of their clients from an analytic perspective, it is critical that they adopt a stance of flexibility. Group counselors need to exercise vigilance lest they misuse their power by turning the group into a forum for pushing clients to adjust by conforming to the dominant cultural values at the expense of losing their own worldviews and cultural identities. Group practitioners also need to be aware of their own potential sources of bias. The concept of countertransference can be expanded to include unacknowledged bias and prejudices that may be conveyed unintentionally through the techniques used by group therapists.

Evaluation of the Psychoanalytic Approach to Groups

CONTRIBUTIONS AND STRENGTHS OF THE APPROACH

There is much in psychoanalytic theory that I consider of great value. All of the theoretical orientations presented in this text have some relationship to the psychoanalytic approach, even if in some cases the theory is a reaction against some of the basic ideas of this foundational theory. The analytic model provides a conceptual framework for understanding an individual's history, and in this regard group practitioners can learn to *think* psychoanalytically even if they do not *practice* psychoanalytically. Although some psychoanalytic techniques may have limited utility for the group counselor in some settings, many analytic concepts help explain the dynamics operating both in individuals and in the group as a whole.

I am convinced that it is important to consider the past to fully understand present behavior. Many of the conflicts brought to a group are rooted in early childhood experiences. Although I am not advocating a preoccupation with the past by excessively dwelling on it, my contention is that ignoring the influence of the past can lead to superficial group work. Understanding this influence gives people more control over their present behavior.

A psychoanalytic concept I find of particular importance is resistance. Even when members are in a group by their own choice, I observe resistances, especially during the early development of the group. These resistances are manifestations of various fears; unless they are dealt with, they are likely to interfere with the progress of a group. In fact, I typically ask members to share with the group the ways in which they expect their behavior patterns to interfere with their group work. Even though resistance is typically unconscious, group members will often be surprisingly revealing. Some members seem to know quite well that they may sabotage their best efforts and resist change by intellectualizing, by being overly nurturing or overly critical with fellow members, or by convincing themselves that their problems are not as pressing as the problems of others in the group. If members can recognize their avoidant behaviors when they occur, they have a chance to change them. Some of the more subtle forms of defense may become evident over time, such as displacing feelings and projecting.

The psychoanalytic concepts of anxiety and the ego-defense mechanisms that emerge as a way to cope with this anxiety are most useful for group practitioners. Although in some groups the leader may not interpret and work through these defensive structures, it is essential to learn to respect defenses and to recognize how they develop and how they manifest themselves in group interactions. Dealing with the defenses against anxiety provides a useful framework for intense group work. Members have the opportunity to challenge some of their defensive strategies, and in the process of learning how to communicate in nondefensive ways, they can also learn new ways of responding.

Transference and countertransference have significant implications for group work. Although not all feelings between members and the leader are the result of these processes, a leader must be able to understand their value and role. I find the analytic concept of projection quite useful in exploring certain feelings within the group. Projections onto the leader and onto other members are valuable clues to unresolved conflicts within the person that can be productively worked through in the group.

The group can also be used to re-create early life situations that are continuing to have an impact on the client. A basic tenet of psychodynamic therapy groups is the notion that group participants, through their interactions within the group, re-create their social situation, implying that the group becomes a microcosm of their everyday lives (Rutan et al., 2007). In most groups individuals elicit feelings of attraction, anger, competition, avoidance, aggression, and so forth. These feelings may be similar to those that members experienced toward significant people in the past. Thus members will most likely find symbolic mothers, fathers, siblings, and lovers in their group. These transferences within the group and the intense feelings that often characterize them are fruitful avenues to explore and to work through.

MODIFICATIONS OF CLASSICAL ANALYTIC PRACTICE

An approach that integrates Freud's psychosexual stages of development with Erikson's psychosocial stages is, in my view, most useful for understanding key themes in the development of personality. Working solely on an insight level will not result in changes; it is essential to explore sociocultural factors as they pertain to the struggles of individuals at the various phases of their development. Unless group practitioners have a good grasp of the major tasks and crises of each stage, they have little basis for determining whether developmental patterns are normal or abnormal. Also, a synthesis of Freud's and Erikson's theories offers a general framework for recognizing conflicts that participants often explore in groups.

The more recent developments—object relations theories, self psychology, and relational psychoanalysis—offer valuable conceptions for group therapists.

There have been a number of breakthroughs in working with borderline and narcissistic dynamics in group therapy, and the group offers some unique advantages over the one-to-one relationship in working with people manifesting borderline personality characteristics.

Many practitioners who were trained in classical psychoanalysis have modified analytic concepts and techniques to fit group situations. I have encountered a number of therapists who think in psychoanalytic terms but use techniques drawn from other therapeutic models. Many practitioners work with psychodynamic concepts such as the unconscious, defenses, resistances, transference, and the significance of the past. Some analytically oriented group therapists demonstrate an openness toward integrating various methods.

LIMITATIONS OF THE APPROACH

From a feminist perspective, there are distinct limitations to a number of Freudian concepts, especially the notion of the Oedipus and Electra complexes and the assumptions about the inferiority of women. In her review of feminist counseling and therapy, Enns (1993) notes that the object relations approach has been criticized for its emphasis on the role of the mother–child relationship as a determinant of later interpersonal functioning. This approach gives great responsibility to mothers for deficiencies and distortions in development, whereas fathers are conspicuously absent from the hypothesis. Enns writes that some feminist therapists have addressed the limitations of psychoanalysis by incorporating family systems work within their psychoanalytic model.

In addition to the criticisms of psychoanalysis from feminist writers, the approach has been accused of failing to adequately address the social, cultural, and political factors that result in an individual's problems. Psychoanalytic therapy is less concerned with short-term problem solving than it is with long-term personality reconstruction. In his critique of long-term psychodynamic therapy, Strupp (1992) acknowledges that this approach will clearly remain a luxury for most people in our society. Low-income clients generally do not have the time, resources, or inclination to begin and maintain the extended and expensive journey of psychoanalytic self-exploration. Instead, they are likely to be motivated more by the need to have psychological security and provide for their family. This is not to imply that all approaches to psychotherapy are inappropriate for people of limited means. Smith (2005) contends that psychotherapists' willingness and ability to work with poor people is compromised by unexamined classist attitudes and that these attitudes constitute a significant obstacle for practitioners' success in working with the poor. Smith seems to making a case for alternative therapeutic models such as psychoeducation, counseling, preventive psychology, and community psychology rather than traditional psychotherapy for the poor.

Where to Go From Here

If you would like to learn more about psychoanalytic groups, you would do well to join the American Group Psychotherapy Association (AGPA). Membership includes a subscription to an excellent journal, the *International*

Journal of Group Psychotherapy, which is published four times a year. The journal contains a variety of articles dealing with both the theory and practice of group therapy, and many of the articles relate to psychoanalytic groups. Each year in February the AGPA sponsors a five-day meeting that features a variety of institutes, seminars, open sessions, and workshops. Although psychodynamic groups are featured, other group orientations are offered as well. Many of these full-day and half-day workshops are directed toward issues of interest to psychodynamic practitioners. The AGPA has a student-member category. For further information about journal subscriptions and membership requirements contact:

American Group Psychotherapy Association, Inc.
25 East 21st Street, 6th Floor
New York, NY 10010
Telephone: (212) 477-2677 or Toll Free: (877) 668-2472
Fax: (212) 979-6627
E-mail: memberservices@agpa.org
Website: www.agpa.org

AUTHOR LECTURES

Watch *Gerald Corey's Perspectives on Theory and Practice of Group Counseling* DVD or visit the *Theory and Practice of Group Counseling* CourseMate website at www.cengagebrain.com/shop/ISBN/0840033869 to watch videos of Dr. Gerald Corey presenting lectures for each chapter. Also available are unique eAudio lectures for each chapter and quiz questions for self-study.

RECOMMENDED SUPPLEMENTARY READINGS

Psychodynamic Group Psychotherapy (Rutan, Stone, & Shay, 2007) presents a comprehensive discussion of various facets of psychodynamic group therapy. This book addresses topics such as the stages of group development, the role of the group therapist, therapeutic factors accounting for change, working with difficult groups and difficult group members, and time-limited psychodynamic groups. If you were to select a single source on the psychodynamic approach to group therapy, I recommend this book.

Brief Dynamic Therapy (Levenson, 2010) describes a model of psychodynamic therapy that fits the reality of time-limited therapy and outlines the steps toward clinical work that is focused and deep. The author clearly explains how psychoanalytic concepts and techniques can be modified to suit the needs of many clients who cannot participate in long-term therapy.

Object Relations and Self Psychology: An Introduction (St. Clair, 2004) provides an overview and critical assessment of two streams of psychoanalytic theory and practice: object relations theory and self psychology. The book looks at how different theorists vary from one another and how they depart from the classical Freudian model. This is a good place to start if you want an update on the contemporary trends in psychoanalysis.

Psychoanalytic Theory: An Introduction (Elliott, 1994) provides thorough coverage of the psychoanalytic implications for "postmodern" theories, systems approaches, and feminist thought.

*American Psychiatric Association. (2000). *Diagnostic and statistical manual of mental disorders* (4th ed., text revision). Washington, DC: Author.

Aviv, A. (2010). Where intersubjectivity and group analysis meet. *International Journal of Group Psychotherapy, 60*(1), 91–109.

Bemak, F., & Epp, L. (2001). Countertransference in the development of graduate student group counselors: Recommendations for training. *Journal for Specialists in Group Work, 26*(4), 305–318.

Bowlby, J. (1988). *A secure base.* New York: Basic Books.

Brabender, V. M. (1987). Vicissitudes of countertransference in inpatient group psychotherapy. *International Journal of Group Psychotherapy, 37*(4), 549–567.

Clarkin, J., Yeomans, F., & Kernberg, O. (2006). *Psychotherapy for borderline personality: Focusing on object relations.* Washington DC: American Psychiatric Press.

Comas-Diaz, L. (2011). Multicultural theories of psychotherapy. In R. Corsini & D. Wedding (Eds.), *Current psychotherapies* (9th ed., pp. 536–567). Belmont, CA: Brooks/Cole, Cengage Learning.

*DeAngelis, T. (1996). Psychoanalysis adapts to the 1990s. *APA Monitor, 27*(9), 1, 43.

Durkin, H. (1964). *The group in depth.* New York: International Universities Press.

*Earley, J. (2000). *Interactive group therapy: Integrating interpersonal, action-oriented, and psychodynamic approaches.* Philadelphia, PA: Brunner/Mazel (Taylor & Francis Group).

*Elliott, A. (1994). *Psychoanalytic theory: An introduction.* Cambridge: Blackwell.

Enns, C. Z. (1993). Twenty years of feminist counseling and therapy: From naming biases to implementing multifaceted practice. *The Counseling Psychologist, 21*(1), 3–87.

Erikson, E. H. (1963). *Childhood and society* (2nd ed.). New York: Norton.

Erikson, E. H. (1968). *Identity: Youth and crisis.* New York: Norton.

Erikson, E. H. (1982). *The life cycle completed.* New York: Norton.

Flores, P. J. (2008). Attachment theory and group psychotherapy. *International Journal of Group Psychotherapy, 58*(1), 127–132.

Fonagy, P. (2001). *Attachment theory and psychoanalysis,* New York: Other Press.

Foulkes, S. H. (1965). *Therapeutic group analysis.* New York: International Universities Press.

Freud, S. (1955). *The interpretation of dreams.* New York: Basic Books.

Gabbard, G. O. (2000). *Psychodynamic psychiatry in clinical practice* (3rd ed.). Washington, DC: American Psychiatric Press.

Gelso, C. J., & Hayes, J. A. (2002). The management of countertransference. In J. C. Norcross (Ed.), *Psychotherapy relationships that work* (pp. 267–283). New York: Oxford University Press.

Hayes, J. A. (2004). Therapist know thyself: Recent research on countertransference. *Psychotherapy Bulletin, 39*(4), 6–12.

Henderson, D. A., & Gladding, S. T. (2004). Group counseling with older adults. In J. L. DeLucia-Waack, D. Gerrity, C. R. Kalodner, & M. T. Riva (Eds.), *Handbook of group counseling and psychotherapy* (pp. 469–478). Thousand Oaks, CA: Sage.

Kauff, P. F. (2009). Transference in combined individual and group psychotherapy. *International Journal of Group Psychotherapy, 59*(1), 29–46.

Kernberg, O. F. (1975). *Borderline conditions and pathological narcissism.* New York: Aronson.

Kernberg, O. F. (1976). *Object-relations theory and clinical psychoanalysis.* New York: Aronson.

---

* Books and articles marked with an asterisk (*) are suggested for further study.

*Kernberg, O. F. (1997). Convergences and divergences in contemporary psychoanalytic technique and psychoanalytic psychotherapy. In J. K. Zeig (Ed.), *The evolution of psychotherapy: The third conference* (pp. 3–22). New York: Brunner/Mazel.

Kohut, H. (1971). *The analysis of the self.* New York: International Universities Press.

Kohut, H. (1977). *The restoration of the self.* New York: International Universities Press.

Kohut, H. (1984). *How does psychoanalysis cure?* Chicago: University of Chicago Press.

Kolb, G. E. (1983). The dream in psychoanalytic group therapy. *International Journal of Group Psychotherapy, 33*(1), 41–52.

Levenson, H. (2010). *Brief dynamic therapy.* Washington, DC: American Psychological Association.

Linehan, M. M. (1993a). *Cognitive-behavioral treatment of borderline personality disorder.* New York: Guilford Press.

Linehan, M. M. (1993b). *Skills training manual for treating borderline personality disorder.* New York: Guilford Press.

Locke, N. (1961). *Group psychoanalysis: Theory and technique.* New York: New York University Press.

*Luborsky, E. B., O'Reilly-Landry, M., & Arlow, J. A. (2011). Psychoanalysis. In R. J. Corsini & D. Wedding (Eds.), *Current psychotherapies* (9th ed., pp. 15–66). Belmont, CA: Brooks/Cole, Cengage Learning.

Mahler, M. S. (1968). *On human symbiosis and the vicissitudes of individuation.* New York: International Universities Press.

Marshall, J. L., & Fitch, T. (2009). Group counseling theories. In American Counseling Association (Ed.), *The ACA encyclopedia of counseling* (p. 249). Alexandria, VA: American Counseling Association.

*Masterson, J. F. (1997). The disorders of the self and intimacy: A developmental self and object relations approach. In J. K. Zeig (Ed.), *The evolution of psychotherapy: The third conference* (pp. 37–52). New York: Brunner/Mazel.

*Messer, S. B., & Warren, C. S. (2001). Brief psychodynamic therapy. In R. J. Corsini (Ed.), *Handbook of innovative therapies* (2nd ed., pp. 67–85). New York: Wiley.

*Mitchell, S. A., & Black, M. J. (1995). *Freud and beyond: A history of modern psychoanalytic thought.* New York: Basic Books.

Morgan, B., & MacMillan, P. (1999). Helping clients move toward constructive change: A three-phase integrative counseling model. *Journal of Counseling and Development, 77*(2), 153–159.

*Mullan, H., & Rosenbaum, M. (1978). *Group psychotherapy: Theory and practice* (2nd ed.). New York: Free Press.

Peluso, P. R., Peluso, J. P., White, J. F., & Kern, R. M. (2004). A comparison of attachment theory and individual psychology: A review of the literature. *Journal of Counseling and Development, 82*(2), 139–145.

Pistole, C., & Arricale, F. (2003). Understanding attachment: Beliefs about conflict. *Journal of Counseling and Development, 81*(3), 318–328.

*Rutan, J. S., Stone, W. N., & Shay, J. J. (2007). *Psychodynamic group psychotherapy* (4th ed.). New York: Guilford Press.

St. Clair, M. (with Wigren, J.). (2004). *Object relations and self psychology: An introduction* (4th ed.). Belmont, CA: Brooks/Cole, Cengage Learning.

Scheidlinger, S. (1987). On interpretation in group psychotherapy: The need for refinement. *International Journal of Group Psychotherapy, 37*(3), 339–352.

Schermer, V. (2009). On the vicissitudes of combining individual and group psychotherapy. *International Journal of Group Psychotherapy, 59*(1), 149–162.

Smith, L. (2005). Psychotherapy, classism, and the poor. *American Psychologist, 60*(7), 687–696.

Strupp, H. H. (1992). The future of psychodynamic psychotherapy. *Psychotherapy, 29*(1), 21–27.

Tuttman, S. (1986). Theoretical and technical elements which characterize the American approaches to psychoanalytic group psychotherapy. *International Journal of Group Psychotherapy, 36*(4), 499–515.

Wolf, A. (1963). The psychoanalysis of groups. In M. Rosenbaum & M. Berger (Eds.), *Group psychotherapy and group function.* New York: Basic Books.

Wolf, A. (1975). Psychoanalysis in groups. In G. M. Gazda (Ed.), *Basic approaches to group psychotherapy and group counseling* (2nd ed.). Springfield, IL: Charles C Thomas.

Wolf, A. (1983). Psychoanalysis in groups. In H. I. Kaplan & B. J. Sadock (Eds.), *Comprehensive group psychotherapy* (2nd ed.). Baltimore: Williams & Wilkins.

Wolf, A., & Kutash, I. L. (1986). Psychoanalysis in groups. In I. L. Kutash & A. Wolf (Eds.), *Psychotherapist's casebook* (pp. 332–352). San Francisco: Jossey-Bass.

Wolf, A., & Schwartz, E. K. (1962). *Psychoanalysis in groups.* New York: Grune & Stratton.

Yalom, I. D. (with Leszcz, M.). (2005). *The theory and practice of group psychotherapy* (5th ed.). New York: Basic Books.

Zaretsky, S. (2009). The conversation group: Using group psychoanalytic techniques to resolve resistances of recently immigrated Chinese students to learning English in a high school setting. *International Journal of Group Psychotherapy, 59*(3), 335–356.

CHAPTER SEVEN

Adlerian Group Counseling

COAUTHORED BY JAMES ROBERT BITTER AND GERALD COREY

Introduction

While Freud was developing his system of psychoanalysis, a number of other psychiatrists also interested in the psychodynamic approach were independently studying the human personality. One of these was Alfred Adler. In contrast to Freud's sexual repression theory, Adler (1996a, 1996b) contended that neurosis was the result of a person's retreat from the required tasks in life with the symptoms serving a safeguarding function to protect the individual from perceived failure in a life task. If a person is depressed, we might ask, "What is she or he avoiding?" Is this person facing a challenge at work or with friendships, or is there conflict in an intimate relationship? We often know the purpose of a symptom by how the person *uses* it. Adler focused on the struggle of individuals to become all that they might be. Adler's growth model was the foundation for his *psychology of use*. We are born with certain building blocks (heredity and environment); what we do with them determines what kind of people we become.

Adler was a politically and socially oriented psychiatrist who showed great concern for the common person. Indeed, many of his early clients were working-class people who struggled to make a living, raise and educate their children, and make a difference in society. Part of Adler's mission was to bring psychological understanding to the general population and to translate psychological concepts into practical methods for helping a varied population meet the challenges of everyday life.

Alfred Adler made significant contributions to contemporary therapeutic practice. Adler believed in the social nature of human beings, and he was interested in working with clients in a group context. He established more than 30 child guidance clinics in which he pioneered live demonstrations by interviewing children, adults, teachers, and parents in front of community groups. He was the first psychiatrist to use group methods in a systematic way in child guidance centers in the 1920s in Vienna (Christensen, 2004).

To fully appreciate the development of the practice of Adlerian psychology, one must recognize the contributions of Rudolf Dreikurs, who was largely responsible for extending and popularizing Adler's work and transplanting Adler's ideas to the United States. He did a great deal to translate Adlerian principles into the practice of group psychotherapy, and he used group psychotherapy in his private practice for more than 40 years (see Dreikurs, 1960, 1967, 1997). Dreikurs developed and refined Adler's concepts into a clear-cut, teachable system with practical applications for family life, education, preventive mental health, and, especially, group psychotherapy (Terner & Pew, 1978). Dreikurs was a key figure in developing the Adlerian family education centers in the United States. Work with children and their parents in a group setting paved the way for Dreikurs's pioneering group psychotherapy. It is believed that Dreikurs was the first person to use group therapy in a private practice.

Adlerian interventions have been widely applied to diverse client populations of all ages in many different settings. Adlerian group therapy is an integration of key concepts of Adlerian psychology with socially constructed, systemic, and brief approaches based on the holistic model developed by Dreikurs (Sonstegard & Bitter, 2004).

Key Concepts

OVERVIEW OF THE ADLERIAN VIEW OF THE PERSON

Adler's socioteleological approach provides an ideal foundation for group work (Sonstegard & Bitter, 2004). Adler's system emphasizes the social determinants of behavior rather than its biological aspects; its goal directedness rather than its origins in the past; and its purposeful rather than its unconscious nature. This "socioteleological" approach implies that people are primarily motivated by social forces and are striving to achieve certain goals. Adler's view is that we create for ourselves an idiosyncratic view of self, life, and others from which we then create goals, both short- and long-term, that motivate our behavior and influence our development. It is especially our long-term goals, which Adler called life goals, that guide our movement toward an envisioned completion and sometimes even toward perfection. The search for significance is related to our basic feelings of inferiority with regard to others, which motivates us to strive toward ever greater mastery, superiority, power, and, ultimately, perfection. Inferiority feelings can thus be the wellspring of creativity; perfection, though never reached, is the ultimate goal of life. Because most of us do not reach completion or perfection, our goals are always fictions—pictures of personal fulfillment that we adopt "as if" they were true.

Adler's system stresses self-determination and consciousness—rather than the unconscious posited by Freud—as the center of personality. We are not the victims of fate but creative, active, choice-making and meaning-making beings whose every action has purpose and is directed toward some goal. Movement toward goals and our anticipation of the future are far more important than what has happened to us in the past. Behavior can be understood only if one takes a holistic approach and looks at all actions from the perspective of the individual's chosen style of living. Each of us has a unique lifestyle, or personality, which starts to develop in early childhood to compensate for and overcome some perceived inferiority. Our lifestyle orders our experiences of life and guides interactions with others. It consists of our views about ourselves, others, and the world, and the distinctive behaviors we use to pursue our goals.

The Adlerian approach is basically a growth model: our destiny is never fixed as we are always in the process of becoming (Carlson & Englar-Carlson, 2008). Adlerians reject the idea that some individuals are psychologically "sick" and in need of a "cure." Milliren and Clemmer (2006) capture this notion: "We need to think in terms of people moving forward with resilience rather than being stuck in some kind of pathology" (p. 18). Adlerians view their work as primarily an educational process—helping people learn better ways to meet the challenges of life tasks, providing direction, helping people change their mistaken notions, and offering encouragement to those who are discouraged.

HOLISM

The Adlerian approach, also known as **Individual Psychology,** is based on a **holistic** view of the person. Adler used the word *individual* to describe an indivisible unit. The focus is on understanding whole persons within their socially embedded contexts of family, school, and work. Individuals are always more than the sum of their parts. Thoughts, feelings, beliefs, behavioral patterns, traits and characteristics, convictions, attitudes, and personal creativity are all expressions of the uniqueness of the person.

One implication of this holistic view is that the client is seen as an integral part of a social system. More attention is given to interpersonal factors than to intrapersonal ones. The therapist is oriented toward understanding the client's social situation and the attitudes he or she has about it. Viewing people in relation to social systems is basic to group and family therapy.

Adler's theory is, in essence, a field theory of personality that deals with how the individual attempts to find his or her place within the social environment. Adler saw behavior as inherently social; therefore, behavior is understandable only with reference to its function within the social context in which the behavior occurs. The group reflects how members behave in other real-life social situations. Members often seek the same position in a group that they held in their family constellation. For example, if Joe assumed the role of caretaker for all of his siblings, he might put most of his energy into taking care of others in the group, neglecting to ask for time for himself. Furthermore, it is in a group that people often manifest their faulty beliefs with ineffective ways of meeting the tasks of life (Carlson, Watts, & Maniacci, 2006). Group counseling is a natural setting for addressing relationships because members can experiment with interactions that result in transforming the mistaken goals and notions they are pursuing (Sonstegard & Bitter, 2004).

TELEOLOGY

Individual Psychology contends that we can be understood best by looking at where we are going and what we are striving to accomplish. According to Adler, all forms of life are characterized by a trend toward growth and expansion. He rejected Freud's causal determinism in favor of **teleology:** humans live by goals and purposes. Adlerians relate the past to the present only to indicate the continuity of the maladaptive lifestyle, not to show a causal connection between the past and the present (Mosak & Maniacci, 2011). In contrast to the Freudian psychoanalytic emphasis on the past, Adlerians are more interested in the future. The three aspects of time are dynamically interrelated: our behavioral decisions are based on the conclusions we have made from what we have experienced in the past, which we use to then provide a framework for understanding our present situation, and for choosing, albeit unconsciously, the goals toward which we move. In short, Adlerians look for continuity or a pattern in a client's life, but the emphasis is always on the goal-directed nature of behavior. The individual's movement through life is unified and directed by the person's self-selected life goal.

PHENOMENOLOGY

Adler was perhaps the first major theorist to stress a **phenomenological orientation** toward therapy. His psychological approach pays attention to the subjective fashion through which people perceive their world. This personal perspective includes the individual's views, beliefs, perceptions, and conclusions. From the Adlerian perspective, objective reality is less important than how we interpret reality and the meanings we attach to what we experience. Humans are creative beings who decide on their actions based on their subjective perceptions.

As you will see in later chapters, many contemporary theories have incorporated this notion of the client's subjective perception of reality, or personal worldview, as a basic factor explaining behavior. Some of the other group approaches that have a phenomenological perspective are psychodrama, existential therapy, person-centered therapy, Gestalt therapy, reality therapy, and solution-focused brief therapy.

CREATIVITY AND CHOICE

From the Adlerian perspective, humans are not defined solely by heredity and environment; rather, these are the foundations, or building blocks, of life. The **socioteleological approach** is grounded on the notion that we are self-determining beings, which implies that we have the capacity to influence and create events. We express ourselves in diverse ways that are consistent with our past experiences, present attitudes, and anticipations about the future (Sonstegard & Bitter, 2004). Adler believed that what we are born with is not as crucial as the use we make of our natural endowment. Adlerians do recognize, however, that biological and environmental conditions limit our capacity to choose and to create. Although Adlerians reject the deterministic stance of Freud, they do not go to the other extreme by maintaining that individuals can become whatever they want to be. This approach is based on the premise that within a framework of limitations a wide range of choices is open to us.

Adlerians base their practice on the assumption that people are creative, active, and self-determining. Adlerians have developed a style of challenging clients to become aware of the ways in which they were active participants in situations they perceived as problematic. Sonstegard and Bitter (2004) report a case in which an adolescent feels his parents are always antagonizing him. After noting that the boy, Erv, often provokes his parents, Sonstegard asks the group if they know why:

> Erv, . . . you are quite a bright boy, but you have some doubts about yourself. You are not sure you are as good as you want to be. So you go about reassuring yourself by proving others wrong. You feel so much better by comparison. What do you think about that? (p. 47)

In this sense, Adlerians explore with individuals how they are part of a circular pattern of causality and thus capable of breaking that pattern. Dreikurs's therapy was aimed at showing clients that, although they could not directly change the behavior of others, they did have the power to change their own reactions and attitudes toward others.

COMMUNITY FEELING AND SOCIAL INTEREST

Community feeling and **social interest**, derived from the German word *Gemeinschaftsgefühl*, are fundamental tenets of Individual Psychology (Watts & Eckstein, 2009). **Community feeling** embodies the feeling of being connected to all of humanity—past, present, and future—and to being involved in making the world a better place. **Social interest** refers to the individual's positive attitude toward other people in the world; it involves the capacity to cooperate and contribute (Milliren & Clemmer, 2006). Adlerians believe this connecting, community feeling is innate and that, when developed, it expresses an active, social interest (Sonstegard & Bitter, 2004). As an antidote to social isolation and self-absorption, social interest leads to courage, optimism, and a true sense of belongingness. Adler equates social interest with a sense of identification and empathy with others.

Individual Psychology rests on a central belief that our happiness and success are largely related to social connectedness. Because we are embedded in a society, we cannot be understood in isolation from that social context. We are primarily motivated by a desire to belong. Only within the group can we actualize our potentialities. As social beings, we have a need to be of use to others and to establish meaningful relationships in a community. As socially embedded individuals, our lives and contributions flourish when we experience a sense of belongingness to the community. It is out of this social embeddedness that we discover who we are (Milliren & Clemmer, 2006).

Adler (1964) notes that we have strong needs to feel united with others and that only when we do so can we act with courage in facing and dealing with life's problems. He contends that we must successfully master at least three *universal life tasks*. All people need to address these life tasks, regardless of age, gender, time in history, culture, or nationality. These tasks are building friendships (*social task*), establishing intimacy (*love/marriage task*), and contributing to society (*occupational task*). These life tasks are so fundamental to human living that dysfunction in any one of them is often an indicator of a psychological disorder (American Psychiatric Association, 2000). Each of these tasks requires the development of psychological capacities for *friendship* and *belonging*, for *contribution* and *self-worth*, and for *cooperation* (Bitter, 2006). Most members have core beliefs surrounding key life tasks such as work, love, self-acceptance, belonging, and friendship. For example, Susan has a core belief that most of her worth as a person hinges on her productivity at work. When she is not working and achieving, she has a difficult time thinking well of herself. These beliefs can be critically examined within the group, and it is possible to eliminate faulty beliefs and replace them with more constructive or useful beliefs.

These key concepts of community feeling and social interest have significant implications for group counseling; the general goals of the group are to increase self-esteem and to develop social interest. The group focuses on discovering the members' mistaken assumptions that keep them from feeling adequate and from being oriented toward and engaged with others. This concept is applied to group counseling by structuring the group so that members can meet some of their needs for affiliation with others.

Self-centeredness and the alienation it produces are the opposite of social interest and are seen as a major problem in contemporary society. It is hoped that one of the outcomes of a group experience will be that members grow to accept themselves and others, even though all of us are imperfect. For this reason, most Adlerians reject the idea of prescreening in groups. They believe the process tends to destroy heterogeneity and works against accepting different levels of imperfection common in the larger society. Sonstegard and Bitter (2004) assert that, generally, prescreening excludes the very people who could most use a group experience—those who are self-absorbed, disruptive, noncommunicative, and isolated. Such people may best find solutions to their problems in a group setting. Adlerians contend that refusing to give an individual the opportunity to participate in a group experience is antidemocratic. Adlerians believe groups ought to welcome all who want to join and not exclude the people who need it most.

INFERIORITY/SUPERIORITY

From our earliest years, we recognize that we are helpless or less capable than we need to be, which is characterized by feelings of inferiority or of being less than we should be. **Inferiority feelings** are based on our appraisal of deficiency that is subjective, global, and judgmental (Carlson et al., 2006). This sense of inferiority is not a negative force. On the contrary, our basic inferiority is the springboard for our attempts to master our environment. To compensate for feelings of inferiority, we strive for a better position in life. In Adler's words, we **strive for superiority,** or to move from a felt minus position in life to a perceived plus position. It is through this striving that we find ways to control the forces in our lives rather than being controlled by them.

Inferiority feelings can be the wellspring of creativity; and life goals of perfection, though never reached, can draw us into new possibilities for which our past has not otherwise prepared us. Since inferiority feelings and striving for success are two sides of the same coin, both are key ingredients of group work. Rather than attempting to make members feel better quickly, it is useful to explore the basis of feelings of inferiority. It is also useful for members to explore their own current strategies for managing their personal feelings of insignificance and inferiority. Members are encouraged to talk about any inferiority feelings and feelings of insignificance they may be experiencing within the group context itself. This can lead to very productive work with early recollections where members have made assumptions about their personal worth based all too often on remembered failure experiences. The group experience provides members with an opportunity to see these experiences in a new light and to put a new ending to a painful story.

ROLE OF THE FAMILY

Adlerians place great emphasis on family processes, which play a significant role in the development of the personality during childhood. The climate of relationships among family members is known as the **family atmosphere.** The **family constellation** is the social configuration of the family group, the system of relationships in which self-awareness develops. This system includes and is maintained by the individual, the parents and siblings, and any others living in the household (Powers & Griffith, 1987).

Children incorporate many of the personal characteristics of their parents, and they learn a great deal about life by observing and interacting with their parents (Christensen, 2004; Sherman & Dinkmeyer, 1987). Dreikurs (1967) takes the position, however, that sibling relationships are more influential in personality development than relationships between children and parents. In addition, the meaning that people give to their own position in the family constellation and the positions of their siblings are more important than the actual chronological ages of the siblings. The personality characteristics of each person in the family, the emotional bonds between family members, the size of the family, and the sex of the siblings are all factors in the family constellation. The child's position and role in the family influence later personality development (Powers & Griffith, 1987).

Powers and Griffith believe young family members rehearse a way of relating to others that will become a vital part of their style of life. They add that the family is not an encapsulated system apart from the community. Once material is gathered about the client's family constellation, a summary is developed so that interpretations can be made. The summary contains the client's strengths and weaknesses, and it is used in helping clients gain a fuller understanding of the current influence of their family on them. It is also important to take into account the ethnic, religious, social, and economic milieu reported by the client. These factors serve as the material for one's self-perception and one's view of the world, but they are not causal factors.

STYLE OF LIFE

Our basic concept of self in relation to the world—our personal orientation toward social living—is expressed in a discernible pattern that characterizes our existence. Bitter (1995) says that this pattern is called the lifestyle, or the "story of our life." He contends that the purpose of counseling is to help enlarge the client's story by making it fuller and richer. Carlson and Englar-Carlson (2008) state that lifestyle is the characteristic way that we move toward our life goals. They add: "Created in early childhood within a social context, life-style serves as a blueprint for coping with the tasks and challenges of life" (p. 108). The formative experiences within the family, particularly among siblings, contribute to establishing guidelines for understanding life that eventually make up the style of life (Sherman & Dinkmeyer, 1987). No two people develop exactly the same style of life. In striving for the goal of success, some people develop their intellect, others develop their physical being, and so on.

Adlerians contend that we are what we think. In striving for goals that are meaningful to us, our behavior is influenced by our core beliefs about self, others, and the world (Ansbacher, 1974). Our style of life is built on **private logic,** firmly held personal beliefs that we develop in early childhood, which may or may not be appropriate later in life (Carlson & Englar-Carlson, 2008). Our private logic provides the lens through which we view the world (Milliren & Clemmer, 2006). Sometimes our convictions get in the way of social interest and do not facilitate useful, constructive belonging (Carlson et al., 2006). This concept of private logic helps explain how all of our behavior fits together, providing consistency to our actions.

Everything we do is related to our fictional goal of perfection. Adlerians re-fer to this process as **fictional finalism**, which is the imagined central goal that gives direction to behavior and unity to the personality. It is an image of what people would be like if they were perfect and perfectly secure. Adlerian group counselors work with both the patterns for living and the logic supporting it as a way to facilitate a more socially useful life (Sonstegard & Bitter, 2004).

Although our style of life is created primarily during the first six years of life, other events that occur later can have a profound effect on our development. It is not childhood experiences in themselves that count but our *interpretation* of these events, which may lead us to develop a faulty style of life based on mistaken notions in our private logic. Although we are not determined by our past, we are significantly influenced by our perceptions and interpretations of past events. Once we become aware of the patterns and continuity of our lives, especially of certain mistaken, self-defeating or self-limiting notions that we have developed, then we are in a position to modify those faulty assumptions and make basic changes. We can reframe childhood experiences and *consciously* create a new style of life.

Role and Functions of the Group Leader

Adlerian group leaders promote an egalitarian, person-to-person relationship, which is basic to the Adlerian approach to groups. Group leaders serve as models for the members, who often learn more from what leaders *do* in the group than from what they *say*.

A number of specific personal attributes are essential for Adlerian group counselors and are prerequisites for effectively fulfilling their role and func-tion in a group. Some of these characteristics include presence, self-confi-dence, demonstrating the courage to be imperfect, willingness to take risks, acceptance, caring, willingness to model, collaborative spirit, sense of humor, listening for purposes and motives, and belief in the usefulness of the group process. For optimum results, counselors need to have a clear sense of their own identity, beliefs, and feelings. They must also be aware of the basic con-ditions essential for the growth of the group members (Sonstegard & Bitter, 2004).

Adlerian group counselors have the role of tending to the group process. Group practitioners have the task of creating a structure that promotes open interaction, involvement, nonjudgmental acceptance, confrontation, and com-mitment. Adlerian group counselors tend to be quite active, especially dur-ing the initial group session. They provide structure for the sessions by assist-ing members to define personal goals, conduct psychological assessments of individuals in the group, offer interpretations, and guide group assessment (Carlson et al., 2006; Sonstegard & Bitter, 2004).

Stages of the Adlerian Group

Like the psychoanalytic approach to groups, Adlerian group counseling in-volves the investigation and interpretation of one's early life. As the follow-ing discussion indicates, however, there are some fundamental differences between Adlerians and psychoanalysts. Sonstegard and Bitter (2004) outline the four stages of group counseling, which correspond to the four goals of counseling listed previously and which overlap to some extent:

Stage 1: Establishing and maintaining cohesive relationships with members

Stage 2: Initiating a psychological investigation emphasizing the motivation in understanding the individual (assessment)

Stage 3: Communicating to the individual an understanding of self (insight)

Stage 4: Seeing new alternatives and making new cognitive and behavioral choices (reorientation)

Let's examine each of these stages in more detail.

STAGE 1: ESTABLISHING AND MAINTAINING COHESIVE RELATIONSHIPS WITH MEMBERS

In the initial stage the emphasis is on establishing a good therapeutic relationship based on cooperation, collaboration, egalitarianism, and mutual respect. By attending to the relationship from the first session, counselors are laying a foundation for cohesiveness and connection (Sonstegard, Bitter, Pelonis-Peneros, & Nicoll, 2001). Adlerians hold that the successful outcomes of the other group stages are based on establishing and maintaining a strong therapeutic relationship at the initial stage of counseling (Watts & Eckstein, 2009). Group participants are encouraged to be active in the process because they are responsible for their own participation in the group. The group situation provides ample opportunity to work on trust issues and to strengthen the relationship between member and leader. Also, by witnessing positive changes in peers, participants can see how well the group works.

The Adlerian therapeutic relationship is one between social equals, and a democratic atmosphere prevails. This does not mean that members do anything they please, however, for firmness in a spirit of kindness is necessary in all group counseling. Nor does social equality mean that everyone in the group is the same. What democracy and social equality imply is mutual respect and involvement.

Winning the client's cooperation is essential for effective group counseling. The process of creating a therapeutic relationship supports the development of common tasks to which the group counselor needs to win the cooperation of the members. Both the leader and the members work together toward mutually agreed-upon goals. Adlerians believe that counseling, individual or group, progresses only when the therapeutic process focuses on what participants see as personally significant and on areas that they want to explore and change.

STAGE 2: ANALYSIS AND ASSESSMENT (EXPLORING THE INDIVIDUAL'S DYNAMICS)

The aim of the second stage is twofold: understanding one's lifestyle and seeing how it is affecting one's current functioning in all the tasks of life (Mosak & Maniacci, 2011). During this assessment stage, emphasis is on the individual in his or her social and cultural context. Adlerians do not try to fit clients into a preconceived model; rather, they allow salient cultural identity concepts to emerge and attend to a clients' personal meaning of culture (Carlson &

Englar-Carlson, 2008). The leader may begin by exploring how the participants are functioning at work and in social situations and how they feel about themselves and their gender-role identities.

According to Dreikurs (1969), the individual's goals and current lifestyle become much more obvious in interactions with others in the group. Adlerian group counselors use any number of assessment techniques. Process assessment techniques include examining such areas as the member's family constellation, birth order, relationship difficulties, early recollections, dreams, and artwork, all of which produce clues to each person's goals, purposes, and lifestyle. Each of these approaches to psychological investigation can reveal a group member's interpretations of self, life, and the world as well as any mistaken notions that may be connected to these interpretations. Analysis and assessment rely heavily on exploration of the client's family constellation, which includes evaluating the conditions that prevailed in the family when the person was a young child in the process of forming lifestyle convictions and basic assumptions.

Another assessment procedure is asking clients to report their **early recollections** (ERs), the "stories of events that a person *says* occurred before he or she was 10 years of age" (Mosak & Di Pietro, 2006, p. 1). ERs are *specific* incidents that clients recall, along with the feelings and thoughts that accompanied these childhood incidents. These recollections are quite useful in getting a better understanding of the client. Early memories cast light on the "story of our life," for they are more like metaphors for our current views on life rather than what actually happened long ago. Early recollections are a series of small mysteries that can be woven together and provide a tapestry that leads to an understanding of how we view and feel about ourselves, how we see the world, what our life goals are, what motivates us, what we believe in, and what we value; they also prepare us for our future (Mosak & Di Pietro, 2006).

From a series of early memories, it is possible to get a clear sense of our mistaken notions, guiding goals in life, present attitudes, social interests, and possible future behavior. Exploring early recollections involves discovering how mistaken notions based on faulty goals and values fly in the face of social interest and create problems in people's lives. Mosak and Di Pietro (2006) capture the therapeutic value of ERs thusly:

> Early recollections help us to determine what is important to a client. Early recollections, once told, tell on a person. They provide evidence of a person's priorities, goals, and methods in achieving goals. They are the solvable mysteries of who one is, where one stands, and where one is heading. (p. 6)

Adlerian counselors elicit early recollections by asking group members to think back to when they were much younger, before the age of 8, and to tell the group about some *specific event* they recall happening at one time: "One time, I _____." Early recollections are different from reports, which are typically generalizations such as "My parents argued a lot and I sat by quietly."

Early recollections represent a significant contribution for group counselors who use a variety of techniques. They are easy to obtain, and because of their projective nature, they offer practitioners a wealth of information that can be used in both the assessment and intervention phases of group counseling.

Dreikurs maintains that it is essential to obtain a thorough social history of the client to understand his or her lifestyle and to provide a foundation for treatment. This social history is made up of both objective and subjective dimensions. The subjective interview precedes the objective interview and involves carefully listening to the client's story. The counselor attends to the client's presentation and questions follow from the client's answers, which helps the client develop a complete picture of who he or she is (Carr & Bitter, 1997; Dreikurs, 1997).

An integral aspect of the subjective interview is the use of "The Question." A question Dreikurs typically asked was, "How would your life be different if you didn't have these problems, concerns, or symptoms?" Other ways of posing the question are "What would change in your life if you could have a pill that would make you completely well?" or "What would be different in your life if you woke up one morning and no longer had this problem?" The client's answer is crucial to the assessment process; it is used as a basis to determine whether an illness is due to organic or psychological factors. The answer clearly indicates the purpose and the direction of the symptoms. If the answer is that life would not be different, except that the symptom, concern, or problem would be gone, then the cause of the problem is probably physiological (Dreikurs, 1997). However, if a group member were to say, "I would be doing better in school or have more friends if it were not for my anxiety," Dreikurs believed the client's anxiety was serving a functional purpose of justifying lack of success or lack of friends (Sonstegard et al., 2001).

During the assessment stage, the group counselor's main task is to integrate and summarize data from the lifestyle investigation and to interpret how the mistaken notions and personal mythology are influencing the client. This is done in a clear and concise way so that clients can recognize their own dynamics and pinpoint their assets. The analysis of the lifestyle is an ongoing process and helps the client and the counselor develop a plan for counseling.

STAGE 3: AWARENESS AND INSIGHT

Whereas the classical analytic position is that personality cannot change unless there is insight, the Adlerian view is that insight is a special form of awareness that facilitates a meaningful understanding within the counseling relationship and acts as a foundation for change. Yet this awareness is not, in and of itself, enough to bring about significant change. It is a means to an end, not an end in itself. According to Carlson and Englar-Carlson (2008), the Adlerian approach is both insight oriented and action oriented. Although insight into our problems can be useful, it is essential that this awareness leads to constructive movement toward desired goals. It is to be noted that people can make abrupt and significant changes without much insight. Mosak and Maniacci (2011) define **insight** as "understanding translated into constructive action" (p. 89). Mosak and Maniacci contend that the psychoanalytic notion that insight must precede behavioral change frequently results in extended treatment and encourages clients to postpone taking action to change. This notion often results in increased self-absorption rather than expanded self-awareness. Mere intellectual insight can lead to the endless "Yes, but" game of "I know I should stop, but _____." Adlerians believe change begins with present-centered awareness, a recognition that one has options or choices in regard to both perception and behavior.

According to Sonstegard and Bitter (2004), groups are more effective than individual counseling in helping people gain awareness and redirect their *mistaken goals* and *mistaken notions*. The interaction within a group provides an ideal setting for learning about oneself. In groups, awareness is heightened by the feedback and support of other members, which may carry more weight than what the group leader says. Group members accept feedback from each other because they feel that a certain equality exists among them. Furthermore, the sense of social connectedness that develops in groups enables members to see parts of themselves in others. In a group context the awareness and insight stage is concerned with helping participants understand why they are functioning as they are.

Interpretation is a technique that facilitates the process of gaining insight into one's lifestyle. Interpretation deals with members' underlying motives for behaving the way they do in the here-and-now. Interpretations are never forced on the client; they are presented tentatively in the form of hypotheses: "Could it be that _____?" "I have a hunch that I'd like to share with you." "It seems to me that _____." "Perhaps _____." "I get the impression that _____."

Interpretations are open-ended sharings that can be explored in group sessions. Interpretations are best achieved collaboratively within groups with group members offering hunches about possible meanings. Sonstegard (1998b) states that the beauty of offering interpretations in this collaborative manner is that group members are free to consider what they hear without feeling that an expert has handed down a final dogma. If the interpretation fits, members tend to respond with statements that give a new understanding. If it does not fit, the group often looks for a more accurate interpretation. Members themselves can be invited to make their own interpretations. The ultimate goal of this process is that participants will come to a deeper psychological understanding of themselves. The aim is for members to acquire deeper awareness of their own role in creating a problem, the ways in which they are maintaining the problem, and what they can do to improve the situation.

STAGE 4: REORIENTATION AND REEDUCATION

The end product of the group process is reorientation and reeducation. The **reorientation stage** consists of both the group leaders and the members working together to challenge erroneous beliefs about self, life, and others. The emphasis is on considering alternative beliefs, behaviors, and attitudes. During this stage, members put insight into action, making new choices that are more consistent with their desired goals (Carlson & Englar-Carlson, 2008).

There is a change in members' attitudes toward their current life situation and the problems they need to solve. This reorientation is an educational experience. Adlerian groups are characterized by an attempt to reorient faulty living patterns and teach a better understanding of the principles that result in cooperative interaction (Sonstegard & Bitter, 2004). One of the aims is teaching participants how to become more effective in dealing with the tasks of life. Another aim is challenging and encouraging clients to take risks and make changes.

During the reorientation phase, members are encouraged to take action based on what they have learned from their group participation. The group becomes an agent of change because of the improved interpersonal relations among members. The group process allows members to see themselves as others do and to recognize faulty self-concepts or mistaken goals that they are pursuing. Change is facilitated by the emergence of hope. Members can gain hope from attempting some course of action that they did not believe was possible (Mosak & Maniacci, 2011). Members accept that there are options; others have shown they can be different and life can work out well. This sense of faith and hope contradicts the negative social influences members are imbued with in daily life (Sonstegard & Bitter, 2004).

Encouragement refers to the "building of courage," and it is derived from strengths and resources of the client. Adlerians use encouragement throughout the counseling process to assist clients to create new patterns of behavior, and to develop strengths, assets, resources, and abilities (Watts, Lewis, & Peluso, 2009). Encouragement entails showing faith in people, expecting them to assume responsibility for their lives, and valuing them for who they are (Carlson et al., 2006). The process of encouragement involves respect, trust, a belief in oneself and others, and a deep sense of caring for others. If encouragement is absent, the counseling efforts will not take root. Encouragement is a basic aspect of all stages but is essential during reorientation where it serves to bring about change (Carlson & Englar-Carlson, 2008). Through encouragement, group participants begin to experience their own inner resources and the power to choose for themselves and direct their own lives. Peer encouragement often plays the most significant role in this reorientation and reeducation. The greatest encouragement comes from feeling that the members have found a place in the group. Members are encouraged when they realize they are accepted through their differences as well as for the common ground they share (Sonstegard & Bitter, 2004).

Reorientation is the action stage of a group, new decisions are made, and goals are modified. To challenge self-limiting assumptions, members are encouraged to act *as if* they were already the person they would like to be. Adlerians often use action-oriented techniques such as **acting as if** as a way to facilitate shifting one's viewing of a situation, enabling members to reflect on how they could be different. Members are encouraged to enact new behaviors, which tend to invoke their strengths, assets, and abilities (Watson, Lewis, & Peluso, 2009; Watts, Peluso, & Lewis, 2005).

Group members may be asked to "catch themselves" in the process of repeating old patterns that have led to ineffective or self-defeating behavior. The technique of **catching oneself** involves helping individuals identify signals associated with their problematic behavior or emotions. Members can then make decisions that stop their symptoms from taking over (Watts, Lewis, & Peluso, 2009). If participants hope to change, they need to set tasks for themselves and do something specific about their problems. Commitment is needed to translate new insights into concrete action.

Application: Therapeutic Techniques and Procedures

RATIONALE FOR A GROUP APPROACH

Adlerians believe that the problems of individuals are mainly of a social nature. Based on this assumption, group work takes on special significance from both diagnostic and treatment perspectives. The group provides the social context in which members can develop a sense of belonging, social connectedness, and community. Inferiority feelings can be challenged and counteracted effectively in groups, and the mistaken concepts and values at the root of social and emotional problems can be deeply influenced by the group because it is a value-forming agent (Sonstegard & Bitter, 2004). Members come to see that many of their problems are interpersonal in nature, that their behavior has social meaning, and that their goals can best be understood in the framework of social purposes. Carlson, Watts, and Maniacci (2006) identify the essence of a group:

> The group environment provides a safe milieu in which individuals can learn how to have a voice in life. Group members learn how to understand and accept differences as well as to identify and understand universal thoughts and feelings. (p. 206)

APPLICATIONS TO BRIEF GROUP THERAPY

Carlson, Watts, and Maniacci (2006) define **brief therapy** as an approach "that is concise, deliberate, direct, effective, efficient, focused, planned, purposeful, and time limited" (p. 155). Adlerian group counseling lends itself to brief interventions and to short-term formats. From the beginning, both Adler and Dreikurs developed and used group methods as a way to reach a greater number of people in a shorter period of time. The core characteristics associated with brief group therapy include rapid establishment of a strong therapeutic alliance, clear problem focus and goal alignment, rapid assessment, emphasis on active and directive therapeutic interventions, a focus on strengths and abilities of clients, an optimistic view of change, a focus on both the present and the future, and an emphasis on tailoring treatment to the unique needs of clients in the most time-efficient manner possible (Carlson et al., 2006).

Bitter and Nicoll (2000) identify five characteristics that form the basis for an integrative framework in brief therapy: time limitation, focus on desired outcomes, counselor directiveness, symptoms as solutions, and the assignment of behavioral tasks. One advantage of the time limitation concept is that it conveys to clients the expectation that change will occur in a short period of time. Specifying the number of sessions can motivate both client and therapist to stay focused on desired outcomes and to work as efficiently as possible. Bitter and Nicoll claim that practitioners of Adlerian brief therapy strive to make a difference in the lives of their clients by staying focused on what is therapeutically possible in each engagement they have with their clients. Because there is no assurance that a future session will occur, brief therapists tend to ask themselves: "If I had only one session to be useful in this person's life, what would I want to accomplish?" (p. 38).

What are the implications of these brief therapy concepts for the practice of group counseling? Adlerian group leaders recognize that many of the changes in the members take place between the group sessions, and leaders create a structure that will help both them and the members stay focused on specific personal goals. Self-selected goals formulated once a group convenes become the focus of group work. Members can decide how they want to best use the time available to them, and they can establish a set of guidelines that will provide direction for their group.

Those groups that are time limited require at least a session or two for accomplishing the tasks of closure, completing unfinished business, suggesting referrals, and scheduling follow-up meetings. Bitter and Nicoll (2000) suggest that some time-limited groups consider meeting on a short-term basis at a later time (perhaps six months or a year after the initial sessions). This arrangement, which is structured with formal follow-up meetings, allows members to check in with one another, and the group may never officially terminate. This kind of group is an example of a form of brief, intermittent therapy.

Adlerians recognize that *focus*, combined with time limits and encouragement, helps group members gain hope that change is possible, and relatively soon (Bitter & Nicoll, 2000). Group leaders focus on empowerment, generating new behaviors from existing internal and external resources. They want group members to leave in better shape than when they came.

Applying the Adlerian Approach to Group Work in Schools

Many Adlerian concepts, techniques, and procedures can be incorporated in groups for children in school settings where the entire history of the group may be limited to as few as six sessions. Because Adlerians focus on conscious aspects, on goals and motives, and deal with the present rather than exploring the past, short-term groups can be designed for a variety of populations in the schools. Adlerians do group work with parents, teachers, and students (Dinkmeyer & Carlson, 2006).

Many Adlerian concepts and themes fit with counseling children and adolescents in various types of group counseling formats. School counselors will find that Adlerian theory and therapeutic techniques are highly applicable to their work (Fallon, 2004). One such example, an intervention based on the family constellation, is to invite children and adolescents to talk about their position in their family. Group members can be asked these questions: "How many children are in your family, and what is your birth order? Are you an only child? the first born? the last born? Which sibling do you feel the closest to? the most distant from? How do you think your relationship with your siblings influences your personality?"

The concept of encouragement has relevance for group work with children and adolescents, for many of them feel a profound sense of discouragement. The group process allows members to express the ways in which they experience their discouragement, and they also come to learn that they are not alone with their feelings. Groups using Adlerian basic concepts can be applied with at-risk high school students who are especially vulnerable to losing a sense of hope that life can be better. The four-stage model of Adlerian groups discussed earlier can be applied to adolescents who are lacking a sense of purpose. Through the reorientation process, at-risk adolescents are able to find a renewed sense of hope that they can change the direction of their lives. Bauer, Sapp, and Johnson's (2000) study provides quantitative and qualitative data that support the use of group counseling in a rural high school environment.

A concept that has great significance for group counseling in schools is social interest, which involves empathy, concern for others, cooperation, the ability to listen well, belonging, mutuality, and relatedness to others.

Social interest is related to Goleman's (1995) notion of **emotional intelligence,** which pertains to the ability to control impulses, empathize with others, form responsible interpersonal relationships, and develop intimate relationships. Emotionally competent children and adolescents can be said to possess a high degree of social interest. Such people are able to express and control a range of emotions, they are accepting of the emotions of others, they strive for connections with others, and they have an interest in increasing both their self- and other-esteem (Hwang, 2000).

The focus of many counseling programs and self-improvement courses is the development of self-esteem. Adlerian groups are ideally suited to this context and can be of great assistance to children and adolescents who struggle with feeling worthwhile, likable, and competent. Henderson and Thompson (2011) state that for children to achieve a feeling of self-esteem, they need to feel good about finding a place in life and about their progress in overcoming the unpleasant sense of inferiority typically associated with dependence and vulnerability, which often begins in early childhood. A well-adjusted child respects the rights of others, has tolerance for others, is cooperative and encouraging of others, has a positive self-concept, feels a sense of belonging, and identifies with socially acceptable goals. Because the problems of most children stem from their interactions in groups, these problems can best be addressed in a counseling group. Participating in a group can be instrumental in understanding others who may think, feel, and act differently. In a productive group, young people not only acquire increased self-esteem but also enhance the interest and esteem in others.

Children are often sent by a teacher to a counseling group because of misbehavior. Adlerians believe that children with a pattern of misbehavior are usually in pursuit of mistaken goals such as attention getting, power struggle, revenge, or a demonstration of inadequacy or withdrawal (Albert, 2003; Dreikurs, 1967). Adlerian group counseling with children deals with these mistaken goals and with changes in the motivations that account for children's behavior. A group can provide a context for understanding the goal for which the child is striving, as well as the purpose underlying a "behavior problem," and can provide a basis for corrective action (Henderson & Thompson, 2011).

Applying the Adlerian Approach With Multicultural Populations

Adlerian theory is well suited to working with culturally diverse clients because of its emphasis on understanding the individual within a social context (Fallon, 2004). Although the Adlerian approach is called Individual Psychology, the emphasis is on the person-in-the-environment, and culture can help define clients in a manner respectful of individual and cultural diversity (Carlson & Carlson, 2000). Mosak and Maniacci (2011) believe that therapists can learn a great deal about their clients through the lifestyle assessment. By asking clients to describe their early family situation, therapists are able to learn about cultural values and traditions, family dynamics, social conventions, and religious background. According to Mosak and Maniacci the lifestyle assessment process typically provides "a quick course in multiculturalism during which the client teaches the therapist about his or her culture" (p. 99).

Carlson and Englar-Carlson (2008) claim that Adlerian therapy not only considers multicultural and social justice issues but is "alive, well, and poised to address the concerns of a contemporary global society" (p. 100). Adlerians' interest in helping others, in social interest, in pursuing meaning in life, in belonging, and in the collective spirit fits well with the group process. This approach respects the role of the family as influential in personality development and stresses social connectedness and establishing meaningful relationships in a community. Adlerian therapists tend to focus on cooperation and socially oriented values as opposed to competitive and individualistic values (Carlson & Carlson, 2000). The Native American, Latino, African American, and Asian American cultures likewise stress collectivism over the individual's welfare and emphasize the role of the family and the extended family. Many of the Adlerian key concepts have been applied to working with people from diverse cultures, for example, Latinos (Frevert & Miranda, 1998), Native Americans (Kawulich & Curlette, 1998), Vietnamese refugee women (Chung & Bemak, 1998), Hindu women (Reddy & Hanna, 1998), and people of the Islamic faith (Johansen, 2005).

In Native American cultures spirituality is highly valued, and health and spirituality are generally viewed as inseparable (Kawulich & Curlette, 1998). A key component of group counseling with Native Americans is respect for the spiritual dimensions of their culture (Dufrene & Coleman, 1992). Adlerian psychology espouses a holistic view of the person that involves a unity of mind, body, and spirit (Sweeney, 1998), which gives this approach some usefulness in working with Native Americans. However, Kawulich and Curlette (1998) state that it is rare for Native Americans to seek formal counseling. Seeking counseling from a Western-oriented program over a traditional healer is not considered the Indian way. It is not uncommon for Native Americans to be cautious in choosing those with whom they become open and trust. If they are referred to group counseling, they may be very reluctant to participate in the group discussions, or they may avoid sharing information that is likely to cast their family in a bad light. Likewise, Dufrene and Coleman (1992) indicate that there is general suspicion by Native Americans of non-Native populations, and group counseling may be seen as an intrusion. They also state that Native Americans tend not to disclose personal or family matters with outsiders. Although some of the philosophy of Individual Psychology may fit for working with Native Americans in groups (Kottler, Carlson, & Keeney, 2004), the group leader needs to assess the degree of congruence with the values of the Native American culture and the group.

Counseling Latinos from an Adlerian perspective has both strengths and limitations. The Adlerian emphasis on the family is congruent with the Latino cultural value given to family connections and social networks. Latinos derive most of their personal identity from their family and social networks (Frevert & Miranda, 1998). However, the Adlerian counselor who values equality and democracy may find that few Latinos are interested in equality in relationships, especially when it comes to parent–children relationships.

Johansen (2005) examines the philosophical overlap between Adlerian psychology and the Islamic faith and concludes that there are many ways that Adlerian principles can be applied in counseling Muslims. Johansen states that Adlerian philosophical assumptions of teleology, striving for superiority, cooperation between people, and social interest are all very applicable to counseling people of the Islamic faith. The concept of life tasks are discussed in detail throughout the Koran, which provides guidelines for how Muslims should meet the various tasks and expects Muslims to strive, cooperate, and work toward the prosperity of the community. The concepts of equality and democracy are fundamental to Adlerian practice, but Islamic theology does not embrace them. Islamic theology holds that men are superior to women because of the qualities that God has granted to them. This inequality between men and women is a key dividing point, and Johansen states that Muslims who seek help for emotional or interpersonal problems will often seek guidance from their spiritual leaders first. Mental health problems are believed to be a result of loss of faith or weakness. Muslims may not trust mental health professionals because they are concerned that these professionals will not take seriously their religious values. Thus it is essential that group counselors who work with Muslims demonstrate understanding, appreciation, and respect for the Islamic faith and be willing to incorporate religious and spiritual values in the therapeutic venture.

Although the Adlerian approach has some advantages in addressing diversity in a counseling group and in helping members apply what they learn in a group to create a therapeutic community where they live and work, there are also some potential limitations from a multicultural perspective. For example, the focus on the future may not fit with all cultural worldviews. If future striving is not central in the client's cultural context, more emphasis may need to be placed on the present or the past.

In many respects Adlerian psychotherapy offers an ideal fit with Asian American clients. Carlson and Carlson (2000) note that a therapist's sensitivity and understanding of a client's culturally constructed beliefs about disclosing family matters are of paramount importance. If the therapist demonstrates an understanding of and respect for a client's cultural values, the client is likely to show more openness to the assessment and treatment process. Carlson and Carlson maintain that aspects of Adlerian psychotherapy conducive to therapeutic work with Asian Americans are the emphasis on the client's social and cultural context, the value placed on collaborative goal setting, the importance given to the family environment, and the role of social interest in healthy functioning. Adlerian therapists encourage clients to define themselves within their social environments. To their credit, Adlerians operate in flexible ways from a theory that can be tailored to work with individually and ethnically diverse clients. Employing this tailored approach, the therapeutic process is grounded within a client's culture and worldview. Instead of attempting to fit clients into preconceived models, they value fitting techniques to the particular needs of the individuals and families with whom they are working.

If the Adlerian approach is practiced appropriately and competently, it is difficult to find limitations from a multicultural perspective. The phenomenological nature of the Adlerian approach lends itself to understanding the worldview of clients, and Adlerians investigate culture in much the same way that they approach birth order and family atmosphere. Culture is a vantage point from which life is experienced and interpreted; it is also a background of values, history, convictions, beliefs, customs, and expectations that must be addressed by the individual. Adlerians do not decide for clients what they should change or what their goals should be; rather, they work cooperatively to enable clients to reach their self-defined goals.

Evaluation of the Adlerian Approach to Groups

CONTRIBUTIONS AND STRENGTHS OF THE APPROACH

My group practice has been influenced by several Adlerian concepts, including emphasis on the social forces that motivate behavior and the search for mastery, superiority, and power. The patterns that people develop out of their relationships with their parents and siblings and the notion that we create a unique style of life as a response to our perceived inferiority also interests me.

The Adlerian approach deviates in many ways from the psychoanalytic model. Most Adlerians maintain that much of Adler's work was done independently of Freud. There are, however, some important commonalities between the two approaches, including a focus on critical periods of development, an interest in early recollections, and an emphasis on interpretation. The difference lies in Adler's social constructivist view of these areas as opposed to Freud's deterministic perspective.

A major Adlerian contribution to group counseling is the use of early recollections. They hold the key to understanding how we see ourselves and the world and what we value in life. Adlerians maintain that what we selectively attend to from the past reflects on how we behave in the present and what we anticipate for our future (Watts et al., 2009).

One of the strengths of the Adlerian approach is its integrative nature. It is a holistic approach that encompasses the full spectrum of human experience, and practitioners have great freedom in working with clients in ways that are uniquely suited to their own therapeutic style. Adlerians select from a wide variety of techniques in various theoretical perspectives based on the client's presenting problems and specific needs. One such technique is the use of the family constellation as a means of learning the client's identity interpretations. Other techniques Adlerians frequently use are encouragement, lifestyle analysis, the question, acting as if, catching oneself, role playing, and other action methods (Watts et al., 2009).

Even though all Adlerians accept the same theoretical concepts, they do not have a monolithic view of the therapeutic process. The methods of assessment and treatment differ substantially among Adlerian practitioners. Some Adlerian group practitioners are very directive, and others are not. Some are willing to disclose themselves, and others rarely make personal disclosures to clients. Adlerians who were trained by Adler tend to ask for 1 early recollection, whereas those who were trained by Dreikurs might routinely ask for as many as 6 to 12 recollections as part of the lifestyle interview. Adlerian group practitioners are not bound to follow a specific procedure, nor are they limited to using certain techniques, nor do they have to be totally in agreement with all of Adler's views. In short, there can be almost as many techniques and approaches as there are Adlerian therapists. The basic criterion is that therapeutic techniques fit the theory and the client. Therapists are encouraged to grow both personally and professionally by being inventive in developing their own therapeutic style.

INTEGRATION WITH OTHER APPROACHES

One of the strengths of the Adlerian approach is that its concepts have group applications in both clinical and educational settings. As we have seen, its emphasis on social factors accounts for its success with individuals in groups, including parent education groups, teacher groups, and families—and also its widespread applicability to diverse client populations.

It is difficult to overestimate the contributions of Adler to contemporary therapeutic practice. Adler's influence has extended beyond group counseling into the community mental health movement, including the use of paraprofessionals. Abraham Maslow, Viktor Frankl, Rollo May, Aaron Beck, and Albert Ellis have all acknowledged their debt to Adler. Both Frankl and May see Adler as a forerunner of the existential movement because of his position that human beings are free to choose and are entirely responsible for what they make of themselves. This view also makes Adler a forerunner of the subjective, phenomenological approach to psychology, which focuses on the internal determinants of behavior: values, beliefs, attitudes, goals, interests, personal meanings, perceptions of reality, and strivings toward self-actualization.

Furthermore, the Adlerian view is congruent with many other current psychological schools, such as Gestalt therapy, existential therapy, social learning theory, transactional analysis, reality therapy, rational emotive behavior therapy, cognitive behavior therapy, solution-focused brief therapy, and the person-centered approach. All these approaches are based on a similar concept of the person as purposive and self-determining and as always striving for growth, value, and meaning in this world. In several important respects, Adler seems to have paved the way for the current developments in the cognitive behavior therapies. A basic premise in Adlerian practice is that if therapists can encourage clients to change their thinking, clients will then change their feelings and behavior. These connections to such a wide range of current theories and psychotherapies make the use of the Adlerian model ideal for integration purposes.

Some Adlerian scholars mention the integrative promises of Adlerian therapy and also address the challenges of continual evolution and development of this approach. Bitter (2006), in his keynote address, emphasized the point that orthodoxy does not lend itself to development and that practitioners must be concerned with the *development* of the model. According to Bitter, Adlerian core concepts provide a solid foundation for integration of new ideas and practices. When new knowledge does not easily fit within the Adlerian model, Bitter contends that it is then necessary to develop, and even challenge, the ideas of Adler and Dreikurs so that they fit the contemporary world.

LIMITATIONS OF THE APPROACH

The Adlerian approach to group work shares some of the basic limitations of the psychoanalytic approach. Leaders of more structured groups may have difficulty incorporating some of the procedures geared toward understanding members' lifestyles and showing them how earlier experiences are influencing their current functioning. Members in structured or short-term groups may not appreciate the value of exploring their childhood dynamics based on a comprehensive assessment.

Adlerian therapy, like most of the other therapeutic models in this book, was developed with a Western orientation. This focus on individuality and the premise that change and responsibility rests with the individual may be problematic for clients from collectivistic cultures (Carlson & Englar-Carlson, 2008). Furthermore, the notion of choice and individual responsibility may not be a good fit for clients from an oppressed group.

Another basic limitation pertains to the practitioner. Unless group leaders are well trained, they can make significant mistakes, especially if they engage in interpreting members' dynamics. Group leaders who have only a general understanding of Adlerian concepts could overstep the boundaries of their competence in attempting to teach members about the meaning of factors such as birth order and the family constellation. Using many of the procedures described in this chapter requires training.

Where to Go From Here

If you find that your thinking is allied with the Adlerian approach, consider seeking training in Individual Psychology or becoming a member of the North American Society of Adlerian Psychology (NASAP). To obtain information on NASAP and a list of Adlerian organizations and institutes, contact:

North American Society of Adlerian Psychology (NASAP)
614 Old West Chocolate Avenue
Hershey, PA 17033
Telephone: (717) 579-8795
Fax: (717) 533-8616
E-mail: nasap@msn.com
Website: www.alfredadler.org

The society publishes a newsletter and a quarterly journal and maintains a list of institutes, training programs, and workshops in Adlerian psychology. The *Journal of Individual Psychology* presents current scholarly and professional research. Columns on counseling, education, and parent and family education are regular features. Information about subscriptions is available by contacting the society.

If you are interested in pursuing training, postgraduate study, continuing education, or a degree, contact NASAP for a list of Adlerian organizations and institutes. A few Adlerian training institutes are listed here:

Adler School of Professional Psychology
65 East Wacker Place, Suite 2100
Chicago, IL 60601-7298
Telephone: (312) 201-5900
Fax: (312) 201-5917
E-mail: information@adler.edu
Website: www.adler.edu

Adlerian Training Institute
P. O. Box 881581
Port St. Lucie, FL 34988
Telephone: (954) 650-0637
Website: www.alfredadler.org

The Alfred Adler Institutes of San Francisco and Northwestern Washington
2565 Mayflower Lane
Bellingham, WA 98226
Telephone: (360) 647-5670
E-mail: HTStein@att.net

The Alfred Adler Institute of Quebec
4947 Grosvenor Avenue
Montreal, QC H3W 2M2
Canada
Telephone: (514) 731-5675
Fax: (514) 731-9242
E-mail: aaiq@total.net

The International Committee for Adlerian Summer Schools
and Institutes (ICASSI)
Betty Haeussler
9212 Morley Road
Lanham, MD 20706
Telephone: (301) 577-8243
Fax: (301) 595-0669
E-mail: bettyicassi@aol.com
Website: http://icassi.net

AUTHOR LECTURES

Watch *Gerald Corey's Perspectives on Theory and Practice of Group Counseling* DVD or visit the *Theory and Practice of Group Counseling* CourseMate website at www.cengagebrain.com/shop/ISBN/0840033869 to watch videos of Dr. Gerald Corey presenting lectures for each chapter. Also available are unique eAudio lectures for each chapter and quiz questions for self-study.

RECOMMENDED SUPPLEMENTARY READINGS

Adlerian Group Counseling and Therapy: Step-by-Step (Sonstegard & Bitter, 2004) represents a distillation of the most significant ideas of Alfred Adler and Rudolf Dreikurs as applied to group work. This excellent book illustrates the development of a group from the formation to the final stage, giving a clear picture of what is important to accomplish at each stage of a group. The authors describe and use an active style of group leadership that offers a structure for group members to get the most from a counseling group.

Adlerian Therapy: Theory and Practice (Carlson, Watts, & Maniacci, 2006) is a very useful resource that clearly presents a comprehensive overview of Adlerian therapy in contemporary practice. Particularly relevant is Chapter 10, which is devoted to group therapy.

Early Recollections: Interpretive Method and Application (Mosak & Di Pietro, 2006) is an extensive review of the use of early recollections as a way to understand an individual's dynamics and behavioral style. This book addresses the theory, research, and clinical applications of early recollections.

Understanding Life-Style: The Psycho-Clarity Process (Powers & Griffith, 1987) is one of the best sources of information for doing a lifestyle analysis. This book comes alive with many good clinical examples. Separate chapters deal with interview techniques, lifestyle assessment, early recollections, the family constellation, and methods of summarizing and interpreting information.

REFERENCES AND SUGGESTED READINGS

Adler, A. (1964). *Social interest: A challenge to mankind.* New York: Capricorn.

Adler, A. (1996a). The structure of neurosis. *Individual Psychology, 52*(4), 318–333. (Original work published in 1935)

Adler, A. (1996b). What is neurosis? *Individual Psychology, 52*(4), 363–371.

Albert, L. (2003). *Cooperative discipline: A Teacher's Handbook.* Circle Pines, MN: American Guidance Service.

American Psychiatric Association. (2000). *Diagnostic and statistical manual of mental disorders* (4th ed., text revision). Washington, DC. Author.

Ansbacher, H. L. (1974) Goal-oriented Individual Psychology: Alfred Adler's theory. In A. Burton (Ed.), *Operational theories of personality* (pp. 99–142). New York: Brunner/Mazel.

Bauer, S. R., Sapp, M., & Johnson, D. (2000). Group counseling strategies for rural at-risk high school students. *The High School Journal, 83*(?), 41–50.

Bitter, J. R. (1995, May 27). *The narrative study of lives: Lifestyle assessment as qualitative research.* Program presented at NASAP Annual Conference, Minneapolis, MN.

Bitter, J. R. (2006, May 26). *Am I an Adlerian?* Keynote address, Ansbacher Lecture at the 54th annual convention of the North American Society of Adlerian Psychology (NASAP), Chicago, IL.

*Bitter, J. R., Christensen, O. C., Hawes, C., & Nicoll, W. G. (1998). Adlerian brief therapy with individuals, couples, and families. *Directions in Clinical and Counseling Psychology, 8*(8), 95–112.

*Bitter, J. R., & Nicoll, W. G. (2000). Adlerian brief therapy with individuals: Process and practice. *Journal of Individual Psychology, 56*(1), 31–44.

Carlson, J., & Slavik, S. (1997). *Techniques in Adlerian psychology.* Philadelphia: Taylor & Francis.

*Carlson, J., Watts, R. E., & Maniacci, M. (2006). *Adlerian therapy: Theory and practice.* Washington, DC: American Psychological Association.

Carlson, J. D., & Englar-Carlson, M. (2008). Adlerian therapy. In J. Frew & M. Spiegler (Eds.), *Contemporary psychotherapies for a diverse world* (pp. 93–140). New York: Lahaska Press

*Carlson, J. M., & Carlson, J. D. (2000). The application of Adlerian psychotherapy with Asian-American clients. *Journal of Individual Psychology, 56*(2), 214–225.

Carr, C. N., & Bitter, J. R (1997). Dreikurs' holistic medicine: An introduction. *Individual Psychology: The Journal of Adlerian Theory, Research & Practice, 53*(2), 122–126.

*Christensen, O. C. (Ed.). (2004). *Adlerian family counseling* (3rd ed.). Minneapolis, MN: Educational Media Corporation.

Chung, R. C-Y., & Bemak, F. (1998). Lifestyle of Vietnamese refugee women. *Journal of Individual Psychology, 54*(3), 373–384.

Corey, G. (1999). Adlerian contributions to the practice of group counseling: A personal perspective. *Journal of Individual Psychology, 55*(1), 4–14.

Dinkmeyer, D., & Carlson, J. (2006). *Consultation: Creating school-based interventions* (3rd ed.). New York: Routledge.

---

* Books and articles marked with an asterisk (*) are suggested for further study.

Dreikurs, R. (1960). *Group psychotherapy and group approaches: The collected papers of Rudolf Dreikurs.* Chicago: Alfred Adler Institute.

Dreikurs, R. (1967). *Psychodynamics, psychotherapy, and counseling: Collected papers.* Chicago: Alfred Adler Institute.

Dreikurs, R. (1969). Group psychotherapy from the point of view of Adlerian psychology. In H. M. Ruitenbeek (Ed.), *Group therapy today: Styles, methods, and techniques* (pp. 37–48). New York: Atherton.

*Dreikurs, R. (1997). Holistic medicine. *Individual Psychology, 53*(2), 127–205.

Dufrene, P. M., & Coleman, V. D. (1992). Counseling Native Americans: Guidelines for group process. *Journal for Specialists in Group Work, 17*(4), 229–234.

Fallon, M. K. (2004). Adlerian therapeutic techniques for professional school counselors. In B. T. Erford (Ed.), *Professional school counseling: A handbook of theories, programs & practices* (pp. 113–122). Austin, TX: CAPS Press.

Frevert, V. S., & Miranda, A. O. (1998). A conceptual formulation of the Latin culture and the treatment of Latinos from an Adlerian psychology perspective. *Journal of Individual Psychology, 54*(3), 291–309.

Goleman, D. (1995). *Emotional intelligence.* New York: Bantam.

Henderson, D., & Thompson, C. L. (2011). *Counseling children* (8th ed.). Belmont, CA: Brooks/Cole, Cengage Learning.

*Hwang, P. O. (2000). *Other esteem: Meaningful life in a multicultural society.* Philadelphia, PA: Accelerated Development (Taylor & Francis).

Johansen, T. M. (2005). Applying Individual Psychology to work with clients of the Islamic faith. *Journal of Individual Psychology, 61*(2), 174–184.

Kawulich, B. B., & Curlette, W. L. (1998). Life tasks and the Native American perspective. *Journal of Individual Psychology, 54*(3), 359–367.

Kottler, J. A., Carlson, J., & Keeney, B. (2004). *American shaman: An odyssey of global healing traditions.* New York: Brunner-Routledge.

Milliren, A., & Clemmer, F. (2006). Introduction to Adlerian psychology: Basic principles and methodology. In S. Slavik, & J. Carlson (Eds.), *Readings in the theory and practice of Individual Psychology* (pp. 17–43). New York: Routledge (Taylor & Francis).

Mosak, H. H., & Di Pietro, R. (2006). *Early recollections: Interpretative method and application.* New York: Routledge.

*Mosak, H. H., & Maniacci, M. P. (2011). Adlerian psychotherapy. In R. J. Corsini & D. Wedding (Eds.), *Current psychotherapies* (9th ed., pp. 67–112). Belmont, CA: Brooks/Cole, Cengage Learning.

*Powers, R. L., & Griffith, J. (1987). *Understanding life-style: The psycho-clarity process.* Chicago: Americas Institute of Adlerian Studies.

Reddy, I., & Hanna, F. J. (1998). The lifestyle of the Hindu woman: Conceptualizing female clients of Indian origin. *Journal of Individual Psychology, 54*(3), 385–398.

Sherman, R., & Dinkmeyer, D. (1987). *Systems of family therapy: An Adlerian integration.* New York: Brunner/Mazel.

*Slavik, S., & Carlson, J. (Eds.). (2006). *Readings in the theory and practice of Individual Psychology.* New York: Routledge (Taylor & Francis).

*Sonstegard, M. A. (1998a). A rationale for group counseling. *Journal of Individual Psychology, 54*(2), 164–175.

*Sonstegard, M. A. (1998b). The theory and practice of group counseling and group psychotherapy. *Journal of Individual Psychology, 54*(2), 217–250.

*Sonstegard, M. A., & Bitter, J. R. (with Pelonis, P.). (2004). *Adlerian group counseling and therapy: Step-by-step.* New York: Brunner-Routledge (Taylor & Francis).

*Sonstegard, M. A., Bitter, J. R., Pelonis-Peneros, P. P., & Nicoll, W. G. (2001). Adlerian group psychotherapy: A brief therapy approach. *Directions in*

Clinical and Counseling Psychology, 11(2), 11–12.

*Sweeney, T. J. (1998). *Adlerian counseling: A practitioner's approach* (4th ed.). Philadelphia: Accelerated Development (Taylor & Francis).

Terner, J., & Pew, W. L. (1978). *The courage to be imperfect: The life and work of Rudolf Dreikurs.* New York: Hawthorn Books.

Watts, R. E., & Eckstein, D. (2009). Individual Psychology. In American Counseling Association (Ed.), *The ACA encyclopedia of counseling* (pp. 281–283). Alexandria, VA: American Counseling Association.

Watts, R. E., Lewis, T. F., & Peluso, P. R. (2009). Individual Psychology counseling techniques. In American Counseling Association (Ed.), *The ACA encyclopedia of counseling* (pp. 283–285). Alexandria, VA: American Counseling Association.

Watts, R. E., Peluso, P. R., & Lewis, T. F. (2005). Expanding the acting as if technique: An Adlerian/constructive integration. *Journal of Individual Psychology,* 61(4), 380–387.

CHAPTER EIGHT

Psychodrama in Groups

Introduction

J. L. Moreno realized that some aspects of the mind cannot be adequately accessed through words. Some feelings are best expressed through action, interpersonal interaction, or imagery, and improvisational theater can provide a channel for understanding and healing in this context. **Psychodrama** is primarily an action approach to group therapy in which clients explore their problems through role playing, enacting situations using various dramatic devices to gain insight, discover their own creativity, and develop behavioral skills. The scenes are played as if they were occurring in the here-and-now, even though they might have their origins in a memory or an anticipated event. This approach was created in the mid-1930s by J. L. Moreno (1889–1974) and later developed by his wife, Zerka Toeman Moreno, and by many other followers. Psychodrama weaves together imagination, intuition, physical action, and various dramatic devices to explore a wide range of psychological problems.

Classical psychodrama is a complex and intense method that involves warm-up, protagonist-centered work, and sharing. These phases are discussed later in this chapter. This method should be conducted only by highly training practitioners, but most types of psychotherapy could be enhanced by integrating selected psychodramatic techniques and their underlying principles (Blatner, 2005b). Group workers with diverse theoretical orientations use various forms of role playing, for example, and this and other psychodramatic methods can foster problem solving, communication, and self-awareness (Blatner, 2001). This process does not require excessive emotionality or theatrics. Instead, the key idea of drama is using enactment as a rehearsal for living, an opportunity to rework the responses as if we were the codirector as well as the principal player of our life.

Psychodrama's roots lie in Moreno's experiments around 1921 with an improvisational drama troupe he called the "Theater of Spontaneity." The actors didn't memorize any scripts, but enacted scenes in an impromptu fashion based on events drawn from the daily newspaper or topics suggested by the audience. Occasionally, people in the audience were invited to react to these scenes and come up and demonstrate how they might have played one or another of the roles differently. Moreno found that both the actors and the audience members experienced a psychological release of pent-up feelings (catharsis) as a result. The Theater of Spontaneity led him to develop the group methods and specialized therapeutic techniques that in the mid-1930s evolved into psychodrama.

Psychodrama allows group members to explore various roles and aspects of themselves, and to experience their perception of others with whom they have a relationship. The techniques of psychodrama encourage people to express themselves more fully, explore both intrapsychic conflicts and interpersonal problems, get constructive feedback on how they come across to others, reduce feelings of isolation, and experiment with novel ways of approaching significant others in their lives. This approach certainly helps to enliven group interactions. Z. T. Moreno (1983) writes that "psychodrama represents a major turning point away from the treatment of the individual in isolation and toward the treatment of the individual in groups, from treatment by verbal methods toward treatment by action methods" (p. 158). Rather than have individuals *talk about* their hopes, dreams, and struggles, J. L. Moreno asked people he worked with to *show* their feelings and situations in the unfolding group setting (Blatner, 1996).

Key Concepts

J. L. Moreno's ideas should be recognized as involving not merely techniques, however useful, but also very important insights about the nature of human relationships. There is considerable value in incorporating these perspectives in an integrative approach to group work.

CREATIVITY

Moreno was unique in his belief that a major function of the therapeutic process is to promote the client's creativity in exploring life, expanding oneself, and in coping with life. Creativity often emerges best not from careful, reasoned planning but as surges of inspired action, and creativity is often generated through active experimentation (Blatner, 2001). Psychodrama aims at fostering creativity in the individual, the group, and ultimately in the culture as a whole. Psychodrama entails the idea that each person is responsible for becoming more creative and for promoting creativity in others (Blatner, 2000). Psychodrama can be thought of as a kind of laboratory for psychosocial experimentation and enhanced creativity (Blatner, 2005b).

SPONTANEITY

According to Blatner (2000), one of Moreno's significant insights is that the best way to promote creativity is through spontaneous exploratory activities; *doing* activates the imagination and intuition. Moreno made *spontaneity* one of his most important concepts. It stands out because so many of life's activities tend to inhibit spontaneity. Moreno sought to reverse this trend by creating contexts and activities that would maximize the courage to improvise.

Moreno observed that children, in contrast to adults, were relatively more able to enter into role-playing and fantasy situations and to express their feelings freely. As people grow older, they tend to become less and less spontaneous. To remedy this tendency, Moreno developed methods for training spontaneity aimed at freeing people from limiting "scripts" and rigid and stereotyped responses. He considered spontaneity training to be a prime way of enabling people to meet new situations from a fresh perspective.

From Moreno's perspective, **spontaneity** is an adequate response to a new situation or a novel response to an old situation. Spontaneity should not be thought of as impulsive behavior or as a license to act out; spontaneity involves reflection and gives people the ability to act according to the situations they face. Instead of encountering a new situation with anxiety, spontaneity fosters a sense of being capable of approaching a challenging situation (Z. T. Moreno, Blomkvist, & Ruetzel, 2000). Blatner (2000) believes that in spontaneity there are elements of courage, liveliness, engagement, openness, the willingness to take risks, and a stretching of the mind. "Spontaneity involves an inclination towards questioning, challenging, re-thinking, re-evaluating, taking a fresh look—it is a shift in attitude" (pp. 83–84).

It is important to create a climate that will facilitate the unfolding of spontaneity—part of an activity that Moreno called "warming up." People cannot will themselves to be spontaneous and cannot effectively be pushed into being spontaneous. We rely on physical, mental, emotional, and relational "starters" to help us warm up our innate spontaneity. In psychodrama, the group leader helps facilitate group members' spontaneity by modeling spontaneous behavior and a sense of playfulness. Sometimes the leader also creates structured activities to help reduce anxiety and promote a climate of safety, trust, risk-taking, and playfulness. To be able to create a climate that fosters the development of spontaneity, group practitioners must be aware of their own feelings and draw upon them in intuitive ways. In psychodrama, play is recognized as a valid need, a part of health, so that people can enjoy a wider range of experiences than they might in everyday life. Play involves imagination, creativity, spontaneity, and self-expression (Blatner, 2007).

WORKING IN THE PRESENT MOMENT

Working in the present moment is a concept closely related to creativity and spontaneity. Pioneered by Moreno years before it became fashionable, action in the *here-and-now* is an important element of psychodrama. Clients *talk about* situations in the past or the future to distance and defend themselves against experiencing their feelings. By re-creating those difficult situations as if they were happening in the present moment, encountering each other in the here-and-now, the actual encounter is brought into consciousness. When the protagonist (group member) slips into narrating, or begins to talk about a problem, the director steers the protagonist into action by saying, "Don't tell me *about* it, show me what happened, as if it's happening now." Members may be asked to "Show us what happened when you were a young child and you found out your parents were divorcing" (Blatner, 2001).

A basic tenet of psychodrama is that reliving and reexperiencing a scene from the past gives the participants both the opportunity to examine how that event affected them at the time it occurred and a chance to deal differently with the event *now.* By replaying a past event "as if" it were happening in the present, the individual is able to assign new meaning to it. Through this process, the client works through unfinished business and reframes that earlier situation.

Psychodrama can deal with a present conflict: "Show us the conflict you are now experiencing between staying in college versus quitting." And psychodrama enables members to bring the future into the now: "Show us how you'd like to be able to talk with your partner one year from now." The past, present, and future are all significant tenses, yet the action is played out in the present moment. When members engage in *showing others* what they are thinking or feeling, they move toward concrete experiencing and cut through defenses. They also move away from abstract and intellectual discussions about a topic when they plunge into personal enactment of a concern.

ENCOUNTER

The underlying goals of immediacy and involvement were further supported when Moreno taught the principle of encounter, which he started writing about in 1914, long before the encounter group movement began in the 1960s. An **encounter** occurs when individuals connect with one another in a meaningful and authentic way. This encounter occurs in the context of the here-and-now, regardless of whether the enactment relates to a past event or to an anticipated future event. It involves a great degree of both directness of communication and self-disclosure. There is great power in encountering. Even when done only symbolically in the form of role playing, it is still more effective than merely reporting an incident.

A psychodrama encounter is not a full encounter because the protagonist is encountering the significant other as portrayed by an auxiliary. In that sense it is an incomplete encounter, whereas a complete encounter involves two protagonists meeting "eye to eye, face to face," as Moreno explained in his works. However, encountering someone playing the role of a significant other in psychodrama is still powerful and healing. For example, if I can change the "father" that resides inside me through psychodramatic work, then my perception of my actual father may change, my behavior toward him may change, and, ultimately, my actual father may change due to the way that I am relating to him differently.

In addition to directness of self-expression, Moreno envisioned an ideal encounter as involving both parties opening their minds and hearts to the viewpoint of each other through role reversal, imagining what it might be like to be in the other's predicament. Encountering is at the very core of psychodrama; through this process people not only meet but also understand one another on a deep and significant level.

Most clients with some psychological-mindedness need to be helped to reverse roles with those in their lives whose behavior may have caused them pain. Group members should have a number of opportunities to feel validated in their own experience before this is attempted. There comes a time, however, when true maturity requires an exercise of empathy for others.

TELE

Tele refers to degrees of feeling of attraction and is Moreno's term for a dynamic similar to rapport. It is a two-way flow of feelings between people (J. L. Moreno, 1964). He calls it a "feeling of individuals into one another, the cement which holds groups together" (p. xi). For many people, this dynamic operates at a preconscious or even unconscious level. Tele and helping people to become more explicitly aware of their interpersonal preferences is a major component of developing self-awareness.

Tele is a therapeutic factor related to change that promotes healing through a reciprocal empathic feeling. The level of positive tele in a group correlates with its cohesiveness. People naturally, or for not-so-obvious reasons, feel attracted to certain people and are put off by others. Addressing the shifting tone of interest (attraction or lack of attraction) of the people in a group is essential to understanding the dynamics of a group. Moreno believed the therapeutic relationship required the development of positive tele. When this rapport is positive and reciprocal, the people involved tend to be more accurately empathic with each other. When tele is negative, misunderstandings multiply and are inclined to be compounded (Blatner, 2000, 2006).

SURPLUS REALITY

Psychotherapy helps people to become more conscious of their deeper attitudes and motives, and sometimes it is useful to bring unspoken and unfulfilled fantasies into explicit awareness. Instead of talking only about what actually happened or what might in fact yet occur, it is often more important to help the client become clear about what was hoped for or feared, even if it is not realistic. Psychodrama includes the portrayal of such scenes, and Moreno gave the name **surplus reality** to these enactments that reflect the psychological world of the client apart from any concern for the limits of ordinary reality (Z. T. Moreno et al., 2000).

These concrete expressions of the imagination enable psychotherapeutic exploration of dimensions of events that do not occur in actuality. Therapists often ask clients questions such as these: "What if you could have spoken up?" "What if she hadn't died?" "What if you could have a new mother or father?" In psychodrama this "what if" perspective is made more explicit by being physically enacted in the present, going beyond the limits of being realistic to acknowledge the way emotions work in the realm of "what could have been *if only* _____." For example, a son can talk to a father who died before they had a chance to say good-bye to each other. A woman can encounter her wiser self from 20 years in the future. A man can go back and experience the perfect seventh birthday to counter memories of what had been a humiliating or disappointing actual event. Using surplus reality, individuals can encounter lost others to talk out previously unexpressed emotions and ask and answer questions. Surplus reality can also be used to replay an unfortunate or even traumatic event so that the individual experiences a more empowered or satisfactory ending.

Moreno called psychodrama a "theater of truth" because the most poignant and central truths in the minds and hearts of people often go beyond ordinary reality and involve the extra dimension of what could have been or what might have happened if things were different. Helping clients to become conscious of their own repressed emotions and implicit beliefs and attitudes requires a context that evokes spontaneous responses and bypasses tendencies to defend oneself through verbal distancing, narration, describing circumstances, and explaining. All these are forgotten when the protagonist engages in a direct encounter with another.

Using surplus reality, clients are helped to discover viewpoints they had not otherwise entertained. Alternative basic assumptions can then be considered from a different perspective. Psychodrama offers a way for clients to express and reflect on their hopes, fears, expectations, unexpressed resentments, projections, internalizations, and judgmental attitudes. Clients are assisted in ventilating these feelings and are able to symbolically live through them. They are generally encouraged to maximize all expression, action, and verbal communication rather than to reduce it (Z. T. Moreno, 1965). The stage offers a way to symbolically live through so much that ordinarily remains suppressed in life, to maximize rather than dampen expression and action in the service of becoming more self-aware.

CATHARSIS AND INSIGHT

Although psychodrama has been considered a therapy that works because of the catharsis it engenders, this may be somewhat misleading. It isn't necessary for therapists to press for catharsis itself. Indeed, in many enactments this may be contraindicated. However, when an individual needs to rediscover repressed emotions, techniques that facilitate this reconnection of conscious and unconscious functions tend to evoke catharsis just as exercising tends to evoke sweat.

People tend to compartmentalize their emotions and attitudes, a main function of most ego-defense mechanisms. When these complexes reconnect, emotions tend to be released—tears, laughter, anger, vulnerability, guilt, hope—and this is the catharsis that often accompanies the experiential aspect of therapy. Catharsis is a natural part of the psychodramatic process, but it is not in itself a goal. Simply rediscovering buried emotions will not bring about healing; these feelings must be worked through for integration to occur. For those who have lost awareness of the roots of their feelings, emotional release may lead to insight, or to an increased awareness of a problem situation.

Insight is the cognitive shift that connects awareness of various emotional experiences with some meaningful narrative or some growing understanding. Insight adds a degree of understanding to the catharsis. There are times in psychodrama when it is inappropriate to have protagonists verbalize their insight explicitly, especially when group members are doing intense emotional work. The experience itself often provides sufficient "action insight." J. L. Moreno did not find it necessary for his patients to have verbal insight in order to get well. Instead he talked about *action learning* and *action insight* and saw healing as an internal state not always attainable by verbal means. For Moreno, learning was more affective than cognitive (Z. T. Moreno, personal communication, January 28, 2010).

It should be noted that protagonists can be helped to find the words that express their feelings through the use of various psychodramatic techniques and so achieve insight in this fashion. Insight might also occur following the enactment when others in the group are sharing with the protagonist their own feelings and reactions to what happened on the stage. Often the other players (auxiliaries) and audience members also experience varying degrees of insight regarding their own life situations. There are many routes to achieving insight, and it is much more than an intellectual understanding of a problem or a situation.

Once people allow themselves the freedom to release intense emotions that have been controlling them and come to a cognitive and emotional (or experiential) understanding that they no longer have to continue living as they did before, they can begin the critical process of gaining control over inappropriate modes of either suppressing or expressing those feelings.

REALITY TESTING

The psychodramatic group offers an opportunity to find out how others feel and what the results of certain behaviors might be. The group is like a laboratory that offers a relatively safe setting for **reality testing,** or trying out behaviors that may not generally be socially acceptable in "real life" situations.

For example, a young woman is in great emotional pain over what she sees as her father's indifference to her and the ways in which he has passed up opportunities to demonstrate whatever love he has for her. After concluding a psychodramatic enactment in which the young woman "tells" her father of her feelings of missing this love, she may still be angry with him and expect him to make the first move to change matters. During the discussion phase, the leader or the members can point out that she is making the assumption that he must be the person to initiate a closer relationship. In reality, the father may well be fearful of showing her affection and attention, thinking that she is not interested in such a relationship with him. The group can be instrumental in helping her see that she may have to make the first move if she wants to change her relationship with him. Then psychodrama can again be used as a reenactment for her to practice this new approach, which will facilitate translating insight into action. This enactment maximizes the process of interpersonal learning.

ROLE THEORY

In the 1930s Moreno was one of the originators of social role theory, a way of thinking and talking about psychological phenomena that has many practical implications. Using psychodrama, we can examine the roles we play, renegotiate them, and choose different ways to play these roles. In psychodrama the members are given the freedom to try out a diversity of roles, thereby getting a sharper focus on parts of themselves that they would like to present to others. Playing roles also enables participants to get in contact with parts of themselves that they were not aware of. They can recognize and explore stereotyped ways of responding to people and break out of behaving within a rigid pattern, creating new dimensions of themselves.

Moreno's **role theory** taught that we are all improvisational actors on the stage of life, creating our parts without scripts. We thus become not only actors but also playwrights. By thinking of our behavior patterns as roles in a drama, we are encouraged to bring a measure of reflection to the task, much as an actor stands back during rehearsal and considers how best to play the role assigned. We can go further and question which roles we want to take on or which roles are to be played out. More than merely performing social roles, we are able to actively modify certain roles. Indeed, we have the capacity to break out of roles when we discover that they no longer serve us.

Role playing, which is largely an extension of psychodrama, involves the sense of "playing with" the role, bringing a measure of spontaneity and creativity to it, refining it, and at times even redefining or radically renegotiating the role. Psychodrama is one way to help people become more conscious and creative in how they play the various roles in their lives.

Role and Functions of the Psychodrama Group Leader

The psychodrama **director** (or main group therapist who facilitates the psychodrama) has a number of roles. According to J. L. Moreno (1964), the director has the role of producer, catalyst/facilitator, and observer/analyzer. Directors help in the selection of the protagonist and then decide which of the special psychodramatic techniques is best suited for the exploration of the person's problem. They organize the psychodrama, play a key role in warming up the group, and pay careful attention to what emerges in the drama. Directors function as catalysts and facilitators in that they assist the protagonist in developing a scene or series of scenes and facilitate the free expression of feelings. Only occasionally will they make therapeutic interpretations to help the protagonist gain a new understanding of a problem.

One of the main skills of the psychodramatist involves appreciating the protagonist's reluctance as insufficient warm-up rather than "resistance." Pushing the protagonist at this point would further reduce spontaneity. Instead, the director works to bring into explicit expression those concerns that might induce hesitation, such as a worry that the group might think a given feeling is "weird." The director can then weave these ideas into a supportive exploration with the group, enabling the protagonist to feel an increase in the *tele* with the other group members and thus be ready to courageously disclose yet another facet of his or her inner truth. Blatner (1996) cites Moreno's advice on this issue: "We don't tear down the protagonist's walls; rather, we simply try some of the handles on the many doors, and see which one opens" (p. 78).

The Basic Elements of Psychodrama

Classical psychodrama involves a *director*, a main player or *protagonist*, supporting players or *auxiliary egos*, other group members in the role of *audience*, a stage, and a number of psychodramatic techniques that are used to further the action.

THE PROTAGONIST

The **protagonist** is the person who is the focus of the psychodramatic enactment—the one who presents a problem to be explored. As members interact with each other, a group member may raise an issue. If that person, the therapist, and the group agree that a psychodramatic exploration is warranted, the person for whom the issue is most relevant generally becomes the protagonist of the ensuing psychodrama. The protagonist's role is assumed voluntarily although it may be suggested by the therapist or by the group. In general, it is important that members feel free to decline to be placed in the position of increased demand for disclosure.

The protagonist selects the event to be explored. He or she, in negotiation with the director, chooses a scene from the past, the future, or an alternative present, and that scene is played as if it is happening in the here-and-now. In the case of a past event, it is not necessary to remember exact words but rather to portray the essential elements as experienced by the protagonist. The protagonist is the source of the imagery but requires the assistance of the director to explore a problem and to create a psychodrama. As soon as possible, the director encourages the protagonist to move spontaneously into action rather than merely talking about the event.

As the protagonist acts out a situation, it is important that he or she have the freedom to explore any aspect of the scene (and related relationships) that seems significant. Although the director may encourage the protagonist to re-enact a situation or deal with an anticipated event, the protagonist decides whether he or she is willing to follow the director's suggestions. In this sense, the director *follows* rather than *leads* the protagonist. The protagonist's preferences, readiness for engaging in a given theme, and decisions should be given priority over the director's or the group's desires. If this is done, there is a greater chance that the protagonist will feel supported in going as far as he or she chooses. It is essential to respect the protagonist's process and decisions. Directors function best when they accurately sense and work with the protagonist's flow. Also, the director may employ a particular technique, but protagonists always have the right to say that they don't want to move in that direction. Effective psychodrama never involves coercion; the auxiliaries and the director are there to serve the protagonist.

THE AUXILIARY EGOS

Auxiliary egos (often simply called "auxiliary," "auxiliaries," or "supporting players") are those in the group other than the protagonist and the director who take part in the psychodrama, usually by portraying the roles of significant others in the life of the protagonist. These persons may be living or dead, real or imagined. Auxiliaries may also play the roles of inanimate objects, pets, or any emotionally charged object or being that is relevant to the protagonist's psychodrama.

Z. T. Moreno (1987) notes four functions of the auxiliary: (1) to play out the perceptions held by the protagonist, at least in the beginning; (2) to investigate the interaction between the protagonist and their own roles; (3) to interpret this interaction and relationship; and (4) to act as therapeutic guides in helping the protagonist develop an improved relationship. Effective auxiliary egos can give a psychodrama greater power and intensity. A few ways in which they do this are by helping the protagonist warm up, by intensifying the action, and by encouraging the protagonist to become more deeply involved in the here-and-now of the drama.

The protagonist generally selects the group members who will serve as supporting players. These choices are made for both conscious and unconscious reasons. Some choices are made on the basis of characteristics of group members that are perceived as similar to those of the other figures in the scene. When a choice is made on this basis, the interaction between the protagonist and auxiliary egos is likely to be more spontaneous, real, and effective. Directors may make an exception to this rule if they want a group member to assume an auxiliary role with particular therapeutic potential. Although the protagonist has ideas about a problem, both the protagonist and the director have the function of coaching auxiliaries in how to play their roles. This task sometimes entails giving an auxiliary some background on the person he or she is to play and a feeling for the style of that person. Protagonists may teach or coach an auxiliary on how best to portray the behavioral style of a significant other.

The director has the task of assessing whether the auxiliary's role playing is working more for the protagonist's benefit or meeting the auxiliary's needs. In the latter case, the auxiliary may be redirected by the director. The director needs to discuss this development during the sharing phase of the group, because it usually has significant therapeutic implications for the auxiliary. It is important to remember that psychodrama is a *group process* and that auxiliary work has great therapeutic potential. Playing someone else's role often serves as a vehicle for getting in touch with parts of the self not uncovered while playing one's own role. At times, it is a good idea to permit auxiliaries some freedom of expression in their role portrayals. This can introduce novel elements that are surprisingly evocative. At other times, the director may help the auxiliary to restrain his or her performance so it fits the protagonist's perception. Z. T. Moreno (1987) warns about possible dangers when the protagonist's psychodrama and the auxiliary's drama combine. She cautions both the auxiliary and the director to avoid doing their own psychodrama, thus taking the focus away from the protagonist's drama.

THE AUDIENCE

The **audience** includes others in the group before whom the problem is explored. Even group members who are not engaged in the action play a role. As members witness the self-disclosure of others, they function psychologically as a kind of externalized "mirror." This gives the protagonist the experience of knowing that others share in looking at the world from his or her point of view. The audience also functions in the ongoing improvisational process as the source of people who will volunteer or be chosen to enter the scene as auxiliaries, or as people who will share with the protagonist in an enactment on a future occasion.

Psychodrama benefits the whole group, not just the protagonist. Almost always some group members find a particularly moving resonance in the enactment, identifying with either the protagonist or one of the other roles. Usually, group members feel at least some empathy, and they can experience a release of their own feelings through their identification with others; they thus gain insight into some of their own interpersonal conflicts. These other group members—the audience—provide valuable support and feedback to the protagonist.

THE STAGE

The **stage** is the area where the enactment takes place. It represents an extension of the life space of the protagonist, and as such it should be large enough to allow for movement of the protagonist, the auxiliary egos, and the director. The stage is generally empty, but it is helpful to have available as props a few chairs, perhaps a table, a variety of pieces of colored fabrics for costuming and other uses, and other items. Props can be used to intensify the dramatic function. When a protagonist emerges from the group, he or she moves to this area to create the psychodrama. In most cases, a special psychodrama stage is not available, but a section of the room can be designated for "as if" action, a dedicated area in which those involved in the action are not expected to be particularly reflective or to function as interactive group members at the same time.

Phases of the Psychodrama Process

Psychodrama consists of three phases: (1) warm-up, (2) action, and (3) sharing and discussion. These phases are not absolute but are general intellectual constructs that help the practitioner build the spontaneity, apply it, and integrate the enactment with the group process.

Certain principles underlie the use of psychodrama action methods. First, it is not appropriate to move into action without warming people up lest they feel overwhelmed by the ambiguity of the situation. Second, after an action segment, the protagonist and other group members need time to share what they have experienced to optimally integrate their feelings and insights. The following discussion of phases of the psychodrama process applies not only to classical psychodrama but also to the use of these approaches within most forms of group therapy.

THE WARM-UP PHASE

Warming up consists of the initial activities required for a gradual increase in involvement and spontaneity. This is aimed at encouraging maximum involvement. It includes the director's warm-up, establishing trust and group cohesion, identifying a group theme, finding a protagonist, and moving the protagonist onto the stage (Blatner, 1996, 2001). It is essential that participants be helped to get ready for the methods used during the action phase. Such readiness involves being motivated enough to formulate one's goals and feeling secure enough to trust the others in the group. Physical techniques for warming up a group are commonly introduced and may include using music, dancing, and movement or other nonverbal exercises.

Early in a psychodrama certain group members may emerge who appear ready to benefit from an experiential exploration of a problem. It may be an individual's relationship to a personal situation outside of the group or some group members needing to clarify their own interactions within the group. In these instances, the flow of group process serves as a warm-up enactment. In settings in which a psychodrama is to be the primary mode for exploration, the following warm-up methods have been used:

- The director gives a brief talk about the nature and purpose of psychodrama, and participants are invited to ask questions.
- Each member is briefly interviewed by the director. A lead question may be, "Is there a present or past relationship that you'd like to understand better?" As each person in the group responds to this question, a basis for group cohesion is being established.
- Members can form several sets of dyads and spend a few minutes sharing a conflict that they are experiencing and that they'd like to explore in the session.

- The go-around technique, in which each member is asked to make some brief comments about what he or she is experiencing in the moment, can facilitate group interaction. Making the rounds can also focus members on personal work they would like to do during the session.
- In a long-term group with functional people, a nondirective warm-up is often used to get members ready for a session. Members may be asked to briefly state what they were aware of as they were coming to the session or to make any comments about their readiness to work.

Leveton (2001) states that the message of a successful warm-up to the members of the group is to actively participate and that all contributions will be rewarded. The warm-up is aimed at creating an atmosphere of spontaneity that eases resistive tendencies within members. Scores of structured experiences can work as warm-ups, and Leveton describes a wide variety of both verbal and nonverbal warm-up techniques. In addition to structured techniques aimed at warming up a group for action, unstructured warm-ups such as the process by which a protagonist emerges from the spontaneous interaction at the beginning of a group session, may be used. The leader needs to pay close attention to verbal and nonverbal cues as the protagonist describes the issue to be explored.

During the warm-up phase, members need to be reassured that the working environment is a safe one, that they are the ones to decide *what* they will reveal and *when* they will reveal it, and that they can stop whenever they want to. The techniques are less important than the spirit and purpose of the warm-up; anything that facilitates the cohesion of the group, establishes trust, and enhances individual and group spontaneity is a useful tool for the initial phase of a psychodrama.

According to Blatner (1996), the most important task during the warm-up phase consists of creating an atmosphere that fosters spontaneity. In his view, these four conditions are necessary for spontaneous behavior to occur:

- A sense of trust and safety
- A receptivity to intuitions, images, and feelings
- An element of playfulness
- A willingness to take risks and engage in novel behavior

Blatner (1996) emphasizes the importance of the director's own warm-up as a key factor in creating a climate that encourages spontaneous behavior. It is during the warm-up period that directors are developing their own spontaneity. By communicating a sense of authenticity and warmth, they foster confidence and trust. Similarly, modeling risk-taking, self-disclosure, humor, spontaneity, creativity, empathy, and the acceptability of expressing emotions and acting them out contributes to the group's cohesion. A theme may begin to emerge, and a protagonist may be selected and move onto the stage for action.

THE ACTION PHASE

The **action phase** includes the enactment and working through of a past or present situation or of an anticipated event. The goal of this phase is to assist members in bringing out underlying thoughts, attitudes, and feelings of which they are not fully aware. It is useful to facilitate the process so that the protagonist can move into action as soon as possible. In doing this, the leader can draw on important cues that the protagonist gave in presenting his or her situation, including facial expressions, figures of speech, and body posture. The director helps the protagonist get a clear focus on a particular concern. Rather than having the protagonist give lengthy details and risk losing the energy of the psychodrama, the director can ask the protagonist focusing questions or make statements such as these:

- With whom in your life are you having the most trouble at this time? [Pick the one with whom you need to do some work. Show us a scene.]
- Be your father [mother]. What would he [she] typically say to you? [Show us a scene.]
- Show us how you would want to respond to your mother [father].
- Show us a scene of how you'd like your partner to behave.
- Give us a few lines you'd like your son to hear.
- Tell us what you would most like to hear from your daughter.

The point of these interventions is to avoid commentaries and instead to plunge the protagonist back into a direct encounter and to try out alternative approaches in action.

Once the protagonist has a clear sense of what he or she would like to explore, it is possible to create the scene and coach the auxiliary egos. After this focusing process, protagonists act out their problems and relationships on the stage. A single action phase may consist of one to several scenes. Scenes are constructed and enacted as they relate to the protagonist's issues. They may be interpersonal or intrapersonal in nature and usually progress from peripheral issues (presenting problems) to more central issues (the real or deeper problems). For example, if a member identifies a time when she felt abandoned, the leader might say: "Let's do a scene of an earlier time when you felt isolated and abandoned. Let's set it up." The enactment would then follow. At the end of a scene the protagonist or the director may suggest that the protagonist assume a different role in the same scene to determine whether he or she can respond more effectively. Another suggestion is that the protagonist fantasize about the future by acting out how things might be a year afterward, thus sharing private thoughts with the audience. The duration of the action phase varies and depends on the director's evaluation of the protagonist's involvement and on the level of involvement of the group.

At times most of a session may be devoted to the group as a whole working through interpersonal issues among members. At other times a common theme such as loneliness, fear of intimacy, or feelings of rejection seems to touch everyone in the group. With skillful facilitation by the group leader, the work of many group members can be linked and a common theme can be pursued.

At the end of the action phase, it is important to help protagonists acquire a sense of closure for any work they have accomplished. One useful way to facilitate closure is to arrange for **behavioral practice** to help the protagonist translate group learning to everyday life. The function of behavioral practice is to create a climate that allows for experimentation with a variety of new behaviors. Later the person can implement some of these new behaviors with significant others outside the group and cope with situations more effectively. To facilitate behavioral practice, the protagonist presents the situation as it was originally presented in the action stage and then can try out alternative ways of behaving. Role reversal, future projection, mirroring, and feedback are often used to help the protagonist get a clearer idea of the impact of his or her new behavior. (These techniques are described later in the chapter.)

THE SHARING AND DISCUSSION PHASE

The third phase of psychodrama involves sharing and discussion. Sharing, which comes first, consists of nonjudgmental statements about oneself; a discussion of the group process follows. After a scene is enacted, the psychodrama leader invites all the group members to express how the enactment affected them personally. Those who took roles as auxiliaries may share in two ways. First, they may be encouraged to share what they found themselves feeling or thinking in their roles. Second, they can de-role further and share something from their own life that was touched by the enactment.

Z. T. Moreno (Moreno et al., 2000) believes that both members and leaders need to be taught to have an open heart, not just an open mind. Sharing is a deeply personal process, not a cognitive reflection, and Moreno has some excellent guidelines for making the sharing session a therapeutic experience:

- Group members should not offer advice or analysis to the protagonist but instead talk about themselves and how they were affected by the enactment.

- The protagonist has engaged in open sharing, and he or she deserves more than an analysis or critique.

- Sharing has healing effects. The disclosure of others' experiences gives people a sense that they are not alone and leads to bonding.

- Interpretation and evaluation come later, when the protagonist is not so vulnerable.

During the sharing phase of psychodrama, the director's function is to initiate and lead a discussion that includes as many participants as possible to maximize feedback. The sharing phase gives all the members in a psychodrama group the chance to express their feelings. It is important that protagonists be given an opportunity for some form of closure of their experience. If they have opened themselves up and expressed deep feelings, they need to be able to count on the support of the group to integrate through sharing and some exploration of the meaning of the experience. If no such opportunity is available, protagonists may leave the session feeling rejected and lost instead of feeling freer and more purposeful.

The director must reinforce the kind of sharing that entails self-disclosure, support, and emotional involvement on the part of the members. The sharing is best structured so that members discuss how they were affected by the session, and in this way their own involvement, transparency, and growth are fostered. If participants attempt to analyze or to provide solutions, the director needs to intervene, for example, by asking questions such as these:

- How has Kanesha's drama affected you?

- Who or what most touched you in what you just saw?

- What experiences in your life relate to Kanesha's situation?

- Are there any feelings you had toward Kanesha that you'd like to share with her?

Sharing has another use for the director, especially in ongoing groups. New information group members reveal should be noted because this might well become the source for further therapeutic exploration, which the director could use with the relevant person's prior permission. During the sharing time, group cohesion is typically increased, for members are able to see commonalities. The participation in universal struggles is a way for members to bond; after effectively sharing experiences, protagonists are not left feeling as though they are alone in an unfriendly universe. They have a basis for feeling accepted, and the feedback from other members acts as a reinforcement for them to continue revealing and exploring personal concerns.

Leveton (2001) stresses the importance of the director in helping the protagonist, auxiliaries, and other members find closure after a piece of work. **Closure** does not necessarily mean that a concern is resolved, but all who were involved in a psychodrama should have an opportunity to talk about how they were affected and what they learned. A key aspect of closure is the process of shedding the roles (debriefing) of protagonist and auxiliaries.

Closure depends on the client, the situation, and the group. The length of the session, the degree of cohesion, and the intensity of the work are other factors that determine what kind of closure is appropriate. If the group will not meet again, closure is particularly important. A period of discussion can be useful for "winding down" the emotional pitch to a more cognitive level and for helping the protagonist and the audience integrate key aspects of the session.

Although the emotional aspects of an enactment are of great therapeutic value, a degree of cognitive integration will maximize the value of experiencing emotions. Protagonists can be asked to express what they have learned from the particular enactment and the insights they have acquired. It is also a good practice to encourage protagonists to talk about the personal meaning of reliving a situation. They can be stimulated to think of a possible course of action that will permit them to cope with repressed feelings and of practical ways of dealing more effectively with similar problem situations in the future. Here are some of the tasks for closing a session that Blatner (1996) lists:

- Assist members in applying what they've learned in the group to daily living.
- Summarize some of the highlights of the session.
- Invite members to raise questions about the group process.
- Identify unfinished business.
- Make plans for the next session or identify future themes.
- Provide additional support.
- Engage in some kind of closing ritual (if appropriate).
- Deal with feelings about separation.

It is important to deal with unfinished business during the final stage of a psychodrama (Blatner, 1996; Leveton, 2001; Z. T. Moreno, 1987). Before ending a session, the director typically encourages members to verbalize any unspoken feelings that have developed during the psychodrama. As mentioned earlier, it is not always necessary to work things out, but it is important that the existence of unfinished business be mentioned before the session closes. Some problems will probably be opened up and fruitfully explored, yet the protagonist may be far from having resolved the issue. After a successful sharing session, new work is likely to be shaping up as other members identify with what they just experienced. Of course, it is not wise to undertake further work in a given session if there is not ample time to address the issue adequately.

Members need to be warned of the danger of attempting premature and forced closure of an issue. It is essential that protagonists have ample opportunities to express their feelings, experience their conflicts, and explore the meaning of their emotional release. Clinicians, out of their own anxiety for wanting to see problems solved, sometimes suggest behavioral practice and an action plan before members have had a chance to ventilate and identify an area of personal concern.

Leveton (2001) notes that some practitioners expect perfection. Unless everything is settled, these leaders feel that they have failed. To avoid such feelings, they may try to force closure in situations where participants are better off if they continue reflecting on what has occurred. One of the most challenging tasks for the director is learning to bring closure to a session without curtailing members' further self-exploration, which is necessary for an in-depth resolution of their problems.

Application: Therapeutic Techniques and Procedures

Psychodrama uses a number of specific techniques designed to intensify feelings, clarify confusions and implicit beliefs, increase insight and self-awareness, and practice new behaviors. These techniques should be used for specific purposes related to what the protagonist and other group members need to experience to optimize relearning. Drama itself is not the goal (J. L. Moreno, 1978).

Blatner (2001) points out that **classical psychodrama** is a powerful approach that requires specialized training on the director's part, adequate time for orientation and follow-up, a supportive group atmosphere, and members who are appropriate for these methods. For those who do not practice classical psychodrama, many small role-playing enactments using some of the principles and techniques described later can be integrated with other approaches discussed in this book. Psychodrama is an integrative approach that provides a context for applying its methods in a variety of therapeutic group settings (such as outpatient clinics, inpatient units, residential treatment centers, and private practice). Psychodrama methods can also be applied in groups designed for training counselors.

Directors have latitude to invent their own techniques or to modify standard psychodramatic ones. It is of the utmost importance that group leaders bring caution and commitment to the practice of their technical skills, and they need to know when and how to apply these methods. Effective psychodrama consists of far more than the mere use of certain techniques. Practitioners must learn to know, and work with, the members' psychological worlds in an educated, trained, sensitive, caring, and creative manner. The techniques mentioned here are described in detail in the following sources: Blatner (1996, 1999), Horvatin and Schreiber (2006), Leveton (2001), J. L. Moreno (1964), J. L. Moreno and Moreno (1958), Z. T. Moreno (1959, 1965, 1969, 1983, 1987), and Z. T. Moreno, Blomkvist, and Ruetzel (2000).

Some principles of psychodramatic techniques serve as useful guidelines for the practitioner (Blatner, 2000, pp. 227–228):

- Whenever possible, use physical action rather than talking about a situation.
- Promote authentic encounters as much as possible. Group members should speak directly to each other rather than explaining to the director.
- Look for ways to promote the active behavior of other members by getting them involved in an enactment as much as possible.
- Make abstract situations more concrete by working with specific scenes.
- Encourage participants to make affirmative statements about themselves by using sentences beginning with "I."
- Encourage members to deal with situations in the past or the future as if they were happening in the present moment.
- Recognize and tap the potential for redecisions, renegotiations, and corrective experiences in the present.
- Pay attention to the nonverbal aspects of communication.
- Work toward increasing levels of self-disclosure and honesty.
- When appropriate, weave in a degree of playfulness, humor, and spontaneity in a situation.
- Utilize symbols and metaphors, personifying them and making them more vivid.
- Include other artistic principles and vehicles, such as movement, staging, lighting, props, poetry, art, and music.
- Exaggerate or amplify behavior to explore a wider range of responses.
- Recognize and use the warming-up process as a prelude to facilitating creative and spontaneous behavior.
- Utilize the therapeutic factors of a group.
- Integrate psychodrama with other therapeutic approaches and the creative arts.

SELF-PRESENTATION

In the **self-presentation** technique, the protagonist gives a self-portrait to introduce the situation. Let us say that in the group Jack wants to explore his relationship with his daughter, Laura. The group is interested in this and wants to have it enacted. The director (group leader) has Jack stand up and come onto the stage area, and they begin to establish a scene in which Jack interacts with Laura. Jack picks someone from the group to be the auxiliary playing his daughter. Jack states the problem as he sees it, and the director helps to translate the narrative into an action so that "talking about" becomes "show us how you and your daughter interact."

ROLE REVERSAL

Role reversal, considered one of the most powerful tools of psychodrama, involves looking at oneself through another individual's eyes. In role reversal the protagonist takes on the part of another personality portrayed in his or her drama. For example, the father can play the daughter's part, while the daughter plays the father. As an alternative, the father can be asked: "What does your daughter say or do?"

Through role reversal, people are able to get outside of their own frame of reference and enact a side of themselves they would rarely show to others (Z. T. Moreno et al., 2000). Once an enactment is set up, the director may wish to have the protagonist use this technique (1) to better portray how he or she imagines or remembers the other personality, and (2) to reach a fuller understanding of the viewpoint or situation of the other. Through reversing roles with a key person in the psychodrama, the protagonist is able to formulate significant emotional and cognitive insights into the situation of others. This technique builds empathy with others.

In setting a scene, the auxiliary ego chosen to play a particular part (mother, father, sibling, lover, close friend, teacher, or relative) does not know how to enact either the nonverbal or the verbal components of the assigned role. The protagonist is asked to reverse roles to demonstrate this. As the scene unfolds, if the auxiliary ego begins to take the role in a direction that does not apply to the protagonist, the director can again invite a role reversal so that the auxiliary can get back on track. The leader needs to intervene to reduce the chances that the auxiliary will contaminate the process with his or her own dynamics. The auxiliary is instructed to keep the drama true to the protagonist's perception of events.

The second and more important function of role reversal is to encourage protagonists to empathize with a significant person in their life. In assuming the role of that person in the psychodrama, they begin to develop a deeper appreciation for the person's world. This reversal allows them to experience the environment from a different perspective. Typically, the director suggests a role reversal when it appears that the protagonist would benefit by attempting to "walk in the shoes" of the person with whom he or she is experiencing conflict. The art of this technique lies in the director's ability to warm up the protagonist as if he or she were the other person (Blatner, 2005b).

Z. T. Moreno (1983) makes the point that protagonists must act out the truth as they feel it and from their own subjective stance, regardless of how distorted their presentation may appear to the other members or the leader. For example, Jack presents his daughter, Laura. Preferably, he plays the role of Laura and demonstrates how she typically responds. As Jack "becomes" his daughter, another member can assume the role of Jack as father. By playing the role of Laura as he experiences her, Jack may begin to come to a clearer understanding of how she feels. To warm the protagonist up to this role shift, the director can interview Jack as he plays the role of his daughter. This technique also gives the director and the group a clearer picture of how Jack perceives his daughter and how he thinks she perceives him.

Z. T. Moreno (1983) maintains that this technique encourages maximum expression in conflict situations. Protagonists' distortions of these relationships can be brought to the surface, explored, and corrected in action. First, clients must "own" their emotions through ventilation, or catharsis. Then, by reversing roles, protagonists can reintegrate, redigest, and grow beyond situations that constrain them. Role reversal allows members to fully express their perceptions of reality, to get feedback from others in the group about their subjective views, and to make modifications of their perceptions to the extent that they discover distortions. It can be used throughout the drama to correct or modify the principal auxiliary's role portrayal and to present additional information to the auxiliary.

Role reversal is a useful psychodramatic technique that has many applications outside of group work. For example, it can be applied to supervision and can enable trainees to get an experiential sense of what it is like to be one of their "difficult clients."

DOUBLE

The double involves an auxiliary playing a special role—that of the protagonist's "inner self." The double represents another part of the protagonist by expressing the thoughts and feelings that might otherwise go unexpressed. Doubling performs the function of the "voice over" in cinema or television. The double stands to the side of the protagonist (so as to be able to see and mirror the protagonist's nonverbal communications and yet not intrude on the protagonist's perceptual field) and says the words that aren't being spoken. The director may introduce the technique by saying: "This is your double. If she says what you're thinking, repeat it. If it's not what you're thinking, correct it." It is often wise to ask the protagonist if he or she wants a double. It is important that the protagonist accept the double. Then, as the encounter proceeds, the director might ask: "Is this double right for you? Is this what you are trying to express?" Doing this empowers the protagonist. Even if the protagonist wants someone to stand in as a double, it is important that the double not overwhelm or take over for the protagonist (Z. T. Moreno et al., 2000).

As an auxiliary, the double assists with the specific job of finding a part of the protagonist that is below the surface. Doubling is not an avenue for the auxiliary to vent personal emotions unless those emotions are intuitively sensed as being what the protagonist is probably feeling. The double needs to pay close attention to cues given by the protagonist and to follow the lead of the protagonist rather than doing the leading. Doubling is one of the most powerful tools in psychodrama, and it must be used cautiously (Leveton, 2001).

Doubling is aimed at expressing preconscious, not unconscious, material and facilitating the client's awareness of internal processes, which often leads to an expression of unvoiced thoughts and feelings. The double also acts as a support of the protagonist and as a link between the director and the protagonist. Once an alliance is developed between the double and the protagonist, the director may coach the double to insert some expansions or confrontive statements as a way of facilitating expression of feeling and the clarification process. It is useful for the double to assume both the posture and the attitude of the protagonist as this can help the protagonist increase his or her awareness of inner conflicts and repressed feelings and even express them.

The double attends to process events and the immediate moment and is available to the protagonist in role reversals and in other roles. In Jack's case, the double technique might be used if he felt stuck or felt overwhelmed by his symbolic work with his daughter. The double would then help Jack stay in contact with and express his feelings. Effective doubling often results in the escalation of an interaction, and it is likely to provide the protagonist with the needed catalyst to say things that until now have remained unexpressed.

Multiple doubles may be used to represent and embody the various sides of the protagonist. They can represent the protagonist's different conflicting sides or various roles he or she plays in life. With Jack, one double may represent the side of him that misses his daughter and wants to express love, and the other double can be the "cold father" who really wants to have nothing to do with her. The doubles may speak at the same time, or they may take turns. If the doubles are effective, the father's ambivalent feelings toward his daughter can be successfully portrayed on the stage, and Jack may come to see which side within him is stronger. Also, he may get a clearer picture of the feelings and attitudes he'd like to express to Laura.

SOLILOQUY

At times protagonists are asked to imagine themselves in a place alone where they can think out loud (soliloquize). The director may ask a protagonist to stop the action at some point, turn aside, and express her feelings at the moment. Or the director, on sensing ambivalence on the part of another protagonist, may stop the action and ask him to walk around the stage and say what he is thinking and feeling. Or the protagonist may be engaged in a solitary activity, such as walking home. As a variation, the protagonist may soliloquize by having an inner dialogue with a double as the two walk together.

Like the doubling technique, **soliloquy** facilitates an open expression of what the protagonist may be thinking and feeling but not verbally expressing. For example, Jack may be asked to verbalize his thoughts during the course of a role reversal. This soliloquy gives him the chance to get a sense of what he believes Laura is thinking and feeling, but perhaps not expressing directly.

THE EMPTY CHAIR

Jacob Moreno originated the **empty chair** technique and suggested this procedure to Rosemary Lippitt, calling it the *auxiliary chair* technique (see Lippitt, 1958). The empty chair technique was later incorporated into Gestalt therapy by Fritz Perls, the founder of Gestalt therapy. Basically, the empty chair is a vehicle for the technique of role reversal when an auxiliary ego may not be available, or the actual person is too threatening to engage in an encounter. The empty chair is most easily adaptable to working in one-to-one therapy sessions. This technique is useful in bringing into consciousness the fantasies of what the "other" might be thinking or feeling. There are many applications of this technique. One can imagine a part of the self, such as the critical parent or the vulnerable child in an externalized format, and engage in a dialogue. The therapist acts as coach, facilitating bringing out hidden underlying assumptions or feelings. One of the more important uses consists of exploring what another person in one's social network might actually be feeling, and what that person's more realistic predicament might be.

The empty chair can be a useful technique when a psychodrama involves someone who is absent or who is dead. A group member, Adeline, can put her mother, who suddenly died, in the empty chair. Adeline can tell her mother what she meant to her and say many of the things that she did not get a chance to let her know before her death. During this time the director might sit or stand next to Adeline for support, or another member with a similar issue could be next to Adeline. A variation of this technique involves an extension of role reversal. Here Adeline is asked to sit in the empty chair, "become her mother," and speak to Adeline. This role reversal gives Adeline a chance to verbalize what she would like to have heard from her mother. In this way the empty chair technique can serve as a way to complete unfinished emotional work (Leveton, 2001).

MIRROR TECHNIQUE

The **mirror** technique is aimed at fostering self-reflection. It involves another member mirroring the protagonist's postures, gestures, and words as they appeared in the enactment. If Jack (as protagonist) observes his own behavior as reflected by another person, he can see himself as others do. It is as if Jack had access to a live equivalent of videotape playback. This process may help Jack develop a more accurate and objective self-assessment. The feedback for protagonists may help them come to understand discrepancies between their self-perception and what they communicate of themselves to others. For example, if another member portrays Jack as demanding, critical, aloof, and cold, he is likely to wonder whether that's the way his daughter perceives him. This technique may be particularly useful if others in the group see Jack differently from the way he sees himself, or if he has difficulty presenting himself verbally or in action. Blatner (2000) cautions that mirroring can be a powerful confrontation technique and must be used with discretion. It must be given in the spirit of concern and empathy rather than making the protagonist the object of ridicule.

FUTURE PROJECTION

The technique of **future projection** is designed to help group members express and clarify concerns they have about the future. In future projection, an anticipated event is brought into the present moment and acted out. These concerns may include wishes and hopes, dreaded fears of tomorrow, and goals that provide some direction to life. Members create a future time and place with selected people, bring this event into the present, and get a new perspective on a problem. Members may act out either a version of the way they hope a given situation will ideally unfold or their version of the most horrible outcome.

Z. T. Moreno (1983) contends that the future has typically been a neglected dimension in therapeutic practice. When participants in psychodrama enact anticipated events as though they were taking place in the here-and-now, they achieve an increased awareness of their available options. Rehearsals for future encounters, coupled with constructive and specific feedback, can be of real value to those members who want to develop more effective ways of relating to significant people in their lives.

Once members clarify their hopes for a particular outcome, they are in a better position to take specific steps that will enable them to achieve the future they desire. To return to the case of Jack, he can be asked to carry on the kind of dialogue with his daughter that he would ideally like one year hence. He may even reverse roles, saying all those things that he hopes she will say to him. He can also project himself forward and tell her how he has acted differently toward her during the previous year. If he gets a clearer sense of the kind of relationship that he would like with her, and if he accepts his own responsibility for the quality of this relationship, he can begin to modify some of the ways in which he approaches his daughter.

THE MAGIC SHOP

The magic shop is occasionally used as a warm-up technique and may also be elaborated on throughout the action phase. The **magic shop** technique involves imagining and "creating" a shop that has many bottles and other exotic containers on the various shelves, each containing a different kind of personal quality. These qualities in their imagined containers can be obtained like magic wishes, but only if there is an exchange for some other quality that the protagonist already possesses. The key device is the bargaining the protagonist does with the auxiliary playing the "shopkeeper" for some imagined quality in one of the containers on the shelves. Jack, for example, may want to exchange his competitive style for the ability to open up to his daughter in a loving way. This technique can help him assess his priorities and see what is keeping him from getting what he wants from his relationship with Laura. The magic shop technique may be useful for protagonists who are unclear about what they value, who are confused about their goals, or who have difficulty assigning priorities to their values. This is a powerful technique, but Leveton (2001) indicates that it is of limited use: it must be timed appropriately, and it cannot be repeated very often with the same group.

REPLAY

One obvious technique, used widely in musical or dramatic rehearsals, is that of simply redoing an action— refining it, replaying it with more expressiveness, or varying it in some other fashion. If you make a mistake, you might simply say, "That didn't work well enough. May I please do it over?" In psychodrama the **replay** technique may be used to accentuate the sense of awareness in an action, to intensify the sense of ownership and responsibility, or to broaden the protagonist's role repertoire. Replay is a fundamental technique that has been modified and used in other approaches, especially in behavior therapy and Gestalt therapy.

ROLE TRAINING

Role training involves a more systematic use of techniques such as replay, mirror, role reversal, and feedback and modeling from the group to help clients develop more skill and confidence in dealing with situations that had previously felt awkward or threatening. This is similar to *behavioral rehearsal*, a component of behavioral group therapy; however, the technique was developed by Moreno in the 1930s and it spread from there.

Psychodramatic methods aren't used only to bring out emotions or even to foster insight. Sometimes they can be applied in the service of expanding or refining an individual's role repertoire. *Role training* allows a person to experiment with new behaviors in the safety of the group. Protagonists have many opportunities for replaying a scene until they discover a response that fits them personally. They are given support, reinforcement, and feedback on the effectiveness of their new behaviors. As a part of working through a problem, the director typically focuses on acquiring and rehearsing specific interpersonal skills, which are often learned through the modeling of other members.

Participants are likely to be coached and to receive role training in situations such as a job interview, with the aim of learning how to manage their anxiety. Not only can they come into contact with their feelings, but they can also gain insight into behaviors that are likely to impede an effective interview. They can get feedback on the way they present themselves in the interview, and they can practice various behavioral styles to prepare themselves psychologically for what they see as a stressful experience. Members work on developing and practicing concrete social skills that will help them deal effectively with a range of interpersonal situations.

Applying Psychodrama to Group Work in Schools

Psychodrama produces insight through action and is designed to bring into consciousness and expression the underlying attitudes, thoughts, and emotions of individuals (Blatner, 2001). Classical psychodrama is too intense for use with children and adolescents, but role playing, which is derived from psychodrama, can be very effective for developing psychosocial skills that are essential for adapting to contemporary life. Role playing is an experiential mode that involves active integration of the imaginative and emotional dimensions of human experience, and it is widely used in education from preschool to professional graduate programs (Blatner, 2007).

Certain other psychodrama methods also can be useful with children and adolescents who are experiencing a conflict or a problem situation that can be enacted or dramatized in some form. Not only does the young person who is the focus of the action benefit, but other students in the group benefit as well. These action-oriented methods build group cohesion, offering opportunities for young people to become aware that their struggles are shared by others.

School groups are generally time limited and structured around a topical theme, and many of the techniques described in this chapter can enliven the work of both children and adolescents. Dramatic role play of previous or anticipated situations can be in vivo or can utilize dolls, puppets, or masks with younger elementary school students. Just as cathartic release can occur as children reenact painful experiences, feelings of self-confidence and self-efficacy can emerge from successful rehearsals of future challenges.

Role reversal gives a young person a chance to understand the world of others by experiencing his or her situation through others' eyes. This method expands a member's vision and assists in the development of empathy. The future projection technique has many possibilities for children and adolescents, especially as a vehicle for clarifying their concerns about their future. In a group situation the members can create the kind of relationships that they would hope for with others, they can rehearse for future encounters, and they can get helpful feedback on how they are coming across to others. The magic shop technique can assist young people in identifying some of their core values and clarifying how their values are related to their behavior.

Depending on what is going on within the group, other action-oriented techniques can tap the creativity, spontaneity, and imagination of the members. Of course, whatever methods group leaders draw from with this approach, it is essential that these methods be appropriate for the specific purpose of the group and for the school context. Leaders need to exert caution that they do not open up material that cannot adequately be dealt with within the limits imposed by the school setting or that exceeds their competence. The topic of training and supervision in psychodrama is addressed in detail later in this chapter.

Applying Psychodrama With Multicultural Populations

If practitioners take seriously the cautions that have been mentioned in this chapter, psychodrama can make unique contributions in helping ethnically and culturally diverse populations. Psychodrama is being used by thousands of professionals worldwide (Blatner, 2005b). Rather than having a mother merely *talk about* her problems in relating to her children, for example, she can take on the roles of her children during therapeutic sessions.

For many people who have English as a second language, psychodrama has some interesting applications. My colleagues and I have often asked group members to speak to a significant other in their native language as they are engaged in a role-playing situation in a group session (Corey, Corey, Callanan, & Russell, 2004). When they do so, their emotions quickly come to the surface. I recall a German-born group member who was speaking in English to her "father" in a role-playing situation. She did this in a detached manner, and what she said had a rehearsed quality to it. We asked her to continue talking to her father, but to speak in German. She did so and was quickly overcome with emotion. It was difficult for her to keep up her defenses against experiencing her intense feelings when she used her native tongue. It was not important for the leaders or the other members to understand the exact words spoken. They could understand the underlying emotional message through the protagonist's nonverbal cues and tone of voice. After she finished her psychodrama, we asked her to put some English words to what she had been experiencing. She said that speaking in German had vividly brought back early images, which led to a powerful experience of reliving scenes from her childhood. This helped others who did not understand German to be more tuned into her work, and it also helped her put her emotional work into a cognitive perspective.

In the DVD program *Groups in Action* (Corey, Corey, & Haynes, 2006), Casey speaks symbolically to her mother in Vietnamese, and through role reversal that is also done in Vietnamese, the mother talks back to Casey. In another group program in the same DVD, Maria speaks to each member in the group about her thoughts and feelings in her first language, which is Spanish. These examples give experiential evidence of the therapeutic value of inviting members to speak in their first language at certain times.

If group members are very uncomfortable in talking about personal issues, let alone displaying their emotions in front of others, some psychodrama techniques are most likely not appropriate. However, some of these techniques can be adapted to a problem-solving approach that makes use of cognitive and behavioral principles. It is possible to combine both didactic and experiential methods in structured groups with multicultural populations. All psychodrama techniques do not have to be used to elicit emotions and to encourage members to express and explore their feelings. Role-playing techniques can be productively adapted to structured situations dealing with trying on a new set of specific behaviors.

For those members who have grave cultural injunctions against talking about their family in a group, role playing that involves "talking" to their mother or father may be met with reluctance. This reluctance can be lessened with adequate warm-up procedures and by creating a sufficient level of trust and safety. Before attempting such techniques, the leader should fully explore the clients' cultural values and any hesitation to participate in certain techniques. This demands a high level of training and skill on the leader's part. It is easy to see that an untrained and culturally unaware leader could make group interventions that are counterproductive.

Evaluation of Psychodrama

CONTRIBUTIONS AND STRENGTHS OF THE APPROACH

The action-oriented methods that have been described in this chapter can be integrated into the framework of other group approaches. Increasing numbers of practitioners are creating their own synthesis of psychodramatic techniques within their theoretical orientation. I value psychodrama's active techniques and role playing mainly because these methods lead participants to the direct experience of real conflicts to a much greater degree than is the case when members *talk about* themselves in an objective and storytelling manner.

Psychodrama offers a dynamic approach to life's problems and provides members with alternative ways of coping with their concerns. People often do not see alternatives for dealing with the significant people in their lives. In psychodrama, group members can demonstrate other ways of responding and thus provide the person with different frames of reference. In a role-playing situation, for example, Noreen approaches her partner, Sylvia, with a list of her shortcomings: In talking about her she says that Sylvia is selfish, she doesn't care, and she doesn't show her feelings or truly share her life with her. Through some variation of role playing, another member can demonstrate for Noreen a different way of relating to her partner that is not accusatory and that is less likely to cause Sylvia to become defensive and ignore her complaints.

POTENTIAL FOR INTEGRATION WITH OTHER APPROACHES

The concepts and methods of psychodrama offer imagery, action, and direct interpersonal encounters to psychodynamic, humanistic, and cognitive behavioral approaches. Most of the approaches covered in this book can be enriched by making the group process more experientially meaningful. In turn, psychodramatists have integrated concepts and techniques from other approaches (Baim, Burmeister, & Maciel, 2007). For example, discussion, cognitive processing, modeling, and feedback may aid in working through the feelings and aligning attitudes brought to the surface by the cathartic experience of psychodrama.

As was discussed earlier, psychodrama frequently involves catharsis, yet this catharsis is not the main goal of psychodrama. Instead, catharsis is a natural product of the process of integration or healing. Although there is value in catharsis, my experience with groups has taught me time and again how essential it is to provide a context in which members can come to an understanding of how their bottled-up emotions have affected both themselves and their relationships. J. L. Moreno taught that every emotional catharsis should be followed by a catharsis of integration (Blatner, 2000).

Psychodrama can foster a healing catharsis when that is what is needed, and it can also be a useful force in integrating insights and developing and practicing more effective behaviors. From my perspective, deep personal changes will come about only if members are taught how to transfer what they have learned in their sessions to everyday situations, which is a vital part of psychodrama. It is also critical to teach members how to maintain these positive emotional and behavioral changes. This can be done by helping them plan ways of coping effectively when they meet with frustration in the world. An excellent time for this cognitive work and formulation of action plans is toward the end of the sharing session after the psychodrama has been brought to a close. One useful way to help members achieve closure on some of their emotional issues is to have them begin to think about the meaning of heightened emotional states. Members can be encouraged to reflect on how their beliefs and decisions may be contributing to some of the emotional turmoil they reexperienced in the psychodrama.

A major contribution of psychodrama is that it supports the growing trend toward technical integration in psychotherapy. Although psychodrama can be usefully applied to various types of individual therapy, it is most powerful when used within the group context. Practitioners are challenged to draw on whatever tools will be useful in a given situation. Yet psychodrama is best viewed as an optional set of tools rather than a single approach that in itself can address all of the group members' problems (Blatner, 1996).

Psychodrama is the ideally suited for groups. In addition to group therapy, psychodrama can be adapted to individual, couple, and family therapy as well. Variations of psychodrama can work quite well in groups with people of all ages. Psychodrama techniques can also be readily integrated with most of the other types of therapy covered in this book—Adlerian therapy, transactional analysis, cognitive behavior therapy, rational emotive behavior therapy, reality therapy, solution-focused therapy, and Gestalt therapy, to mention a few. Psychodramatic methods can synergistically enhance techniques from those group approaches that stress a cognitive behavioral orientation. (See Blatner 1996, 2000, 2005b, for a more detailed discussion of integrations with other therapies.) As you read about other group therapeutic approaches, you will see how many of the basic concepts and techniques of psychodrama appear in what are sometimes referred to as "innovative therapies."

Keep in mind that the field of psychodrama is characterized by evolution. Psychodrama has continued to develop with significant refinements in theory and practice beyond the seminal work of J. L. Moreno (see Baim, Burmeister, & Maciel, 2007; Dayton, 2005; & Gershoni, 2003). Z. T. Moreno has made significant contributions to psychodramatic methodology, along with scores of other psychodramatists who have added their own significant innovations and applications. Horvatin and Schreiber's (2006) anthology, *The Quintessential*

Zerka: Writings by Zerka Moreno on Psychodrama, Sociometry and Group Psychotherapy, compiles much of Zerka Moreno's work in one volume.

LIMITATIONS OF THE APPROACH

Blatner (1996) emphasizes that psychodrama is no panacea and that it must be used with good judgment and in a balance with other group therapy skills. Indeed, because enactment can evoke powerful emotions, therapists need to exercise humility in their commitment to continuing their professional and emotional education and in refining their own skills in the understanding and use of this most valuable method. Although spontaneity is one of the basic concepts of psychodrama, it can be misused. It is imperative that a group leader's spontaneity, inventiveness, and courage to try new techniques be tempered with a measure of caution, respect for the members, and concern for their welfare.

Practitioners who use psychodrama need to exercise caution in working with people who manifest acting-out behaviors and with individuals with serious disturbances. It is critical that leaders have the experience, competence, and knowledge to deal with underlying psychopathology. In addition, they must have considerable sensitivity so that they do not push clients with disturbances past a point that is therapeutic. It is also important to use good judgment in structuring situations so that members are not likely to open up old wounds without getting some closure to their problems. For example, in exploring memories of people who have experienced PTSD, Hudgins (2002) has developed a complex adaptation of psychodrama that is structured with a number of specific techniques for safety and containment to avoid retraumatization.

As with other approaches to psychotherapy, it is important that leaders using the powerful methods of psychodrama also become aware of how their own personal problems and unmet needs might interfere with their professional functioning. In this regard, countertransference issues must be understood and explored before leaders can hope to have a therapeutic impact on the group. For example, some group leaders may easily become impatient with what they perceive as the "slow progress" of clients. Out of their desire to see more immediate results, they may resort to a variety of manipulations designed to stir up emotions for the sake of drama. Group leaders also need to become aware of how they experience, express, and manage intense feelings. If they are uncomfortable with emotions, they are likely to steer members away from expressing their feelings. A continued commitment to the director's own personal development is essential. Becoming aware of countertransference is as relevant in psychodrama as it is in psychoanalysis (Blatner, 1996).

The underlying philosophy of psychodrama is consistent with many of the premises of existential therapy, person-centered therapy, and Gestalt therapy (see Chapters 9, 10, and 11), all of which emphasize understanding and respecting the client's experience and the importance of the therapeutic relationship as a healing factor. Although group counselors who employ psychodramatic methods assume an active and directive role in facilitating a group, these methods will be most effective when the leader maintains the person-centered spirit (Blatner, 1996). Group leaders who are authentic, who are successful in making good contact with members, who are able to be psychologically present, who demonstrate empathy, and who exhibit a high level of respect and positive regard for their clients are most effectively able to implement a range of psychodrama techniques. One of the best safeguards for using these techniques appropriately is for a leader's practice to be grounded on a person-centered philosophical foundation.

TRAINING AS A SAFEGUARD

To minimize the limitations and potential problems that might be associated with psychodrama, those who practice psychodrama must have the necessary training and supervision in this approach. Leveton (2001) warns about the irresponsible use of psychodramatic procedures. Skilled directors, she says, are willing to devote the time necessary to develop their skills, and they have undergone a training program under the supervision of an experienced clinician. Psychodrama works best with clinicians who are well grounded in professional judgment and open to drawing methods from various approaches. It is important to remember that practitioners can use certain aspects of psychodrama without employing the full classical enactment for many populations.

The director's function is complicated and involves a combination of art and science, requiring several years of training (Z. T. Moreno, 1987). However, completing the requirements for the psychodrama practitioner certification can take much longer. The more fully the director lives, the better he or she will be able to fulfill the functions demanded in a psychodrama. Orchestrating the many variables in psychodrama is not simply a matter of learning a technique at a weekend workshop. Although some psychodramatic methods can be acquired at a beginning level of competence in this fashion, the skills of an effective psychodramatist require many hundreds of hours of training and supervision.

Blatner (1996) contends that it is essential that directors have theoretical, technical, and practical knowledge of psychodramatic techniques. To appreciate fully the potential values and risks inherent in these techniques, directors need to have participated in the process of experientially learning these techniques. The training required for full certification as a psychodramatist includes having at least a master's degree in counseling or a related field and more than 780 hours of didactic and experiential work plus supervised experience directing psychodrama sessions. Certification involves an examination based on ethical issues, knowledge of theory and practice, and an observation of the candidate's skills in leading psychodrama (Blatner, 2001).

Students of psychodrama need to experience the process in all available roles: auxiliary ego, audience, director, and especially protagonist. By getting personally involved in the psychodrama process, trainees not only learn a great deal more about themselves but develop sensitivity toward the role of the client. Inept leadership—manifested, for instance, in forcing people into situations with which they are not ready to deal—can have serious negative consequences for the participants. The sensitivity and expertise of the director are crucial if the experience is to be therapeutic.

Group practitioners who are interested in incorporating psychodrama into their style of leadership should realize that they do not have to be perfect in their first attempts to apply its methods. With supervised practice, experience as a member of a psychodramatic group, and specialized training, group practitioners are in a good position to acquire competence in applying psychodramatic techniques in their groups.

Where to Go From Here

If you are interested in learning more about the practical values and applications of psychodrama, you can make a good beginning by reading about the approach in journals and books. Also, consider seeking out advanced training and supervision and attending reputable workshops led by certified psychodramatists where you can experience psychodrama as a group member. Not only will you learn how this approach works in a group, but you will also be able to work on some personal concerns and find new ways of dealing with them.

The American Society for Group Psychotherapy and Psychodrama (ASGPP) is geared to the needs of professionals who want to learn about the latest developments in the field. It is an interdisciplinary society with members from all of the helping professions. The goals of the organization are to establish standards for specialists in group therapy and psychodrama and to support the exploration of new areas of endeavors in research, practice, teaching, and training. The ASGPP holds national and regional conferences and offers a number of membership benefits. For further information, contact ASGPP directly:

American Society for Group Psychotherapy and Psychodrama (ASGPP)
301 N. Harrison Street, Suite 508
Princeton, NJ 08540
Telephone: (609) 737-8500
Fax: (609) 737-8510
E-mail: asgpp@asgpp.org
Website: www.asgpp.org

For information on the journal of the ASGPP contact:

Mental Health Resources
44 West Bridge Street
Catskills, NY 12414
Telephone: (518) 943-3559
E-mail: brian.mhr@verizon.net

The American Board of Examiners in Psychodrama, Sociometry and Group Psychotherapy was formed in 1975 to establish national professional standards in the fields of psychodrama, sociometry, and group psychotherapy and to certify qualified professionals on the basis of these standards. Two levels of certification have been established by the Board: Certified Practitioner (CP), and Trainer, Educator, and Practitioner (TEP). Applicants must be certified at the first level before becoming eligible for certification at the second. The board website provides information on certification standards, application materials, fees, and how to find certified psychodramatists and psychodrama trainers in your area.

American Board of Examiners in Psychodrama, Sociometry, and Group Psychotherapy
P.O. Box 15572
Washington, DC 20003-0572
Telephone: (202) 483-0514
E-mail: abepsychodrama@yahoo.com
Website: http://www.psychodramacertification.org/

Adam Blatner, M.D., is a doubly-board–certified adult and child-adolescent psychiatrist and the author of some of the most widely used works on psychodrama. Although retired from active practice, he continues writing, editing, and teaching. A wide variety of papers on psychodrama and psychotherapy can be accessed through his website. In addition, you can learn about the current practice of psychodrama, find lists of currently available books and CDs, and view a photo gallery of Moreno and other historical and contemporary leaders in the field.

Adam Blatner, M.D.
E-mail: adam@blatner.com
Website: www.blatner.com/adam/

A series of three DVDs featuring the work of Zerka Moreno has been produced. In *Psychodrama in Action,* Zerka conducts an actual psychodrama session with a group of psychodrama practitioners. *Zerka on Psychodrama* describes the basics of psychodrama, and *Psychodrama, Sociometry and Beyond* is an extended interview by a panel of psychodrama practitioners.

Website: www.psychotherapy.net
Telephone: (800) 577-4762

AUTHOR LECTURES

Watch *Gerald Corey's Perspectives on Theory and Practice of Group Counseling* DVD or visit the *Theory and Practice of Group Counseling* CourseMate website at www.cengagebrain.com/shop/ISBN/0840033869 to watch videos of Dr. Gerald Corey presenting lectures for each chapter. Also available are unique eAudio lectures for each chapter and quiz questions for self-study.

RECOMMENDED SUPPLEMENTARY READINGS

The Quintessential Zerka: Writings by Zerka Toeman Moreno on Psychodrama, Sociometry and Group Psychotherapy (Horvatin & Schreiber, 2006) documents the origins and development of the theory and practice of psychodrama, sociometry, and group psychotherapy through the work and innovation of its cocreator, Zerka Toeman Moreno. This anthology contains all of the articles by Zerka Moreno cited in this chapter, as well as many of her writings from the early 1940s to the present.

Interactive and Improvisational Drama: Varieties of Applied Theatre and Performances (Blatner, 2007) is an anthology describing more than 30 approaches to using drama in community building, education, therapy, personal and group empowerment, and recreation.

Psychodrama: Advances in Theory and Practice (Baim, Burmeister, & Maciel, 2007) is an anthology that contains some of the current thinking in the field of psychodrama.

Acting-In: Practical Applications of Psychodramatic Methods (Blatner, 1996) is an excellent introduction and a guide for practitioners interested in using psychodramatic techniques in a group setting. This brief book is written very clearly and deals with the basic elements of psychodrama—its methods, stages, principles, and applications— as well as some of its pitfalls. This has become one of the most widely used basic textbooks for this approach, and it has been updated with extensive references. If you have time to read only one source, this would be my recommendation.

A Clinician's Guide to Psychodrama (Leveton, 2001) offers an excellent and eclectic view of psychodrama. The writing is clear, vivid, and interesting. A number of psychodramatic techniques are described and illustrated through case examples that attest to the author's skills and creativity in applying these techniques.

REFERENCES AND SUGGESTED READINGS

*Baim, C., Burmeister, J., & Maciel, M. (Eds.). (2007). *Psychodrama: Advances in theory & practice*. London: Routledge.

*Blatner, A. (1996). *Acting-in: Practical applications of psychodramatic methods* (3rd ed.). New York: Springer.

*Blatner, A. (1999). Psychodramatic methods in psychotherapy. In D. J. Wiener (Ed.), *Beyond talk therapy: Using movement and expressive techniques in clinical practice* (pp. 125–143). Washington, DC: American Psychological Association.

*Blatner, A. (2000). *Foundations of psychodrama: History, theory, and practice* (4th ed.). New York: Springer.

*Blatner, A. (2001). Psychodrama. In R. J. Corsini (Ed.), *Handbook of innovative therapies* (2nd ed., pp. 535–545). New York: Wiley.

Blatner, A. (2005a). Beyond psychodrama. *New Therapist, 36*, 15–21.

Blatner, A. (2005b). Psychodrama. In R. J. Corsini & D. Wedding (Eds.), *Current psychotherapies* (7th ed., pp. 405–438). Belmont, CA: Brooks/Cole, Cengage Learning.

Blatner, A. (2006). *Tele: The dynamics of rapport*. Retrieved March 17, 2006, from http://www.blatner.com/adam/pdntbk/tele.htm

Blatner, A. (2007). Psychodrama, sociodrama, and role playing. In A. Blatner (Ed.), *Interactive and improvisational drama: Varieties of applied theatre and performance*. Lincoln, NE: iUniverse.

*Blatner, A. (with Wiener, D. J.). (Ed.). (2007). *Interactive and improvisational drama: Varieties of applied theatre and performance*. Lincoln, NE: iUniverse.

*Corey, G., Corey, M., Callanan, P., & Russell, J. M. (2004). *Group techniques* (3rd ed.). Belmont, CA: Brooks/Cole, Cengage Learning.

*Corey, G., Corey, M., & Haynes, R. (2006). *Groups in action: Evolution and challenges, DVD and workbook*. Belmont, CA: Brooks/Cole, Cengage Learning.

*Dayton, T. (2005). *The living stage: A step-by-step guide to psychodrama, sociometry, and experiential group therapy*. Deerfield Beach, FL: Health Communications, Inc.

*Gershoni, J. (Ed.). (2003). *Psychodrama in the 21st century: Clinical and educational applications*. New York: Springer.

*Horvatin, T., & Schreiber, E. (Eds.). (2006). *The quintessential Zerka: Writings by Zerka Toeman Moreno on psychodrama, sociometry and group psychotherapy*. New York: Routledge (Taylor & Francis).

Hudgins, M. K. (2002). *Experiential treatment for PTSD: The therapeutic spiral model*. New York: Springer.

*Leveton, E. (2001). *A clinician's guide to psychodrama* (3rd ed.). New York: Springer.

Lippitt, R. (1958). The auxiliary chair technique. *Group Psychotherapy, 11*, 8–23.

Moreno, J. L. (1964). *Psychodrama: Vol. 1* (3rd ed.). Beacon, NY: Beacon House.

* Books and articles marked with an asterisk (*) are suggested for further study.

Moreno, J. L. (1978). *Who shall survive?* (3rd ed.). Beacon, NY: Beacon House.

Moreno, J. L., & Moreno, Z. T. (1958). *Psychodrama: Vol. 2.* Beacon, NY: Beacon House.

Moreno, J. L., & Moreno, Z. T. (1969). *Psychodrama: Vol. 3.* Beacon, NY: Beacon House.

Moreno, Z. T. (1959). A survey of psychodramatic techniques. *Group Psychotherapy, 12,* 5–14.

Moreno, Z. T. (1965). Psychodramatic rules, techniques, and adjunctive methods. *Group Psychotherapy, 18,* 73–86.

Moreno, Z. T. (1969). Practical aspects of psychodrama. *Group Psychotherapy, 22,* 213–219.

Moreno, Z. T. (1983). Psychodrama. In H. I. Kaplan & B. J. Sadock (Eds.), *Comprehensive group psychotherapy* (2nd ed., pp. 158–166). Philadelphia: Lippincott, Williams & Wilkins.

Moreno, Z. T. (1987). Psychodrama, role theory, and the concept of the social atom. In J. K. Zeig (Ed.), *The evolution of psychotherapy* (pp. 341–366). New York: Brunner/Mazel.

*Moreno, Z. T., Blomkvist, L. D., & Ruetzel, T. (2000). *Psychodrama, surplus reality and the art of healing.* Philadelphia: Routledge (Taylor & Francis).

CHAPTER NINE

The Existential Approach to Groups

Introduction

Existential therapy can best be considered as a way of thinking rather than as a particular style of practicing group therapy. It is not a separate school or a neatly defined, systematic model with specific therapeutic techniques. Universal human concerns and existential themes constitute the background of most groups. This chapter deals with the practical implications of existential themes that have relevance to a wide variety of therapy groups, counseling groups, and support groups.

The existential approach rejects the deterministic views of traditional psychoanalysis and behaviorism and emphasizes our freedom to choose what to make of our circumstances. It is a dynamic approach that focuses on the underlying givens or the four ultimate concerns that are rooted in human existence: freedom, existential isolation, meaninglessness, and death (Yalom, 1980; Yalom & Josselson, 2011). Existential therapy is grounded on the assumption that we are *free* and therefore *responsible* for our choices and actions. We need to be the pioneers of our lives and to find models that will give us meaning. Even though we sometimes cannot control things that happen to us, we have complete control over how we choose to perceive and handle them. Although our freedom *to act* is limited by external reality, our freedom *to be* relates to our internal reality. One of the goals of the therapeutic process is to challenge clients to discover alternatives and to choose among them. Schneider and Krug (2010) state that existential therapists are mainly concerned about helping people to reclaim and reown their lives. Schneider and Krug identify four essential aims of existential-humanistic therapy: (1) to help clients become more present to both themselves and others; (2) to assist clients in identifying ways they block themselves from fuller presence; (3) to challenge clients to assume responsibility for designing their present lives; and (4) to encourage clients to choose more expanded ways of being in their daily lives.

As van Deurzen (2002a) has indicated, existential therapy is ultimately a process of exploring clients' values and beliefs that give meaning to living. She adds that the aim of existential therapy is to invite clients to take action that grows out of their honest appraisal of their life's purpose. The therapist's basic task is to encourage clients to consider what they are most serious about so they can pursue a direction in life. The existential approach assumes the individual's capacity to make well-informed choices about his or her life. Group leaders cannot assume that they alone know the purpose of the group; rather, it is up to each participant to create this purpose.

THE FOCUS OF EXISTENTIAL PSYCHOTHERAPY

Existentialism is a branch of philosophical thought that began in Europe. Key existential writers, such as Martin Heidegger (1889–1976) and Jean-Paul Sartre (1905–1980), did not address themselves to psychotherapeutic concerns directly. The existential tradition seeks a balance between recognizing the limits and tragic dimensions of human existence on one hand and the possibilities and opportunities for humans to transcend those limits to achieve a vital existence on the other hand. It grew out of a desire to help people engage the dilemmas of contemporary life, such as isolation, alienation, and meaninglessness. The focus is on the individual's experience of being in the world alone and facing the anxiety of this isolation.

Rollo May brought existential thinking from Europe and translated key concepts into psychotherapeutic practice in the United States. May's writings (1953, 1961, 1981, 1983) have had a significant impact on existentially oriented practitioners throughout the world. According to May, becoming a person is not an automatic process, yet people do have a desire to fulfill their potential. It takes courage to be, and our choices determine who we become. There is a constant struggle within us. Although we want to grow toward maturity and independence, we realize that expansion is often a painful process. Hence, the struggle is between the security of dependence and the delights and pains of growth. Along with May, another significant contemporary advocate for existential therapy in the United States is Irvin Yalom.

Significant developments in the existential approach in Britain are due largely to the efforts of Emmy van Deurzen, who is currently developing academic and training programs at the New School of Psychotherapy and Counselling. For a description of the historical context and development of existential therapy in Britain, see van Deurzen (2002b) and Cooper (2003); for an excellent overview of the theory and practice of existential therapy, see van Deurzen (2002a) and Schneider and Krug (2010).

The existential perspective focuses on understanding the person's subjective view of the world. As such, it is a phenomenological approach. Therapy is a journey taken by therapist and client into the world as perceived and experienced by the client. But this quest demands that the therapist also be in contact with his or her own phenomenological world. Existential therapists are personally engaged in their work and are willing to be affected by their clients' experiences in therapy. The human dilemmas that grow out of the therapeutic relationship have as much relevance for the therapist as for the client (van Deurzen, 2002b). Bugental (1987) writes about life-changing psychotherapy, which is the effort to help clients examine how they have answered life's existential questions and to invite them to revise their answers and begin to live authentically.

Existential therapists are concerned with the deepest and most vexing problems clients present in therapy. Yalom and Josselson (2011) describe existential psychotherapy as "an attitude toward human suffering [that] has no manual.

It asks deep questions about the nature of the human being and the nature of anxiety, despair, grief, loneliness, isolation, and anomie. It also deals centrally with the questions of meaning, creativity, and love" (p. 310).

Existential therapy provides a rigorous, intensive forum for the full-lived, awe-informed life (Zur, 2009). This approach does not focus on merely applying problem-solving techniques to the complex task of authentic living, nor does it aim to cure people in the traditional medical sense. People are not viewed as being ill but as being sick of playing certain roles or being clumsy at living. Clients need assistance in surveying the terrain so that they can decide which path to pursue, and therapists help clients come to terms with life in all its contradictions. One of the aims of existential therapy is to challenge people to stop deceiving themselves regarding their lack of responsibility for what is happening to them and their excessive demands on life (van Deurzen, 2002b).

May (1981) views the aim of existential therapy as setting clients free. Through the experience of existential therapy, people enlarge their vision of themselves as being free to engage in action that aims at change, tempered by the wisdom to acknowledge that we are (as Heidegger puts it) "thrown" into a world we didn't create. Clients gradually learn how to accept life in all its complexities and paradoxes. This process involves learning to face the inevitable problems, difficulties, crises, and disappointments that are a part of living. Clients come to realize that they are not imprisoned by their responses but have the ability to achieve authentic freedom. They are better able to live with the givens and find the courage within themselves to deal with uncertainty. Therapy provides them with the opportunity to contemplate a life that is worthy of commitment (van Deurzen, 1990a, 2002a).

THE PURPOSE OF AN EXISTENTIAL GROUP

The existential group represents a microcosm of the world in which participants live and function. Over time the interpersonal and existential problems of the participants become evident in the here-and-now interactions within the group (Yalom & Josselson, 2011). A guiding purpose of the group is to enable members to discover themselves as they are by sharing their existential concerns. In an existential group participants make a commitment to a lifelong journey of self-exploration with these goals: (1) enabling members to become truthful with themselves, (2) widening their perspectives on themselves and the world around them, (3) clarifying what gives meaning to their present and future life, (4) successfully negotiating and coming to terms with past, present, and future crises, and (5) understanding themselves and others better and learning better ways of communicating with others (van Deurzen, 2002b). An open attitude toward life is essential, as is the willingness to explore unknown territory. Van Deurzen (2010) captures this idea well:

> Embarking on our existential journey requires us to be prepared to be touched and shaken by what we find on the way and to not be afraid to discover our own limitations and weaknesses, uncertainties and doubts. It is only with such an attitude of openness and wonder that we can encounter the impenetrable everyday mysteries, which take us beyond our own preoccupations and sorrows and which by confronting us with death, make us rediscover life. (p. 5)

The therapeutic process involves encouraging members to begin listening to themselves and paying attention to their subjective experience. A group can assist members in addressing their deepest human concerns. Attention is given to clients' immediate, ongoing experience with the aim of helping them develop greater presence in their quest for meaning and purpose (Sharp & Bugental, 2001). This phenomenological self-searching emphasizes what members discover within their own stream of awareness when this stream is not directed by the therapist. By openly sharing and exploring universal personal concerns, members develop a sense of mutuality. The group becomes a place where people can be together in deeply meaningful ways.

Key Concepts

Key concepts of the existential approach include self-awareness, self-determination and responsibility, existential anxiety, death and nonbeing, the search for meaning, the search for authenticity, and aloneness/relatedness. These key existential concepts guide the practice of group work by providing a way to view and understand individuals in the group. Although existentially oriented group practitioners may incorporate many techniques from other models, these interventions are made within the context of striving to understand the subjective world of the members. In this spirit, rather than focusing on group techniques, I will stress the implications of these key concepts for group work.

SELF-AWARENESS

The capacity for self-awareness separates us from other animals and enables us to make free choices. The greater our awareness, the greater our possibilities for freedom. Schneider (2008) explains that the core existential position is that we are both *free* (willful, creative, expressive) and *limited* by environmental and social constraints. We are all subject to the deterministic forces of sociocultural conditioning and to the limitations imposed by our genetic endowment, but we are still able to choose based on our awareness of these limiting factors. According to May (1961), regardless of how great the forces victimizing us are, we have the capacity to know that we are being victimized, which allows us to take a stand on this situation. Furthermore, through self-awareness we come to recognize the responsibility associated with the freedom to choose and to act.

Implications for Group Work In group work, the basic existential goal of expanding self-awareness and thereby increasing the potential for choice is pursued by helping members discover their unique "being-in-the-world." By asking key questions, participants seek to define themselves and become aware of the central dimensions of their existence: "To what degree am I aware of who I am and where I am going?" "How do I experience my world?" "What meanings do I attach to the events I experience?" "How can I increase my self-awareness?" "In what concrete ways does expanded consciousness increase my range of alternatives?" The task for group members is to become aware of their existence as fully as possible, which includes realizing their possibilities and learning to act on the basis of them. A central theme of the existential approach is taking existence seriously.

In the group situation participants have the opportunity to express their own unique feelings and their subjective views of the world. They are also explicitly confronted by others, and they learn to deal with the anxiety that arises from being without the security of their everyday roles. As we will see in detail later in the chapter, existentialists view anxiety in positive terms. Anxiety helps "individuate" us by awakening us to the inauthenticity of merely being who others want us to be, and it reflects the understanding that we are unique.

I believe group leaders need to alert the members of their groups to the price that is involved in seeking greater self-awareness. As people become more aware, they find it increasingly difficult to "go back home again." While living in ignorance of the quality of one's existence can lead to staleness, it can also provide a certain degree of contentment or, at least, security. As we open doors that were previously closed, we can expect to encounter more struggles as well as the potential for enhancing the quality of our living. The experience can be exciting and joyful but also frightening and, at times, depressing. This is an issue that should be mentioned during the early phases of a group.

A higher degree of self-awareness permits us to recognize that we can make choices for ourselves. For example:

- We can choose to expand our awareness or to limit our vision of ourselves.
- We can determine the direction of our own lives or allow other people and environmental forces to determine it for us.
- We can use our potential for action or choose not to act.
- We can choose to establish meaningful ties with others or choose to isolate ourselves.
- We can search for our own uniqueness or allow our identity to be lost in conformity.
- We can create and find meaning in our life or lead an empty and meaningless existence.
- We can engage in certain risks and experience the anxieties that accompany deciding for ourselves or choose the security of dependence.
- We can make the most of the present by accepting the inevitability of our eventual death or hide from this reality because of the anxiety it generates.

Example Here is an example that illustrates how participants in a group can gradually achieve a higher level of awareness. When Crystal first entered the group, she could see no value in expressing intense emotions and insisted that she had to be rational no matter what. She tried very hard to keep her feelings harnessed at all times because she was afraid that she'd "go crazy" if she allowed herself to feel intensely. This need to tightly control her feelings manifested itself in several ways. For example, when other group members relived painful emotional events, Crystal panicked and tried to leave the room, and she often attempted to defuse the expression of intense emotions by others in the group. During one session, however, another person's work triggered some painful memories in Crystal that were associated with her childhood memories of her parents' divorce. Suddenly she became that frightened child again, pleading with her parents to stay together and letting herself "go emotionally out of control."

This unexpected experience made Crystal aware that she had been keeping a lid on her strong feelings and that her defenses against "hurting too much" had resulted in her difficulty in getting close to others, in expressing anger, and in manifesting the love she claimed she felt for her family now. She also learned that she did not "go crazy" by permitting herself to experience the depth of her feelings. After that experience, Crystal chose to open herself to feelings and not to run out of the room when she was afraid of the intense emotions of other members.

SELF-DETERMINATION, FREEDOM, AND PERSONAL RESPONSIBILITY

Another existential theme is that we are self-determining beings, free to choose among alternatives and therefore responsible for directing our lives and shaping our destinies. Although we are thrust into the world, the existentialist view is that how we live and what we become are the result of our own choices. As Sartre (1971) put it, our existence is a given, but we do not have, and cannot have, a fixed, settled "nature," or "essence." We are constantly faced with having to choose the kind of person we want to become, and as long as we live, we must continue to choose. Sartre remarks: "Man being condemned to be free carries the weight of the whole world on his shoulders; he is responsible for the world and for himself as a way of being" (p. 553). For Sartre, we are free in that we are nothing but what we do, and what we do is not the result of our past. However, we are much given to making excuses for our behavior, thus acting in "bad faith." Schneider and Krug (2010) write that existential therapy embraces three values: (1) the *freedom to become* within the context of natural and self-imposed limitations; (2) the capacity to *reflect* on the meaning of our choices; and (3) the capacity to *act* on the choices we make.

Viktor Frankl, an existential psychiatrist, stresses the relationship between freedom and responsibility and insists that ultimate freedom can never be taken from us because we can at least choose our attitude toward any given set of circumstances. To support this statement, Frankl (1963) draws from his own experiences in a German concentration camp, where the prisoners were stripped of every semblance of outward freedom. He contends that even in a situation of such extreme powerlessness, people can ultimately be their own master because the attitude they assume toward their suffering is of their own choosing: "Life ultimately means taking responsibility to find the right answer to its problems and to fulfill the tasks which it constantly sets for each individual" (p. 122). Frankl believes human freedom is not freedom from conditions but the ability to take a stand in the face of conditions.

Frankl's brand of existential therapy, **logotherapy** (*logos* = meaning), teaches that meaning in life cannot be dictated but can only be discovered by searching in our own existential situation. Indeed, we have the will to meaning, and we have the freedom to find meaning in how we think and in what we do. Frankl believes the goal is not to attain peace of mind but to experience meaning in a healthy striving. This search for meaning, which is our central quest, enables us to make sense of our existence despite guilt, suffering, and the inevitability of death (Gould, 1993). We are also responsible for (but not to blame for) the symptoms that restrict our ability to live freely and fully. It is essential that we recognize and accept our part in creating the quality of our existence, for life does not simply happen to us. We are capable of actively influencing our thoughts, feelings, and actions. Until we accept our capacity for freedom, we will not change. If we wait around for others to change or for the environment to change, we may well increase our misery and hopelessness instead of taking action to make something happen differently.

Implications for Group Work The members of an existential group are confronted over and over again with the fact that they cannot escape from freedom and that they are responsible for their existence. Accepting this freedom and responsibility generates anxiety, and so does the risk associated with making choices. Another goal of the existential group is to help participants face and deal with these anxieties. The main task for the group leader is to confront members with the reality of their freedom and of the ways in which they are restricting or denying it. Group participants sometimes present themselves as victims, talk about their feelings of helplessness and powerlessness, and place the blame for their unhappiness on others and on external circumstances. A good place for members to start on the road to greater self-determination is to become aware of the roles they have chosen to play. When people come to believe they can make choices, they can direct their own destiny, and ultimately assume control of their life.

Yalom and Josselson (2011) contend that the group provides the optimal conditions for therapeutic work on personal responsibility. Members are responsible for the interpersonal position they assume in the group, which also provides a glimpse of how they behave in real-life situations. Through feedback, members learn to see themselves through others' eyes, and they learn how their behavior affects others. Building on these discoveries, members can take responsibility for making changes in their everyday lives. The group work "not only allows individuals to change their way of relating to one another but also brings home to them in a powerful way the extent to which they have created their own life predicaments—clearly an existential therapeutic mechanism" (p. 334). The existential group leader encourages members to assume genuine responsibility for their functioning in the group and to carry these changes into daily life.

Example Edward reluctantly joined one of my groups. I say "reluctantly" because he had serious misgivings about the value of participating in a group. At 62, Edward had settled into a passive, predictable, but comfortable and safe life as a successful business executive. When he joined, he presented himself with this statement: "I don't know if this group will do me any good or not. Frankly, I think that I'm too old to change and that what I have is the most I can hope to get from life. I believe that things will probably stay as they are." In spite of his own statement and in spite of the fact that his life was orderly and safe, he felt that he was "drying up" and that life had lost zest. He was ready for a change, even though he was not sure whether change was possible.

Through his involvement in the group, Edward began to realize that he did have options—many more than he had thought possible. All along, he had blamed his wife, his three sons, and his daughter for the fact that he couldn't change jobs and live the kind of life he wanted for himself. He was avoiding responsibility for his own problems by focusing on what his family expected, often without ever verifying whether they did expect what he thought they did.

The other members and I challenged Edward to begin thinking for himself about how he wanted his life to be different. I asked him these questions: "If you were to continue living for the rest of your life as you are now, with no basic changes, how would you feel about it?" "Assume that your family would be willing to make the changes in lifestyle that you want to make. How would your life be different a year from now? five years from now?" "What steps can you take today that will help you make some of the changes you want to make?"

The safety within a group allows members like Edward to explore the meaning of crisis as a place for rediscovering opportunities and challenges that have been forgotten. An existential group leader could help Edward face the actual process of decay that he is allowing to take place. Once he recognizes his ways of engaging in self-deception and sees that he is choosing to rest on his laurels, he can decide to take a different direction.

EXISTENTIAL ANXIETY

Existential therapists view anxiety as providing potentially instructive signals that can assist individuals to live more authentically. Existential anxiety is the unavoidable product of being confronted with the **givens of existence:** death, freedom, existential isolation, and meaninglessness (Vontress, 2008; Yalom, 1980). **Existential anxiety** is the basic unease that we experience when we become aware of our vulnerability and our inevitable death (van Deurzen, 2002a). From the existential viewpoint, **anxiety** is an invitation to freedom and not just a symptom to be eliminated or "cured." Anxiety results from having to face choices without clear guidelines and without knowing what the outcome will be, and from being aware that we are ultimately responsible for the consequences of our actions. In the words of the Danish philosopher Søren Kierkegaard (1813–1855), existential anxiety is "the dizziness of freedom." In the context of group work, it is expected that we will feel anxious! At some level we know that for new dimensions of ourselves to emerge, old parts of ourselves must die. The knowledge that to grow we must exchange familiar and secure ways for new and unknown ones is in itself a source of anxiety.

From the perspective of van Deurzen (2002a), existential anxiety is basic to living with awareness and being fully alive. In fact, the courage to live fully entails accepting the reality of death and the anxiety associated with uncertainty. Although we may not welcome this anxiety, it is the price we must pay for becoming what we are capable of becoming. Some people dull their sensitivity as a way of avoiding the basic challenges of life, and others find different ways of disguising their anxiety. Yet underneath the surface of their coping styles, people experience anxiety as an ever-present threat. Paradoxically, it is equally a source of transformation.

Implications for Group Work At the core of therapy, clients eventually come to terms with the underlying conditions of being human. These sources of existential anxiety must be faced and worked through in therapy; they involve recognition of our separateness and our need to be with others, of our guilt over not living authentically, of the emptiness in the universe and lack of meaning, of the burden of responsibility associated with choosing for ourselves, and of our fear of death and nonbeing. As therapy progresses, group members often painfully recognize how much energy they have put into maintaining an idealized image of themselves that is impossible to achieve. They also see that they must let go of static images of themselves that lead to a restricted existence. As group participants give up their inauthentic roles, they are able to bring a renewed quality to their living. This process typically results in anxiety because clients are giving up ways of being that are familiar.

In existential group therapy, members are assisted in coming to terms with the paradoxes of existence: that life can be undone by death, that success is precarious, that we are determined to be free, that we are responsible for a world we didn't choose, that we have the capacity to make choices and to accept the burdens that come with it, and that these choices are decisive in the face of doubt and uncertainty. Anxiety arises as members recognize the realities of their mortality, their confrontation with pain and suffering, their need to struggle for survival, and their basic fallibility. Thus anxiety is an indicator of the level of awareness that group participants allow. Existential anxiety is exposed in a group, especially when members explore ways in which they have adjusted too comfortably to a status quo style of living designed to mask basic insecurity and anxiety. Van Deurzen (1991, 2010) maintains that a main aim of existential therapy is not to make life seem easier or safer but to encourage clients to be more receptive to recognizing and dealing with the sources of insecurity and anxiety. Facing existential anxiety involves viewing life as an adventure rather than hiding behind securities that seem to offer protection. As van Deurzen (1991) puts it: "We need to question and scrape away at the easy answers and expose ourselves to some of the anxiety that can bring us back to life in a real and deep way" (p. 46).

It is essential for the group leader to recognize existential anxiety and guide group members in finding ways of exploring it constructively. The purpose of an existential group is not to eliminate anxiety, for doing so would cut off a source of vitality. The optimal use of anxiety is one of the goals of existential therapy. Leaders have the task of encouraging members to deal with their existential anxiety and to develop the courage to face life squarely (van Deurzen, 2002a, 2002b).

Once group members face and fully accept their anxieties, the next step is to encourage them to make a commitment to action. Through the support of the leader and of other participants in the group, the individual can be motivated to explore unknown paths and to investigate new dimensions of self. This search can lead to even greater anxiety for a time, but if the person is in the process of growth, he or she knows that anxiety doesn't have to be devastating and that it is the price one must pay for breaking out of constricting modes of existence.

Example For much of her life, Ann had allowed others to make decisions for her. She had uncritically accepted her parents' religious values and had become dependent on her church to make decisions for her. At this time in her life, she was struggling with following the values she had grown up with. Through her work in a group, she came to see more and more clearly that if she wanted to change she needed to take more responsibility for her choices. Ann decided to look within herself for strength and direction. It took Ann some time to begin to trust herself and even longer to let go of the need to rely on external authority for her answers and security. Making decisions for herself were fraught with anxiety and self-doubt. Although some of her values have changed, she now has a sense that these are her own values.

The task of existential therapy is to teach Ann how to understand the feelings that surfaced as she became aware that she is responsible for deciding who she will be. As Ann realizes she does not have to continue being her "old self," she begins to experience the uneasiness that accompanies not having the familiar structure to which she was accustomed.

DEATH AND NONBEING

The existential therapist considers death as essential to the discovery of meaning and purpose in life. Life has meaning precisely because it must end, and life is enhanced when we take seriously the reality of the life we do have. The reality of our finiteness can stimulate us to look at our priorities and to ask what we value most. The present is precious because it is all we really have. It is our temporal nature that makes us feel the urgency to do something with our life, to make a choice between affirming life by trying to become the person we are capable of becoming or allowing life to slip by us and eventually realizing that we've never given ourselves a chance to be different. Frankl (1963) believes that it is not how long we live but *how* we live that determines the quality and meaningfulness of our life. When we emotionally accept the reality of our mortality, we realize more clearly that our actions do count, that we do have choices, and that we must accept the ultimate responsibility for how we are living (Corey & Corey, 2010).

As the only creatures with a strong sense of the future, humans need to deal with the end of life, which Heidegger (1962) calls "cessation of possibility." Because many of us are afraid of facing the reality of our own death and the anxiety that goes with it, we might attempt to escape the awareness of this reality. But the price for trying to flee from the confrontation with nonbeing results in self-alienation. Vontress (1996) suggests that counselors should address the implications of the fact that we are all mortal beings: "Counseling is a human encounter in which counselors accept their clients as fellow travelers, en route to the same destination, death" (p. 161). Vontress stresses that people all over the world are engaged in a lifelong quest to make sense out of life and of their significance in the world. Human mortality is a catalyst for giving meaning to life.

Death awareness is an awakening experience that can be a useful catalyst for making significant life changes. Confronting the idea of one's personal death can result in a massive shift in the way one lives in the world (Yalom & Josselson, 2011). We can turn our fear of death into a positive force when we accept the reality of our mortality. We can wisely and resolutely use our time on this earth to live courageously and fully (Vontress, 2008).

Implications for Group Work Awareness of death and the anxiety it generates has significant implications for the practice of group work. The concern with living life fully, rather than merely existing, is a recurrent theme in many groups. Generally, I address this theme by encouraging group members to ask themselves honestly how they feel about the quality of their lives. Then I ask them to answer this same question as if they knew that they were about to die. How do the two answers differ? Have they made decisions that were not carried through? Have they ignored opportunities for change? By reflecting on their unfinished business, participants may come to realize that they are not living the kind of life they'd like to live, and they may be able to identify the reasons for this unsatisfactory existence. Sometimes dreams about one's dying may symbolize the coming to a close of one phase of life, of some interest, work, or relationship.

I find it valuable to expand the concept of physical death to other kinds of death. Even though we are physically alive, we may be dead or dying in important areas of life. Perhaps we are numb to our feelings or caught up in deadening roles. We may have lost our intellectual curiosity and wonderment about life. Perhaps our relationships with significant people are characterized by routine and ritual. What we do may have little meaning. In fact, the end of the group is itself a sort of "death" that is often avoided. A group can be a good place to recognize the areas in which we have grown stale and to confront ourselves with what we are willing to do to change.

The process of change always entails allowing parts of us to die to make room for new growth. Growth often demands that we be willing to let go of familiar ways of being. We may need to experience a period of mourning over our losses before we can move forward and establish new patterns. Groups offer a safe place to express this sadness, to explore the ambivalence that generally accompanies change, and to experiment with new ways of being.

Example The stoics of ancient Greece proclaimed, "Contemplate death if you would learn how to live." Indeed, we can learn a great deal from those who have faced death or those with near-death experiences. People who are terminally ill often develop a new appreciation for the gift of life and remark on how a "death sentence" awakened them to living as fully as possible. Their confrontation with death results in their getting the most from a relatively brief period of time. The pressure of time forces them to choose how they will spend whatever time they have left. Kinnier, Tribbensee, Rose, and Vaughan (2001) conducted interviews with people who experienced life-threatening situations and found some common themes: less materialism, more spirituality, and more caring for and serving others. Kinnier and his colleagues found that people who have faced death worry less about mundane issues and become more optimistic about the future of humankind.

This framework can be applied to group work, including those who are very young and those who have not experienced a life-threatening event. Members can be challenged to look at how they are living right now, and if they are not satisfied with the direction they are moving, they can make new choices. If they accept the reality that they have only a limited time to achieve their personal goals, they may discover a freshness in living.

Irvin Yalom (1980) found that cancer patients in group therapy had the capacity to view their crisis as an opportunity to bring about changes in how they were living. After discovering they had cancer, many of these individuals experienced the following inner changes that enabled them to find a powerful focus on life:

- A rearrangement of life's priorities; avoiding getting caught up in insignificant matters
- A sense of liberation; being able to choose the things they most wanted to do
- An increased sense of living in the present moment; living less for the future
- A vivid appreciation of the basic facts of life; noticing various aspects of nature
- A deeper communication with loved ones than before the crisis
- Fewer interpersonal fears, less concern over security, and more willingness to take risks (p. 35)

Group members do not have to wait until they are diagnosed with a terminal illness to begin living the way they would like. Members and leaders of a variety of groups can, however, learn a great deal from groups for cancer patients and others who are exploring end-of-life challenges.

For an existential perspective on addressing death in the therapeutic setting, Barnett's (2008) book, *When Death Enters the Therapeutic Space*, provides many useful insights. In Irvin Yalom's (2005) work, *The Schopenhauer Cure: A Novel*, a group therapist is confronted with his own mortality and is forced to examine the meaning of his life and work. In *Staring at the Sun: Overcoming the Terror of Death*, Yalom (2008) develops the idea that confronting death enables us to live in a more compassionate way.

THE SEARCH FOR MEANING

The struggle for a sense of significance and purpose in life is a distinctively human characteristic. We have the capacity to cultivate meaning and awe in our lives. We can also conceptualize, imagine, invent, communicate, and physically and psychologically enlarge our world (Zur, 2009). We search for meaning and personal identity, and we raise existential questions: "Who am I? How did I get here? Where am I going and why? Why am I here? What gives my life purpose and meaning?" For the existential thinker, life does not have positive meaning in itself; it is up to us to create meaning. Vontress (1996) believes that people all over the world try to understand life. As we struggle in a world that often appears meaningless and even absurd, we challenge long-held values, discover new facets of ourselves, and try to reconcile conflicts and discrepancies. In so doing, we create meaning for ourselves. Vontress (2008) captures the idea that meaning in life is an ongoing process we struggle with throughout our life: "What provides meaning one day may not provide meaning the next, and what has been meaningful to a person throughout life may be meaningless when a person is on his or her deathbed" (p. 158).

Frankl (1963) has devoted his career to developing an existential approach to therapy that is grounded on the role of meaning in life. According to him, the central human concern is to discover meaning that will give one's life direction. On the basis of his clinical work and study, Frankl has concluded that a lack of meaning is the major source of existential stress and anxiety in modern times. He views **existential neurosis** as the experience of meaninglessness. Many people come to therapy because of an **existential vacuum**, a feeling of inner void that results from not fully addressing issues of meaning. Therefore, according to Frankl, the function of therapy is to help clients create meaning in their lives.

There are many ways of creating meaning—through work, through loving, through suffering, or through doing for others. According to Frankl, the therapist's task is not to tell clients what their particular meaning in life should be but to encourage clients to develop meaning for themselves. He believes that even suffering can be a source of growth and that if we have the courage to experience our suffering we can find meaning in it. Suffering can be turned into achievement by the stand we take in the face of it. Frankl discovered this in his own experience in the death camps. By confronting pain, despair, and death, and by trying to understand their meaning for us, we turn the negative sides of life into triumph.

Implications for Group Work It is common for groups to explore both the issue of creating meaning and the related question of examining and perhaps discarding values that are no longer meaningful. Many participants are concerned about leaving old values without finding new and more suitable ones to replace them. Some people live by a value system that they have never critically evaluated, one that was handed down to them. Others have lost their identity by conforming to social mores. This issue comes alive within the group, where there is considerable pressure to conform to the expectations of others.

One of the tasks of the therapeutic process is to confront group members with evidence of the fact that they are living by unexamined values that no longer contribute to a meaningful existence. We may not be responsible for having acquired values that don't give us a sense of meaning, but we are certainly responsible for clinging to them and for failing to find new ones. Some useful questions that can be explored in a group setting are these:

- Do you like the direction of your life? If not, what are you doing about it?
- What are the aspects of your life that satisfy you most?
- What is preventing you from doing what you really want to do?

With the support of the group, participants can find the strength to create an internally derived value system that is consistent with their way of being. This process will likely generate anxiety, at least for a time, and they may flounder in the absence of clear-cut values. The leader's job is to remind members that learning to develop the self-trust necessary to look within, discover one's own values, and live by them is a long and difficult process that requires determination and patience.

Group work is especially valuable for older persons as a way of assisting them in putting their lives into perspective, in consolidating the meaning of their life experiences, and in finding new meaning. Finding meaning in life takes on special urgency as we experience the losses associated with aging.

> Loss is the existential given of old age. We wake every day to face a way of being for which we are never prepared. Our minds, our bodies, our loved ones, our surroundings, our habitual ways of dealing with difficulties, our place in our social network, our status, our work, our self-definitions disintegrate in our hands as we struggle to hold them together. (Bugental, 2008, p. 334)

Elizabeth Bugental (2008) describes a group for elders she leads as "swimming together in a sea of loss." Her groups are composed of eight elders between the ages of 65 and 90 who meet once a week for eight weeks. The group sessions are loosely structured around existential themes concerning personal experiences with aging and loss. The themes are presented in the form of questions such as the following that group members explore together:

- How did I get to be this old?
- How can I create a new old age?
- Who am I now?
- How can I stay connected?
- How can I fill my life with beauty, goodness, wonder, and truth?
- Do I have the courage to find new possibilities in the midst of loss?

Although this is not a therapy group, it is very therapeutic. Members share their stories, especially those surrounding many different kinds of loss. Members are asked to stay in the here-and-now as much as possible. As group members express their feelings and receive understanding, they discover common bonds with one another. An overall theme guiding the group is "How do we choose to live during our final phase of life?"

Example Priscilla was reared with conventional values, and she had never really questioned them. She felt compelled to be a "proper lady" at all times, as if her parents were watching over her shoulder. Whenever Priscilla was doing something she thought her parents wouldn't approve of, she seemed to "hear mother and father speaking," telling her what she *should* do and what she *ought* to feel. In various group exercises, Priscilla "became" her parents and spoke for them by lecturing each of us about how we ought to change our ways.

At one point I urged her to act as if she had no choice but to remain forever the nice and proper lady her parents expected her to be and asked her to exaggerate this ladylike behavior in the group for several sessions. Afterward she reported that it "made me sick" to be so rigid and so ready to conform. She decided she would change, no matter how difficult the task was going to be. Although Priscilla still respected some of the core values she had learned at home, she wanted the freedom to discard others even if it resulted in her feeling guilty. Her work in the group and outside of it gave her new freedom to develop her own set of values—values that were meaningful to her and that freed her to live by her own expectations rather than by those of others.

THE SEARCH FOR AUTHENTICITY

The theologian Paul Tillich (1952) uses the phrase "the courage to be" to define a courage that can take all forms of "nonbeing" into itself because it is based on the ground of being. Such a grounding both centers our being and gives us the power to be self-transcending. It is a courage that "allows us to accept our acceptance."

Discovering, creating, and maintaining the core deep within our being is a difficult and never-ending struggle. Van Deurzen (2002a) suggests that such authentic living is more of a process than a static end result. Living authentically entails engagement in doing what is worthwhile as we see it. Briefly put, it means that we are true to ourselves. This kind of living can provide a deep sense of inner peace, yet authenticity is no easy matter. It is only when we stop trying to be cured of the paradoxes of life, van Deurzen reminds us, that we can be truly alive.

When we lead an *authentic existence,* we are constantly becoming the person we are capable of becoming. Living authentically also entails knowing and accepting our limits. The "Serenity Prayer" offers a good example of this knowledge and acceptance: "God grant me the serenity to accept the things I cannot change, courage to change the things I can, and wisdom to know the difference."

A quote with a different twist that Frankl (1963) is fond of using is Goethe's admonition: "If we take man as he is, we make him worse; but if we take him as he should be, we help him become what he can be." Frankl sees it as the therapist's task to challenge clients to become their full and authentic selves by engaging in life and making commitments. Logotherapy, being concerned with people's spiritual dimensions and higher aspirations, provides inspiration to continually seek the meaning that is necessary to live authentically. This idea is captured in an adage I discovered in a church in Hawaii: "Who you are is God's gift to you; what you make of yourself is your gift to God."

Those who typically ignore their inner promptings in a perennial quest for conformity lose themselves in the values and standards of others. One of the most common fears expressed by people in groups is that if they take an honest look at themselves they will discover they are empty shells with no core and no substance. Therefore, they are afraid of shedding masks and pretenses because, once those are gone, nothing will be left.

Existential guilt is rooted in the realization that we inevitably fall short of becoming what we could become, which means that we are always in debt to life to some extent. Existential guilt grows out of a sense of incompleteness and the realization that we are viewing life through someone else's eyes. Ultimately, the loss of the sense of being becomes psychological sickness. To the extent that we allow others to design our lives, we experience a restricted existence.

Implications for Group Work A group provides a powerful context in which to look at oneself, decide the degree to which one is a fully functioning person as opposed to reflecting what others expect, and consider what choices might be more authentically one's own. Members can openly share their fears related to living in unfulfilling ways and come to see how they have compromised their integrity. The group offers many opportunities for tackling the tasks of life. Members can gradually discover ways in which they have lost their direction and can begin to be more true to themselves. They will learn that the easy answers others give them to the problems of living do not work well for them. Certainly, existential group leaders will not prescribe simple solutions, for they know that this is inconsistent with helping members live in authentic ways. It is also important for group leaders to be vigilant for members who may try to persuade others in the group to live in a certain way.

A major part of the group counseling experience involves members sorting out for themselves who they are and what identities they have assumed without conscious thought. When people live by outworn identities, their lives lose meaning. An existential group can be instrumental in assisting members to come to a full appreciation of themselves in relation to others. Through the group experience, members see that their identity is not cast in stone but that they can shape their own lives. Group leaders who themselves continue to reshape their personal meanings are an encouragement to the members.

Example Martha, who at 45 had devoted a major portion of her life to her family, is typical of many women who have been members of my groups and personal growth workshops. For most of her life, Martha had depended almost totally on her roles as wife, mother, and homemaker as sources of identity. As her daughters and sons entered high school and then college and finally left home, she asked herself more and more frequently: "Is there more to life than what I've done so far? Who am I besides all the roles I've responsibly filled? What do I want to do with the rest of my life?"

Martha returned to the university and obtained a degree in human services, a critical turning point in her life that opened many new doors for her. She engaged in a number of projects that enriched her life, including specialized work with the elderly. Through her program of studies, Martha joined several intensive personal growth workshops, which gave her the opportunity to pose and debate questions such as "Do I have the courage to find out if I can create a new identity for myself? Will I be able to withstand pressures from my family to remain the way they want me to be? Can I give to others and at the same time give to myself?" These questions indicated Martha's growing awareness that she needed to be a person in her own right and that she wanted to live an authentic existence. Martha's self-questioning also showed that she knew that making choices entails doubts and struggles that one must resolve for oneself.

ALONENESS AND RELATEDNESS

Existential group practitioners believe that even though we have close friends we are ultimately alone—that only we can give a sense of meaning to our lives, decide how we will live, find our own answers, and decide whether we will be or not be. *Existential isolation* refers to our aloneness in the universe. Even though we find meaning in connections with others, we enter the world alone and we leave the world alone. We must manage the tension between our wish for relatedness with others and the reality of our aloneness (Yalom & Josselson, 2011). Because awareness of our *ultimate aloneness* can be frightening, some of us try to avoid it by throwing ourselves into casual relationships and frantic activities, trusting that they will numb us to our fears and anguish.

We also have the choice of experiencing our aloneness and trying to find a center of meaning and direction within ourselves. When we make this choice and succeed at establishing our own identity, we can relate genuinely and meaningfully to others. We must stand alone before we can truly stand with another. **Solitude**, unlike aloneness, is something that we can choose for ourselves. In solitude, we make time to be with ourselves, to discover who we are, and to renew ourselves (Corey & Corey, 2010).

There is a paradox in the proposition that we are existentially both alone and related. Yet it is this very paradox that describes the human condition. Zur (2009) reminds us that we come to terms with our sense of loneliness, even in the midst of community. We are social beings, and we depend on interpersonal relationships for our humanness. We have a desire for meaningful connections, a hope to be significant in another's world, and a desire to feel that another's presence is important in our world. But unless we can find our own strength within ourselves, we cannot have nourishing relationships with others based on fulfillment rather than deprivation.

Implications for Group Work Group participants have the opportunity to relate to others in meaningful ways, to learn to be themselves in the company of other people, and to find reward and nourishment in the relationships they establish. They also learn that it is not in others that they find the answers to questions about significance and purpose in life. If their struggle for self-awareness is successful, they come to realize that no matter how valuable their relationships are they are ultimately on their own.

The relationships that participants establish within the group are valuable also because they teach people how to relate to others outside of the group. In a group, people recognize their own struggles in others, and this often results in a bond. Even though they may accept that ultimately they are existentially alone, they also come to realize that they are not alone in their struggles and that others, too, are courageously looking at themselves and trying to establish their own identities. In short, groups offer distinct possibilities for members to intimately relate to one another that individual therapy does not offer.

Example The case of Zeke shows that a person can be with others and at the same time be very much alone. In a group session, Zeke said that he felt cut off from everyone in the group and described himself as a "spectator who seems out of place." I asked him if he would be willing to experiment with really separating himself from the group and observing us from a distance. He agreed to leave the room, sit outside on the balcony, and observe what was going on through the window. I asked him to be aware of what he was thinking and feeling as he sat out there observing. He was told to return to the group when he was ready to talk about what he had experienced sitting on the outside.

When he returned, Zeke said that for the first time he had realized how safe it was for him to keep himself in a spectator role and that he was ready to do something different. I asked him if he would go around to each person in the group and complete these two sentences: "One way I have kept you at a distance is by _____." and "One way I could be closer to you is by _____." After he had "made the rounds," Zeke described the circumstances in which he typically felt alone, even when surrounded by many people. He spoke of his desire to achieve intimacy and of his fears of approaching people. His work in the group had intensified his attempts to keep himself separate, which finally resulted in a desire to change.

Role and Functions of the Group Leader

According to Schneider and Krug (2010), existential-humanistic therapists assist clients in addressing their concerns, not just behaviorally and intellectually but experientially, by maximizing their capacity to transform themselves. To achieve these aims, existential practitioners draw upon existential conditions through which experiential liberation and profound transformation can take root. In the existential view, therapy is a partnership and a shared venture between the therapist and the client. To develop this collaborative partnership, therapists focus on the person-to-person relationship. Existential therapists must bring their own subjectivity into their work, and it is essential that they demonstrate presence if they are to develop an effective working relationship with members. High priority is given to the quality of the therapeutic relationship as a healing force, with an emphasis on I/Thou encounters and dialogue (Cain, 2002). A central role of existential leaders is to create a therapeutic alliance, for it is assumed that change comes from the relationship itself. (As you will see in Chapters 10 and 11, the relationship is also the core of the person-centered approach and of Gestalt therapy.)

Bugental (1997) sees the main task of existential therapy as being to increase both the range and the depth of clients' awareness. He adds that a therapist's function is to display to clients the ways in which they constrict their awareness and the cost of such constrictions. This climate for change will not come about if the leader maintains a strictly objective orientation, is psychologically absent from the group, and is merely a skilled but impersonal technician.

Change is brought about not only by the relationship with the leader but also by relationships with other members. A primary role of the leader is to foster meaningful relationships among participants by having members focus on key existential concerns and by providing a climate in which these concerns can be fully explored. According to Yalom and Josselson (2011) existential group therapists value being real and are willing to make themselves known through appropriate self-disclosure. Group leaders are *fellow travelers* in the sense that they must come to terms with the ultimate existential concerns of life. A therapeutic community is thus established based on the commonality of universal struggles.

Existential group leaders assume a basic role of encouraging members to assess ways their freedom may be restricted, reflect on how they might increase their choices, and assume responsibility for their choices. Cain (2002) writes: "Clients are challenged to wrestle with the basic question of how they are living, face the givens of their existence, confront the associated anxiety, and learn to live more fully, authentically, and responsibly" (p. 24). Van Deurzen (2010) claims that existential therapists do not have the role of addressing the practical aspects and problems of a person's life; rather, "we focus on the person's struggle with human existence and elucidate the parameters of the human condition that the person is trying to come to terms with. We help them to get better at reflecting on their situation, deal with their dilemma, face their predicament and think for themselves" (p. 236).

Sharp and Bugental (2001) emphasize that the cornerstone of existential therapeutic work is the attention that is paid to *presence*. The therapist's job is to draw attention to what interferes with the client's presence and to invite him or her to recognize and deal with resistances to change. A group can be instrumental in helping members see how some of the self-constricting patterns they manifest in the group are paralleled in their everyday life. By gaining a better understanding of how they are in the group, members have a basis for increasing their awareness of their way of being in the world.

Application: Therapeutic Techniques and Procedures

Unlike many other group approaches, the existential model puts more emphasis on experiencing and understanding the group member in the present moment than on using a particular set of techniques. May (1983) emphasizes that technique follows understanding. Overemphasis on technique can block the therapist's ability to understand the client's subjective world. There are no "right" techniques in this approach; the task is accomplished through the therapeutic encounter and dialogue between client and therapist. It is not theories and techniques that heal, but the encounter that occurs between client and therapist as they work together (Elkins, 2007). Emphasis is on understanding and exploring the client's subjective reality rather than diagnosis, treatment, and prognosis (van Deurzen (2002b).

The interventions therapists employ are based on philosophical views about the essential nature of human existence. Vontress (1996) uses the phrase "Socratic dialogue" to describe his holistic intervention strategy, which addresses simultaneously the psychological, sociological, physical, and spiritual dimensions of human existence. Rejecting the term *eclectic*, Vontress will sometimes draw on phenomenological, cognitive, behavioral, and psychoanalytic insights during a single session with a client. Existential group therapists may incorporate a variety of techniques from various therapeutic approaches, but they do not employ an array of unintegrated techniques. A set of assumptions and attitudes guide their interventions.

Van Deurzen (2010) stresses the importance of therapists reaching sufficient depth and openness in their own lives to enable them to venture into their clients' subjective world without losing their own sense of identity. Van Deurzen reminds us that existential therapy is a collaborative adventure in which both client and therapist will be transformed if they allow themselves to be touched by life. She encourages therapists to use interventions that reflect their own personality and style but to remain flexible in relation to what their clients need.

Van Deurzen (2010) suggests several kinds of interventions, including the therapeutic use of silence, questions, and making interpretations:

- *Silence* is one of the most significant interventions a therapist can make. There needs to be a breathing space in between dialogue. Therapists have the task of listening with a receptive attitude so that clients can move forward in a way of their choosing.

- *Questions* have a place in therapy, yet they need to be based on what clients are saying rather than probing for more information. It is best for therapists to ask open-ended questions that are implied in the client's words and in the subtext of their messages.

- *Interpretations* are used in existential therapy as a way to make sense of the client's overall story by connecting individual statements and experiences to enhance meaning. Van Deurzen (2010) sums up the essence of this intervention thusly: "The duty of the existential therapist is to see to it that interpretations are made within the framework of meaning of the client, rather than within the framework of meaning of the therapist. The puzzle to be completed is the client's, not our own" (p. 293). Because existential counseling is a philosophical investigation, van Deurzen (2002a) views the existential practitioner as a mentor in the art of living, one who is more of a sage than a brilliant technician.

Group practitioners who work within an existential framework often use many of the techniques described in this book. Many of the procedures used by Adlerians and the techniques used by psychodramatists fit with an existential philosophy beautifully. Furthermore, it is possible to have an existential orientation that guides the interventions of a group leader and still rely heavily on techniques from transactional analysis, cognitive behavior therapy, rational emotive behavior therapy, reality therapy, and solution-focused brief therapy. The techniques of these action-oriented therapeutic approaches can be grounded on existential concepts. However, existential group counselors never use techniques as the main menu. Instead, primary consideration is given to the nature of the relationships being formed in the group. When the deepest self of the group therapist meets the deepest part of the individual group members in the I/Thou encounter, the group process is at its best.

The leader sets the tone for the group not by introducing techniques and *doing something* but rather by *being* and *becoming* somebody. The group experience can shake up the conventional ways in which members view the world. When their status quo is shaken, members have a better chance of facing themselves and of changing.

Phases of an Existential Group

A therapeutic group is characterized by a creative, evolving process of discovery, which is conceptualized in three general phases. During the initial phase, group counselors assist the participants in identifying and clarifying their assumptions about the world. Group members are invited to define and question the ways in which they perceive and make sense of their existence. They examine their values, beliefs, and assumptions to determine their validity. For many group members this is a difficult task because they may initially present their problems as resulting almost entirely from external causes. They may focus on what other people "make them feel" or on how others are largely responsible for their actions or inaction. The group leader teaches members how to reflect on their own existence and to examine their role in contributing to their problems in living.

During the middle phase of existential group counseling, the members are encouraged to more fully examine the source and authority of their present value system. This process of self-exploration typically leads to new insights and some restructuring of their values and attitudes. Group members get a better idea of what kind of life they consider worthy to live. They develop a clearer sense of their internal valuing process. Van Deurzen (2010) states that existential exploration addresses a spiritual dimension of finding meaning. The focus is on core life issues, and clients deal with moral issues of living.

The final phase focuses on helping members put what they are learning about themselves into action. The aim of a group experience is to empower the participants to implement their examined and internalized values in concrete ways. Through a therapeutic group experience, members are able to discover their strengths and put these capabilities to the service of living a meaningful existence.

Existential group counseling focuses on exploring options to help members create a meaningful life. For many of us, recognition of the ways in which we have kept ourselves in a victimlike stance marks the beginning of change. Through the group process, we begin to understand that we can choose to consciously become the authors of our lives.

Applying the Existential Approach to Group Work in Schools

The existential approach has a great deal to offer when counseling adolescents in groups because they face so many existential challenges today. From elementary to high school level, violence is becoming more commonplace, and school counselors are called upon for crisis intervention and to devise programs to prevent violence. When tragedies do occur, these young people are certainly awakened to the reality of death. Such occurrences are a stark reminder that we do not know how much time we have on this earth and that we may not be able to accomplish our dreams. A crisis-oriented group gives students opportunities to verbally express their shock, grief, anger, and fear.

During a period of crisis, existential themes involving death and nonbeing, life's meaning, and existential anxiety become very real. It is not necessary for those who conduct a school group to process feelings surrounding violence to come up with answers or to bring closure to such issues; rather, the leader can provide a valuable function by encouraging students to give full expression to their feelings and thoughts. Group members can acknowledge their common concerns and provide support in a time when it is sorely needed. Such a group can be a catalyst for young people to assess their lives and do what they can to make life-affirming choices. Groups can be a rich source of healing, for both young people in the group and the counselor who facilitates the open expression of reactions. Exploring the existential anxiety surrounding the unknown is a main task of a group with a crisis-oriented focus.

Existential concepts can be incorporated in groups with adolescents in other ways as well. One of my colleagues, Conrad, is a social worker at a middle school. He facilitates several different kinds of groups, including a bereavement group that he started in response to a number of students who had to cope with the death of a parent. Conrad finds that these junior high students are able to process a wide range of feelings and reactions associated with a significant loss, that they can be a genuine source of support for one another, and that they are able to begin healing from losses. As is the case for crisis-oriented groups, the members of Conrad's groups are challenged to reflect on their own mortality, to talk about their fears of death, and to explore what really counts in their lives. Conrad reports that his level of presence and compassion with the students is far more important than any techniques or exercises he might introduce.

Most key concepts of the existential approach have relevance for a wide variety of groups with both children and adolescents. Young people struggle with issues of freedom and responsibility, existential anxiety around the unpredictable nature of life, the reality of death, question the true purpose of their lives, and reflect on striving for authenticity. Even a psychoeducational group or a short-term school group can reach more depth if the group leader learns to listen for the existential underpinnings that form the concerns of the members. In addition to teaching coping skills or acquiring certain information, a group can be instrumental in beginning a reflection process that encourages young people to take seriously the existential challenges of their existence. In working with school-age students, the emphasis needs to be placed on personal responsibility and the choices they make. In talking about members' changes within the group, it is important to build an internal locus of control by processing the choices members make and the actions they take.

Applying the Existential Approach With Multicultural Populations

The existential approach emphasizes presence, the I/Thou relationship, and courage. As such, it can be effectively applied with diverse client populations with a range of specific problems and in a wide array of settings (Schneider & Krug, 2010). Van Deurzen (2010) points out that existential therapists are willing to shift their stance when the situation requires it, especially in cross-cultural counseling situations. Existential therapists attempt to free themselves of their preconceptions and prejudices as much as possible. They respect the uniqueness of the particular situation of each client and do not impose their cultural values on the client. Assuming an existential orientation does not mean that we have to preach to group members about the values of self-awareness, choice, and responsibility.

The existential approach is particularly relevant for multicultural situations because it does not impose particular values and meanings; rather, it investigates the values and meanings of group members. Existential group counselors respect the different elements that make up a member's philosophy of life. With this understanding of different worldviews, group practitioners are in a position to establish mutually agreed-upon goals with individuals that will provide a direction for change.

Vontress (2008) believes existential therapy is especially useful in working with culturally different populations because of its focus on universality, or the similarities we all share. He encourages counselors-in-training to focus on the universal commonalities of clients first and secondarily on areas of differences. He believes that is it essential to recognize and address both the ways we are alike and the ways we are different.

Those people who are willing to participate in a group are frequently experiencing psychological pain. Faced with a crisis and feeling helpless, they often experience their lives as being out of their control. Some individuals simply believe that they do not have a choice or that choice is mainly a middle-class notion. Even if they do have some freedom, societal factors (such as racism, discrimination, and lack of opportunity) may severely restrict their ability to choose for themselves. Existentially oriented group leaders would do well to take into account the sociocultural factors that restrict choices. Clients who come from the barrio or an inner-city environment, for example, may be motivated primarily by the need for safety and survival and may be seeking help in getting these basic needs met. Simply *telling* people they have a choice in making their life better will not help, and it is likely to have a negative impact. Premature assurances that we are all free to give meaning to our lives will seem like insensitive clichés. It is real-life issues that provide grist for the mill for group work, assuming that the leader is willing to deal with them. Developing interventions that can help the group member take action, even if it is only small steps toward change, can have a significant impact on a client's life in the long run (van Deurzen, 2010).

Pack-Brown, Whittington-Clark, and Parker (1998) maintain that existential approaches will resonate with many African American women, mainly because they encounter many difficult realities, suffering, and pain. Here are a few specific existential factors that often resonate with African American women:

- Life can be unfair and unjust.
- Ultimately there is no escape from pain and death.
- In spite of intimacy with others, one must still face life alone.
- The core challenge is to face and deal with basic issues of life and death.
- We must assume the ultimate responsibility for how we are living, regardless of the support and guidance we may get from others.

These authors state that the Afrocentric approach addresses the illumination and liberation of the spirit and focuses on the principles of harmony within the universe as a natural order of existence.

In an individual's search for a meaningful existence, spiritual values should be viewed as a potential resource. For many clients, spirituality can be a powerful force in fostering healing through an exploration of self by learning to accept oneself, forgiving others and oneself, admitting one's shortcomings, accepting personal responsibility, letting go of resentments, and dealing with guilt. Clearly, spirituality is an existential issue in group work.

Wide-ranging international interest is currently focused on the existential approach (van Deurzen, personal communication, February 8, 2009). The International Collaborative of Existential Counsellors and Psychotherapists (ICECAP) meets online and hosts international conferences. Existential organizations and training programs have emerged in Israel, Portugal, China, Singapore, and Australia. Several Scandinavian societies (Sweden, Denmark, and Norway) are dedicated to promoting existential therapy, and the existential movement is gaining in popularity throughout eastern European society (including Estonia, Latvia, Lithuania, Russia, Ukraine, and Belarus). Mexican and South American societies also have been established to promote the existential approach. The existential movement in the United Kingdom is thriving, and several doctoral programs are offered. These international developments confirm that existential therapy has wide appeal for diverse populations in many parts of the world.

Evaluation of the Existential Approach to Groups

CONTRIBUTIONS AND STRENGTHS OF THE APPROACH

I value many features of the existential approach and have incorporated them in my practice. I work on the basic assumption that people have the capacity to become increasingly self-aware and that expansion of awareness results in greater freedom to choose their own direction in life. I share the existentialists' view that we are not driven by instinctual forces, nor are we merely the products of conditioning. I base my group work on the assumption that people do not have to remain victims of their past or of the external world and that they have the power to decide for themselves and take action, at least to some extent. The existential approach is useful in a wide range of groups for victims of rape, battering, crime, and various other forms of abuse. Although I agree that people can indeed be victims of forces outside of themselves, I also believe that existential therapy can help such individuals reclaim or acquire a sense of power so they can be survivors rather than remaining victims. This approach is largely about empowerment of individuals.

I value the existential perspective because it has brought the person back into a central place and because it addresses itself to the basic question of what it means to be human. This approach humanizes psychotherapy and reduces the chances of its becoming a mechanical process in the hands of technicians. I especially value the emphasis on the therapist's being fully present in the therapeutic encounter. Bugental (1987) maintains that through the therapist's concern, sensitivity, and presence, individuals are invited to disclose the core life issues with which they are struggling. If therapists are not personally involved in their work, their clients will not be supported as they endure the painful and frightening self-confrontations that are necessary for major life changes to occur.

This approach allows me as a group leader to bring my own experiences and my very humanness to my group work. I cannot help group participants face their existential concerns without doing the same in my own life. I like the notion of the group leader being a fellow traveler who struggles with existential concerns just as do the members. My willingness to remain open to my own struggles determines the degree to which I can be a significant and positive influence for others in a group.

An important contribution of the existential approach is the notion that techniques follow understanding. In my view, this basic concept lessens the danger of misusing techniques. Too often leaders use techniques merely to "get things going" in a group. When the emphasis is on understanding the world of the participant, the leader's first concern is with genuinely grasping the core struggles of others and then drawing on certain techniques to help participants explore these struggles more fully. Because existentially oriented group leaders can draw from the techniques of most of the other approaches discussed in this book, they can develop a highly flexible therapeutic style that is suitable for a variety of groups. Not only do I view the relationship-oriented and experiential approaches as being compatible with an existential orientation, but I also think **cognitive behavioral therapies** (the Adlerian approach, transactional analysis, cognitive behavior therapy, rational emotive behavior therapy, reality therapy, and solution-focused brief therapy) can be productively used along with an existential foundation.

Van Deurzen (2002a, 2002b) identifies the clients and problems most suited to an existential approach as those who are interested in and committed to dealing with their problems about living. The approach has particular relevance for people who feel alienated from the current expectations of society or for those who are searching for meaning in their lives. It tends to work well with people who are at a crossroads, coping with the changes of personal circumstances such as bereavement or loss of employment. Van Deurzen (2002b) believes existential therapy works better with individuals who are willing to challenge the status quo in the world. She maintains that this approach can be useful for people who are on the edge of existence: those who are dying, those working through a developmental or situational crisis, those who no longer feel they belong in their surroundings, or those who are starting a new phase of life.

A particular strength of the existential approach is its focus on spirituality and meaning in life. Some group members cannot be understood without appreciating the central role their religious or spiritual beliefs and practices exert in daily life. Universal concerns about freedom and responsibility, anxiety, guilt, and the relationship of death to finding purpose in life can all be explored in an existential group. If spirituality or religious values are important in the group members' lives, then such concerns should be addressed and can be integrated with other therapeutic tools to enhance the process of a therapeutic group. However, these values should never be imposed on the group by the leader.

Bugental and Bracke (1992) write that the value and vitality of a psychotherapeutic approach depend on its ability to help clients deal with the sources of pain and dissatisfaction in their lives. They contend that the existential orientation is particularly suited to offering meaningful assistance to individuals who are experiencing a lack of a centered awareness of being. Cushman (1990) has written about the *empty self*—whose emptiness results from failing to listen to our internal voice or from not trusting our sense of direction. This emptiness is manifested in several ways: through depression, through the absence of a purpose for life, through a lack of clear priorities, through addiction to food or drugs, and through other means of striving to fill the void. Frankl (1963) refers to this condition of emptiness as an "existential vacuum." Many group members describe feeling as if there is a hole in their lives, and even though they attempt to fill this emptiness of self, they are not successful. Unless they confront their fears and the sources that are blocking their ability to live fully, they are likely to strive in vain to numb the pain created by this inner void. An existential group can be instrumental in encouraging members to face themselves courageously and deal with the inauthentic aspects of their lives. Group members can learn that the greatest peace of mind comes from listening to themselves and being true to themselves (Vontress, 2008).

Group work has a distinct advantage over dyadic existential therapy. Existential group counseling is comprehensive; it includes a consideration of the "worlds" in which people live. One of the most important of these worlds is the *Mitwelt,* the interpersonal environment in which we relate to others. The idea of human connectedness is universal (Vontress, 2008). From infancy to old age, we need others and develop a sense of empathy with others. We are fulfilled by fellowship with other people and are influenced by continued contact with others. People who learn to relate to others usually have little trouble relating to themselves. However, before people can relate meaningfully to others, they need to know and have a good relationship with themselves. The interpersonal perspective of the existential approach to group work is well suited to this process of discovery (Vontress, 1996).

Exploring the deeper layers of human existence is an involved process best suited for a long-term group, but the basic concepts of the existential approach can form the foundation of a short-term, structured group. The existential themes of death and mortality challenge members to examine what they are doing in their lives. Likewise, the reality of a time-limited group can be a catalyst for members to become actively and fully involved in each group session. Strasser and Strasser (1997), who are connected to the British school of existential analysis, maintain that there are clear benefits to time-limited therapy, which mirrors the time-limited reality of human existence. In a time-limited group, the members can be challenged to examine how they are relating to the here-and-now aspect of the group experience. They can be asked to evaluate the degree to which they are fully utilizing the resources within the group and the degree to which they are active in the group. A short-term group can actually help members keep their focus clearly in mind and can encourage them to make optimal use of the limited time they have to accomplish their personal goals.

J. Bugental (2008) indicates that short-term work in existential therapy requires a clearly defined purpose and a limited goal of treatment. A carefully thought out structure is required to maintain maximum gain from such a limited opportunity. Members are asked to present their concerns in a succinct form, and a contract might be designed to work toward resolution of a particular concern. Sharp and Bugental (2001) believe that this short-term focus is often a compromise necessitated by managed care programs, which are characterized by cost containment, brevity, and quantifiable behavioral change. Zur (2009) has observed that this focus emphasizes instant results and appearances. However, existential psychology teaches us that speed and quick-fixes will not provide us with freedom and meaning in life. Most of the existential themes considered in this chapter would be viewed as being too abstract, complex, and amorphous to fit within a managed care context.

Yalom and Josselson (2011) capture the essence of the contemporary value of the existential approach: "Our present age is one of disintegration of cultural and historic mores, of love and marriage, the family, the inherited religions, and so forth. Given these realities, the existential emphasis on meaning, responsibility, and living a finite life fully will become increasingly important" (p. 340).

LIMITATIONS OF THE APPROACH

Many existentialist concepts are quite abstract and difficult to apply in practice. Existential theorists such as Kierkegaard, Heidegger, and Sartre were not writing for group counselors and therapists! Existentialism began as a formal philosophical movement, and although it eventually led to existential approaches within both psychology and psychiatry, its philosophical nature still dominates. Both beginning and advanced group practitioners who are not of a philosophical turn of mind tend to find many of the existential concepts lofty, abstract, and elusive. Even those group counselors who are sympathetic to the core ideas of this perspective sometimes struggle with knowing how to apply these concepts to the practice of group work. It is not so much a matter of applying existentialist philosophy as it is a matter of educating group leaders on the concrete and practical issues of life that are relevant to all human beings.

As van Deurzen (1990a) points out, some existential therapists tend to emphasize the cognitive aspects of a client's concerns, and some clients are attracted to the approach believing that they can avoid tapping their senses, feelings, and intuitions. She suggests that a good existential therapist would address all these different levels of human experience, believing that openness to exploring these aspects of being is a requisite for self-understanding. Van Deurzen has identified some other limitations of the existential approach:

- It is not particularly relevant for people who are uninterested in examining their basic assumptions and who would rather not explore the foundation of their human existence.

- Those clients who want relief from specific symptoms or who are seeking problem-solving methods will generally not find much value in this orientation.

- The existential therapist functions in the role of a consultant who can provide clients with support in facing up to the truth of their lives. For those who are looking for a therapist who will direct them or who will function as a substitute parent, this approach will have little to offer.

An effective existential practitioner needs to have a great deal of maturity, life experience, and intensive supervision and training. Therapists themselves provide the most limiting factor in existential group work. Van Deurzen (2002b) believes that "existential therapists are required to be wise and capable of profound and wide-ranging understanding of what it means to be human" (p. 198). It is easy to envision the dangers posed by therapists who have a shallow grasp of this approach and who deceive both themselves and their clients into thinking that they possess the requisite wisdom.

Where to Go From Here

The Existential-Humanistic Institute's (EHI) primary focus is training, and courses in existential-humanistic therapy and theory are offered. A secondary focus is community building. EHI was formed as a nonprofit organization under the auspices of the Pacific Institute in 1997 to provide a home for those mental health professionals, scholars, and students who seek in-depth training in existential-humanistic theory and practice.

The Existential-Humanistic Institute, Dr. Kirk Schneider
Website: www.kirkjschneider.com

The Society for Existential Analysis is a professional organization devoted to exploring issues pertaining to an existential/phenomenological approach to counseling and therapy. Membership is open to anyone interested in this approach and includes students, trainees, psychotherapists, philosophers, psychiatrists, counselors, and psychologists. Members receive a regular newsletter and an annual copy of the *Journal of the Society for Existential Analysis.* The society provides a list of existentially oriented psychotherapists for referral purposes. The School of Psychotherapy and Counselling at Regent's College in London offers an advanced diploma in existential psychotherapy as well as short courses in the field.

Society for Existential Analysis
BM Existential
London WCIN 3XX
England
Telephone: 07000 47 33 37
E-mail: info@existentialanalysis.co.uk/
Website: http://www.existentialanalysis.co.uk/

Other useful websites are listed below:

Dilemma Consultancy Limited
Website: www.dilemmas.org
Psychotherapy Training
Website: www.existentialpsychotherapy.net

The International Collaborative of Existential Counsellors and Psychotherapists (ICECAP) meets online and sponsors international conferences. ICECAP exists to promote the appreciation, understanding, and growth of existential and phenomenological psychotherapy through publications, events, and colloquia. ICECAP provides a platform for the international registration of existential practitioners through the European Association for Psychotherapy and the World Council for Psychotherapy.

International Collaborative of Existential Counsellors and Psychotherapists (ICECAP)
Website: http://www.icecap.org.uk

Septimus is an Internet-based course that is taught in Ireland, Iceland, Sweden, Poland, Czech Republic, Romania, Italy, Portugal, and the United Kingdom.

Psychotherapy Training on the Net—Septimus
Website: www.septimus.info

The New School of Psychotherapy and Counselling (NSPC) is a training institute set up especially for the training of existential therapists, which offers a DPsych in Existential Counselling Psychology and Psychotherapy and a DProf in Existential Psychotherapy and Counselling, both as joint programs with Middlesex University. NSPC offers intensive courses for distance learners (worldwide student body) including e-learning.

New School of Psychotherapy and Counselling
Royal Waterloo House
51-55 Waterloo Road
London SE1 8TX
England
020 7928 43 44
E-mail: Admin@nspc.org.uk
Website: www.nspc.org.uk

For an online course that focuses on contemporary trends within existential-humanistic psychotherapy, consult the Zur Institute.

Zur Institute
E-mail: info@zurinstitute.com

AUTHOR LECTURES

Watch *Gerald Corey's Perspectives on Theory and Practice of Group Counseling* DVD or visit the *Theory and Practice of Group Counseling* CourseMate website at www.cengagebrain.com/shop/ISBN/0840033869 to watch videos of Dr. Gerald Corey presenting lectures for each chapter. Also available are unique eAudio lectures for each chapter and quiz questions for self study.

RECOMMENDED SUPPLEMENTARY READINGS

No books that I am aware of deal explicitly and exclusively with the application of the existential approach to group counseling. However, the books listed here contain related material that you can use to apply this approach to your work with groups.

Everyday Mysteries: A Handbook of Existential Psychotherapy (van Deurzen, 2010) provides a framework for practicing counseling from an existential perspective. The author puts into clear perspective topics such as anxiety, authentic living, clarifying one's worldview, determining values, discovering meaning, and coming to terms with life.

Existential-Humanistic Therapy (Schneider & Krug, 2010) provides a clear presentation of the theory and practice of existential-humanistic therapy. This approach allows for incorporating techniques from other contemporary therapeutic approaches.

Existential-Integrative Psychotherapy (Schneider, 2008) is an edited book that offers recent and future trends in existential-integrative therapy and case illustrations of this model as well.

Existential Therapies (Cooper, 2003) provides a useful and clear introduction to the existential therapies. There are separate chapters on logotherapy, the British school of existential analysis, the American existential-humanistic approach, dimensions of existential therapeutic practice, and brief existential therapies.

When Death Enters the Therapeutic Space: Existential Perspectives in Psychotherapy and Counselling (Barnett, 2008) offers insights into working therapeutically with mortality. This book presents an existential perspective for working with a variety of client groups who have experienced a confrontation with mortality.

Existential Psychotherapy (Yalom, 1980) is a superb treatment of ultimate human concerns of death, freedom, isolation, and meaninglessness as these issues relate to therapy. This book has depth and clarity, and it is rich with clinical examples that illustrate existential themes. If you were to select just one book on existential therapy, this would be my recommendation.

The Schopenhauer Cure: A Novel (Yalom, 2005) describes the work of a group run along existential parameters in the form of a novel. Key points such as lack of commitment to the group, intragroup sexual relationships, envy and anger, and facing the death of the group therapist are dealt with in this made-up group.

I Never Knew I Had a Choice (Corey & Corey, 2010) is a self-help book written from an existential perspective. It contains many exercises and activities that leaders can use for their group work and that they can suggest as "homework assignments" between sessions. The topics covered include our struggle to achieve autonomy; the roles that work, love, sexuality, intimacy, and solitude play in our lives; the meaning of loneliness, death, and loss; and the ways in which we choose our values and philosophy of life.

REFERENCES AND SUGGESTED READINGS

*Barnett, L. (Ed.). (2008). *When death enters the therapeutic space: Existential perspectives in psychotherapy and counselling.* New York: Routledge.

Brown, L. S. (2008). Feminist therapy as a meaning-making practice: Where there is no power, where is the meaning? In K. J. Schneider (Ed.), *Existential-integrative psychotherapy: Guideposts to the core of practice* (pp. 130–140). New York: Routledge.

Bugental, E. K. (2008). Swimming together in a sea of loss: A group process for elders. In K. J. Schneider (Ed.), *Existential-integrative psychotherapy: Guideposts to the core of practice* (pp. 333–342). New York: Routledge.

*Bugental, J.F.T. (1987). *The art of the psychotherapist.* New York: Norton.

*Bugental, J.F.T. (1997). There is a fundamental division in how psychotherapy is conceived. In J. K. Zeig (Ed.), *The evolution of psychotherapy: The third conference* (pp. 185–196). New York: Brunner/ Mazel.

Bugental, J.F.T. (2008). Preliminary sketches for a short-term existential-humanistic therapy. In K. J. Schneider (Ed.), *Existential-integrative psychotherapy: Guideposts to the core of practice* (pp. 165–168). New York: Routledge.

Bugental, J.F.T., & Bracke, P. E. (1992). The future of existential-humanistic psychotherapy. *Psychotherapy 29*(1), 28–33.

---

* Books and articles marked with an asterisk (*) are suggested for further study.

*Cain, D. J. (2002). Defining characteristics, history, and evolution of humanistic psychotherapies. In D. J. Cain, & J. Seeman (Eds.), *Humanistic psychotherapies: Handbook of research and practice* (pp. 3–54). Washington, DC: American Psychological Association.

*Cooper, M. (2003). *Existential therapies.* London: Sage.

*Corey, G., & Corey, M. (2010). *I never knew I had a choice* (9th ed.). Belmont, CA: Brooks/Cole, Cengage Learning.

Cushman, P. (1990). Why the self is empty: Toward a historically situated psychology. *American Psychologist, 45*(5), 599–611.

*Deurzen, E. van. (1990a). *Existential therapy.* London: Society for Existential Analysis.

Deurzen, E. van. (1990b). What is existential analysis? *Journal of the Society for Existential Analysis, 1,* 6–14.

Deurzen, E. van. (1991). Ontological insecurity revisited. *Journal of the Society for Existential Analysis, 2,* 38–48.

*Deurzen, E. van. (2002a). *Existential counselling & psychotherapy in practice* (2nd ed.). London: Sage.

Deurzen, E. van. (2002b). Existential therapy. In W. Dryden (Ed.), *Handbook of individual therapy* (4th ed., pp. 179–208). London: Sage.

Deurzen, E. van. (2009). *Psychotherapy and the quest for happiness.* London: Sage.

*Deurzen, E. van. (2010). *Everyday mysteries: A handbook of existential psychotherapy* (2nd ed.). London: Routledge.

Deurzen, E. van, & Arnold-Baker, C. (2005). *Existential perspectives on human issues: A handbook for practice.* London: Palgrave, Macmillan.

Deurzen, E. van, & Kenward, R. (2005). *Dictionary of existential psychotherapy and counselling.* London: Sage.

Deurzen, E. van, & Young, S. (2009) *Existential perspectives on supervision: Broadening the horizon of psychotherapy and counselling,* London: Palgrave Macmillan.

Elkins, D. (2007). Empirically supported treatments: The deconstruction of a myth. *Journal of Humanistic Psychology, 47,* 474–500.

*Frankl, V. (1963). *Man's search for meaning.* New York: Washington Square Press.

*Gould, W. B. (1993). *Viktor E. Frankl: Life with meaning.* Belmont, CA: Brooks/Cole, Cengage Learning.

Heidegger, M. (1962). *Being and time* (John Macquarrie & Edward Robinson, Trans.). New York: Harper & Row.

*Kinnier, R. T., Tribbensee, N. E., Rose, C. A., & Vaughan, S. M. (2001). In the final analysis: More wisdom from people who have faced death. *Journal of Counseling and Development, 79*(2), 171–177.

Lantz, J. (1993). Treatment modalities in logotherapy. *International Forum for Logotherapy, 16*(2), 65–73.

*May, R. (1953). *Man's search for himself.* New York: Norton.

May, R. (Ed.). (1961). *Existential psychology.* New York: Random House.

May, R. (1981). *Freedom and destiny.* New York: Norton.

May, R. (1983). *The discovery of being: Writings in existential psychology.* New York: Norton.

Pack-Brown, S. P., Whittington-Clark, L. E., & Parker, W. M. (1998). *Images of me: A guide to group work with African-American women.* Boston: Allyn & Bacon.

Russell, J. M. (1978). Sartre, therapy, and expanding the concept of responsibility. *The American Journal of Psychoanalysis, 38,* 259–269.

*Russell, J. M. (2007). Existential psychotherapy. In A. B. Rochlen (Ed.), *Applying counseling theories: An online case-based approach* (pp. 107–125). Upper Saddle River, NJ: Pearson Prentice-Hall.

Sartre, J. P. (1971). *Being and nothingness.* New York: Bantam.

*Schneider, K. J. (Ed.). (2008). *Existential-integrative psychotherapy: Guideposts to the core of practice.* New York: Routledge.

* Schneider, K. J., & Krug, O. T. (2010). *Existential-humanistic therapy.*

Washington, DC: American Psychological Association.

*Sharp, J. G., & Bugental, J.F.T. (2001). Existential-humanistic psychotherapy. In R. J. Corsini (Ed.), *Handbook of innovative therapies* (2nd ed., pp. 206–217). New York: Wiley.

Strasser, F., & Strasser, A. (1997). *Existential time-limited therapy: The wheel of existence.* Chichester: Wiley.

Tillich, P. (1952). *The courage to be.* New Haven, CT: Yale University Press.

*Vontress, C. E. (1996). A personal retrospective on cross-cultural counseling. *Journal of Multicultural Counseling and Development, 24*(3), 156–166.

*Vontress, C. E. (2008). Existential therapy. In J. Frew & M. D. Spiegler (Eds.), *Contemporary psychotherapies for a diverse world* (pp. 141–176). Boston: Lahaska Press.

*Walsh, R. A., & McElwain, B. (2002). Existential psychotherapies. In D. J. Cain & J. Seeman (Eds.), *Humanistic psychotherapies: Handbook of research and practice* (pp. 253–278). Washington, DC: American Psychological Association.

*Yalom, I. D. (1980). *Existential psychotherapy.* New York: Basic Books.

*Yalom, I. D. (2005). *The Schopenhauer cure: A novel.* New York: HarperCollins.

*Yalom, I. D. (2008). *Staring at the sun: Overcoming the terror of death.* San Francisco: Jossey-Bass.

*Yalom, I. D., & Josselson, R. (2011). Existential psychotherapy. In R. Corsini & D. Wedding (Eds.), *Current psychotherapies* (9th ed., pp. 310–341). Belmont, CA: Brooks/Cole, Cengage Learning.

Zur, O. (2009). *Clinical update: Existential-humanistic psychotherapy revisited.* Retrieved June 15, 2009, from info@zurinstitute.com

CHAPTER TEN

The Person-Centered Approach to Groups

Introduction

The person-centered approach to group counseling was developed by the late Carl Rogers. Of all the pioneers of various approaches to group work, Rogers stands out as the one who most changed the direction of counseling theory and practice. In the early 1940s Rogers developed *nondirective counseling,* a powerful and revolutionary alternative to the directive and interpretative approaches to therapy then being practiced. He caused a furor by challenging the basic assumption that the counselor was the expert and the client had a passive role. Rogers questioned the validity of such widely used therapeutic procedures as diagnosis, interpretation, giving advice, suggestions, and teaching.

In nondirective counseling the therapist's realness and empathy are emphasized, and the therapeutic relationship rather than the therapist's techniques are viewed as the central factors in facilitating change. Rogers's approach was grounded on the assumption that human beings tend to move toward wholeness and self-actualization. He believed that individual members, as well as the group as a whole, could find their own direction with a minimal degree of direction from the group facilitator. Rogers was a *quiet revolutionary;* his ideas challenged the medical model of traditional therapeutic approaches and continue to influence counseling practice today (see Cain, 2010; Kirschenbaum, 2009; Rogers & Russell, 2002).

A common theme in Rogers's early writings, which permeated all of his later works, was a basic trust in the client's ability to move forward if conditions fostering growth are present. According to Rogers, there is a **formative tendency** in nature that both maintains and enhances the organism. This central source of energy seeks fulfillment and actualization. A faith in the emergent nature of reality and his belief that therapy is an emergent relational process differentiates person-centered therapy from almost all other psychological theories. It leads naturally to a faith in subjective experience and a belief in the basic trustworthiness of human nature. This **actualization tendency** suggests an intrinsic source of growth and healing that can be counted on. Clients have capacities for self-understanding and constructive change. There is a tendency toward self-realization, or autonomy, which means that the individual moves inherently toward self-regulation, self-determination, and inner freedom. However, the actualizing tendency does not imply a movement away from relationships, interdependence, and connection (Brodley, 1999a). Rogers's conceptual framework grew out of his experience that human beings become increasingly worthy of trust when they feel they are understood and respected at a deep level (Kirschenbaum, 2009).

HISTORICAL BACKGROUND

Rogers's nondirective approach focused on reflecting and clarifying the feelings of individual clients. Rogers believed that through an accepting relationship clients were able to gain increasing insight into the nature of their problems and then take constructive action based on their new self-understanding. During the 1950s, Rogers developed and refined his basic hypotheses for psychotherapy, and these principles were later applied to therapy groups. He also developed a systematic theory of personality and applied this self-theory to the practice of counseling individuals, which led him to rename his approach *client-centered therapy* (Rogers, 1951). The client-centered approach was broadened to include applications to the teaching/learning situation, affective/cognitive learning in workshops, and organizational development and leadership.

In the 1960s and 1970s Rogers did a great deal to spearhead development of basic encounter groups and personal growth groups. As the fields of application grew in number and variety, the name "client-centered therapy" was changed to the *person-centered approach.* Rogers also broadened his emphasis beyond the therapist's ability to reflect accurately what clients were expressing to include the therapist's congruence and willingness to become increasingly involved in the therapy. The group work that Rogers pioneered was mostly in the form of weekend workshops, although some of his workshops lasted 2 to 3 weeks. These small groups did much to revolutionize the practice of group work.

Bozarth, Zimring, and Tausch (2002) provide a comprehensive review of research in person-centered therapy over the various periods in the evolution of its development. Here are some of their conclusions:

- In the earliest years of the approach, the client rather than the therapist was the person in charge. Research showed that nondirective therapy was associated with increased understanding, greater self-exploration, and improved self-concepts.

- Later the approach was characterized by a shift from clarification of feelings to a focus on the client's frame of reference. Research confirmed many of Rogers's hypotheses, offering strong evidence for the value of the therapeutic relationship and the client's resources as the crux of successful therapy.

- As person-centered therapy developed, research centered on the core conditions of therapy, which were assumed to be both necessary and sufficient conditions for successful therapy. The research strongly supports certain attitudes of the therapist as being basic to successful therapy outcomes.

Although person-centered therapy has changed over the years, this faith in the fundamental actualization tendency of the person has remained at its foundation. The contemporary person-centered approach to group counseling is the result of an evolutionary process begun more than 70 years ago that continues to remain open to change and refinement (see Cain & Seeman, 2002; Cain, 2010). For a detailed review of the development of Rogers's approach over the past 55 years, see Bozarth, Zimring, and Tausch (2002) and Zimring and Raskin (1992).

THE RELATIONSHIP BETWEEN EXISTENTIAL THERAPY AND HUMANISTIC PSYCHOLOGY

Some key concepts of existential therapy overlap with the humanistic themes put forth by Rogers and others. Indeed, Rogers constructed his notions of therapeutic practice on existential principles about what it means to be human, the balance between freedom and responsibility, and the client–therapist relationship as a key to change. Both person-centered therapy and Gestalt therapy (the subject of Chapter 11) are experiential, humanistic, phenomenological, and existentially oriented.

The Focus of Humanistic Psychology A number of humanistic theorists have contributed to a movement often referred to as the "third force" in psychology (in reaction to the psychoanalytic and behavioral forces). They have written on the nature of human existence, on methods for studying human modes of functioning, and on the implications of humanistic assumptions. Synthesizing their theories from many divergent fields and approaches, early humanistic psychologists contended that people could not be studied and understood in segmented fashion. Rather, humans must be studied in complete relation to how they interact with others and with the world. Some key figures in the development of humanistic psychology were Carl Rogers, Rollo May, Abraham Maslow, Fritz Perls, Virginia Satir, Natalie Rogers, Clark Moustakas, Sidney Jourard, and James Bugental. Many of these psychologists have an existential orientation, but they also applied themes to the practice of psychotherapy that focus on the capacities unique to humans: love, freedom, choice, creativity, purpose, relatedness, meaning, values, growth, self-actualization, autonomy, responsibility, ego transcendence, humor, and spontaneity. According to humanistic psychologists, any therapy that aims at growth must take these human capacities into account.

Several authors (Greenberg & Rice, 1997; Page, Weiss, & Lietaer, 2002) address basic concepts shared by the humanistic approaches to psychotherapy: person-centered group therapy, Gestalt group therapy, and existential group therapy. These authors include these three theories under the humanistic umbrella because they all share common assumptions about human nature and what constitutes key therapeutic processes necessary for effective therapeutic outcomes. Basic concepts of primary importance in all of the humanistic approaches to psychotherapy include these ideas:

1. *Importance of self-awareness.* These theories stress the importance of self-awareness in therapy based on the premise that people who are self-aware can make more life-affirming choices.

2. *Commitment to a phenomenological approach.* A belief in the uniquely human capacity for reflective consciousness involves considering the client's subjective world and striving to understand reality from the client's perspective. Emphasis is on the uniqueness and individuality of the person.

3. *Actualization, or growth, tendency.* Both Maslow and Rogers maintained that rather than merely seeking stability human beings strive to grow. People have an innate drive toward realizing their full potential that enables them to benefit from therapy.

4. *Belief that humans are free, self-determining beings.* Individuals may be influenced by their past and by their environment, but they have a role in who and what they become through the choices they make.

5. *Concern and respect for the subjective experience of each person.* Humanistic therapists attempt to understand and grasp the experiential world of their clients. The humanistic approaches all emphasize the notion that people are capable of acting in responsible and caring ways in interpersonal relationships.

Key Concepts

TRUST IN THE GROUP PROCESS

Rogers (1986b) made it clear that the person-centered approach rests on a basic trust in human beings' tendency to realize their full potential. Similarly, person-centered therapy is based on a deep sense of trust in the group's ability to develop its own potential by moving in a constructive direction. For a group to move forward, it must develop an accepting and trusting atmosphere in which the members can show the aspects of themselves they usually conceal and move into new behaviors. For example:

• Members move from playing roles to expressing themselves more directly.

• Members move from being relatively closed to experience to becoming more open to outside reality.

• Members move from being out of contact with internal and subjective experience to becoming aware of it.

• Members move from looking for answers outside of themselves to a willingness to direct their own lives from within.

• Member move from lacking trust and being somewhat closed and fearful in interpersonal relationships to being more open and expressive with others.

Members begin to sense that by being in a group they are part of something larger and are willing to participate in the larger process without giving up their own sense of autonomy. O'Hara and Wood (1984, 2004) maintain that groups only realize their full potential when individuals align their own inner direction with the collective direction that is an emergent phenomenon of the collective consciousness.

THE THERAPEUTIC CONDITIONS FOR GROWTH

The basic tenet underlying the person-centered approach to group work was stated briefly by Rogers (1980): "Individuals have within themselves vast resources for self-understanding and for altering their self-concepts, basic attitudes, and self-directed behavior; these resources can be tapped if a definable climate of facilitative psychological attitudes can be provided" (p. 115).

According to Rogers (1986b), the necessary climate that releases our formative, or actualizing, tendency is characterized by three primary attitudes of the therapist: genuineness (or congruence), unconditional positive regard (also called nonpossessive warmth or acceptance), and empathy. As the facilitator models these attitudes, an accepting and caring climate emerges. Given the establishment of a favorable climate, the group members can be trusted to drop their defenses, to make use of their inner resources, and to work toward personally meaningful goals that will lead to significant personal change. To function effectively in a group, the facilitator must trust the abilities of the group members to grow in a favorable direction. If this is not the case, the group leader is likely to apply more control over the group process than is helpful (Page, Weiss, & Lietaer, 2002).

When a group facilitator experiences genuineness, acceptance, and accurate empathy for the members in their group and when members perceive these conditions, therapeutic personality change and growth will occur (Cain, 2010). Rogers's original conviction was that these core conditions work together rather than operating independently. The core conditions have been put to the test in a wide variety of situations with very divergent groups, different cultures, and different nations (Rogers, 1987d). Rogers stressed that the core conditions are not only *necessary* for effective therapy but also *sufficient.*

Implications for Group Leaders Bozarth, Zimring, and Tausch (2002) assert that the most important aspect of training is to develop the attitude of the therapist to support the client's perception of the world, to demonstrate faith in the client's inner resources, and to attend to the therapeutic relationship. Coghlan and McIlduff (1990) maintain that an important aspect of training group facilitators is teaching them the use of personal power. Because the person-centered approach emphasizes an equalization of power, it is critical that the facilitator's behavior in no way diminish the power of members. Coghlan and McIlduff believe facilitators need to learn how to offer alternatives in sensitive ways to group members so that real choice and increased freedom become the property of the group rather than the instrument of the leader.

Researchers have confirmed that the person-centered assumption that the facilitator's expression of three core therapeutic attitudes—genuineness (or congruence), acceptance, and empathic understanding—is foundational for positive therapeutic outcomes (Cain, 2010; Kirschenbaum, 2009; Raskin, 1986b). Emphasis is best placed on the art of listening and understanding rather than on techniques and strategies. Clients often identify "being understood" as one of the most helpful aspects of their therapy and express appreciation for being carefully listened to (Cain, 2010). Thorne (1992) puts the challenge to clinicians well: "The 'core conditions' of congruence, acceptance, and empathy are simple to state, much more difficult to describe and infinitely challenging to practice" (p. 36).

To fully understand the significance of the person-centered approach, students who are interested in becoming group facilitators need to experience it at a deep psychological level themselves. Students do not learn empathy, congruence, and unconditional positive regard by reading about it or hearing about it in a lecture. For this reason, most person-centered training is best done in the context of intensive experiential workshops and courses (N. Rogers, personal communication, June 17, 2009).

The following sections expand on Rogers's three core therapeutic conditions as they apply to group leaders' behavior.

GENUINENESS

The first element is the **genuineness**, or **congruence**, of the facilitator of the group. The greater the extent to which facilitators become involved in the group as persons, putting up no professional front, the greater the likelihood that the members will change and grow. What the therapist expresses externally must be *congruent* with his or her inner experience, at least during the time of therapy. In other words, genuine therapists do not pretend to be interested when they are not, don't fake attention or understanding, don't say what they don't mean, and don't adopt behaviors designed to win approval. They can perform their professional functions without hiding behind their professional roles.

According to Natiello (1987), to maintain genuineness or congruence, therapists need a high level of self-awareness, self-acceptance, and self-trust. Genuineness is the state of authenticity that results from a deep exploration of self and a willingness to accept the truths of this exploration. Natiello contends that without congruence the other therapeutic conditions are offered inauthentically and become mere techniques, which are meaningless, manipulative, and controlling. Congruence lends credibility to empathy and unconditional positive regard. Clients must first be seen and understood, and then unconditional positive regard becomes believable because the therapist is perceived as congruent.

Implications for Group Leaders Congruent group leaders avoid using their professional role to keep themselves hidden; instead, they are naturally themselves in their way of relating to members in the group. Although group leaders are essentially honest in their encounters in the group, they are not indiscriminately open, and they know the boundaries of appropriate self-revelation. They realize the importance of taking responsibility for any feelings they express in the group and the importance of exploring with clients any persistent feelings, especially those that may be blocking their ability to be fully present. Through their own authenticity, congruent group leaders offer a model that helps their clients work toward greater realness.

Some group leaders have difficulty "being themselves." Often that difficulty stems from the misapprehension that genuineness entails expressing every immediate thought or feeling or being spontaneous without any restraint or consideration of the appropriateness and timeliness of one's reactions. Another difficulty arises when leaders, in the name of being "authentic," make themselves the focal point of the group by discussing their personal problems in great detail. Leaders need to examine their motivations for discussing their personal issues and ask themselves whether the disclosure serves the members' needs or their own. Therapists use self-disclosure to validate a client's reality, normalize experiences, strengthen the alliance, or present alternative ways of thinking or acting (Norcross, 2010). Leader self-disclosure should be done with careful attention to timing and with the purpose of helping the group advance its capacity to support growth.

UNCONDITIONAL POSITIVE REGARD AND ACCEPTANCE

The second core element is the attitude called **unconditional positive regard**, which is an acceptance of and caring for group members. When group facilitators display a positive, nonjudgmental, accepting attitude toward their clients, therapeutic change is more likely (Rogers, 1986b). Positive regard involves communicating a caring that is without conditions and that is not contaminated by evaluation or judgment of the client's feelings and thoughts. By valuing and accepting members' experiences without placing stipulations and expectations on this acceptance, group leaders reduce client defensiveness and enable clients to be more open to all their experiences and more involved in their therapy. Acceptance is not to be confused with approval, however; facilitators can accept and value their group members as separate persons, with a right to their separateness, without necessarily approving of some of their behavior. As clients perceive that they are seen, accepted, and valued for who they are, they tend to move in more positive directions and become more self-accepting (Cain, 2010). The members' perceptions of the leader's positive regard have the strongest association with positive outcomes (Norcross, 2010).

Associated with positive regard is an attitude of nonpossessive caring and warmth, which can be expressed in subtle ways such as through gestures, eye contact, tone of voice, and facial expression. A genuine expression of caring can be sensed by clients and will promote their development. In contrast, artificial warmth can be as readily identified and will not be helpful to group members. If clients sense that the therapist's expression of warmth is more a technique than a genuine feeling, it becomes difficult for clients to trust the genuineness of other reactions of the therapist.

It is a rare group facilitator who can genuinely provide unconditional acceptance for every member on a consistent basis. Unconditional positive regard can best be thought of as an attitude of receptiveness toward the subjective and experiential world of the group member. From Lietaer's (1984) perspective, unconditionality means that the therapist values the deeper core of the person. Through the therapist's attempt at unconditionality, clients sense that the therapist is on their side and that they will not be let down in spite of their current difficulties. In its optimal form, unconditionality expresses a deep belief in another person. For a scholarly treatment of the controversial concept of unconditional positive regard, see Lietaer (1984).

Related to the concept of accepting the individual group member with unconditional positive regard, caring, and warmth is the idea of developing an attitude of acceptance of the group as a whole. Just as Rogers (1970) believed in the capacity of the individual to find his or her own direction, so did he believe in accepting a group where it is, without attempting to impose a direction on it: "From my experience I know that if I attempt to push a group to a deeper level, it is not, in the long run, going to work" (p. 48).

Implications for Group Leaders Group leaders in training often struggle with what they see as the monumental task of being able to feel accepting or being able to demonstrate positive regard. Some burden themselves with the unrealistic expectation that they *must always be accepting* and that they must consistently respond with warmth in all situations. Group leaders need to develop an accepting attitude toward themselves as well as toward their clients. At times they may not feel caring or unconditional positive regard. It is not necessary to feel a high level of warmth and positive regard all the time to be an effective group leader. These attitudes are not an either-or condition; rather, they occur on a graded continuum. Being an effective group leader starts by accepting oneself and continues by bearing in mind that valuing, caring, and accepting group participants leads to greater opportunities to facilitate change.

EMPATHY

The third facilitative aspect is an **empathic understanding** of the members' internal and subjective frame of reference. Facilitators show this empathy when they are able to sense accurately the feelings and personal meanings members are experiencing. Rogers (1961) defined empathy as the capacity to see the world of another by assuming the internal frame of reference of that person: "To sense the client's private world as if it were your own but without ever losing the 'as if' quality—this is empathy, and it seems essential to therapy" (p. 284). But sensing, even understanding, the client's private world is not enough. The facilitator must also be able to communicate this understanding effectively to the group members. A primary means of determining whether members experience a facilitator's empathy is to secure feedback from them (Norcross, 2010).

Rogers (1975) considered empathy as "an unappreciated way of being" for many group practitioners. He regarded empathy as one of the most potent factors in bringing about learning and self-directed change, thus locating power in the person and not in the expert. He summarized some general research findings concerning empathy as follows:

- Therapists of many different orientations agree that attempting sensitively and accurately to understand others from their viewpoint is a critical factor in being effective therapists.

- One of the main functions of empathy is to foster client self-exploration. Clients come to a deeper self-understanding through a relationship in which they feel they are being understood by others. Research has demonstrated that clients who feel understood by their therapists are encouraged to share more of themselves.

- Empathy dissolves alienation; the person who receives empathy feels connected with others. Furthermore, those who receive empathy learn that they are valued, cared for, and accepted as they are.

- The ability to exhibit empathy depends on the personal development of the therapist. Rogers came to the conclusion that "the more psychologically mature and integrated the therapist is as a person, the more helpful is the relationship he provides" (p. 5).

- Being a skilled diagnostician and making interpretations is not related to empathy, which, at its best, is accepting and nonjudgmental. In fact, for Rogers "true empathy is always free of any evaluative or diagnostic quality" (p. 7).

Accurate empathy is central to the practice of person-centered group work. It is a way for facilitators to hear the meanings expressed by the members of their group that often lie at the edge of their awareness. According to Watson (2002), full empathy entails understanding the meaning and feeling of a client's experiencing and being able to communicate that clearly to the person. Watson adds that almost 60 years of research has consistently demonstrated that empathy is the most powerful determinant of client progress in therapy. She puts the challenge to counselors as follows: "Therapists need to be able to be responsively attuned to their clients and to understand them emotionally as well as cognitively. When empathy is operating on all three levels—interpersonal, cognitive, and affective—it is one of the most powerful tools therapists have at their disposal"(pp. 463–464).

Active and sensitive listening was what Rogers (1970) *did* when he facilitated a group: "I listen as carefully, accurately, and sensitively as I am able, to each individual who expresses himself. Whether the utterance is superficial or significant, I listen" (p. 47). It is apparent that Rogers was listening to more than the words; he also heard the meaning behind both the verbal and the nonverbal content. In this regard he was concerned with facilitating the truest expression of the person's subjective experience. Natalie Rogers has called this "listening to the music as well as the words of the client"; it is hearing the undercurrent of emotional statements (personal communication, September 10, 2005).

In a group context, the interpersonal and higher-order aspects of empathy frequently result in bonding among the members and cohesion and alignment in the group as a whole. According to Cain (2010), the potent aspect of empathy that leads to change works this way: Empathy, particularly emotionally focused empathy, helps clients (1) pay attention to and value their experiencing, (2) process their experience both cognitively and bodily, (3) view old experiences in new ways that promote shifts in perceptions of the self and one's view of the world, and (4) increase their confidence in their perceptions and judgment and their ability to make sound decisions and take action. In the context of the safety of a group, members' capacity for effective learning about themselves and how they relate to others is gradually restored. For a scholarly discussion of the role of empathy in the person-centered approach, see Bozarth (1984); for an examination of empathy in and for the group as a whole, see O'Hara (1997); and for a comprehensive treatment of empathy in therapy, see Bohart and Greenberg (1997).

O'Hara and Wood (1984, 2004) have described a more transpersonal level of empathy that can be developed in groups where it is possible for the members to tune into the formative direction of the group as a whole. When that happens, groups can reach extraordinary levels of healing at both individual and collective levels.

Implications for Group Leaders Empathic understanding is essential to foster the climate of acceptance and trust necessary for the success of the group. Empathy is a skill that can be developed—and it is a skill that an effective group leader needs to develop.

In working with group counselors, I have found that many mistakenly assume that they can't be empathic unless they themselves have directly experienced the same problems voiced by group members. Such an assumption can severely limit the leader's effectiveness. Clearly, one need not experience incest to empathize with a group member's anguish over reliving such a painful experience. One need not to have been abandoned by a parent to feel and experience the sadness of abandonment. It is not necessary to have been divorced to share a client's anger, hurt, and sadness about separation. Such experiences come in many forms and, at one level or another, are common to us all. Situations in every life trigger feelings of isolation, rage, resentment, guilt, sadness, loss, or rejection—to name a few of the feelings that will be expressed in groups. Our ability to experience anger, joy, fear, and love makes it possible for us to enter the world of another person, even though this person's circumstances may be different from our own. As group leaders, if we remain open to our own emotions, allow ourselves to be touched by the emotions of others, and are willing to reexperience certain difficult events, we will increase our capacity to be psychologically present for others.

BARRIERS TO EFFECTIVE THERAPY

In the training workshops that my colleagues and I conduct, the participants typically lead groups and then receive feedback from the members and from us. Many of our students and trainees express feelings of inadequacy as group leaders and a sense of frustration and hopelessness. They many times see little change occurring in the members of their groups, and they perceive that their clients are resistant and don't like coming to groups. In many instances the problems besetting these students can be traced back to the fact that the conditions of active listening, empathy, and positive regard are in some measure lacking in their groups. Here is a list of specific problems that work against group progress:

- *Lack of attending and empathy.* Often these prospective group leaders show that they don't really listen; they are preoccupied with a message that they want to impart to their groups and use the group as a vehicle for indoctrination. Or they ask many closed questions and are preoccupied with problem solving rather than problem understanding. They often take on too much responsibility for making things happen. In short, beginning group counselors sometimes talk too much and listen too little.

- *Absence of counselor self-disclosure.* Some agencies and institutions foster, even require, an aloof and undisclosing leader role. Group counselors may be given these messages: "Avoid being personal," "Don't get involved," and "Avoid sharing anything about yourself, even if it affects the relationship." Leaders are expected to change the behavior of members yet keep themselves out of their interactions with group members—clearly an unreasonable and self-defeating expectation.

- *Lack of positive regard, warmth, and acceptance.* Some group counselors are intolerant of the people they are supposedly helping and cling to assumptions that keep their clientele in stereotyped categories. Such prejudice makes client change difficult, if not impossible. Admittedly, it may be hard to maintain positive regard, warmth, and acceptance toward people who are in a treatment program for spousal abuse, child abuse, or murder. Although these actions are not condoned, it is important for leaders to be able to set aside their reactions to these behaviors at least during the course of the group. If that is not possible, leaders need to disqualify themselves from the role of leader.

- *Lack of belief in the therapeutic process.* Underlying the concepts of positive regard and acceptance is the belief that people can change and improve their personal condition. In our in-service group process workshops, we frequently meet practitioners and students who lead groups only because they are required to do so and who question the effectiveness of group therapy. In a climate in which enthusiasm, motivation, and faith in groups is absent, is it surprising that leaders find that their groups are somewhat less than

successful? How can group members be expected to have faith in ?
that the group leader does not have? When group leaders believ
they are doing and value the unique attributes of a group approa'
in a position to educate their clients to the reality that group cou'
optimal choice for many clients, not a second-class treatment.

Implications for Group Leaders It is essential that leaders examine
attitudes and behaviors can be barriers to the progress of a group. Here
some questions that can serve as useful catalysts for self-reflection:

- What personal needs am I meeting by being a group leader?
- Am I authentically myself in a group, or do I hide behind the role of "leader"?
- Am I able to trust the capacity for self-direction of others, or do I need to direct their lives? Do I insist that members look at the world through my eyes? Can I engage equitably with the range of people who attend the group?
- Am I willing to take time to understand others, or do I force them to follow my agenda?
- Do I see my main task as helping members get what they want, or getting them to want what I want for them?

Bohart (2003) states that it is essential in the person-centered therapeutic
process to attend closely to the moment-to-moment unfolding of events in a
session. Paying attention to what the members want to talk about rather than
guiding the exploration of topics the facilitator determines to be important
moves the group forward. Bohart believes that most of the mistakes a person-
centered therapist might make are likely to come about because of not being
warm, empathic, and congruent; imposing an agenda on the client; or failing
to be in tune with the unfolding moment-by-moment process.

Role and Functions of the Group Leader

The person-centered approach emphasizes the personal qualities of the group
leader rather than the techniques of leading. The primary function of the
facilitator is to create an accepting and healing climate in the group. This therapy is best considered as a "way of being" rather than a "way of doing." Rogers
(1986b) wrote that the therapist's role is to be a companion to clients in their
journey toward self-discovery. When facilitators can achieve this level of
"being" rather than "doing," they can enter a state of integration of their actions that resembles that of master practitioners in the arts and sciences.

The group leader is called a *facilitator*, which reflects the importance of interactions between group members and the leader's ability to assist members in
expressing themselves. Person-centered group facilitators use themselves as
instruments of change in a group. Their central function is to establish a therapeutic climate in which group members will interact in increasingly authentic
and honest ways. Boy and Pine (1999) believe the therapist's role is closely tied
to *who* and *what* the therapist is as a person: his or her values, lifestyle, life

experiences, and basic philosophy of life. Clearly, the therapist's attitudes and behavior are powerful determinants of the accepting group atmosphere that is conducive to real communication. Boy and Pine put this emphasis well:

> A person-centered approach to group counseling puts far greater emphasis on the facilitative quality of the counselor *as a person* rather than emphasizing the counselor's knowledge and use of specific and predesigned procedures. It views the counselor's presence as the basic catalyst that prompts group participants to make progress. (p. 150)

Rogers did his best to become a person to the members of his groups rather than assuming the role of an expert. In his work as a group facilitator, he functioned somewhat like a guide on a journey. Rogers (1970) emphasized the following characteristics of group facilitators:

- They have a great deal of trust in the group process and believe the group can move forward without their directive intervention.
- They listen carefully and sensitively to each member.
- They do all that is possible to contribute to the creation of a climate that is psychologically safe for the members.
- They attempt to be empathically understanding and accept individuals and the group; they do not push the group to a deeper level.
- They operate in terms of their own experience and their own feelings, which means that they express here-and-now reactions.
- They offer members feedback and, if appropriate, challenge members on specifics of their behavior; they avoid judging and, instead, speak about how they are affected by others' behavior.

The person-centered group approach emphasizes certain attitudes and skills as a necessary part of the facilitator's style: listening in an active and sensitive way, accepting, understanding, respecting, reflecting, clarifying, summarizing, sharing personal experiences, responding, encountering and engaging others in the group, going with the flow of the group rather than trying to direct the way the group is going, and affirming a member's capacity for self-determination. Other relational qualities and attitudes embraced by person-centered therapists include receptivity to experience, contact and engagement, a therapeutic alliance, authentic dialogue, understanding the client's experience, and hopefulness regarding the client's capacity for the relationship (Cain, 2008, 2010). The facilitator encourages members to explore the incongruities between their beliefs and behaviors and to move toward the inclinations of their inner feelings and subjective experiencing. As the members become more aware of these incongruities within themselves, their view of themselves expands.

Similar to his belief in the actualizing tendency within individuals, Rogers (1970) had faith in the capacity of a group to move on its own initiative. However, he acknowledged that anxiety and irritation among group members may result from the lack of a clear and shared structure, especially during the early phase of a group. He believed it was important for the group to determine for themselves how they would spend their time, and he might open a session by saying, "I wonder how you might like to spend the time in the group today?" Or he might say, "Welcome. We have set aside (a certain amount of) time today to meet in the group. I'm not sure what we will end up talking or thinking about, but I'm looking forward to seeing how it unfolds." Bohart and Tallman (2010) emphasize that clients' active involvement is critical to successful therapy. This involvement encompasses openness and a willingness to engage in the tasks of therapy, cooperative participation, and a collaborative stance.

Rogers believed members have the resourcefulness for positive movement without the facilitator assuming an active and directive role. The facilitator's nondirectiveness allows members to demonstrate their typical interpersonal style within the context of the group. The premise is that members will generally reveal their typical behavior if the group is unstructured. Group members, who are accustomed to following authorities, are challenged to rely on themselves to formulate a purpose and a direction. Members are helped to increasingly listen to themselves and other members by a facilitator who will not act as an expert and give them direction. They are challenged to struggle and to express themselves, and out of this struggle they have a basis for learning how to trust themselves. If the facilitator assumes a role of being too directive or relies on group exercises to get things going in the group, then the members' natural manner of interacting will not evolve as readily.

Because person-centered practitioners have a basic trust in the process of a group, they view their job as facilitating this process. Here are some specific ways a group counselor might facilitate the group process:

- Encourage members to express their feelings and expectations openly.
- Teach members to focus on themselves and their feelings.
- Work to create a climate of safety that encourages members to take risks.
- Provide support for members as they try new behaviors.
- Foster a member-to-member rather than a member-to-leader interaction style.
- Assist members in overcoming barriers to direct communication.
- Help members integrate what they are learning in the group, and find ways to apply it to their everyday lives.
- Encourage members to make an ongoing assessment of what is going in their group and determine whether they want to change anything.

According to Boy and Pine (1999), the facilitator is challenged to deal with a complexity that is not evident in the more structured and leader-centered process models. The emphasis of a person-centered group is on the natural emergence of the self of each of the participants. Tallman and Bohart (1999) maintain that the client is the primary agent of change and that the relationship members have with the facilitator provides a supportive structure within which clients' self-healing capacities are activated. "Clients then are the 'magicians' with the special healing powers. Therapists set the stage and serve as assistants who provide the conditions under which this magic can operate" (p. 95).

Stages of a Person-Centered Group

CHARACTERISTICS OF THE GROUP

The person-centered group may meet weekly for about 2 hours for an unspecified number of meetings. Another format consists of a personal growth workshop that meets for a weekend, a week, or longer. The residential aspect of such small personal growth groups affords members opportunities to become a community as a group.

There are few rules or procedures for the selection of members when organizing and conducting a person-centered group. If both the facilitator and the group participant agree that a group experience would be beneficial, the person is included. When the group initially meets, the facilitator does not present ground rules by which members must abide or provide a great deal of information or orientation. It is up to the group members to formulate the rules for their sessions and to establish norms that they agree will assist them in reaching their goals.

UNFOLDING OF THE GROUP PROCESS

On the basis of his experience with numerous groups, Rogers (1970) delineated 15 process patterns that occur in groups that employ the person-centered approach. These process patterns, or trends, do not occur in a clear-cut sequence, and they may vary considerably from group to group.

1. *Milling around.* The lack of leader direction inevitably results in some initial confusion, frustration, and "milling around"—either actually or verbally. Questions such as "Who is responsible here?" or "What are we supposed to be doing?" are characteristic and reflect the concern felt at this stage.

2. *Resistance to personal expression or exploration.* Members initially present a public self—one they think will be acceptable to the group. They are fearful of and resistant to revealing their private selves.

3. *Description of past feelings.* Despite doubts about the trustworthiness of the group and the risk of exposing oneself, disclosure of personal feelings does begin—however hesitantly and ambivalently. Generally, this disclosure deals with events outside of the group; members tend to describe feelings in a "there-and-then" fashion.

4. *Expression of negative feelings.* As the group progresses, there is a movement toward the expression of here-and-now feelings. Often these expressions take the form of criticism of the group leader, usually for not providing the needed direction.

5. *Expression and exploration of personally meaningful material.* If the expression of negative reactions is seen by the members as acceptable to the group, a climate of trust is likely to emerge. Members are then able to take the risks involved in disclosing personal material. At this point the participants begin to realize that the group is what they make it, and they begin to experience freedom.

6. *Expression of immediate interpersonal feelings in the group.* Members tend to express a full range of feelings toward one another.

7. *Development of a healing capacity in the group.* Next, members begin to spontaneously reach out to one another, expressing care, support, understanding, and concern. At this stage helping relationships are often formed within the group that offer members aid in leading more constructive lives outside of the group.

8. *Self-acceptance and the beginning of change.* Participants begin to accept aspects of themselves that they formerly denied or distorted; they get

closer to their feelings and consequently become less rigid and more open to change. As members accept their strengths and weaknesses, they drop their defenses and welcome change.

9. *Cracking of facades.* Here individual members begin to respond to the group demand that masks and pretenses be dropped. This revealing of deeper selves by some members validates the theory that meaningful encounters can occur when people risk getting beneath surface interaction. At this stage the group strives toward deeper communication.

10. *Feedback.* In the process of receiving feedback, members acquire a lot of data concerning how others experience them and what impact they have on others. This information often leads to new insights that help them decide on aspects of themselves that they want to change.

11. *Confrontation.* Here members confront one another in what is usually an emotional process involving feedback. Confrontation can be seen as a stepping up of the interactions described in earlier stages.

12. *The helping relationship outside the group sessions.* By this stage members have begun making contacts outside the group. Here we see an extension of the process described in number 7.

13. *The basic encounter.* Because the members come into closer and more direct contact with one another than is generally the case in everyday life, genuine person to person relationships occur. At this point members begin to experience how meaningful relationships occur when there is a commitment to work toward a common goal and a sense of community.

14. *Expression of feelings of closeness.* As the sessions progress, an increasing warmth and closeness develops within the group because of the realness of the participants' expression of feelings about themselves and toward others.

15. *Behavior changes in the group.* As members experience increased ease in expressing their feelings, their behaviors, mannerisms, and even their appearance begin to change. They tend to act in an open manner; they express deeper feelings toward others; they achieve an increased understanding of themselves; and they work out more effective ways of being with others. If the changes are effective, the members will carry their new behaviors into their everyday lives.

SOME OUTCOMES OF THE GROUP EXPERIENCE

Based on his vast experience in conducting groups and workshops, as well as his process and outcomes studies, Rogers (1987d) identified and summarized a number of changes that tend to occur within individuals in a successful group experience. Members become more open and honest. They learn to listen to themselves and increase their self-understanding. They gradually become less critical and more self-accepting. As they feel increasingly understood and accepted, they have less need to defend themselves, and therefore they drop their facades and are willing to be themselves. Because they become more aware of their own feelings and of what is going on around them, they are more realistic and objective. They tend to be more like the self that they wanted to be before entering a group experience. They are not as easily threatened because the safety of the group changes their attitude toward themselves

' others. Within the group there is more understanding and acceptance of
others are. Members become more appreciative of themselves as they are,
ey move toward self-direction. They empower themselves in new ways,
they increasingly trust themselves. The members become more creative
because they are willing to accept their own uniqueness. They become more
empathic, accepting, and congruent in their relationships with others, and in
doing so engage in more meaningful relationships (Cain, 2010).

Person-Centered Expressive Arts in Groups*

Natalie Rogers, daughter of Carl Rogers, expanded on her father's theory of
creativity using the expressive arts to enhance personal growth for individuals and groups. Group facilitators, counselors, and psychotherapists trained in
person-centered expressive arts offer their clients or groups the opportunity to
create movement, visual art, journal writing, and sound and music to express
their feelings and gain insight from these activities (N. Rogers, 1993).

PRINCIPLES OF EXPRESSIVE ARTS THERAPY

Expressive arts therapy is a multimodal approach integrating mind, body,
emotions, and spiritual inner resources through the use of various art forms—
movement, drawing, painting, sculpting, writing, music, and improvisation—
in a supportive setting for the purpose of growth and healing. This therapy is
in addition to talking about feelings. Any art form generated from deep emotions aids in the process of self-discovery, and the raw and spontaneous
product—as is—is part of the therapeutic process. This therapy is *not* about
creating a "pretty" picture, a dance ready for the stage, or a poem written and
rewritten to perfection.

Natalie Rogers's methods of expressive arts therapy are based on the following humanistic principles:

- All people have an innate ability to be creative.
- The creative process is healing. The expressive product supplies important
  messages to the individual. However, it is the process of creation that is
  profoundly transformative.
- Personal growth and higher states of consciousness are achieved through
  self-awareness, self-understanding, and insight.
- Self-awareness, understanding, and insight are achieved by delving into
  our emotions. The feelings of grief, anger, pain, fear, joy, and ecstasy are the
  tunnel through which we must pass to get to self-awareness, understanding, and wholeness.
- Our feelings and emotions are an energy source. That energy can be chan-
  neled into the expressive arts to be released and transformed.

* Much of the material in this section is based on key ideas that are more fully developed in
Natalie Rogers's (1993) book, *The Creative Connection: Expressive Arts as Healing.* This section was
written in close collaboration with Natalie Rogers.

- The expressive arts lead us into the unconscious. This often allows us to express previously unknown facets of ourselves, thus bringing to light new information and awareness.

- Art modes interrelate in what Natalie Rogers calls the "creative connection." When we move, it affects how we write or paint. When we write or paint, it affects how we feel and think. During the creative connection process, one art form stimulates and nurtures the other, bringing us to an inner core or essence that is our life energy.

- A connection exists between our life force—our inner core, or soul—and the essence of all beings. As we journey inward to discover our essence or wholeness, we discover our relatedness to the outer world and the inner and outer become one (N. Rogers, 1993, p. 7).

Natalie Rogers's work is based on the philosophy and methods of person-centered therapy, which she expanded by incorporating nonverbal forms of creative expression. The same conditions that Carl Rogers and his colleagues found basic to fostering a facilitative client–counselor relationship also help support creativity. Personal growth takes place in a safe, supportive environment created by facilitators (teachers, therapists, group leaders, parents, colleagues) who are genuine, warm, empathic, open, honest, congruent, and caring—qualities that are best learned by first being experienced. Taking time to reflect on and evaluate these experiences allows for personal integration at many levels: intellectual, emotional, physical, and spiritual (N. Rogers, 1993).

CONDITIONS THAT FOSTER CREATIVITY

In his book *On Becoming a Person,* Carl Rogers (1961) discussed our innate striving for creativity: "The mainspring of creativity appears to be the same tendency which we discover so deeply as the curative force in psychotherapy—*man's tendency to actualize himself, to become his potentialities*" (p. 351). According to N. Rogers (1993), this deep faith in the individual's innate drive to become fully oneself is basic to the work in person-centered expressive arts. Individuals have a tremendous capacity for self-healing through creativity if given the proper environment. When one feels appreciated, trusted, and is given support to use individuality to develop a plan, create a project, write a paper, or to be authentic, the challenge is exciting, stimulating, and gives a sense of personal expansion. N. Rogers believes the tendency to actualize and become one's full potential, including innate creativity, is undervalued, discounted, and frequently quashed in our society. Traditional educational institutions tend to promote conformity rather than original thinking and the creative process.

In fostering creativity, it is important to recognize that both internal and external conditions need attention. Carl Rogers (1961) defined the internal conditions as *openness to experience* and *internal locus of evaluation.* He named the external conditions as *psychological safety* and *psychological freedom.* According to Rogers, **openness to experience** is a lack of defensiveness, and an ability to perceive the existential moment as it is without prejudgment. This includes a lack of rigidity, openness to new concepts and beliefs, and a tolerance for ambiguity. Being fully open to any experience and seeing its many facets is not easy. Most of us screen out what we don't want to see or experience. To expand our ability to be creative, we need to practice being open to experience *as it is* rather than viewing it through filtered lenses.

Rogers claimed that when we are able to listen to the response of others but are not overly concerned with their reactions, we are able to develop an **internal locus of evaluation**. Because most of us have a strong need for approval, gaining that sense of self-evaluation is a challenging task. Also, many of us are more critical of ourselves than of others. As we develop an internal locus of evaluation, we are able to give ourselves credit and appreciation when it is due. Having a keen sense of our talents and abilities goes along with developing a sense of self-esteem. As we become able to assess ourselves honestly, we are less in need of continual praise from others.

OFFERING STIMULATING AND CHALLENGING EXPERIENCES

Certain external conditions foster and nurture the internal conditions for creativity. Carl Rogers (1961) outlined two such conditions: *psychological safety,* consisting of accepting the individual as of unconditional worth, providing a climate in which external evaluation is absent, and empathic understanding; and *psychological freedom.* Natalie Rogers (1993) adds a third condition: offering *stimulating and challenging experiences.* Psychological safety and psychological freedom are the soil and nutrients for creativity, but seeds must be planted. What N. Rogers found lacking as she worked with her father were stimulating experiences that would motivate and allow people time and space to engage in the creative process. People could sit in therapy and talk about being creative without actually experiencing the creative process. Our culture is particularly geared to verbalizing, and according to N. Rogers, it is necessary to stimulate the client or group participant by offering challenging experiences. Carefully planned experiments or experiences designed to involve participants in the expressive arts (if they chose to take the opportunity) help clients focus on the process of creating.

The expressive arts are an ideal means for expression through symbols and metaphors. Symbolically expressing feelings toward any hated person, for instance, releases pent-up feelings without damaging that person. Using drawing, painting, and sculpting to express feelings about that person gives a tremendous relief and a new perspective. Also, symbols carry messages that go beyond the meanings of words (N. Rogers, 1993).

N. Rogers believes most people have experienced their attempts at creativity in an unsafe environment. They are offered art materials in a classroom or studio where the teacher says or implies there is a right or a wrong way to do it. Or they dance or sing only to be corrected, evaluated, or graded. To be offered an opportunity to explore and experiment with a wide variety of materials in a supportive, nonjudgmental space is an entirely different experience for most people. Such a setting gives participants permission to be authentic, to be childlike, and to delve deeply into themselves. It is possible to put out the materials and simply say, "Go to it." However, N. Rogers (1993) says that it is helpful to most participants to suggest projects or experiences that have no right or wrong outcome but that stimulate the creative juices.

WHAT HOLDS US BACK?

In Natalie Rogers's (1993) work there are many stories from clients and group participants who can pinpoint the exact moment they stopped using art, music, or dance as a form of pleasure and self-expression. A teacher gave them a poor grade, others ridiculed them as they danced, or someone told them to mouth the words while others sang. They felt misunderstood and judged negatively. The self-image that remained was, "I can't draw," "I'm not musical," "It's no fun anymore." Music and drawing then were confined to singing in the shower or doodling on a note pad.

N. Rogers believes our society has squeezed the tasty juice of the creative process right out of most of us. We need to find ways to recapture spontaneous freedom of expression without looking to others for approval. We cheat ourselves out of a fulfilling and joyous source of creativity if we cling to the idea that an artist is the only one who can enter the realm of creativity. We all can use the arts to focus on self-expression and personal growth.

GUIDELINES FOR CREATIVE EXPRESSION IN GROUPS AND IN COMMUNITY BUILDING

N. Rogers's (1993) group work differs from her father's in that she offers group guidelines at the beginning of any workshop or experiential class so that participants understand the concepts of creative expression and the basic guidelines for group behavior. Group evaluations and feedback over 25 years revealed that participants consistently felt that the following guidelines were helpful:

- Be aware of your feelings and your own body, and take care of yourself, including talking with the facilitators.
- There is no right or wrong way to do art.
- All instructions are *always* suggestions.
- Do not judge others, and keep the general bounds of confidentiality.

N. Rogers also developed guidelines for community group behavior. Because most of these courses are 4- to 8-day intensive experiential groups, the group process has some predictable stages. These guidelines have proven helpful in addressing each stage.

Facilitators have a key role in establishing trust in a group that will allow for creative expression. Although facilitators cannot *make* participants trust the group process, they can do much to *earn* that trust from the participants by being respectful and caring. As is true for any form of person-centered therapy, being an effective facilitator has a lot more to do with one's "way of being" than with one's techniques. No technique or intervention can create trust unless the facilitator is fully present, respectful, caring, authentic, and responsive.

N. Rogers (personal communication, June 17, 2009) believes that people have to enter into expressive arts work in a group at their own pace, when they feel safe enough to share. She thinks that expressive arts is useful for people who are shy or defended. She finds that if group participants can create a piece of art, then write about it, they are likely to share this with one other person in the group, which is a big step for many. The next step is to share the meaning of their art in the whole group.

Trust in a group situation also depends of the attitudes and actions of the members of that group. According to N. Rogers, any group that lives or works together over time becomes a community. Whether the community provides a safe, supportive environment depends on each person in the community as well as the facilitators. Each has feelings about being an insider or outsider, about recognition or lack of it, and about being seen, heard, and understood within the community. To enhance trust in the community, these feelings must be discussed openly. The co-created community is an important factor in the ability to learn.

SUMMARY COMMENTS

Person-centered expressive arts therapy utilizes the arts for spontaneous creative expression that symbolizes deep and sometimes inaccessible feelings and emotional states. Conditions that foster creativity occur both within the participants and within the group environment. The conditions for free expression require acceptance of the participants, a nonjudgmental setting, empathy, psychological freedom, and the availability of stimulating and challenging experiences. Participants respond with nondefensive openness to experience and an internal locus of evaluation that receives but is not overly concerned with the reactions of others. Offering guidelines to participants at the beginning of the process is helpful and stays within the person-centered framework because the guidelines place the responsibility and authority with the participants. Using the person-centered philosophical base of Carl Rogers, Natalie Rogers has developed an active group approach to personal growth and emotional health.

Application: Therapeutic Techniques and Procedures

DIVERSITY OF METHODS AND THERAPEUTIC STYLES

Rogers's original emphasis was on methods of reflecting feelings. As his view of psychotherapy developed, its focus shifted away from therapeutic techniques toward the therapist's personal qualities, beliefs, and attitudes and toward the relationship with the client. Attitudes and qualities critical in creating a favorable relationship include the therapist's congruence, transparency, nonjudgmental caring, prizing, presence, empathy, respect, and unconditional positive regard (Cain, 2010). It is of the utmost importance to remember that techniques do not function separately from the person of the group facilitator. Any intervention must be an honest expression of the group facilitator. Carl Rogers's style of reflective response is not the only acceptable way of being a group facilitator. Rogers emphasized that there are many ways to be facilitative, and he did not expect others to imitate him. Those who facilitate groups need to find their own way and discover their unique personal style.

Person-centered therapy has evolved through diversity, inventiveness, creativity, and individualization in practice (Cain, 2010). In newer versions of the person-centered approaches, group facilitators have greater freedom to participate in the relationship, to share their reactions, to confront clients in a caring way, and to be active in the therapeutic process (Bozarth, Zimring, & Tausch, 2002; Kirschenbaum, 2009; Lietaer, 1984). Current formulations of the approach assign more importance to therapists' bringing in their own here-and-now experiences, which can stimulate members to explore themselves at a deeper level. These changes from Rogers's original view of the counselor have encouraged the use of a wider variety of methods and a considerable diversity of therapeutic styles.

Although the therapist's receptive attitude is still viewed as being of central importance, this does not exclude the therapist from taking the initiative at times to stimulate a client's experiential process. Lietaer (1984) mentions that even "homework" and other auxiliary techniques may be used in a person-centered manner if the experience of the client remains the touchstone. Bohart (2003) claims that person-centered therapists are not banned from using techniques. What is important is *how* they suggest techniques. Bohart points out that some person-centered therapists incorporate dream work, Gestalt techniques, and behavioral techniques. With the emphasis on genuineness, person-centered therapists can practice in a more flexible and creative way suited to their personality. They can also tailor their relationship style to suit different clients (Bohart, 2003).

Today relatively few practitioners adhere to the classic client-centered model (Cain, 2010). Practitioners have adapted the approach to their personal convictions and personal style, integrating their own life experiences and ideas into their work with groups. Integrative personal-centered therapists subscribe to a fundamental philosophy but may blend concepts and methods from existential, Gestalt, and experiential approaches in facilitating their groups.

Although Rogers affirmed the value of diverse styles of facilitation, he disliked leaders who manipulated the group toward some unspoken agenda or who seemed to thrive on dramatics (MacMillan & Lago, 1999). Rogers (1970) took a dim view of the use of techniques or exercises to get a group moving. He also suggested that facilitators avoid making interpretive comments because such comments are apt to make the group self-conscious and slow the process down. Group process observations should come from members, a view that is consistent with Rogers's philosophy of placing the responsibility for the direction of the group on the members.

Using this approach, members are at the center of the group. The commitment of the therapist to empathically experience the client's frame of reference creates a loyalty to the client's direction and pace. It is the therapist's attitudes and belief in the inner resources of the client that create the therapeutic climate for growth (Bozarth, Zimring, & Tausch, 2002). Members of the person-centered group are often as helpful to the other members as is the leader, and they direct and orchestrate the process and progress.

Whatever techniques one employs or avoids, whatever style one adopts or refrains from, the approach should be adapted to the needs of the group and its members. The diverse range of client populations and the individual differences that characterize members of a group require that any approach be flexibly applied. Some clients function better with a high degree of structure, whereas others need very little structure. In addition to the needs of the members, the leadership approach should fit the personality and style of the leader.

AREAS OF APPLICATION

People without advanced psychological education are able to benefit by translating the therapeutic conditions of genuineness, empathic understanding, and unconditional positive regard into both their personal and professional lives. The approach's basic concepts are straightforward and easy to comprehend, yet they are not always easy to practice. The approach is based on locating power in the person rather than fostering an authoritarian structure in which control and power are denied to the person. These core skills can be used by many people in the helping professions and are the foundation for virtually all of the other theoretical orientations discussed in this book. If group workers are lacking in relationship and communication skills, they will not be effective in carrying out their role and functions in a group.

The person-centered approach to groups has been applied to diverse populations including therapy clients, counselors, staff members of entire school systems, administrators, medical students, groups in conflict, drug users and their helpers, people representing different cultures and languages, and job training groups. As the group movement developed, the person-centered approach became increasingly concerned with reducing human suffering, with cross-cultural awareness, and with conflict resolution on an international scale (Raskin, 1986a).

Applying the Person-Centered Approach to Group Work in Schools

In the foreword to *Freedom to Learn* (Rogers & Freiberg, 1994), Natalie Rogers summarizes the philosophy and values of educational systems that foster creativity:

> This philosophy includes: encouraging curiosity and experimentation, valuing individual freedom and responsibility, giving support and constructive criticism instead of judgment and grades, valuing the creative process more than the product, choosing to pursue one's own interests and goals rather than predetermined goals of the teacher, and having respect for the inner truth of each individual. (p. vi)

This philosophy forms the foundation for transforming traditional schools into schools where children are free to learn and where the human dimensions of the student–teacher relationship are prized. When these key values are applied to education at all levels, Rogers and Freiberg demonstrate that a transformation of education can take place. They summarize research that has been done on person-centered education and conclude "that a human approach is a fundamental precondition and foundation to learning and, in a great many ways, is more appropriate than traditional approaches to learning" (p. 248).

Both research and experience show that more learning, more problem solving, and more creativity can be found in classrooms that operate within a person-centered climate. The key elements of a person-centered environment include the following features:

- Teachers assume the role of facilitators of learning rather than mainly giving information.

- Teachers, from elementary school classrooms to graduate schools, discover ingenious ways to help students learn and make decisions.

- Students develop responsibility, self-discipline, and the ability to work cooperatively.

- Teachers move in the direction of becoming more genuine, more understanding, and more caring toward their students.
- Learners become increasingly self-directing and are able to assume more responsibility for the consequences of their choices.

Rogers and Freiberg (1994) describe journeys taken by different teachers who have moved from being controlling managers to facilitators of learning. Each of these teachers has discovered his or her own pathway to freedom.

In a person-centered group with children, play therapy is often the medium of expression. Axline's (1964) classic book, *Dibs: In Search of Self,* is an excellent example of a person-centered approach adapted to play therapy. In reading about Dibs, the power of listening, empathy, warmth, and engagement becomes evident. Axline (1964, 1969) demonstrates the healing power of play with children. There are many ways to adapt Axline's basic ideas and methods of person-centered play therapy in small group work. Play can be the medium through which children express their feelings, bring their conflicts to life, explore relationships, and reveal their hopes and fears.

In addition to play, other expressive techniques, which are an outgrowth of the person-centered approach, can be used in group work with children such as art, music, and movement. Because children's verbal communication skills may be limited, these nonverbal and expressive approaches can provide clues to what children are feeling and trying to communicate (Henderson & Thompson, 2011). The essence of person-centered play therapy is captured by Boy and Pine (1999):

> The focus of child-centered play therapy is on the child rather than the problem, the present rather than the past, feelings rather than thoughts or acts, understanding rather than explaining, accepting rather than correcting, the child's direction rather than the therapist's instruction, and the child's insight rather than the therapist's knowledge. (p. 172)

It is possible to create a group using these key principles and, at the same time, bring some degree of structure into the group. Depending on the ages of the children and the main purpose of the group, a facilitator may want to assume a more active role rather than being highly nondirective. Generally, if children sense the counselor understands and accepts them, they are likely to open up and become quite responsive. This approach allows for therapist flexibility in working with children in groups.

Play group therapy can be appropriately applied to counseling children in elementary school (Landreth, 2002). Child-centered group play therapy can help children learn to become responsible in interpersonal relationships, to explore their behavior, to cope with stress and anxiety, and to find satisfaction in living with others. The group experience allows children to process their personal concerns on both an intrapersonal and interpersonal level (Landreth, 2002; Sweeney & Homeyer, 1999). Baggerly and Parker (2005) describe how child-centered group play therapy with African American boys in the elementary school setting honors the African worldview and builds the self-confidence of boys. Baggerly and Parker found that during group play therapy the younger participants tended to identify with the older children, gained courage, and demonstrated newfound strength and skills. Those children who were timid frequently overcame their hesitancy by watching other children succeed at tasks. According to Baggerly and Parker, "child-centered group play therapy is an innovative strategy that fosters positive growth in African American boys' racial cultural identity" (p. 394).

Applying the Person-Centered Approach With Multicultural Populations

Rogers's interests evolved from working with individuals, to groups, to communities, and to world peace. During the last 15 years of his life, Rogers developed a passion for addressing broader social issues, especially peace. He sought ways to reduce psychological barriers that impinge on communication between factions (see Kirschenbaum, 2009; Rogers, 1987c; Rogers & Malcolm, 1987).

In 1974, Rogers and some of his colleagues initiated a new form of person-centered group known as the *large community group.* These groups, which began at the Center for Studies of the Person in La Jolla, California, eventually were offered in many communities and places around the world. These large groups, whose size often reached 75 to 800 people, worked and lived together for 2 to 3 weeks (Cain, 2002). Raskin (1986a) writes that these workshops were designed to build community, to facilitate the members' self-exploration, and to resolve tensions between members representing diverse cultures. These large community groups provided data for understanding how cross-cultural and international differences can be resolved through the application of conditions advocated by the person-centered approach. For more on large groups, I recommend Lago and MacMillan (1999).

The person-centered approach, more than other models, has been applied to bringing people of diverse cultures together for the purpose of developing mutual understanding. One of Rogers's hopes was that people from different cultures would be able to listen to one another and find the common ground that unites them. In 1948 Rogers began developing a theory of reducing tension among antagonistic groups, and he continued this work until his death in 1987.

Shortly before his death, Rogers conducted 4-day workshops with Soviet psychologists, educators, and researchers. He maintained that these sessions had demonstrated that the concerns expressed differed little from those felt by a similar professional group in the United States. He found that a psychological climate produced certain predictable results in the United States, Latin America, European countries, and South Africa as well as Russia (Rogers, 1987a).

As we've seen, the person-centered approach is grounded on the importance of hearing the deeper messages that participants bring to a group. Empathy, being present, and respecting the values of group participants are particularly important attitudes and skills in groups with culturally diverse individuals. These attitudes are not limited to any one cultural group but transcend culture. Cain (2008, 2010) states that the core therapist conditions of empathy, unconditional positive regard, and congruence are universal or near universal and are likely to have a constructive impact on all clients. Thus, person-centered therapy has much to offer a wide range of client populations. Cain adds that although person-centered therapists are aware of diversity factors, they do not make initial assumptions about individuals. They realize that each client's journey is unique and appreciate the importance of tailoring their methods to fit each individual.

Therapist empathy has moved far beyond simple "reflection," and therapists now draw from a variety of empathic response modes (Bohart & Greenberg, 1997). Empathy is a pathway to making significant connections with persons of color, and it can be expressed and communicated either directly or indirectly. Clients coming from certain cultures may not be comfortable with a direct expression of empathy by the therapist, but there are many ways to demonstrate an empathic grasp of the client's subjective world and inner experiencing.

Glauser and Bozarth (2001) remind us to pay attention to the cultural identity that resides within the client. They caution against making assumptions about clients based on their cultural background or the specific group to which they belong and recommend waiting for the cultural context to emerge from the client. Glauser and Bozarth maintain that the use of specific techniques often results in a "specificity myth" that concentrates on specific treatments for particular groups of people. They believe there has been too much emphasis on how to *do* counseling rather than how to *be* a counselor.

Although the person-centered approach has made significant contributions to working with groups representing diverse social, political, and cultural backgrounds, there are also some limitations to practicing exclusively within this framework in community agency settings and outpatient clinics. Many of the clients who come to a community mental health clinic or who are involved in some other type of outpatient treatment may desire or need a more structured group experience. This is especially true of short term groups, open groups with a rapidly changing membership, task-oriented groups, and groups composed of culturally diverse populations. Clients from a lower socioeconomic status often seek professional help to deal with some current crisis, to alleviate psychosomatic symptoms, to learn certain coping skills (such as stress management), or to find solutions for pressing problems. These clients may expect a directive leader who functions in an expert role as an authority, who offers advice and recommends a specific course of action, and they may experience difficulty with a leader who does not provide the structure they want. Bohart (2003) makes the point that the person-centered therapist is not an expert who is going to tell the client the "right way of being." Instead, the therapist is a "fellow explorer" who strives to deeply understand the experiential world of the client. In addition, the person-centered approach extols the value of an internal locus of control and prizes self-determination and autonomy, whereas some cultures place a value on an external locus of evaluation and do not place a high priority on autonomy and self-direction.

More preparation and orientation may be called for than is usually the case in a person-centered framework, especially in a group. As I have mentioned previously, group members can benefit from some orientation by the leader on what the group is about and how best to participate. For example, in her expressive arts groups, Natalie Rogers provides a general orientation for members, which includes guidelines for their participation. Group members stand a better chance of using the group process in a constructive way if they understand what behavior is useful in the context of the group. Members can profit from a discussion of the general goals and procedures of group process and of how the group might help them deal with their concerns.

Although there may be some distinct limitations to working exclusively within a person-centered perspective with some groups, it should not be concluded that this approach is unsuitable for ethnically and culturally diverse populations. Cain (2010) notes that rigid insistence on nondirectiveness may be too constricting for the therapist and the client. The personal preferences and learning styles of various members need to be taken into consideration. Some people prefer a directive and active style; others respond well to a less directive leader.

Evaluation of the Person-Centered Approach to Groups

CONTRIBUTIONS AND STRENGTHS OF THE APPROACH

Because the person-centered approach is very much a phenomenological one, based on the subjective worldview of the client, I consider it an excellent foundation for the initial stages of any type of group. Many person-centered practitioners would argue that this approach is sufficient for all the stages of a group's development. The approach encourages members from the outset to assume responsibility for determining their level of investment in the group and deciding what personal concerns they will raise. A main strength of this approach is the emphasis on truly listening to and deeply understanding the clients' world from their internal frame of reference. Empathy is the cornerstone of this approach, and it is a necessary foundation upon which any theory rests (Bohart, 2003; Bohart & Greenberg, 1997; Cain, 2010). Critical evaluation, analysis, and judgment are suspended, and attention is given to grasping the feelings and thoughts being expressed by the others. I see this form of listening and understanding as a prerequisite to any group approach, particularly during the early stages when it is essential that members feel free to explore their concerns openly. Unless the participants feel that they are being understood, any technique or intervention plan is bound to fail.

I appreciate the core values and principles upon which the person-centered approach rests, and I am convinced that many of its principles can be incorporated into other approaches to group work. This approach emphasizes each person's ability to find the answers for his or her own problems. By creating an egalitarian environment in which the facilitator functions not as an authority figure with answers but as a person creating a safe place for exploration, the participants are able to empower themselves. Being a facilitator in a person-centered group entails finding rewards in seeing people take charge of their own lives (Natalie Rogers, personal communication, June 17, 2009).

Many of the problems of group leaders in training stem from their failure to reach an understanding of the members' subjective world, an understanding that can be achieved only by very careful listening and attending and by restraining the tendency to solve members' problems. A major strength of this approach is the central importance placed on the group counselor as a person, and the assumption that the client is the major change agent in a therapy group—both of these assumptions have a great deal to do with determining the outcomes of a group. Client contributions to the therapeutic process continue to be neglected in most theoretical models, with very few exceptions (see Bohart & Tallman, 1999, 2010). The therapist's personal development goes hand in hand with mastering the ability to respond with heartfelt empathy. Furthermore, faith in the client's capacity for self-healing is in stark contrast with many theories that view the therapist's techniques and procedures as the most powerful agents that lead to change (Tallman & Bohart, 1999).

The leader must develop the ability to be present for members and to encourage them to interact openly. If the leader can encourage the creation of an open and accepting climate within the group, the members' self-healing forces and the healing forces present in the group as a community will become operant, and members will engage in the kind of individual and interpersonal work that will enable them to find their own resolutions that lead to self-acceptance. Ultimately, group members make their own choices and bring about change for themselves. Yet with the presence of the facilitator and the support of other members, participants realize that they do not have to experience the change process alone and that groups as collective entities have their own source of transformation.

Rogers and his colleagues engaged in research with personal growth groups when the group movement had reached its zenith in the 1960s, but Page, Weiss, and Lietaer (2002) indicate that there was a decline in the volume of person-centered research in the United States in the 1970s as American interests turned to more cognitive approaches. Elsewhere during the past two decades, however, numerous studies of person-centered group therapy have emerged, especially in Europe. The findings of these studies generally support a strong relationship between empathy, warmth, and genuineness and positive therapeutic outcomes in a group setting. Indeed, the quality of the therapeutic relationship is considered to be the single most important factor in the person-centered approach (Bohart, 2003). According to Cain (2010), an enormous body of research, conducted over a period of 70 years, supports the effectiveness of the person-centered approach and "clearly shows that humanistic therapies are as effective or more effective than other major therapeutic approaches in treating a wide range of client problems" (Cain, 2002, pp. 48–49). This research is ongoing in many parts of the world and continues to expand and refine our understanding of what constitutes effective psychotherapy.

In summarizing the studies on person-centered group therapy, Page and his colleagues (2002) make a number of important points about the efficacy of this approach. Research supports the notion that people with serious problems, such as substance abuse, can assume responsibility for making personal gains in these groups. Hospitalized patients and counseling center clients have also made significant improvement by participating in groups. It is clear that humanistic therapy groups can be used to help clients with a wide range of problems to function better interpersonally and to deal more effectively with their problems. However, humanistic group therapy is an underutilized approach in the managed care era in which practitioners are required to demonstrate concrete and measurable outcomes. Many practitioners are unaware of the research that demonstrates the effectiveness of these kinds of groups with clinical populations.

LIMITATIONS OF THE APPROACH

Although I deeply appreciate the person-centered philosophy, this approach provides little structure for group members. Both active support and directive interventions can be extremely helpful in promoting client change. Person-centered group leaders typically do not employ directive strategies, nor do they believe it is the facilitator's job to devise and introduce techniques and exercises as a way of helping the group do its work (Boy, 1990). I prefer the value of action; of therapeutic direction, if it is needed by clients; and of more directive skills than are generally found in this approach.

The way Natalie Rogers and her colleagues work is an exception as they do offer structured experiences to group members, giving them the opportunity to use movement, visual arts, music, and journal writing to go on their inner journey. The facilitator responds to the art in a person-centered way by honoring the world of the group member and by reflecting the deep feelings that are stirred by these art experiences. There is also a profound difference in the group process in that each group member can be going on his or her inner journey through art at the same time. When the participants are finished with their creative work, they share in dyads, and later they also share with the entire group.

Cain (1990b) believes nondirectiveness does not necessarily translate to "freedom" for many participants; rather, it may become a barrier. Given the freedom to choose their own direction, members do not always move toward productive work. For example, a group may be characterized by low energy, and members may choose to stay largely on a superficial and impersonal level. Ultimately, group members have the power to move or not move to a deeper level, yet the leader can encourage them to look at their behavior and decide what they might do differently. Not all persons do well when left primarily to draw on their intrinsic resources. It is essential that therapists modify their therapeutic approach to accommodate the specific needs of each client and the group as a whole. This may be especially true in some community mental health groups with the chronically mentally ill. A guiding question Cain (2010) asks of himself and of his clients is "Does it fit?" Cain believes that, ideally, therapists will continually monitor whether what they are doing "fits," especially whether their therapeutic style is compatible with their clients' way of viewing and understanding their problems. Cain believes person-centered practitioners must adapt their therapy approach to their clients rather than expecting clients to adopt the therapist's approach and style.

In keeping with a person-centered spirit, Lazarus (1996) asserts that *relationships of choice* are no less important than *techniques of choice*. I am in basic agreement with Lazarus on the importance of being able to draw upon various relationship styles as a way to facilitate movement within a group and to promote member change. I generally use techniques to enhance and to highlight the existing material in the group rather than to get things moving. For example, when members talk about a lonely time of their lives and sadness comes up naturally, I am inclined to ask them to do any number of things: Look at another person in the room and talk directly to this person about the sadness, talk to a person as though he or she were a significant other, or reenact a past event as though it were happening now. I continue to find that when members bring a struggle or some unfinished business with significant people in their lives into the present, whatever they are experiencing is intensified. Providing some therapeutic structure affords members the encouragement and support they need to fully experience their personal pain and make a crucial breakthrough. However, I do not have an outcome in mind for the group member.

Instead, I endeavor to facilitate the work of members so that they will find their own solutions. I am not leading them in a direction that I think they should go but taking my cues from them in selecting interventions.

As you will see in Chapter 11, I favor the active style afforded by the Gestalt approach, which involves creating experiments aimed at heightening the awareness level of group members. This is what Cain (2010) refers to as integrative person-centered therapy. I strive to pay close attention to the core conditions that are an integral part of person-centered approach and, at the same time, to use a variety of techniques to bring about cognitive, affective, and behavioral change. I believe members can benefit from leader intervention in translating their insights into action programs, and I collaborate with group members in designing homework assignments that will encourage them to do difficult things. My style is to ask members to come up with their own homework, but I may make suggestions for them to consider.

Concluding Commentary As with any theoretical orientation, there are limitations to the person-centered approach to group counseling. However, the longevity of the person-centered approach is certainly a factor to be considered in evaluating its impact. From Cain's (1990a) perspective, the most important contribution of the person-centered approach to group work is that it challenges group therapists to trust the resources of group members and to trust the relational characteristics of leaders (and other members) to cultivate these resources. In an age when practitioners are increasingly looking for immediate cures and the techniques that produce quick fixes, the person-centered approach reminds us that it is people who heal people, not techniques (David Cain, personal communication, July 11, 2001). Therapists need to evolve as persons rather than being intent on expanding their repertoire of techniques. However, it is important to remember that effective group facilitators need to be therapeutic persons, *and they need to have the knowledge and skills required to assist members in reaching their personal goals in a group.*

The scope and influence of Rogers's work has continued well beyond his death; the person-centered approach is alive, well, and expanding (Kirschenbaum, 2009). "It is a vibrant international movement with burgeoning publications, organizations, research, theories, orientations, applications, and adherents. It has significant challenges to face if its renaissance is to continue, but clearly, it has survived its founder" (p. 607). Today there is not one version of person-centered therapy but a number of continuously evolving person-centered psychotherapies (Cain, 2010). Although few psychotherapists claim to have an exclusive person-centered theoretical orientation, the philosophy and principles of this approach permeate the practice of many, if not most, therapists. Other schools of therapy are increasingly recognizing the centrality of the therapeutic relationship as a route to therapeutic change (Kirschenbaum, 2009).

Where to Go From Here

MAJOR ASSOCIATIONS: THE PERSON-CENTERED APPROACH

You might consider joining the Association for the Development of the Person-Centered Approach (ADPCA), an interdisciplinary and international organization. Membership includes a subscription to *The Person-Centered*

Journal, the association's newsletter, a membership directory, and information about the annual meeting. It also provides information about continuing education and supervision and training in the person-centered approach.

Association for the Development of the Person-Centered Approach
2865 Shimmering Bay Street
Laughlin, NV 89029
Telephone: (702) 298-9215
E-mail: adpca@cmaaccess.com
Website: http://adpca.org

For information about *The Person-Centered Journal*, contact:

Jon Rose, editor
E-mail: jonmrose@aol.com

The Association for Humanistic Psychology (AHP) is devoted to promoting personal integrity, creative learning, and active responsibility in embracing the challenges of being human in these times.

Association for Humanistic Psychology
1516 Oak Street #320
Alameda, CA 94501-2947
Telephone: (510) 769-6495
Fax: (510) 769-6433
E-mail: AHPOffice@aol.com
Website: http://ahpweb.org

Person-centered practitioners are working in many countries, including Australia, Canada, Korea, Israel, Jamaica, Russia, New Zealand, and South Africa. Active associations of person-centered practitioners can be found in many countries, including Argentina, Brazil, Chile, France, Germany, Greece, Hungary, Japan, the Netherlands, Belgium, Austria, Switzerland, Slovakia, and the United Kingdom. The World Association for Person Centered and Experiential Psychotherapy and Counselling (WAPCEPC) publishes a quarterly journal and promotes international conferences and international forums.

World Association for Person Centered and Experiential Psychotherapy and Counselling
Website: www.pce-world.org

Many new books on the person-centered approach have been published in the United Kingdom in recent years. The principal publisher behind this vigorous development is PCCS Books, but other UK publishers include Sage, Radcliffe, Routledge, Palgrave-McMillan, and Whurr.

PCCS Books
Ross-on-Wye, Herefordshire
Website: www.pccs-books.co.uk

TRAINING IN THE PERSON-CENTERED APPROACH

The Center for Studies of the Person (CSP) in La Jolla offers workshops, training seminars, experiential small groups, and sharing of learning in community meetings. The Distance Learning Project and the Carl Rogers Institute for Psychotherapy Training and Supervision provide experiential and didactic training and supervision for professionals interested in developing their own person-centered orientation.

Center for Studies of the Person
1150 Silverado Street, Suite #112
La Jolla, CA 92037
Telephone: (858) 459-3861
E-mail: centerfortheperson@yahoo.com
Website: www.centerfortheperson.org

TRAINING IN THE PERSON-CENTERED APPROACH TO EXPRESSIVE ARTS

For training in expressive art therapy, you could join Natalie Rogers, PhD, and Shellee Davis, MA, faculty of the certificate program at Saybrook graduate school in their course, "Expressive Arts for Healing and Social Change: A Person-Centered Approach." A 16-unit certificate program requires 6 weeks of study spread over 2 years at a retreat center north of San Francisco. Rogers and Davis offer expressive arts within a person-centered counseling framework. They use counseling demonstrations, practice counseling sessions, readings, discussions, papers, and a creative project to teach experiential and theoretical methods.

Saybrook University
E-mail: registrar@saybrook.edu

CARL ROGERS: A DAUGHTER'S TRIBUTE

This Carl Rogers CD-ROM is a visually beautiful and lasting archive of the life and works of the founder of humanistic psychology. It includes excerpts from his 16 books, over 120 photographs spanning his lifetime, and award-winning video footage of two encounter groups and Carl's early counseling sessions. It is an essential resource for students, teachers, libraries, and universities. It is a profound tribute to one of the most important thinkers, influential psychologists, and peace activists of the 20th century. *Carl Rogers: A Daughter's Tribute* was developed for Natalie Rogers by Mindgarden Media, Inc.

Carl Rogers: A Daughter's Tribute
Website: www.psychotherapy.net

AUTHOR LECTURES

Watch *Gerald Corey's Perspectives on Theory and Practice of Group Counseling* DVD or visit the *Theory and Practice of Group Counseling* CourseMate website at www.cengagebrain.com/shop/ISBN/0840033869 to watch videos of Dr. Gerald Corey presenting lectures for each chapter. Also available are unique eAudio lectures for each chapter and quiz questions for self-study.

RECOMMENDED SUPPLEMENTARY READINGS

The Life and Work of Carl Rogers (Kirschenbaum, 2009) is a definitive biography of Carl Rogers that follows his life from his early childhood through his death. This book illustrates the legacy of Carl Rogers and shows his enormous influence on the field of counseling and psychotherapy. *Carl Rogers on Encounter Groups* (Rogers, 1970) is an excellent introduction to person-centered groups. It is a readable account of their process and outcomes, changes as a result of them, and glimpses of the subjective struggles and experiences of those who participate in these groups.

Experiences in Relatedness: Groupwork and the Person-Centered Approach (Lago & MacMillan, 1999) is the only other book devoted to group work from the person-centered perspective. The book includes a discussion of training and development, research, applications, and large groups.

On Becoming a Person (Rogers, 1961) is an important work addressing the characteristics of the helping relationship, the philosophy of the person-centered approach, and practical issues related to therapy. I especially recommend Chapters 2–9, 16, and 17.

A Way of Being (Rogers, 1980) contains a series of updated writings on Rogers's personal experiences and perspectives, as well as chapters on the foundations and applications of a person-centered approach. Especially

useful are the chapters on person-centered communities, large groups, and perspectives on the world and person of tomorrow.

The Creative Connection: Expressive Arts as Healing (N. Rogers, 1993) is a practical, spirited book lavishly illustrated with colorful action photos. Filled with fresh ideas to stimulate creativity, self-expression, healing, and transformation, Natalie Rogers combines the philosophy of her father with the expressive arts to enhance communication between client and therapist.

Humanistic Psychotherapies: Handbook of Research and Practice (Cain & Seeman, 2002) is a comprehensive discussion of person-centered therapy, Gestalt therapy, and existential therapy. This book provides research evidence for person-centered theory.

Person-Centered Psychotherapies (Cain, 2010) provides a comprehensive overview of the development of the person-centered approach. This volume contains abundant current research supporting the core concepts of this approach.

REFERENCES AND SUGGESTED READINGS

Axline, V. (1964). *Dibs: In search of self.* New York: Ballantine.

Axline, V. (1969). *Play therapy* (rev. ed.). New York: Ballantine.

Baggerly, J., & Parker, M. (2005). Play therapy with African American boys at the elementary school level. *Journal of Counseling and Development, 83*(4), 387–396.

Bohart, A. C. (2003). Person-centered psychotherapy and related experiential approaches. In A. S. Gurman & S. B. Messer (Eds.), *Essential psychotherapies: Theory and practice* (2nd ed., pp. 107–148). New York: Guilford Press.

*Bohart, A. C., & Greenberg, L. S. (Eds.). (1997). *Empathy reconsidered: New*

directions in psychotherapy. Washington, DC: American Psychological Association.

*Bohart, A. C., & Tallman, K. (1999). *How clients make therapy work: The process of active-self healing.* Washington, DC: American Psychological Association.

*Bohart, A. C., & Tallman, K. (2010). Clients: The neglected common factor in psychotherapy. In B. L. Duncan, S. D. Miller, B. E. Wampold, & M. A. Hubble (Eds.), *The heart and soul of change: Delivering what works in therapy* (2nd ed., pp. 83–111). Washington, DC: American Psychological Association.

Boy, A. V. (1990). The therapist in person-centered groups. *Person-Centered Review, 5*(3), 308–315.

*Boy, A. V., & Pine, G. J. (1999). *A person-centered foundation for counseling and* *psychotherapy* (2nd ed.). Springfield, IL: Charles C Thomas.

*Bozarth, J. D., Zimring, F. M., & Tausch, R. (2002). Client-centered therapy: The evolution of a revolution. In D. J. Cain & J. Seeman (Eds.), *Humanistic psychotherapies: Handbook of research and practice* (pp. 147–188). Washington, DC: American Psychological Association.

Bozarth, J. D. (1984). Beyond reflections: Emergent modes of empathy. In R. F. Levant & J. M. Shlien (Eds.), *Client-centered therapy and the person-centered approach: New directions in theory, research, and practice* (pp. 59–75). New York: Praeger.

Braaten, L. J. (1986). Thirty years with Rogers's necessary and sufficient conditions of therapeutic personality change: A personal evaluation. *Person-Centered Review, 1*(1), 37–50.

Brodley, B. T. (1996). Empathic understanding and feelings in client-centered therapy. *The Person-Centered Journal, 3*(1), 22–30.

Brodley, B. T. (1997). The nondirective attitude in client-centered therapy. *The Person-Centered Journal, 4*(1), 18–30.

Brodley, B. T. (1998). Congruence and its relation to communication in client-centered therapy. *The Person-Centered Journal, 5*(2), 83–106.

Brodley, B. T. (1999a). The actualizing tendency concept in client-centered theory. *The Person-Centered Journal, 6*(2), 108–120.

Brodley, B. T. (1999b). Reasons for responses expressing the therapist's frame of reference in client-centered therapy. *The Person-Centered Journal, 6*(1), 4–27.

Brodley, B. T. (2000). Personal presence in client-centered therapy. *The Person-Centered Journal, 7*(2), 139–149.

Bugental, J.F.T. (1987). *The art of the psychotherapist.* New York: Norton.

Cain, D. J. (1990a). Fifty years of client-centered therapy and the person-centered approach. *Person-Centered Review, 5*(1), 3–7.

Cain, D. J. (1990b). Further thoughts about nondirectiveness and client-centered therapy. *Person-Centered Review, 5*(1), 89–99.

*Cain, D. J. (2002). Defining characteristics, history, and evolution of humanistic psychotherapies. In D. J. Cain & J. Seeman (Eds.), *Humanistic psychotherapies: Handbook of research and practice* (pp. 3–54). Washington, DC: American Psychological Association.

Cain, D. J. (2008). Person-centered therapy. In J. Frew & M. Spiegler (Eds.), *Contemporary psychotherapies for a diverse world* (pp. 177–227). New York: Lahaska Press.

*Cain, D. J. (2010). *Person-centered psychotherapies.* Washington, DC: American Psychological Association.

*Cain, D. J., & Seeman, J. (Eds.). (2002). *Humanistic psychotherapies: Handbook of research and practice.* Washington, DC: American Psychological Association.

Coghlan, D., & McIlduff, E. (1990). Structuring and nondirectiveness in group facilitation. *Person-Centered Review, 5*(1), 13–29.

*Glauser, A. S., & Bozarth, J. D. (2001). Person-centered counseling: The culture within. *Journal of Counseling and Development, 79*(2), 142–147.

*Greenberg, L. S., & Rice, L. N. (1997). Humanistic approaches to psychotherapy. In P. L. Wachtel & S. B. Messer (Eds.), *Theories of psychotherapy: Origins and evolution* (pp. 97–129). Washington, DC: American Psychological Association.

Henderson, D. A., & Thompson, C. L. (2011). *Counseling children* (8th ed.). Belmont, CA: Brooks/Cole, Cengage Learning.

*Kirschenbaum, H. (2009). *The life and work of Carl Rogers.* Alexandria, VA: American Counseling Association.

*Lago, C., & MacMillan, M. (Eds.). (1999). *Experiences in relatedness: Groupwork and the person-centred approach.* Herefordshire, UK: PCCS Books.

Landreth, G. L. (2002). *Play therapy: The art of relationship* (2nd ed.). New York: Brunner-Routledge.

Lazarus, A. A. (1996). Some reflections after 40 years of trying to be an effective psychotherapist. *Psychotherapy, 33*(1), 142–145.

Lietaer, G. (1984). Unconditional positive regard: A controversial basic attitude in client-centered therapy. In R. F. Levant & J. M. Shlien (Eds.), *Client-centered therapy and the person-centered approach: New directions in theory, research, and practice* (pp. 41–58). New York: Praeger.

MacMillan, M., & Lago, C. (1999). PCA groups: Past, present . . . and future? In C. Lago & M. MacMillan (Eds.), *Experiences in relatedness: Groupwork and the person-centred approach* (pp. 29–45). Herefordshire, UK: PCCS Books.

Natiello, P. (1987). The person-centered approach: From theory to practice. *Person-Centered Review, 2*(2), 203–216.

*Norcross, J. C. (2010). The therapeutic relationship. In B. L. Duncan, S. D. Miller, B. E. Wampold, & M. A. Hubble (Eds.), *The heart and soul of change: Delivering what works in therapy* (2nd ed., pp. 113–141). Washington, DC: American Psychological Association.

O'Hara, M. (1984). Person-centered gestalt: Towards a holistic synthesis. In R. F. Levant & J. M. Shlien (Eds.), *Client-centered therapy and the person-centered approach: New directions in theory, research, and practice* (pp. 203–221). New York: Praeger.

O'Hara, M. (1997). Relational empathy: Beyond modern egocentricism to postmodern holistic contextualism. In A. C. Bohart & L. S. Greenberg (Eds.), *Empathy reconsidered: New directions in psychotherapy* (pp. 295–319). Washington, DC: American Psychological Association.

O'Hara. M., & Wood, J. K. (1984) Patterns of awareness: Consciousness and the group mind. *The Gestalt Journal, 6*(2), 103–116.

O'Hara, M., & Wood, J. K. (2004). Transforming communities. Person-centered encounters and the creation of integral conscious groups. In B. Banathy & P. Jenlink (Eds.), *Dialogue as a means of collective communication* (pp. 105–136). New York: Kluwer Academic/Plenum.

*Page, R. C., Weiss, J. F., & Lietaer, G. (2002). Humanistic group psychotherapy. In D. J. Cain & J. Seeman (Eds.), *Humanistic psychotherapies: Handbook of research and practice* (pp. 339–368). Washington, DC: American Psychological Association.

Raskin, N. J. (1986a). Client-centered group psychotherapy, Part 1: Development of client-centered groups. *Person-Centered Review, 1*(3), 272–290.

Raskin, N. J. (1986b). Client-centered group psychotherapy, Part 2: Research on client-centered groups. *Person-Centered Review, 1*(4), 389–408.

Raskin, N. J., & Rogers, C. R. (2011). Client-centered therapy. In R. Corsini & D. Wedding (Eds.), *Current psychotherapies* (9th ed., pp. 148–195). Belmont, CA: Brooks/Cole, Cengage Learning.

Rogers, C. (1951). *Client-centered therapy.* Boston: Houghton Mifflin.

Rogers, C. (1957). The necessary and sufficient conditions of therapeutic personality change. *Journal of Consulting Psychology, 21*, 95–103.

*Rogers, C. (1961). *On becoming a person.* Boston: Houghton Mifflin.

*Rogers, C. (1970). *Carl Rogers on encounter groups.* New York: Harper & Row.

Rogers, C. (1975). Empathic: An unappreciated way of being. *The Counseling Psychologist, 5*(2), 2–9.

*Rogers, C. (1980). *A way of being.* Boston: Houghton Mifflin.

Rogers, C. (1986a). Carl Rogers on the development of the person-centered approach. *Person-Centered Review, 1*(3), 257–259.

Rogers, C. (1986b). Client-centered therapy. In I. L. Kutash, & A. Wolf (Eds.), *Psychotherapist's casebook* (pp. 197–208). San Francisco: Jossey-Bass.

Rogers, C. R. (1987a). Inside the world of the Soviet professional. *Counseling and Values, 32*(1), 46–66.

Rogers, C. R. (1987b). Rogers, Kohut, and Erikson: A personal perspective on some similarities and differences.

In J. K. Zeig (Ed.), *The evolution of psychotherapy* (pp. 179–187). New York: Brunner/Mazel.

Rogers, C. R. (1987c). Steps toward world peace, 1948–1986: Tension reduction in theory and practice. *Counseling and Values, 32*(1), 12–16.

Rogers, C. R. (1987d). The underlying theory: Drawn from experience with individuals and groups. *Counseling and Values, 32*(1), 38–45.

Rogers, C. R., & Freiberg, H. J. (1994). *Freedom to learn* (3rd ed.). Upper Saddle River, NJ: Prentice Hall.

Rogers, C. R., & Malcolm, D. (1987). The potential contribution of the behavioral scientist to world peace. *Counseling and Values, 32*(1), 10–11.

Rogers, C. R., & Russell, D. E. (2002). *Carl Rogers: The quiet revolutionary.* Roseville, CA: Penmarin Books.

Rogers, N. (1993). *The creative connection: Expressive arts as healing.* Palo Alto, CA: Science & Behavior Books.

Rogers, N. (1995). *Emerging woman: A decade of midlife transitions.* Manchester, UK: PCCS Books.

Sweeney, D. S., & Homeyer, L. E. (Eds.). (1999). *The handbook of group play therapy.* San Francisco: Jossey-Bass.

*Tallman, K., & Bohart, A. C. (1999). The client as a common factor: Clients as self-healers. In M. A. Hubble, B. L. Duncan, & S. D. Miller (Eds.), *The heart and soul of change: What works in therapy* (pp. 91–131). Washington, DC: American Psychological Association.

*Thorne, B. (1992). *Carl Rogers.* Newbury Park, CA: Sage.

*Watson, J. C. (2002). Re-visioning empathy. In D. J. Cain & J. Seeman (Eds.), *Humanistic psychotherapies: Handbook of research and practice* (pp. 445–471). Washington, DC: American Psychological Association.

Zimring, F. M., & Raskin, N. J. (1992). Carl Rogers and client/person-centered therapy. In D. K. Freedheim (Ed.), *History of psychotherapy: A century of change* (pp. 629–656). Washington, DC: American Psychological Association.

Gestalt Therapy in Groups

Introduction

Gestalt therapy was developed by Fritz Perls and his wife, Laura, in the 1940s. It is based on the assumption that we are best understood in the context of our environment. The basic goal of a Gestalt group is to provide a context that will enable members to increase their awareness of what they are experiencing and the quality of the contact they are making with others. Moment-to-moment awareness of one's experiencing, together with the almost immediate awareness of one's blocks to such experiencing, is seen as therapeutic in and of itself.

Gestalt therapy is *existential* in that it is grounded in the here-and-now and gives primacy to existential dialogue. Awareness, choice, and responsibility are cornerstones of practice. Gestalt therapy gives special attention to existence as people experience it and affirms the human capacity for growth and healing through interpersonal contact and insight (Yontef, 1995). This approach is *phenomenological* in that it emphasizes how we see the world, how we contribute to creating our experience, and how we organize our world and ourselves. Gestalt therapy is also an *experiential* approach, and group members are able to come to grips with *what* and *how* they are thinking, feeling, and doing as they interact with others in the group. Members are encouraged and guided in experimenting with new behaviors as a way to increase self-understanding (Yontef, 1995).

As clients acquire present-centered awareness and a clearer perception of the limitations of their style of interpersonal relating, significant unfinished business emerges. To live more fully in the present, clients need to identify and deal with anything from the past that interferes with current functioning. By reexperiencing past conflicts as if they were occurring in the present, clients expand their level of awareness and are able to integrate denied and fragmented parts of themselves, thus becoming unified and whole.

The Gestalt view is that experiencing is more powerful than the therapist's interpretations (Strumpfel & Goldman, 2002). Therefore, the approach of the Gestalt group therapist is fundamentally noninterpretive. Gestalt group therapists do not try to explain to members why they do things, nor do therapists interpret the true meaning of members' experiences (Frew, 2008). Instead, group leaders encourage members to discover their own meaning.

Group members are encouraged to try on a new style of behavior, to give expression to certain dimensions of their personality that are dormant, and to test out alternative modes of behavior to widen their ability to respond in the world. According to Zinker (1978), Gestalt experiments are anchored in the experiential life of the members as they present themselves in the situation and grow out of a living context for the group.

THE EVOLUTION OF GESTALT GROUP THERAPY

Fritz Perls, one of the founders of Gestalt therapy, was highly influential in promoting his style of therapeutic practice. Perls developed many of the key concepts of Gestalt therapy, but Perls never claimed to be doing group therapy. In the 1950s and early 1960s, Perls devoted much of his time to conducting workshops to train mental health practitioners in Gestalt theory and techniques as they applied to individual therapy. He emphasized one-to-one work—using the "hot seat" style—and discouraged any group interaction. Perls made frequent use of the "empty chair" technique, which was originated by J. L. Moreno (see Chapter 8). Miriam Polster (1997) points out that Perls's work was clearly focused on interaction between himself and a client who volunteered to work *in front of* a group, but not *within* the group. She adds that Perls was not particularly interested in or adept at working with groups, and he rarely recognized the group as a presence in his work. The audience was viewed almost entirely as background for the encounter between the leader and the individual participant (Feder & Frew, 2008).

Perls challenged clients to see how they were avoiding responsibility or avoiding feeling, and his therapeutic style was characterized by theatrics, abrasive confrontation, and intense catharsis. Yontef (1993) suggests that this flamboyant style may have met more of Perls's own narcissistic needs than the needs of his clients. Yontef is critical of the anti-intellectual, individualistic, dramatic, and confrontive flavor that characterized Gestalt therapy in the "anything goes environment" of the 1960s. Yontef (1999) claims that contemporary forms of Gestalt practice have moved away from the harsh and dramatic style of the 1960s and 1970s to an approach that "combines sustained empathic inquiry with crisp, clear, and relevant awareness focusing" (p. 10). Frew (2008) agrees that Gestalt therapy has evolved to focus more on attention to awareness and to interpersonal contact. Increased attention also has been given to the families and communities, which are an integral part of an individual's life. Polster (2008) writes about *life focus communities,* which is a way of taking therapy from the office into ordinary life in small groups.

Contemporary Gestalt practice in the United States is very different from the style popularized by Perls (Schoenberg & Feder, 2005). This newer version, called **relational Gestalt therapy,** includes more support and increased kindness and compassion in therapy as compared to the confrontive and dramatic style of Perls (Yontef, 1999). Erving and Miriam Polster (1973, 1999), pioneers in relational Gestalt therapy, have made many significant theoretical and practical contributions to the development of contemporary Gestalt therapy. As therapists, supervisors, and trainers, the Polsters employ a style that is supportive, accepting, challenging, and less confrontational than the traditional Gestalt therapy practiced by Perls.

Today few Gestalt practitioners use the empty chair technique as their *primary* method of conducting groups (Cain, 2002; Feder & Frew, 2008; Frew, 1988;

Kepner, 2008). One survey found that only 19% of Gestalt group leaders endorsed using such an exclusively intrapersonal approach (Feder & Frew, 2006). The essence of current Gestalt therapy involves supporting the client to become more aware of his or her experience without pushing or blaming. The practice of Gestalt therapy has softened and shifted its emphasis toward the quality of the therapist–client relationship, dialogue, empathic attunement, and tapping the client's wisdom and resources (Cain, 2002). In keeping with this evolution of Gestalt therapy, in this chapter I emphasize the contemporary developments that characterize this approach in the post-Perls era.

Key Concepts

THERAPEUTIC GOALS

The basic goal of Gestalt therapy is increased awareness, which by and of itself is seen as curative or growth producing. **Awareness** requires self-knowledge, responsibility for choices, contact with the environment, immersion in current experience, self-acceptance, and the ability to make contact (Yontef & Jacobs, 2011). With awareness, clients have the capacity to find within themselves the resources necessary to solve their problems and to discover the conditions that will make change possible. Without awareness, they do not possess the tools for personality change.

Gestalt therapy aims not at analysis but at integration of conflicting dimensions within the individual. This step-by-step process involves "reowning" parts of oneself that have been disowned and then unifying these disparate parts into an integrated whole. As clients become more fully aware, they can carry on with their own personal growth, make informed choices, and live a meaningful existence.

A basic assumption of Gestalt therapy is that individuals can self-regulate, especially if they are fully aware of what is happening in and around them. Because the environments in which individuals are embedded are never completely responsive to their needs, creative adjustments occur, and aspects of the individual are lost to awareness. Therapy, individual or group, attempts to awaken the lost parts to the possibilities in the current set of field conditions.

The Gestalt theory of change posits that the more we attempt to be who or what we are not, the more we remain the same. According to Beisser's (1970) **paradoxical theory of change**, personal change tends to occur when we become aware of *what we are* as opposed to trying to become *what we are not.* Stated slightly differently, it is important that we accept *who* and *what* we are rather than striving to become what we "should be." What we are is always the starting point for the path we might take. Erving Polster (1995) states that the therapist is called on to see clients as they are, hear them as they are, talk to them as they are, and sense them as they are—to identify with them and create a union. When we face and become what we are, we open rich possibilities for change. The challenge for group therapists is not to directly change group participants but to engage participants and assist them in developing their own awareness of how they are in the present moment.

The question of therapeutic goals can be considered from the point of view of personal goals for each member and of group process goals for the group as a whole. Zinker (2008) describes the following *individual* goals:

- Integrating polarities within oneself
- Enriching and expanding awareness
- Achieving contact with self and others
- Learning to provide self-support instead of looking to others for this support
- Defining one's boundaries with clarity
- Translating insights into action
- Being willing to learn about oneself by engaging in creative experiments
- Learning to flow smoothly through the awareness-excitement-contact cycle without serious blockage

At the *group level,* Zinker (2008) lists the following goals for members:

- Learning how to ask clearly and directly for what they want or need
- Learning how to deal effectively with interpersonal conflicts
- Learning how to give support and energy to one another
- Being direct with each other and speaking in the first person
- Finding ways to challenge members to grow while respecting their needs for space and boundaries
- Creating a community that is based on trust that allows for a level of deep and meaningful work
- Learning how to give each other feedback
- Learning not to give advice
- Using the resources within the group rather than relying on the group leader as the director

The goals of a Gestalt group involve equal attention to both process and content. As Frew (2008) puts it, "Gestalt therapy embraces the inseparable yin and yang of process and content, but it is primarily a process-oriented counseling approach" (p. 258).

Miriam Polster (1997) points to the importance of allowing members to talk about aspects of their lives that concern or baffle them and also their way of relating to one another within the group. She states that although it is essential for a member to be able to tell his or her story, the story itself is not enough. What is important is *how* the member tells the story and the way in which others in the group listen and are affected by the story. Polster gives an example of a man in one of her groups who let his sentences simply trail off in such a way that even he was not interested in what he was saying. She asked him to end his sentences with the phrase, "and I *really* mean that!" This led him to put more animation into his speech, which kept the rest of the group interested in what he was saying. As a way to enhance the possibilities for interpersonal learning, the group leader might ask members to let this man know how they are affected by being in his presence. Other members can share some ways they reduce their power in their daily lives and within the group context. They can also talk of ways they could become more animated. In other words, an individual's work can be enlarged upon by bringing in the interpersonal dimension so that members become more keenly aware of how they are functioning in the group situation. Doing this will give members a better sense of how they function out of the group as well.

SOME PRINCIPLES OF GESTALT THERAPY THEORY

A number of basic principles underlie the theory of Gestalt therapy. These principles include holism, field theory, the figure-formation process, and organismic self-regulation.

Holism Holism is one of the foundational principles of Gestalt therapy (Latner, 1986) and is expressed by this dictum: The whole is greater than the sum of its parts. We can only be understood to the extent that we take into consideration all dimensions of human functioning. Because Gestalt therapists are interested in the whole person, they place no superior value on a particular aspect of the individual. Gestalt practice attends to a client's thoughts, feelings, behaviors, body, and dreams as they become figural or move into the foreground for clients (Frew, 2008). The emphasis is on the aspects of the individual that are most "figural" or salient at any moment and to integration, how the parts fit together, and how the individual makes contact with the environment.

Field Theory Gestalt therapy is based on **field theory**, which is grounded on the principle that the organism must be seen in its environment, or in its context, as part of the constantly changing field. Everything is relational, in flux, interrelated, and in process, and Gestalt therapists pay particular attention to and explore what is occurring at the boundary between the person and the environment.

The Figure-Formation Process Originally developed in the field of visual perception by a group of Gestalt psychologists, this process describes how the individual organizes experiences from moment to moment. In Gestalt therapy the field differentiates into figure (the emerging focus of attention) and ground (the background environment). The **figure-formation process** tracks how some aspect of the environmental field emerges from the background and becomes the focal point of the individual's attention and interest (Latner, 1986). The needs of an individual at a given moment influence this process (Frew, 1997).

Organismic Self-Regulation The figure-formation process is intertwined with the principle of **organismic self-regulation**, which describes the nature of the relationship between the individual and the environment. When equilibrium is "disturbed" by the emergence of a need, a sensation, or an interest, the organism will distinguish the means required to gratify this need. Organisms do their best to regulate themselves, given their own capabilities and the resources of their environment (Latner, 1986), and individuals will take actions and make contacts that will both restore equilibrium and contribute to growth and change.

Frew (1997) describes the implications of the principles of figure formation and organismic self-regulation for the therapy group. Members attempt to self-regulate in the group context by attending to what becomes figural moment to moment. A main method Gestalt therapists use in working with group members involves directing participants' awareness to the "figures" that emerge from the background during a group session. What emerges for each group member is associated with what is of interest or what he or she needs to be able to regain a sense of equilibrium or a measure of personal growth. The therapist uses the figure-formation process as the guide for the focus of exploration and work in the group.

AWARENESS

The task of members of a Gestalt group is to pay attention to the structure of their experience and to become aware of the *what* and *how* of such experiencing. The psychoanalytic approach is interested in *why* we do what we do; the Gestalt leader asks "what" and "how" questions but rarely "why" questions. By attending to the **continuum of awareness**—that is, by staying with the moment-to-moment flow of experiencing—group members discover how they are functioning in the world.

Gestalt group leaders employ the figure-formation process when they assist members in paying attention to what becomes figural for them. To help members gain a sharper awareness of what they are thinking, feeling, and doing, the Gestalt group therapist asks questions like the following, which lead to present-centeredness:

- What are you experiencing now?
- What's going on inside you as you're speaking?
- How are you experiencing your anxiety in your body?
- How are you attempting to withdraw at this moment, and how are you avoiding contact with unpleasant feelings?
- What's your feeling at this moment as you sit there and try to talk?
- What do you hear in your voice as you talk to your father now?

To attain present-centered awareness of our existence, Gestalt therapy focuses on the surface of behavior by concentrating on the group member's movements, postures, language patterns, voice, gestures, and interactions with others. There is value in attending to observable behavior and creating a climate in which group members can come into contact with their changing awareness from moment to moment.

THE HERE-AND-NOW

One of the most important contributions of Gestalt therapy is the emphasis on learning to appreciate and fully experience the present. The past is gone, and the future has not yet arrived, whereas the present moment is lively and exciting. The past is important, but only insofar as it is related to our present functioning. Gestalt therapy's focus on the here-and-now encompasses the past and helps influence the future (Melnick & Nevis, 2005). Gestalt therapists have developed a methodology that helps individuals discover and experiment with new possibilities. Gestalt group process provides many opportunities for using present-centeredness to increase awareness and bring about change, and the group process offers a greater chance to awaken unfinished business in members through their present-centered interactions (Schoenberg & Feder, 2005).

In Gestalt groups the participants bring past problem situations into the present by reenacting the situation as if it were occurring now. For example, if a group member (Leslie) begins to talk about the difficulty she had when she was younger and attempted to live with her father, the therapist could intervene with a request that Leslie "be here now" with her father and speak directly to him. The therapist might say: "Bring your father into this room now, and let yourself go back to the time when you were a child. Tell him now, as though he were here and you were that child, what you most want to say." The leader might make use of the empty chair technique by suggesting that Leslie imagine that her father is sitting in an empty chair and asking her to talk directly to him. The leader has many ways to encourage this client to attend to the present moment, for example, she might be asked to look at someone in the group and talk to that person as she would if her father were present. Another alternative that a group leader might suggest to enhance the group process is to involve other members in Leslie's work. Leslie might select a group member to actually play the role of her father. This brings an interpersonal dimension to the Gestalt work and encourages other members to get involved by expressing their reactions to others in the group.

Most Gestalt experiments are designed to put clients into closer contact with their ongoing experiencing from moment to moment, and some Gestalt groups have a very tight focus on the here-and-now. A basic ground rule of Feder's (2008a) interactive, here-and-now approach is that participants agree to devote their attention and efforts to their experiences that directly pertain to what is taking place within the group. There are disadvantages to this exclusive here-and-now focus if the past and the future are discarded. E. Polster (1987a) observes that too tight a focus, with a highly concentrated emphasis on the here-and-now, will foreclose on much that matters, such as continuity of commitment, the implications of one's acts, dependability, and responsiveness to others.

UNFINISHED BUSINESS

Unfinished business includes unexpressed feelings—such as resentment, hate, rage, pain, hurt, anxiety, guilt, shame, and grief—and events and memories that linger in the background and clamor for completion. Unless these unfinished situations and unexpressed emotions become figural and are dealt with, they will interfere with present-centered awareness and with our effective functioning.

Because we don't sense the internal and environmental support to confront and fully experience our uncomfortable emotions, the emotions become a nagging undercurrent that prevents us from being fully alive. The Gestalt therapist might encourage expressing in the therapeutic session feelings never directly expressed before. If a client says to the group that she is afraid of experiencing her feelings of hatred and spite, she may be encouraged by the therapist to stay with what is truly figural—"I am afraid." The therapist can then design an experiment in which she can deepen her awareness of her fear. For example, she could talk to group members out of her fear, or she might tell each member one of her fears. Once this member has explored her fears, other members can react to her and share their fears in daily life and in the group itself. This intervention is one way to involve several members in exploring their fears.

During a group session, a member says that he feels empty and powerless. The therapist is likely to encourage him to stay with these uncomfortable feelings, even to exaggerate them—to "be empty," to "be powerless." If this person can endure and truly experience the depth of his feelings, with the support of the group, he will probably discover that whatever expectations he has with regard to those feelings are more of a fantasy than a reality and that his helplessness and emptiness will shift at least slightly. By going beyond our creative adjustments, we make it possible to effectively address unfinished business that interferes with our present life, and we move toward health and integration.

CONTACT AND DISTURBANCES TO CONTACT

In Gestalt therapy **contact** is made by seeing, hearing, smelling, touching, and moving. When we make optimal contact with the environment, change is inevitable. Effective contact means fully interacting with nature and with other people without losing one's sense of individuality. It is the continually renewed creative adjustment of individuals to their environment (M. Polster, 1987). Prerequisites for good contact are clear awareness, full energy, and the ability to express oneself (Zinker, 1978). Miriam Polster (1987) claims that contact is the lifeblood of growth. It entails zest, imagination, and creativity. There are only moments of this type of contact, so it is most accurate to think of levels of contact rather than a final state to achieve. After a contact experience, there is typically a separation or withdrawal to integrate what has been learned.

The Gestalt therapist also focuses on disturbances to contact. From a Gestalt perspective, contact with the environment is diminished in ways that prevent us from experiencing and staying with the present in a full and real way. Polster and Polster (1973) describe five contact boundary disturbances or phenomena that are articulated in Gestalt therapy: introjection, projection, retroflection, confluence, and deflection.

Introjection involves the tendency to accept others' beliefs and standards uncritically without assimilating them and making them congruent with who we are. These introjects are alien to us because we have not analyzed and restructured them. When we introject, we passively incorporate what the environment provides, spending little time on clearly understanding what we want or need. During the early stages of a group, introjection is common because the members tend to look to the leader to provide structure and direction. At this phase of a group's development, members typically do not question the leader's interventions or rules. As the group reaches a working stage, members are less inclined to swallow whole the suggestions of the group leader.

Projection is the reverse of introjection. In projection we disown certain aspects of ourselves by ascribing them to the environment. When we are projecting, we have trouble distinguishing between the inside world and the outside world. Those attributes of our personality that are inconsistent with our self-image are disowned and put onto other people. By seeing in others the very qualities that we refuse to acknowledge in ourselves, we avoid taking responsibility for our own feelings and the person who we are. Of course, projection is the basis of transference. When transference feelings surface early in a group, these dynamics can be fruitfully explored. As members attempt to get a sense of both the leader and other members, they often attribute characteristics to these individuals that really belong to significant others in their lives. During the transition stage, when issues such as the struggle for control and power become central, projection continues to be a primary contacting style. Now participants may disown their own needs to control the group. The conflicts that occur at this phase are difficult to resolve unless those members who are projecting their need to control recognize and own their projections (Frew, 1986).

Retroflection consists of turning back to ourselves what we would like to do to someone else. For example, if we lash out and injure ourselves, we are often directing aggression inward that we are fearful of directing toward others. Typically, these maladaptive styles of functioning are done outside of our awareness; part of the process of Gestalt therapy is to help us discover a self-regulatory system so that we can deal realistically with the world. During the initial phase of a group, retroflection is easily observed in the tendency of some members to "hold back" by saying very little and expressing little emotion.

Confluence involves the blurring of awareness of differentiation between the self and the environment. For people who are confluent, there is no clear demarcation between internal experience and outer reality. Confluence in relationships involves an absence of conflicts, or a belief that all parties experience the same feelings and thoughts. It is a style of contact that is characteristic of group members who have a high need to be accepted and liked. Conflicts can be very anxiety producing for individuals who rely on confluence as a style of contact (Frew, 1986). Confluence makes it difficult for people to have their own thoughts and to speak for themselves and makes genuine contact next to impossible.

Deflection is the interruption of awareness so that it is difficult to maintain a sustained sense of contact. People who deflect attempt to diffuse contact through the overuse of humor, abstract generalizations, and questions rather than statements (Frew, 1986). Deflection involves a diminished emotional experience. People who deflect speak through and for others.

Introjection, projection, retroflection, confluence, and deflection represent styles of contact. These styles can be either healthy or unhealthy, depending on the situation and the group member's level of awareness. Terms such as *interruptions in contact* or *boundary disturbance* are used to characterize people who attempt to control their environment. The premise in Gestalt therapy is that contact and withdrawal are both normal and healthy. Therefore, a discussion of these styles of contact focuses on the degree to which these processes are in the individual's awareness and serve adaptive purposes. Clients are encouraged to become increasingly aware of their dominant style of blocking contact.

ENERGY AND BLOCKS TO ENERGY

Unexpressed emotions can create a kind of blockage within the body. Gestalt therapists pay attention to bodily experience on the assumption that unexpressed feelings may result in some physical sensations or problems. Because members need energy to work in group sessions, Gestalt leaders pay special attention to where energy is located, how it is used, and how it can be blocked. **Blocks to energy** show up in the body in a number of ways. One member will experience tension in his neck and shoulders, and another member will experience shortness of breath. Another person will typically speak with a restricted voice, holding back power. A few other ways that these blocks to energy will manifest themselves are keeping one's mouth shut tightly (as though one were afraid what might slip out); slouching; looking at the ground or in the air as a way of avoiding contact with others' eyes; keeping one's body tight and closed; talking in a fast and staccato fashion; being emotionally flat; or experiencing body sensations such as a lump in the throat, a quivering of the mouth, a hot and flushed feeling, shaking movements of the hands and legs, or dizziness.

Group members may not be aware of their energy or where it is located and may experience it in a negative way. Zinker (1978) suggests that therapy at

its best is "a lively process of stoking the client's inner fires of awareness and contact" (p. 24). This process involves a therapeutic relationship that awakens and nourishes the client in such a way that the therapist does not become sapped of his or her own energy. Zinker maintains that it is the therapist's job to help clients locate the ways in which they are blocking energy and to help them transform this blocked energy into more adaptive behaviors. Group therapists can learn to welcome these blocks and use them as a way of deepening therapeutic work. Members can be encouraged to recognize how their energy is being expressed or constricted in their body. Rather than trying to rid themselves of certain bodily symptoms, they can actually delve fully into tension states. By allowing themselves to exaggerate their tight mouth and shaking legs, they are able to discover for themselves how they are diverting energy and keeping themselves powerless.

Experiments can be designed that allow members to try out various body positions. For example, if a member sits with a closed posture, the leader can invite him or her to uncross and experience the feeling, and then cross again. By inviting individuals to move out of a particular posture and experiment with a new posture, leaders can facilitate awareness. Members who slouch and who also complain about low self-esteem can be invited to stand and walk erect. In a like way, members can be asked to exaggerate a particular gesture or posture as a way of learning more about themselves. In short, paying attention to the body and energy blockages within the body can be a productive way to explore the meaning of a member's experience and perhaps reveal unspoken issues.

Role and Functions of the Group Leader

Although Gestalt leaders encourage members to heighten their awareness and attend to their contact styles, leaders can nevertheless take an active role in creating experiments to help members tap their resources. Gestalt leaders focus on conscious awareness, contact, and experimentation. The therapist models the process of useful interactions by disclosing his or her own awareness and experience (Yontef & Jacobs, 2011). Leaders are actively engaged with group members and may use self-disclosure as a way to enhance relationships and create a sense of mutuality within the group. Leaders can share a great deal about themselves by sticking to what they are experiencing in the moment in the group, without revealing much about themselves outside of the group. When leaders sharing their personal reactions to what is going on in the group, including how they are being affected by what they are hearing and observing, this can be especially helpful. Disclosure of personal problems or life outside of the group should be done with intentionality and serve the needs of the group.

The group therapist, functioning much like an artist, invents experiments with clients to augment their range of behaviors. The leader's function is to create an atmosphere and structure in which the group's own creativity and inventiveness can emerge (Zinker, 1978). For example, a theme of loneliness may come up in a group. Here a central task of the leader is to orchestrate this theme by connecting members with one another and finding ways to involve the group as a whole in exploring loneliness.

Gestalt therapists assume an active role by employing a wide range of interventions and experiments to help group members gain awareness and experience their internal and interpersonal conflicts fully. Gestalt therapy uses both a supportive therapeutic relationship and active methods to help members discover how they block their awareness and personal functioning (Yontef & Jacobs, 2011). Gestalt therapists frequently invite clients to engage in experiments that lead to fresh emotional experiencing and new insights (Strumpfel & Goldman, 2002). It should be made clear, however, that an equally important function of the Gestalt group therapist is to promote and create a nurturing environment within the group. Unless the group atmosphere is perceived as being safe, members will keep themselves hidden, and therapeutic work will be limited (Feder, 2008b). Yontef (1993) contends that although the therapist functions as a guide and a catalyst, suggests experiments, and shares observations, the basic work of exploration is done by the client. Yontef maintains that the therapist's role is to create a climate in which clients will feel free enough to try out new ways of being and behaving.

THE ROLE OF THE RELATIONSHIP

Therapists have latitude to invent their own experiments, which are basically an extension of their personality. Thus therapists must be grounded and in tune with themselves as well as being present for their clients. They warn of the dangers of becoming technique-bound and losing sight of their own being as they engage the client. The therapist's attitudes and behavior and the relationship that is established are what really count (Frew, 2008; Hycner & Jacobs, 1995; Jacobs, 1989; E. Polster, 1987a, 1987b; M. Polster, 1987; Polster & Polster, 1999; Yontef, 1993, 1995, 1999; Yontef & Jacobs, 2011). These writers point out that current Gestalt therapy has moved beyond earlier therapeutic practices. Many contemporary Gestalt therapists place increasing emphasis on factors such as presence, authentic dialogue, gentleness, more direct self-expression by the therapist, decreased use of stereotypic exercises, a greater trust in the client's experiencing, and more interest in making full use of the Gestalt group process. Frew (2008) believes "the client–counselor relationship is the heart and soul of Gestalt therapy. . . . The client and counselor are partners in an endeavor that involves increasing awareness, identifying figures of interest, and restoring contacting functions" (p. 258).

Many who write about Gestalt therapy give central importance to a dialogic relationship marked by an "I/Thou" attitude. If clients are to become authentic, they need contact with an authentic therapist on a genuine I/Thou basis. Because Gestalt therapy is part of the existential approach, the mutuality of the I/Thou encounter is seen as essential for therapy to succeed. Healing results from these nonexploitive encounters. The best experiments grow out of the trusting relationship that the leader creates. This approach encourages genuine experimentation and allows for a great deal of creativity on the part of leaders and members (see Zinker, 1978, 2008).

In a seminal article, "Dialogue in Gestalt Theory and Therapy," Jacobs (1989) explored the role of the therapeutic relationship as a factor in healing and the extent to which the client–therapist relationship is the focus of therapy. She shows how Martin Buber's philosophy of dialogue, which involves a genuine and loving meeting, is congruent with Gestalt concepts of contact, awareness, and the paradoxical theory of change. Jacobs asserts that a current trend in

Gestalt practice is toward greater emphasis on the client–therapist relationship rather than on techniques divorced from the context of this encounter. She believes a therapist who operates from this orientation establishes a present-centered, nonjudgmental dialogue that allows the client to deepen awareness and to find contact with another person. The experiments therapists employ evolve out of this process of engagement. Experiments must always be a phenomenological part of the therapeutic process. The experiments that we consider later in this chapter are aimed at awareness, not at simple solutions to a client's problem. If therapists use experiments when they are frustrated with a client and want to change the person, they are misusing the experiments and will probably thwart rather than foster the client's growth and change (see Hycner & Jacobs, 1995).

Polster and Polster (1973) see the therapist as nothing less than an artist involved in creating new life. Yet in Gestalt, as in most other approaches, the danger exists that the therapist will lose sight of the true meaning of the therapeutic process and become a mere technician. Therapists should use their own experience as an essential ingredient in the therapy process and never forget that they are far more than mere responders, givers of feedback, or catalysts who don't change themselves (Polster & Polster, 1973).

Creative therapists possess a rich personal background, having opened themselves to a range of life experiences and become able to celebrate life fully (Zinker, 1978, 2008). In short, they are able to use themselves as a person as they function as a therapist. In addition to being mature and integrated people, creative therapists also possess certain capacities, abilities, and technical skills. Out of their experimental attitude, they use themselves, other group members, and objects and events in the group environment in the service of inventing novel visions of the members.

From this discussion of the role and functions of the Gestalt group leader, it should be apparent that who the leader is as a person and how he or she functions in the group, creatively drawing on technical expertise, are the critical factors that determine the potency of leadership. There are different styles of practicing Gestalt therapy, but all share these common elements: direct experiencing and experimenting, the use of direct contact and personal presence, attention to *what* and *how*, and a *here-and-now* focus (Yontef & Jacobs, 2011).

Stages of a Gestalt Group

One way of conceptualizing the role of the Gestalt group leader is to consider the stage of development of the group. Kepner (2008) presents a model that calls for different roles of the leader in working with different dimensions of group process. Gestalt group process aims to create conditions for learning about what it means to be a member of a group. Kepner notes that Gestalt group therapy can accentuate one of three contact boundaries: (1) the *intrapsychic* or *intrapersonal* (the individual's thoughts, sensations, and feelings), (2) the *interpersonal* (the interactions between and among group members), or (3) the *group level* (the processes that involve the whole group). She maintains that the choice of boundary emphasis is often defined by the leader's choice of role: *therapist* for the intrapersonal dimension, *facilitator* of interpersonal processes, and *consultant* to the group as a whole. In writing about the Gestalt group process, Kepner emphasizes that the leader is committed to working with both the individual and the group for the enhancement of both. She describes the various roles of the leader in the Gestalt process group using a three-stage model.

FIRST STAGE

In the first stage (initial stage) of a group, the key characteristics are identity and dependence. Each member of the group is dependent on the way he or she is perceived and responded to by other members and the leader. The leader, functioning as a therapist, helps individuals explore questions members have about their identity in the group. The leader's activities are directed toward providing a climate of trust that will support risk-taking and making connections between individuals. Once members discover what they have in common with each other, the group is ready to work on differentiation.

SECOND STAGE

In the second stage (which is similar to the transition stage) the key characteristics are influence and counterdependence. During this time of transition, the group grapples with issues of influence, authority, and control. The leader's task is to work for increasing differentiation, divergence, and role flexibility among members. The leader assumes the role of facilitator to help members work through reactions they are having toward what is taking place in the group. Some of these facilitative activities include heightening the awareness of the norms operating in the group, encouraging members to challenge norms and openly express differences and dissatisfaction, and differentiating roles from persons.

THIRD STAGE

In the third stage (which is similar to the working stage) intimacy and interdependence are the key themes. At this stage of the group's development, real contact occurs within and among members of the group. Now that the members have worked through the issues of influence, power, and authority, they are ready for a deeper level of work, both individually and with the group as a whole. During this stage a high level of cohesiveness encourages members to take risks by engaging in experiments for the sake of new learning. "Experiment modifies the group members' perceptions of their own inner lives as well as the lives of others" (Zinker, 2008, p. 107). Group members utilize the experiment as a way to make significant discoveries.

The group leader is no longer the ultimate authority but now assumes the role of an experienced resource or consultant. The leader helps the group to arrive at closure and also assists members in recognizing unfinished business not worked through in the group. It is clear that Kepner's (2008) model accounts for the reality that the roles and functions of the group leader are rooted in three types of processes that occur simultaneously in groups: intrapersonal, interpersonal, and the group as a system. Gestalt leaders have the advantage of being able to intervene at all three of these levels: the *intrapersonal level* is aimed at heightening awareness, the *interpersonal level* is mainly used to promote interpersonal contact, and the *group level* is aimed at supporting and illuminating the group's journey through the stages of development (Jon Frew, personal communication, February 19, 2009).

Application: Therapeutic Techniques and Procedures

Gestalt therapy employs a rich variety of interventions designed to intensify what group members are experiencing in the present moment for the purpose of leading to increased awareness. Melnick and Nevis (2005) state that "Gestalt methodology combines an Eastern focus on awareness and being in the here and now with a Western emphasis on action and doing" (p. 114). Gestalt therapy encourages direct experience and actions as opposed to merely *talking about* conflicts, problems, and feelings. Moving from talking about to action is often done by the use of experiments. These experiments need to be tailored to each individual and used in a timely manner; they also need to be carried out in a context that offers a balance between support and risk. Experiments should be the outgrowth of the therapeutic encounter—an encounter grounded in the mutual experiencing of the group member and the group therapist. There are no prescribed techniques that Gestalt group leaders must follow.

THE ROLE OF EXPERIMENTS

It is important to distinguish between *techniques* and *experiments* because the two terms are not synonymous. Techniques are exercises or procedures that are often used to bring about action or interaction, sometimes with a prescribed outcome in mind. Generally, they are not invented in the moment as an integral part of the client's process or the group environment. In contrast, **experiments** are phenomenologically based; that is, they evolve out of what is occurring within a member or members in the present moment, and the outcome is unknown. Frew (2008) defines the experiment as "a method that shifts the focus of counseling from talking about a topic to an activity that will heighten the client's awareness and understanding through experience" (p. 253). In Gestalt group experiments, members are invited to try out some new behavior and to pay attention to what they experience. Experiments grow out of the therapeutic relationship and provide a safe context for members to increase their awareness and try out new ways of thinking and behaving. The purpose of an experiment is to assist a member in active self-exploration (Melnick & Nevis, 2005). A Gestalt-oriented group leader is encouraged to be creative in designing and implementing a wide range of interventions, always using as a guide the participant's most pressing need or interest.

It is also useful to differentiate between a *group exercise* and a *group experiment.* Leaders prepare **group exercises** prior to the group meeting. Members might be asked to pair up and talk, or a catalyst might be introduced into the group to provide a specific focus for work during a session. In contrast, a **group experiment** is a creative happening that grows out of the group experience; as such it cannot be predetermined, and its outcome cannot be predicted (Zinker, 1978). M. Polster (1987) states that experiments are "aimed at restoring momentum to the stuck points of a person's life. It is one way to recover the connection between deliberation and spontaneity by bringing the possibilities for action right into the therapy room" (p. 318). Frew (2008) indicates that experiments are always one of a kind: "Experiments emerge organically and seamlessly in the moment-to-moment contact between a counselor and a client, and they are discovered within that dialogic process" (p. 253).

Some forms that Gestalt experiments might take include dramatizing a painful memory, imagining a dreaded encounter, playing one's parent, creating a dialogue between two parts within oneself, attending to an overlooked gesture, or exaggerating a certain posture (M. Polster, 1987). One of the therapist's functions is to observe whether the experiment appears too safe or too risky. The Polsters (1990) call for sensitivity and careful attention on the therapist's part so that clients are "neither blasted into experiences that are too threatening nor allowed to stay in safe but infertile territory" (p. 104).

Polster (1995) writes that a diversity of Gestalt experiments is available, and therapists can create their own on-the-spot experiments that evolve from therapeutic engagements with clients as well. A loud-voiced client can be asked to experiment with speaking softly. A client grieving over the home she left may be asked to imagine herself walking into her home and report what she sees and feels. M. Polster (1997) describes the experiment as the "safe emergency" that provides group members with the opportunity to explore beyond ways of behaving that have become restrictive and habitual:

> Interactions and experiments within the group setting are not to be taken as scripts or dress rehearsals to be put to use indiscriminately. Within the Gestalt group there are options that a person might not have available in everyday circumstances or might not think of—or dare—to do. (p. 235)

On a similar note, Feder (2008b) pays close attention to the balance of safety and danger in the Gestalt group. An experiment is always done within the context of support. Members will not be able to engage in the kind of risk-taking that an experiment entails unless they feel safe in going beyond their comfort zone and venturing into new territory. Feder is particularly concerned about creating a nurturing atmosphere within the group as a whole, and any signs that this safety is lacking warrants the leader's attention.

If members experience the group as being a safe place, they will be inclined to move into the unknown and challenge themselves. It is useful for leaders to provide members with a general understanding of the role of experiments in the group process. To increase the chances that members will benefit from Gestalt methods, group leaders need to communicate the general purpose of these interventions and to create an experimental climate. "Let's try something on for size and see how it fits" or "try it and see what you might learn" conveys this experimental attitude on the part of the leader. The message also says that the leader is not trying to prove a point and that the members are free to try something new and determine for themselves whether it's going to work.

Many problems that members bring to the group relate to unfinished situations with significant people in their lives. Consider the woman who learned to be cautious around men, based largely on her earlier relationship with her father. She may harbor feelings of resentment and mistrust toward men, based on her convictions that men will simply not be there for her in time of need. She may connect this present feeling to old feelings associated with her alcoholic father, who continually let her down and brought much pain into her life. Based on her early decision not to trust men, she may be projecting her negative feelings toward all men now. Concluding that if her own father could not be counted on for love and protection then surely other men will not be more trustworthy, she now looks for evidence to support her hypothesis. The Gestalt group leader might invite her to deal with her father symbolically in the here-and-now. She might have a dialogue with him, becoming both her father and herself. She could now say all the things that she wanted to say to her father as a child but, because of her fear, kept deep inside herself.

Of course, there are many creative possibilities within the group. She could look at the men in the group, expressing to each some of her resentments. In making contact with each man in the group, she could share her fantasies of all the ways in which they would let her down or of what she would like from them now yet is afraid to ask for. The theoretical rationale for this experiment is rooted in the assumption that the emotions that were overwhelming to her as a child were dealt with by some form of distortion or denial. The Gestalt leader encourages her to reexperience these past events by reliving them in the here-and-now so that emotions that were repressed can come to the surface. With the support of the leader and the group members, she can allow herself to experience feelings that she has sealed off from awareness, and she can now work through some of these feelings and beliefs that are keeping her stuck. By challenging her assumptions of how men are, she is able to establish a new basis for relating to men.

Experiments can be applied to future events as well as dealing with present conflicts and unfinished situations from the past. If the above group member is afraid of a future confrontation with her father, she can be asked to live her expectations in the here-and-now by speaking directly to her father in the group in a symbolic way and by expressing her fears and hopes. She may say to her father: "I want to tell you how much I'd like to be close to you, but I'm afraid that if I do so, you won't care. I'm afraid of saying the wrong things and pushing you even further away from me."

In this example the possibilities are almost endless if there is good contact between the group leader and members, and if there is a climate of safety that encourages trying on a host of ways to deal with unexpressed thoughts and feelings. The emphasis is on inviting (not ordering) members to examine their behaviors, attitudes, and thoughts. Leaders can encourage members to look at certain incongruities, such as gaps between their verbal and nonverbal expression. The Gestalt group is characterized by assisting members to pay attention to what they are doing and experiencing in the here-and-now. Asking members to make this kind of examination of what is in the forefront for them could be perceived as challenging to some clients at times. Any time a member is encouraged to take a risk, this must be done in a caring manner. Also, a leader's challenge does not necessarily have to be aimed at weaknesses or negative traits; members can be asked to pay attention to the ways in which they are blocking their strengths and ways in which they are not living as fully as they might. In this sense the leader is expressing a genuine interest in the member, that, if timed well, is likely to be perceived as supportive and therapeutic, not confrontational or abrasive.

Members must be prepared for taking part in experiments. They need to know that they can choose to go along and that they can also decide to stop when they want to. Rather than pushing them into experimenting, the spirit is always one of inviting them to discover something new about themselves. It is essential that leaders begin where the group member is. By drawing on the support within the members and the group environment, experiments can be designed so that members can move in the direction of becoming more spontaneous.

Keep these introductory comments in mind as you read the following pages, which describe several Gestalt interventions, their rationales, and their applications to group situations. My discussion is based on a variety of sources, including Frew (2008), Levitsky and Perls (1970), Passons (1975), E. Polster (1997), Polster and Polster (1973, 1999), M. Polster (1997), and Zinker (1978). I have modified some techniques to fit the needs of the group situation.

PAYING ATTENTION TO LANGUAGE

Gestalt therapy emphasizes the relationship between language patterns and personality. Our speech patterns are often expressions of our feelings, thoughts, and attitudes; by focusing on our overt speaking habits, we can increase our self-awareness (Passons, 1975). Words can bring us closer to what we are experiencing or distance us from what we are thinking and feeling. Becoming more aware of our speech patterns can enhance self-awareness. It should be noted, however, that paying attention to a client's language patterns requires a great deal of skill on the part of the leader. Unless the members, through the leader's help, are able to see the value of paying attention to the impact of their language style, they will come to feel that everything they say and do is subject to unnecessary scrutiny. Any one of these interventions based on language may or may not be appropriate with a particular client. These experiments grow out of the phenomenological work with the member; they are not techniques to use in routine and stereotyped ways.

It "It" talk is a way of depersonalizing language. By using "it" instead of "I," we maintain distance from our experience. When group members say, "It's frightening to come to this group," they can be asked to change the sentence to, "I'm frightened to come to this group." Substituting personal pronouns for impersonal ones is a way of assuming responsibility for what we say.

You Group participants often say things like "You feel hurt when someone rejects you." By using "you" talk, people detach themselves from whatever they may be feeling. Ask members to pay attention to the differences between this "you" statement and saying, "I feel hurt when someone rebuffs me." By changing a "you" statement to an "I" statement, we reveal ourselves, and we take responsibility for what we are saying. Beginning a sentence with the word "you" tends to put others on the defensive and allows us to disown our own experience.

Questions In a Gestalt group, members are discouraged from asking questions. Questions direct attention to other people and can easily put others on the defensive. Also, questions often demand that those being questioned reveal themselves whereas those who ask questions remain safe behind their interrogation. Group members who tend to ask too many questions can be asked to experiment with any of the following:

• Instead of asking a question, make a direct statement to the person and share your own motivation for your question.

- Avoid "why" questions because they lead to a chain of "why/because" exchanges. Try "how" and "what" questions instead.
- Practice making "I" statements. By doing so, you take responsibility for your position, your opinions, and your preferences.

Qualifiers and Disclaimers By paying attention to the qualifiers they attach to their statements, group members can increase their awareness of how they diminish the power of their messages. A common example is the use of "but": "I like you, *but* your mannerisms drive me up the wall"; "I often feel depressed, *but* I don't know what to do to change the situation"; "I think this group is helping me, *but* people outside are so different from those in here." In each of these cases the word "but" essentially discounts the statement that precedes it. Without making group members excessively self-conscious, the leader can encourage members to pay attention to the impact of the use of qualifiers and disclaimers.

"Can't" Statements Group members often say "I can't" when they really mean "I won't." Sally says, "I simply can't talk to my father and tell him what I feel; he'd never understand me." It would be more precise and more honest for Sally to say that she won't make the attempt to talk with her father. Essentially, Sally is unwilling to (won't) take the risk or sees it as not being worth the effort. If a group leader consistently and gently insists that members substitute "won't" for "can't," he or she is helping them own and accept their power by taking responsibility for their decisions.

"Shoulds" and "Oughts" Some group members seem to be ruled by "shoulds" and "oughts": "I should be interested in what others say in this group"; "I ought to care for everyone, and if I don't, I feel terrible"; "I should express only positive feelings"; and so on. The list of "shouldisms," both in daily life and in a group situation, is endless. Members can at least become aware of the frequency of their "should" and "ought" remarks and of the feelings of powerlessness that accompany their use. One way of increasing one's awareness of the limitations imposed by a "should" standard is to experiment with changing phrases such as "I have to" or "I should" to "I choose to."

In working with language, it is important to consider the stage of a group's development. If a leader or a member challenges someone's language during the early stages of a group, this can interfere with a sense of safety. Challenging the language of some members may result in their feeling criticized, judged, and not understood. Therefore, sensitivity and appropriate timing are essential as the leader explores with members their language patterns.

NONVERBAL LANGUAGE

Skilled group counselors listen not just to the verbal level of communication but also, and even more keenly, to the message behind the words, which is often conveyed in the voice tone, pitch, and volume, in the speed of delivery, and so forth.

The group setting offers many opportunities to explore the meaning of nonverbal messages. Such explorations are especially useful when participants exhibit nonverbal cues that are incongruent with what they are saying verbally. For example, Dwight tells the group leader that he is angry with him for passing him over, but as he utters his angry words, he is smiling. The leader is likely to call to Dwight's attention the discrepancy between his angry words and his smile. Dwight may then be asked to carry on a dialogue between his words and his smile, or he may be asked to "become his smile" and give this smile a voice: "What is your smile saying?" This procedure gives Dwight the opportunity to discover for himself the meaning of the discrepancy. In fact he may be saying, "I want to let you know that I'm upset that you passed me by, yet I don't want to risk your disapproval by letting you know how angry I am."

Here are some other examples of how the exploration of nonverbal expressions can increase members' awareness of what they are really experiencing in the moment.

- Conrad typically carries himself in a slouched posture. The leader says: "Become aware of your posture; go around the group and tell what your posture says about yourself to each member of the group. Complete the sentence 'I am my posture, and what I am telling you about me is _____!'"

- Maiko tends to speak in a soft voice and with a very tight mouth. The leader invites her to give a speech to the group and consciously exaggerate these mannerisms. She could "become her tight mouth" and say something like: "I'm holding my words and myself back from you. I'm not going to be open, and if you want something from me, you'll have to pry me open."

- Manuel comes across as though he were always delivering a lecture to an audience. Group members have told him that his voice and his style of speaking create a barrier between him and others. He could be asked to stand before the group and give a lecture, perhaps on the value of lecturing people.

Examples of how people deal with nonverbal cues are endless. Creative group leaders can invent a wide variety of experiments designed to help participants become increasingly aware of what they are communicating through their eye contact, mannerisms, subtle gestures, tone of voice, and hand movements, as well as through their whole bodies. Keep in mind that experiments are presented as invitations rather than as dictates that members must follow. Group leaders would do well to avoid making bold interpretations—for example, that keeping one's arms crossed means that one is closed—and instead encourage members to merely pay attention to the nonverbal cues they emit. It is especially important for leaders to avoid making interpretations of nonverbal behavior in cross-cultural contexts. For example, it may be a mistake to assume that lack of direct eye contact indicates a lack of confidence. It may be a cultural message that direct eye contact is a confrontational act that should be avoided.

EXPERIMENTS WITH INTERNAL DIALOGUES

Because a goal of Gestalt therapy is to achieve integrated function and the acceptance of aspects of one's personality that have been disowned and denied, therapists pay close attention to splits and polarities in personality function. Fantasy dialogues are meant to promote awareness of internal splits and eventual personality integration. These dialogues can take many forms, for example, dialogues between opposing sides or polarities within oneself (like tender/tough, brave/scared, masculine/feminine, loving/hateful, active/passive) or dialogues with a parent or other significant person, fantasized others, or inanimate objects.

Understanding how polarities are related to inner conflicts is central to Gestalt therapy. A variety of experiments with dialogues can help members increase their awareness of the dichotomies within themselves and help them come to terms with dimensions of their personality that seem to oppose each other. Our self-concept often excludes painful awareness of the polarities within us. We prefer to think of ourselves as bright rather than dull, as kind rather than cruel, as loving rather than unloving, and as sensitive rather than indifferent. Typically, we may resist "seeing" in ourselves those parts that we don't want to accept as being part of who we are. Although we can recognize the altruistic side of ourselves, we might have trouble coming to terms with our self-centered nature. Ideally, as we move closer to becoming psychologically mature and healthy, we are aware of most of the polarities within ourselves, including those thoughts and feelings that society does not sanction. As we become more tolerant of the complexities and seeming contradictions within us, there is less of a tendency to expend energy on fighting to disown those parts of our nature that we don't want to accept.

Dialogue experiments are a powerful method of contacting parts of our nature that we work hard at keeping secret from both ourselves and others. Learning how to carry on a conversation between our feminine and masculine sides, for instance, is one way of bringing to the surface inner conflicts we might have with these polarities. Alternately becoming each side as fully as we can is a way to *experience* both of these facets of our personality.

Dialogue experiments are typically used to heighten awareness of introjections and projections. In introjection, we uncritically take in aspects of other people, especially parents, and incorporate them into our personality. The danger of uncritical and wholesale acceptance of another's values as our own is that it can prevent personality integration. Gestalt experiments are aimed at getting these introjections out in the open, so that we can take a good look at what we have been swallowing whole without digesting it.

For example, by experimenting with fantasy dialogues, Joaquin becomes aware of some of the messages he has internalized without question: I must be practical; I ought to cling to security and never set out on a new path unless I have carefully assessed all the odds; only irresponsible people seek fun for the sake of fun—in other words, a long list of "dos" and "don'ts," "shoulds," and "shouldn'ts" that keep him from enjoying life. At last, Joaquin begins to realize that he has listened to these directives from others and given others the power to direct his life. Through dialogues with the different facets of himself, Joaquin becomes aware that he wants to reclaim this power for himself.

MAKING THE ROUNDS

Making the rounds can be a useful technique to help a group member recognize a hidden fear. The member is encouraged to go around to each of the group members and say something that he or she usually does not communicate verbally. For example, assume that Larry sees himself as a self-made man who needs nothing from others. Although he may not say this about himself, the theme of "I can do it by myself" runs through much of his life. To better understand how this theme actually determines what he does, Larry could be asked to stand before each member in the group and tell that person something about himself and then add, "and [or but] I can do everything by myself." First, Larry goes to Yesenia and says, "I never ask for emotional support from others, and at times I feel lonely . . . but I can do everything by myself." He then goes to Michael and says, "I make all the decisions in my business . . . and I can do everything by myself." The aim of this experiment is to have Larry feel fully what it's like for him to be so self-reliant, to the extent that he will not ask for help from anyone. Ultimately, he may decide to continue to do things for himself, but with the awareness of the price he pays for doing so. Or he may come to see that he doesn't have to be totally self-reliant and that he can be independent while letting others do things for him from time to time.

Here are a few more examples of the use of making the rounds:

- Paul says that he is afraid of women. He could make the rounds and say to each woman, "I'm afraid of you because _____." or "If I were to get close to you _____."

- Adriana worries about boring people in the group. She might be asked to make the rounds and, for each person, complete the sentence, "One way I could bore you is by _____." or "You would be bored if I _____."

- Nisha says that she feels distant from the rest of the group, even though she would like to have a sense of identification. She could make the rounds and experiment with completing the sentence, "One way I feel distant from you is _____." or "The way I am different from you is _____."

FANTASY APPROACHES

Experimenting with a diversity of fantasy situations in a group can lead to significant growth. Fantasy can promote personal awareness in a number of ways, as the following brief list suggests.

- Fantasy can be used when members are too threatened to deal with a problem in concrete terms. For example, members who are afraid to be assertive can imagine themselves in situations in which they are assertive. Then they can compare what they feel when they are passive with what they feel when they are able to ask for what they want.

- Fantasy approaches are useful in dealing with negative expectations, which often result in a sense of paralysis. Members who are afraid to express what they think and feel to someone they love can be guided through a fantasy situation in which they say everything they want to say but are afraid to express. Essentially the person speaks in the here-and-now to the loved one (as if he or she were present) in front of the group. The leader may say: "Pick someone in this group to be your mother [or some other significant person]. Borrow this member's eyes, and tell your mother what you most want her to hear." There is a possible psychological value in working through these feelings in the safety of the fantasy approach, because the person may be able to release submerged feelings that have become split off. Note that it is not necessary for the person to express these feelings in real life; as a matter of fact, to do so could be unwise.

- Fantasy is a useful and safe way to explore members' fears about involving themselves in the group. For example, members can be asked to imagine the thing they most fear occurring in the group. If, for example, some members are afraid of being rejected by the group, they can be directed to imagine that everyone is systematically rejecting them and then work with the feelings associated with this fantasy.

Once a fantasy has been tried in the group, it can be carried outside of it. At times members can be invited to picture themselves as they wish they were in interpersonal situations. They might share their fantasies aloud in the group as they experience themselves in powerful, alive, creative, and dynamic ways. Then they can be asked to try acting in the group as if they were the person they imagined themselves to be. If the experiment is successful, members may feel encouraged enough to try the new behavior in real-life situations.

REHEARSAL

In everyday life we often rehearse for roles we think we are expected to play, and we worry that we may not say the "right" thing and perform "properly." Internal rehearsing consumes much energy and frequently inhibits spontaneity. By participating in a **rehearsal,** members say *out loud* what they are thinking silently. This technique can be especially useful when it is obvious that members are doing a lot of blocking and censoring and when what they say seems carefully measured out for a certain effect. Again, suggesting a rehearsal technique must be timed properly, and it must emerge from the situation in which a member is struggling in some way. Rehearsals are not designed to stir up emotions but to bring into sharper awareness a process that is typically done without awareness. For example, during the initial stages of one of my groups, Sherry was quite silent and appeared to be developing an observer's stance. When I asked her if she was indeed saying everything she wanted to say, she shook her head in denial. So I asked her to express aloud some of the random thoughts she had as she was sitting there in silence.

Rehearsing can also be productive when a member is anticipating some future confrontation. Assume that Klaus wants to tell his boss that he doesn't feel appreciated and that he wants to be recognized for his accomplishments. Klaus can, in fantasy, picture himself standing before his boss, ready to tell him what he wants to say. Klaus's out-loud rehearsal could go something like this: "I'm standing here like a fool. What if I mess up? He won't listen to me, and I don't really have anything to say. How can I let him know what I'm thinking? Right now I feel like running away and apologizing."

In a Gestalt group the participants share their rehearsals with one another to become more aware of the many preparations they go through in performing their social roles. By doing so, they become more aware of how they strive to please others, of the degree to which they want to be accepted and approved, and of the extent of their efforts to avoid alienating others. And then they can decide whether this role playing is worth the effort.

THE EXAGGERATION TECHNIQUE

This technique involves becoming more aware of the subtle signals and cues we send through body language. Group members are asked to repeat and intensify a particular behavior for the purpose of bringing out-of-awareness emotional processes to awareness (Strumpfel & Goldman, 2002). Movements, postures, and gestures are exaggerated so that the meanings they communicate become clearer. By exaggerating the movement or gesture repeatedly, the person experiences the feelings associated with the behavior more intensely and becomes more aware of the inner meaning of that behavior.

For example, if the leader notices that Sandy consistently nods her head in an approving way when people speak, the leader could ask Sandy to go before each group member and intentionally exaggerate nodding her head while, at the same time, putting words with this action. Other examples of behaviors that lend themselves to exaggeration are habitually smiling while expressing painful or negative emotions, trembling, clenching one's fists, tapping one's foot, crossing one's arms tightly, and pointing a finger at someone.

Berrin, a group member, said, "I feel burdened by listening to everyone's problems in this group!" At an earlier session, Stephen had confronted Berrin for intervening so quickly and trying to make him feel better when he was working on conflicts he was having with his family. She then revealed that during her childhood years she typically assumed the role of family arbitrator, always doing her best to smooth over the battles in her family. Berrin eventually said that she was sick and tired of carrying everyone's burdens; it weighed her down and gave her a heavy feeling.

The leader suggested that Berrin pick up some heavy objects and hold them as she looked at each person in the group. She could be invited to allow herself to get into the experience of the heaviness and being burdened. For example, while holding the heavy objects, she might make the rounds and complete the sentence, "Looking at you I am burdened by _____." Or she might say something to each member such as, "Here, let me take on all your burdens. I really enjoy carrying everyone's problems, and I just wouldn't know what to do if I didn't have all these burdens weighing me down!" Even though she said that she was sick and tired of carrying around everyone's burdens, we encouraged her to allow herself to give in to the part of herself that felt burdened and experiment with telling others all the benefits of being this way. The rationale here was that if she could fully experience being burdened there was a good chance she could allow herself to experience shedding these burdens and being light, at least for a few moments. Often the best way to discover the aspect of ourselves that we say we'd like to experience more of is to allow ourselves to stay with that part of us that we want to avoid.

DREAM WORK IN GROUPS

Consistent with its noninterpretive spirit, the Gestalt approach does not interpret and analyze dreams. Instead, the intent is to bring the dream back to life, to re-create it, and to relive it as if it were happening now. If you are interested in a detailed presentation of the Gestalt approach to dream work, good sources are Coven (2004), Downing and Marmorstein (1973), Perls (1969a), Polster and Polster (1973), Rainwater (1979), and Zinker (1978). Here is a brief description of this approach.

Group members don't report their dreams or talk about them in the past tense. Instead, they are asked to tell the dream as if it were happening in the present. Dreamers become immersed in their dreams with more vitality when they narrate dreams as though they are happening now. Members can be asked to identify with a segment of the dream and to narrate their dream from a subjective perspective. Group members may be asked to transform key elements of the dream into a dialogue and become each part of the dream. The group context allows them to play out parts of the dream as present events.

Dreams contain existential messages; they represent our conflicts, our wishes, and key themes in our lives. By making a list of all the details in a dream—remembering each person, event, and mood—and then acting out ("becoming") each of these parts as fully as possible, one becomes increasingly aware of one's opposing sides and of the range of one's feelings. Eventually the person appreciates and accepts his or her complexities and integrates the conflicting forces;

each piece of work on a dream leads to further assimilation and integration. By avoiding analyzing and interpreting the dream and focusing instead on becoming and experiencing it in all its aspects, the client gets closer to the existential message of the dream. Freud calls the dream "the royal road to the unconscious"; Perls (1969a) calls it "the royal road to integration" (p. 66).

The Polsters (1973) see dreams as a projection of the dreamer. All aspects of the dream are representations of the dreamer. They also view dreams as a road to contact. As dreamers acknowledge their kinship with the many aspects of their dream, they are also extending their own sense of diversity, broadening the experience of self, and centering themselves in the world. Dreams can be used in groups quite creatively "as a starting point for discoveries about present relationships with other group members or the therapist or with a recognition of an existential position which bears exploration using the dream only as a point of departure" (p. 273).

The Polsters give the example of a man (Fred) in a group who dreams a large frog is always watching him and is ready to jump. The group leader can suggest a number of creative experiments to increase contact between Fred and others in the group. The leader might ask Fred to describe his experience of the group as he relates his dream in the present tense. Fred might be asked, "What would you like to say to the members in this group?" If Fred were to indicate that they might see something in him that he doesn't want them to see, he could be asked to imagine what each person sees in him as they watch him. The dream work is an interactive process that enables Fred to experience more intensely his sense of being watched and his fears of being jumped on. It could be that Fred has some unfinished business with the group about a time when he thought they jumped on him.

Here are some suggestions to group leaders for helping members explore their dreams in a group:

- The member can be asked to relive the dream as though it were happening right now.

- After dreamers have had an opportunity to recount a dream in the present tense, they can be asked any one of these questions: "What are you experiencing now?" "What was it like for you to recount your dream?" "What interests you most about the dream?"

- Have members choose an element of the dream that seems most like them and ask, "What element of the dream has the most energy?"

- It is useful to inquire if there is a troublesome part of the dream. If there is, it is important to address it early so that there is time to work on it.

- Members can be encouraged to "become" different parts of a dream. For example, members become all the people in the dream. Are any of them significant people? They can "become" objects in the dream, especially objects that link and join, such as telephone lines and highways. They can identify any powerful force, such as a storm.

- A way for members to become a part of a dream is for them to assume the identity of a person or an object by giving voice and personality to this dream element.

Rainwater (1979) suggests that you notice how you feel when you wake up from a dream. Do you feel fear, joy, sadness, frustration, surprise, anger?

Identifying the feeling tone may be the key to finding the meaning of the dream. In working with dreams in Gestalt style, dreamers can focus on questions such as "What are you doing in the dream?" "What are you feeling?" "What do you want in the dream?" "What are your relationships with other objects and people in the dream?" "What kind of action can you take now?" and "What is your dream telling you?"

Group experiments can emerge out of the dream work of individuals in a group. Zinker (1978) has developed an approach he calls *dream work as theater,* which goes beyond working with an individual's dream. After a dream is reported and worked through by a participant, a group experiment is created that allows other members to benefit therapeutically from the original imagery of the dreamer. Each plays out a part of the dream. This offers the group participants many opportunities for enacting certain dimensions of the dream that relate both to the dreamer and to their own life.

For example, assume that Kara has had a dream that contains a broken-down car, a man shooting at people in the car, and a woman trying to save the passengers. One member may choose to take on the identity of the person doing the shooting, another can take on the role of one of the people in the car being shot at, and still another can be the car that doesn't function. Each of the members can play out his or her part, and the dreamer can help them understand the characters or objects in the dream. The group leader can facilitate the production of the dream as a dramatic and therapeutic experience for the entire group. There are many advantages to this approach in increasing group cohesion and linking one member's work with others.

The dreams of group participants may have implications for how they feel in their group. For example, Kara may discover that she feels frightened in the group and would like to escape. She may feel attacked (shot at) by one or more members, with a woman coming to her rescue. In this case she can act out her dream in the group by selecting the person by whom she feels most seriously attacked and talking to that person directly. She can then become the broken-down car—her powerless vehicle of escape—and see what insights this association brings. She can also pick out the woman in the group by whom she feels most supported and have a dialogue with her. She might reverse roles, becoming the person doing the shooting. Working with the dream in this way has great potential for dealing with unfinished business with others in the group.

Arnold Coven (2004) describes Gestalt group dream work demonstrations that he conducted at two Taiwan universities. In one of these workshops, Coven reports that there was a high level of energy and excitement among the 40 or 50 group members, comprised of undergraduate, master's and doctoral students, and a few professors. Coven gave a brief presentation of Gestalt dream theory, and then initiating a group warm-up exercise. He then facilitated role-playing enactments of dreams in the group. Coven emphasizes the importance for the participants who explore a dream and the observers of sharing their reactions to the dream enactments. Through this sharing the group as a whole became closer and the experience enhanced their already cohesive learning experience. During the dream enactment, Coven was challenged to pay attention to the member enacting a dream, to the other participants in the role-playing enactment, and to the group as a whole. To intensify the experience, Coven made use of a number of Gestalt interventions including encouraging members to stay in the here-and-now, facilitating members in taking ownership of their dreams

by using the personal pronoun, and increasing interpersonal contact by asking participants to speak directly to one another.

Coven initially had doubts that doing Gestalt dream work in a group with Taiwanese students and professors would be effective. The research literature supports the perception that Asians are generally hesitant to share personal problems and display emotions in a group, and Coven wondered if participants would be willing not only to share their dreams, but to role-play and act out their dreams. Contrary to expectations that the Taiwanese participants would be cognitive and reserved, Coven discovered that they readily enacted roles, were personally open, and expressed intense feelings.

Applying Gestalt Therapy to Group Work in Schools

Gestalt therapy is grounded on existential principles. The genuineness of the group leader and the quality of the therapeutic relationships between the leader and members (and among the members themselves) are given primary emphasis. This emphasis on creating quality therapeutic relationships fits well with what is required for conducting successful groups with both children and adolescents. More than the techniques group leaders employ, it is the personal dimensions that leaders are able to bring to a group that increase the involvement of young people. According to Coker (2004), Gestalt counseling, although not generally viewed as a school-based approach to counseling, has many developmentally appropriate techniques that work effectively with both children and adolescents in brief counseling contexts. Gestalt counseling offers school counselors a theoretically based approach that is conducive to brief interventions that can lead to both insight and behavior change.

As you have learned in this chapter, Gestalt group work places a premium on the quality of the contact between the individual and the group (M. Polster, 1997). In this respect the Gestalt approach has some common denominators with both the existential and person-centered approaches. I think this is a main strength of Gestalt therapy, and children and adolescents are likely to respond to this collaborative spirit. Specific applications of Gestalt interventions with children can be seen in the works of Lambert (2003), Lederman (1969), Oaklander (1988), and Owmby (1983). In her book, *Anger in the Rocking Chair*, Lederman (1969) describes her Gestalt awareness work with children by asking them to put people into the rocking chair and express their feelings. Not only are the children able to experience a catharsis if they have feelings of resentment, but they are also able to begin to see options other than blaming others for their problems.

Although Lederman applies Gestalt techniques with children in a special education setting, the Gestalt awareness interventions she describes can be productively adapted to working with children and adolescents in other school settings as well. In her book, *Windows to Our Children*, Oaklander (1988) describes various Gestalt techniques for children that can be adapted to group work. She describes various creative activities she uses that are aimed at helping children experience their feelings, their relationship with people in their environment, and approaches to help children develop a sense of responsibility for their actions. Oaklander sees value in projection through art and storytelling as ways of increasing a child's self-awareness. Like Lederman, Oaklander often uses the empty chair technique as a way to assist children in understanding and dealing with frustration, anger, resentment, and other unfinished business.

Techniques from Gestalt therapy may be limited in working with some adolescent groups, especially in the case of involuntary members. Middle school and high school students are often highly self-conscious and may not take kindly to what they perceive as "weird" techniques. Adolescents who may be reluctant to participate in certain Gestalt activities can be invited by a skillful group leader to take the risk of engaging in here-and-now experiments. The manner in which group leaders introduce role-playing interventions has a great deal to do with enlisting a cooperative spirit among these group members. Instead of adolescents merely talking about problems they have in their relationships, they might be surprised by how real the interactions become when they bring interpersonal difficulties to life by using present-centered methods advocated in Gestalt therapy.

Applying Gestalt Therapy With Multicultural Populations

There are certain advantages in using a Gestalt approach with culturally diverse client populations. Gestalt therapy pays attention to how clients view their world, and therapists attend to what is figural for members out of their diverse backgrounds. Because Gestalt therapy is practiced with a phenomenological attitude, therapists are less likely to impose their own values and cultural standards on their clients. Frew (2008) notes that Gestalt therapy can be a useful and effective approach with clients from diverse backgrounds because it takes the clients' context into account.

There are many opportunities for Gestalt leaders to apply their creativity with diverse client populations. People in many cultures give attention to expressing themselves nonverbally rather than emphasizing the content of oral communication. Some clients may express themselves nonverbally to a greater extent than they do with words. For example, group leaders may ask members to focus on their gestures, facial expressions, and the experience within their own body. If a group member, Eduardo, says that he is feeling threatened, the leader may invite him to pay attention to his bodily reactions. Some very creative work can emerge from work with people's gestures and body sensations. One of the advantages of drawing on Gestalt experiments is that they can be tailored to fit the unique way in which an individual member perceives and interprets his or her culture. Of course, before Gestalt procedures are introduced, especially with culturally different group members, it is essential that the clients have been adequately prepared.

The use of imagery and fantasy has much potential if members are well prepared and if there is a high degree of trust within the group. Assume that Anita is dealing with unfinished business pertaining to guilt surrounding the death of a loved one. She can make significant inroads into completing this unfinished business by bringing this dead person symbolically into the room and dealing with her in the present. If English is her second language, Anita can be asked to speak in her original language. However, such an exercise may be resisted by the client on two counts: it may be difficult for her to talk about the dead person, let alone "speak directly" to her; she may also argue that it would be more comfortable for her if she spoke in English.

There are some cautions in too quickly utilizing some Gestalt experiments with ethnic minority clients. As is evident from this chapter, these interventions often lead to emotional expression. Focusing on affect has some limitations with those clients who have been culturally conditioned to be emotionally reserved, or at least not to publicly express their emotions, because doing so is viewed as a sign of weakness and a display of one's vulnerability. Certainly, an effective Gestalt leader would invite such clients to explore their feelings, thoughts, and attitudes surrounding being vulnerable. Ineffective leaders who push for catharsis are likely to find certain clients becoming increasingly uncooperative, and these members may eventually terminate. For instance, clients who are reluctant to experience and express their emotions will probably not take kindly to the therapist's suggestion that they "talk to the empty chair."

Henderson and Thompson (2011) point out further limitations of applying Gestalt therapy to diverse cultural groups. People who have experienced oppression may perceive the emphasis on individual responsibility as a minimization of the role of societal factors in contributing to their problems. For example, group members from Latino and Asian cultures may not appreciate the Gestalt emphasis on experiencing and expressing feelings. American Indian clients may object to what they perceive as discounting the past. Although these limitations can be escalated by ill-timed interventions on the leader's part, timely Gestalt interventions can be one approach in helping clients work through some of their deeper resistances and struggles. More than the methods themselves, the manner in which these interventions are presented to members determines the outcomes. The criticisms of Gestalt therapy's value with multicultural populations are often based on misconceptions of this approach as being confrontational and of being a technique-oriented therapy.

Although some raise concerns about using Gestalt interventions with diverse cultural groups, I think we do a disservice to group members if we decide in advance that experiential approaches will not be effective because of our expectations based on a person's cultural background. Coven's (2004) group demonstration exploring dreams with Taiwanese students does not support research findings that Asians are reserved and are not willing to actively participate in experiential group work. Participants in his workshops demonstrated unexpected behavioral and affective responses. By conducting these group demonstrations, Coven increased his awareness and appreciation of the universality of life issues.

In training workshops in group counseling that Marianne Schneider Corey and I conducted in Korea, we found group participants to be very open and willing to share themselves emotionally. As we do with any person we work with in our groups, but especially members who are obviously culturally different from ourselves, we begin with a not-knowing position. We are not quick to make assumptions about the clients, nor do we impose our worldview or values on them. Instead, we approach clients with respect, interest, compassion, and presence. We work collaboratively with our clients to discover how to best help them resolve the difficulties they experience internally, interpersonally, and in the context of their social environment. It is unrealistic to think you need to know everything about different cultures. What is important is to have an attitude of respect and appreciation for cultural differences.

Evaluation of the Gestalt Approach to Groups

CONTRIBUTIONS AND STRENGTHS OF THE APPROACH

Perls originally conceived of Gestalt therapy primarily as an individual approach, but the practice of Gestalt therapy has evolved and expanded into group work over the years. Feder and Frew's (2006) survey data indicate that Gestalt therapists rely heavily on group work today, with the most popular applications being in psychotherapy, training, and supervision groups.

In his discussion of the distinctive characteristics of Gestalt therapy, Cain (2002) identifies these ideas as being the most significant contributions of this approach:

- The critical importance of contact with oneself, others, and the environment
- The central role of authentic relationship and dialogue in therapy
- The emphasis on field theory, phenomenology, and awareness
- The therapeutic focus on the present; the here-and-now experiencing of the client
- The creative and spontaneous use of active experiments as a pathway to experiential learning

One of the strengths of this approach is the attempt to integrate theory, practice, and research. Strumpfel and Goldman (2002) note that both process and outcome studies have advanced the theory and practice of Gestalt therapy. Process research is appropriate for the process orientation of Gestalt therapy. Strumpfel and Goldman summarize a number of significant findings based on outcome research:

- Gestalt therapy has been shown to be of equal or greater benefit than other therapies for a variety of psychological disorders.
- Gestalt therapy has beneficial effects for people with personality disturbances, psychosomatic problems, and substance addictions.
- The effects of therapy tend to be stable in follow-up studies 1 to 3 years after termination of treatment.

Gestalt therapy is a humanistic, existential, and holistic model that brings a fresh and creative perspective to the practice of group work. I find that Gestalt experiments are powerful and often lead to the expression of immediate emotions and the reexperiencing of old feelings. As is the case with psychodramatic techniques, the Gestalt present-centered methods of reenacting early life experiences bring vitality both to an individual's work and to the participants of the group.

Another distinctive feature of Gestalt therapy is its focus on the body. In an excellent book dealing with the role of the body in psychotherapy, Kepner (1993) demonstrates how a client's posture, movements, and bodily experiences can be incorporated into the practice of Gestalt therapy. Without making interpretations for members, leaders can encourage them to pay attention to what they are experiencing bodily. This focus can provide rich clues to areas members want to avoid, and it also offers a way for members to come in contact with their anxiety. If the leader avoids telling members the meaning of their gestures, postures, and body symptoms, members are more able to stay with what they are experiencing and eventually find their own meaning.

LIMITATIONS OF THE APPROACH

Gestalt interventions frequently elicit participants' emotions, which may make it tempting for a leader to focus on feelings and sometimes give less attention to cognitive factors. Helping participants discover the meaning of their emotional experiences is a significant factor in producing personality changes that will extend beyond the group. Although the earlier phase of Gestalt therapy's development did not focus on cognitive processes, more recent versions of Gestalt therapy address cognitive factors and integrate the affective and cognitive dimensions of human experiencing (see Yontef, 1993; Yontef & Jacobs, 2011). Also, contemporary Gestalt therapy focuses more on relationships and less on techniques.

A major concern I have about the way Gestalt therapy could be practiced is the potential misuse of power. Typically, Gestalt therapists are very active, and if they do not have the characteristics mentioned by Zinker (1978)—sensitivity, timing, inventiveness, empathy, and respect for the client—the experiments can easily boomerang. Also, the members can grow accustomed to the leader's assuming the initiative in creating experiments for them instead of coming up with some of their own experiments. Ideally, experiments in a group are co-created by the leader and the members.

With an approach that can have powerful effects on members, either constructive or destructive, ethical practice requires adequate training and supervision for leaders. The most immediate limitation of Gestalt therapy or any other therapy is the skill, knowledge, training, experience, and judgment of the therapist. Yontef (1995) indicates that therapists who are poorly trained in Gestalt therapy are likely to use techniques without knowing the goals of therapy, what is central to the client's experience, and what alternative methods might be appropriate. Some leaders assume an imposing style, which increases the potential for abuse of power. Those leaders who impose on members are more interested in what they want than in what the members want from them. In the imposing stance, group leaders are less concerned with understanding and respecting the members' experience than they are with making something happen (Frew, 1992).

Inept therapists may use powerful interventions to stir up emotions and open up problems that members have kept from full awareness, only to abandon the members once they have managed to have a dramatic catharsis. Such leaders fail to help members work through what they have experienced and bring some closure to it. It is essential that leaders are able to be psychologically present as members express emotions. If leaders are threatened by emotional intensity, they might also abandon members who are experiencing emotion. Leaders need to learn to manage powerfully expressed emotions.

It is easy to see that the misapplication of Gestalt methodology could provide a tempting place for group leaders to hide their personal responses and forget about the I/Thou relationship, especially those leaders who adopt an imposing style. Through the use of confrontive techniques, without a clear understanding of the theory of Gestalt therapy, leaders can do more damage than good. Contemporary Gestalt therapists make use of facilitative interventions that highlight interpersonal processes, as opposed to relying on a coercive and hard-hitting style (Schoenberg & Feder, 2005). It is essential for Gestalt practitioners to learn how to intervene in a manner that respects the client's reluctance and the lack of internal and environmental support to do more at that moment. A blend of support and the invitation to risk go a long way in creating the kind of relationship that enables clients to explore a universal tension—I want to change versus I want to stay the same.

Gestalt group leaders who have truly integrated their therapeutic approach are sensitive enough to practice in a flexible way. They have solid training in Gestalt theory and practice, which allows them to design experiments that will deepen the work of members. They strive to help members experience themselves as fully as possible in the present, yet they are not rigidly bound by dictates, nor do they routinely intervene with a directive whenever members stray from the present. Sensitively staying in contact with a member's flow of experiencing entails the ability to focus on the person and not on the mechanical use of techniques for a certain effect.

Where to Go From Here

If you have become interested in learning more about Gestalt theory and practice, I encourage you to attend a workshop led by a competent professional. You might consider pursuing Gestalt training, which would include attending workshops, seeking out personal therapy from a Gestalt therapist, and enrolling in a Gestalt training program that would involve reading, practice, and supervision. Here are a few resources for training in Gestalt therapy:

Gestalt Institute of Cleveland, Inc.
1588 Hazel Drive
Cleveland, OH 44106-1791
Telephone: (216) 421-0468
Fax: (216) 421-1729
E-mail: gestaltclv@aol.com
Website: www.gestaltcleveland.org

Gestalt Therapy Institute of the Pacific
1626 Westwood Blvd., Suite 104
Los Angeles, CA 90024
Telephone: (310) 446-9720
Fax: (310) 475-4704
E-mail: info@gesetalttherapy.org
Website: www.gestalttherapy.org

Gestalt Therapy Training Center, Northwest
757 SE 34th Avenue
Portland, OR 97214
Telephone: (503) 230-0900
Fax: (360) 696-4811
E-mail: gttcnw@aol.com
Website: gttcnw.org

The Center for Gestalt Development, Inc. publishes *The Gestalt Directory*, which includes information about Gestalt practitioners and training programs throughout the world. The training center's program is described in detail, including admission requirements, costs, length of the program, certifications, and other pertinent data. Single copies of *The Gestalt Directory* are free of charge. Requests for a copy must be in writing or from the website. Also available are books, audiotapes, and videotapes dealing with Gestalt practice.

The Center for Gestalt Development, Inc.
Website: www.gestalt.org

JOURNALS

The International Gestalt Journal, which is devoted to the theory and practice of Gestalt therapy, is available from the Center for Gestalt Development, Inc. Published biannually, it offers articles, reviews, and commentaries of interest to the practitioner, theoretician, academician, and student. For subscription information, contact:

International Gestalt Journal
P. O. Box 278
Gouldsboro, ME 04607-0278
Website: www.international-gestalt-journal.org

Two other journals are:

Gestalt Review
P. O. Box 515
South Wellfleet, MA 02663
Website: www.gestaltreview.com

British Gestalt Journal
P. O. Box 420
Bristol, BS99 7PQ
England
Website: www.britishgestaltjournal.com

AUTHOR LECTURES

Watch *Gerald Corey's Perspectives on Theory and Practice of Group Counseling* DVD or visit the *Theory and Practice of Group Counseling* CourseMate website at www.cengagebrain.com/shop/ISBN/0840033869 to watch videos of Dr. Gerald Corey presenting lectures for each chapter. Also available are unique eAudio lectures for each chapter and quiz questions for self-study.

RECOMMENDED SUPPLEMENTARY READINGS

Beyond the Hot Seat Revisited: Gestalt Approaches to Group (Feder & Frew, 2008) is one of the few books exclusively devoted to Gestalt approaches to group work, and I highly recommend it. Separate chapters are devoted to Gestalt group process,

family therapy, training groups, intensive workshops, and other clinical applications.

Gestalt Group Therapy: A Practical Guide (Feder, 2006) provides a good discussion of what Gestalt group therapy is and how a Gestalt group progresses.

Gestalt Therapy: History, Theory, and Practice (Woldt & Toman, 2005) introduces the historical underpinnings and key concepts of Gestalt therapy and features applications of those concepts to therapeutic practice. This is a significant publication in the field of Gestalt therapy and contains pedagogical learning activities and experiments, review questions, and photographs of all contributors.

REFERENCES AND SUGGESTED READINGS

Beisser, A. R. (1970). The paradoxical theory of change. In J. Fagan & I. L. Shepherd (Eds.), *Gestalt therapy now* (pp. 77–80). New York: Harper & Row (Colophon).

*Cain, D. J. (2002). Defining characteristics, history, and evolution of humanistic psychotherapies. In D. J. Cain & J. Seeman (Eds.), *Humanistic psychotherapies: Handbook of research and practice* (pp. 3–54). Washington, DC: American Psychological Association.

Coker, J. K. (2004). Using Gestalt counseling in a school setting. In B. T. Erford (Ed.), *Professional school counseling: A handbook of theories, programs & practices* (pp. 131–138). Austin, TX: CAPS Press.

Coven, A. (2004). Gestalt group dreamwork demonstrations in Taiwan. *Journal for Specialists in Group Work, 29*(2), 175–184.

Downing, J., & Marmorstein, R. (Eds.). (1973). *Dreams and nightmares: A book of Gestalt therapy sessions.* New York: Harper & Row.

*Feder, B. (2006). *Gestalt group therapy: A practical guide.* Metairie/New Orleans, LA: Gestalt Institute Press.

*Feder, B. (2008a).Gestalt group therapy: An interactive approach. In B. Feder & J. Frew (Eds.), *Beyond the hot seat revisited: Gestalt approaches to group* (pp. 157–166). Metairie/ New Orleans, LA: Gestalt Institute Press.

*Feder, B. (2008b). Safety and danger in the Gestalt group. In B. Feder & J. Frew (Eds.), *Beyond the hot seat revisited: Gestalt approaches to group* (pp. 67–84). Metairie/New Orleans, LA: Gestalt Institute Press.

Feder, B., & Frew, J. (2006). A survey of the practice of Gestalt group therapy. *Gestalt Review, 10*(3), 242–248.

*Feder, B., & Frew, J. (Eds.). (2008). *Beyond the hot seat revisited: Gestalt approaches to groups.* Metairie/ New Orleans, LA: Gestalt Institute Press.

Fernbacher, S., & Plummer, D. (2005). Cultural influences and considerations in Gestalt therapy. In A. L. Woldt & S. M. Toman (Eds.), *Gestalt therapy: History, theory and practice* (pp. 117–132). Thousand Oaks, CA: Sage.

Frew, J. E. (1986). The functions and patterns of occurrence of individual contact styles during the development phase of the Gestalt group. *The Gestalt Journal, 9*(1), 55–70.

*Frew, J. E. (1988). The practice of Gestalt therapy in groups. *The Gestalt Journal, 11*(1), 77–96.

Frew, J. E. (1992). From the perspective of the environment. *The Gestalt Journal, 15*(1), 39–60.

*Frew, J. E. (1997). A Gestalt therapy theory application to the practice of group leadership. *Gestalt Review, 1*(2), 131–149.

*Frew, J. E. (2008). Gestalt therapy. In J. Frew & M. Spiegler (Eds.), *Contemporary psychotherapies for a diverse world* (pp. 228–274). New York: Lahaska Press.

---

* Books and articles marked with an asterisk (*) are suggested for further study.

Henderson, D., & Thompson, C. L. (2011). *Counseling children* (8th ed.). Belmont, CA: Brooks/Cole, Cengage Learning.

*Hycner, R., & Jacobs, L. (1995). *The healing relationship in Gestalt therapy.* Highland, NY: The Center for Gestalt Development.

*Jacobs, L. (1989). Dialogue in Gestalt theory and therapy. *The Gestalt Journal, 12*(1), 25–67.

*Kepner, E. (2008). Gestalt group process. In B. Feder & J. Frew (Eds.), *Beyond the hot seat revisited: Gestalt approaches to group* (pp. 17–37). Metairie/New Orleans, LA: Gestalt Institute Press.

Kepner, J. I. (1993). *Body process: Working with the body in psychotherapy.* San Francisco: Jossey-Bass.

Lambert, R. (2003). *A child's view: Gestalt therapy with children, adolescents, and their families.* Highland, NY: Gestalt Journal Press.

Latner, J. (1986). *The Gestalt therapy book.* Highland, NY: Center for Gestalt Development.

Lederman, J. (1969). *Anger in the rocking chair.* New York: McGraw-Hill.

Levitsky, A., & Perls, F. (1970). The rules and games of Gestalt therapy. In J. Fagan & I. Shepherd (Eds.), *Gestalt therapy now.* New York: Harper & Row (Colophon).

Melnick, J., & Nevis, S. (2005). Gestalt therapy methodology. In A. L. Woldt & S. M. Toman (Eds.), *Gestalt therapy: History, theory, and practice* (pp. 101–116). Thousand Oaks, CA: Sage.

Oaklander, V. (1988). *Windows to our children: A Gestalt therapy approach to children and adolescents.* Highland, NY: Center for Gestalt Development.

Owmby, R. L. (1983). Gestalt therapy with children. *Journal of Gestalt Therapy, 6,* 51–58.

Passons, W. R. (1975). *Gestalt approaches in counseling.* New York: Holt, Rinehart & Winston.

*Perls, F. (1969a). *Gestalt therapy verbatim.* New York: Bantam. (Note: In 1992, published by The Gestalt Journal Press, Highland, NY)

Perls, F. (1969b). *In and out of the garbage pail.* New York: Bantam.

Polster, E. (1987a). Escape from the present: Transition and storyline. In J. K. Zeig (Ed.), *The evolution of psychotherapy* (pp. 326–340). New York: Brunner/Mazel.

*Polster, E. (1987b). *Every person's life is worth a novel.* New York: Norton.

*Polster, E. (1995). *A population of selves: A therapeutic exploration of personal diversity.* San Francisco: Jossey-Bass.

*Polster, E. (1997). The therapeutic power of attention: Theory and technique. In J. K. Zeig (Ed.), *The evolution of psychotherapy: The third conference* (pp. 221–229). New York: Brunner/Mazel.

Polster, E. (2008). Life focus communities. In B. Feder & J. Frew (Eds.), *Beyond the hot seat revisited: Gestalt approaches to group* (pp. 345–370). Metairie/New Orleans, LA: Gestalt Institute Press.

*Polster, E., & Polster, M. (1973). *Gestalt therapy integrated: Contours of theory and practice.* New York: Brunner/Mazel.

*Polster, E., & Polster, M. (1999). *From the radical center: The heart of Gestalt therapy.* Cambridge, MA: The Gestalt Institute of Cleveland Press.

Polster, M. (1987). Gestalt therapy: Evolution and application. In J. K. Zeig (Ed.), *The evolution of psychotherapy* (pp. 312–322). New York: Brunner/Mazel.

*Polster, M. (1997). Beyond one-to-one. In J. K. Zeig (Ed.), *The evolution of psychotherapy: The third conference* (pp. 233–241). New York: Brunner/Mazel.

Polster, M., & Polster, E. (1990). Gestalt therapy. In J. K. Zeig & W. M. Munion (Eds.), *What is psychotherapy? Contemporary perspectives* (pp. 103–107). San Francisco: Jossey-Bass.

Rainwater, J. (1979). *You're in charge! A guide to becoming your own therapist.* Los Angeles: Guild of Tutors Press.

Schoenberg, P., & Feder, B. (2005). Gestalt therapy in groups. In A. L. Woldt & S. M. Toman (Eds.), *Gestalt therapy: History, theory and practice* (pp. 219–236). Thousand Oaks, CA: Sage.

*Strumpfel, U., & Goldman, R. (2002). Contacting Gestalt therapy. In D. J. Cain & J. Seeman (Eds.), *Humanistic psychotherapies: Handbook of research and practice* (pp. 189–219). Washington, DC: American Psychological Association.

*Yontef, G. (1993). *Awareness, dialogue and process: Essays on Gestalt therapy.* Highland, NY: The Gestalt Journal Press.

*Yontef, G. (1995). Gestalt therapy. In A. S. Gurman & S. B. Messer (Eds.), *Essential psychotherapies: Theory and practice* (pp. 261–303). New York: Guilford Press.

Yontef, G. (1999). Awareness, dialogue and process: Preface to the 1998 German edition. *The Gestalt Journal, 22*(1), 9–20.

*Yontef, G., & Jacobs, L. (2011). Gestalt therapy. In R. Corsini & D. Wedding (Eds.), *Current psychotherapies* (9th ed., pp. 342–382). Belmont, CA: Brooks/Cole, Cengage Learning.

Woldt, A. L., & Toman, S. M. (Eds.). (2005). *Gestalt therapy: History, theory and practice.* Thousand Oaks, CA: Sage.

*Zinker, J. (1978). *Creative process in Gestalt therapy.* New York: Random House (Vintage).

*Zinker, J. C. (2008). The developmental process of a Gestalt therapy group. In B. Feder & J. Frew (Eds.), *Beyond the hot seat revisited: Gestalt approaches to group* (pp. 85–109). Metairie/New Orleans, LA: Gestalt Institute Press.

CHAPTER TWELVE

Transactional Analysis in Groups

Introduction

Transactional analysis (TA) is a theory of personality, a language of behavior, and an organized system of interactional therapy. It is grounded on the assumption that we make current decisions based on our early experiences. Early in life we may have felt powerless or even experienced ourselves as struggling for survival. Decisions made then about how to behave may not be valid, useful, or empowering today. These early decisions may, in fact, be self-sabotaging. The TA therapist focuses on helping clients rethink and redecide these early decisions in light of present circumstances. TA emphasizes the cognitive and behavioral aspects of the therapeutic process. Within TA there are three recognized schools—classical, Schiffian (or reparenting), and redecisional—and unofficial schools identified as self-reparenting and restructuring or corrective parenting. The redecisional school has gained in prominence and is the focus of this chapter.

TA therapists strive to create a meaningful relationship with clients within which transformation can occur. The goal of transactional analysis is **autonomy**, which is defined as awareness, spontaneity, and the capacity for intimacy (Tudor & Hobbes, 2002). In achieving autonomy people have the capacity to make new decisions (redecide), thereby empowering themselves and altering the course of their lives. Specific client goals are mutually arrived at and agreed upon. In therapy groups, TA participants learn how to recognize the three ego states—Parent, Adult, and Child—in which they function. Group members also learn how their current behavior is being affected by the rules and regulations they received and incorporated as children and how they can identify the life script they decided upon, which is determining their actions. Ultimately, they come to realize that they can now redecide and initiate a new direction in life, changing what is not working while retaining what serves them well. To turn their desires into reality, clients are required to actively change their behavior.

TA provides an *interactional* and *contractual* approach to groups. It is interactional in that it emphasizes the dynamics of transactions between people,

323

and it is contractual in that group members develop clear statements of what they will change and how they will be different as a result of being in a group. Members establish their goals and direction and describe how they will be different when they complete their contract. Contracting allows for a more equal footing between client and therapist and demonstrates that the responsibility for change is shared between group member and therapist. Contracting for change also minimizes potential power struggles between therapist and client.

HISTORICAL BACKGROUND

Transactional analysis was originally developed by the late Eric Berne (1961), who was trained as a Freudian psychoanalyst and psychiatrist. TA evolved out of Berne's dissatisfaction with the slowness of psychoanalysis in helping people solve their problems. Berne's major objections to psychoanalysis were that it was time consuming, complex, and poorly communicated to clients. Historically, TA developed as an extension of psychoanalysis with concepts and techniques especially designed for group treatment. Berne discovered that by using TA his clients were making significant changes in their lives. As his theory of personality evolved, Berne parted ways with psychoanalysis to devote himself full time to the theory and practice of TA (Dusay, 1986).

Berne formulated most of the concepts of TA by paying attention to what his clients were saying with their accompanying behavior. He began to see an ego state emerge that correlated to the childhood experiences of his patients. He concluded that there was a Child ego state that was different from the "grown-up" ego state. Later, he postulated that there were two "grown-up" states: one, which seemed to be a copy of the person's parents, he called the Parent ego state; the other, which was the rational part of the person, he named the Adult ego state. One of Berne's contributions is his perspective on how young children develop a personal plan for their life as a strategy for physical and psychological survival. A personal **life script** is an unconscious life plan made in childhood, reinforced by the parents, "justified" by subsequent events, and culminating in a chosen alternative (Stewart & Joines, 1987). Berne's view is that people are shaped from their first few years by that life script, which they follow sporadically during the rest of their lives.

Contemporary TA practitioners have moved in various directions and modified many of the basic concepts Berne formulated, and it is difficult to discuss practices that apply to all of them. This chapter highlights the expansion of Berne's approach by the late Mary and Robert Goulding (1979), leaders of the redecisional school of TA. The Gouldings differ from the classical Bernian approach in a number of ways. They have combined TA with the principles and techniques of Gestalt therapy, family therapy, psychodrama, and behavior therapy. The redecisional approach helps group members experience their impasse, or the point at which they feel stuck. They relive the context in which they made earlier decisions, some of which were not functional, and they make new decisions that are functional. **Redecision therapy** is aimed at helping people challenge themselves to discover ways in which they perceive themselves in victimlike roles and to take charge of their lives by deciding for themselves how they will change. With its emphasis on personal responsibility and freedom, TA can be considered an existential approach to psychotherapy. Both existential therapy and TA emphasize the importance of clients assuming responsibility for their lives (Widdowson, 2010).

BASIC ASSUMPTIONS AND RATIONALE FOR A GROUP APPROACH

Underlying the practice of TA group work is the premise that awareness is an important first step in the process of changing our ways of thinking, feeling, and behaving. In the early stages of a group, techniques are aimed at increasing participants' awareness of their problems and their options for making substantive changes in their lives. Another basic assumption of TA is that all of us are in charge of what we do, of the ways in which we think, and of how we feel. Others do not make us feel a certain way; rather, we respond to situations largely by our choices (R. Goulding, 1987).

The practice of TA is ideally suited for groups. Berne believed that group therapy yielded information about one's personal plan for life much more quickly than individual therapy. Redecision therapy, as introduced by the Gouldings, is conducted in a group context in which members can experience elements of their scripts by relating current issues to early scenes in their lives when a decision was initially made. From a redecisional perspective, group therapy is the treatment of choice. Group participants tend to change more rapidly than they can in individual therapy, and groups seem to add a human quality to therapy (R. Goulding, 1987).

There are many avenues of self-understanding through analyzing transactions within the group. In the same way that Gestalt groups function in the here-and-now, TA groups bring past issues into the present. Group members facilitate action by representing both family members from the past and contemporaries. Because of the interaction within the TA group, members have easier access to their life script content by seeing it reflected back to them through the words and behavior of other group members. By identifying early decisions and appreciating how valuable they were at the time they were made, members are challenged to see what they would prefer given the reality of today. For Robert Goulding, one rationale for a group is that it provides a living experience that members can take out to their family, friends, and community.

Key Concepts

THE EGO STATES

An **ego state** is a set of related thoughts, feelings, and behaviors in which part of an individual's personality is manifested at a given time (Stewart & Joines, 1987). All transactional analysts work with ego states, which encompass important facets of the personality and are considered to be essential and distinguishing characteristics of TA therapy (Dusay, 1986). Each person has a basic trio of Parent, Adult, and Child (P-A-C). According to TA, people are constantly shifting from one of these ego states to another, and their behavior at any one time is related to the ego state they are in at the moment. People operate from the ego state that has the most energy and make decisions from that ego state. One definition of autonomy is the capacity to move with agility and intention through ego states and to operate in the one most appropriate to the reality of the given situation.

The **Parent** ego state contains the values, morals, core beliefs, and behaviors incorporated from significant authority figures, primarily one's parents. Outwardly, this ego state is expressed toward others in critical or nurturing behavior. Inwardly, it is experienced as old parental messages that continue to influence the inner Child. When we are in the Parent ego state, we react to situations as we imagine our parents might have reacted, or we may act toward others the way our parents acted toward us. The Parent contains all the "shoulds" and "oughts" and other rules for living. When we are in that ego state, we may act in ways that are strikingly similar to those of our parents or other significant people in our early life. We may use some of their very phrases, and our posture, gestures, voice, and mannerisms may replicate those that we experienced in our parents.

The Parent ego state is divided into **Nurturing Parent** (NP) and **Controlling Parent** (CP), both of which have positive and negative aspects. The positive aspect of Nurturing Parent is to affirm individuals for both being and doing. The negative aspect of the Nuturing Parent involves discounting others with phrases such as, "Oh, you poor thing." The positive aspect of Controlling Parent is to provide structure intended for the benefit or success of the individual, such as "Finish your homework before you watch television." The negative aspect of Controlling Parent is to be critical and often to discount the Child ego state in others.

The **Adult** ego state is the objective and computer-like part of our personality that functions as a data processor; it computes possibilities and, like the other two ego states, makes decisions, and represents what we have learned and thought out for ourselves. The state is not related to chronological age. The Adult is a thinking state oriented toward current reality; the Adult is objective in gathering information, is nonemotional, and works with the facts of the external reality as perceived by that individual. The Adult often negotiates between the Child's wants and the Parent's shoulds.

The **Child** ego state is the original part of us and is most naturally who we are. It is the part of ourselves we use to form long-lasting relationships. The Child ego state consists of feelings, impulses, and spontaneous actions and includes "recordings" of early experiences. The Child ego state is divided into Natural Child (NC) and Adapted Child (AC), both of which have positive and negative aspects. The positive aspects of the Natural Child are the spontaneous, ever so endearing, loving and charming parts of all of us. The negative aspect of the Natural Child is to be impulsive to the degree that our safety is compromised. The positive aspect of the Adapted Child is that we respond appropriately in social situations. The negative aspect of the Adapted Child involves overadapting and giving up our power and discounting our value, worth, and dignity. Some TA theorists include the Rebellious Child in the domain of Adapted Child because one who continuously attempts to solve problems by rebelling is overadapting. Both overadapting and rebelling are life script issues considered necessary for survival.

In a TA group, members are first taught how to recognize in which of the five ego states they are functioning at any given time: Nurturing Parent, Controlling Parent, Adult, Nurturing Child, or Adapted Child. The aim is to enable them to decide consciously whether that state or another state is most appropriate or useful. For example, a member who typically responds to others in a Controlling Parent style and who has contracted to become more tolerant toward others must recognize his or her habitual ego state before any steps can be taken to change. Participants in a group learn that when something is not working, the wrong ego state is in charge.

THE NEED FOR STROKES

Humans need to be stimulated physically, socially, and intellectually. As we grow and develop, we need to be recognized for who we are and what we do. This need for stimulation and recognition is referred to as a need for **strokes** (a stroke is a unit of recognition). A stroke is any act of recognition or source of stimulation.

A basic premise of the TA approach is that humans need to receive both physical and psychological "strokes" to develop a sense of trust in the world and a basis for loving themselves. There is ample evidence that lack of physical contact can impair infant growth and development and, in extreme cases, can lead to death. **Psychological strokes**—verbal and nonverbal signs of acceptance and recognition—are also necessary to people as confirmations of their worth. The strokes a child receives early in life have a significant influence on the development of the child's life script.

Strokes can be classified as verbal or nonverbal, unconditional (being) or conditional (doing), and positive or negative. *Positive strokes* that express warmth, affection, or appreciation verbally or with a look, smile, touch, or gesture are necessary for the development of psychologically healthy people. *Negative strokes* can be useful in that they set limits: "I don't like it when you use my computer without asking." Negative strokes are a way to give feedback to people about their behavior. They are sometimes essential in protecting children: "Stop right there! Don't go out into the street until I get to the curb and take your hand." Interestingly, negative strokes are considered preferable to no strokes at all—that is, to being ignored. We are all familiar with instances when children's actions elicit negative strokes from their parents. Even these responses are preferable to being ignored, dismissed, or emotionally neglected. Strokes are life giving; they are fuel for the psyche in the same way that food is fuel for the body. To be able to live effectively, people need strokes.

Steiner (1974) describes strokes as exchanges. They can be offered, accepted or taken in, refused or rejected, and directly requested, such as "Will you tell me that you appreciate that I cooked dinner for you?" Another way strokes are exchanged is to self-stroke or even brag, such as "I did the best I could in putting my kids through college." TA group members are introduced to how they live the "stroke economy" and can then examine whether they have incorporated any of these five self-sabotaging rules about stroking:

- Don't give positive strokes when you have them to give.
- Don't ask for strokes when you need them.
- Don't accept strokes when you want them (and they are offered).
- Don't reject (negative) strokes when you don't want them.
- Don't give yourself strokes.

When group members understand how these exchanges affect their behavior, they can choose the kinds of exchanges they want to make. For example, Sabrina continually puts herself down with self-deprecating remarks, exercising the third restrictive rule in the preceding list. She either doesn't hear or soon forgets the positive feedback she gets from others in her group. When paid a sincere compliment, Sabrina finds some way to play it down or make a joke of it. If she is the focus of positive attention or receives any display of tenderness, affection, or caring, she becomes extremely uncomfortable, yet she remembers and stores up any critical remarks and feels depressed. As Steiner (1974) would put it, Sabrina collects the "cold pricklies" rather than the "warm fuzzies."

In her TA group Sabrina is made aware that she discounts or declines positive strokes offered by others. She is encouraged to explore what that is about in relation to her own sense of value and worth as a prelude to deciding something different about herself. If she wants to change, she will courageously explore her discomfort in listening to acknowledgments and where that may have started. For example, how might she not feel safe in accepting a compliment?

INJUNCTIONS AND COUNTERINJUNCTIONS

The Gouldings' redecision work is grounded in the TA concepts of injunctions and early decisions (M. Goulding, 1987). When parents are excited by a child's behavior, the messages given are often *permissions,* or reinforcement for the behavior. However, when parents feel threatened by a child's behavior, the messages expressed are often **injunctions**, which are issued from the parents' own Child ego state. Such messages—expressions of disappointment, frustration, anxiety, and unhappiness—establish the "don'ts" by which children learn to live. Out of their own pain, parents can issue this short, but profound list of general injunctions: "Don't." "Don't be." "Don't be close." "Don't be separate from me." "Don't be the sex you are." "Don't want." "Don't need." "Don't think." "Don't feel." "Don't grow up." "Don't be a child." "Don't succeed." "Don't be you." "Don't be sane." "Don't be well." "Don't belong" (M. Goulding, 1987; M. Goulding & Goulding, 1979). These messages are predominantly given nonverbally and at the psychological level between birth and 7 years of age.

According to Mary Goulding (1987), children decide either to accept these parental messages or to fight against them. If they do accept them, they decide precisely *how* they will accept them. The decisions children make about these injunctions become a basic part of their permanent character structure. When a child accepts the emotionally transmitted injunction, communicated by the fervor of the Child of the significant grown-up, the child will bury it deep within and not let his or her own internal Parent and Adult know what it is (Ray Quiett, personal communication, May 24, 2009). This becomes a matter of survival. Group members often have the misconception that if an injunction is discovered and changed in any way, they will not survive. For example, Tom exhibits nervous, fidgeting behavior during his first meeting with the group. Outside of his conscious awareness, Tom is afraid the injunction segment of his script will be discovered, and he will perish. The life script doesn't match reality, but it matches his perception of reality in the Child ego state. This becomes a challenge for the group leader. The leader, from his Nurturing Parent, must ally with the member's scared internal Child and build a safe environment in the group to facilitate change.

When parents observe their sons or daughters not succeeding, or not being comfortable with who they are, they attempt to "counter" the effect of the earlier messages with **counterinjunctions.** These messages come from the parents' Parent ego state and are given at the social level. They convey the "shoulds," "oughts," and "dos" of parental expectations. Examples of counterinjunctions are "Be perfect." "Try hard." "Hurry up." "Be strong." "Please me." "Be careful."

The problem with these counterinjunctions is that no matter how much we try to please we feel as though we still are not doing enough or being enough. This demonstrates the rule that the messages given at the psychological level are far more powerful and enduring than those given at the social level.

In TA groups the members explore the "shoulds" and "shouldn'ts," the "dos" and "don'ts" by which they have been trained to live. The first step in freeing oneself from behaviors dictated by the often irrational and generally uncritically received parental messages is awareness of the specific injunctions and counterinjunctions that one has accepted as a child. Once group participants have identified and become aware of these internalized "shoulds," "oughts," "dos," "don'ts," and "musts," they are in a better position to critically examine them to determine whether they are useful or self-sabotaging.

DECISIONS AND REDECISIONS

As indicated earlier, transactional analysis emphasizes the cognitive and behavioral dimensions, especially our ability to become aware of decisions that govern our behavior and of the capacity to make new decisions that will beneficially alter the course of our life. This section addresses the decisions made in response to parental injunctions and counterinjunctions and explains how TA group members learn to relive these early decisions and make new ones.

Let's look at an example of decision making that has been dictated by parental injunctions. A TA group member, Alejandro, apparently received the parental injunction, "Don't trust anybody." The decisions about behavior resulting from this injunction were implicit in many of Alejandro's characteristic pronouncements: "If you don't let yourself care, you won't be hurt." "If I keep to myself, I won't need anything from anyone." "Whenever I've wanted something from another, I've been hurt. It's just not worth getting involved with, or even close to, others." Indeed, it became clear in group that by accepting his parents' injunctions against trusting people, Alejandro consistently made decisions that caused him to avoid others. To support these decisions, Alejandro was able to find plenty of data—both in the group and in his everyday life—to maintain his view that trust would inevitably lead to hurt. Consequently he continued, often unwittingly, to abide by his parents' injunction.

In the TA group Alejandro not only had the opportunity to become aware of his decisions and of the injunctions behind them but was also helped to investigate whether these decisions were still appropriate. At one time the decisions to avoid people might have been necessary for Alejandro's physical and psychological safety—a matter of sheer survival. In group Alejandro was able to question whether such decisions were serving any purpose now, or whether they were, instead, interfering with him getting what he really wanted and needed from and with others. In doing a piece of personal work where he decides to trust others, he could experiment with his decision in the safety of the therapy group.

Even though injunctions and counterinjunctions carry the weight of parental authority, the Gouldings (1978, 1979) point out that the child must accept these messages if they are to have an impact on his or her personality. The Gouldings add that many childhood injunctions are not issued by the parents but derive instead from the children's own fantasies and misinterpretations. It is important to note that a single parental injunction may foster a variety of decisions on the part of the child, ranging from reasonable to pathological. For example, one child may respond to the injunction "Don't be sane or well" by deciding she'll become a psychiatrist; another may decide she actually is crazy and later collapse as a grown person and need residential care. Similarly, the injunction "Don't be you" may evoke decisions ranging from "I'll hide who I really am" to "I'll be someone else" to "I'll be a nobody" to "I'll kill myself, and then they'll accept me and love me." The injunction "Don't be you" is sometimes offered and taken as "Don't be the gender you are," resulting in gender-role confusion. Another form of expressing this injunction is, "Don't be who you are; be who I wanted to be when I was young." This might result in a young woman choosing a career in medicine when her real love was architecture.

Whatever injunctions people have received, and whatever the resulting life decisions were, transactional analysis maintains that people can change by changing their decisions—by redeciding in the moment. A basic assumption of TA is that anything that has been learned can be relearned. In their groups the Gouldings developed an atmosphere in which members were challenged from the outset to change. Robert Goulding (1975) started each group session by asking members this question: "What do you want to change today?" Early in the course of a group, R. Goulding also asked, "What did you decide to do to screw up your life, and what are you going to decide now to unscrew it?" (p. 246).

The group work related to making new decisions frequently requires members to return to the childhood scenes in which they arrived at self-limiting decisions. The group leader may facilitate this process with any of the following interventions: "As you are speaking, how old do you feel?" "Is what you are saying reminding you of any times when you were a child?" "What pictures are coming to your mind right now?" "Could you exaggerate that frown on your face? What are you feeling? What scene comes to mind as you experience your frowning?" Mary Goulding (1987) believed that there are many ways of assisting a member to return to some critical point in childhood. Once the client is there, he or she reexperiences the scene, reliving it in the here-and-now, only this time with a different outcome. The redecision is a decision that is truly empowering. After members experience a redecision from being in an old scene, they design experiments so that they can practice new behavior to reinforce their redecision both in and out of group. Members typically leave group sessions with homework assignments aimed at reinforcing the new decision.

Consider Helga, for example, who relives scenes with her parents when she was positively stroked for failing or was negatively stroked for succeeding. It was apparently at those times that she accepted the injunction "Don't succeed." The group can encourage her to examine whether the decision, which may have been functional or even necessary in the past, is currently appropriate. She may redecide that "I will make it, and I am successful, even though it is not what you want from me."

Another group member, Kieran, is able to see that he responded to his father's injunction "Don't grow up" by deciding to remain helpless and immature. He recalls learning that when he was independent his dad shouted at him and, when he was helpless, he was given his father's attention. Because he wanted his father's approval, Kieran decided, "I'll remain a child forever." During a group session, Kieran goes back to a childhood scene in which he was stroked for his helplessness, and he talks to his father now in a way that he never did as a child: "Dad, even though I still want your approval, I don't need it to exist. Your acceptance is not worth the price I'd have to pay. I'm capable of

deciding for myself and of standing on my own two feet. I'll be the man that I want to be, not the boy that you want me to be."

In this redecision work Helga and Kieran enter the past and re-create old scenes in which they can safely give up old and currently inappropriate early decisions because both are armed with an understanding in the present that enables them to relive the scene in a new way. According to the Gouldings, it is possible to construe a *new ending* to the scenes in which original decisions were made—a new ending that often results in a *new beginning* that allows clients to think, feel, and act in revitalized ways.

GAMES

A transaction, which is considered the basic unit of communication, consists of an exchange of strokes between two or more people. A **game** is an ongoing series of transactions that ends with a negative payoff called for by the script that concludes the game and advances some way of feeling badly. The basic nature of the game is to get negative strokes and reinforce the script. By their very nature, games serve the function of preventing intimacy. Games consist of three basic elements: a series of complementary transactions that on the surface seem plausible; an ulterior transaction that is the hidden agenda; and a negative payoff that concludes the game and is the real purpose of the game. When a person becomes stroke starved, it is normal to engage in a game to build up a stroke reserve—even though doing so is negative (Ray Quiett, personal communication, May 24, 2009).

Stephen Karpman (1968) assigns three roles to game participants: *persecutor, rescuer,* and *victim.* For example, people who have decided they are helpless may play some version of "Poor me" or "Kick me." A student "loses" or "forgets" her homework for the second time this week and makes the announcement publicly in class. The teacher gets angry, and the student takes the payoff and gets paid attention to in the process. People who feel superior may either persecute or rescue. The persecutor plays some form of "Gotcha" or "Blemish" (looking for the flaw), whereas the rescuer plays some form of "I am only trying to help you." Berne (1964) described an anthology of games, including "Yes, but," "Kick me," "Harassed," "If it weren't for you," "Martyr," "Ain't it awful," "I'm only trying to help you," "Uproar," and "Look what you made me do!" Games always have some payoff (or they wouldn't be perpetuated), and one common payoff is support for the decisions described in the preceding section. For example, people who have decided that they are helpless may play the "Yes, but" game. They ask others for help, and then greet any suggestions with a list of reasons the suggestions won't work, thus remaining free to cling to their helplessness. Those who play the "Kick me" game are often people who have decided to be rejected; they set themselves up to be mistreated by others so that they can play the role of the victim nobody likes.

By engaging in game playing, people receive strokes and also maintain and defend their early decisions. They find evidence to support their view of the world, and they collect bad feelings. The unpleasant feelings people experience after a game are known as **rackets**. A racket feeling is a familiar emotion that was learned and encouraged in childhood and experienced in many different stress situations, but it is maladaptive as an adult means of problem solving (Stewart & Joines, 1987). Rackets are often substitute feelings that replaced feelings the child's parents did not allow. For example, Ed was not allowed to show anger as a child. He was told, "You are not angry, you are just tired! Go to your room and rest." So Ed adopted being tired as a racket feeling for anger, and as an adult Ed is often tired for no apparent reason.

These rackets are maintained by actually choosing situations that will support them. Therefore, those who typically feel depressed, angry, or bored may be actively collecting these feelings and feeding them into long-standing feeling patterns that often lead to stereotypical ways of behaving. People also choose the games they will play to maintain their rackets. Games and rackets can be thought of as the emotional and relational patterns that people create to foster their life script decisions (Tudor & Hobbes, 2002).

A group situation provides an ideal environment for the participants to become aware of the specific ways in which they choose game-playing strategies to avoid genuine contact and choose patterns of thinking, feeling, and behaving that are ultimately self-defeating. Group members bring to the group and act out the very games that they play outside of the group. Group members can learn about their own games and rackets by observing the behavior of others in the group, as well as by analyzing how their responses in the group are connected to their responses to life situations in early childhood. By using the games they are currently playing in the group, members begin to understand that these games often give the appearance of intimacy, but their actual effect is to create distance between people. Later, as members become aware of the more subtle aspects of game playing, they begin to realize that games prevent close human interaction. Consequently, if the members decide that they want to relate more closely to others, they also have to decide not to play games anymore.

Anytime any element of the script, including a game, is interrupted, the person is in a position to redecide an early life script decision. Games start off with the optimal goal of supporting the person's basic life position and script injunction. It is imperative that the leader be aware that group members will be manifesting their games in the group; the leader needs to confront them on what they are doing and to facilitate redecision (Ray Quiett, personal communication, May 24, 2009).

Eventually, members are taught to make connections between the games they played as children and those they play now—for example, how they attempted to get attention in the past and how those past attempts relate to the games they play now to get stroked. The aim of this TA group process is to offer members the chance to drop certain games in favor of responding honestly and authentically—an opportunity that may lead them to discover ways of changing negative strokes and to learn how to give and receive positive strokes.

BASIC PSYCHOLOGICAL LIFE POSITIONS AND LIFE SCRIPTS

Decisions about oneself, one's world, and one's relationships to others are crystallized during the first 5 years of life. Such decisions are basic for the formulation of a life position, which develops into the roles of the life script. Generally, once a person has decided on a life position, there is a tendency for it to remain fixed unless there is some intervention, such as therapy, to change the underlying decisions. Games are often used to support and maintain life positions and to play out life scripts. People seek security by maintaining that which is familiar, even though what is familiar may be highly unpleasant and self-sabotaging. As we have seen earlier, games such as "Kick me" may be unpleasant, but they have the virtue of allowing the player to maintain a familiar position in life, even though this position is negative.

Transactional analysis identifies four **basic life positions,** all of which are based on decisions made as a result of childhood experiences, and all of which determine how people feel about themselves and how they relate to others:

1. I'm OK—You're OK.   or I count—You count.*
2. I'm OK—You're not OK.   or I count—You don't count.
3. I'm not OK—You're OK.   or I don't count—You do count.
4. I'm not OK—You're not OK. or I don't count—You don't count.

The *I'm OK—You're OK* position is game free. It is the belief that people have basic value, worth, and dignity as human beings. That people are OK is a statement of their essence, not necessarily their behavior. This position is characterized by an attitude of trust and openness, a willingness to give and take, and an acceptance of others as they are. People are close to themselves and to others. There are no losers, only winners.

I'm OK—You're not OK is the position of people who project their problems onto others and blame them, put them down, and criticize them. The games that reinforce this position involve a self-styled superior (the "I'm OK") who projects anger, disgust, and scorn onto a designated inferior, or scapegoat (the "You're not OK"). This position is that of the person who needs an underdog to maintain his or her sense of "OKness."

I'm not OK—You're OK is known as the depressive position and is characterized by feeling powerless in comparison with others. Typically such people serve others' needs instead of their own and generally feel victimized. Games supporting this position include "Kick me" and "Martyr"—games that support the power of others and deny one's own.

The *I'm not OK—You're not OK* quadrant is known as the position of futility and despair. Operating from this place, people have lost interest in life and may see the world as a lousy place and life as totally without promise. This self-destructive stance is characteristic of people who are unable to cope in the real world, and it may lead to extreme withdrawal, a return to infantile behavior, various forms of psychotic behavior, or violent behavior resulting in injury or death of themselves or others.

Each of us operates from our favorite position when under stress. The challenge is to become aware of how we are attempting to make life real through our basic existential position and then to create an alternative.

LIFE SCRIPTS AND SCRIPT ANALYSIS

The *life script* is developed early in life as a result of parental teaching (such as injunctions and counterinjunctions) and the early decisions we make. Among these decisions is selecting the basic psychological position, or dramatic role, that we play in our life script. Indeed, life scripts are comparable to a dramatic stage production, with a cast of characters, a plot, scenes, dialogues, and endless rehearsals. In essence, the life script is a blueprint that tells people where they are going in life and what they will do when they arrive.

---

*Virginia Satir suggested to Eric Berne a more mature language for these basic life positions as expressed by using the word "count."

According to Berne (1972), through our early interactions with parents and others we receive a pattern of strokes that may be either supporting or disparaging. Based on this stroking pattern, we make a basic existential decision about ourselves; that is, we assume one of the four life positions previously described. This existential decision is then reinforced by messages (both verbal and nonverbal) that we continue to receive during our lifetime. It is also reinforced by the results of our games, rackets, and interpretations of events. During our childhood years we also decide whether people are trustworthy. Our basic belief system is thus shaped through this process of deciding about ourselves and others. If we hope to change the life course that we are traveling, it helps to understand the components of this script, which to a large extent determine our patterns of thinking, feeling, and behaving.

Through a process known as **script analysis**, the TA group helps members become aware of how they acquired their life script and to see more clearly their life role (basic psychological life position). Script analysis helps members see the ways in which they feel compelled to play out their life script and offers them alternative life choices. Put another way, the group process relieves participants of the compulsion to play games that justify behavior called for in their life script.

Script analysis demonstrates the process by which group members acquired a script and the strategies they employ to justify their actions based on it. The aim is to help members open up possibilities for making changes in their early programming. The participants are asked to recall their favorite stories as children, to determine how they fit into these stories or fables, and to see how these stories fit their current life experiences.

Steiner (1967) developed a life script questionnaire that can be used as a catalyst for script analysis in group situations to help members explore significant components of their life script—among them, life positions and games. In completing this script checklist, members provide basic information such as the general direction of their life, the models in their life, the nature of their injunctions, the payoffs they seek, and the tragic ending they expect from life.

The analysis of the life script of a group member is based on the drama of his or her original family. Through the process of acting out portions of their life script in the group sessions, members learn about the injunctions they uncritically accepted as children, the decisions they made in response to these messages, and the games and rackets they now employ to keep these early decisions alive. The group leader can gather information about the family drama by taking a history of the childhood experiences of the members. Members can be asked the kind of drama that would probably result if their family were put on the stage. Other group members can be given a part to play in this family play.

These and other cognitive and emotive techniques often help group participants recall early events and the feelings associated with them. The group setting provides a supportive place to explore the ways in which these past situations are influencing the participants. By being part of the process of self-discovery of other members, each member increases the opportunities for coming to a deeper understanding of his or her own unfinished psychological business.

The group situation allows members to analyze the positions they often take and the games they play, both in the group and in everyday life. As a result, group participants gain the capacity to take some initial steps to break out of self-defeating patterns. They start a process of becoming autonomous and regaining their personal power. As the group members analyze their own life from a TA perspective, they can check the accuracy of their self-interpretations by asking for feedback from the leader and the other members.

Role and Functions of the Group Leader

Although TA is designed to develop both emotional and intellectual awareness, the focus is clearly on the cognitive aspects. As a teacher, the TA therapist explains concepts such as structural analysis, script analysis, and game analysis. The TA therapist functions as a consultant. As noted earlier, TA stresses the importance of equality in the client–therapist relationship, an equality that is manifested through contractual agreements between the group leader and the individual members, which make them mutual allies in the therapeutic process. Consequently, the role of the group leader is to facilitate the members in fulfilling their contracts. Regardless of what school of TA a practitioner belongs to, the focus is on the establishment, maintenance, and successful ending of the therapeutic relationship (Tudor & Hobbes, 2002).

From the perspective of redecision therapy, the group leader's function is to create a climate in which people can discover for themselves how the games they play are supporting chronic bad feelings and how they hold onto these feelings to support their life script and early decisions. Another function of the TA facilitator is to challenge group members to discover and experiment with more effective ways of being. The role of the leader is to help members acquire the tools necessary to effect change.

The group leader's style in a TA group tends to promote individual work within a group setting rather than facilitating free interaction among the group members. TA group leaders assume an active role and occupy a central position in the group, but a group leader who does most of the talking may be blocking the member from doing the necessary work toward change. Although the transactional analyst is active in structuring the group sessions, is an active catalyst for the redecision, and confronts impasses, the group member does most of the actual work. It is assumed that group members have the power to change negative childhood decisions by developing their positive ego state forces.

Stages of a Transactional Analysis Group

The following summary of the redecisional approach to TA groups is based on an adaptation of some of the chief works of the Gouldings (1976, 1978, 1979; M. Goulding, 1987; R. Goulding, 1982). The core of the work in this approach consists of helping clients make redecisions while they are in their Child ego state. Because the decision was made in the Child ego state in its earliest form, the redecision must be made in the Child ego state in the present. This is done by having members reexperience an early scene as if the situation were occurring in the present. Merely talking about past events or understanding early feelings and decisions from the Adult ego state is not sufficient to push members beyond the places where they are stuck. How the leader helps members get into their Child ego state and make a new decision can best be seen by examining the stages of redecisional group therapy.

The stages described below have primary relevance for a closed group. TA groups are often closed, but some groups are open and allow members to graduate from the group and welcome new members into the group as it continues over time.

THE INITIAL STAGE

The first step in the group process consists of establishing good contact. To a large extent, the outcome for group members depends on the quality of the relationship the group leader is able to establish with the members and on the leader's competence. TA group leaders pay attention to the quality of the therapeutic relationship, for they realize that the therapeutic alliance is central to assisting members in achieving their goals (Widdowson, 2010). Even when the group leader has developed a working alliance with the group, members sometimes avoid addressing their most pertinent problems. Therefore, the leader attempts to get at the chief complaint of the member. It is the leader's responsibility to get the client to reveal *what is not working* in their lives. Obviously, the trust factor in the group has a lot to do with the willingness of clients to get to their chief complaint. It is incumbent on the group leader to provide the necessary ingredients for sustainable change: a safe place, nurturance, adequate structure, and support. The leader needs to encourage members to accept themselves as they are, and at the same time invite them to think about specific ways they want to change.

The next step in the process consists of making an inquiry into the member's actual contract for change. Typical questions are: "What are you going to change about yourself today?" "In your finest vision, in what ways might you be different?" These questions communicate that change is possible immediately. Notice that members are not asked to state what they hope to change or what the leader will do to bring about change; nor are they asked what changes they want in the future. The emphasis is on members taking action in the here-and-now to bring about change.

THE WORKING STAGE

After contracts have been formulated, the Gouldings' approach to group therapy explores rackets the members use to justify their life scripts and, ultimately, their decisions (M. Goulding & Goulding, 1979). The aim is to expose the rackets of group members and have them take responsibility for them. For example, a person with an "anger racket" (one who is chronically angry) may be asked, "What do you do to maintain your anger?" Beginning with recent events, the person is led back through his or her life in an attempt to remember early situations involving anger. Often the person is asked, "When you were a little child, when did you feel anger in the same way?" As in Gestalt therapy, members are asked to be in these situations—to recall them not as observers but as participants in the here-and-now. Members are asked to act out both their own responses and the responses of other significant people in the scene.

During this stage of group work, games are analyzed, mainly to see how they support and maintain rackets and how they fit with one's life script. In this connection much work is devoted to looking for evidence of the participants' early decisions, discovering the original injunction that lies at the base of these early decisions, and determining the kinds of strokes the person received to support the original injunction. Once the person becomes aware of the original injunction, he or she is in a salient position to make a new decision about the injunction. For example, when George discovers a "Don't be you" injunction, he can redecide that "I will be who I am, not who you want me to be."

A major function of the TA group leader is to have the members take responsibility for their thinking, feeling, and behaving. Members are challenged when they use "cop-out language," such as "can't," "perhaps," "if it weren't for," "try," and other words that keep members from claiming their own power. The leader also creates a group climate in which the members rapidly become aware of how they maintain their chronic bad feelings by their behavior and fantasy. It is the therapist's task to challenge them to discover alternate choices.

The Gouldings take the position that clients can change *rapidly*, without years of analysis. It is clear that TA groups can be short term, solution focused, and structured in such a way that members acquire skills in addressing current and future problems. The Gouldings stress the decisional aspects of TA therapy on the assumption that when clients perceive that they are responsible for their early decisions they also have it in their power to change those decisions—and they can make these decisional shifts without drawing out the therapeutic process. This approach emphasizes helping participants reexperience early, highly emotional situations to generate the energy to break through the places where they are stuck (M. Goulding & Goulding, 1979). Such breakthroughs, according to the Gouldings, usually require that participants remember and relive situations involving real parenting figures. Through the use of fantasy, in which group members reexperience how their parents sounded, acted, and looked, the therapist creates a psychological climate that enables members to feel the same emotional intensity they felt when, as children, they made their original decisions. If participants are to be successful in going beyond an impasse, the Gouldings stress that they must be in the Child ego state and allow themselves to psychologically relive earlier scenes. If participants remain in their Adult ego state and merely thinking about new insights, the injunction will maintain its original power.

THE FINAL STAGE

Once a redecision is made from the Child ego state, the changes in one's voice, body, and facial expressions are obvious to everyone in the group. The group process provides support for members who begin to feel and behave in new ways. Group members are encouraged to tell a new story in the group to replace their old story, and they typically receive verbal and nonverbal stroking to support their new decision. Attention is also given to ways that members might devise other support systems outside the group. It is also important for members to plan specific ways in which they will change their thinking, feeling, and behavior.

The focus during the final phase of group work is on challenging members to transfer their changes from the therapy situation to their daily life and then supporting them in these changes. Before members set out on their own, it is important that they imagine how some of their changes are likely to lead to other changes. It is well for them to prepare themselves for the new situations they will face when they leave the group and to develop support systems that will help them creatively deal with new problem situations as they arise.

Widdowson (2010) emphasizes that effective and therapeutic endings are a major part of the therapeutic process. The grieving that is associated with endings is not a single event but a process that needs to be revisited a number of times during the ending phase of a group. It is important for group members to structure their departure with appreciations and claim time to say meaningful good-byes.

Application: Therapeutic Techniques and Procedures

CONTRACTS: THE STRUCTURE OF THE THERAPEUTIC RELATIONSHIP

Transactional analysis is based largely on the capacity and willingness of group participants to understand and design a therapeutic contract that requires them to state their intentions and set personal goals. Contracts are the key to all TA treatment and are the central focus of the initial stage of a group. Widdowson (2010) recommends avoiding premature contracting. If therapists pursue a firm and fully formed contract too early in therapy, clients may terminate prematurely. New group members often do not have a clear sense of their goals, and they need to feel understood if they are to formulate a meaningful contract.

The initiation of a contract begins with group participants creating a vision (from the Child) of how they will be different as a result of their time in group. From the creation of the vision, the **contract** becomes specific and measurable and contains a concrete statement of the objectives group participants intend to attain and how and when these goals are to be met. Contracts place the responsibility on members for clearly defining what, how, and when *they* want to change. The leader is responsible for pointing out flaws and sabotages and must ultimately agree to help the members achieve their contracts. From the very beginning, members learn that group therapy is a shared responsibility and that they cannot passively wait for the leader to direct the group. In short, the members' contracts establish the departure point for group activity.

Group members agree to work on specific issues within the group, although these concerns may change as the group emerges. For example, a woman who reacts to others in a highly critical way can design a contract that will lead to changing such behavior. Her contract describes *what* she will do in the group to change her actions and experiences, *when* she will do it, and *how many times.* The contract can then be expanded to include situations outside the group.

Dusay (1983) asserts that a well-stated treatment contract will make it clear whether clients are obtaining what they want from therapy. The key question is, "How will you know and how will I know when you get what you are coming to the group for?" It is common practice to write down each contract and hang these charts on the wall, clearly identifying the person to whom each belongs. Because everyone in the group knows the other participants' contracts, there is a measure of accountability. The process of TA treatment focuses primarily on change as defined by the contract, and the therapeutic partnership is aimed at accomplishing this mutual goal. The extent to which members have fulfilled their contracts and benefited from group therapy can be measured.

Although contracts are emphasized in TA, they are intended to be practical tools for helping people change themselves; they cannot be rigid and should be open to revision. TA group leaders have the challenge of negotiating a clear contract that leaves room for flexibility and new work to evolve. Widdowson (2010) believes it is possible to do effective TA therapy without establishing a highly specific fixed outcome. For Widdowson, a good therapeutic contract increases options rather than restricting members to a set outcome or course of action from the start of the therapeutic process. Contracts are developed in steps and are subject to modification as members penetrate more deeply into the areas in which they are seeking to change. These short-term contracts fit well with the requirements of limited therapy and brief therapy characteristic of many community agencies. Contracts can guide the course of brief therapy and can provide a basis for evaluation of outcomes.

Applying Transactional Analysis to Group Work in Schools

Many of the basic ideas found in TA groups can easily be understood even by very young children. For example, children are able to understand the concept of the need for human strokes. Even children in the early grades are able to understand that acting-out children are striving to get attention (strokes). Children soon learn that negative strokes are better than receiving no strokes. Both children and adolescents can easily distinguish between a "warm fuzzy" (a pleasant or positive stroke that makes them feel good) and a "cold prickly" (an unpleasant or negative stroke that hurts or feels bad). In children's groups the story *A Warm Fuzzy Tale* (Steiner, 1969) typically leads to lively discussion and interaction.

TA concepts and techniques can be usefully applied in guidance classes in schools or in group counseling sessions with students 5 to 17 years of age (Henderson & Thompson, 2011). For example, exploring parental injunctions can be a useful exercise with both children and adolescent groups. Young people can learn a great deal about the messages they have incorporated from their family of origin. TA provides a structured approach that allows children and adolescents to see connections between what they learned in their family and their attitudes toward others. Many young people are likely to find this type of structure useful because it helps them understand how their family and culture have influenced them. Consider these injunctions, which you may hear from children and adolescents in your groups:

- Don't cry, or at least don't shed tears in public.
- Don't let down your parents and your family.
- Don't make mistakes.
- Don't be too concerned about yourself.
- Don't put your own interests before the interests of others.
- Don't succeed in class.
- Don't do it if they tell you to do it.
- Don't stand out or be noticed.

- Don't brag.
- Think of what is best for your family (or community) rather than focusing on your self-interests.
- Don't talk about your family or about family problems with strangers.

These injunctions provide a good starting place for exploration in groups in the school setting.

It is essential for leaders to be aware of the cultural context that may limit confronting certain cultural injunctions. A competent group leader can create a climate in which the members can begin to question the degree to which they have accepted these messages and how certain injunctions influence their present behavior. A main goal of a TA group with students is to facilitate insight so that they are able to reclaim control of their thoughts, feelings, and actions. As children and adolescents develop this self-understanding, they also acquire the ability to make changes both within themselves and in their transactions with others. If you are interested in group work with young people from preschool through high school, useful resources are Freed and Freed (1998) and Freed (1992, 1998).

Applying Transactional Analysis With Multicultural Populations

The contractual approach used in a TA group has much to offer in a multicultural context. Group members' contracts act as a safeguard against therapists' imposing their cultural values on members. A contract increases the chances that members will become empowered in a group because they eventually must identify specific problem areas they want to bring into the group. The contractual approach helps clients assume more personal responsibility for the outcomes of their therapy.

Henderson and Thompson (2011) suggest a number of multicultural applications of TA, one of which is the user-friendly nature of TA in transcending cultural barriers. The International Transactional Analysis Association is growing rapidly worldwide, and TA has been successfully applied in many different cultures. Individuals who prefer a direct and educational approach to personal development are likely to find TA an appropriate modality because it emphasizes learning practical skills. When TA is used across cultures, the method is generally the same. Ego states are easily understood in many cultures. Members learn the basic terminology and formulate contracts that guide their work in a group.

A number of factors in TA groups make them particularly useful in working with women. Some of these elements are the use of contracts, the egalitarian relationships between the members and the leader, the emphasis on providing members with knowledge of the TA group process, and the value placed on empowering the group members. From a feminist perspective, when women are in groups, they have more opportunities to challenge the therapist's ideas, and they are able to compare their reality with those of other women (Enns, 1993).

A strength of TA is that its concepts are congruent with a gender-sensitive approach to group work. When women and men enter a group, they often are unaware of the role that gender plays in their lives. Furthermore, not all practitioners are aware of the detrimental effects of gender socialization when working with individuals in a group. If leaders hope to avoid reinforcing the cultural status quo, they must learn how traditional gender socialization can hurt both women and men. Both women and men can learn to interact with each other in the group in new ways. Just as they can examine the influence of a host of injunctions and decisions they have made based on certain messages, group members can fruitfully examine how they can free themselves from restrictive gender-role socialization.

In a TA group, both women and men can identify societal messages and stereotypes of what it means to be a female or a male. The book *I Never Knew I Had a Choice* (Corey & Corey, 2010) describes some of these messages that both men and women hear and accept in growing up. Men often hide their feelings of vulnerability and are ever watchful of others' reactions, looking for indications that they might be exposed to ridicule. This theme of men hiding their true nature is characteristic of many men, regardless of their racial, ethnic, and cultural background. It is reinforced by early childhood injunctions such as "Don't feel," and "Don't be close." It is especially common for male children to be taught to be tough and to be told "Don't cry." Many men have become prisoners of a stereotypical role that they feel they must live by. A TA group provides a context where men are able to challenge the restrictions of these traditional roles and where they can take on new attitudes and beliefs that can lead to behavioral change.

Traditional gender stereotypes of women also are alive and well in our culture. Women, too, have been restricted by their cultural conditioning and by accepting gender-role stereotypes that keep them in an inferior position. A TA group lends itself to critically examining the degree to which women have bought into self-limiting messages. Adjectives often associated with women include gentle, tactful, neat, sensitive, talkative, emotional, unassertive, indirect, and caring. Too often women have defined their own preferences as being the same as those of their partners, and they have had to gain their identity by protecting, helping, nurturing, and comforting. These roles are reinforced by injunctions such as "Don't be you" and "Don't think." A TA group is an ideal place for women to increase their awareness of how they have been living by these gender-role expectations and to consider what changes, if any, they may want to make.

In working with a diverse group, leaders need to be aware that the terminology may seem foreign to some members. Even though TA therapists assert that TA is simple and easy to understand, clients may have difficulty with the complexity of concepts such as the structure and dynamics of games and the subcomponents of the various ego states. Before TA group leaders challenge the life scripts of group members, which are frequently rooted in their cultural heritage, it is well for them to make sure that a trusting relationship has been established and that these clients have demonstrated a readiness to question their family traditions. In some cultures it is considered taboo to doubt family traditions, let alone talk about such matters in a nonfamily group or have these traditions challenged by others. The contract approach can be useful in empowering these clients by giving them the responsibility for deciding what aspects of their family life they are willing to share as well as deciding which family values they are ready to question or explore. If group members assume this responsibility for defining clear contracts, the chances of inappropriate confrontations by the leader are lessened.

Evaluation of Transactional Analysis in Groups

CONTRIBUTIONS AND STRENGTHS OF THE APPROACH

Transactional analysis provides a cognitive basis for group process that is often missing in experientially oriented groups. The insistence of this approach on having members get out of their *persecutor, rescuer,* and *victim* positions and realize that they don't have to continue to live by their early decisions is, I believe, crucial to effective therapy. In my opinion TA, especially redecision therapy, provides a useful conceptual framework for understanding how these early decisions are made, and how they are related to present self-defeating life stances.

Many people are restricted by their early decisions: they cling to parental messages, live their lives by unexamined injunctions, and frequently are not even aware that they are living in a psychological straitjacket. Conceptually, redecision therapy offers tools members can use to free themselves from an archaic life script and achieve a successful and meaningful life.

One of the strengths of the TA approach to group counseling is the emphasis on contracts as a way to guide each member's work. Contracts equalize the power base between the leader and the members; they also remove much of the mystery that surrounds what a group is all about. To its credit, TA groups work toward empowerment of members. Members are able to see their responsibility in contributing to their problems, and they also learn new ways of thinking and acting.

Because TA is a structured, psychoeducational approach, the group format lends itself well to agencies within a managed care system. Members identify specific areas they are interested in changing, they formulate a specific contract that guides their work in a group, and they design action plans to reach their goals in the shortest amount of time. This gives TA clear advantages for brief treatment and a focus on specific problems and goals. The emphasis of TA on developing contracts for behavior change enhances the opportunity for bringing about effective changes in brief therapy.

TA groups allow a range of possibilities for both preventive and remedial work; they also provide for both an educational and a therapeutic structure. It is important that the information given in TA groups be balanced by experiential work aimed at involving the members both cognitively and emotionally. Therapy interventions are more likely to succeed and produce enduring change if they involve the emotional realm rather than being aimed purely at a cognitive level (Greenberg, Korman, & Paivio, 2002).

Personally, I favor integrating TA concepts and practices with Gestalt and psychodrama techniques. Doing so can integrate the cognitive and emotive dimensions quite naturally. Many of the specific techniques in psychodrama—such as role reversal, self-presentation, doubling, soliloquy, and future projection—are ideal methods of exploring the affective dimensions of injunctions and early decisions. TA concepts can be brought to life by the enactment methods that are typical of psychodrama.

LIMITATIONS OF THE APPROACH

Like most of the other approaches that have been discussed so far, TA can be criticized on the ground that its theory and procedures have not been adequately subjected to empirical validation. Indeed, many of Berne's concepts were stated in such a manner that it would be impossible to design a research study to test them. It appears that most of the claims of success rest on clinical observations and testimonials. Conducting well-designed research studies to evaluate the process and outcome of group therapy has surely not been one of the strengths of TA.

A limitation of TA is that some group members can use TA concepts in an intellectual way and deceive themselves into believing that they are becoming self-actualized when, in reality, they are only learning new terms to identify old processes. The danger of becoming lost in the structure and vocabulary of TA can be lessened if the therapist is willing to challenge members when they use jargon. Another criticism is that TA is too simplistic. Ego states are simple concepts and easy to learn and often give rise to the claim that TA is a "pop psychology."

Transactional analysis group leaders have the potential of working primarily in a cognitive way and not allowing enough room for exploration of feelings. A further concern relates to the way in which some practitioners use the structure and vocabulary of this system to avoid genuine contact with their clients or to keep from revealing their reactions. A therapist can use the structure of TA to avoid person-to-person interactions and to focus on labeling ego states, devising contracts, and directing traffic between transactions. Widdowson (2010) states that TA therapists sometimes teach TA concepts to their clients with an almost missionary zeal. He suggests that such teaching be used sparingly and that explanations be short and concise. Widdowson acknowledges that explanations are often useful, but they "cannot replace client-generated insight, or the kind of emotional knowing that occurs when important connections emerge in the therapy and both therapist and client make meaning of them" (p. 250).

Where to Go From Here

The *Transactional Analysis Journal* is a good source for keeping current with the developments of TA theory, clinical applications, and research. For information concerning dues for various membership classifications and for journal subscriptions, contact the International Transactional Analysis Association (ITAA) office.

If you want to learn more about TA group work, I encourage you to take an introductory transactional analysis course, known as a TA 101 course, or to participate in a TA group as a member. Experiencing TA as a member could benefit you personally by bringing many of the concepts in this chapter to life in a concrete way. Also, you may want to consider attending an educational workshop where you can apply TA principles in a group setting.

The International Transactional Analysis Association provides information on training and certification in transactional analysis. There are approximately 1,500 members in some 60 countries. TA practitioners are involved in clinical and mental health professions as well as in business, education, and industry. Professional credentials may be obtained for the application of transactional analysis and for teaching and training others in transactional analysis in the following four areas of specialization: (1) psychotherapy, the application of transactional analysis in psychotherapy; (2) educational, the application of transactional analysis to teaching and counseling in academic, family, or community education; (3) organizational, the application of transactional analysis in organizational training, counseling, and consulting; and (4) counseling, the application of transactional analysis in counseling and social fields.

International accreditation as a Certified Transactional Analyst (CTA) is available to individuals who have received training and supervision and passed written and oral examinations. They are then certified by the Board of Certification as competent to practice transactional analysis in their field of specialization. This process generally takes between 3 and 5 years.

International accreditation as a Certified Teaching and Supervising Transactional Analyst (TSTA) is available to individuals who, after becoming a CTA, have received additional training and supervision and passed an oral examination. They are then certified as competent to teach transactional analysis and to supervise others in the application of transactional analysis. This process takes another 5 to 7 years, depending on time devoted.

The International Transactional Analysis Association
2186 Rheem Drive #B-1
Pleasanton, CA 94588
Telephone: (925) 600-8110
Fax: (925) 600-8112
E-mail: itaa@itaa-net.org
Website: www.itaa-net.org

For TA information and training events on a local level, contact the United States Transactional Association.

United States Transactional Association
Website: www.usataa.org

AUTHOR LECTURES

Watch *Gerald Corey's Perspectives on Theory and Practice of Group Counseling* DVD or visit the *Theory and Practice of Group Counseling* CourseMate website at www.cengagebrain.com/shop/ISBN/0840033869 to watch videos of Dr. Gerald Corey presenting lectures for each chapter. Also available are unique eAudio lectures for each chapter and quiz questions for self-study.

RECOMMENDED SUPPLEMENTARY READINGS

Transactional Analysis: 100 Key Points and Techniques (Widdowson, 2010) provides a good overview of the practice of TA. A sample of the various sections includes the therapeutic relationship, diagnosis, contracting, and treatment planning.

TA Today: A New Introduction to Transactional Analysis (Stewart & Joines, 1987) is a comprehensive text on transactional analysis theory.

Changing Lives Through Redecision Therapy (M. Goulding & Goulding, 1979) is the work I would recommend to a practitioner who had time to read only one book on the TA approach to group work. The authors describe their successful integration of Gestalt and behavioral techniques in their TA theoretical framework.

Berne, E. (1961). *Transactional analysis in psychotherapy.* New York: Grove Press.

Berne, E. (1964). *Games people play.* New York: Grove Press.

*Berne, E. (1966). *Principles of group treatment.* New York: Oxford University Press.

Berne, E. (1972). *What do you say after you say hello?* New York: Grove Press.

Corey, G., & Corey, M. S. (2010). *I never knew I had a choice* (9th ed.). Belmont, CA: Brooks/Cole, Cengage Learning.

Dusay, J. M. (1983). Transactional analysis in groups. In H. I. Kaplan & B. J. Sadock (Eds.), *Comprehensive group psychotherapy* (2nd ed.). Baltimore: Williams & Wilkins.

Dusay, J. M. (1986). Transactional analysis. In I. L. Kutash & A. Wolf (Eds.), *Psychotherapist's casebook* (pp. 413–423). San Francisco: Jossey Bass.

Dusay, J. M., & Dusay, K. M. (1989). Transactional analysis. In R. J. Corsini (Ed.), *Current psychotherapies* (4th ed., pp. 405–453). Itasca, IL: F. E. Peacock.

Enns, C. Z. (1993). Twenty years of feminist counseling and therapy: From naming biases to implementing multifaceted practice. *The Counseling Psychologist, 21*(1), 3–87.

Freed, A. (1992). *TA for teens and other important people* (rev. ed.). Rolling Hills Estates, CA: Jalmar Press.

Freed, A. (1998). *TA for tots: And other prinzes.* Rolling Hills Estates, CA: Jalmar Press. (Originally published 1973)

Freed, A., & Freed, M. (1998). *TA for kids: And grown ups too.* Rolling Hills Estates, CA: Jalmar Press. (Originally published 1971)

Goulding, M. M. (1987). Transactional analysis and redecision therapy. In J. K. Zeig (Ed.), *The evolution of psychotherapy* (pp. 285–299). New York: Brunner/Mazel.

*Goulding, M., & Goulding, R. (1979). *Changing lives through redecision therapy.* New York: Brunner/Mazel.

Goulding, R. (1975). The formation and beginning process of transactional analysis groups. In G. Gazda (Ed.), *Basic approaches to group psychotherapy and group counseling* (2nd ed., pp. 234–264). Springfield, IL: Charles C Thomas.

Goulding, R. (1982). Transactional analysis/Gestalt/redecision therapy. In G. Gazda (Ed.), *Basic approaches to group psychotherapy and group counseling* (3rd ed., pp. 319–351). Springfield, IL: Charles C Thomas.

Goulding, R. L. (1987). Group therapy: Mainline or sideline? In J. K. Zeig (Ed.), *The evolution of psychotherapy* (pp. 300–311). New York: Brunner/Mazel.

Goulding, R., & Goulding, M. (1976). Injunctions, decisions, and redecisions. *Transactional Analysis Journal, 6*(1), 41–48.

*Goulding, R., & Goulding, M. (1978). *The power is in the patient.* San Francisco: TA Press.

*Greenberg, L. S., Korman, L. M., & Paivio, S. C. (2002). Emotion in humanistic psychotherapy. In D. J. Cain & J. Seeman (Eds.), *Humanistic psychotherapies: Handbook of research and practice* (pp. 499–530). Washington, DC: American Psychological Association.

Henderson, D., & Thompson, C. L. (2011). *Counseling children* (8th ed.). Belmont, CA: Brooks/Cole, Cengage Learning.

James, M., & Jongeward, D. (1971). *Born to win: Transactional analysis with Gestalt experiments.* Reading, MA: Addison-Wesley.

Karpman, S. (1968). Fairy tales and script drama analysis. *Transactional Analysis Bulletin, 7*(2), 39–43.

Steiner, C. (1967). A script checklist. *Transactional Analysis Bulletin, 6*(22), 38–39.

---

* Books and articles marked with an asterisk (*) are suggested for further study.

Steiner, C. (1969). *A warm fuzzy tale.* Retrieved March 24, 2001, from www.claudesteiner.com/fuzzy.htm

*Steiner, C. (1974). *Scripts people live: Transactional analysis of life scripts.* New York: Grove Press.

*Stewart, I., & Joines, V. (1987). *TA today: A new introduction to transactional analysis.* Nottingham, England: Lifespace.

Tudor, K., & Hobbes, R. (2002). Transactional analysis. In W. Dryden (Ed.), *Handbook of individual therapy* (4th ed., pp. 239–265). London: Sage.

*Widdowson, M. (2010). *Transactional analysis: 100 key points and techniques.* New York: Routledge (Taylor & Francis Group).

CHAPTER THIRTEEN

Cognitive Behavioral Approaches to Groups

Introduction

Cognitive behavioral approaches are becoming increasingly popular for many client groups and work settings. Cognitive behavioral group therapy is an efficient form of treatment for a wide range of specific problems for diverse client populations (Bieling, McCabe, & Antony, 2006; White & Freeman, 2000). The structured nature of a group appeals to many who facilitate psychoeducational groups. Cognitive behavioral practitioners use a brief, active, directive, collaborative, present-focused, didactic, psychoeducational model of therapy that relies on empirical validation of its concepts and techniques (Reinecke & Freeman, 2003).

Cognitive factors have been incorporated into the practice of behavioral group work, and behavior therapists have reformulated their techniques in cognitive and social learning terms rather than traditional conditioning terms. Many groups are designed primarily to increase the client's degree of control and freedom in specific aspects of daily life. For example, cognitive factors are stressed in the self-control and independence of individuals in groups designed for stress management training, social skills training, and self-directed behavior change—all topics addressed later in this chapter.

Behavior therapy refers to the application of diverse techniques and procedures that are rooted in various theories of learning. No single theory undergirds the practice of contemporary behavior therapy, and no single group model, strictly speaking, can be called a "behavioral group." Rather, various types of groups operate using behavioral and learning principles. Behavior therapy is best conceptualized as a general orientation to clinical practice that is based on the experimental approach to changing behavior, not just understanding it. By the mid-1970s **cognitive behavior therapy** (CBT) had replaced the term *behavior therapy*, and most therapists practice CBT today. The cognitive behavioral approach to groups currently represents the mainstream of contemporary behavior therapy.

A basic assumption of the cognitive behavioral perspective is that most problematic behaviors, cognitions, and emotions have been learned and can be modified by new learning. This process is often called "therapy," yet a significant component of the process is *educational*. Members of a group are involved in a teaching and learning process and are taught how to develop a new perspective on ways of learning. They are encouraged to try out more effective behaviors, cognitions, and emotions. Problems may also arise due to a skills deficit—adaptive behaviors or cognitive strategies that have not been learned—and group members can acquire coping skills by participating in this educational experience. An example would be providing social effectiveness skills to people with agoraphobia or social phobias who need to confront their fears.

Another assumption of the cognitive behavioral orientation is that the behaviors that clients express are the problem (not merely symptoms of the problem). Successful resolution of these problematic behaviors resolves the problem, and a new set of problems does not necessarily arise. This orientation is in contrast to the relationship-oriented and insight-oriented approaches that assume that if clients understand the nature and causes of their symptoms they will be better able to control their lives. The cognitive behavioral approach assumes that change can take place without insight into underlying dynamics. Behavior therapists operate on the premise that changes in behavior can occur prior to or simultaneously with understanding oneself and that behavioral changes may well lead to an increased level of self-understanding.

Group practitioners who function within a cognitive behavioral framework may develop techniques and strategies from diverse theoretical viewpoints. However, the effectiveness of these methods in meeting therapeutic goals should be scientifically demonstrated. The cognitive behavioral group leader is both a clinician and a scientist who is concerned with testing the efficacy of his or her techniques. These leaders follow the progress of group members through the ongoing collection of data before, during, and after all interventions. Such an approach provides both the group leader and the members with continuous feedback about therapeutic progress.

During the last decade, behavior therapy has evolved and expanded in the cognitive and behavioral dimensions. *Third-generation behavior therapies* (also called *third wave* approaches) emphasize mindfulness, acceptance, the therapeutic relationship, spirituality, values, meaning and purpose in one's life, meditation, being in the present moment, and emotional expression (Hayes, Follette, & Linehan, 2004). These newer approaches are making an impact on behavior therapy, especially in treating more difficult clinical problems (Spiegler & Guevremont, 2010). The field of behavior therapy has changed significantly, and it continues to evolve. The theoretical foundations of behavior therapy have broadened, and treatment strategies have become more diverse. As behavior therapy continues to expand, it increasingly overlaps with other theoretical approaches to therapy (Wilson, 2011).

In keeping with the developments within this field, this chapter deals more with *cognitive behavior therapy* (CBT) than it does with *traditional behavior therapy*, which emphasized environmental determinism. Approaches such as social skills training, cognitive therapy, stress management training, mindfulness, and acceptance-based practices that are discussed in this chapter all represent the cognitive behavioral tradition. Chapter 14 is devoted to one specific cognitive behavioral branch, rational emotive behavior therapy (REBT), founded by Albert Ellis.

Key Concepts

Cognitive behavior therapy has some unique characteristics that set it apart from most of the other group approaches discussed in this book. It relies on the principles and procedures of the scientific method, and these experimentally derived principles of learning are systematically applied to help people change maladaptive behaviors. The distinguishing characteristic of cognitive behavioral practitioners is their systematic adherence to specification and measurement. Concepts and procedures are stated explicitly, tested empirically, and revised continually. Assessment and treatment occur simultaneously. The specific unique characteristics of behavior therapy include (1) conducting a behavioral assessment, (2) precisely spelling out collaborative treatment goals, (3) formulating a specific treatment procedure appropriate to a particular problem, and (4) objectively evaluating the outcomes of therapy.

BEHAVIORAL ASSESSMENT

Behavioral assessment consists of a set of procedures used to obtain information that will guide the development of a specific treatment plan for each client and help measure the effectiveness of treatment. According to Spiegler and Guevremont (2010), behavioral assessment involves five characteristics that are consistent with behavior therapy. Behavioral assessment (1) is aimed at gathering unique and detailed information about a client's problem, (2) focuses on the client's current functioning and life conditions, (3) is concerned with taking samples of a client's behaviors to provide information about how the client typically functions in various situations, (4) is narrowly focused rather than dealing with a client's total personality, and (5) is integrated with therapy.

PRECISE THERAPEUTIC GOALS

The most unique aspect of CBT with groups is the specific goals of change. A CBT approach to group therapy focuses more concretely on specific target areas of change than any other modality. In most CBT groups, the initial stages of group work are devoted to clients' expanding the final step of their assessment by formulating specific statements of the personal goals they want to achieve. The identification of goals determines the direction of therapeutic movement. Although the group leader guides the discussion of goals and collaborates with the members, the group members themselves select their personal goals (White, 2000b). Group members spell out concrete problematic behaviors they want to change and new skills they want to learn. Personal goals that clients might set include reducing anxiety in test-taking situations, eliminating phobias that interfere with effective functioning, coping with depression, learning communication skills, developing problem-solving strategies to cope with a variety of situations encountered in daily life, losing weight, and getting rid of addictions (to smoking, alcohol, or other drugs). At the beginning of each session an agenda is set to prioritize members' goals and to outline how the time will be spent. This agenda is co-created by members and the group leader. A CBT group at its best is a collaborative endeavor.

The task of the group leader is to help group participants break down broad, general goals into specific, concrete, measurable goals that can be pursued in a systematic fashion. For example, if Albert says that he feels inadequate in social situations, and that he would like to change this, the leader may ask questions such as these:

- What do you mean by "inadequate"?
- What are you doing or not doing that seems to be related to your feeling of inadequacy?
- What are the conditions under which you feel inadequate?
- Can you give me some concrete examples of the situations in which you feel inadequate?
- In what specific ways would you like to change your behavior?

The group can help Albert formulate answers to these difficult questions by giving him an opportunity to explore these questions, practice new behaviors in the group sessions, and get feedback from others in the group.

TREATMENT PLAN

Once members have specified their goals, a treatment plan to achieve these goals is formulated. Cognitive behavioral techniques are action oriented; members are expected to take an active role with tasks, not just reflect passively and talk about their problems. Initially, the group leader generally develops the plans in a collaborative fashion that includes each group member. After an initial assessment, and as the members learn the necessary skills, the group participants together with the group leader brainstorm intervention strategies that might be used or specific actions that might be taken. Ultimately, the person with the problem is the judge of the strategy or actions he or she must take. Some of the most commonly used techniques include modeling, shaping, behavioral rehearsal, coaching, homework, feedback, cognitive restructuring, desensitization, problem-solving, meditation, relaxation training, stress management, and information giving. (These are defined and discussed later in this chapter.)

OBJECTIVE EVALUATION

Once target behaviors have been clearly identified, treatment goals specified, and therapeutic procedures delineated, the outcomes of therapy can be objectively assessed. Because CBT groups emphasize the importance of evaluating the effectiveness of the techniques they employ, assessment of clients' progress toward their goals is ongoing. If a group meets for 10 weeks for social skills training, for example, baseline data on these skills are likely to be taken at the initial session. At every subsequent session an assessment of behavioral changes may be made so members can determine how successfully their objectives are being met. Providing members with feedback is a vital part of cognitive behavioral group therapy.

The decision to use certain techniques is based on their demonstrated effectiveness. The range of these techniques is quite wide, and many CBT group practitioners are very eclectic in their choices of treatment procedures. They are willing to draw techniques from many of the therapeutic approaches in helping members change their patterns of thinking, feeling, and acting.

Role and Functions of the Group Leader

Cognitive behavioral groups have a detailed, concrete, problem-oriented structure. They tend to utilize short-term interventions, and leaders need to be skilled in drawing on a wide variety of brief interventions aimed at efficiently and effectively solving problems and assisting members in developing new skills. Because of their short-term nature, cognitive behavioral groups are most effective when goals are limited and specific. Actually, the time limitation can be a catalyst for members to make the best use of group time to achieve their goals.

Cognitive behavioral group leaders assume the role of teacher and encourage members to learn and practice social skills in the group that they can apply to everyday living. Group leaders are expected to assume an active, directive, and supportive role in the group and to apply their knowledge of behavioral principles and skills to the resolution of problems. Through their conduct in a group, leaders model active participation and collaboration by their involvement with members in creating an agenda, generating adaptive responses, designing homework, and teaching skills (White, 2000a). Group leaders carefully observe and assess behavior to determine the conditions that are related to certain problems and the conditions that will facilitate change. Members in cognitive behavioral groups identify specific skills that they lack or would like to enhance. They proceed through a series of training sessions that involve interventions such as modeling the skill, behavioral rehearsal and coaching, feedback, practicing skills both in the group sessions and through homework, and self-monitoring.

In discussing the social learning that occurs in therapy through modeling and imitation, Bandura (1969, 1977, 1986) suggests that most of the learning that takes place through direct experience can also be acquired by observing the behavior of others. In Bandura's view, one of the fundamental processes by which clients learn new behavior is imitation of the social modeling provided by the therapist. Therefore, group leaders need to be aware of the impact of their values, attitudes, and behaviors on group members, as well as those behaviors that members model to each other. If they are unaware of their power in actually influencing and shaping their clients' ways of behaving, they deny the central importance of their influence as human beings in the therapeutic process.

In addition to these broad functions, the group leader is expected to perform a number of specific educational and therapeutic functions and tasks, some of which include the following:

- Group leaders conduct intake interviews with prospective members during which the preliminary assessment and orientation to the group takes place, and they also conduct an ongoing assessment of members' problems.

- Leaders draw on a wide array of techniques designed to achieve the members' stated goals.

- A major function of leaders is serving as a model of appropriate behaviors. Also, leaders prepare and coach members to model by role playing for one another how an individual might respond in a particular situation.

- Leaders provide reinforcement to members for their newly developing behavior and skills by making sure that even small achievements are recognized.

- Leaders teach group members that they are responsible for becoming actively involved both in the group and outside of therapy. To broaden their repertoire of adaptive behaviors, members are urged to experiment in the group and to practice homework assignments.

- Leaders emphasize a plan for change and an active stance on the part of the members and help members understand that verbalizations and insight are not enough to produce change.

- Leaders help members prepare for termination well ahead of the group's ending date so that members have adequate time to discuss their reactions, to consolidate what they have learned, and to practice new skills to apply at home and work. Appropriate referrals are made when reasonable goals have not been achieved.

A basic assumption of CBT is that a good working relationship between the leader and members is a necessary, but not sufficient condition for change. Most cognitive behavioral practitioners stress the value of establishing collaborative partnerships between members and the leader. For example, Lazarus (1993, 1996a, 2005, 2008) believes a flexible repertoire of relationship styles, plus a wide range of techniques, enhances treatment outcomes. Lazarus emphasizes the need for therapeutic flexibility and versatility above all else. He suggests that it is appropriate to discuss the client–therapist relationship whenever there is reason to think relationship issues are getting in the way of therapeutic progress.

More than simply drawing on a variety of cognitive, affective, and behavioral techniques, group leaders need to make choices regarding different styles of relating to group members. Lazarus (2005, 2008) stresses that care must be taken to avoid fitting group members into a preconceived treatment mode. Leaders need to carefully analyze precisely what relationship with the therapist and what therapeutic methods will work best for each client and under what particular circumstances. Group therapists must constantly adjust their interventions to help clients accomplish their goals. Leaders must decide when and how to be directive or supportive, formal or informal, and tough or tender. The ability to blend appropriate and effective techniques with the most suitable relationship style is one of the most difficult challenges therapists face (Lazarus, 1996a). In short, cognitive behavioral group leaders must be skilled technicians who also possess the human qualities that lead to the climate of trust and care necessary for the effective application of these therapeutic techniques.

Stages of a Cognitive Behavioral Group

The "multimethod group approach" was developed by Rose and his associates (see Rose, 1998; Rose & Edleson, 1987) and uses various coping strategies for dealing with specific problems: training group members in systematic problem solving, cognitive restructuring, assertion training, relaxation training, behavioral rehearsal, and other strategies that are appropriate for specific problems. This approach involves gradually increasing members' participation and involvement in setting specific goals, planning, decision making, and mutual helping of others. The process progresses from a high to a low degree of leader structure. Each client is helped to establish individualized goals and coping skills. CBT groups often have a common theme, such as stress management, anger control, or pain management. The goal goes beyond demonstrating change within the group setting. The ultimate goal is the transfer of change into the real world. Later group sessions are structured to make this generalization of learning more likely. How this transfer and generalization are facilitated is addressed in the section describing the final stage of a group.

The following discussion of the stages of a CBT group is based partly on the works of Sheldon Rose (1998) and Rose and Edleson (1987); Ledley, Marx, and Heimberg (2005); Bieling, McCabe, and Antony (2006); Antony and Roemer (2003); and Reinecke and Freeman (2003). Whether the stages described below accurately reflect CTB groups remains an empirical question, but Bieling, McCabe, and Antony (2006) state that their clinical experience shows that CBT groups evolve over time in repeatable and predictable sequences.

INITIAL STAGE

Prospective group members generally know very little about cognitive behavioral programs, so it is important that they be given all the pertinent information about the group process before they join. Pregroup individual interviews and the first group session are devoted to exploring the prospective members' expectations and to helping them decide whether they will join the group. Those who decide to join negotiate a treatment contract, spelling out what the group leader expects from the member over the course of the group, as well as what the client can expect from the leader. Ledley, Marx, and Heimberg (2005) emphasize the importance of helping clients make an informed decision about CBT. Group members should be informed about what CBT is, how it works, and what is unique about this therapeutic approach. Ledley and colleagues specify four key points that can be a part of the informed consent process in a group. First, group members need to know the meaning of *collaborative empiricism,* which involves a partnership between the group therapist and the members in addressing the problems they bring to a group. Second, group members should be informed that CBT is generally a time-limited form of treatment. Third, it is useful to let members know that generally their goals can be accomplished relatively quickly because CBT is an active, structured, directive, problem-focused, and present-focused approach to helping people deal with psychological problems. Finally, group members can be informed that cognitive behavioral practitioners rely upon techniques that have proven to be effective. Part of the informed consent process entails exploring the meaning of confidentiality and its limits in a group context.

During the initial phase of a group, members learn how the group functions and how each of the sessions is structured. Key tasks at this stage deal with helping members get acquainted, orienting members, increasing the motivation of group members, providing a sense of hope that change is possible, identifying problem areas for exploration, creating a sense of safety, and establishing the beginnings of cohesion. Building cohesion is the foundation for effective work during each stage of a group's development, and the leader has a central role in establishing trust and creating a climate of safety. Generally, each session opens with group members checking in by stating significant developments during the week, reporting on their homework, and identifying topics or issues they would like to put on the agenda for the session. If the leader does not pay attention to the group process, this homework review may become deenergizing as each person simply reports on how his or her homework went.

Reinecke and Freeman (2003) suggest that each session conclude with a review or a summary of the session. This process, which is best done by the group members, offers participants an opportunity to clarify their goals and identify insights and skills that have been explored. In addition to a summary, members also can be asked for their reactions to the session. Homework, which ideally grows out of the group session, can then be collaboratively developed. Formulating homework is a group process, and members are encouraged to suggest potential homework assignments for each other (Bieling et al., 2006).

Rose (1998) emphasizes that the leader must initially strive to make the group attractive to its members, create group situations that require social competence on the part of the members, create many functional roles that members can play in the group, delegate the leadership responsibility to the members in a gradual and appropriate manner, present situations in which the members function as therapeutic partners for each other, control excessive group conflict, and find ways of involving all members in group interactions. As the group evolves, leaders move from being directive to training the members in performing these functions for themselves.

WORKING STAGE: TREATMENT PLAN AND APPLICATION OF TECHNIQUES

Treatment planning involves choosing the most appropriate set of procedures from among specific strategies that have been demonstrated to be effective in achieving behavioral change. Assessment and evaluation continue throughout the working stage, and group leaders must continually evaluate the degree of effectiveness of the sessions and how well treatment goals are being attained. To make this evaluation during the working stage, leaders continue to collect data on matters such as participation, member satisfaction, attendance, and completion of agreed-upon assignments between sessions. These assessments also include gathering data to determine whether problems exist within the group and the degree to which group goals are being attained. Throughout the course of a group, individuals monitor their behaviors and the situations in which they occur. In this way they can quickly determine those strategies that are effective or ineffective. By means of this continuing evaluation process, both the members and the leader have a basis for looking at alternative and more effective strategies. Some of the strategies typically used during the working stage are discussed next.

Modeling Modeling refers to a process in which clients learn through observation and imitation of both the leader and the other members. Verbal instruction alone is usually not sufficient to bring about behavior change. Modeling procedures can be useful in demonstrating specific skills to be learned (Naugle & Maher, 2003). Role modeling is one of the most powerful teaching tools available to the group leader. As we have seen with other approaches, an advantage of group counseling over individual counseling is that it offers members a variety of social and role models to imitate. Modeling is incorporated in a number of cognitive behavioral groups, especially in skills training groups and assertion training groups. As much as possible, models should be reinforced in the presence of the observer, and observers should be reinforced for their imitation of the behavior that is modeled.

Modeling specific behavior is carried out in role playing during the sessions and practiced in vivo. For example, Henry has difficulty initiating contacts with men and would like to feel freer in approaching them in his college classes. He can observe another member modeling at least one way of effectively starting conversations in the group. Henry can then practice in the sessions, using skills he has learned from the person modeling. Then he can make a contract to initiate several conversations with different men in his classes. Modeling is especially useful in social skills training groups and in teaching clients how to make more constructive self-statements and change cognitive structures.

Behavior Rehearsal Practicing in a group session a new behavior that will be used in everyday situations is called **behavioral rehearsal.** The aim of behavior rehearsal is to prepare members to perform the desired behaviors outside the group, when modeling cues will not be available. Behavioral rehearsal is an integral part of modeling as members are typically asked to participate by performing the behavior immediately after it has been modeled for them. This allows the therapist to reinforce and later shape client performance of the target skill (Naugle & Maher, 2003). New behaviors are practiced in a safe context that simulates the real world. Not only are members protected from adverse consequences while they are learning, but they can also benefit from positive reinforcement, which is likely to increase their willingness to experiment with the new behavior in their daily life (Rose, 1998). The rehearsal of desirable behaviors should take place under conditions that are as similar as possible to the situations that occur in the client's environment so that maximum generalization from the group to the real world will take place.

Behavior rehearsal, which can be thought of as a gradual shaping process, is useful in teaching social skills. Feedback is a useful mechanism of change during behavior rehearsals. Once members achieve successful performance in the group situation, they need to be made aware that application in real life is a basic part of behavior rehearsal. This can be accomplished by reminding members of the importance of completing homework assignments, by devoting some time in each session to deciding on appropriate assignments, and by routinely beginning each group session by checking on the assignments of each member.

Coaching In addition to modeling and behavior rehearsal, group members sometimes require coaching. This process consists of providing the members with general principles for performing the desired behavior effectively. Coaching seems to work best when the coach sits behind the client who is rehearsing. When a member gets stuck and does not know how to proceed, another group member can whisper suggestions. After one or two coached rehearsals, the coaching is reduced in subsequent role playing. Members rehearse independently before trying out a new role in the real world (Rose, 1998).

Homework Therapeutic homework is aimed at putting into action what members explore during a group session, which, in essence, is the crux of the matter. Homework affords many opportunities for members to practice new skills in the real world. At its best, homework should integrate what goes on within the group with everyday life.

In cognitive behavioral groups, homework is an essential part of the process. One practitioner survey demonstrated that 98% of practicing psychologists use homework in their clinical practice (Kazantzis & Deane, 1999). Recent research on the use of homework has shown that it has become increasingly valued as an instrument to ensure change of behavior (Kazantzis & Lampropoulos, 2002). The more time group members are willing to commit to working on their problems outside of the therapeutic context, the more likely it is that they will make positive gains (Ledley, Marx, & Heimberg, 2005).

How can group counselors increase the chances of homework being an effective intervention? How can compliance in completing homework be fostered? In addressing the role of homework in psychotherapy, Kazantzis and Lampropoulos (2002) mention that compliance with homework assignments is a consistently significant predictor of treatment outcome. They write that therapists' clarity in describing the homework, providing a rationale, and enlisting client involvement are key factors that determine the effectiveness of homework.

Unless group members participate in designing their own homework assignments, it is unlikely that they will retain a cooperative spirit and keep the motivation needed to carry out the homework. This is particularly important because collaboration is a key element of a CBT group. If group members feel they are being forced to do homework, White (2000b) believes the homework is probably going to fail. White suggests that it takes artistic skill on the part of the group leader to guide members in finding homework they are willing to do. Following up on the homework is essential, for all group members can benefit from the homework experiences of each other. Difficulty in completing homework tasks may also be viewed as resistance and needs to be addressed appropriately (Dattilio, 2002, 2003). One way of doing this is by asking members what makes it difficult to complete their homework and to explore the degree to which they are committed to make certain changes. Leaders might also inquire about both obstacles to completing homework and ways that members may be engaging in self-sabotage.

Feedback After members practice a new behavior in a group session or report on their homework assignments in daily life, fellow group members or the group leader can provide verbal reactions to these performances. **Feedback** typically has two aspects: praise and encouragement for the behavior and specific suggestions for correcting or modifying errors. Feedback is a useful part of learning new behaviors, especially if it is constructive, specific, and positive. Refer to Chapter 5 for specific guidelines that help members effectively give and receive feedback.

Reinforcement The term **reinforcement** refers to a specified event that strengthens the tendency for a response to be repeated. In behavioral groups, social reinforcement is a major intervention provided by the group leader and by other members. In addition to the reinforcement provided by the group leader, other members reinforce one another through praise, approval, support, and attention. It is a good idea to begin each session with members reporting their successes rather than their failures. This sets a positive tone in the group, provides reinforcement to those who did well in everyday life, and reminds the group that change is possible. Reports of success, no matter how modest, are especially important when the members are improving but are still falling short of their expectations and when their changing behavior is being met with disapproval in their everyday environments. In these cases the reinforcement and support of the group are critical if members are to maintain their gains.

Social reinforcement is a powerful method of shaping desired behaviors. In addition, self-reinforcement is a key method of helping members change. Participants are taught how to reinforce themselves to increase their self-control and become less dependent on others.

Cognitive Restructuring An individual's cognitive processes have implications for behavior change. Indeed, group members often reveal self-defeating thoughts and negative self-talk when they find themselves in stressful situations. **Cognitive restructuring** is the process of identifying and evaluating one's cognitions, understanding the negative behavioral impact of certain thoughts, and learning to replace these cognitions with more realistic, appropriate, and adaptive thoughts. Members are expected to identify self-defeating cognitions and to monitor their self-talk. Cognitive restructuring is a basic component of most cognitive behavioral procedures (Cormier, Nurius, & Osborn, 2009). Both cognitive therapy and rational emotive behavior therapy use cognitive restructuring as a core procedure in changing an individual's interpretations and thinking processes, which have a powerful effect on his or her feelings and actions. Later in this chapter, cognitive therapy groups are briefly discussed.

Initially, members may be taught through group exercises how to differentiate between self-defeating and self-enhancing statements. Typically, members provide one another with feedback and various models of a cognitive analysis. After clients decide on a set of realistic cognitive statements, cognitive modeling is used, in which the members imagine themselves in stressful situations and substitute self enhancing statements for self-defeating remarks. In cognitive rehearsal, members imitate the model and get feedback from others in the group. After several trials in the group, they are given the assignment to practice a new set of statements at home before they try out a new style in the real world. In the final step of cognitive restructuring, homework is assigned at the end of each session and then monitored at the beginning of the following session. As members make progress, assignments can be developed at successive levels of difficulty.

Problem Solving Problem-solving therapy is a cognitive behavioral strategy that teaches individuals ways to deal with problems in their daily lives. The main goal is to identify the most effective solution to a problem and to provide systematic training in cognitive and behavioral skills so the client can apply them and also cope effectively with future problems. The seven stages in the problem-solving process are described by Spiegler and Guevremont (2010):

1. *Adopt a problem-solving orientation.* Clients are helped in assessing, defining, and understanding the problem. They need to understand that it is essential to identify problems when they occur so that action can be taken. Clients must also be convinced that skills can be acquired to cope with daily problems. Finally, it is important to carefully assess alternative courses of action when problem solving.

2. *Define the problem.* Clients are helped to understand why certain problem situations are likely to occur and are given the expectation that they can learn ways to cope.

3. *Set goals.* Client goals can focus on the problem situation, reactions to the problem situation, or both. The question clients explore is: "What must happen so that I no longer have the problem?"

4. *Brainstorm alternative solutions.* The objective is to think of as many solutions as possible to maximize the chances of finding an adequate solution to a problem. Clients are discouraged from evaluating any of the possible solutions until all the suggestions have been presented.

5. *Make a decision.* Based on the alternatives generated in the fourth stage, clients examine the potential consequences of each course of action and make their choice.

6. *Implement the solution.* This may be the most important stage because the best solutions will be effective in dealing with a problem situation only if these solutions are implemented appropriately.

7. *Evaluate the effectiveness of the action.* This verification phase consists of having clients observe and evaluate the consequences of their actions in everyday life situations.

In group therapy problem-solving skills are typically introduced didactically, and the entire group may participate in working through some problems that group members are experiencing (Bieling et al., 2006). Procedures such as modeling, coaching, and reinforcement are used during problem-solving training. Throughout the therapy process, clients are taught self-control techniques, and they are encouraged to reinforce their own successful performance. Further, once clients have had an opportunity to observe the therapist (or other models) demonstrate effective problem-solving procedures, they are expected to assume a more active role. At this time the therapist functions largely as a consultant, providing guidance, giving feedback, and encouraging and evaluating real-life applications (Rose, 1998). Members are then encouraged to practice the skills they are learning as they encounter problem situations during the week.

The Buddy System Rose (1998) describes the **buddy system** as a form of therapeutic alliance between members. Typically, a client is assigned or chooses another member as a monitor and coach throughout the group treatment process. The members monitor each other's behavior in the group and remind each other between meetings to stick to their commitments and practice their assignments. In this way they play a supportive role both in and out of the group. Buddies are trained in giving reinforcement for achievements and in giving and receiving feedback. The most important part of treatment occurs outside of the group with the practice of homework assignments. Members assist each other in designing these tasks and monitoring their completion. This arrangement offers members opportunities to be helpful to others and to practice their newly learned leadership skills. The buddy system becomes a self-help network that functions after the group terminates (Rose & Edleson, 1987).

FINAL STAGE

During the final stage of a cognitive behavioral group, the leader is primarily concerned with having members transfer the changes they have exhibited in the group to their everyday environment. Practice sessions involving simulations of the real world are used to promote this transfer. Members rehearse what they want to say to significant people in their life and practice new behaviors. Feedback from others in the group, along with coaching, can be most useful at the final stage. Sessions are systematically designed so that new behaviors are gradually carried into daily life. Although preparation for generalization and maintenance of change is given a special focus in the final stage, it is a characteristic of all phases of the group.

Consolidation of learning and developing strategies for transferring what was learned in the group to daily life are key goals of the final stage. The following tasks are characteristic of the final phase of a group:

- Giving and receiving feedback
- Providing many opportunities to practice new and more effective behaviors
- Carrying learning further by developing a specific plan of action to continue applying changes to situations outside of the group
- Preparing members for dealing with possible setbacks
- Assisting members in reviewing the group experience and the meaning it holds for them

Self-responsibility is emphasized throughout the life of the group, but it is especially critical in planning for termination. As the group progresses, the members should be given increased responsibility for implementing an action plan that they have collaboratively developed with the group leader. One of the main goals of successful therapy is to teach clients the skills they will need in becoming their own therapists (Ledley et al., 2005). The leader's role shifts from a direct therapist to a consultant in the final stage. Members are typically encouraged to apply their newly learned skills to new situations with others outside of their group. In addition, they are taught self-help cognitive skills such as self-reinforcement and problem solving as a way of preparing them for situations they have not encountered in the group. It is critical for members to know what to do if problematic symptoms reemerge. The move toward member independence from the group is essential if clients are to gain confidence in their ability to cope effectively with new problems. Ledley and colleagues (2005) state that a main therapeutic goal is helping members to acquire new skills that will enable them to deal with residual difficulties after therapy as well as new problems that may arise in the future. As the time of termination approaches, many of the initial assessment instruments are repeated as a way of evaluating the effectiveness of the group program.

Termination and follow-up are issues of special concern to CBT group practitioners. Short- and long-term follow-up interviews are scheduled, at which time data are collected to determine the outcomes of a group. Follow-up interviews can serve as "booster sessions" that help members maintain the changed behaviors and continue to engage in self-directed change. Follow-up group sessions provide opportunities for members to review what they have learned, to update the group on how they are doing, and to encourage members to be accountable for their changes or lack of them. Knowing that they will be accountable, members often are motivated to maintain and use the newly acquired skills they learned in the group.

An important advantage of scheduling follow-up sessions is that doing so provides a way to predict and plan for the setbacks members may encounter after terminating a group. *Relapse prevention* helps members think about ways to deal with the potential problems they may face when they no longer have the support of a group. This is an essential part of terminating a therapy group. It is easy for members to revert to ingrained patterns of old learning, especially when they are faced with a new crisis or when stress escalates. Follow-up group sessions assist members in keeping up with their commitments and plans (White, 2000b).

Application: Therapeutic Techniques and Procedures

There is a growing trend toward "giving psychology away"—that is, a tendency to teach people how to apply interpersonal skills to their everyday life. This trend implies that practitioners will share their knowledge with consumers so that people can lead increasingly self-directed lives and not be dependent on the experts for the effective management of the problems they encounter.

Cognitive behavioral approaches to groups offer great promise for those who want to learn the skills necessary for self-management. Areas in which one can learn to control behavior and bring about self-directed change are controlling excessive eating, drinking, and smoking and learning self-discipline at work or in school. Some people cannot accomplish certain goals in their work because their efforts are hindered by lack of organization; they do not know where to begin with a project, how to sustain their efforts, or how to avoid the crippling discouragement they experience when they fail to attain their goals. It is in these and similar areas that behavioral groups for self-directed change can provide the guidelines and planning necessary to bring about change.

This section deals with some common behavioral and cognitive techniques that are applicable to group work. For the purpose of this discussion, the techniques have been grouped under four general approaches that can be applied to the practice of cognitive behavioral groups: (1) social skills training groups, (2) cognitive therapy groups, (3) stress management groups, and (4) mindfulness and acceptance-based cognitive behavior therapy.

SOCIAL SKILLS TRAINING GROUPS

Social skills training (SST) is a broad category that deals with one's ability to interact effectively with others in a variety of social situations. *Social skills* involve being able to communicate with others in a way that is both appropriate and effective. Individuals who experience psychosocial problems that are partly caused by interpersonal difficulties are good candidates for social skills training. The goal of SST is to enhance a person's functioning in social and performance situations (Bieling et al., 2006). Social skills training in groups involves the application of many of the behavioral techniques discussed earlier in this chapter.

Group members identify particular social skills deficits or communication-related problems that they would like to change, then target these social skills in the group sessions. This process often includes learning basic skills essential to effective communication, becoming more assertive, and performing more effectively in a job interview. Generally, social skills training includes strategies such as psychoeducation, modeling, behavioral rehearsal, role playing, and feedback (Bieling et al., 2006).

Social Effectiveness Training One model of social skills training is **social effectiveness training** (or SET), which is a multifaceted treatment program designed to reduce social anxiety, improve interpersonal skills, and increase the range of enjoyable social activities (Turner, Beidel, & Cooley, 1994). The primary components of this program are exposure to reduce social anxiety and social skills training to improve general social skills and social deficits. This treatment is based on over a decade of both clinical experience and empirical literature. The social skills training component is conducted in weekly small group sessions over a 12-week period. This group experience focuses on training in three areas: (1) social environment awareness, (2) interpersonal skill enhancement, and (3) presentation skill enhancement. In these three areas, participants are taught the nuances of interpersonal interactions and conversations, including the verbal and nonverbal *dos* and *don'ts* of successful social encounters as well as the presentation of communication skills in public speaking. Didactic instruction, modeling, behavior rehearsal, corrective feedback, and positive reinforcement are utilized in the group process to achieve these outcomes. Turner and colleagues (1994) emphasize that the SET program is primarily for use by mental health professionals who are either under supervision or who are trained in general clinical skills, who have a knowledge of social anxiety and phobia, and who are familiar with behavioral intervention strategies.

Assertion Training A group format offers unique advantages over individual counseling for the development of new social skills. One specialized form of social skills training is teaching people how to be assertive in a variety of social situations. The basic assumption underlying the practice of **assertion training** is that people have the right—but not the obligation—to express their feelings, thoughts, beliefs, and attitudes. Assertiveness training can be especially useful for people who cannot ask others for what they want; who are unable to resist demands; and who have difficulty expressing feelings of love, gratitude, and approval as well as feelings of irritation, anger, and disagreement. Alberti and Emmons (2008) identify three particularly difficult barriers to self-expression: (1) people may not believe they have the right to have or express their thoughts and feelings, (2) people may be anxious about being assertive, and (3) people may sometimes lack the skills for effectively expressing themselves.

The goal of assertion training is to increase the group members' behavioral repertoire so that they can make the choice of being assertive or not. Another goal of assertion training is teaching people how to express themselves in a way that reflects sensitivity to the feelings and rights of others. Truly assertive individuals do not rigidly stand up for their rights at all costs, riding roughshod over the feelings and opinions of others. Assertion training attempts to equip clients with the skills and attitudes necessary to deal effectively with a wide range of interpersonal situations. These are some specific outcome goals of this type of training:

- Recognize and change self-defeating or faulty beliefs concerning one's right to be assertive.
- Develop an attitude that places value on one's right to express oneself and on respect for the rights of others.
- Learn how to identify and discriminate among assertive, aggressive, and nonassertive behaviors.
- Be able to apply newly learned assertive skills to specific interpersonal situations.

Most assertion training programs focus on clients' negative self-statements, self-defeating beliefs, and faulty thinking. Effective programs aimed at teaching assertiveness do more than give people skills and techniques for dealing with difficult situations. These programs challenge people's beliefs that accompany their lack of assertiveness and teach them to make constructive self-statements and to adopt a new set of beliefs and self-talk that will result in assertive behavior.

For those who are interested in learning the specifics of planning, setting up, conducting, and evaluating assertion training groups, I recommend Alberti and Emmons (2008).

COGNITIVE THERAPY GROUPS

Cognitive behavioral therapy utilizes a group dynamics format, in conjunction with standard cognitive behavioral techniques, to change maladaptive and dysfunctional beliefs, interpretations, behaviors, and attitudes (Petrocelli, 2002). Some of the most common interventions include automatic thought records, disputing beliefs, monitoring moods, developing an arousal hierarchy, monitoring activities, problem solving, Socratic questioning, relaxation methods, risk assessment, and relapse prevention (Petrocelli, 2002; White, 2000b). Two of the best-known models of cognitive behavioral group therapy are based on the theories of Albert Ellis's rational emotive behavior therapy (the subject of Chapter 14) and Aaron Beck's cognitive therapy, which is described next.

Aaron Beck (1976, 1997), a practicing psychoanalytic therapist for many years, grew interested in his clients' **automatic thoughts** (personalized notions that are triggered by particular stimuli that lead to emotional responses). Beck asked his clients to observe negative automatic thoughts (or faulty beliefs) that persisted even though they were contrary to objective evidence, and from this he developed the most comprehensive theory on depression in the world.

Beck (1976) and J. Beck (1995, 2005) contend that people with emotional difficulties tend to commit characteristic "logical errors" that tilt objective reality in the direction of self-deprecation. **Cognitive therapy** perceives psychological problems as stemming from commonplace processes such as faulty thinking, making incorrect inferences on the basis of inadequate or incorrect information, and failing to distinguish between fantasy and reality.

The cognitive model of group therapy is based on a theory that emphasizes the interaction of thoughts, feelings, and behaviors; these components are interrelated and multidirectional (White, 2000b). The most direct way to change dysfunctional emotions and behaviors is to modify inaccurate and dysfunctional thinking. To change how we feel about events, we need to change the way we think about them (Neenan & Dryden, 2004).

In this model of group therapy, a sound therapeutic relationship that emphasizes collaboration and active participation is the foundation for effective practice. The cognitive therapist teaches group members how to identify these distorted and dysfunctional cognitions through a process of evaluation. The group leader assists members in forming hypotheses and testing their assumptions, which is known as **collaborative empiricism.** Through a collaborative effort, group members learn to discriminate between their own thoughts and events that occur in reality. They learn the influence that cognition has on their feelings and behaviors and even on environmental events, particularly the distortions that they have acquired. In a group counseling context, members are taught to recognize, observe, and monitor their own thoughts and assumptions, especially their negative automatic thoughts.

Group members often engage in catastrophic thinking by choosing to dwell on the most extreme negative scenarios in many situations. Group leaders can assist members in detecting those times when they get stuck imagining the worst possible outcome of a situation by asking these questions: "What is the worst thing that could occur?" and "If this happens, what would make this such a negative outcome?"

Group members can learn to engage in more realistic thinking, especially if they consistently notice times when they tend to get caught up in catastrophic thinking. Guiding group members to look for evidence to support or refute some of their core beliefs and faulty thinking can also be useful. As individuals identify a number of self-defeating beliefs, they can begin to monitor the frequency with which these beliefs intrude in situations in everyday life. This simple question can be frequently asked, "Where is the evidence for _____?" If this question is raised often enough, members are likely to make it a practice to ask themselves this question, especially as they become more adept at spotting dysfunctional thoughts and paying attention to their cognitive patterns. Once members discover those beliefs that are not accurate, they are encouraged to try out a different set of beliefs to determine whether the new beliefs are more accurate and functional (Beck & Weishaar, 2011).

After group members have gained insight into how their unrealistically negative thoughts are affecting them, they are trained to test these automatic thoughts against reality by examining and weighing the evidence for and against them. This process involves empirically testing their beliefs by actively participating in a variety of methods, such as engaging in a *Socratic dialogue* with the therapist, carrying out homework assignments, gathering data on assumptions they make, keeping a record of activities, and forming alternative interpretations (Freeman & Dattilio, 1994). Members in a cognitive therapy group are expected to form hypotheses about their behavior and eventually learn to employ specific problem-solving and coping skills. Through a process of *guided discovery*, they acquire insight about the connection between their thinking and the ways they feel and act. In guided discovery, the group therapist helps to illuminate the meaning of thoughts and problems in logic and also helps members to acquire new information and different ways of thinking, acting, and feeling (Bieling et al., 2006). Group members, not the group leader, then determine the usefulness of their beliefs.

In a cognitive therapy group, the emphasis is on the present and the approach is time limited. Group sessions are focused on current problems, regardless of diagnosis. The past may be brought into group work under certain circumstances: when the member expresses a strong desire to talk about a past situation; when work on current problems results in little or no cognitive, behavioral, and emotional change; and when the therapist considers it essential to understand how and when certain dysfunctional beliefs originated and how these ideas have a current impact on the group member. In addressing the role of the past in CBT, Ledley, Marx, and Heimberg (2005) state that clinicians using this approach have an interest in the connection between past experiences and current beliefs and behaviors. The role of the past is considered throughout treatment, especially in understanding more about a client's core beliefs. They stress that merely understanding the origin of a problem is not enough; clients must act on this knowledge to change dysfunctional beliefs and behaviors that are maintaining present problems. With this present-centered focus, cognitive group therapy tends to be both brief and task oriented. The therapeutic goals that guide group interventions include providing symptom relief, assisting members in resolving their most pressing problems, and teaching them relapse prevention strategies.

STRESS MANAGEMENT TRAINING IN GROUPS

Stress is a basic part of contemporary life. Although it is not realistic to assume that we can eliminate stress, it is realistic for us to learn how to control how we view and cope with stressful events. **Stress management training** has potentially useful applications for a wide variety of problems and client populations, both for remediation of stress disorders and for prevention. Stress management training is especially useful in dealing with anger, anxiety, phobias, and medical problems; the training is appropriate for victim populations and for professional groups. Stress management can be used both as a primary focus of treatment and as an adjunctive treatment for people who experience significant problems in the biopsychological sphere (Kaplan & Laygo, 2003). Stress management groups are helping military personnel and their families cope with the stresses of war zone deployments today.

The goal of stress management programs is not to eliminate stress but to educate clients about its nature and effects and to teach them a variety of intrapersonal and interpersonal skills to deal with stress constructively (Meichenbaum, 1985). A basic assumption of stress management programs is that we are not simply victims of stress; rather, what we do and what we *think* actively contribute to how we experience stress. In other words, how we appraise events in life determines whether stress will affect us positively or negatively.

Kaplan and Laygo (2003) describe how stress management works. The training begins with a brief assessment of the client's lifestyle, including identifying aspects that may cause stress. Participants in the program are then presented with a psychoeducational overview of stress from a psychosocial perspective and learn to use behaviors and thoughts for coping with a variety of stressful situations. Clients make a concrete behavioral plan for implementing lifestyle changes that will lead to a better quality of life.

Meichenbaum's Stress Inoculation Training Meichenbaum (1985, 1986, 1993, 1994, 2003) is concerned with more than merely teaching people specific coping skills. His program is designed to prepare clients for interventions and motivate them to change, and it deals with issues such as resistance and relapse. **Stress inoculation training** (SIT) consists of a combination of elements of information giving, Socratic discussion, cognitive restructuring, problem solving, relaxation training, behavioral and imagined rehearsals, self-monitoring, self-instruction, self-reinforcement, and environmental change. Meichenbaum (2003) contends that SIT can be used for both preventive and treatment purposes with a broad range of people who experience stress responses. This approach is designed to teach coping skills that can be applied to both present problems and future stressors when they are encountered. If clients do not have an opportunity to apply coping skills to situations other than their present problems, their coping skills may not generalize to new situations. Cormier, Nurius, and Osborn (2009) report that "stress inoculation training is one of the most comprehensive therapeutic treatments presently in use" (p. 437).

Meichenbaum (1985, 1993, 2003) has designed a three-stage model for SIT: (1) conceptual-educational, (2) skills acquisition, consolidation, and rehearsal, and (3) application and follow-through. During the initial stage of SIT (conceptual-educational), the primary focus is on creating a working relationship with clients by educating them to gain a better understanding of the nature of stress and to reconceptualize it in social interaction terms. During this phase, clients are educated about the transactional nature of stress and coping. They learn about the role that cognitions and emotions play in creating and maintaining stress. They also learn how their reactions to stress emanate from their perception of events rather than from the events themselves. In a collaborative fashion, clients identify the determinants of their presenting problems. After an assessment process in which they take an active role, they determine specific goals that will guide treatment. Self-monitoring, which begins at this time, continues throughout the training. Clients typically keep an open-ended diary in which they systematically record their specific thoughts, feelings, and behaviors. Training includes teaching clients to become aware of their own role in creating their stress and to identify their coping strengths and resources. This provides clients with a rationale for treatment and a basis for learning ways to reduce the negative effects of stress.

During the second phase of SIT (skills acquisition, consolidation, and rehearsal), clients learn and rehearse coping strategies. Some of these specific techniques include cognitive restructuring; problem solving; social skills training; time management; self-instructional training; guided self-dialogue; relaxation training; and lifestyle changes such as reevaluating priorities, developing support systems, and taking direct action to alter stressful situations. As a part of this phase of SIT, clients are introduced to a variety of methods of relaxation and are taught to use these skills to decrease arousal due to stress. Through teaching, demonstration, and guided practice, they learn the skills of progressive relaxation. Clients rehearse skills by means of imagery and behavioral practice, which they are expected to practice regularly. These activities may include meditation, yoga, tensing and relaxing muscle groups, and breath-control techniques. They can also include walking, jogging, gardening, knitting, or other physical activities. Meichenbaum stresses that it is essential that both clients and trainers understand that relaxation is as much a state of mind as a physical state.

Another method used to teach coping skills is a graded task assignment—a shaping strategy in which clients are encouraged to perform small sequential steps leading to a goal. In treating stress-related problems, SIT uses three core techniques: (1) eliciting the client's thoughts, feelings, and interpretations of events; (2) gathering evidence with the client to either support or disprove these interpretations; and (3) designing homework assignments to test the validity of the interpretations and to gather more data for discussion.

In *cognitive restructuring,* clients become aware of the role that their cognitions and emotions play in creating and maintaining stress. The cognitive restructuring approach used in SIT is based on Beck's (1976) cognitive therapy, which was described earlier. Therapists systematically use strategies such as modeling and behavior rehearsal in teaching constructive cognitive and coping skills. Through cognitive therapy techniques, clients learn to detect negative and stress-engendering thoughts and to challenge their "automatic thoughts," which compound their stress. Clients are also given self-instructional training, which teaches them to instruct themselves, often silently, in coping with problematic situations. Clients learn and practice a new set of cognitive coping strategies that they can apply when they encounter stressors. If our thinking can make us worse, it is assumed that we can adopt a different set of self-statements to reduce, avoid, or constructively use stress.

In the third phase of SIT (application and follow-through), the focus is on carefully arranging for transfer and maintenance of change from the therapeutic situation to daily life. The assumption is that coping skills that are practiced in the clinic will not automatically generalize to everyday life situations. To consolidate the lessons learned in the training sessions, clients participate in a variety of activities, including imagery and behavior rehearsal, role playing, modeling, and graduated in vivo practice. Clients are asked to write down the homework assignments, or personal experiments, that they are willing to complete. The outcomes of these assignments are carefully checked at subsequent meetings; if clients do not follow through with them, the trainer and the members collaboratively consider the reasons for these failures. Clients are provided with training in relapse prevention, which consists of procedures for dealing with the inevitable setbacks they are likely to experience as they apply their learning to daily life. A more detailed discussion of the techniques typically used during this phase of treatment was presented in the section describing the final stage of a behavioral group.

MINDFULNESS AND ACCEPTANCE APPROACHES IN COGNITIVE BEHAVIOR THERAPY

Over the past decade or so, third-generation behavior therapies have been developed that center around five interrelated core themes: (1) an expanded view of psychological health, (2) a broad view of acceptable outcomes in therapy, (3) acceptance, (4) mindfulness, and (5) creating a life worth living (Spiegler & Guevremont, 2010). These third-generation therapeutic approaches include a host of new interventions that are gaining ground and popularity for a number of disorders (Bieling et al., 2006). They have their roots in group practice and represent an expansion of the cognitive behavioral tradition.

Mindfulness is a process that involves becoming increasingly observant and aware of external and internal stimuli in the present moment and adopting an open attitude toward accepting what is rather than judging the current situation (Kabat-Zinn, 1994; Segal, Williams, & Teasdale, 2002). Mindfulness can be defined as "using awareness and thoughts to bring consciousness fully into the present moment" (Wills, 2009, p. 69). The essence of mindfulness is becoming aware of one's mind from one moment to the next, with gentle acceptance (Germer, Siegel, & Fulton, 2005). In mindfulness practice clients

train themselves to focus on their present experience. Mindfulness-based approaches tend to be group-based.

Acceptance is a process involving receiving one's present experience without judgment or preference, but with curiosity and kindness, and striving for full awareness of the present moment (Germer, 2005b). The concept of acceptance does not imply resigning oneself to life's problems. Instead, acceptance is best viewed as a willingness to choose to experience negative thoughts or feelings without defense (Wilson, 2011).

An increasing amount of literature on mindfulness-based interventions and acceptance-based cognitive behavioral treatment as a potentially powerful clinical method has resulted in an expansion of the cognitive behavioral tradition (Hayes et al., 2004). The four major approaches include (1) *dialectical behavior therapy* (Linehan, 1993a, 1993b), which has become a recognized treatment for borderline personality disorder; (2) *mindfulness-based stress reduction* (Kabat-Zinn, 1990), which involves an 8- to 10-week group program applying mindfulness techniques to coping with stress and promoting physical and psychological health; (3) *mindfulness-based cognitive therapy* (Segal et al., 2002), which is aimed primarily at treating depression; and (4) *acceptance and commitment therapy* (Hayes, Strosahl, & Wilson, 1999; Hayes, Strosahl, & Houts, 2005; Roemer & Orsillio, 2009), which is based on encouraging clients to accept, rather than attempt to control or change, unpleasant sensations. All four of these approaches are based on empirical data, which certainly is a hallmark of the behavioral tradition.

Behavior therapists are increasingly recognizing that in many cases optimal treatment may require more than one behavioral approach. Moreover, the growing trend toward psychotherapeutic integration involves incorporating treatment strategies from two or more orientations. In keeping with this trend, CBT practitioners are now incorporating nonbehavioral methods in the treatment plans they devise (Spiegler & Guevremont, 2010). Likewise, non-CBT practitioners are borrowing from and using many of the methods from mindfulness and acceptance approaches.

Dialectical Behavior Therapy (DBT) This approach makes use of mindfulness and was developed to help clients regulate emotions and behavior associated with depression. This is a paradoxical treatment aimed at helping clients to accept their emotions as well as to change their emotional experience (Morgan, 2005). DBT is a particularly promising blend of cognitive behavior and psychoanalytic techniques. Linehan (1993a, 1993b) formulated DBT for clients whose symptoms include behaviors resulting in nonfatal self-harm. These symptoms are most typical of an individual diagnosed as having a borderline personality disorder but may also be encountered with other clients. Like analytic therapy, DBT emphasizes the importance of the psychotherapeutic relationship, validation of the client, and the etiologic importance of the client having experienced an "invalidating environment" as a child. The learning emphasis in DBT is an "empirically validated" treatment approach. DBT integrates cognitive behavioral concepts not only with analytic notions but also with the mindfulness training of "Eastern psychological and spiritual practices (primarily Zen practice)" (Linehan, 1993b, p. 6). Over the past 15 years, a significant body of research has demonstrated that DBT is an empirically supported treatment for people exhibiting characteristics of borderline personality disorders

(Spiegler & Guevremont, 2010). Although DBT was developed primarily for treating borderline personality disorders, the basic concepts and strategies of DBT are now being applied to treatment with a wide range of problems including anxiety disorders, depression, and eating disorders (Hayes et al., 2004).

DBT involves teaching clients both mindfulness and acceptance. The practice of acceptance involves being in the present moment, seeing reality as it is without distortions, without judgment, without evaluation, and without trying to hang on to an experience or to get rid of it. It involves entering fully into activities of the present moment without separating oneself from ongoing events and interactions.

In DBT clients are taught skills for accepting life as it is (Robins, Schmidt, & Linehan, 2004). Mindfulness skills are taught over two or three group sessions and then reviewed later. Some of these skills include focusing on breathing, staying with a present activity, identifying and describing feelings, attending to emotions without trying to avoid them when they are painful, letting thoughts flow, assuming a nonjudgmental stance, focusing on one thing at a time, and accepting all feelings.

DBT is not a quick fix approach for it generally involves a minimum of one year of treatment. The group work must be accompanied by individual therapy. Linehan (1993b) allows for the "integration of DBT skills training with individual psychodynamic therapy" in some settings (p. 14). Clearly, to practice DBT requires intensive training and supervision.

Mindfulness-based Stress Reduction (MBSR) Basically, all the skills that are taught in the MBSR program, such as sitting meditation and mindful yoga, are aimed at cultivating mindfulness. The program includes a body scan meditation that helps clients to observe all the sensations in their body. This attitude of mindfulness is encouraged in every aspect of daily life including standing, walking, and eating. Those who are involved in the program are encouraged to practice formal mindfulness meditation for 45 minutes daily. The MBSR program is mainly designed to teach participants to relate to external and internal sources of stress in constructive ways. The program aims to teach people how to live more fully in the present rather than ruminating about the past or being overly concerned about the future.

Mindfulness-based Cognitive Therapy (MBCT) This is a comprehensive integration of the principles and skills of mindfulness applied to the treatment of depression (Segal et al., 2002). MBCT is an 8-week group treatment program adapted from Kabat-Zinn's (1990) mindfulness-based stress reduction program and includes components of cognitive behavior therapy. In this manualized treatment program, clients suffering from depression are taught how to become aware of their thoughts and feelings without concluding that they are objective facts (Morgan, 2005). Clients learn that their thoughts are not facts and that we can allow thoughts to come and go rather than attempting to dispute them out of existence as might be done in traditional CBT. MBCT aims at changing clients' awareness of and relation to their negative thoughts (Germer, 2005b). MBCT integrates aspects of cognitive therapy and mindfulness-based stress reduction procedures. Initial research on the efficacy of MBCT in treating depression is promising, yet more research needs to be done. The brevity and group format of MBCT make this approach an efficient and cost-effective treatment (Spiegler & Guevremont, 2010).

Acceptance and Commitment Therapy (ACT) Another mindfulness-based approach is *acceptance and commitment therapy* (Hayes et al., 1999, 2005), which involves fully accepting present experience and mindfully letting go of obstacles. In this approach "acceptance is not merely tolerance—rather it is the active nonjudgmental embracing of experience in the here and now" (Hayes, 2004, p. 32). In the practice of ACT there is a conscious stance of openness and acceptance toward psychological events. *Acceptance* is not a specific technique; rather, it is a stance or posture from which to conduct therapy and from which a client can conduct life (Hayes & Pankey, 2003). ACT is designed to help clients learn that suppressing negative or unwanted thoughts or painful feelings does not work. Avoidance is part of the problem rather than the solution (Wilson, 2011). The goal of ACT is to allow for increased psychological flexibility. Values are a basic part of the therapeutic process, and ACT practitioners might ask clients "What do you want your life to stand for?" ACT emphasizes action, and it makes use of concrete homework and behavioral exercises as a way to create larger patterns of effective action that will help clients live by their values (Hayes, 2004). *Commitment* refers to making mindful decisions about what clients most value and what they are willing to do in order to live a valued and meaningful life (Wilson, 2011).

Germer (2005b) states that there are more than 100 ACT skills to choose from, which are individualized for each client. Some acceptance exercises include contemplating the Serenity Prayer, journaling about painful events, saying one's thoughts very slowly, writing difficult thoughts on a card and carrying them around, and doing something different and noting what happens. The focus of ACT is allowing experience to come and go while pursuing a meaningful life. Hayes and Pankey (2003) contend that "there is a growing evidence base that acceptance skills are central to psychological well-being and can increase the impact of psychotherapy with a broad variety of clients" (p. 8).

Future Directions The new behavior therapies have brought many new ideas into the behavioral tradition. This evolution of the field reflects the commitment of cognitive behavior therapists to follow the data in their practices. Hayes (2004) summarized this developmental process:

> It is truly new for empirical clinical approaches to embrace the kind of deep clinical and human issues that have previously been the province of nonempirical approaches. If the new behavior therapies continue down this road, the entire field of behavioral health seems bound to change in a fundamental way. (p. 25)

All of the mindfulness and acceptance-based approaches share one important feature that enables them to fit under the general behavioral umbrella: they are all based on empirical data. In addressing ways that mindfulness might continue to influence the practice of cognitive behavior therapy, Germer (2005a) suggests that these developments may result in a more unified model of psychotherapy. He believes that we are likely to see more research that identifies mindfulness as a key element in treatment protocols and as a crucial ingredient in the therapy relationship: "Mindfulness might become a construct that draws clinical theory, research, and practice closer together, and helps integrate the private and professional lives of therapists" (p. 11).

For a more in-depth discussion of the role of mindfulness in psychotherapeutic practice, three highly recommended readings are *Mindfulness and*

Acceptance: Expanding the Cognitive-Behavioral Tradition (Hayes et al., 2004); *Mindfulness and Psychotherapy* (Germer et al., 2005); and *Mindfulness and Acceptance-Based Behavioral Therapies in Practice* (Roemer & Orsillio, 2009).

Applying the Cognitive Behavioral Approach to Group Work in Schools

The framework of present-centered, short-term, action-focused, reeducative, cognitive behavioral approaches are a good fit in working with a diverse range of students from the elementary to the high school level. A variety of behavioral methods are useful tools for cognitive behavioral group counseling with K–12 students. One of the most compelling reasons for employing CBT groups in schools is that they can be used for both remediation and prevention (Vernon, 2004). Vernon provides some reasons for the effectiveness of cognitive behavioral therapies with school-aged populations:

- CBT principles are easy to understand, and they can be adapted to children of most ages and from many cultural backgrounds.

- CBT groups tend to be short term and employ brief interventions, which fits in school settings where time is limited.

- The teachable concepts can be translated into acquiring life skills.

- Children and adolescents can learn emotional and behavioral self-control through understanding the connection between thoughts, feelings, and behaviors.

- CBT groups help participants to cope with what they can change and to accept what they cannot change.

- The cognitive principles empower young people to deal with both present concerns and future problems.

Sheldon Rose's (1998) *Group Therapy With Troubled Youth: A Cognitive-Behavioral Interactive Approach* is particularly useful for group leaders of adolescent groups. Rose describes how a group for adolescents and preadolescents can be structured to address several general targets of intervention: interpersonal skills, problem-solving skills, cognitive coping skills, and self-management skills. Rose shows how behavioral assessment and treatment interventions can be applied to working with adolescents. He makes the assumption that the behavior of youth is not due solely to their beliefs but is a product of their immediate environment, family, community, gender, race, and ethnicity as well. A broad-based treatment provides the greatest benefit to young people. The group methods that Rose describes in various settings can be applied to group work with students in middle schools and high schools.

Shechtman (2002) reviewed existing studies in counseling and psychoeducation groups with children in the school setting and found that the cognitive behavioral approach is the most popular theoretical base for interventions in children's groups. This is due to a number of factors: the structured nature of cognitive behavioral interventions, the emphasis given to a time-limited framework, and the demonstrated accountability of this approach. Shechtman states that the results of process research indicate that children and adolescents are generally willing to engage in self-disclosure, even during the early stages of a group. In addition, children tend to react negatively to confrontation, but they react positively to feedback given in a caring and supportive manner. Adolescents are interested in interpersonal learning that they can apply to their social interactions; they also express a need for practical guidance and training. For these reasons, the school setting is very suitable for a variety of behavioral groups with both children and adolescents.

Applying the Cognitive Behavioral Approach With Multicultural Populations

Cognitive behavioral group therapy has some clear advantages in work with multicultural populations. Spiegler (2008) contends that cognitive behavior therapy is inherently suited for treating diverse client populations due to its emphasis on individualized treatment and the external environment, its psychoeducational focus, and the active nature of the approach. CBT groups deal more with patterns of thinking and behaving than with experiencing and expressing intense feelings. Group members who might find catharsis distasteful, due to cultural inhibitions against displaying emotions, are less likely to be immediately put off by this approach. In addition, CBT groups are often short term and highly structured, and clients will know what they are getting into when they agree to participate. Cognitive behavioral practitioners typically spend time preparing members to participate in a group experience. The group process is demystified and norms are made clear. This approach may appeal to clients who are somewhat suspicious of the value of a group experience but are interested in learning practical ways of coping with immediate problems.

Most important, this approach tends to be culturally sensitive because it uses the individual's belief system as part of the method of self-challenge. Beck and Weishaar (2011) point out that cognitive therapy begins with an understanding of a client's beliefs and values, which exist within a cultural context. The therapist's attention is on the degree to which these beliefs are adaptive for the client. Cognitive therapists do not impose their beliefs on the group members; rather, they help members assess whether a given belief fosters emotional well-being. CBT group practitioners acknowledge the environmental contributors of problems many clients face, such as stress, inequality, and social injustice (Cormier et al., 2009).

Hays (2009) contends that there is an "almost perfect fit" between CBT and multicultural therapy. Both perspectives share common assumptions that facilitate their integration:

- Both emphasize the need to tailor interventions to the unique needs and strengths of the individual.
- Both emphasize empowerment: CBT teaches clients specific skills that they can apply in daily life; multicultural therapy emphasizes cultural influences that contribute to a client's uniqueness.
- Both emphasize a strength model wherein the inner resources of the client are activated to bring about change.
- CBT's behavioral roots call attention to the influence of environment, which fits well with the multicultural emphasis on cultural influences.

Other factors that contribute to the usefulness of cognitive behavioral approaches to group work with diverse client populations include its specificity, task orientation, focus on objectivity, emphasis on collaboration, focus on cognition and behavior, action orientation, dealing with the present more than the past, emphasis on brief interventions, and problem-solving orientation. The attention given to transfer of learning and the principles and strategies for maintaining new behavior in daily life are crucial. Because CBT fits into a short-term group format, it is applicable to a variety of practical problems that certain client populations face, and the time frame makes it possible to deal with day-to-day concerns that these clients bring to therapy.

According to Organista (2000), Latinos who are a part of a cognitive behavioral therapy group are likely to find some of the interventions consistent with their expectations. The emphasis on symptom relief, guidance and advice, directiveness, the expert role of the leader, a focus on dealing with problems, brevity, and tailoring treatment to the client's particular circumstances are all facets they may appreciate and find useful. Group members from many different cultures are likely to find that this approach suits their preferences for direction and a focus on present problems.

CBT's emphasis on assertiveness, independence, verbal ability, rationality, cognition, and behavioral change may limit its use in cultures that value subtle communication over assertiveness, interdependence over personal independence, listening and observing over talking, acceptance over behavior change, and a less linear cognitive style (Hays, 2009). In addition, the focus on the present in CBT can result in neglecting the past. Cognitive behavioral assessments involve the investigation of a client's *personal* history. If therapists are unaware of a client's *cultural* beliefs, they may have difficulty in interpreting a client's personal experiences. Another limitation of CBT from a multicultural perspective involves its individual orientation, which emphasizes the influence of the physical and social environment. An inexperienced therapist may overemphasize cognitive restructuring to the neglect of environmental interventions.

Organista (2000) indicates that cognitive behavioral models of assertiveness training have some limitations when groups include members who come from a traditional Latino culture. The basic concepts of assertive behavior might well be foreign to the nonegalitarian family and friendship systems of Latino clients. Assertive communication can be oppositional to the Latino cultural emphasis on communication that is polite, nonconfrontational, deferential, and even purposefully indirect.

Organista proposes an alternative way to motivate Latino members of a group to consider potential values of being assertive in certain situations. These members can be asked to describe what happens to them when they hold negative feelings inside. Latino clients who hold in anger often describe the experience of a range of physical symptoms such as high blood pressure, heart disease, and other somatic symptoms. Once group members become clearer about the price they are paying for denying expression of some of their thoughts and feelings, they might be more likely to consider ways of expressing themselves in a way that is congruent with their cultural framework.

It is important for group leaders to help their clients assess the possible consequences of some of their newly acquired social skills within a particular cultural context. Fukuyama and Coleman (1992) describe Asian cultural norms that may influence levels of assertiveness, such as deference to authority, interpersonal harmony, modesty, and avoidance of public shame. Chinese culture places a premium on compliance with tradition, and being assertive can lead to problems. Individuals who grow up in a traditional Chinese family may have little opportunity to develop assertiveness or decision-making skills. Instead, the parents and the elderly are invested with the power to make decisions; children are expected to be obedient and respectful. It is clear that assertion training groups had better take into consideration cultural values and norms. Group leaders need to be mindful of how cultural values can influence the behaviors of clients, and they will also do well to help these members assess the advantages and disadvantages of developing a more assertive style. Members can learn to use what they already have to their advantage. It is also important that members have opportunities to talk about the problems they encounter as they acquire new attitudes and behaviors in their home and at work.

Evaluation of the Cognitive Behavioral Approaches to Groups

CONTRIBUTIONS AND STRENGTHS OF THE APPROACH

One of the strengths of the cognitive behavioral approaches is the emphasis given to education and prevention. CBT is precise in specifying goals, target behaviors, and therapy procedures, which are defined in unambiguous and measurable terms. This specificity allows for links among assessment, treatment, and evaluation strategies. Because of this specificity, explicit criteria for evaluating the success of treatment can be established (Spiegler & Guevremont, 2010).). Although cognitive behavioral practitioners are characterized by a diversity of therapeutic styles, CBT is unified by its empirical foundation, its reliance on the theory and science of cognition and behavior, and its problem-focused orientation (Craske, 2010).

A unifying aspect in the practice of CBT is the attention given to replacing maladaptive cognitions, behaviors, and emotions with more adaptive ones (Craske, 2010). The cognitive behavioral tradition seeks to tailor specific strategies to each client. Consider how specificity applies to a stress management group. Because cognitive behavioral group leaders favor specificity, they take a general term such as "stress" and break it down into its component parts. A group leader would not say, "I'm treating Alfonso for stress." Rather, the group leader might say, "I'm addressing Alfonso's unassertiveness at work, his tendency to catastrophize, his habit of placing demands on himself, and his fears of rejection, all of which contribute to his feeling stressed out." Leaders attempt to fit the treatment to the client's primary processing style.

Behavioral treatments have been subjected to more rigorous experimental investigation than any other psychological therapy (Wilson, 2011). CBT is to be credited for conducting research to determine the efficacy of its techniques. There is a commitment to the systematic evaluation of the procedures used in a group. Those interventions that do not work are eliminated, and techniques are continually being improved. CBT practitioners are open to integrating techniques from various theoretical models into their group work. Cognitive behavioral interventions can be incorporated effectively into both heterogeneous and homogeneous groups and can be used with groups that have a wide variety of specific purposes. Cognitive behavioral groups have been extensively used with inpatient populations with demonstrated success in teaching social skills (Klein, Brabender, & Fallon, 1994).

CBT is broadly applied, serving a diverse range of client populations who exhibit a wide array of psychological disorders (Spiegler & Guevremont, 2010). Cognitive behavioral group therapy has been demonstrated to have beneficial applications for depression, social anxiety, panic and phobia, eating disorders, bipolar disorder, substance abuse, personality disorders, and schizophrenia (see Bieling et al., 2006; Velasquez, Maurer, Crouch, & DiClemente, 2001). A wide range of emotional and behavioral problems are the focus of treatment in cognitive behavioral groups, and there is growing empirical support for the utility of various components of behavioral and cognitive behavioral group therapy (Petrocelli, 2002; White & Freeman, 2000).

A cognitive behavioral group is a concrete example of a humanistic approach in action. The third-generation behavior therapies that have ushered in mindfulness and acceptance-based approaches is evidence of the openness of cognitive behavioral practitioners to incorporating a broader range of techniques in their practice. Certainly, topics such as values, spirituality, relationship, focusing on the present moment, meditation, and mindfulness were all explored in humanistic psychology, and such topics are now being included in contemporary CBT.

Another way that CBT has humanistic dimensions is that group members are collaboratively involved in the selection of both goals and treatment strategies. In many groups, the leader helps members move toward independence by delegating leadership functions to them. Members in a cognitive behavioral group typically carry out part of the therapy independently of the group in homework assignments and in transferring what they are learning in the sessions to everyday living. Therapy then becomes a place where members learn how to learn and become motivated to develop the skills necessary to solve future problems.

A cognitive behavioral approach allows for evaluation of intervention methods. With the focus on research, these techniques are made more precise so that they can be used with specific clients with a variety of specific problems. The cognitive behavioral approaches to group work fit well with the context of the evidence-based practice movement (Craske, 2010). More than any theoretical model in this book, CBT relies on using therapeutic strategies that have the support of empirical evidence, and its effects carry across a wide array of clinical disorders. CBT is very popular with practitioners, with some surveys showing that the majority of clinicians identify themselves with a CBT orientation (Craske, 2010). To a large extent, this popularity is due to strong empirical support for its theoretical framework and to the large number of outcome studies with clinical populations (Beck & Weishaar, 2011). CBT is problem-focused, time-limited, and available in manualized form (Craske, 2010). Regardless of which models influence our style of group leadership, the spirit of CBT can encourage us to strive for accountability rather than simply relying on faith and intuition that our practices are working.

Advantages of a Group Approach According to Brabender and Fallon (1993), even though the focus of a cognitive behavioral group is on individual goals, the group setting permits and augments individual behavior changes in ways that are not possible in individual therapy. They add that the group facilitates progress toward individual goals by providing enhanced reinforcement options. Given the protected group environment, the members are encouraged to practice their newly acquired or modified behaviors spontaneously without fear of negative consequences.

Group leaders can derive practical benefits from the use of specific behavioral techniques, regardless of their theoretical orientation. As a matter of fact, certain experiential and humanistic models can be enhanced by systematically incorporating some of the cognitive behavioral techniques into their relationship-oriented frameworks. Moreover, many behavioral principles can be applied to any kind of group. For example, modeling and reinforcement are essential factors in any successful group. Members are supported (reinforced) in their attempts to be honest, to take risks, to experiment with new behavior, to be active, to take the initiative, and to participate fully in the group. Behavioral principles are instrumental in fostering group cohesion, which enables members to feel that they are not alone with their problems. The mutual learning and exploration of personal concerns bind the members of a group in a meaningful way.

Another strength of the cognitive behavioral approaches is the wide range of techniques that participants can use to specify their goals and to develop the skills needed to achieve these goals. The specificity of the CBT approaches helps group members translate fuzzy goals into concrete plans of action, which helps the members keep these plans clearly in focus. Techniques such as role playing, behavioral rehearsal, coaching, guided practice, modeling, feedback, learning by successive approximations, mindfulness skills, and homework assignments can be included in any group leader's repertoire regardless of theoretical orientation. In addition, specific cognitive behavioral strategies for specific clinical problems are supported by research evidence. These cognitive behavioral principles and techniques lend themselves to short-term groups, which is certainly a factor contributing to the widespread use of CBT groups. Bieling and colleagues (2006) contend that both efficiency and cost factors have contributed to the popularity of cognitive behavioral group therapy.

LIMITATIONS OF THE COGNITIVE BEHAVIORAL APPROACH

Cognitive behavioral groups do have their disadvantages. For example, when groups are too highly structured, as cognitive behavioral groups can often become, individual clients may be prevented from meeting their personal needs. CBT groups have a didactic emphasis, which can be both a strength and a limitation. Groups have an educative function, yet this didactic aspect needs to be balanced with the experiential aspects of group work. A cognitive behavioral group therapist needs to be aware of a range of group process issues, a few of which include observing connections between group members, encouraging open dialogue, promoting expression of feelings, and encouraging useful feedback between group members (Bieling et al., 2006).

When CBT is too rigidly applied, the group leader may lose sight of the people in the group by focusing exclusively on techniques or on solving specific problems. In my opinion, this focus on problems and symptoms can result in a failure to understand the meaning behind an individual's behavior. This is not to say that group therapy should focus on the "underlying causes" of behavior. However, I prefer to deal with factors both in one's external situation that may be eliciting behavioral problems and with one's internal reactions to these environmental variables. For example, in working with Henry, who has great anxiety over relating to men he perceives as being confident, I would be interested in knowing what particular situations in his environment lead to this anxiety, and I would be concerned about his reactions to these situations. How does Henry feel when he is in the presence of confident men? What are some things he tells himself when he meets confident people? What thoughts does Henry have about his own level of confidence? What are some historical roots of his fear? I would not simply employ techniques to eliminate his anxiety; rather, I would want to explore with him the meaning of this anxiety and how it might be related to his lack of self-confidence. I might also encourage Henry to relive some earlier painful experiences in dealing with men and facilitate deeper expression of his feelings and self-exploration. We might explore what significant people in his life told him about what it means to be confident.

In fairness, most cognitive behavior therapists now look at the situation and the response. They are interested in exploring cognitions and, to some extent, the affective elements in the context of the client's problem. In other words, cognitive behavior therapists are interested in more than merely eliminating symptoms of problem behaviors. Certainly, practitioners from any orientation are able to profit from drawing on behavioral interventions and incorporating them in their group work.

Where to Go From Here

If you have an interest in further training in behavior therapy and cognitive behavior therapy, the Association for Behavioral and Cognitive Therapies (ABCT) is an excellent resource. This group was formerly known as the Association for Advancement of Behavior Therapy (AABT). ABCT is a membership organization of more than 4,500 mental health professionals and students who are interested in empirically based behavior therapy or cognitive behavior therapy. ABCT's website provides information on membership services, publications, conventions, careers, resources, and much more.

Association for Behavioral and Cognitive Therapies
305 Seventh Avenue, 16th Floor
New York, NY 10001-6008
Telephone: (212) 647-1890 or (800) 685-AABT
Fax: (212) 647-1865
E-mail: membership@abct.org
Website: www.abct.org

The International Association for Cognitive Psychotherapy (IACP) is a professional, scientific, interdisciplinary organization whose mission is to facilitate the utilization and growth of cognitive psychotherapy as a professional activity and scientific discipline. In addition, the association serves as a resource and information center for matters related to cognitive psychotherapy.

The *Journal of Cognitive Psychotherapy: An International Quarterly*, edited by John Riskind, also provides information on theory, practice, and research in cognitive behavior therapy. Information about the journal is available from IACP.

International Association for Cognitive Psychotherapy
Website: http://www.the-iacp.com/

AUTHOR LECTURES

Watch *Gerald Corey's Perspectives on Theory and Practice of Group Counseling* DVD or visit the *Theory and Practice of Group Counseling* CourseMate website at www.cengagebrain.com/shop/ISBN/0840033869 to watch videos of Dr. Gerald Corey presenting lectures for each chapter. Also available are unique eAudio lectures for each chapter and quiz questions for self-study.

RECOMMENDED SUPPLEMENTARY READINGS

Cognitive-Behavioral Therapy in Groups (Bieling, McCabe, & Antony, 2006) offers ideas on how to structure and lead cognitive behavioral groups. This comprehensive text emphasizes general principles and the practice of CBT groups, discussion of group process concepts from a CBT perspective, cognitive and behavioral strategies useful in groups, and discussion of evidence-based approaches. There are separate chapters for specific disorders including panic disorder, obsessive-compulsive disorder, depression, eating disorders, substance abuse, and personality disorders.

Cognitive Therapy for Challenging Problems (J. Beck, 2005) is a comprehensive account of cognitive therapy procedures applied to clients who present a multiplicity of difficult behaviors. There are chapters dealing with topics such as the therapeutic alliance, setting goals, structuring sessions, homework, identifying cognitions, modifying thoughts and images, modifying assumptions, and modifying core beliefs.

Contemporary Behavior Therapy (Spiegler & Guevremont, 2010) is a comprehensive and up-to-date treatment of basic principles and applications of the behavior therapies. It also contains a fine discussion of ethical issues. Specific chapters deal with procedures that can be usefully applied to group counseling, a few of which are behavioral assessment, modeling therapy, systematic desensitization, cognitive restructuring, cognitive coping skills, and third-generation behavior therapies.

Interviewing and Change Strategies for Helpers: Fundamental Skills and Cognitive Behavioral Interventions (Cormier, Nurius, & Osborn, 2009) is a comprehensive and clearly written textbook dealing with training experiences and skill development. Its excellent documentation offers group practitioners a wealth of material on a variety of topics, such as assessment procedures, selection of goals, development of appropriate treatment programs, and methods of evaluating outcomes. There are useful chapters on a variety of cognitive behavioral strategies, including modeling, reframing, problem solving, cognitive restructuring, stress management, meditation and relaxation, exposure therapy, and self-management strategies.

Mindfulness and Psychotherapy (Germer, Siegel, & Fulton, 2005) is a practical book that provides a comprehensive introduction to mindfulness as it is applied to contemporary therapeutic practice.

Mindfulness and Acceptance: Expanding the Cognitive-Behavioral Tradition (Hayes, Follette, & Linehan, 2004) addresses a new set of behavior therapies that emphasize nontraditional themes such as mindfulness, acceptance, values, spirituality, being in relationship, living in the present moment, and emotional deepening. Included is a useful appendix devoted to resources (books, websites, and training centers) on the application of mindfulness and acceptance practices to therapy.

*Alberti, R. E., & Emmons, M. L. (2008). *Your perfect right: Assertiveness and equality in your life and relationships.* (9th ed.). Atascadero, CA: Impact.

Antony, M. M., & Roemer, L. (2003). Behavior therapy. In A. S. Gurman & S. B. Messer (Eds.), *Essential psychotherapies: Theory and practice* (2nd ed., pp. 182–223). New York: Guilford Press.

Bandura, A. (1969). *Principles of behavior modification.* New York: Holt, Rinehart & Winston.

Bandura, A. (1977). *Social learning theory.* Englewood Cliffs, NJ: Prentice Hall.

Bandura, A. (1986). *Social foundations of thought and action: A social cognitive theory.* Englewood Cliffs, NJ: Prentice Hall.

*Beck, A. T. (1976). *Cognitive therapy and the emotional disorders.* New York: New American Library.

Beck, A. T. (1997). Cognitive therapy: Reflections. In J. K. Zeig (Ed.), *The evolution of psychotherapy: The third conference* (pp. 55–67). New York: Brunner/Mazel.

*Beck, J. S. (1995). *Cognitive therapy: Basics and beyond.* New York: Guilford Press.

*Beck, J. S. (2005). *Cognitive therapy for challenging problems.* New York: Guilford Press.

*Beck, A. T., & Weishaar, M. E. (2011). Cognitive therapy. In R. J. Corsini & D. Wedding (Eds.), *Current psychotherapies* (9th ed., pp. 276–309). Belmont, CA: Brooks/Cole, Cengage Learning.

*Bieling, P. J., McCabe, R. E., & Antony, M. M. (2006). *Cognitive-behavioral therapy in groups.* New York: Guilford Press.

*Bond, F., & Flaxman, P. (2010). *Acceptance and commitment therapy: Distinctive features.* New York: Routledge (Taylor & Francis Group).

Brabender, V., & Fallon, A. (1993). *Models of inpatient group therapy.* Washington, DC: American Psychological Association.

*Cormier, S., Nurius, P. S., & Osborn, C. J. (2009). *Interviewing and change strategies for helpers: Fundamental skills and cognitive behavioral interventions* (6th ed.). Belmont, CA: Brooks/Cole, Cengage Learning.

*Crane, R. (2008). *Mindfulness-based cognitive therapy: Distinctive features.* New York: Routledge (Taylor & Francis Group).

*Craske, M. G. (2010). *Cognitive-behavioral therapy.* Washington, DC: American Psychological Association.

Dattilio, F. M. (2002). Using homework assignments in couple and family therapy. *Journal of Clinical Psychology, 58*(5), 570–585.

Dattilio, F. M. (2003). Family therapy. In R. L. Leahy (Ed.), *Roadblocks in cognitive behavior therapy* (pp. 236–252). New York: Guilford Press.

Dobson, D., & Dobson, K. S. (2009). *Evidence-based practice of cognitive-behavioral therapy.* New York: Guilford Press.

Dobson, K. S. (2009). *Handbook of cognitive-behavioral therapies* (3rd ed.). New York: Guilford Press.

Enns, C. Z. (1993). Twenty years of feminist counseling and therapy: From naming biases to implementing multifaceted practice. *The Counseling Psychologist, 21*(1), 3–87.

*Freeman, A., & Dattilio, F. M. (1994). Cognitive therapy. In J. L. Ronch, W. Van Ornum, & N. C. Stilwell (Eds.), *The counseling sourcebook: A practical reference on contemporary issues.* (pp. 60–71). New York: Continuum Press.

Fukuyama, M. A., & Coleman, N. C. (1992). A model for bicultural assertion training with Asian-Pacific American college students: A pilot study. *Journal for Specialists in Group Work, 17*(4), 210–217.

---

* Books and articles marked with an asterisk (*) are suggested for further study.

Germer, C. K. (2005a). Mindfulness: What is it: What does it matter? In C. K. Germer, R. D. Siegel, & P. R. Fulton (Eds.), *Mindfulness and psychotherapy* (pp. 3–27). New York: Guilford Press.

Germer, C. K. (2005b). Teaching mindfulness in therapy. In C. K. Germer, R. D. Siegel, & P. R. Fulton (Eds.), *Mindfulness and psychotherapy* (pp. 113–129). New York: Guilford Press.

*Germer, C. K., Siegel, R. D., & Fulton, P. R. (Eds.). (2005). *Mindfulness and psychotherapy.* New York: Guilford Press.

*Gilbert, P., & Leahy, R. L. (2009). *The therapeutic relationship in the cognitive behavioral psychotherapies.* New York: Routledge (Taylor & Francis Group).

Goldfried, M. R., & Davison, G. C. (1994). *Clinical behavior therapy* (expanded ed.). New York: Wiley Interscience.

Hayes, S. C. (2004). Acceptance and commitment therapy and the new behavior therapies: Mindfulness, acceptance, and relationship. In S. C. Hayes, V. M. Follette, & M. M. Linehan (Eds.), *Mindfulness and acceptance: Expanding the cognitive-behavioral tradition* (pp. 1–29). New York: Guilford Press.

*Hayes, S. C., Follette, V. M., & Linehan, M. M. (Eds.). (2004). *Mindfulness and acceptance: Expanding the cognitive-behavioral tradition.* New York: Guilford Press.

*Hayes, S. C., & Pankey, J. (2003). Acceptance. In W. O'Donohue, J. E. Fisher, & S. C. Hayes (Eds.), *Cognitive behavior therapy: Applying empirically supported techniques in your practice* (pp. 4–9). Hoboken, NJ: Wiley.

*Hayes, S. C., Strosahl, K. D., & Houts, A. (Eds.). (2005). *A practical guide to acceptance and commitment therapy.* New York: Springer.

Hayes, S. C., Strosahl, K. D., & Wilson, K. G. (1999). *Acceptance and commitment therapy: An experiential approach to behavior change.* New York: Guilford Press.

Hays, P. A. (2009). Integrating evidence-based practice, cognitive-behavior therapy, and multicultural therapy: Ten steps for culturally competent practice. *Professional Psychology: Research and Practice, 40*(4), 354–360.

Henderson, D., & Thompson, C. L. (2011). *Counseling children* (8th ed.). Belmont, CA: Brooks/Cole, Cengage Learning.

*Kabat-Zinn, J. (1990). *Full catastrophe living: Using the wisdom of your body and mind to face stress, pain, and illness.* New York: Dell.

Kabat-Zinn, J. (1994). *Wherever you go there you are: Mindfulness meditation in everyday life.* New York: Hyperion.

Kaplan, A., & Laygo, R. (2003). Stress management. In W. O'Donohue, J. E. Fisher, & S. C. Hayes (Eds.), *Cognitive behavior therapy: Applying empirically supported techniques in your practice* (pp. 411–416). Hoboken, NJ: Wiley.

Kazantzis, N., & Deane, F. P. (1999). Psychologists' use of homework assignments in clinical practice. *Professional Psychology: Research and Practice, 30,* 581–585.

*Kazantzis, N., Deane, F. P., Ronan, K. R., & L'Abate, L. (2005). *Using homework assignments in cognitive behavior therapy.* New York: Routledge (Taylor & Francis Group).

Kazantzis, N., & Lampropoulos, G. K. (2002). The use of homework in psychotherapy: An introduction. *Journal of Clinical Psychology, 58*(5), 487–488.

*Klein, R., Brabender, V., & Fallon, A. (1994). Inpatient group therapy. In A. Fuhriman & G. Burlingame (Eds.), *Handbook of group psychotherapy: An empirical and clinical synthesis* (pp. 370–415). New York: Wiley.

*Lazarus, A. A. (1989). *The practice of multimodal therapy.* Baltimore: Johns Hopkins University.

*Lazarus, A. A. (1993). Tailoring the therapeutic relationship, or being an authentic chameleon. *Psychotherapy, 30,* 404–407.

Lazarus, A. A. (1996a). Some reflections after 40 years of trying to be an effective psychotherapist. *Psychotherapy, 33*(1), 142–145.

Lazarus, A. A. (1996b). The utility and futility of combining treatments in psychotherapy. *Clinical Psychology: Science and Practice, 3*(1), 59–68.

Lazarus, A. A. (2005). Multimodal therapy. In J. C. Norcross & M. R. Goldfried (Eds.), *Handbook of psychotherapy integration* (2nd ed., pp. 105–120). New York: Oxford University Press.

*Lazarus, A. A. (2008). Multimodal therapy. In R. J. Corsini & D. Wedding (Eds.), *Current psychotherapies* (8th ed., pp. 368–401). Belmont, CA: Brooks/ Cole, Cengage Learning.

Ledley, D. R., Marx, B. P., & Heimberg, R. G. (2005). *Making cognitive-behavioral therapy work: Clinical processes for new practitioners.* New York: Guilford Press.

Linehan, M. M. (1993a). *Cognitive-behavioral treatment of borderline personality disorder.* New York: Guilford Press.

Linehan, M. M. (1993b). *Skills training manual for treating borderline personality disorder.* New York: Guilford Press.

Meichenbaum, D. (1985). *Stress inoculation training.* New York: Pergamon Press.

Meichenbaum, D. (1986). Cognitive behavior modification. In F. H. Kanfer & A. P. Goldstein (Eds.), *Helping people change: A textbook of methods* (3rd ed.). New York: Pergamon Press.

Meichenbaum, D. (1993). Stress inoculation training: A 20-year update. In P. M. Lehrer & R. L. Woolfolk (Eds.), *Principles and practice of stress management* (2nd ed., pp. 373– 406). New York: Guilford Press.

Meichenbaum, D. (1994). *A clinical handbook/practical therapist manual for assessing and treating adults with posttraumatic stress disorder (PTSD).* Waterloo, Ontario, Canada: Institute Press.

*Meichenbaum, D. (2003). Stress inoculation training. In W. O'Donohue, J. E. Fisher, & S. C. Hayes (Eds.), *Cognitive behavior therapy: Applying empirically supported techniques in your practice* (pp. 407–410). Hoboken, NJ: Wiley.

Miller, W. R., & Rollnick, S. (2002). *Motivational interviewing: Preparing people for change* (2nd ed.). New York: Guilford Press.

Miltenberger, R. G. (2004). *Behavior modification: Principles and procedures* (3rd ed.). Belmont, CA: Wadsworth, Cengage Learning.

Morgan, S. P. (2005). Depression: Turning toward life. In C. K. Germer, R. D. Siegel, & P. R. Fulton (Eds.), *Mindfulness and psychotherapy* (pp. 130–151). New York: Guilford Press.

Naugle, A. E., & Maher, S. (2003). Modeling and behavioral rehearsal. In W. O'Donohue, J. E. Fisher, & S. C. Hayes (Eds.), *Cognitive behavior therapy: Applying empirically supported techniques in your practice* (pp. 238–246). Hoboken, NJ: Wiley.

* Neenan, M., & Dryden, W. (2004). *Cognitive therapy: 100 key points and techniques.* New York: Routledge (Taylor & Francis Group).

*Organista, K. (2000). Latinos. In J. R. White & A. Freeman (Eds.), *Cognitive-behavioral group therapy for specific problems and populations* (pp. 281– 303). Washington, DC: American Psychological Association.

Petrocelli, J. V. (2002). Effectiveness of group cognitive-behavioral therapy for general symptomatology: A meta-analysis. *Journal for Specialists in Group Work, 27*(1), 92–115.

Reinecke, M. A., & Freeman, A. (2003). Cognitive therapy. In A. S. Gurman & S. B. Messer (Eds.), *Essential psychotherapies: Theory and practice* (2nd ed., pp. 224–271). New York: Guilford Press.

Robins, C. J., Schmidt, H., & Linehan, M. M. (2004). Dialectical behavior therapy: Synthesizing radical acceptance with skillful means. In S. C. Hayes, V. M. Follette, & M. M. Linehan (Eds.), *Mindfulness and acceptance: Expanding the cognitive-behavioral tradition* (pp. 30–44). New York: Guilford Press.

*Roemer, L., & Orsillio, S. M. (2009). *Mindfulness and acceptance-based behavioral therapies in practice.* New York: Guilford Press.

*Rose, S. D. (1998). *Group therapy with troubled youth: A cognitive-behavioral interactive approach.* Thousand Oaks, CA: Sage.

Rose, S. D., & Edleson, J. (1987). *Working with children and adolescents in groups.* San Francisco: Jossey-Bass.

*Segal, Z. V., Williams, J. M. G., & Teasdale, J. D. (2002). *Mindfulness-based cognitive therapy for depression: A new approach to preventing relapse.* New York: Guilford Press.

Shechtman, Z. (2002). Child group psychotherapy in the school at the threshold of a new millennium. *Journal of Counseling and Development, 80*(3), 293–299.

Spiegler, M. D. (2008). Behavior therapy II: Cognitive-behavioral therapy. In J. Frew & M. D. Spiegler (Eds.), *Contemporary psychotherapies for a diverse world* (pp. 320–359). Boston: Lahaska Press.

*Spiegler, M. D., & Guevremont, D. C. (2010). *Contemporary behavior therapy* (5th ed.). Belmont, CA: Wadsworth, Cengage Learning.

*Swales, M. A., & Heard, H. L. (2008). *Dialectical behaviour therapy: Distinctive features.* New York: Routledge (Taylor & Francis Group).

*Turner, S., Beidel, D., & Cooley, M. (1994). *Social effectiveness therapy.* Charleston, SC: Turndel.

Velasquez, M. M., Maurer, G. G., Crouch, C., & DiClemente, C. C. (2001). *Group treatment for substance abuse: A stage-of-change therapy model.* New York: Guilford Press.

Vernon, A. (2004). Using cognitive behavioral techniques. In B. T. Erford (Ed.), *Professional school counseling: A handbook of theories, programs & practices* (pp. 91–99). Austin, TX: CAPS Press.

*Watson, D. L., & Tharp, R. G. (2007). *Self-directed behavior: Self-modification for personal adjustment* (9th ed.). Belmont, CA: Brooks/Cole, Cengage Learning.

*White, J. R. (2000a). Depression. In J. R. White & A. Freeman (Eds.), *Cognitive-behavioral group therapy for specific problems and populations* (pp. 29–61). Washington, DC: American Psychological Association.

*White, J. R. (2000b). Introduction. In J. R. White & A. Freeman (Eds.), *Cognitive-behavioral group therapy for specific problems and populations* (pp. 3–25). Washington, DC: American Psychological Association.

*White, J. R., & Freeman, A. (Eds.). (2000). *Cognitive-behavioral group therapy for specific problems and populations.* Washington, DC: American Psychological Association.

*Wills, F. (2009). *Beck's cognitive therapy: Distinctive features.* New York: Routledge (Taylor & Francis Group).

Wilson, G. T. (2011). Behavior therapy. In R. J. Corsini & D. Wedding (Eds.), *Current psychotherapies* (9th ed., pp. 235–275). Belmont, CA: Brooks/Cole, Cengage Learning.

CHAPTER FOURTEEN

Rational Emotive Behavior Therapy in Groups

Introduction

Albert Ellis founded **rational therapy** in the mid-1950s and was one of the first therapists to emphasize the influential role of cognition in behavior. In the early 1960s Ellis changed the name to **rational emotive therapy (RET)**, and later still to **rational emotive behavior therapy (REBT)**, because of his contention that the model had always stressed the reciprocal interactions among cognition, emotion, and behavior. REBT was one of the first cognitive behavior therapies, and today it continues to be a major cognitive behavioral approach.

Based in part on his own experiences conquering emotional problems and their consequent inhibited behavior during his youth, Ellis pioneered a large number of thinking, feeling, and activity-oriented methods (Ellis, 1996, 2001a, 2004a). One of Ellis's problems, for example, was a fear of speaking in public. To overcome his anxieties, Ellis developed a cognitive philosophical approach combined with in vivo desensitization and homework assignments, which involved speaking in public regardless of how uncomfortable he might initially be. With these cognitive behavioral methods, Ellis said, he had conquered some of his worst fears. At age 19 he also feared meeting women, so he forced himself to use behavioral methods to overcome his shyness. He gave himself "one lousy minute" to talk to each of 100 women. Ellis (1996) reports: "I made verbal overtures to 100 different women sitting on park benches in the Bronx Botanical Gardens, got rejected for dating by all of them (one woman kissed me in the park, and made a date for later that evening, but never showed up!)" (p. 109). Ellis believed that taking these actions helped him to overcome his fear of talking to women.

In his clinical practice, Ellis developed active and direct ways of working. He combined humanistic and behavior therapy, and his pioneering efforts earned him the right to be known as the father of REBT and the grandfather of cognitive behavioral therapy. Ellis lived a very active life until his death in 2007 at age 93. As he put it, "I am busy spreading the gospel according to St. Albert." If you are interested in learning more about the life and work of

Albert Ellis, I recommend two of his books: *Rational Emotive Behavior Therapy: It Works for Me—It Can Work for You* (Ellis, 2004a) and *All Out! An Autobiography* (Ellis, 2010).

REBT is based on the assumption that we are not disturbed solely by our early or later environments but that we have strong inclinations to disturb ourselves consciously and unconsciously. We do this largely by taking our goals and values, which we mainly learn from our families and culture, and changing them into absolute "shoulds," "oughts," and "musts" (Ellis, 1992). To overcome this self-indoctrination, which has resulted in irrational thinking, REBT therapists employ active/directive techniques such as teaching, suggestion, persuasion, and homework assignments, and they challenge clients to substitute a rational belief system for an irrational one (Ellis, 2001a, 2004a; Dryden, 2009b).

The rational emotive behavior approach to group therapy considers the relationship between the group leader and the members to be important mainly as a means to an end—that is, of getting results. It emphasizes the group therapist's ability and willingness to challenge, confront, and convince the members to practice activities (both in and outside of the group) that will lead to constructive changes in thinking and behaving. The approach stresses action—doing something about the insights one gains in the therapy group. Change, it is assumed, will come about mainly by a commitment to practice new behaviors consistently. The most efficient way to bring about lasting emotional and behavioral change is for group members to change their way of thinking (Dryden, 2007).

Ellis (2011) contends that REBT is particularly applicable to group therapy and is frequently the treatment of choice. The group leader, and members as well, can help others to learn and apply the principles and procedures of REBT in group sessions. Ellis notes that group work affords many opportunities to agree on homework assignments, to practice assertiveness skills, to take risks by practicing different behaviors, to challenge self-defeating thinking, to learn from the experiences of others, and to interact therapeutically and socially with each other in after-group sessions. REBT lends itself to short-term group-oriented procedures, and group members are often able to make significant changes with brief therapy (10 to 20 sessions).

Key Concepts

SOME HYPOTHESES AND ASSUMPTIONS OF REBT

A few of the basic assumptions of REBT can be categorized under these main postulates (Ellis, 2004a, 2004b, 2011):

- Thinking, feeling, and behaving continually interact with and influence one another. We disturb ourselves cognitively, emotionally, and behaviorally. REBT uses various techniques to show us how to minimize our self-sabotaging thoughts, feelings, and behaviors.

- When unfortunate events occur, we tend to create irrational beliefs about these events characterized by absolutist and dogmatic thinking. It is not unfortunate events by themselves that cause emotional disturbance; rather, irrational beliefs about these events often lead to psychological problems.

- If we hope to change, we need to (1) acknowledge that we are mainly responsible for our own disturbed thoughts, emotions, and actions; (2) look at how we are thinking, feeling, and behaving when we needlessly disturb ourselves; and (3) commit ourselves to the hard work that it will take to change.

ORIGINS OF EMOTIONAL DISTURBANCE

A central concept of REBT is the role that absolutist "shoulds," "oughts," and "musts" play when people become and remain emotionally disturbed. We forcefully, rigidly, and emotionally subscribe to many grandiose "musts" that result in our needlessly disturbing ourselves. According to Ellis (2001a, 2001b), feelings of anxiety, depression, hurt, shame, rage, and guilt are largely initiated and perpetuated by a belief system based on irrational ideas that were uncritically embraced, often during early childhood. In addition to taking on dysfunctional beliefs from others, Ellis stresses that we also invent "musts" on our own. Ellis (1994, 1997; Ellis & Dryden, 2007; Ellis & Harper, 1997) contends that most of our dysfunctional beliefs can be reduced to three main forms of "*mustur*bation":

1. "I *absolutely must* do well and be approved of by significant others. I must win their approval or else I am an inadequate, worthless person."

2. "You *must* under all conditions and at all times treat me considerately, kindly, lovingly, and fairly. If you don't, you are no damned good and are a rotten person."

3. "Conditions under which I live *absolutely must* be comfortable so that I can get what I want without too much effort. If not, it is *awful*; I *can't* stand it and life is no good."

Rational emotive behavior therapy is grounded on existential principles in many respects. Although parents and society play a significant role in contributing to our emotional disturbance, we do not need to be victims of this indoctrination that takes place in our early years. We may not have had the resources during childhood to challenge parental and societal messages. As psychological adults now, however, we can become aware of how adhering to negative and destructive beliefs actually hampers our efforts to live fully, and we are also in a position to modify these beliefs.

THE A-B-C THEORY

The **A-B-C theory** of personality and emotional disturbance is central to REBT theory and practice. The A-B-C theory maintains that when we have an emotional reaction at point C (the emotional Consequence), after some Activating event that occurred at point A, it is not the event itself (A) that causes the emotional state (C), although it may contribute to it. It is the Belief system (B), or the beliefs that we have about the event, that mainly creates C. For example, if you feel depressed (C) over not getting a promotion at work (A), it is not the fact that you weren't promoted that causes your depression; it is your belief (B) about the event. By believing that you absolutely should have been promoted and that not receiving it means that you are a failure, you "construct" the emotional consequence of feeling depressed. Thus, we are largely responsible for creating our own emotional disturbances through the beliefs we associate with the events of our lives.

Ellis (2011) maintains that we have the capacity to significantly change our cognitions, emotions, and behaviors. We can best accomplish this goal by avoiding preoccupying ourselves with the activating events at A and by acknowledging the futility of dwelling endlessly on the emotional consequences at C. We can choose to examine, challenge, modify, and uproot B—the irrational beliefs we hold about the activating events at A.

CONFRONTING IRRATIONAL BELIEFS

REBT group leaders begin by teaching group members the A-B-C theory. When they have come to see how their irrational beliefs are contributing to their emotional and behavioral disturbances, they are ready to Dispute (D) these beliefs. D represents the application of scientific principles to challenge self-defeating philosophies and to dispose of unrealistic and unverifiable hypotheses. *Cognitive restructuring*, a central technique of cognitive therapy, teaches people how to make themselves less disturbed (Ellis, 2003). One of the most effective methods of helping people reduce their emotional disturbances is to show them how to actively and forcefully dispute these irrational beliefs until they surrender them. This process of disputation involves three other Ds: (1) *detecting* irrational beliefs and seeing that they are illogical and unrealistic, (2) *debating* these irrational beliefs and showing oneself how they are unsupported by evidence, and (3) *discriminating* between irrational thinking and rational thinking (Ellis, 1994, 1996).

After D comes E, or the Effect of disputing—the relinquishing of self-destructive ideologies, the acquisition of effective new beliefs, and a greater acceptance of oneself, of others, and of the inevitable frustrations of everyday life. This new philosophy of life has, of course, a practical side—a concrete F, if you wish. In the previous example, E would translate into a rational statement such as this: "I'd like to have gotten the job, but there is no reason I have to get what I want. It is unfortunate that I did not get the job, but it is not terrible." According to REBT theory, the ultimate desired result is that the person experiences a healthy negative emotion, in this case, disappointment and sadness, rather than depression.

Group members learn to separate their rational (or functional) beliefs from their irrational (or dysfunctional) beliefs and to understand the origins of their emotional disturbances as well as those of other members. Participants are taught the many ways in which they can (1) free themselves of their irrational life philosophy so that they can function more effectively as an individual and as a relational being and (2) learn more appropriate ways of responding so that they won't needlessly feel disturbed about the realities of living. The group members help and support one another in these learning endeavors.

SELF-RATING AND LEARNING SELF-ACCEPTANCE

According to Ellis (2001b; Ellis & Harper, 1997), we have a strong tendency not only to rate our acts and behaviors as "good" or "bad," "worthy" or "unworthy," but also to rate ourselves as a total person on the basis of our performances. Self-rating stems from rigid demands. Ellis contends that we oftentimes rate our performances as ineffectual and then illogically overgeneralize by rating ourselves as incompetent and worthless. This self-rating process—"If I fail at something, I'm a failure in life."—constitutes one of the main sources of our emotional disturbances. The opposite of self-rating is learning to accept ourselves unconditionally in spite of our imperfections. REBT group leaders teach members the importance of self-acceptance by showing them how to separate the evaluation of their behaviors from the evaluation of themselves—their essence and their totality—and how they can accept themselves in spite of their imperfections.

GOALS OF A REBT GROUP

The basic goal of REBT is to help clients replace rigid demands with flexible preferences. According to Ellis (2001b; 2011), two of the main goals of REBT are to assist clients in the process of achieving *unconditional self-acceptance* (USA) and *unconditional other acceptance* (UOA), and to see how these are interrelated. To the degree that group members are able to accept themselves, they are able to accept others. The process of REBT involves a collaborative effort on the part of both the group leader and the members in choosing realistic and self-enhancing outcome goals. The therapist's task is to help group participants to differentiate between realistic and unrealistic goals and self-defeating and self-enhancing goals (Dryden, 2007). Further goals are to teach members how to change their dysfunctional emotions and behaviors into healthy ones and to cope with almost any unfortunate event that may arise in their lives (Ellis, 2001b).

REBT aims at providing group members with tools for experiencing healthy emotions (such as sadness and concern) about negative activating events rather than unhealthy emotions (such as depression and anxiety) about these events so that they can live richer and more satisfying lives. To accomplish this basic objective, group members learn practical ways to identify their underlying irrational beliefs, to critically evaluate such beliefs, and to replace them with rational beliefs.

Basically, group members are taught that they are largely responsible for their own emotional reactions; that they can minimize their emotional disturbances by paying attention to their self-verbalizations and by changing their irrational beliefs; and that if they acquire a new and more realistic philosophy, they can cope effectively with most of the unfortunate events in their lives. Although the therapeutic goals of REBT are essentially the same for both individual and group therapy, the two differ in some of the specific methods and techniques employed, as you will see in the discussion that follows.

Role and Functions of the Group Leader

The therapeutic activities of an REBT group are carried out with a central purpose: to help participants internalize a rational philosophy of life, just as they internalized a set of dogmatic and extreme beliefs derived from their sociocultural environment and from their own invention. In working toward this ultimate aim, the group leader has several specific functions and tasks. The first task is to show group members how they have largely created their own emotional and behavioral disturbances. The leader helps group members to identify and challenge the irrational beliefs they originally unquestioningly accepted, demonstrates how they are continuing to indoctrinate themselves with these beliefs, and teaches them how to modify their thinking by developing rational alternative beliefs. It is the group leader's task to teach members how to stop the vicious circle of the self-blaming and other-blaming process.

REBT assumes that people's irrational beliefs are so deeply ingrained that they will not change easily. Thus, to bring about a significant cognitive change, leaders employ a variety of active cognitive and emotive techniques (Ellis, 1996, 2001b; Ellis & Dryden, 2007). REBT group practitioners favor interventions such as questioning, confronting, negotiating homework assignments, and helping members experiment with new ways of thinking, feeling, and doing. REBT group leaders are active in teaching the theoretical model, proposing methods of coping, and teaching members strategies for testing hypotheses and solutions.

REBT group leaders assume the role of a psychological educator, and they tend to avoid relating too closely to their members and thus avoid having them increase their dependency tendencies. They provide unconditional acceptance rather than warmth and approval (Dryden, 2009b). However, REBT group practitioners demonstrate respect for the members of their groups and also tend to be collaborative, encouraging, supportive, and mentoring.

REBT practitioners employ a directive role in encouraging members to commit themselves to practicing in everyday situations what they are learning in the group sessions. They view what goes on during the group as important, but they realize that the hard work between sessions and after therapy is terminated is even more crucial. The group context provides members with tools they can use to become self-reliant and to accept themselves unconditionally as they encounter new problems in daily living.

Application: Therapeutic Techniques and Procedures

Ellis originally developed REBT to try to make psychotherapy shorter and more efficient than most other systems of therapy; hence, it is intrinsically a brief therapy. As applied to groups, REBT mainly employs interventions that teach group members how to tackle practical problems of living in a brief and efficient way (Ellis, 2001b).

From the origin of the approach, REBT has utilized a wide range of cognitive, emotive, and behavioral methods with most clients. Like other cognitive behavioral therapies, REBT blends techniques to change clients' patterns of thinking, feeling, and acting. It is an integrative therapy, selectively adapting various methods that are also used in existential, humanistic, phenomenologically oriented therapeutic approaches, but the emphasis is on the cognitive and behavioral dimensions (Ellis, 2001b). REBT focuses on specific techniques for changing a client's self-defeating thoughts in concrete situations. In addition to modifying beliefs, this approach helps group members see how their beliefs influence what they feel and what they do; thus, there is also a concern for changing feelings and behaviors that flow from rigid and extreme beliefs. This model aims to minimize symptoms by bringing about a profound change in philosophy. REBT practitioners are flexible and creative in their use of methods and tailor their techniques to the unique needs of group members (Dryden, 2007).

COGNITIVE METHODS OF REBT IN GROUPS

From a cognitive perspective, REBT demonstrates to clients that their irrational beliefs and the self-talk that is derived from these beliefs are keeping them disturbed. Various techniques are used to dispel these self-defeating cognitions and teach people how to acquire a rational approach to living. As mentioned earlier, in an REBT group there is an emphasis on thinking, disputing, debating, persuading, interpreting, explaining, and teaching. Some of the cognitive techniques often used in REBT groups are described below.

Teaching the A-B-Cs of REBT The A-B-C theory is taught to clients undergoing individual or group therapy. Group members are taught that no matter how or where they originally acquired their absolute "shoulds," "oughts," and "musts," they have the power now to begin to surrender these dysfunctional beliefs. They are shown ways to apply the A-B-C theory to practical problems they encounter in everyday life. Group members can quickly learn how they disturb themselves. The A-B-Cs of their problems can be clearly and simply shown, easily grasped, and quickly put to use in therapy.

Active Disputation of Irrational Beliefs Group participants are taught how to check and modify their rigid and extreme beliefs about themselves, others, and life conditions. For example, a member may cling to the extreme belief that everyone must think well of her or her self-esteem will be damaged beyond repair. Therapists show group members how to detect their demands, "awfulizing beliefs, and their "self- and other-downing beliefs." In their active and didactic role, REBT leaders focus on disputing the rigid and extreme ideas of individuals. They demonstrate how such ideas bring about unnecessary disturbances, and they persuade clients to change or surrender these dysfunctional beliefs. For best results, active disputation needs to go beyond the cognitive level and include emotional disputing. Members challenge their faulty thinking, and they also engage in a number of emotive methods (described later) as a way of extending the impact of disputing beliefs.

Teaching Coping Self-Statements Group members are taught how self-destructive beliefs can be countered by sensible, rational, coping self-statements. They are expected to monitor their manner of speaking by writing down and analyzing the quality of their language. For example, a member might tell herself: "I *must* perform well, which means being perfect. People will give me approval and love only when I'm perfect, and I *absolutely* need this acceptance from others to feel worthwhile." By becoming aware of the absolutist and demanding quality of her internal and external speech, she can learn how what she tells herself is setting her up for failure. It is possible for her to learn that her demands of being perfect will inevitably result in psychological disturbance, disillusionment, and heartache. She can replace these self-defeating statements with coping statements: "I can still accept myself in spite of my imperfections. I don't have to do everything perfectly well to feel worthwhile as a person."

Psychoeducational Methods REBT and most cognitive behavior therapy programs take an educational approach with clients. Therapists educate group members about the nature of their problems and how treatment is likely to proceed. In REBT groups the members acquire skills in generalizing what they are learning in the group to present and future problems. Ultimately, group leaders teach members how to become their own therapists (Dryden, 2009b). Rather than merely lecturing to group members, therapists strive to ask members how particular concepts apply to them. Group members are more likely to cooperate with a treatment program if they understand how the group therapy process works and if they understand why particular techniques are being used (Ledley, Marx, & Heimberg, 2005). REBT offers many resources for dealing with general emotional problems and specific concerns such as overcoming addictions, dealing with depression, managing anger, understanding and coping with weight problems, becoming assertive, and overcoming procrastination.

Cognitive Homework Those who participate in REBT groups are given cognitive homework assignments, which consist of ways of applying the A-B-C theory to many of the problems in daily life. Members may be given the "REBT Self-Help Form" (reproduced in the *Student Manual* that accompanies this text), on which they list their irrational beliefs. In an adjoining column they write down a disputing statement for each irrational belief. In another column they record an effective rational belief to replace the irrational belief. Finally, they record the feelings and behaviors that they experienced after arriving at an effective rational belief. During the week, group members make the time to record and think about how their beliefs contribute to their personal problems, and they work hard at uprooting these self-defeating cognitions. When they return to the group, they can bring up specific situations in which they did well or in which they experienced difficulty.

EMOTIVE METHODS IN REBT GROUPS

As we have seen, REBT is almost always a multimodal approach, using several cognitive, behavioral, and emotive methods to bring about change (Dryden, 2007, 2009b; Dryden & Neenan, 2006; Ellis, 2001a; Ellis & MacLaren, 2005). Emotive techniques include unconditional acceptance, rational-emotive imagery, the use of humor, and shame-attacking exercises. Emotive techniques tend to be vivid and evocative in nature, yet the main purpose is to dispute clients' irrational beliefs. Group leaders teach members that once they have achieved intellectual insight they can use a variety of methods in changing their thoughts, behavior, and feelings (Dryden, 2007, 2009b). These techniques are explored in more detail in the following sections.

Unconditional Acceptance Group members often burden themselves with fears of being "discovered" for what they really are and then being rejected. Group leaders can model an accepting attitude that goes beyond what members have done or felt. This kind of REBT-flavored unconditional acceptance creates a group atmosphere that allows members to feel personally accepted, even though some of their beliefs and behaviors will likely be challenged.

Rational-Emotive Imagery Using the technique of **rational-emotive imagery (REI)**, group members are asked to vividly imagine one of the worst things that might happen to them. They imagine themselves in specific situations where they experience disturbing feelings. Then they are shown how to train themselves to develop healthy emotions in place of disruptive ones. Members work actively to implicitly exchange their irrational beliefs for rational ones, thereby changing their behavior in the situation. The group therapist's role is to verify that these emotional changes are in fact produced by implicit belief changes. For example, leaders can encourage group members to imagine vividly that they keep failing and keep getting criticized and can thereby produce in them extreme feelings of inadequacy. Then members are shown how to change their feelings to regret and disappointment instead of feelings of worthlessness. Members practice this process for at least 30 days in a row until they have trained themselves to feel regretful and disappointed automatically when they experience failure instead of feeling devastated. Members might imagine some of their worst fears coming true. Within the group, they can share these fears, gain some emotional insight on how such fears control much of what they do and say, and eventually learn to respond in different ways. Imagery work is a safe prelude to actually confronting one's fears in daily life. (For a more detailed discussion of REI, see Ellis, 2001a.)

Use of Humor Humor has both cognitive and emotional benefits in bringing about change. When people disturb themselves, Ellis (2001a) believes they usually lose their sense of humor and take themselves far too seriously. As one of its main techniques to combat the kind of exaggerated thinking that leads people into trouble, REBT employs a good deal of humor. It teaches group members to laugh—not at themselves but at their self-defeating beliefs. Leaders use humor to show group members how ridiculous some of their irrational ideas actually are (Dryden, 2009b). Although introducing humor inappropriately or too soon in a group can present problems, once trust has been established, the members are generally far more ready to see the folly of some of their ways and can actually enjoy laughing at some of their behaviors. (For a more detailed discussion of humor and comical songs, see Ellis, 2001a.)

Shame-Attacking Exercises The rationale underlying **shame-attacking exercises** is that emotional disturbance related to the self is often characterized by feelings of shame, guilt, anxiety, and depression. The more that people directly face and deal with the irrational beliefs behind these feelings, the less likely they are to remain emotionally disturbed. Members in REBT groups are often encouraged to participate in risk-taking activities as a way to challenge their fears of looking foolish, but leaders discourage members from doing anything that is illegal, immoral, or that will unduly alarm other people. Practitioners employ shame-attacking exercises to teach group participants to accept themselves in spite of reactions from others. These exercises are aimed at increasing self-acceptance and mature responsibility, as well as helping members to see that much of what they think of as being shameful has to do with the way they define reality for themselves. The main thing clients learn from shame-attacking exercises is that disapproval does not have to affect their worth or change them, nor does the fear of disapproval have to prevent them from doing things they consider right. In the course of doing "shameful" things in a group, members move toward unconditional self-acceptance.

Group members frequently admit that they are inhibiting themselves from doing many things they would like to do because of their fear of what others might think. In a group situation other members might exert therapeutic pressure and also provide support for individuals to experiment with risky behaviors, first in the group and then in daily life situations. Ellis (2002) describes a few exercises that clients might be induced to perform in public. These include wearing outlandish clothes, borrowing money from a stranger, or shouting out the stops in the train or bus. If clients do some of these acts and also work on not feeling ashamed, they are likely to overcome their fear of looking foolish that keeps them from doing things they would like to do. Ellis suggests that it is better to combine cognitive homework with these in vivo shame-attacking exercises. Here are a few other examples of possible shame-attacking exercises:

- Walk through a park singing at the top of your voice.
- In a crowded elevator, tell people that you are glad they could attend this important meeting that you have called.
- Talk to animals, and pretend that they are talking back to you.
- Ride in a crowded elevator facing the rear wall.
- Tie a ribbon around a banana and "walk it" down a street.
- In public, shout out the exact time by saying, "The time is 11:11 and 20 seconds."
- Go to a drugstore, and in a loud voice say to the pharmacist, "I want a gross of condoms, and since I use so many of them, you should give me a special discount!" (This is one of Ellis's favorites.)
- After finishing a meal in a restaurant, say, "Ah, I feel a fart coming on!" (This is one of my favorites.)

BEHAVIORAL METHODS IN REBT GROUPS
REBT group practitioners can employ the entire range of cognitive behavioral techniques described in Chapter 13. According to Ellis (1996, 2001a), the behavioral methods of REBT work best when they are used in combination with emotive and cognitive methods. Also, self-management methods work best when clients control their own behavior rather than allowing themselves to be controlled by the leader.

Role Playing There are emotional, cognitive, and behavioral components in role playing. One way of assisting group members to experience and cope with feelings of fear is to ask them to reverse roles. For example, if a member is experiencing anxiety over an upcoming job interview, he can assume the role of the interviewer. He can also play himself in both a fearful stance and in a confident manner. Rather than having members simply talk about their problems or think about their beliefs, they can become emotionally involved if they allow themselves to role-play. Of course, some members will be faced with challenging their fears of looking foolish during the role playing or of not engaging in the activity as they think they should. Not only can role playing free members up emotionally, but it can also provide them with opportunities to experiment with a host of new behaviors. Indeed, role playing can result in modifying a member's way of thinking, feeling, and behaving.

In an REBT group, role playing also involves a cognitive evaluation of the feelings and beliefs that are experienced. Thus, if a member is trying to deal more effectively with a rejecting father who demands perfection, he can adopt a role quite different from his usual one, a role in which he no longer feels victimized by his father's lack of approval. Afterward, this person undertakes a cognitive analysis of the feelings experienced during the role enactment. To that effect, he may try to answer questions such as these:

- Do I need my father's approval to survive?
- Will I ever be able to attain the level of perfection that my father demands?
- Can I accept myself although I'll never be perfect?
- Can I avoid destructive self-rating and self-blaming because of my imperfection?
- Do I really have to be perfect before I can accept myself?

Ellis believes role playing is more effective if it entails a cognitive restructuring of the attitudes revealed by the experience.

Homework Assignments Members of REBT groups are encouraged to practice and work hard outside of the therapy sessions as a pathway to personal change. Activity-oriented homework assignments are frequently negotiated to help group participants make the changes they desire. Negotiating homework assignments is more effective than unilaterally prescribing tasks to carry out. It is also important to ask members to clarify what they are going to do, how often they will do tasks, and in which contexts (Dryden & Neenan, 2006). Working outside of the group sessions can actually be more valuable for clients than work done during the sessions (Ledley et al., 2005). Group leaders assist members in rehearsing these assignments in their head, through the imagination process, and then encourage members to carry them into real life. REBT favors *in vivo desensitization* and strongly encourages members to do repetitively the very things they are afraid of doing as a way to overcome their fears (Ellis, 2001b).

Group participants engage in the PYA (*Push Your Ass*) technique, deliberately forcing themselves to confront "dangerous" pursuits until they can learn how to cope when they encounter fearful situations. Partly by doing the fearful thing many times in carrying out their homework assignments, they eventually conquer their fears. These assignments, which are suggested by the leader as well as by other group members, may be carried out in the group itself or outside of it; in the latter case, the person is supposed to report the results to the group. Here are some examples of in-group assignments:

- A man who is shy around women is encouraged to approach the female group members and systematically challenge his fears and expectations by talking about them.
- A woman who is very quiet during the group sessions because she is self-conscious about her accent can be asked to disclose and explore her fears and embarrassment about speaking out. She can also work on changing her beliefs about her inability to contribute something of value because of her accent.
- A group member who is convinced that others in the group will reject her if they know about her shameful side can be encouraged to disclose some of the fears that are keeping her hidden.

In addition to these in-group assignments, leaders strongly encourage members to carry out homework assignments. Individuals who are afraid of riding in the subway, flying on airplanes, or riding in elevators are encouraged to engage repeatedly in these activities about which they feel anxious. In his lectures,

Ellis has given the example of helping people with a fear of elevators to over-come this fear. He would encourage them to enter an elevator daily for one month while forcefully telling themselves that they can stand it even if the damn elevator gets stuck.

A typical group session often begins with members checking in on their homework assignments during the week. After homework is reviewed and discussed, members generally bring up some problem they want to explore, discuss their goals and plans, or report on their progress. During a group session members' dysfunctional core beliefs are identified, they are challenged to dispute them vigorously, and they learn rational coping statements. Then another homework assignment is formulated from members to continue prac-ticing new beliefs and behaviors in everyday life.

For an excellent resource on the use of homework assignments in cognitive behavior therapy, see Kazantzis, Deane, Ronan, and L'Abate (2005).

Reinforcement and Penalties Both reinforcers and penalties are used to help group members change. Reinforcements can involve reading a novel, watching a movie, going to a concert, or eating a favorite food. People can be taught to re-inforce themselves with something they like, but only after they have carried out a specific homework assignment that they have promised themselves to do but that they tend to avoid doing. One of REBT's goals is to teach individuals better methods of self-management; compliance of members is essential to the suc-cess of this technique. Members' ultimate success depends on how effectively they can take charge of their lives beyond the group sessions. Using principles of reinforcement often helps members develop consistency in applying rational principles to the new problems they encounter. In this sense, they become their own therapists and continually teach themselves how to manage their lives.

Skills Training Training clients in specific skills in which they are deficient has long been espoused as a technique in group work. The assumption is that by acquiring skills they formerly lacked, members will feel more confident about themselves and will experience significant changes in the way they think, feel, and behave. Group members have opportunities to learn and practice impor-tant interpersonal skills in the group sessions. They are encouraged to acquire personal and interpersonal skills by taking courses and practicing outside of the group (Ellis, 2001b).

ADVANTAGES OF REBT APPLIED TO GROUP WORK

Ellis (2001b) has identified many of the advantages of applying REBT tech-niques to groups, some of which are briefly summarized here:

- The activity-oriented homework assignments that are a vital component of REBT are more effectively carried out in the group context than in one-to-one therapy, mainly because members often feel a sense of accountability to others in the group to follow through on their commitments.

- The group offers an effective milieu for several active/directive procedures, such as role playing, assertion training, behavior rehearsal, modeling, and risk-taking exercises.

- The group serves as a laboratory in which behavior can be directly observed in action. Because the group exists in a social context, many problems of members can be more easily assessed and explored than they might be in individual therapy.

- REBT is highly educational and didactic and typically includes information giving and discussion of problem-solving strategies. Economically and practically, this is better done in a group than in an individual setting.

- Group procedures are especially useful for people who are rigidly bound by old patterns of dysfunctional behavior; the group setting assists members in reevaluating these patterns and adopting healthier behaviors.

The points above discussed by Ellis can be usefully considered by any group practitioner who is in the process of developing a rationale for a group counseling program, regardless of his or her theoretical orientation.

Applying Rational Emotive Behavior Therapy to Group Work in Schools

REBT uses a variety of methods to reeducate clients, which has a number of direct applications to group counseling with students from grades K–12. REBT has been applied to children for a wide spectrum of problems, some of which include anxiety, anger, depression, school phobia, acting out, perfectionism, and underachievement (Vernon, 2004). The principles and methods of REBT are aimed at prevention of emotional and behavioral problems, which makes it an ideal model for structuring psychoeducational groups. Vernon (1989a, 1989b, 1998a, 1998b, 1998c) has created programs based on REBT principles to help both children and adolescents apply rational skills to promote social, emotional, and cognitive development. Vernon's programs can be used in the classroom and also in counseling groups.

Groups for children or adolescents in alcoholic families are found in the schools. A main benefit of groups in a school setting is that they help members deal with situations beyond their control. Quite often children and adolescents in school-related groups feel personally responsible for the disruptions in their family, when in reality the adults' substance abuse is the primary cause of the family turmoil. School counselors leading these groups can assist members in identifying and changing beliefs that put the main blame on themselves and can help members create new self-talk. According to Vernon (2004), REBT groups can promote skill acquisition and help children acquire practical coping skills. Because these groups teach children how to think better, youngsters make gains because they can modify their faulty thinking.

The educational aspects of REBT hold promise as a preventive intervention for children, adolescents, and adults who are inclined to exaggerate negative events (Henderson & Thompson, 2011). Consider the faulty beliefs that many adolescents harbor that would provide grist for the mill in an REBT high school group. Adolescents often tell themselves that they cannot stand rejection. They may believe that if they fail at something important they are basically worthless. Cognitive interventions, such as learning to dispute certain faulty beliefs that are held tenaciously, can be most useful in helping adolescents to think differently. A group is an ideal place to work on unconditional self-acceptance and also to increase one's acceptance of others, which are pressing concerns for adolescents.

Groups oriented around key concepts in REBT can be useful in dealing not only with problems at school but also those in a student's interpersonal relationships and home environment. The general purpose of the group is to teach the participants coping skills for daily living and to assist students in modifying certain cognitions, emotions, and behaviors. In these educational groups, participants soon learn that change is the result of practice and hard work outside of the group meetings. Useful resources for teaching REBT concepts to students in both developmental and remedial groups are Ann Vernon's series of books (Vernon 1989a, 1989b, 1998a, 1998b, 1998c).

Applying Rational Emotive Behavior Therapy With Multicultural Populations

REBT has certain advantages in working with multicultural populations. If members are not challenged too quickly, they can be invited to examine the premises on which they behave. Consider a group composed of members from a culture that stresses doing one's best, cooperation, interdependence, respect for the family, and working hard. Some members of this group may be struggling with feelings of shame and guilt if they perceive that they are not living up to the expectations set for them by their parents and families. Leaders who confront the cultural values of such clients too quickly are likely to see counterproductive results. In fact, these clients may drop out of therapy, based largely on feeling misunderstood. A sensitive REBT group practitioner can encourage clients to begin to question how they may have uncritically accepted as truth all of the messages from their culture. It is not the cultural values that should be confronted, but rigid adherence to such values. Without encouraging them to abandon respect for their cultural heritage, the therapist can still challenge them to examine their beliefs and understand their consequences.

The REBT group leader, as does any CBT leader, functions in the role of a teacher. This image would seem ideal for certain cultural groups because it detracts from the stigma of being mentally ill and focuses on problems of living. Life can be more fulfilling if group participants learn better ways to think about the issues that confront them. With the help of the leader and other group members, participants learn new ways of thinking and behaving, which result in new feelings.

Examining faulty beliefs and the cognitive restructuring process involve confronting group members with their self-defeating thinking and certain of their core beliefs. In using these cognitive interventions with Latino group members, Organista (2000) indicates the value of empathy in softening the A-B-C-D approach so frequently used in REBT groups. Organista teaches Latino group members the difference between "helpful" thoughts that ameliorate symptoms and lead to constructive thinking and adaptive behavior and "unhelpful" thoughts that do the opposite. Rather than provoking defensiveness by labeling client beliefs "irrational" or "distorted," in this context it is well for therapists to demonstrate that client thought patterns may be understandable in light of their circumstances.

REBT can be a forceful approach, and the group leader must exert caution in interpreting certain beliefs as being irrational. Active/directive practitioners might adopt an authoritarian style, which is likely to result in neglecting important individual and multicultural influences (Ellis, 2001b). What may seem like an irrational belief to therapists may be a long-cherished value that influences the individual. It is critical that group leaders not err by imposing their standards on group members.

Ellis (2001b) takes the position that an essential part of people's lives consists of group living and that their happiness depends largely on the quality of their functioning within their community. Thus individuals can make the mistake of being too self-centered and self-indulgent. REBT stresses the relationship of individuals to the family, community, and other systems. This orientation is consistent with valuing diversity and the interdependence of being an individual and a productive member of the community.

Evaluation of Rational Emotive Behavior Therapy in Groups

CONTRIBUTIONS AND STRENGTHS OF THE APPROACH

A strength of REBT groups is the wide range of disorders that can be addressed: anxiety, depression, anger, marital problems, poor interpersonal skills, perfectionism, morbid jealousy, parenting skills, character disorders, obsessive/compulsive disorders, eating disorders, psychosomatic disorders, addictive behaviors, posttraumatic stress disorders, and psychotic disorders (Ellis, 2001b; Ellis & Blau, 1998; Ellis & Crawford, 2000).

I consider numerous aspects of REBT valuable enough to use in my own approach to group practice. Although I believe that events and significant persons in our past play a critical role in shaping our present beliefs about ourselves, I agree with the REBT perspective that we are responsible for maintaining self-destructive and faulty convictions. True, we may have learned that unless we were everything others expected us to be we could never hope to be loved and accepted. But the fact that at one time we uncritically accepted certain premises does not have to stop us now from critically evaluating these faulty assumptions and replacing them with more effective beliefs, which will lead to different and more functional behavior. In this sense, REBT is based on the existential assumption that we are ultimately free and responsible rather than being controlled by our past conditioning. Groups are a particularly useful format both for exploring the ways in which we have bought into self-defeating beliefs and for providing a climate where we can try out new and constructive beliefs and behaviors.

I often ask group members to identify and explore the beliefs or assumptions that underlie the problems they are experiencing. I am likely to raise some of these questions: "Does this belief really make sense to you now? What would your life be like if you continued to live by these assumptions? How do you think you'd be different if you could change some of these basic beliefs? What actions can you take now, in this group and in your everyday life, that will help you change some of the beliefs you hold?"

Another contribution of REBT relates to training group leaders. REBT can be used effectively in helping trainees learn how to identify and challenge their internal dialogue, which sometimes gets in the way by creating self-doubt and blocking optimal functioning. Corey, Ellis, and Cooker (1998) provide some examples of the self-talk that blocks the effectiveness of students who are learning how to facilitate groups:

- I *must* have love and approval from all the members in my group and from my coleader and my supervisor. My worth as a counselor and as a person is dependent on the affirmation of all of these people.

- As a group facilitator, I *must* always perform competently and perfectly. There is absolutely no room for serious mistakes, for this implies failing, and notable failure always means that I am a failure.

- If I do not get what I want from each member, it is terrible and I *cannot stand it.* The group *must* act exactly the way I want when I want it.

- I absolutely should always know what to say, and it is *essential* that I have the right answers.

- I *must* be the perfect role model for all my group members.

- I fear that I may look foolish, and this *must* never happen!

- I *must* have the right technique for each situation, or else everything might fall flat, and the consequences would be a disaster.

It is likely that in your work as a group leader you will discover a core of dysfunctional beliefs that affect both your personal life and the manner in which you lead your groups. By using some of the concepts and methods of REBT, you can learn how to transform dysfunctional thinking into more productive beliefs. The more capable you are of exploring your own self-limiting thoughts, the more able you will be to challenge the thought patterns of the members of your groups (Corey et al., 1998).

Like any other action-oriented approach, REBT emphasizes that our newly acquired insights must be put into action. REBT's use of the homework method is an excellent avenue for translating insights into concrete action programs. In my own groups I often suggest assignments that can be carried out outside the group and that allow group members to practice new behaviors and experiment with a different style of being. These assignments do not have to be "given" by the leader; members can be encouraged to set personally meaningful tasks for themselves. From my perspective, it is essential that homework assignments be tailored to members' specific problems and that these activities be collaboratively developed by both the member and the leader.

Once members have identified unsupported conclusions and faulty beliefs, they can be encouraged to record and think about how their beliefs contribute to their personal problems. In this way members can work diligently at critically examining their self-defeating cognitions. When members come to the next group session, they can bring up specific situations in which they did well or in which they experienced difficulty. As members consistently question the actual evidence for situations they encounter, they become more effective in evaluating their beliefs and behavior. By working outside of the group, members are using the group as a means to an end. Members learn how to generalize their learning from one problem to another and how to apply what they are learning in the group to everyday life.

LIMITATIONS OF THE APPROACH

A major reservation I have with regard to REBT concerns the dangers inherent in the therapist's confrontive and persuasive stance and the possibility of imposing the leader's values on the members. Coercion of members is more possible in REBT than in less directive approaches. Cormier, Nurius, and Osborn (2009) suggest that therapists be careful about the language they use when describing clients' cognitions, avoiding terms such as *rational* and *irrational* or *maladaptive* and *dysfunctional*. This is especially important when interacting with group members who feel marginalized by the mainstream culture. Cormier and her colleagues further recommend adapting the language presented in cognitive restructuring to the client's primary language, age, and educational level. They emphasize avoiding jargon and using respectful language. These guidelines can certainly be applied to REBT leaders who might do well to reflect on the kinds of words they use and the tone of their language, especially when they are zeroing in on members' core beliefs.

A leader using REBT would do well to enlist the members' input in making determinations about what they consider to be constructive or problematic beliefs. The leader can guide the process so that members can question certain beliefs and assume an active role in the therapeutic process. Members may be subjected to group pressure from the group leader and from other members to change their thinking, even if they are not yet convinced that they hold faulty beliefs. An effective REBT group leader is alert and guards against this happening. It is important to get feedback from the member being engaged. Ultimately it is really up to the person receiving the feedback to decide what to do about it.

Ellis (2011) has stated: "REBT practitioners often employ a rapid-fire active-directive-persuasive philosophical methodology. In most instances, they quickly pin clients down to a few basic dysfunctional beliefs" (p. 214). Some group members may depend on the leader to determine for them what constitutes rational thinking; others may be intimidated by a leader's confrontive style. Ellis (2001b) acknowledges that among the possible disadvantages of an active/directive therapy is that clients may be pressured to adopt goals and values that the therapist puts forth as opposed to operating within the framework of their own value system. Furthermore, active/directive therapy can result in the therapist exercising excessive amounts of power and responsibility, which will disrupt a collaborative and cooperative client–therapist relationship. Some group leaders may make it their task to decide for members what specific beliefs are irrational and what needs to be changed, and doing so can be unethical. Dryden (2007) cautions that the skills of the practitioner are critical in determining the quality of the therapy. REBT is easy to practice poorly, which means that there is no substitute for adequate training and supervision in this approach.

It is critical that REBT practitioners be keenly aware of themselves and their own motivations. The therapist's level of knowledge, training, perceptiveness, and accuracy of judgment are particularly important. Perhaps one ethical safeguard is for group leaders using REBT procedures to discuss the issue of values openly and to caution members to beware of pressure to change in a definite direction, one that might be alien to their value system.

It is well to underscore that REBT can be done by many people in a manner different from Ellis's style. It is worth distinguishing between the principles and techniques of REBT and Ellis's somewhat confrontational way of using them. A therapist can be soft-spoken and gentle and still use REBT concepts and methods. REBT is not prescriptive when it comes to therapeutic style, except that the therapist needs to be active-directive (Dryden, 2009b). Different group members will require different therapeutic styles. Even with the same person it is often necessary to tailor the approach at different times. To use a fixed interpersonal style with all group participants is not a route to effective practice (Dryden & Neenan, 2006).

Where to Go From Here

For information about REBT, check out the following resources:

REBT Network
Website: www.rebtnetwork.org
Dr. Debbie Joffee Ellis
Website: www.debbiejoffeeellis.com
Friends of Albert Ellis
Website: www.albert-ellis-friends.net

The Centre for Rational Emotive Behaviour Therapy at the University of Birmingham is the only training center in the United Kingdom accredited by the Albert Ellis Institute. Currently the center offers two accredited courses, both aimed at individuals who already have a core profession in psychology, counseling, psychotherapy, or another allied mental health profession. The primary certificate takes place over 3 days and includes live demonstrations of REBT and 12 hours of supervised peer counseling. The center also offers an advanced certificate, which follows the same lines as the primary certificate and includes a further 12 hours of supervised peer counseling.

Centre for Rational Emotive Behaviour Therapy
Website: www.rebt-uk.org/

AUTHOR LECTURES
Watch *Gerald Corey's Perspectives on Theory and Practice of Group Counseling* DVD or visit the *Theory and Practice of Group Counseling* CourseMate website at www.cengagebrain.com/shop/ISBN/0840033869 to watch videos of Dr. Gerald Corey presenting lectures for each chapter. Also available are unique eAudio lectures for each chapter and quiz questions for self-study.

RECOMMENDED SUPPLEMENTARY READINGS

Overcoming Destructive Beliefs, Feelings, and Behaviors (Ellis, 2001b) brings REBT up to date and shows how this approach helps neurotic clients and those suffering from severe personality disorders.

Rational Emotive Behavior Therapy: It Works for Me—It Can Work for You (Ellis, 2004a) is a personal book that describes the many challenges Ellis has faced in his life and how he has coped with these realities by applying REBT principles.

The Road to Tolerance: The Philosophy of Rational Emotive Behavior Therapy (Ellis,

2004b) is a companion book to the book listed above. Ellis demonstrates that tolerance is a deliberate, rational choice that we can make, both for the good of ourselves and for others.

The Practice of Rational Emotive Behavior Therapy (Ellis & Dryden, 2007) contains a chapter on group therapy and REBT intensives and marathons.

Rational Emotive Behaviour Group Therapy (Dryden & Neenan, 2002) provides comprehensive coverage of group REBT in different contexts and with different client populations.

Corey, G., Ellis, A., & Cooker, P. G. (1998). Challenging the internal dialogue of group counselors. *Journal of the Mississippi Counseling Association, 16*(1), 36–44.

*Cormier, S., Nurius, P. S., & Osborn, C. J. (2009). *Interviewing and change strategies for helpers: Fundamental skills and cognitive behavioral interventions* (6th ed.). Belmont, CA: Brooks/Cole, Cengage Learning.

*Dryden, W. (2006). *Getting started with REBT: A concise guide for clients.* New York: Routledge (Taylor & Francis Group).

Dryden, W. (2007). Rational emotive behaviour therapy. In Dryden, W. (Ed.), *Dryden's handbook of individual therapy* (5th ed., pp. 352–378). London: Sage.

*Dryden, W. (2008). *Understanding emotional problems: The REBT perspective.* New York: Routledge (Taylor & Francis Group).

*Dryden, W. (2009a). *How to think and intervene like an REBT therapist.* New York: Routledge (Taylor & Francis Group).

*Dryden, W. (2009b). *Rational emotive behavior therapy: Distinctive features.* New York: Routledge (Taylor & Francis Group).

*Dryden, W., & Neenan, M. (Eds.). (2002). *Rational emotive behaviour group therapy.* London: Whurr.

*Dryden, W., & Neenan, M. (2006). *Rational emotive behaviour therapy: 100 key points and techniques.* New York: Routledge (Taylor & Francis Group).

Ellis, A. (1988). *How to stubbornly refuse to make yourself miserable about anything—Yes, anything!* Secaucus, NJ: Lyle Stuart.

Ellis, A. (1992). Group rational-emotive and cognitive-behavioral therapy. *International Journal of Group Psychotherapy, 42*(1), 63–80.

*Ellis, A. (1994). *Reason and emotion in psychotherapy* (rev. ed.). New York: Kensington.

*Ellis, A. (1996). *Better, deeper, and more enduring brief therapy: The rational emotive behavior therapy approach.* New York: Brunner/Mazel.

Ellis, A. (1997). The evolution of Albert Ellis and rational emotive behavior therapy. In J. K. Zeig (Ed.), *The evolution of psychotherapy: The third conference* (pp. 69–82). New York: Brunner/Mazel.

*Ellis, A. (1999). *How to make yourself happy and remarkably less disturbable.* Atascadero, CA: Impact.

*Ellis, A. (2000). *How to control your anxiety before it controls you.* New York: Citadel Press.

*Ellis, A. (2001a). *Feeling better, getting better, and staying better.* Atascadero, CA: Impact.

*Ellis, A. (2001b). *Overcoming destructive beliefs, feelings, and behaviors.* Amherst, NY: Prometheus Books.

*Ellis, A. (2002). *Overcoming resistance: A rational emotive behavior therapy integrated approach* (2nd ed.). New York: Springer.

Ellis, A. (2003). Cognitive restructuring of the disputing of irrational beliefs. In W. O'Donohue, J. E. Fisher, & S. C. Hayes (Eds.), *Cognitive behavior therapy: Applying empirically supported techniques in your practice* (pp. 79–83). Hoboken, NJ: Wiley.

*Ellis, A. (2004a). *Rational emotive behavior therapy: It works for me— It can work for you.* Amherst, NY: Prometheus Books.

*Ellis, A. (2004b). *The road to tolerance: The philosophy of rational emotive behavior therapy.* Amherst, NY: Prometheus Books.

Ellis, A. (2010). *All out! An autobiography.* Amherst, NY: Prometheus Books.

Ellis, A. (2011). Rational emotive behavior therapy. In R. Corsini & D. Wedding (Eds.), *Current*

* Books and articles marked with an asterisk (*) are suggested for further study.

psychotherapies (9th ed., pp. 196–234). Belmont, CA: Brooks/Cole, Cengage Learning.

Ellis, A., & Blau, S. (Eds.). (1998). *The Albert Ellis reader.* New York: Kensington.

*Ellis, A., & Crawford, T. (2000). *Making intimate connections: Seven guidelines for great relationships and better communication.* Atascadero, CA: Impact.

*Ellis, A., & Dryden, W. (2007). *The practice of rational-emotive therapy* (3rd. ed.). New York: Springer.

*Ellis, A., & Harper, R. A. (1997). *A guide to rational living* (3rd ed.). North Hollywood, CA: Melvin Powers/Wilshire Books.

Ellis, A., & MacLaren, C. (2005). *Rational emotive behavior therapy: A therapist's guide* (2nd ed.). Atascadero, CA: Impact.

Henderson, D., & Thompson, C. L. (2011). *Counseling children* (8th ed.). Belmont, CA: Brooks/Cole, Cengage Learning.

*Kazantzis, N., Deane, F. P., Ronan, K. R., & L'Abate, L. (2005). *Using homework assignments in cognitive behavior therapy.* New York: Routledge (Taylor & Francis Group).

*Ledley, D. R., Marx, B. P., & Heimberg, R. G. (2005). *Making cognitive-behavioral therapy work: Clinical processes for new practitioners.* New York: Guilford Press.

*Organista, K. (2000). Latinos. In J. R. White & A. Freeman (Eds.), *Cognitive-behavioral group therapy for specific problems and populations* (pp. 281–303). Washington, DC: American Psychological Association.

Sapp, M. (1994). Cognitive-behavioral counseling: Applications for African American middle school students who are academically at-risk. *Journal of Instructional Psychology, 21*(2), 161–171.

Vernon, A. (1989a). *Thinking, feeling, and behaving: An emotional education for children.* Champaign, IL: Research Press.

Vernon, A. (1989b). *Thinking, feeling, and behaving: An emotional education for adolescents.* Champaign, IL: Research Press.

Vernon, A. (1998a). *The passport program: A journey through social, emotional, cognitive, and self-development (grades 1–5).* Champaign, IL: Research Press.

Vernon, A. (1998b). *The passport program: A journey through social, emotional, cognitive, and self-development (grades 6–8).* Champaign, IL: Research Press.

Vernon, A. (1998c). *The passport program: A journey through social, emotional, cognitive, and self-development (grades 9–12).* Champaign, IL: Research Press.

Vernon, A. (2004). Using cognitive behavioral techniques. In B. T. Erford (Ed.), *Professional school counseling: A handbook of theories, programs & practices* (pp. 91–99). Austin, TX: CAPS Press.

Reality Therapy in Groups

Introduction

Like many of the founders of other therapeutic approaches described in this book, William Glasser was immersed in Freudian psychology during his training. He quickly became disenchanted with this approach, however, and began to experiment with innovative methods, which later came to be called reality therapy. The essence of reality therapy, now taught all over the world, is that we are responsible for what we choose to do. Because all problems are in the present, reality therapy spends very little time delving into the past. Glasser believes we can only control what we are presently doing. We may be the product of our past, but we are not the victims of our past unless we so choose.

Reality therapy is based on the assumption that people strive to gain control of their lives to fulfill their needs. Like transactional analysis, cognitive behavior therapy, rational emotive behavior therapy, and solution-focused brief therapy, reality therapy is active, directive, structured, psychoeducational, and focuses on *doing* and *action plans.* Attitudes, feelings, insight, transference, one's past, or unconscious motivations are not emphasized. Reality therapy deals with helping clients solving problems and cope with the demands of reality by making more effective choices. People can improve the quality of their lives through honestly examining their wants, needs, and perceptions. Group members are challenged by the leader and other members to evaluate their current behavior, formulate plans for change, commit themselves to their plans, and follow through with their commitments.

From the 1960s to the late 1970s, reality therapy was aimed at putting a few basic concepts of the approach to work in a variety of settings, such as correctional institutions, schools, private practice, marital and family therapy, group work, and counseling in community clinics. In the early 1980s Glasser developed control theory as an explanation for human behavior, which served as the foundation for the practice of reality therapy. In March 1996 he renamed this theory **choice theory.**

Glasser's (2001, 2005) basic premise is that the source of almost all clients' problems is the lack of satisfying present relationships. In short, Glasser believes the core problem most of us experience is an inability to get along with others as well as we want to. Furthermore, because the core of choice theory is that everything we do is chosen, we can learn to make better choices. **Reality therapy** is the methodology for implementing the key concepts of choice theory. The focus of this chapter is on applying key concepts of choice theory to the practice of reality therapy in groups.

Key Concepts

HUMAN NEEDS AND PURPOSEFUL BEHAVIOR

Choice theory is built on the notion that human behavior is purposeful and originates from within the individual rather than from external forces. We are motivated by innate forces, and all of our behavior is aimed at fulfilling basic needs. Glasser (1998, 2001, 2005) and Wubbolding (2008) identify five essential human needs: survival, love and belonging, power, freedom, and fun. *Survival,* or self-preservation, is concerned with maintaining life and good health. *Love and belonging* is the need for involvement with people and the need for loving others and being loved. *Power,* or inner control, is the need for achievement and accomplishment, or the need for a sense of being in charge of one's own life. *Freedom,* or independence, is the need to make choices. *Fun,* or enjoyment, involves the need to enjoy life, to laugh, and to experience humor. Choice theory is based on the premise that all our behavior is basically an attempt to control the world around us for the purpose of satisfying these five basic needs, which are built into our genetic structure.

Robert Wubbolding (personal communication, April 7, 2009) has recently added a new idea to choice theory. He believes that behavior is a language whose purpose is to help us get what we want from the world. Therapists can ask clients what messages they are sending into the world by way of their actions with questions like these:

- What message do you want others to get?
- What message are others getting whether you want them to or not?

By considering the messages that clients send to others, counselors can indirectly help clients come to a greater appreciation of these unintended messages.

We each fulfill the five basic needs in our own way. For example, we all have a need for love, but some people need more love than others. We develop an inner **picture album** (or "quality world") of specific wants as well as precise ways to satisfy these wants. We are attempting to choose to behave in a way that gives us the most effective control over our lives, which means being able to behave in a way that reasonably satisfies the pictures in our quality world (Glasser, 1998).

People behave with purpose, molding their environment, as a sculptor molds clay, to match their own inner pictures of what they want. An essential part of reality therapy consists of teaching people about their needs and how to more effectively meet these needs. These goals are achievable only through hard work (Wubbolding, 2000, 2008). We have a significant degree of control over our lives, and the more effectively we put this control into action, the more fulfilled we will be. The essence of reality therapy in groups consists of teaching members to help each other to accept responsibility through effective choices.

Choice theory explains that we do not satisfy our needs directly. What we do, beginning shortly after birth and continuing all our lives, is to keep close track of anything we do that feels very good and to store this knowledge in a special place in our brain called our quality world. Also included are systems of belief that give us pleasure, such as our religious, political, or personal beliefs. This world is our personal Shangri-La—the world we would like to live in if we could. Although based on the general needs we all share, this world is very specific. We need love, but we put the actual people we want to love in our quality world. People are, by far, the most important components of this world, and these are the people we most want to connect with.

Choice theory provides an explanation for human motivation; reality therapy is the delivery system. If choice theory is the highway, reality therapy is the vehicle delivering the product (Wubbolding, 2011). Choice theory and reality therapy, with their emphases on connection and interpersonal relationships, are well suited for various kinds of group counseling. Groups provide members with many opportunities for exploring ways to meet their needs through the relationships formed within the group.

EXISTENTIAL/PHENOMENOLOGICAL ORIENTATION

In many ways choice theory is grounded on phenomenological and existential premises. We perceive the world in the context of our own needs, not as it really is. It is important for group counselors to teach members the difference between the world as they perceive it and the world as other people perceive it. Choice theory is based on the existential assumption that it is possible for people to learn to replace external control psychology with internal control psychology. Glasser (2005, p. 21) talks about the seven deadly habits that are based on external control and that destroy our relationships: criticizing, blaming, complaining, nagging, threatening, punishing, and rewarding to control. He suggests that people replace these deadly habits with these seven caring habits to improve relationships: supporting, encouraging, listening, accepting, trusting, respecting, and negotiating differences.

In addition to the focus on internal control and on the subjective world, contemporary choice theory continues to have a strong existential orientation. We are viewed as choosing our own goals and as being responsible for the kind of world we create for ourselves. We are not helpless victims, and we can create a better life. Glasser (1997, 1998, 2001) and Wubbolding (2011) do not accept the notion that misery simply happens to us; rather, it is something that we sometimes choose, not because we want to suffer but because suffering may give us more control over our lives. Suffering often appears to be the only choice available, and people are quick to complain that they are upset because others are not behaving as they would like them to. It is a powerful lesson for people to recognize that they choose their behaviors, including feeling miserable and thinking that they are victims. Some psychological pain can be lessened by making more effective choices.

Glasser (1998, 2001, 2003) speaks of people *depressing* or *angering* themselves rather than being depressed or being angry. With this perspective, depression can be explained as an active choice that we make rather than the result of being a passive victim. This process of "depressing" keeps anger in check, and it also allows us to ask for help. As long as we cling to the notion that we are victims of depression and that misery is something that happens to us, Glasser contends that we will not change for the better. By adding the "ing" word ending, Glasser replaces a static state with an active one and emphasizes that feelings are behaviors that are generated. If we want to stop choosing a painful behavior such as depressing, we can change what we want, change what we are doing, or change both.

Robert Wubbolding (personal communication, April 7, 2009) believes people have trouble accepting that there is an element of choice when it comes to depressing. When he asks clients if they could make their lives worse, they typically say that they could. Then he leads them to the conclusion that if they can make their situation worse, they could make it better, which results in empowerment.

TOTAL BEHAVIOR

According to Glasser's current formulation of choice theory (1998, 2001, 2005), we always have control over what we do. This basic premise is clarified in the context of understanding our **total behavior**, which includes four inseparable, but distinct, components: *acting* (things that we do such as talking or jogging), *thinking* (voluntary thoughts and self-statements), *feeling* (such as anger, joy, depression, anxiety), and *physiology* (such as sweating, "headaching," or developing other psychosomatic symptoms). Although these behaviors are interrelated, one of them is often more prominent than the others.

If we think of our behavioral choices as analogous to a car, the motor represents the basic needs, the steering wheel allows us to steer the car in the direction of our quality world; acting, thinking, feeling, and physiology are the wheels. Acting and thinking, both obviously chosen, are the front wheels; they steer the car. Feeling and physiology are the back wheels, which have to follow the front wheels. They can't be independently or directly steered any more than we can directly choose how we feel or our physiology.

Choice theory is grounded on the assumption that it is impossible to choose a total behavior and not choose all of its components. Although all total behavior is chosen, we have direct control over only the *acting* and *thinking* components. If we hope to change a total behavior (such as experiencing the emotional and physiological consequences of depressing ourselves), it is necessary to change what we are doing and what we are thinking. Reality therapists accept that people feel badly or that their physiology may not be healthy, as in a psychosomatic disease. However, they do not focus on these components because they cannot be directly changed. For example, we might feel upset and then depress ourselves if we fail to get a job that we applied for. We do not have the ability to directly change how we are feeling independently of what we are doing or thinking. But we can change what we are doing, and we have some ability to change what we are thinking, in spite of how we might be feeling. Therefore, the best way of changing a total behavior lies in choosing to change how we are acting, for these are the behaviors we can control. If we markedly change what we are doing, then it is more likely that the thinking, feeling, and physiological components will change as well (Glasser, 1998, 2001; Wubbolding & Brickell, 2005).

THE ESSENCE OF CHOICE THEORY

Choice theory teaches that the only person whose behavior we can control is our own. The only way we can control events in our environment is through what we choose to do. How we feel is not controlled by others or by events. We are not psychological slaves to others, nor are we trapped by our past or present—unless we choose to be. By focusing on the past or on their symptoms, clients can avoid talking about their present unhappy relationships. An axiom of choice theory is that although the past may have contributed to a current problem the past is never the problem. Regardless of what occurred in the past, to function effectively we need to live and plan in the present.

Glasser (2005) contends that almost all symptoms are caused by a present unhappy relationship. Our task is to do what we can to correct our present relationships (Glasser, 1998, 2001, 2005). For example, if we have had an unsatisfying relationship in the past—perhaps due to being abandoned by a parent as a child—what actually happened cannot be changed. All we have control over is our own behavior, and all we can do is try to change our present behavior so that we can get along with people we now need. Reality group therapists often say to members: "Because the past is over, it can't be changed. Instead of talking about the past, let's face your current problems and search for solutions."

What are the implications of choice theory for the practice of reality therapy group counseling? Group leaders can help members recognize that what they are doing is not working for them, help them accept themselves as they are, and guide them in making realistic plans to do better and to help others in the group to do the same. Practitioners provide help through skillful questioning that is aimed at getting members to assess what they want. If group leaders are not skillful enough to get clients to see that their total behavior is not getting them what they want, therapy will not be effective.

Leaders need to confront members frequently with this basic reality therapy question: "Is what you are now choosing to do (your actions and thoughts) getting you what you want?" Here are some other questions often posed to members:

- Do you want to change?
- How would you most like to change your life?
- What do you want in your life that you are not getting?
- Is your current behavior getting you closer or further from people in your environment?
- If you changed, how would you feel better?
- What would you have in your life if you were to change?
- What do you have to do now to make the changes happen?

Members can more easily choose better behavior if they come to realize that what they are doing, thinking, and feeling is not simply happening to them but that they are, indeed, making choices.

Role and Functions of the Group Leader

Group leaders strive to establish an empathic and trusting therapeutic alliance, which is the foundation for the effective use of reality therapy. Once an effective therapeutic relationship has been established, reality therapists teach clients the basics of choice theory and its applications to their lives (Wubbolding,

2008). Reality therapy teaches that people are most able to gain effective control of their lives when they recognize and accept accountability for their own chosen behaviors and make better choices. The group leader helps participants understand that they have some control over their feelings by choosing to act and think differently. The group leader functions as a mentor by encouraging members to consider different choices in the following ways:

- Promotes discussion of members' current behavior and actively discourages excuses for irresponsible or ineffective behavior
- Helps members make an evaluation of their present behavior
- Introduces and fosters the process of evaluating which wants are realistically attainable
- Teaches members to formulate and carry out plans to change their behavior
- Helps participants evaluate their level of commitment to their action plans
- Encourages members to identify how to continue making the changes they want once the group ends

Reality therapy group leaders assume a verbally active and directive role in the group. In carrying out their functions, they focus on the strengths and potentials of the members rather than on their misery. They assume that dwelling on limitations, problems, and failures tends to reinforce clients' low self-esteem and ineffective control. Therefore, they challenge members to look at their unused potential and to discover how to work toward more effective choices and, thus, more effective control.

Application: Therapeutic Techniques and Procedures

The practice of reality therapy consists of two major components: (1) the counseling environment and (2) specific procedures that lead to changes in behavior. The art of counseling is to weave these components together in ways that encourage clients to evaluate their lives and decide to move in more effective directions. Wubbolding (1988, 2000, 2010) describes these two elements as the "cycle of counseling." The cycle illustrates that there is an overall sequence to translating reality therapy's theory into practice. The counseling environment, which consists of specific guidelines for implementing interventions, is the foundation from which the procedures are built.

Several points are important to keep in mind. First, although the concepts discussed here may seem clear and simple as they are presented in written form, they are difficult to translate into actual therapeutic practice. It takes skill and creativity to apply these concepts successfully in group work. Although the principles will be the same when used by any certified reality therapist, the manner in which they are applied does vary depending on the therapist's style and personal characteristics.

Reality therapy is a process, and it is a mistake to apply these methods in a rigid, step-by-step, or "cookbook" fashion. There are no absolute patterns, questions, techniques, or timing that the therapist must follow. Guided by the principles of choice theory, group counselors tailor their interventions to what the group members present as topics they want to discuss. Although the leader does not operate with preordained techniques, the move in the direction of satisfying relationships is kept in the foreground.

The discussion that follows is an integrated summary and adaptation of material from various sources (Glasser, 1992, 1998, 2001; Wubbolding, 1988, 1991, 2000, 2008, 2009, 2011). In addition, the *Student Manual* that accompanies this textbook contains a chart by Wubbolding (2010) that highlights issues and tasks to be accomplished at each of the stages of a reality therapy group. This discussion provides a look at reality therapy in group work, but it should not be thought of as a replacement for the extensive training that is needed to counsel effectively using this approach.

STAGES OF A REALITY THERAPY GROUP

The stages of group development, discussed in detail in Chapters 4 and 5, are quite applicable to reality therapy groups. During the initial stage of a reality therapy group, key leader functions include developing a safe psychological atmosphere, discussing informed consent, and exploring rules and boundaries. When a group is in transition, the leader will have to be prepared to deal effectively with anxiety, conflict, control issues, and resistance. At the working stage, the role of the leader includes encouraging feedback among members, helping members to evaluate their level of commitment, assisting members in reframing failure, encouraging the development of action plans, and teaching members how to confront without criticism. As is the case during the final stage of any group, important functions of the reality therapy group leader center around consolidation and termination issues, such as dealing with feelings and thoughts about the ending of the group, completing unfinished business, and carrying learning further. Other aspects of the leader's role during the final stage involve helping members to evaluate their action program, to develop a future map that will help members deal with new problems, and to assist members in summarizing their perceptions of the future. For a more detailed discussion of the role of group leaders at the various stages of a reality therapy group, see Wubbolding and Brickell (1999, 2005).

THE COUNSELING ENVIRONMENT

Establishing Safety Within a Group The practice of reality therapy begins with the group counselor's efforts to establish a safe climate as the basis for effective use of interventions. To create this therapeutic climate, counselors need to establish good working relationships with the members of a group, which implies taking an interest in their lives and creating the rapport that will be the foundation of the therapeutic relationship. It is essential for the group leader to see the world as the members see it. In a sense, this is the most important and demanding aspect of a group, for in the absence of personal involvement there can be no effective therapy. When reality group therapy is ineffective, it is usually because genuine involvement has not been established. Caring on the part of the group leader can go a long way toward building the bonds of trust that will be needed for clients to commit themselves to the challenges of making positive changes. When a working relationship is established, members are generally able to evaluate both what they want and the total behavior they are presently choosing.

For a sense of safety to grow, the leader must have certain personal qualities, including warmth, understanding, acceptance, concern, respect for the client, openness, and the willingness to be challenged by others. One of the best ways to develop this goodwill and therapeutic friendship is simply by listening to group members. Yet, as Wubbolding (2011) mentions, this high level of empathy is shown more by skillful questioning than by reflective listening. Involvement is also promoted by talking about a wide range of topics that have relevance for group members, topics that relate to the members' current everyday behaviors and experiences and that play down misery and past failures.

In his description of the **cycle of counseling**, Wubbolding (2000, 2010) identifies specific ways for counselors to create a climate that leads to involvement with clients, emphasizing that the cycle of counseling cannot be applied in the same way with every client. Some of the approaches to establishing a therapeutic environment include using attending behavior, showing empathy, suspending judgment, doing the unexpected, using humor appropriately, being oneself as a counselor, engaging in facilitative self-disclosure, listening for metaphors in the client's mode of self-expression, listening for themes, summarizing and focusing, and being an ethical practitioner. The basis for therapeutic interventions to work rests on a fair, firm, friendly, and trusting environment.

Counselor Attitudes and Behaviors That Promote Change In addition to the positive attributes of counselors to establish a climate conducive to positive change, counselors who hope to create a therapeutic alliance avoid arguing, attacking, accusing, blaming, criticizing, coercing, condemning, demeaning, demanding, encouraging excuses, finding fault, and giving up easily (Wubbolding, 2010). Instead, the emphasis is on accepting clients as they are and encouraging them to focus on what they can control.

Group counselors hope to teach the members to value the attitude of accepting responsibility for their total behaviors. Thus, they accept no excuses for harmful choices such as not doing what they said they would do. If members do not follow through with their plans for change, leaders do not ask fruitless questions about why the plan failed. Instead, they teach members that excuses are a form of self-deception that may offer temporary relief but will ultimately lead to failure and to the cementing of a failure identity. Counselors allow members to learn the consequences of their choices but never give up on clients or on the WDEP system.

PROCEDURES IN A REALITY THERAPY GROUP: THE WDEP SYSTEM

Wubbolding (2000, 2008, 2009, 2010, 2011) uses an acronym—WDEP—to illustrate key procedures that can be applied in the practice of reality therapy groups. Grounded in choice theory, the WDEP system assists people in satisfying their basic needs. Each of the letters refers to a cluster of strategies designed to promote change: W = wants; D = direction and doing; E = self-evaluation; and P = planning. The WDEP framework involves a collaborative approach in which therapist and client join together in determining goals and plans of action (Wubbolding & Brickell, 2005). Glasser and Glasser (2008) stress the centrality of learning to use the WDEP system: "We wish to state publicly that teaching the procedures (the WDEP system) continues to be an integral part of training participants wishing to learn choice theory and reality therapy" (p. 1).

Wants (W) Reality therapists assist clients in discovering their wants, needs, perceptions, hopes, and dreams. They ask, "What do you want?" Through the therapist's skillful questioning, clients are encouraged to recognize, define, and refine how they wish to meet their needs. The use of questioning is basic to the practice of this form of therapy. Well-timed and strategic questions can get members to think about what they want and to evaluate whether their behavior is leading them in the direction they want to go. Because reality therapy makes use of questioning to a greater degree than many other counseling approaches, it is important for group leaders to develop extensive questioning skills. The art of group counseling requires that leaders know *what* questions to ask, *how* to ask them, and *when* to ask them.

Questioning is often misused by group leaders. Some leaders' questions appear to have no point other than to keep the members talking. Those leaders use the question-and-answer technique mainly because they don't know what else to do. Excessive questioning can result in resistance and defensiveness on the part of group members. If questioning becomes the main technique a leader uses, it tends to create distance and keep the leader anonymous. Relationships are enhanced when questioning is combined with reflective thinking, checking perceptions, and other techniques.

Part of counseling consists of an exploration of clients' picture albums— their **quality worlds**—and the ways in which their behavior is aimed at moving the external world closer to their inner world of wants. It is essential that this exploration continue throughout the entire group counseling process because the client's pictures change. Group members are given the opportunity to explore every facet of life, including what they want from their family, friends, and work. Furthermore, it is useful for members to define what they expect and want from the counselor and from themselves (Wubbolding, 2008; Wubbolding & Brickell, 1999).

In a group, members explore what they want, what they have, and what they are not getting. Throughout the process, the focus is on getting members to make a self-evaluation to determine the direction in which their behavior is taking them. This assessment provides a basis for making specific changes that will enable the members to reduce their frustrations. Useful questions can help them pinpoint what they want: "What kind of person do you wish you were?" "What would your family be like if your wants and their wants matched?" "What would you be doing if you were living the way you wished?" "Is this choice to your best short-term and long-term advantage, and is it consistent with your values?" Wubbolding and Brickell (2009) now also include questions that focus on perceptions: "How do you look at the situation? Where do you see your control?" (p. 51). The purpose of such questions is to help clients move from a sense of external control to a sense of internal control. This line of questioning sets the stage for the application of other procedures in reality therapy.

Doing and Direction (D) After members explore their quality world (wants) and needs, they are asked to look at their current behavior to determine if what they are doing is getting them what they want. The group therapist assists members in describing in detail their total behavior (doing, thinking, feelings, and physiology). This heightened awareness and self-insight is a key step toward making changes. Wubbolding (1991) writes that the therapist holds a mirror before group members and asks: "Will this choice get you where you want to go? Is your destination truly helpful to you?" (p. 93).

The leader encourages discussion of past behaviors only if these events can be easily related to present situations or to help them plan for a better tomorrow. Although problems may originate in the past, they all occur in the present. Therefore, problems must be solved either in the present or through a plan for the future. When problems are solved, it is the result of clients learning how to modify their thinking and choosing better ways of acting than when they began therapy.

Reality therapists avoid endless discussions of clients' feelings or their physiological reactions as though these were separate from their total behavior. It is actions that result in an alteration of total behavior. Members are encouraged to discuss feelings in tandem with actions and thinking because reality therapists believe changing ways of acting and thinking is easier than changing feelings and of greater value in the therapeutic process. When members change their actions, their feelings and their thoughts will tend to change.

Part of this exploration involves a discussion of the internal self-talk that often relates to the choices an individual has made (Wubbolding, 2008). The group counselor relates members' feelings or physical symptoms to their concurrent actions and thoughts, over which they have more direct control. Although the counselor might encourage members to discuss feelings, the focus would clearly be on encouraging them to identify actions that accompany or support the feelings.

The aim of the emphasis on current behavior is to help group members understand their responsibilities for their own feelings. As a way of encouraging clients to look at what they are actually doing to contribute to their feelings, these questions might be asked:

- What are you doing now?
- What did you actually do this past week?
- What did you want to do differently this past week?

Getting members to focus on what they are doing has the aim of teaching them that they can gain conscious control over their behavior, can make choices, and can change their lives. Although they may want to talk in detail about how others are not living up to their expectations and how, if only the world would change, they could be happy, such talk will only solidify their victimlike position.

Self-Evaluation (E) It is the group leader's task to assist members in exploring their total behavior. Leaders confront members with the consequences of their behavior and get them to judge the quality of their actions. Members will not change their behaviors or make better choices until they evaluate their own behavior and make the determination that their current course of action is not helpful (Wubbolding, 2011). **Self-evaluation** is the cornerstone of reality therapy procedures. After group members make an evaluation about the quality of their behavior, they can determine what may be contributing to their failures and what changes they can undertake to promote success.

It is important that group leaders remain nonjudgmental about members' behavior and do not assume the responsibility for the individual in making these value judgments. Instead, they best serve members when they challenge them to stop, look, and listen. If therapists can stimulate client self-questioning, the member will be more likely to begin to make changes. Asking members to evaluate each component of their total behavior is a major task in reality therapy. The skillful group leader directs and instructs members to help them learn how to evaluate their own behavior. Members might be asked questions such as these: "Is what you are doing helping or hurting you?" "Is your current behavior satisfying or unsatisfying to you?" "To what degree is what you are doing enhancing your relationships?"

Reality therapists sometimes express what they think will be helpful. In treating children of alcoholics and even alcoholics themselves, for example, it is necessary to say straightforwardly what will work and what will not work. Certain clients do not have the thinking behavior skills that are necessary to make consistent evaluations. These individuals are likely to have blurred pictures and may not always be aware of what they want or whether their wants are realistic. As members grow and continually interact with the other members and with the leader, they learn to make evaluations with less help.

Planning (P) Much of the work in reality therapy consists of helping members identify specific ways to change their failure choices into success choices. Once an individual has made an evaluation about his or her behavior and decided to change it, the group counselor is in a position to assist the member in developing a plan for behavioral changes. The best plan is one that is initiated by the individual. The second best plan is one that is initiated by the therapist and the individual client. And the third best plan is one that is initiated by the therapist (Wubbolding, 2000, 2009). Regardless of who initiates the plan, the art of planning is to establish practical short-term goals that have a high probability of being successfully attained; these successes will positively reinforce the member's efforts to achieve long-range goals.

Planning for responsible behavior is an essential part of the process of a reality therapy group. This is clearly a teaching phase of therapy. Therefore, therapy is best directed toward providing members with new information and helping them discover more effective ways of getting what they want. A large portion of the therapy time consists of making plans and then checking to determine how these plans are working. In a group context, members learn how to plan realistically and responsibly through contact with both the other members and the leader. The members are encouraged to experiment with new behaviors, to try out different ways of attaining their goals, and to carry out an action program. It is important that these plans not be too ambitious because people need to experience success. The purpose of the plan is to arrange for successful experiences. Once a plan works, feelings of self-esteem will increase. It is clear that helpful plans are modest in the beginning and specify what is to be done, when it will be done, and how often. In short, plans are meant to encourage clients to translate their talk and intentions into actions.

A plan that fulfills wants and needs is central to effective group counseling. The process of creating and carrying out plans enables people to gain effective control over their lives. Wubbolding (2008) summarizes the characteristics of a good plan as being simple, attainable, measurable, immediate, consistently implemented, controlled by the planner, and committed to. Wubbolding (2000, 2011) describes the characteristics of effective planning:

- Good plans are simple and easy to understand, realistically doable, positive rather than negative, dependent on the planner, specific, immediate, and repetitive.

- Effective planning involves process-centered activities. For example, members may say that they can do any of the following: pay their child three compliments, jog 30 minutes a day, devote 2 hours a week to volunteer work, or take a vacation that they have been wanting.

- In groups, the plan can be brought to the here-and-now by practicing a new way to relate to someone, by practicing saying "no," or by practicing assertive behavior.

- Before members carry out a plan, it is a good idea to evaluate the plan in the group and get feedback from other members and the leader. After the plan has been carried out in real life, it is useful to evaluate it again. Members can return to the group and talk about the degree to which their plan has been successful. With input from the group, they can figure out what the plan might be lacking, how it needs to be more specific, or how it might need to be modified in some other way.

- For members to commit themselves to their plan, it is useful for them to firm it up by writing it down. Both the group leader and other members can help by providing reinforcement for an effective plan.

Most members do not formulate an ideal plan like the one just described. The better the plan, however, the better the chances are that members will attain their wants. Toward this end, it is essential that they commit themselves to following through with their plans.

Commitment Clearly, formulating even the most reasonable and practical plan is a waste of time if the client lacks the willingness to implement it. As is true for transactional analysis groups, plans can be put in the form of a contract that will assist group members in holding themselves and others accountable for carrying them out.

Once individual members make plans and announce them, the group is in a position to help members evaluate and review these plans and to offer support and encouragement when needed. If individual members fall short of their commitments or in any way fail to implement their plans, that fact cannot be hidden from others or, more important, from themselves. If some members are able to follow through with their plans, they serve as models for the rest of the group. If their peers can do what they have set out to do, others may realize that they can succeed too.

Asking group participants to determine what they want for themselves, to make a self-evaluation, and to follow through with action plans includes assisting them in determining how intensely they are willing to work to attain the changes they desire. Wubbolding (2000, p. 142) describes five levels of commitment:

Level 1: "I don't want to be here. You can't help me."

Level 2: "I want the outcome. But I don't want to exert any effort."

Level 3: "I'll try. I might. I could."

Level 4: "I will do my best."

Level 5: "I will do whatever it takes."

Commitment is not an all-or-nothing matter; it exists in degrees. Leaders can encourage members who have a low level of commitment to move in the direction of increasing their level of commitment to do what it takes to bring about change. It is essential that members who are reluctant to make a commitment be helped to express and explore their fears of failing. Members can be encouraged to begin each group session by reporting on the activities of the week, including the difficulties they encountered in sticking with their plans as well as the successes they had in trying out new behaviors in the real world. Just as in behavioral groups, where the buddy system is used, reality therapy can encourage members to make contacts with each other during the week if they have trouble sticking by their commitments.

Some group members may be unwilling to make any commitments. Therapists cannot force change, but they can help such group members look at what is stopping them from making a commitment to change. Sometimes people are convinced that they cannot change, that they cannot stick to any decision, and that they are destined to remain a failure. In such cases it is important that the group member be helped to see clearly the consequences of not changing and then be guided to formulate very short-range, limited plans with goals that are easy to reach.

Commitment places the responsibility for changing directly on the clients. If members say over and over that they want to change and hope to change, they can be asked the question, "Will you do it, and when will you do it?" The danger, of course, is that the member's plan may not be carried out, which leads to an increase of frustrations and adds to the person's failures. Reality therapy tries to avoid this problem by not asking for any commitment that is unreasonable or impossible.

Applying Reality Therapy to Group Work in Schools

Generally, Glasser has been well received by educators interested in applying the basic ideas of reality therapy to the classroom (Wubbolding & Brickell, 1999). Glasser's (1969) first book on applying reality therapy to groups in the classroom was *Schools Without Failure*. In *Control Theory in the Classroom*, Glasser (1986) showed how teachers could be managers whose main task was to motivate students by empowering them with the responsibility for their learning. Later developments of ways that reality therapy could be applied to schools are found in *The Quality School: Managing Students Without Coercion* (Glasser, 1990), *The Quality School Teacher* (Glasser, 1993), and *Every Student Can Succeed* (Glasser, 2000).

Currently about 25 schools worldwide qualify as Glasser Quality Schools and structure their school programs using choice theory and reality therapy (Wubbolding & Brickell, 1999). The quality school models a democratic structure as opposed to an autocratic structure. In "boss management" teachers use coercion and punishment in an attempt to get children to learn; in "lead management" teachers function in democratic and straightforward ways. Lead management involves all individuals in decisions that affect them. All viewpoints are considered before decisions are made. Teachers and counselors who use lead management are mainly interested in empowering students. Glasser (1998) believes a quality school will reduce the problems that characterize so many schools today. He states: "In a quality school, where students are led instead of bossed, they acquire a lot of knowledge by using what they learn, and they retain it" (p. 239). Wubbolding (1997, 2007) writes about ways to improve the school environment by empowering students by (1) creating a curriculum that aims to fulfill the basic needs of survival, belonging, power, freedom, and fun; (2) emphasizing the rights of students to make choices for themselves and to accept the consequences that result from their choices; (3) teaching students the art of self-evaluation; (4) conducting class meetings that encourage students to provide input in the formulation of class rules; and (5) creating and consistently enforcing schoolwide rules and policies that are clear, simple, reasonable, and known by all students. According to Wubbolding (2004), school counselors have the challenge of wearing many hats and managing various overlapping roles including counselor, group facilitator, parent educator, consultant, in-service trainer, advocate, and community leader. Wubbolding (2004) believes that "professional school counselors adopting the WDEP system of reality therapy have a comprehensive and programmatic basis for school improvement" (p. 218).

Although much of what has been written about applying choice theory and reality therapy to schools pertains to working with the classroom and the overall structure of a school system, the basic philosophy of choice theory is highly applicable to group counseling with both children and adolescents. Any counseling group can be designed to assist students in exploring the degree to which they are meeting their needs for survival, love and belonging, power, freedom, and fun.

Using the WDEP system described earlier in this chapter, children and adolescents can be invited to explore their wants, needs, and perceptions. They can be asked to take an honest look at what they are doing and to clarify whether their behavior is getting them what they say they want. The emphasis on present behavior is a plus when it comes to school counseling because groups are generally time limited in the school context. Depending on their developmental level, children and adolescents can be taught how to make evaluations of what they are doing and how to use self-evaluation to determine if they want to behave in any different ways. Once young people get a clearer picture of what they want, they can begin to make plans that will help them attain their goals. Much of the time in a counseling group can be devoted to assisting students in designing useful action plans to change their behavior. The key concepts of choice theory and the interventions used in reality therapy are effective tools for counseling students of varying ages in many different kinds of groups.

Henderson and Thompson (2011) consider the best validation of reality therapy to be Glasser's success early in his career in conducting both individual and group counseling at the Ventura School for Girls. Before he became associated with this institution, the school's recidivism rate approached 90%. Shortly after his work with the girls, this rate fell to 20%. It is crucial for group counselors who work in school settings to create a trusting climate within their groups. The personal characteristics of the group leader really matter in creating an open climate and in establishing and maintaining a safe atmosphere that will facilitate productive work in school groups.

Applying Reality Therapy With Multicultural Populations

Wubbolding (1990, 2000) and Wubbolding and his colleagues (2004) have expanded the practice of reality therapy to both group counseling and multicultural situations. Wubbolding believes reality therapy needs to be modified to fit the cultural context of people from areas other than North America. After a 7-year effort, the European Association for Psychotherapy (EAP), representing 120,000 psychotherapists in 41 European countries, endorsed reality therapy as a scientifically based theory. Wubbolding (2011) asserts that this as one reason for believing that reality therapy has a bright multicultural future.

Wubbolding's experiences conducting reality therapy workshops in many parts of the world have taught him the difficulty of making generalizations about other cultures. Based on these experiences, Wubbolding (1990, 2000) adapted the cycle of counseling to working with Japanese clients. He points to some basic language differences between Japanese and Western cultures. North Americans are inclined to say what they mean, to be assertive, and to be clear and direct in asking for what they want. In Japanese culture, assertive language is not appropriate between a child and a parent or between an employee and a supervisor. Ways of communicating are less direct. Because of this indirect style, some specific adaptations are needed to make the practice of reality therapy relevant to Japanese clients.

First, it is not necessary to have clients verbally define their specific wants or express their goals. Also, the reality therapist's tendency to ask direct questions may need to be softened. Questions could be posed more elaborately and indirectly and confrontation used less frequently. For example, in counseling American students the counselor might ask, "Is what you are doing helping or hurting you?" However, in counseling an Asian youth in Singapore, more emphasis would be placed on questions such as "What does your family think about your actions?" or "Do your actions bring shame or honor on your parents?" The teaching and the practice of reality therapy must be adjusted to people's values, wants, and manner of expression (Robert Wubbolding, personal communication, April 7, 2009).

Second, there is no exact Japanese translation for the word *plan*, nor is there an exact word for the term *accountability*, yet both of these are key dimensions in the practice of reality therapy. Finally, as counselors present dimensions such as wants of the client, the evaluation process, making plans, and committing to them, it is useful to employ a more indirect style of communication than is typically practiced in the Western version of reality therapy. For example, in working with Western clients, counselors would not settle for a response of "I'll try." In Japan, however, the counselor is likely to accept "I'll try" as a firm commitment.

These are but a few illustrations of ways in which reality therapy might be adapted to non-Western clients. Although reality therapy assumes that the basic needs (survival, belonging, power, freedom, and fun) are universal, the ways in which these needs are expressed depend largely on the cultural context. When working with culturally diverse clients, it is essential that group leaders allow latitude for a diverse range of acceptable behaviors to satisfy these needs.

It is a sign of respect that the group leader refrains from deciding what behavior should be changed. Through skillful and sensitive questioning, the leader can help members determine the degree to which they have acculturated into the dominant society. Members can then make a personal assessment of the degree to which their wants and needs are being satisfied by having made this decision. It is possible for them to find their own balance of retaining their ethnic and cultural identity and at the same time integrating some of the values and practices of the dominant group. Again, the group leader does not determine this for these clients but challenges them to arrive at their own answers based on their own value system. This focus clearly empowers clients.

Practitioners who lead groups composed of culturally diverse members may find such clients reluctant to share their feelings during the early phase of the group. Because of their cultural values, some clients are likely to react more positively and to cooperate to a greater degree if the focus is on what they are doing and wanting rather than on what they are feeling. For example, some clients may be experiencing depression and anxiety, and they may hope to gain relief from these symptoms by being in a group. Thinking of these symptoms from a reality therapy perspective, the leader could guide the members to look at what they are doing (or not doing) that is contributing to their emotional state. There is no pressure to experience a catharsis and to do emotional work within the group. Yet members eventually realize that they are "depressing" and "anxietying" rather than having these things simply happen to them. Once they realize that certain behaviors are not functional for their purposes, they are in a better position to make changes that will lead to different outcomes.

As is true for the cognitive behavioral approaches, reality therapy often utilizes contracts. In this way the group members eventually specify particular problems that are causing them difficulty and that they would like to explore in the group. Group counseling is typically cast in the framework of a teaching/learning process, which appeals to many ethnically diverse client groups. A specific focus—namely, a certain behavioral pattern—becomes the target for intervention. The reality therapy group leader is interested in helping members discover better ways to meet their needs. To its credit, choice theory and reality therapy provide group members with tools for making the desired changes, especially during the planning phase. With the support and help of other members and the group leader, clients can develop specific and workable plans for action. Within this context, members can be assisted in taking specific steps to move the external world closer to the inner world of their wants. If their plans do not meet with success in everyday reality, these members can then bring concrete situations back to the group sessions. This type of specificity, and the direction provided by an effective plan, is certainly an asset in working with minority clients in groups.

One of the limitations of using choice theory and reality therapy with ethnic minorities, gay and lesbian individuals, and women is that these clients may not feel that real environmental forces that are operating against them in everyday life are being taken into consideration. For example, discrimination, racism, sexism, homophobia, heterosexism, ageism, and negative attitudes toward disabilities are unfortunate realities, and these forces do limit many minority clients in getting what they want from life. If the group leader does not accept these environmental restrictions or is not interested in social change as well as individual change, members are likely to feel misunderstood. There is a danger that some reality therapists may overstress the ability of these clients to take charge of their lives and not pay enough attention to systemic and environmental issues. Such clients may interpret the group leader's line of questioning as "If you try hard enough, you can pull yourself up by your bootstraps and become anything you choose." Group members who get such messages may prematurely leave the group in the belief that the leader and other members are not fully appreciating their everyday struggles. Rather than being a fault of choice theory and reality therapy, this is more a limitation of some who practice it.

In writing about the multicultural applications of reality therapy, Wubbolding and his colleagues (2004) note that reality therapy is based on universal principles and is practiced and taught in many cultures and countries. Effective reality therapists learn to adapt the methodology to individuals and groups from many cultures. Wubbolding and his colleagues (1998) put forth the following ethical principles for adapting reality therapy to culturally diverse client populations:

- Reality therapy is most ethically and effectively practiced in a multicultural setting when its principles and procedures are adapted to the individual client.

- Because of the need for adaptation, reality therapy should not be viewed as a rigid and closed system that is applied in the same manner to everyone or to every cultural group but as an open system that allows for flexibility in application.

- The skill in this adaptation process requires more than knowing the concepts and procedures of reality therapy. It requires an understanding of how to apply these principles and procedures to the client's culture and worldview.

- Practitioners are advised to examine their own attitudes, knowledge, and skills with a view to learning more about how other cultural values influence the behaviors of individuals.

In summary, the specific skills that are a part of the WDEP system should be viewed as flexible procedures to be adapted to the personality of the leader and to the specific wants of members of various cultures. The challenge is to find ways of adapting reality therapy to the diversity we encounter in our groups rather than expecting (or forcing) these clients to adapt to and neatly correspond with the theory. As with other theories and the techniques that flow from them, flexibility is a foremost requirement.

Evaluation of Reality Therapy in Groups

CONTRIBUTIONS AND STRENGTHS OF THE APPROACH

A characteristic of reality therapy that I especially favor is its stress on accountability. When a group participant indicates a desire to change certain behaviors, for example, the leader confronts the member with a question about what is keeping the person from doing so. I appreciate the fact that it is the members, not the leader, who evaluate their own behavior and decide whether they want to change. It seems to me that many group leaders meet with resistance because they have suggestions and plans for how the members should best live their lives. To their credit, reality therapists keep asking the members to evaluate for themselves whether what they are doing is getting them what they want. If the members concede that what they are doing is not working for them, their resistance is much more likely to melt, and they tend to be more open to trying different behaviors.

Once the members make some change, reality therapy provides the structure for them to formulate specific plans for action and to evaluate their level of success. In most of my groups I have found it useful to employ these action-oriented procedures to help members carry what they are learning in the group into their everyday lives. I also ask members to state the terms of their contract clearly in the group and to report to the group the outcome of their efforts to fulfill it.

Other aspects of reality therapy that I especially support include the idea of not accepting excuses for failure to follow through with contracts and the avoidance of any form of punishment and blaming. As I see it, if people don't carry out a plan, it is important to discuss with them what stopped them. Perhaps they set their goals unrealistically high, or perhaps there is a discrepancy between what they *say* they want to change and the steps they are willing to take to bring about change.

I also like reality therapy's insistence that change will not come by insight alone; rather, members have to begin doing something different once they determine that their behavior is not working for them. I am skeptical about the value of catharsis as a therapeutic vehicle unless the release of pent-up emotions is eventually put into some kind of cognitive framework and followed up with an action plan. In the groups that I facilitate, I challenge members to look at the futility of waiting for others to change. I ask them to assume that the significant people in their life may never change, which means that they will have to take a more active stance in shaping their own destiny. Their own changes may, in fact, influence another's change, but I appreciate the emphasis of reality therapy on teaching clients that the only life they can control is their own. The focus is not on what others are doing or on getting others to be different; instead, it is on helping clients change their own patterns of acting and thinking.

Group members are encouraged to look inward and search for alternatives. Since other members and the group leader will not accept rationalizations for their failing behavior, the members are forced to face the challenge of change. I consider the skillful questioning by reality therapists to be a major strength of this approach. Of course, it is important for leaders to ask open-ended questions that get members to search inwardly and to avoid the "district attorney" style of questioning.

Reality therapy encourages clients to look at the range of freedom they do possess, along with the responsibilities of this freedom. In this sense reality therapy is based on concepts from existential therapy. As it is currently practiced, the emphasis is on the inner needs, wants, self-evaluation, and choices made by clients (Wubbolding, 2011). Because of this focus on the perceptual and behavioral systems, reality therapy can also be considered as a cognitive behavioral approach. A strength of this approach is its emphasis on understanding the subjective inner world of individuals. This phenomenological view helps the group counselor understand more fully how group members perceive their world. A group leader who consistently maintains a sense of hope that people can change is often the catalyst for instilling and activating a sense of optimism.

One of the appealing aspects of reality therapy is that it is a straightforward and clear approach. Although its key principles are simple and basic, applying these methods in group counseling situations requires skill and practice. Using the methods effectively in groups requires training and supervision—the kind that is provided by the resources listed at the end of this chapter.

Reality therapy has much to offer groups of parents, groups composed of children and adolescents who are having behavioral problems and who continually get in trouble at school, and groups of teachers who work with a variety of students (Wubbolding, 2004). It is also applicable to groups of people who recognize that their lifestyle is not working for them, and to groups of people in institutions for criminal behavior. The approach is well suited to brief interventions in crisis counseling situations. Because reality therapy deals with what clients are presently doing—and asks clients to make an evaluation of what they want to change—the approach fits into the managed care programs that restrict the number of sessions. Group members are expected to identify specific problem areas they want to explore, which also lends this approach to short-term methods. Groups designed on reality therapy principles can fit into a 10- to 12-week format.

Groups based on choice theory can be useful in working with clients who see themselves as the victims of the abusive actions of others. Reality therapy has been effectively used in addiction treatment and recovery programs for over 30 years (Wubbolding & Brickell, 2005). In many situations with these populations, it would be inappropriate to embark on long-term therapy that delves into unconscious dynamics and an intensive exploration of one's past. Reality therapy focuses on making changes in the present and is an effective, short-term approach that fits into the structure of many kinds of psychoeducational groups.

Choice theory and reality therapy work effectively for a variety of practitioners in a diversity of groups, and this approach has been successfully used in educational settings, in correctional institutions, in various mental health agencies, and in private practice. Choice theory can be used by parents, social welfare workers, counselors, marriage and family therapists, school administrators, the clergy, health practitioners, and youth workers. Reality therapy can help clients increase their inner sense of control and self-determination as they learn to satisfy their own needs (Wubbolding, 2008). Glasser (1992, 2001, 2005) has successfully applied reality therapy principles and procedures with schools, youth custodial institutions, drug addiction clinics, rehabilitation centers, and public health settings.

LIMITATIONS OF THE APPROACH

A concern I have about this approach is the tendency of certain group leaders who may assume the role of a "preacher," or moral expert, who judges for the members how they should change. Clearly, if group members accept the leader's standards of behavior instead of questioning and making their own evaluation, they don't have to look within themselves to discover their own values, which is a very undesirable outcome. People need more than advice or solutions to problems; they need to learn how to draw upon their own resources to find creative ways of living fully.

Though I agree that an action program is essential for changes in behavior, my personal preference is to give more attention to the realm of expressing and exploring feelings than is found in choice theory and reality therapy. Once involvement is attained in a group, my inclination is to give members many opportunities to express emotions that they may have kept buried for years. As I've mentioned several times, I believe therapeutic work is deepened by paying attention to the realm of feelings. Therefore, I draw heavily on techniques from the experiential approaches as a way of helping the members fully experience their feelings. However, I go along with transactional analysis, rational emotive behavior therapy, and the other cognitive behavioral therapies in placing emphasis on the role of thinking as a key determinant of behavior. Reality therapy emphasizes self-evaluation, which is a cognitive function. Many problems that show up behaviorally have a connection to the self-defeating statements that we often repeat to ourselves. In addition to encouraging members to come into full contact with the range of their feelings, I also try to get them to look at the thoughts and beliefs that are contributing to their emotional and behavioral problems.

Glasser's (1998) perspective on the past is also limiting. Glasser writes: "What happened in the past that was painful has a great deal to do with what we are today, but revisiting this painful past can contribute little or nothing to what we need to do now: improve an important present relationship" (p. 334). Although it is true that dwelling on the past can constitute avoidance of present responsibility, discounting the role of the past can easily lead to a superficial treatment of certain problems. Many therapeutic approaches are based on the assumption that adequate functioning in the present demands an understanding of our past. Some theories are grounded on the premise that unless we revisit our past we can't understand it. Glasser (1998) maintains that we should discard the notion that it is important to know our past before we can deal with the present. He adds, "It is good to revisit the parts of our past that were satisfying, but leave what was unhappy alone" (p. 334).

From my perspective, Glasser's view of the past is flawed. As I have maintained throughout the critiques of each approach, unrecognized and unexplored issues from our past will bring a shadow to our present experiencing and behavior. I believe it is critical to explore the ways in which our experiences are manifested in our present and in our future. However, some reality therapists do make it a practice to talk about the past if it is tied to the present (Wubbolding, 2000, 2011). For example, they are likely to help an adult who was abandoned by a parent as a child to talk about it, for this is not really purely a past event, even though it happened many years ago. If a group member has never discussed this rejection with anyone, then this is still currently influencing behavior. The event results in a present source of pain, and therefore it is present behavior rather than past behavior.

Although I have pointed out what I consider to be several limitations of reality therapy, I see some unique values and strengths of this approach. Most of its principles can be fruitfully integrated into several of the other systems that have been discussed in this book. As is true of all models, as a group counselor, you will need to examine the concepts of choice theory and the procedures of reality therapy to determine what elements can be effectively incorporated into your individual therapeutic style of facilitating groups.

Where to Go From Here

The programs offered by the William Glasser Institute are designed to teach the concepts of choice theory and the practice of reality therapy. The institute offers a certification process, which starts with a 3-day introductory course known as "basic training" in which participants are involved in discussions, demonstrations, and role playing. For those wishing to pursue more extensive training, the institute offers a five-part sequential course of study leading to certification in reality therapy, which includes basic training, a basic practicum, advanced training, an advanced practicum, and a certification week.

The William Glasser Institute
Dr. William Glasser, President and Founder
22024 Lassen Street, Suite #118
Chatsworth, CA 91311-3600
Telephone: (818) 700-8000 Toll Free: (800) 899-0688
Fax: (818) 700-0555
E-mail: wginst@wglasser.com
Website: www.wglasser.com

A useful videotape, *Using Reality Therapy in Group Counseling,* has been prepared by Robert Wubbolding. The first part of this 2-hour video consists of an explanation of the basic concepts of choice theory and of the stages involved in a reality therapy group. The second part is a demonstration of a group, with a commentary from the perspective of a practicing reality therapist. Another source is Dr. Wubbolding's 2005 DVD entitled, *Dealing With Blaming, Resisting, Whining, Avoiding, and Excuse-Making: A Group Reality Therapy Approach.* The video and DVD are both available through the Center for Reality Therapy.

Center for Reality Therapy
Dr. Robert E. Wubbolding, Director
7672 Montgomery Road #383
Cincinnati, OH 45236-4258
Telephone: (513) 561-1911
Fax: (513) 561-3568
E-mail: wubsrt@fuse.net
Website: www.realitytherapywub.com

The *International Journal of Reality Therapy* publishes manuscripts concerning research, theory development, and specific descriptions of the successful application of reality therapy principles in field settings.

International Journal of Reality Therapy
Dr. Tom Parish
4606 SW Moundview Drive
Topeka, Kansas 66610
Telephone: (785) 862-1379
E-mail: Parishts@gmail.com

AUTHOR LECTURES

Watch *Gerald Corey's Perspectives on Theory and Practice of Group Counseling* DVD or visit the *Theory and Practice of Group Counseling* CourseMate website at www.cengagebrain.com/shop/ISBN/0840033869 to watch videos of Dr. Gerald

Corey presenting lectures for each chapter. Also available are unique eAudio lectures for each chapter and quiz questions for self-study.

Glasser has written little on group counseling; however, the principles and concepts discussed in his books easily translate to group work.

Counseling With Choice Theory: The New Reality Therapy (Glasser, 2001) uses many cases to give readers a sense of how choice theory principles can actually be applied in helping people establish better relationships. He develops the existential theme that because we are responsible for our behavior we are capable of acquiring more effective coping styles.

Warning: Psychiatry Can Be Hazardous to Your Mental Health (Glasser, 2003) addresses the dangers involved in diagnosing mental illness and using medication treatments. Glasser develops the thesis that unhappiness causes symptoms more than brain pathology.

Reality Therapy for the 21st Century (Wubbolding, 2000) is a comprehensive and practical book that represents the major developments of reality therapy. If you were to select only one book to extend your understanding of reality therapy, this would be my choice. The practical formulation of the WDEP system of reality therapy is highlighted, much of which can be adapted to group counseling. Included are multicultural adaptations and summaries of research studies validating the theory and practice of reality therapy.

Reality therapy: Theories of Psychotherapy Series (Wubbolding, 2011) updates and extends previous publications on choice theory and reality therapy. This book contains additions to choice theory and applications of reality therapy to cross-cultural situations.

Glasser, W. (1965). *Reality therapy: A new approach to psychiatry.* New York: Harper & Row.

Glasser, W. (1969). *Schools without failure.* New York: Harper & Row.

Glasser, W. (1986). *Control theory in the classroom.* New York: Harper & Row.

Glasser, W. (1990). *The quality school: Managing students without coercion.* New York: Harper & Row.

Glasser, W. (1992). Reality therapy. *New York State Journal for Counseling and Development, 7*(1), 5–13.

Glasser, W. (1993). *The quality school teacher.* New York: Harper & Row.

Glasser, W. (1997). Teaching and learning reality therapy. In J. K. Zeig (Ed.), *The evolution of psychotherapy: The third conference* (pp. 123–133). New York: Brunner/Mazel.

*Glasser, W. (1998). *Choice theory: A new psychology of personal freedom.* New York: HarperCollins.

Glasser, W. (2000). *Every student can succeed.* Chatsworth, CA: Author.

*Glasser, W. (2001). *Counseling with choice theory: The new reality therapy.* New York: HarperCollins.

*Glasser, W. (2003). *Warning: Psychiatry can be hazardous to your mental health.* New York: HarperCollins.

Glasser, W. (2005). *Defining mental health as a public health issue: A new leadership*

* Books and articles marked with an asterisk (*) are suggested for further study.

role for the helping and teaching professions. Chatsworth, CA: William Glasser Institute.

Glasser, W., & Glasser, C. (2008). Procedures: The cornerstone of institute training. *The William Glasser Institute Newsletter,* Summer, p. 1.

Henderson, D., & Thompson, C. L. (2011). *Counseling children* (8th ed.). Belmont, CA: Brooks/Cole, Cengage Learning.

*Wubbolding, R. (1988). *Using reality therapy.* New York: Harper & Row (Perennial).

Wubbolding, R. (1990). *Expanding reality therapy: Group counseling and multicultural dimensions.* Cincinnati, OH: Center for Reality Therapy.

*Wubbolding, R. (1991). *Understanding reality therapy.* New York: Harper & Row (Perennial).

Wubbolding, R. (1997). The school as a system: Quality linkages. *Journal of Reality Therapy, 16*(2), 76–79.

*Wubbolding, R. (2000). *Reality therapy for the 21st century.* Philadelphia, PA: Brunner-Routledge (Taylor & Francis Group).

*Wubbolding, R. (2004). Professional school counselors and reality therapy. In B. Erford (Ed.), *Professional school counseling: A handbook of theories, programs & practices* (pp. 211–218). Austin, TX: CAPS Press.

Wubbolding, R. (2007). Glasser quality school. *Group Dynamics: Theory, Research and Practice. 11*(4), 253–261.

Wubbolding, R. (2008). Reality therapy. In J. Frew & M. Spiegler (Eds.), *Contemporary psychotherapies for a diverse world* (pp. 360–396). New York: Lahaska Press.

Wubbolding, R. (2009). *Reality therapy training manual* (15th rev.). Cincinnati, OH: Center for Reality Therapy.

Wubbolding, R. (2010). *Cycle of psychotherapy, counseling, coaching, managing and supervising* (chart, 17th rev.). Cincinnati, OH: Center for Reality Therapy.

*Wubbolding, R. (2011). *Reality therapy: Theories of psychotherapy series.* Washington, DC: American Psychological Association.

Wubbolding, R., Al-Rashidi, B., Brickell, J., Kakitani, M., Kim, R. I., Lennon, B., Lojk, L., et al. (1998). Multicultural awareness: Implications for reality therapy and choice theory. *International Journal of Reality Therapy, 17*(2), 4–6.

*Wubbolding, R., & Brickell, J. (1999). *Counselling with reality therapy.* London: Winslow.

*Wubbolding, R., & Brickell, J. (2001). *A set of directions for putting and keeping yourself together.* Minneapolis, MN: Educational Media Corporation.

Wubbolding, R., & Brickell, J. (2005). Reality therapy in recovery. *Directions in Addiction Treatment and Prevention, 9*(1), 1–10.

Wubbolding, R., & Brickell, J. (2009). Perception: The orphaned component of choice theory. *International Journal of Reality Therapy, 28*(2), 50–54.

Wubbolding, R., Brickell, J., Imhof, L., In-za Kim, R., Lojk, L., & Al-Rashidi, B. (2004). Reality therapy: A global perspective. *International Journal for the Advancement of Counseling, 26*(3), 219–228.

Solution-Focused Brief Therapy in Groups

Introduction

Solution-focused brief therapy (SFBT) is a future-focused, goal-oriented therapeutic approach to brief therapy developed initially by Steve de Shazer and Insoo Kim Berg at the Brief Family Therapy Center in Milwaukee in the early 1980s. This approach shifts the focus from problem solving to an emphasis on solutions. SFBT emphasizes strengths and resiliencies of the individual by focusing on exceptions to their problems and their conceptualized solutions. Through a series of interventions, therapists encourage clients to increase those behaviors that have worked for them in the past (de Shazer & Dolan, 2007).

Having grown dissatisfied with the constraints of existing therapy models, in the 1980s de Shazer collaborated with a number of therapists, including Eve Lipchik, John Walter, Jane Peller, and Michele Weiner-Davis, who each wrote extensively about solution-focused therapy and started their own solution-focused training institutes. Later Scott Miller joined forces with Insoo Kim Berg, and Michele Weiner-Davis later joined Bill O'Hanlon, who had been trained by Milton Erickson. Together this group of practitioners expanded the foundation originated by de Shazer (Nichols, 2007, 2008) and applied their ideas to diverse client populations in a variety of settings. As a result, various terms are currently used when referring to this therapeutic approach.

Key Concepts

POSITIVE ORIENTATION

Solution-focused brief therapy, or **solution-focused counseling** as it is sometimes called, is grounded on the optimistic assumption that people are resourceful and competent and have the ability to construct solutions that can change the direction of their lives. The role of the counselor is to help clients recognize the resources they already possess, such as resilience, courage, and ingenuity. Solution-focused counselors engage in conversations with their clients about what is going well, future possibilities, and what will likely lead to a sense of accomplishment.

This respectful and hopeful counseling orientation builds on existing positive dimensions such as the strengths of the person and solutions under construction that are already working for the person in other circumstances. Solution-focused counseling has parallels to **positive psychology**, which concentrates on what is right and what is working for people rather than dwelling on deficits, weaknesses, and problems (Murphy, 2008). By emphasizing positive dimensions, clients quickly become involved in resolving their problems, which makes this a very empowering approach.

Because clients often come to therapy in a "problem-oriented" state, even the few solutions they have considered are wrapped in the power of the problem orientation. Clients often have a story that is rooted in a deterministic view that what has happened in their past will certainly shape their future. In fact, their problem orientation is reinforced by retelling this story over and over to themselves. Solution-focused practitioners counter this negative client presentation with optimistic conversations that highlight a belief in achievable and usable goals. One of the goals of SFBT is to shift clients' perceptions by reframing what White and Epston (1990) refer to as clients' *problem-saturated stories* through the counselor's skillful use of language. Solution-focused practitioners are mainly concerned with eliciting a rich description of the client's solution rather than listening to the client's detailed account of the problem. Together client and counselor construct solutions, and counselors encourage clients to write a different story that can lead to a new ending (O'Hanlon, cited in Bubenzer & West, 1993). SFBT counselors can be instrumental in assisting people in making a shift from a static problem state to a world with new possibilities that lead to creative solutions.

FOCUS ON SOLUTIONS, NOT PROBLEMS

Solution-focused brief therapy differs from traditional therapies by eschewing the past in favor of both the present and the future. Solution-focused practitioners are so interested in what is possible they have little interest in wrestling with the presenting problem or exploring past issues. The past is considered only to identify times when the presenting problem occurred less often. When counselors encourage clients to create a picture of what their world will look like when they are functioning successfully, this sends a clear message to clients about their abilities to overcome pressing problems and adversities (Sklare, 2005). The solution-focused philosophy rests on the assumption that people can become mired in unresolved past conflicts and blocked when they focus on past or present problems rather than on future solutions. de Shazer (1988, 1991) suggests that it is not necessary to know the cause of a problem to solve it and that there is no necessary relationship between problems and their solutions. Gathering information about a problem is not necessary for change to occur. If knowing and understanding problems are unimportant, so is searching for "right" solutions. Any person might consider multiple solutions, and what is right for one person may not be right for another (O'Hanlon & Weiner-Davis, 2003). Clients choose the goals they wish to accomplish, and little attention is given to diagnosis, history taking, analysis of dysfunctional interactions, or exploration of the problem (Bertolino & O'Hanlon, 2002; Murphy, 2008; O'Hanlon & Weiner-Davis, 2003).

LOOKING FOR WHAT IS WORKING

Individuals bring stories to their counseling sessions. Some are used to justify their belief that life can't be changed or, worse, that life is moving them farther and farther away from their goals. Counselors assist clients in paying attention to the *exceptions* to their problem patterns or their *instances of success* (Miller, Hubble, & Duncan, 1996). Solution-focused counseling emphasizes finding out what people are doing that is working and then helps them to apply this knowledge to eliminate problems in the shortest amount of time possible. Identifying what is working for clients and encouraging them to replicate these patterns is extremely important (Murphy, 2008; Sklare, 2005). A key concept is, "Once you know what works, do more of it." If something is not working, clients are encouraged to do something different. In a similar vein, Metcalf (1998) often begins a group session by saying, "Look back over your week and tell me what seemed to go slightly better for each of you."

There are various ways to assist clients in thinking about what has worked for them. de Shazer (1991) prefers to engage clients in conversations that lead to progressive narratives whereby people create situations in which they can make steady gains toward their goals. de Shazer might say, "Tell me about times when you felt a little better and when things were going your way." It is in these stories of life worth living that the power of problems is deconstructed and new solutions are manifest and made possible.

BASIC ASSUMPTIONS GUIDING PRACTICE

Walter and Peller (1992, 2000) think of solution-focused therapy as a model that explains how people change and how they can reach their goals. Here are some of their basic assumptions about the solution-focused approach as modified for the context of group counseling:

- There are advantages to a positive focus on solutions and on the future. If group members can reorient themselves in the direction of their strengths using solution-talk, there is a good chance group counseling can be brief. By concentrating on successes, beneficial changes are likely to occur.

- Individuals who come to a counseling group have the capability of behaving effectively, even though this effectiveness may be temporarily blocked by negative cognitions and negative language. Problem-focused thinking prevents people from recognizing effective ways they have dealt with problems.

- There are exceptions to every problem, or times when the problem was minimal or even absent. By talking about these exceptions, or instances of success, members can get control over what had seemed to be an insurmountable problem. The climate of these exceptions allows for the possibility of creating solutions. When the group leader asks, "What have you done in the past that worked?" group participants develop a new perspective on their situation.

- Participants often present only one side of themselves. Solution-focused group leaders invite members to examine another side of the story they are presenting.

- No problem is constant, and change is inevitable. Small changes pave the way for larger changes. Once a change has been made, it will lead to other small changes. Any problem is solved one step at a time.

- People want to change, have the capacity to change, and are doing their best to make change happen. Group leaders should adopt a cooperative stance with members rather than devising strategies to control resistive patterns.
- Group members can be trusted in their intention to create solutions to their problems. There are no universal solutions to specific problems that can be applied to all people. Each individual is unique and so, too, is each solution.

Walter and Peller (2000) have moved away from the term *therapy* and refer to what they do as *personal consultation.* They facilitate *conversations* around the preferences and possibilities of their clients to help them create a positive future. By avoiding the stance of the expert, Walter and Peller believe they can be interested, curious, and encouraging in jointly exploring the desires of their clients. Because SFBT is more preventive than remedial, the model is especially useful for group counseling that stresses developmental concerns.

Role and Functions of the Group Leader

A NOT KNOWING POSITION

Clients are much more likely to fully participate in the therapeutic process if they perceive themselves as determining the direction and purpose of the conversation (Walter & Peller, 1996). Much of what the therapeutic process is about involves clients thinking about their future and what they want to be different in their lives. Solution-focused group counselors adopt a *"not knowing" position* (Anderson & Goolishian, 1992) as a route to putting group members into the position of being the experts about their own lives. In this approach, the therapist-as-expert is replaced by the client-as-expert, especially when it comes to what he or she wants in life. This is accomplished by group counselors continuously deflecting questions asked of them to the other group members. The group leader's task is to follow the lead of the group members. Although group participants are viewed as experts on their own lives, they are often stuck in patterns that are not working for them. Solution-focused practitioners prefer a more collaborative or consultative stance and see their job as creating the opportunity for clients to see themselves as experts in their lives. They tend to view themselves as tour guides, as co-discoverers, or as co-constructors of solutions rather than as expert leaders (Metcalf, 1998). De Jong and Berg (2008) put this notion about the therapist's task well:

> We do not view ourselves as expert at scientifically assessing client problems and then intervening. Instead, we strive to be expert at exploring clients' frames of reference and identifying those perceptions that clients can use to create more satisfying lives. (p. 19)

The solution-focused group counselor not only takes on the role of not knowing but shifts the responsibility toward group members noticing exceptions to their problems and instances of success. This allows the group leader to be assisted by members who function as cofacilitators who support and encourage each other and who also keep the focus on exceptions rather than problems (Linda Metcalf, personal communication, November 16, 2009). It is the group counselor's willingness to enter the therapeutic conversation from a not-knowing position that facilitates a caring relationship with the group members. In the **not-knowing position**, group leaders still retain all of the knowledge and personal, experiential capacities they have gained over years of living, but they allow themselves to enter the conversation with curiosity and with an intense interest in discovery. The aim here is to enter a group member's world as fully as possible and to elicit the perspectives, resources, strengths, and unique experiences of each group member.

This model casts the role and functions of a counselor in quite a different light from traditionally oriented mental health practitioners who view themselves as experts in assessment, diagnosis, and treatment. Empathy and the collaborative partnership in the therapeutic process are seen as more important than assessment or technique. Functions such as diagnosis and assessment often grant priority to the practitioner's "truth" over clients' knowledge about their own lives. Solution-focused counselors tend to avoid using language that embodies diagnosis, assessment, and intervention. Instead, they believe that the way problems and solutions are talked about makes a difference. Using language can assume major importance in how problems are conceptualized; indeed, language *creates* reality.

CREATING A THERAPEUTIC PARTNERSHIP

The qualities of the therapeutic relationship are at the heart of the effectiveness of SFBT. Client ratings of the therapeutic relationship and alliance are significantly related to therapeutic outcome (Bertolino, 2010). The term *alliance* pertains to the collaborative partnership between group members and the group facilitator. Many group counselors are giving increased attention to creating a collaborative relationship with members because of their belief that doing so opens up a range of possibilities for present and future change. One way of creating an effective therapeutic partnership is for the group facilitator to show the members how they can use the strengths and resources they already have to construct solutions. Acknowledging that therapists have expertise in creating a context for change, Bertolino (2010) stresses that clients have a good sense of what has or has not worked in the past and, as well, what might work in the future. According to Murphy (2008), counseling works best when clients are actively involved in the therapeutic process, when they experience a positive relationship with the counselor, and when counseling addresses what clients see as being important. If clients are involved in the therapeutic process from beginning to end, the chances are increased that therapy will be successful. In short, collaborative and cooperative relationships tend to be more effective than hierarchical relationships in therapy.

Metcalf (1998) maintains that the solution-focused group practitioner believes that people are competent, and that given a climate where they can experience their competency, they are able to solve their own problems, which will enable them to live a richer life. The group leader might begin the first group session by saying, "This group is different. While we will discuss your reason for being here, we will shift our focus to what you want to accomplish rather than why you are here." Alternatively, a leader might say: "We will focus on what you hope to get out of this group."

The concepts of care, interest, respectful curiosity, openness, empathy, contact, and even fascination are seen as relational necessities. Group leaders create a climate of mutual respect, dialogue, inquiry, and affirmation in which clients are free to create, explore, and coauthor their evolving stories (Walter & Peller, 1996). It is the counselor's role to create opportunities for the members to experience themselves as being resourceful. Because solution-focused counseling is designed to be brief, the leader has the task of keeping group members on a *solution track* rather than a *problem track*. If members concentrate on telling *problem-saturated stories*, it is difficult for them to move in a positive direction.

A counselor's main task involves helping clients imagine how they would like life to be different and what it would take to bring about these changes. One of the functions of the leader is to ask questions of members and, based on the answers, generate further questions. Some of the questions that Walter and Peller (2000, p. 43) find useful are "What do you want from coming here?" "How would that make a difference to you?" and "What might be some signs to you that the changes you want are happening?" The group counselor helps clients construct a preferred story line. The therapist adopts a stance characterized by respectful curiosity and works with clients to explore both the impact of the problem on them and what they are doing to reduce the effects of the problem (Winslade & Monk, 2007).

The Process of the Solution-Focused Group

STEPS IN THE CHANGE PROCESS

Walter and Peller (1992) describe four steps that characterize the process of SFBT, which can also be applied to group counseling: (1) Find out what group members want rather than searching for what they do not want. (2) Do not look for pathology, and do not attempt to reduce members' abilities by giving them a diagnostic label. Instead, look for what they are doing that is already working and encourage them to continue in that direction. (3) If what members are doing is not working, encourage them to experiment with doing something different. (4) Keep therapy brief by approaching each session as if it were the last and only session. Although these steps seem fairly obvious, the collaborative process of the group members and the leader constructing solutions is not merely a matter of mastering a few techniques. The solution-focused group model requires a philosophical stance of accepting people where they are and assisting them in creating solutions. The attitudes of the group leader are crucial to the effectiveness of a group.

de Shazer (1991) believes clients can generally build solutions to their problems without any assessment of the nature of their problems. Given this framework, the structure of solution building differs greatly from traditional approaches to problem solving. I have briefly summarized the steps involved based on Metcalf's (1998) book on solution-focused group therapy.

Setting the Tone for the Group The facilitator sets the mood for focusing on solutions from the beginning. Group members are given an opportunity to describe their problems briefly. The group facilitator listens respectfully and carefully as members answer the facilitator's question, "How can I be useful to you?" Another leader intervention is, "I would like each of you to introduce yourself. As you do, give us a sense of what you are here for." Facilitators help members to keep the problem external in conversations, which tends to be a relief to members because it gives them an opportunity to see themselves as less problem-saturated.

Beginning to Set Goals The group leader works with members in developing well-formed goals as soon as possible. Questions that might be posed include "What will be different in your life when this problem is no longer prominent, has become irrelevant, or has even disappeared?" and "What will be going on in the future that will tell you and the rest of us in the group that things are better for you?" Sometimes members talk about what others will be doing or not doing and forget to pay attention to their own goals or behavior. At times such as this they can be asked, "And what about yourself? What will you be doing differently in that picture?" The process of creating member goals is discussed more fully later in the chapter.

Searching for Exceptions to the Problem The facilitator asks members about times when their problems were not present or when the problems were less severe. The members are assisted in exploring these exceptions, and special emphasis is placed on what they did to make these events happen. One leader intervention might be, "I've been listening to each of you talk about why you are here today. I appreciate you for taking the step in coming to this group to make things better for you. For a change of pace, let's talk about the times before your problem started to interfere in your life. What were you doing at those times that kept the problem at bay?"

The group members engage in identifying exceptions with each other. This improves the group process and promotes a solution focus, which can become quite powerful. For instance, in sexual abuse survivor groups, when group members focus on their resilience skills, the "former victims" see themselves differently, which tends to dramatically increase their confidence and their belief in themselves as being competent. The search for exceptions is discussed in more detail later in this chapter.

Encouraging Motivation Hope is a powerful source of motivation, which is a key therapeutic factor in groups. Facilitators may pose questions like these: "Someday, when your concerns are less problematic to you, what will you be doing?" "As each of you listened to others today, is there someone in our group who could be a source of encouragement for you to do something different?" "In this group session, who did you notice who became less preoccupied with the problem and appeared to be more problem free?"

Assisting Group Members With Task Development At the end of each solution-building conversation, the leader offers members summary feedback, provides encouragement, and suggests what they might observe or do before the next session to further solve their problems. The leader encourages members to give one another feedback, especially on small steps members may have taken. A leader could say, "Many of you have talked about times when the problem bothered you less. Now let's consider what you might do before we meet next time to keep these problems smaller."

If goals have not been established, the facilitator could say, "As we close for today, I want to suggest that each of you monitor your daily activities until our next session. Pay particular attention to situations that are not bothering you as often. Note these instances of success and bring them with you to the next group session."

Before the close of the meeting, the group leader and members can evaluate the progress being made in reaching satisfactory solutions by using a rating scale. Members are also asked what needs to be done before they see their problem as being solved and what their next step will be.

The Next Group Session At the next group meeting the leader might ask, "Who wants to begin today by telling us what has gone better for you since our last meeting?" If some members do not have many improvements to report and want to talk about what did not work, the facilitator could assist them in getting on a solution track. One possible intervention is this: "Let's suppose that more of this continues to happen. What will this be like for you by the time we see you next time? What would you like to have happen that is different?"

CREATING MEMBER GOALS

SFBT reflects some basic notions about change, about interaction, and about reaching goals. The facilitator believes people have the ability to define meaningful personal goals and that they are in the best position to choose the goals they want to accomplish in the group because they know themselves better than anyone else. Thus, it is essential that members address what they want and what concerns they are willing to explore. The group leader believes that the move toward goal setting needs to begin during the initial session, based on the assumption that clients come for change rather than to rehash dismal events. In group therapy, if this does not occur, the group can too easily move backward into a problem focus (Linda Metcalf, personal communication, November 16, 2009).

Leaders concentrate on clear, specific, observable, small, realistic, achievable changes that may lead to additional positive outcomes. Because success tends to build upon itself, modest goals are viewed as the beginning of change. Solution-focused practitioners join with the language of their clients, using similar words, pacing, and tone. Group leaders use questions such as these that presuppose change, posit multiple responses, and remain goal-directed and future-oriented: "What did you do and what has changed since last time?" or "What did you notice that went better?" (Bubenzer & West, 1993).

Walter and Peller (1992) and Murphy (2008) emphasize the importance of assisting clients in creating clear, well-defined goals that are (1) stated in the positive in the client's language, (2) are process or action oriented, (3) are structured in the here-and-now, (4) are attainable, concrete, and specific, and (5) are controlled by the client. However, Walter and Peller (2000) caution against too rigidly imposing an agenda of getting precise goals before clients have a chance to express their concerns. It is essential that members first feel that their concerns have been heard and understood so they will be willing to formulate meaningful personal goals. Sharing concerns assists the group in developing cohesiveness, and that sense of belongingness encourages engagement within the group.

In SFBT there are several forms of goals: *changing the viewing* of a situation or a frame of reference, *changing the doing* of the problematic situation, and tapping client strengths and resources (Murphy, 2008; O'Hanlon & Weiner-Davis, 2003). Members are encouraged to engage in solution-talk, rather than problem-talk, on the assumption that what we talk about most will be what we produce. Talking about problems empowers ongoing problems, and talking about change will empower change. When individuals learn to speak in terms of what they are able to do competently, what resources and strengths they have, and what they have already done that has worked, they are well on their way toward solutions (Murphy, 2008; Nichols, 2008).

TERMINATING

From the very first solution-focused group session, the facilitator is mindful of working toward termination. The initial goal-formation question that a group leader often asks is, "What needs to be different in your life as a result of coming here for you to say that being in this group was worthwhile?" Another question to get members thinking is, "When the problem is solved, what will you be doing differently?" Establishing clear goals from the beginning of a group lays the groundwork for effective termination (Murphy, 2008). The group leader assists group members in monitoring their progress and eventually determining when they have accomplished their personal goals. Prior to ending a group experience, leaders assist members in identifying things they can do to continue the changes they have already made into the future (Bertolino & O'Hanlon, 2002). Members can also be helped to identify hurdles or perceived barriers that could get in the way of maintaining the changes they have made. If such barriers are recognized, the group leader can ask the other group members for solutions, thereby empowering the group members to see past barriers.

Because this model of therapy is brief, present and future centered, and addresses specific complaints, it is very possible that participants in a group will experience other developmental concerns at a later time. Group members can ask for individual sessions if they feel a need to get their life back on track or to update their story, or if the group is an open one, they can return to the group for some sessions.

Application: Therapeutic Techniques and Procedures

Some of the key techniques that solution-focused group practitioners are likely to employ include looking for differences in doing, exception questions, scaling questions, and the miracle question. Murphy (2008) reminds us that these solution-focused techniques should be used flexibly and tailored to the unique circumstances of the members. The group counseling process is best guided by the members' goals, perceptions, resources, and feedback. Techniques should never be given more prominence than the members in a group.

PRETHERAPY CHANGE

Pretherapy change addresses any changes made before the initial session. Simply scheduling an appointment often sets positive change in motion. During the initial therapy session, it is common for solution-focused counselors to ask, "What changes have you noticed that have happened or started to happen since you called to make the appointment for this session?" (de Shazer & Dolan, 2007, p. 5). By asking about such changes, the therapist can elicit, evoke, and amplify what clients have already done by way of making positive changes. These changes cannot be attributed to the therapy process itself, so asking about them tends to encourage clients to rely less on their therapist and more on their own resources to accomplish their treatment goals (de Shazer & Dolan, 2007).

QUESTIONING

Questions become the primary communication tool and main intervention. Solution-focused group leaders use questions as a way to better understand a group member's experience rather than simply to gather information. Group leaders do not raise questions to which they think they know the answer. Questions are asked from a position of respect, genuine curiosity, sincere interest, and openness. These questions are guided by the group members. In the SFBT approach the questions counselors ask are always informed by the answers the client-expert has provided. The group member's answers provide information that stimulates the interest of the leader, and another question proceeds from each answer given. Other group members are encouraged to respond along with the group leader to promote group collaboration. Creating a collaborative group process is critical to the success of a group. As the leader helps members identify exceptions and begin to recognize personal resiliency and competency, group members begin to feel the context as different from that of a problem-focused group. This keeps the group process more solution-focused and on track. Creating a group context in which the members are able to learn more about their personal abilities and resources is key to members learning to solve their own concerns (Linda Metcalf, personal communication, November 16, 2009).

EXCEPTION QUESTIONS

SFBT is based on the notion that there were times in individuals' lives when the problems they identify were not problematic. These times are called *exceptions.* Bateson (1972) argued that we learn by comparing one phenomenon with another and discovering what he called "the news of difference." **Exception questions** direct members to times when the problem does not occur, or occurs less often or less intensely. Exceptions are those past experiences in a member's life when it would be reasonable to have expected the problem to occur, but somehow it did not (de Shazer, 1985; Murphy, 2008). Once identified by a group member, these instances of success can be useful in making further changes. *Change-focused questions* explore what group members believe to be important goals and how they can tap their strengths and resources to reach their goals (Murphy, 2008). This exploration reminds people that problems are not all-powerful and have not existed forever; it also provides a field of opportunity for evoking resources, engaging strengths, and positing possible solutions. Exceptions are actual events that take place outside of the problem context. Solution-focused counselors listen attentively for signs of previous solutions, exceptions, and goals (de Shazer & Dolan, 2007). They believe that life is about *change* and that change is inevitable. The intent of solution-focused counselors is to guide clients in a self-chosen direction based on what has worked previously. Members can be asked what has to happen for these exceptions to their problems to occur more often. In individual counseling, only the therapist and the client are observers of competency. An advantage of group counseling is that the audience widens and more input is possible (Metcalf, 1998).

Some participants in a group want to justify their belief that life can't be changed or, worse, that they are moving farther and farther away from where they would like to be in their life. de Shazer (1991) prefers to engage clients in conversations whereby people create situations in which they can make steady gains toward their goals. In doing this, a counselor might say, "Tell me about times when you feel good, when things are going your way, and when you enjoy your family and friends." It is in these stories of life worth living that the power of problems is deconstructed and new solutions are manifest and made possible.

THE MIRACLE QUESTION

In many groups the participants will come with a "problem-oriented" frame of mind. Even the few solutions they have considered are wrapped in the power of the problem orientation. Group leaders who draw on ideas from a solution-focused perspective tend to intervene by asking people to create optimistic conversations that highlight the belief that it is possible to quickly achieve usable goals. These goals are developed by using what de Shazer (1985, 1988) calls the **miracle question**, which is generally presented as follows: "If a miracle happened and the problem you have disappeared overnight, how would you know it was solved, *and what would be different*?" Group members are then encouraged to enact "what would be different" in spite of perceived problems. Essentially, the miracle question is designed to enable group members to visualize what life would look like if the problem did not exist (Sklare, 2005). If a group member asserts that she wants to feel more confident and secure, the facilitator might say something like this: "Let yourself imagine that you leave the group today and that you are on track to acting more confidently and securely. What will you be *doing* differently?" This process of considering hypothetical solutions reflects O'Hanlon and Weiner-Davis's (2003) belief that change can occur in three ways: (1) by changing what we are doing, (2) by changing how we view the problem situation, and (3) by engaging in a conversation of resources and strengths that we can use to create solutions. In solution-focused counseling, problems are not "solved" as much as solutions are constructed. The eventual solutions group members construct may not have anything to do with the problem that they describe when they enter the group.

It can be most helpful for group counselors to encourage the members to dream, for dreams say a great deal about where people want to go and the kind of life they want. Indeed, members can be invited to dream the impossible dream. If they have the courage to pursue their dreams, they are more likely to meet with success than if they limit their imagination. The miracle question is one example of a future-oriented exception question and is a goal-setting technique that is useful when a member has no clue of what a miracle might look like. The miracle question is a way to discover the client's goal that conveys respect for the client's situation and assists the individual in identifying smaller, more manageable goals (de Shazer & Dolan, 2007). At times it can be helpful to ask other group members to brainstorm with the member who is unclear about his or her goals what they think his or her miracle might look like. This sparks creative conversations and is immensely supportive (Linda Metcalf, personal communication, November 16, 2009). This question has a future focus in that the members can begin to consider a different kind of life that is disentangled from or emancipated from the problem-saturate" story they described at the beginning of group counseling. This intervention shifts the emphasis from both past and current problems toward a more satisfying life in the future.

SCALING QUESTIONS

Solution-focused therapists use **scaling questions** when changes in human experiences are not easily observed, such as feelings, moods, or communication. For example, a group member reporting feelings of panic or anxiety might be asked, "On a scale of zero to 10, with zero being how you felt when you first came to this group and 10 being how you feel the day after your miracle occurs and your problem is gone, how would you rate your anxiety right now?" Even if the group member has only moved away from zero to 1, she has improved. How did she do that? What does she need to do to move another number up the scale? Scaling questions enable clients to pay closer attention to what they are doing and how they can take steps that will lead to the changes they desire. This technique can be creatively applied to tap clients' perceptions about a wide range of experiences, including "self-esteem, pre-session change, self-confidence, investment in change, willingness to work hard to bring about desired changes, prioritizing of problems to be solved, perception of hopefulness, and evaluation of progress" (Berg, 1994, pp. 102–103).

Metcalf (1998) writes about the importance of group therapists evaluating how much leading they are doing in a given group session. She raises this question for group leaders to reflect on: "On a scale of 0 to 10, with 0 meaning I did nothing and 10 meaning I did all of the work for the group, where was I when the session was over? Where was the group as a whole?" If leaders become aware that they are at the 10 mark and the group members are on the low end of the scale, leaders should consider changing the degree of responsibility they are assuming for keeping a group session moving. Group leaders can get feedback by asking participants to rate their leadership performance on the scale, ideally at the end of each group session. This is an example of how group leaders can incorporate practice-based evidence into their group work (see Chapter 2).

FORMULA FIRST SESSION TASK

The **formula first session task (FFST)** is a form of homework a group leader might give members to complete between their first and second sessions. The leader might say, "Between now and the next time we meet, I would like for each of you to observe, so that you can describe to all of us next time, what happens in your (family, life, marriage, relationship) that you want to continue to have happen" (de Shazer, 1985, p. 137). At the second session, members can be asked what they observed and what they would like to have happen in the future. They can also respond to each other's observations as group colleagues. de Shazer believes this intervention tends to increase individuals' optimism and hope about their present and future situation. The FFST technique puts the emphasis on future solutions rather than past problems (Murphy, 2008). Members generally cooperate with the FFST and report change or improvements since their first session (Walter & Peller, 2000). Bertolino and O'Hanlon (2002) suggest that the FFST intervention be used after clients have had a chance to express their present concerns, views, and stories. It is important that group members feel understood before they are directed to make changes.

GROUP LEADER FEEDBACK TO GROUP MEMBERS

Solution-focused practitioners typically allow time in each group session for sharing feedback with one another. This kind of summary feedback assists members in carrying their learning outside of the group sessions into daily living. De Jong and Berg (2008) describe three basic parts to the structure of the summary feedback: compliments, a bridge, and suggesting a task. *Compliments* are genuine affirmations of what clients are already doing (exceptions) that is leading toward effective solutions. These compliments, which are a form of encouragement, create hope and convey the expectation to clients that they can achieve their goals by drawing on their strengths and successes. Compliments can take the form of positive and sincere feedback about exceptions throughout a group session. Second, a *bridge* links the initial compliments to the suggested tasks to carry outside of the group that are always based on identified exceptions. The bridge provides the rationale for the suggestions. The third aspect of feedback consists of *suggesting tasks* to clients, which can be considered as homework. Observational tasks ask clients to simply pay attention to some aspect of their lives. This self-monitoring process helps clients note the differences when things are better, especially what was different about the way they thought, felt, or behaved. Behavioral tasks may be assigned when group members are uncertain of what they want different or what they will be doing when things are better. These tasks require that members actually do something that would likely be useful to them in constructing solutions. SFBT group leaders prefer ending a session by suggesting possible experiments for members based on something the members are already doing (exceptions), thinking, or feeling that is moving them in the direction of their goals. It is best if change ideas and assignments emanate from the group member, rather than the therapist. Oftentimes leaders encourage members to design their own experiments that they are willing to do before the next group session (de Shazer & Dolan, 2007).

Applying Solution-Focused Brief Therapy to Group Work in Schools

Solution-focused counseling offers a great deal of promise for practitioners who want a practical and time-effective approach to interventions in school settings. As a cooperative approach, SFBT shifts the focus from what's wrong to what's working (Murphy, 2008; Sklare, 2005). Rather than being a cookbook of techniques for removing students' problems, this approach offers school counselors a collaborative framework aimed at achieving small, concrete changes that enable students to discover a more productive direction. This model has much to offer to school counselors who are responsible for serving large caseloads of students with a range of problems from preschool through high school (Henderson & Thompson, 2011; Murphy, 2008; Sklare, 2005). Gingerich and Wabeke (2001) report that a number of writers have provided case examples and discussions of successfully employing *solution-focused brief counseling* (SFBC) in the schools.

Charlesworth and Jackson (2004) view solution-focused counseling as appropriate for school settings for a number of reasons:

- Counselors are able to provide effective counseling to more students in less time.
- The model underscores the importance of small changes and co-constructed goals.
- The approach helps students develop positive goals rather than negative "stop doing it" goals.
- SFBC is perceived as effective and practical because it emphasizes "what works" rather than "why" something is a problem.
- The approach encourages the acceptance and accommodation of diverse opinions and beliefs, which is appropriate for many school counselors who work in schools with diverse student groups.
- SFBC is based on clear concepts and is relatively easy to learn.
- It is a strength-based approach rather than a model based on psychological disorders and dysfunctional behaviors.

Sklare (2005) describes fives steps in SFBC that can be applied to counseling students, both individually and in groups:

- Students identify a well-defined goal that has meaning to them.
- Students then say what their lives would be like without the problem that gets in the way of attaining their goals.
- The counselor facilitates students' recognition of times when their problem did not exist and how they brought about exceptions to a problem.
- The counselor asks students to establish a baseline rating that reflects the severity of their situation at the present time, which can be accomplished by asking scaling questions. The counselor then encourages students to think of how they might move slowly up the scale. Tasks are very specific so that students have a clear direction toward change.
- The counselor constructs written messages to students that compliments their efforts and identifies a task to complete.

For a detailed description of 15 steps that can be used to lead group participants through a solution-focused journey, see Sklare (2005, pp. 147–156).

Sklare (2005) gives special attention to the process of goal setting and provides many concrete examples of how counselors can assist students in identifying well-established goals. Positive goals involve what students want to achieve and are stated in observable, specific, measurable, and attainable ways. Counselors assist students in changing negative goals, which are couched in words that imply the absence of something, into positive ones by focusing on desired behaviors. One cannot, for example, describe what "not angry" looks like. Davis and Osborn (2000, p. 64) suggest using the "great instead" question to help students identify a positive future: "So when you are not angry, what are you doing instead?"

The concepts and techniques in the solution-focused approach are applicable to both group and individual counseling (Murphy, 2008). Students in a counseling group can be asked to identify exceptions to their problematic situations and to identify resources that can be useful to them in achieving their goals. In these groups, the students can rate their progress toward their goals and provide feedback to the leader on the usefulness of each session. For more information on the tasks and techniques of solution-focused counseling in schools, see Murphy (2008) and Davis and Osborn (2000). For examples of solution-focused groups in schools, refer to Tollison and Synatschk (2007).

Applying Solution-Focused Brief Therapy With Multicultural Populations

Sklare (2005) contends that many characteristics of solution-focused brief counseling (SFBC) make it an ideal counseling approach with diverse populations: the emphasis on the experience of clients rather than working from the counselor's framework, the discussion of solutions rather than problems, the use of the client's words rather than the counselor's terms and phrases, and the focus on strengths rather than weaknesses. In their discussion of multicultural applications of SFBC, Henderson and Thompson (2011) maintain that SFBC works most effectively with individuals and cultures with preferences for engaging in direct behavior change rather than approaches that focus on feelings and cognitions. This appeals to people who want a practical approach to making things better as soon as possible.

Murphy (2008) claims that the emphasis on strengths and resources in solution-focused counseling supports culturally competent services to students, regardless of ethnicity and cultural background. Some specific aspects of solution-focused counseling that lend themselves to culturally competent practice include (a) treating each client as a unique individual; (b) collaborating on the goals of counseling; (c) tailoring services to each client; and (d) obtaining ongoing feedback from clients on the usefulness of interventions and adjusting them accordingly. Murphy summarizes this message: "Putting clients first and keeping them in the driver's seat throughout the helping process provides built-in safeguards for culturally sound counseling services" (p. 18).

Bertolino and O'Hanlon (2002) do not approach clients with a preconceived notion about their experience. Instead, they learn from their clients about their experiential world. Bertolino and O'Hanlon practice multicultural curiosity by listening respectfully to their clients, who actually become their best teachers. Here are some questions these authors suggest as a way to more fully understand multicultural influences on a client:

- Tell me more about the influence that [some aspect of your culture] has played in your life.
- What can you share with me about your background that will enable me to more fully understand you?
- What challenges have you faced growing up in your culture?
- What, if anything, about your background has been difficult for you?
- How have you been able to draw on strengths and resources from your culture? What resources can you draw from in times of need?

Questions such as these can shed light on specific multicultural influences that have been sources of support or that contributed to a client's problem.

The not-knowing stance the group leader assumes, and the assumption that the client is the expert, can limit the effectiveness of SFBT counseling for some individuals. In some cultural groups the professional is seen as the expert who will offer direction and solutions for the person seeking help. If the group counselor asserts "I am not really an expert; you are the expert; I trust in your resources for you to find solutions to your problems," this is likely to engender lack of confidence in the group leader. To avoid this situation, group counselors need to convey to those in the group that they have expertise in the group process but will not direct members to engage in behaviors that are contrary to their underlying goals. When group members ask for ideas from the leader because this is proper in their culture, the facilitator could engage members in a discussion of what those ideas might be.

Motivational Interviewing

Motivational Interviewing (MI) is a humanistic, client-centered, directive counseling approach that was developed by William R. Miller and Stephen Rollnick in the early 1980s. Over the past 25 years, clinical and research applications of motivational interviewing have grown at a remarkable pace, and this trend is reflected in the more than 800 publications and 200 random clinical trials on MI (Arkowitz & Westra, 2009).

Motivational interviewing was initially designed as a brief intervention for problem drinking, but subsequently this approach has been applied to a wide range of problems including substance abuse, compulsive gambling, eating disorders, anxiety disorders, depression, suicidality, chronic disease management, and health-related practices (Arkowitz & Miller, 2008; Arkowitz & Westra, 2009). MI has been applied to individual counseling more so than to group work, but the practice of group MI (and group motivational enhancement therapy, an adaptation of MI) is gaining momentum as an efficient and cost-effective preventive method and an intervention for court-mandated individuals and college students referred to campus educational programs because of alcohol violations (see LaChance, Ewing, Bryan, & Hutchison, 2009). Lundahl and Burke (2009) caution against relying solely on MI group treatment until more data supporting the effectiveness of group-delivered MI become available.

In this section I highlight ways that group counselors can integrate motivational principles with a number of approaches, especially person-centered therapy, cognitive-behavior therapy, reality therapy, and solution-focused therapy.

THE MI SPIRIT

MI is rooted in the philosophy of client-centered therapy, but with a "twist." The twist is that, unlike the nondirective person-centered approach, MI is deliberately directive and has the specific goals of reducing ambivalence about change and increasing intrinsic motivation (Arkowitz & Miller, 2008). MI emphasizes being purposeful and getting to the point—the direction, purpose, and point is to guide group members toward positive change (Cynthia Osborn, personal communication, March 2, 2010). In both person-centered therapy and MI, the counselor provides the conditions for growth and change by communicating attitudes of accurate empathy and unconditional positive regard. In MI, the therapeutic relationship is as important in achieving successful outcomes as the specific theoretical model or school of psychotherapy from which the therapist operates (Miller & Rollnick, 2002).

Like solution-focused therapy, MI emphasizes the relational context of therapy, which is known as the "MI spirit." When this MI spirit is applied to group counseling, it involves the group leader establishing collaborative partnerships with members, drawing on the ideas and resources of group members, and preserving the autonomy of the members (recognizing that all choices ultimately rest with the members rather than with the leader). Both MI and SFBT emphasize the internal frame of reference of clients, their present concerns, and discrepancies between values and behavior. Rollnick, Miller, and Butler (2008) describe MI as a "refined form of guiding." MI works by activating clients' own motivation for change and adherence to treatment. Group leaders assist members in becoming their own advocates for change and the primary agents of change in their lives.

There are many possibilities for combining solution-focused therapy and motivational interviewing that group practitioners can adapt for working with a variety of groups. An effective integration of these two approaches facilitates change through a collaborative and respectful therapeutic relationship, by honoring client stories, by recognizing client strengths and preferences, and by enhancing intrinsic motivation. Together SFBT and MI provide multiple ways of addressing the impasses clients often experience during the change process (Lewis & Osborn, 2004).

THE PRINCIPLES AND CLINICAL STRATEGIES OF MOTIVATIONAL INTERVIEWING

Miller and Rollnick (2002) formulated five basic principles of MI, which I have modified here to fit within the context of group counseling.

1. Group leaders strive to experience the world from the members' perspective without judgment or criticism. MI emphasizes reflective listening, which is a way for group practitioners to better understand the subjective world of members. This emphasis on understanding the members' subjective world is not unique to MI as this is a core concept in most of the relationship-oriented therapies.

2. Group leaders using MI reflect discrepancies between the behaviors and values of the members to increase the motivation to change. MI is designed to evoke and explore ambivalence. Leaders pay particular attention to the members' arguments for changing compared to their arguments for not changing. By listening to members' speech as they address both sides of ambivalence, group leaders assist members in emphasizing the argument for change. Leaders elicit and reinforce *change talk* by employing specific strategies to strengthen discussion about change. MI is directive, and leaders steer the conversation in the direction of considering change without persuading members to change. MI group leaders encourage members to determine whether change will occur, and if so, what kinds of changes will occur and when.

3. Leaders operating from an MI orientation support the members' self-efficacy, mainly by encouraging members to use their own resources to take

necessary actions and succeed in changing. MI therapists strive to enhance client agency about change and are interested in the group members' ideas about change. Emphasis is on the right and inherent ability of clients to make their own decisions.

4. Reluctance to change is viewed as a normal and expected part of the therapeutic process. Although members may see advantages to making life changes, they also may have many concerns and fears about changing. During the early phase of MI therapy it is common for members to express ambivalence about changing, and members may have insufficient motivation to bring about change. Group leaders strive to minimize the ambivalence and to build intrinsic motivation. The group leader attempts to understand both sides of this ambivalence from a member's perspective, and this material can be fruitfully explored in group sessions.

5. When clients show signs of readiness to change through decreased resistance to change and increased talk about change, a critical phase of MI begins. In this stage, clients may express a desire and ability to change, show an interest in questions about change, experiment with possible change actions between sessions, and envision a future picture of their life once the desired changes have been made. Therapists shift their focus toward strengthening clients' commitments to change and helping them implement a change plan.

The Stages of Change It is critical for the therapist to understand the client's degree of involvement in each of the stages of change. In the transtheoretical model of change, people are assumed to progress through a series of five identifiable stages in the counseling process (Prochaska & Norcross, 2010). In the *precontemplation stage,* there is no intention of changing a behavior pattern. In the *contemplation stage,* people are aware of a problem and are considering overcoming it, but they have not yet made a commitment to take action to bring about the change. In the *preparation stage,* individuals intend to take action immediately and report some small behavioral changes. In the *action stage,* individuals are taking steps to modify their behavior to solve their problems. During the *maintenance stage,* people work to consolidate their gains and prevent relapse.

People do not pass neatly through these five stages in linear fashion, and if change is initially unsuccessful, individuals may return to an earlier stage (Prochaska & Norcross, 2010). MI therapists strive to match specific interventions with whatever stage of change clients are experiencing. If there is a mismatch between process and stage, movement through the stage will be impeded and is likely to be manifested in reluctant behavior. MI focuses on present and future conditions and empowers clients to find ways to achieve their goals.

The attitudes and skills in MI are based on a person-centered philosophy and include using open-ended questions, employing reflective listening, affirming and supporting the client, summarizing and linking at the end of sessions, and eliciting and reinforcing *change talk*. Therapists guide clients to make a commitment to change and help them clarify where they want to go (Arkowitz & Miller, 2008). In MI the group leader assumes the role of a guide or change consultant and encourages a change plan that comes primarily from the members themselves.

CONCEPTS COMMON TO SOLUTION-FOCUSED BRIEF THERAPY AND MOTIVATIONAL INTERVIEWING

There are many common denominators between motivational interviewing and solution-focused therapy, and, as Lewis and Osborn (2004) have noted, both counseling styles have gained recognition and increased popularity over the past two decades. Lewis and Osborn state that a confluence between these two approaches can enhance clinical practice. I believe that this confluence has implications for group practitioners, regardless of their primary theoretical orientation. Some of these commonalities are discussed in the following sections.

Nonpathological, Health-Promoting Emphasis Both SFBT and MI emerged as a reaction against the prevailing medical model that focuses on problems. Neither approach gives much credence to diagnostic labels because of the dehumanizing aspect of attaching a label to a client. SFBT and MI practitioners believe in client abilities, strengths, resources, and competencies. The assumption is that clients want to be healthy and desire positive change. Group practitioners are mainly interested in exploring what is working well for participants in the group rather than dwelling on members' problems.

Multiple Perspectives Lewis and Osborn (2004) state that both MI and SFBT reflect a social constructionist, postmodern philosophy that argues for the existence of multiple social realities. MI exemplifies a phenomenological approach in which the counselor attempts to see life from the client's perspective and to identify goals from that vantage point. In MI clients are not persuaded to adopt advice by the counselor, rather they are invited to consider a menu of alternative interventions or options.

Reframing "Resistance" Resistance is typically viewed as a phenomenon that resides within the client, and traditional therapy approaches often assume that clients who are "stuck" are resistant to change. If an impasse in therapy is reached, clients are frequently blamed and labeled as "unmotivated." MI and SFBT hold that labeling clients "resistant" gets in the way of understanding clients' behavior and impedes development of a collaborative partnership with clients. MI encourages counselors to reflect on their style of interacting with clients to better understand their own part in creating resistant or noncompliant client behavior. By viewing resistance as something that emerges from the interactions between clients and counselors, the functions resistance serves are illuminated and counselors can adapt their approach to it. People who seek therapy are often ambivalent about change, and their motivation may ebb and flow during the course of therapy. A central goal of MI is to increase internal motivation to change that is based on the personal goals and values of the client (Arkowitz & Miller, 2008). Likewise, SFBT therapists engage clients in choosing goals and strategies for success. Both MI and SFBT group leaders take a respectful view of resistance and work with it therapeutically.

Cooperation Is Key MI was initially developed as a way of working with people with addictions that avoided the confrontational style used by many addictions counselors (Miller & Rollnick, 2002). MI stresses client self-responsibility and promotes an invitational style for working cooperatively with clients to generate alternative solutions to behavioral problems. MI therapists avoid arguing with clients, roll with resistance, express empathy, and listen reflectively. In SFBT therapists also work cooperatively with clients, and clients experience support from therapists, which facilitates openness toward future possibilities and new directions (Lewis & Osborn, 2004). MI and SFBT therapists do not view clients as opponents to be defeated but as allies who play a major role in their present and future success.

Use of Client Strengths and Resources Both MI and SFBT rest on the premise that people have strengths and resources that can be tapped in their efforts to bring about positive change. They emphasize that the responsibility for change lies with clients, not with the counselor. Individuals have within themselves the capacity to generate intrinsic motivation to change, and therapists and clients share a sense of hope and optimism that change is possible. Once clients believe that they have the capacity to change and heal, all sorts of exciting possibilities open up. This hope can lead to enhanced motivation to reach personal goals.

Temporal Sensitivity Both SFBT and MI are time-sensitive counseling approaches, with their respective ties to brief interventions in addiction counseling and to brief therapy. MI was designed from the outset to be a brief intervention aimed at producing results. SFBT also tends to be brief, but it is both present- and future-oriented. SFBT and MI practitioners use time efficiently, keeping themselves and their clients focused without rushing the process (Lewis & Osborn, 2004).

MOTIVATIONAL INTERVIEWING AS AN INTEGRATIVE APPROACH

Motivational interviewing can be integrated with cognitive behavioral and other therapies (Arkowitz, Westra, Miller, & Rollnick, 2008). Constantino, DeGeorge, Dadlani, and Overtree (2009) believe that the ability of MI to work with ambivalence and to address a client's hopes, fears, desires, and possible ambivalence about the therapist are among its main strengths as an integrative psychotherapy approach.

Many of MI's principles are compatible with cognitive behavioral therapy techniques. CBT group practitioners also use a structured approach and have an agenda for helping group members to make behavioral changes. Borrowing more fully from MI strategies, especially in exploring ambivalence and in working with clients to increase intrinsic motivation, could enhance the functioning of cognitive behavioral groups. MI also can be considered as a precursor to more formal treatment, for example, helping to prepare individual clients for cognitive behavioral group therapy.

I also see many possibilities of an integration of MI and reality therapy. As you will recall, reality therapy emphasizes the importance of group members making their own evaluation of their current behavior. Members are asked to determine for themselves the degree to which what they are doing in the present is working for them and is meeting their needs. Once members in a reality therapy group decide that they want to change some of their behaviors, they are ready to create an action plan. Both reality therapy and MI share common notions of how to best establish and implement a change plan.

Research on MI Cormier, Nurius, and Osborn (2009) note that motivational interviewing enjoys an extensive and impressive record of well-conducted and compelling research. Reviews of MI suggest that this counseling style has broad applications across behavioral domains, and the practice of MI (including combining elements of MI with other therapy methods) results in positive client outcomes. MI can be a significant factor in assisting clients in making a commitment to the therapy process, thus improving client involvement, adherence, and retention in cognitive behavioral and other action-oriented therapies. Cormier and colleagues believe that MI and SFBT approaches have earned appeal and relevance among clinicians because of their scholarly and research commitments. They conclude that both MI and SFBT are well-respected methods for helping people in the process of change.

Evaluation of Solution-Focused Brief Therapy in Groups

CONTRIBUTIONS AND STRENGTHS OF THE APPROACH

I especially value the optimistic orientation of SFBT that rests on the assumption that people are competent and can be trusted to use their resources in creating better solutions and more life-affirming stories. Rather than focusing on one's limitations, the emphasis is on possibilities. Many solution-focused practitioners and writers have found that clients are able to make significant moves toward building more satisfying lives in a short period of time (De Jong & Berg, 2008; de Shazer & Dolan, 2007; Metcalf, 1998; Murphy, 2008; O'Hanlon & Weiner-Davis, 2003; Sklare, 2005; Walter & Peller, 1992, 2000; Winslade & Monk, 2007).

I think the nonpathologizing stance characteristic of solution-focused practitioners is a major contribution to the counseling profession. Group participants are not viewed as being sick but rather as being stuck. Group counselors assist members in developing a new level of awareness of aspects of themselves that are underappreciated and overlooked. The emphasis is on what group members are doing when they are not stuck. The orientation is toward developing a fuller appreciation and utilization of human abilities (Hoyt, 2003). As you have seen, these practitioners do not accept the notion that the therapist is the expert who applies treatment interventions to a passive client. Rather than dwelling on what is wrong with a person, this approach views the client in positive ways from a strength-based perspective and thus empowers the person.

To its credit, solution-focused therapy is a brief approach, of about five sessions, that seems to show promising results (de Shazer, 1991). In de Shazer's summary of two outcome studies at the Brief Family Therapy Center, he reports that 91% of the clients who attended four or more sessions were successful in achieving their treatment goals. Brevity is a main appeal of SFBT in an era of managed care, which places a premium on short-term therapy. The orientation is on making each session count and helping clients to see that what happens after a therapy session is critical (Hoyt, 2003).

From a strictly empirical and objective perspective, research is somewhat antithetical to the social constructionist approach. Research should always be conducted from the perspective of the client and not from a generalizable or expert external perspective. With this in mind, the question can be raised, "How effective is solution-focused brief counseling?" Research that supports the successful outcomes of SFBC is increasing (Charlesworth & Jackson, 2004). Regardless of the specific theoretical orientation of the counselor, brief counseling has been shown to be effective for a wide range of problems. Reviews of research literature on psychotherapy outcome reveal that brief and long-term approaches are equally effective, yet brief methods are more cost-effective (Hoyt, 2003).

Other studies that have compared brief therapies with long-term therapies have generally found no difference in outcomes (McKeel, 1996). In a review of research of SFBT, McKeel concludes that when SFBT techniques have been tested the results are generally favorable. Although only a few studies of SFBT exist, outcome studies generally show that most clients receiving SFBT report accomplishing their treatment goals.

In their review of 15 outcome studies of SFBT, Gingerich and Eisengart (2000) found that 5 studies were well-controlled and all showed positive outcomes. The other 10 studies, which were only moderately controlled, supported a hypothesis of the effectiveness of SFBT. The review of these studies provided preliminary support for the efficacy of SFBT, but methodological flaws did not permit a definitive conclusion.

A major strength of the solution-focused approach to group work is the use of questioning, which is the centerpiece of this approach. Open-ended questions about the group member's attitudes, thoughts, feelings, behaviors, and perceptions during the times when the problem occurs less or is less intense are one of the main interventions. As we have seen, skilled group counselors do not barrage clients with questions; instead, by a combination of respectful listening and appropriate questioning it is possible for group participants to make progress. Especially useful are future-oriented questions that encourage group members to think about how they are likely to solve potential problems in the future. An assumption of this approach is that the future is both created and negotiable. The future is a hopeful place, where people are the architects of their own destiny (de Shazer & Dolan, 2007). It is the role of the solution-focused group counselor to create the landscape wherein the members construct their futures together.

LIMITATIONS OF THE APPROACH

A concern that I have about solution-focused brief group therapy pertains to the manner in which some group workers may glorify a technique and make it an end in itself. Several writers and practitioners have emphasized that when it comes to effective practice of SFBT there are no set formulas or recipes to follow (Freedman & Combs, 1996; Monk, Winslade, Crocket, & Epston, 1997; Winslade & Monk, 2007). Lipchik (2002) brings a sense of heart and soul to solution-focused therapy with her emphasis on going beyond technique, working with emotions, and attending to the therapeutic relationship.

To effectively practice solution-focused group therapy, it is essential that group leaders hold the basic belief that group participants have the internal resources to discover their own solutions. Group practitioners also need to possess a range of group and clinical skills that they can use in a timely way. In a relative short time group practitioners must be able to convey the importance of formulating specific goals, and then to effectively use appropriate interventions to assist members in attaining their goals. Some inexperienced or untrained group leaders may be enamored by any number of techniques of the solution-focused approach. But effective group work is not simply a matter of utilizing any of these interventions. Instead, it is the atmosphere created by the group facilitator that moves the group from a problem-focused belief to the belief that each member has the capacity to solve his or her own problems. The attitudes of group counselors and their ability to use questions that are reflective of genuine respectful interest are crucial to the process and outcomes of a group.

Some solution-focused therapists now acknowledge the problem of relying too much on a few techniques, and they are placing increased importance on the therapeutic relationship and the overall philosophy of the approach (Nichols, 2007, 2008). Currently, solution-focused therapists are encouraged to think in a possibility-oriented way, allowing the questions stirred by their curiosity to guide the process. Indeed, these findings have implications for group counselors who apply solution-focused methods. A solution-focused group counselor who can truly embrace the notion of not being the expert and instead can acknowledge the expertise of the group member will be successful with this model and will gain satisfaction from observing members grow through their personal discoveries (Linda Metcalf, personal communication, November 16, 2009).

Key figures of solution-focused therapy often present the theory as something revolutionary and new, yet the similarities between the Adlerian approach and SFBT are striking (Carlson, Watts, & Maniacci, 2006). Many solution-focused writers have criticized traditional theories for their focus on pathology, deficits, exploring the past, and ignoring clients' competencies and resources. However, Adlerians have long objected to the medical model, promoted the values of brief therapy, talked more about growth than curing clients' problems, given more attention to the present and the future than to a client's past, and have made the encouragement process central in therapy. Watts and Pietrzak (2000) make a case for the similarities between SFBT and Adlerian therapy, especially in the area of the encouragement process. They contend that theorists and practitioners of SFBT tend not to give Adler credit for the foundations of their approach.

In spite of these limitations, SFBT has much to offer group practitioners. Many of the basic ideas and techniques of solution-focused brief therapy can be integrated into the other therapeutic orientations addressed in this book. This model offers a framework for group practitioners, regardless of their theoretical orientation, to critically examine the basic assumptions that guide the interventions they make in their groups.

Where to Go From Here

The *Journal of Brief Therapy* is devoted to developments, innovations, and research related to brief therapy with individuals, couples, families, and groups. The articles deal with brief therapy related to all theoretical approaches, but especially to social constructionism, solution-focused therapy, and narrative therapy.

Springer Publishing Company
11 West 42nd Street, 15th Floor
New York, NY 10036
Telephone: (877) 687-7476
E-mail: contactus@springerpub.com
Website: www.springerpub.com

TRAINING IN SOLUTION-FOCUSED THERAPY APPROACHES

Below are several organizations that provide training in solution-focused brief therapy.

Center for Solution-Focused Brief Therapy
John Walter and Jane Peller
1620 W. Thome
Chicago, IL 60660
Telephone: (847) 475-2691
E-mail: j-peller@neiu.edu or walterpeller@aol.com

Bill O'Hanlon, Possibilities
551 Cordova Rd., #715
Santa Fe, NM 87501
Telephone: (800) 381-2374
Fax: (505) 983-2761
E-mail: PossiBill@aol.com
Website: http://www.brieftherapy.com

Therapeutic Collaborations: Consultation and Training (TCCT)
Bob Bertolino
P. O. Box 1175
St. Charles, MO 63302
Telephone/Fax: (314) 852-7274
E-mail: tcctinfo@cs.com

The Solution Focused Institute (SFI) at Texas Wesleyan University was founded in January 2009 in Fort Worth, Texas, to provide training to mental health practitioners and school teachers and counselors who desire to implement a solution-focused approach in their work. The institute provides training on- and offsite and offers supervision to individuals and groups.

Solution Focused Institute
Linda Metcalf, PhD
3001 Avenue D
Fort Worth, TX 76105
Telephone: (817) 690-2229
Fax: (817) 531-4935
E-mail: lmetcalf@txwes.edu
Website: www.Solutionfocusedinstitute.com

Motivational interviewing is a client-centered, directive method for enhancing intrinsic motivation to change by exploring and resolving ambivalence. The motivational interviewing website provides general information about the approach, as well as links, training resources, and information on reprints and recent research.

Motivational Interviewing
Website: www.motivationalinterview.org

AUTHOR LECTURES

Watch *Gerald Corey's Perspectives on Theory and Practice of Group Counseling* DVD or visit the *Theory and Practice of Group Counseling* CourseMate website at www.cengagebrain.com/shop/ISBN/0840033869 to watch videos of Dr. Gerald Corey presenting lectures for each chapter. Also available are unique eAudio lectures for each chapter and quiz questions for self-study.

Interviewing for Solutions (De Jong & Berg, 2008) is an excellent practical text aimed at teaching and learning solution-focused skills. It is written in a conversational and informal style and contains many examples to solidify learning of skills.

Solution-Focused Counseling in Schools (Murphy, 2008) is a clearly written and practical book that provides strategies for dealing with a range of problems from preschool through high school. This work focuses on the foundations of solution-focused counseling and on the tasks and techniques of this approach.

Brief Counseling That Works: A Solution-Focused Approach for School Counselors and Administrators (Sklare, 2005) provides guidelines for using solution-focused methods in schools. The author combines specific instructions with many case examples that offer an overview of basic principles and methods of the solution-focused approach applicable to K–12 school systems.

Solution-Focused Group Therapy: Ideas for Groups in Private Practice, Schools, Agencies, and Treatment Programs (Metcalf, 1998) deals with the practical applications of solution-focused group therapy in various settings.

Becoming Solution-Focused in Brief Therapy (Walter & Peller, 1992) and *Recreating Brief Therapy: Preferences and Possibilities* (Walter & Peller, 2000) are clearly written books that contain a great deal of useful information on basic ideas of brief therapy and ways of implementing solution-focused brief therapy.

Motivational Interviewing: Preparing People for Change (Miller & Rollnick, 2002) explains current thinking on the process of behavior change, present the principles of MI, and provides detailed guidelines for putting these principles into practice. Case examples illustrate key points and demonstrate the benefits of MI in addictions treatment and other clinical contexts. The authors also discuss the process of learning MI.

REFERENCES AND SUGGESTED READINGS

Anderson, H., & Goolishian, H. (1992). The client is the expert: A not-knowing approach to therapy. In S. McNamee & K. J. Gergen (Eds.), *Therapy as social construction* (pp. 25–39). Newbury Park, CA: Sage.

*Arkowitz, H., & Miller, W. R. (2008). Learning, applying, and extending motivational interviewing. In H. Arkowitz, H. A. Westra, W. R. Miller, & S. Rollnick (Eds.), *Motivational interviewing in the treatment of psychological disorders* (pp. 1–25). New York: Guilford Press.

Arkowitz, H., & Westra, H. A. (2009). Introduction to the special series on motivational interviewing and psychotherapy. *Journal of Clinical Psychology, 65*(11), 1149–1155.

*Arkowitz, H., Westra, H. A., Miller, W. R., & Rollnick, S. (Eds.). (2008). *Motivational interviewing in the treatment of psychological problems.* New York: Guilford Press.

Bateson, G. (1972). *Steps to an ecology of mind.* New York: Ballantine.

Berg, I. K. (1994). *Family based services: A solution-focused approach.* New York: Norton.

*Bertolino, B. (2010). *Strengths-based engagement and practice: Creating effective helping relationships.* Boston, MA: Allyn & Bacon/Pearson Education.

---

* Books and articles marked with an asterisk (*) are suggested for further study.

*Bertolino, B., & O'Hanlon, B. (2002). *Collaborative, competency-based counseling and therapy.* Boston: Allyn & Bacon.

*Bitter, J. R. (2009). *Theory and practice of family therapy and counseling* (chap. 10). Belmont, CA: Brooks/Cole, Cengage Learning.

Bubenzer, D. L., & West, J. D. (1993). William Hudson O'Hanlon: On seeking possibilities and solutions in therapy. *The Family Journal: Counseling and Therapy for Couples and Families, 1*(4), 365–379.

*Carlson, J., Watts, R. E., & Maniacci, M. (2006). *Adlerian therapy: Theory and practice.* Washington DC: American Psychological Association.

Charlesworth, J. R., & Jackson, M. (2004). Solution-focused brief counseling: An approach for professional school counselors. In B. T. Erford (Ed.), *Professional school counseling: A handbook of theories, programs & practices* (pp. 139–148). Austin, TX: CAPS Press.

Constantino, M. J., DeGeorge, J., Dadlani, M. B., & Overtree, C. E. (2009). Motivational interviewing: A bellwether for context-responsive psychotherapy integration. *Journal of Clinical Psychology, 65*(11), 1246–1253.

*Cormier, S., Nurius, P. S., & Osborn, C. J. (2009). *Interviewing and change strategies for helpers: Fundamental skills and cognitive behavioral interventions* (6th ed.). Belmont, CA: Brooks/Cole, Cengage Learning.

*Davis, T. E., & Osborn, C. J. (2000). *The solution-focused school counselor: Shaping professional practice.* Philadelphia, PA: Accelerated Development (Taylor & Francis Group).

*De Jong, P., & Berg, I. K. (2008). *Interviewing for solutions* (3rd ed.). Belmont, CA: Brooks/Cole, Cengage Learning.

*de Shazer, S. (1985). *Keys to solutions in brief therapy.* New York: Norton.

*de Shazer, S. (1988). *Clues: Investigating solutions in brief therapy.* New York: Norton.

*de Shazer, S. (1991). *Putting difference to work.* New York: Norton.

*de Shazer, S. (1994). *Words were originally magic.* New York: Norton.

*de Shazer, S., & Dolon, Y. (with Korman, H., McCollum, E., Trepper, T., & Berg, I. K.). (2007). *More than miracles: The state of the art of solution-focused brief therapy.* New York: Haworth.

*Freedman, J., & Combs, G. (1996). *Narrative therapy: The social construction of preferred realities.* New York: Norton.

Gingerich, W. J., & Eisengart, S. (2000). Solution-focused brief therapy: A review of the outcome research. *Family Process, 39*(4), 477–498.

Gingerich, W. J., & Wabeke, T. (2001). A solution-focused approach to mental health intervention in school settings. *Children & Schools, 23*, 33–41.

Henderson, D. A., & Thompson, C. L. (2011). *Counseling children* (8th ed.). Belmont, CA: Brooks/Cole, Cengage Learning.

Hoyt, M. F. (2003). Brief psychotherapies. In A. S. Gurman, & S. B. Messer (Eds.), *Essential psychotherapies: Theory and practice* (2nd ed., pp. 350–399). New York: Guilford Press.

LaChance, H., Ewing, S.W.F., Bryan, A. D., & Hutchison, K. E. (2009). What makes group MET work: A randomized controlled trial of college student drinkers in mandated alcohol diversion. *Psychology of Addictive Behaviors, 23*, 598–612.

*Lewis, T. F., & Osborn, C. J. (2004). Solution-focused counseling and motivational interviewing: A consideration of confluence. *Journal of Counseling and Development, 82*(1), 38–48.

Lipchik, E. (2002). *Beyond technique in solution-focused therapy: Working with emotions and the therapeutic relationship.* New York: Guilford Press.

Lundahl, B., & Burke, B. L. (2009). The effectiveness and applicability of motivational interviewing: A practice-friendly review of four meta-analyses. *Journal of Clinical Psychology, 65*(11), 1232–1245.

McKeel, A. J. (1996). A clinician's guide to research on solution-focused brief therapy. In S. D. Miller, M. A. Hubble, &

B. L. Duncan (Eds.), *Handbook of solution-focused brief therapy* (pp. 251–271). San Francisco: Jossey-Bass.

*Metcalf, L. (1998). *Solution focused group therapy: Ideas for groups in private practice, schools, agencies, and treatment programs.* New York: Free Press.

*Miller, S. D., Hubble, M. A., & Duncan, B. L. (Eds.). (1996). *Handbook of solution-focused brief therapy.* San Francisco: Jossey-Bass.

*Miller, W. R., & Rollnick, S. (2002). *Motivational interviewing: Preparing people for change* (2nd ed.). New York: Guilford Press.

Monk, G., Winslade, J., Crocket, K., & Epston, D. (Eds.). (1997). *Narrative therapy in practice: The archeology of hope.* San Francisco: Jossey-Bass.

*Murphy, J. J. (2008). *Solution-focused counseling in schools* (2nd ed.). Alexandria, VA: American Counseling Association.

Nichols, M. P. (with Schwartz, R. C.). (2007). *The essentials of family therapy* (3rd ed.). Boston: Allyn & Bacon.

Nichols, M. P. (with Schwartz, R. C.). (2008). *Family therapy: Concepts and methods* (8th ed.). Boston: Allyn & Bacon.

*O'Hanlon, W. H., & Weiner-Davis, M. (2003). *In search of solutions: A new direction in psychotherapy* (rev. ed.). New York: Norton.

Prochaska, J., & Norcross, J. (2010). *Systems of psychotherapy: A transtheoretical analysis* (7th ed.). Belmont, CA: Brooks/Cole, Cengage Learning.

*Rollnick, S., Miller, W. R., & Butler, C. C. (2008). *Motivational interviewing in health care: Helping patients change behavior.* New York: Guilford Press.

*Sklare, G. B. (2005). *Brief counseling that works: A solution-focused approach for school counselors and administrators* (2nd ed.). Thousand Oaks, CA: Corwin Press.

Tollison, P. K., & Synatschk, K. O. (2007). *SOS: A practical guide for leading solution-focused groups with kids K–12.* Austin, TX: PRO-ED.

*Walter, J. L., & Peller, J. E. (1992). *Becoming solution-focused in brief therapy.* New York: Brunner/Mazel.

*Walter, J. L., & Peller, J. E. (1996). Rethinking our assumptions: Assuming anew in a postmodern world. In S. D. Miller, M. A. Hubble, & B. L. Duncan (Eds.), *Handbook of solution-focused brief therapy* (pp. 9–26). San Francisco: Jossey-Bass.

*Walter, J. L., & Peller, J. E. (2000). *Recreating brief therapy: Preferences and possibilities.* New York: Norton.

Watts, R. E., & Pietrzak, D. (2000). Adlerian "encouragement" and the therapeutic process of solution-focused brief therapy. *Journal of Counseling and Development, 78,* 442–447.

White, M., & Epston, D. (1990). *Narrative means to therapeutic ends.* New York: Norton.

*Winslade, J., & Monk, G. (2007). *Narrative counseling in schools: Powerful and brief* (2nd ed.). Thousand Oaks, CA: Corwin Press (Sage).

PART

3

INTEGRATION AND APPLICATION

CHAPTER SEVENTEEN

Comparisons, Contrasts, and Integration

Introduction

The purpose of this chapter is fourfold: (1) to compare and contrast the various models as they apply to issues special to group work; (2) to raise some basic questions that you'll need to answer now and throughout the course of your practice; (3) to assist you in conceptualizing and integrating the various theoretical perspectives that most appeal to you; and (4) to stimulate your thinking about ways of developing and refining group techniques that reflect your leadership style. This chapter will help you answer these questions:

- Is it possible to achieve some integration of the diverse group models by focusing on their commonalities?

- How would an integrated view of the various perspectives actually help me define my own goals of group counseling?

- How do I go about blending concepts and techniques from several approaches to achieve my own definition of the leader's role and my own unique leadership style?

- How can I best develop collaborative relationships with members so that responsibility for the group is a shared function?

- What kind of structuring do I want to provide for a group? How do I determine how much structure is appropriate?

- How do I develop techniques that fit with my personality and style and are also appropriate for the kinds of groups I lead?

- How can the techniques of the theoretical approaches be modified to fit the cultural backgrounds of various clients?

- What are the advantages and the disadvantages of an integrative approach to group practice?

The Goals of Group Counseling: Various Perspectives

To impart meaningful direction to their groups, leaders need to address themselves to the issue of goals. What should be the specific goals of a given group, and who should determine them? How can the leader help group members develop meaningful goals for themselves? How does the leader's theoretical orientation influence the process of goal setting? Is it possible to set group goals based on a variety of theoretical orientations? To help you find common denominators among the goals stressed by the various theoretical models and to guide you in your attempt to integrate these models, Table 17.1 (p. 471) lists the essential therapeutic goals of each of the group approaches discussed in Part Two. As you read the table, keep in mind that the diversity of goals can be simplified by seeing the goals as existing on a continuum from general, global, long-term objectives to specific, concrete, short-term objectives. Existential and relationship-oriented group approaches tend to deal with broad goals that are formulated by the members, whereas cognitive behavioral approaches focus on short-term, observable, and precise goals that are formulated collaboratively with the members and the leader. The goals at opposite ends of the continuum are not necessarily contradictory; it is just a matter of how specifically the goals are defined. Thus a convergence is possible if practitioners view concrete short-term goals as components of broad, long-range goals.

Most theoretical perspectives agree on the importance of group members' formulating their own specific goals. When leaders decide that they know what is best for the participants and force their own goals on them, they typically encounter resistance. To be sure, leaders need to have some overall goals for the group, and these should be openly disclosed to the members. These general group goals should in no way infringe on the members' freedom to select personal goals that will give direction to their work in the group. Individual goal setting is an ongoing collaborative process that needs to be constantly reevaluated. The leader can be of invaluable assistance in this regard by encouraging members to formulate clear and specific goals and by helping members determine how they can work toward achieving these goals.

A SNAPSHOT OF THE GOALS ASSOCIATED WITH VARIOUS THEORIES

In Argosy University's counseling program (in Atlanta), Dr. Mary Kate Reese and her colleagues asked the question, "How would you describe this group in a screening interview, or in your advertisement, or to the group in the first session?" They developed the following "snapshot" views for each theory from the perspective of the leader.

Psychoanalytic: "In this group I'll be paying a lot of attention to what is going on in the here-and-now, with particular attention on your reactions to one another. I'll look for patterns in the way you relate, and my job is to help you see how your earlier experiences often influence the way you perceive others and react to them. Part of our process will be to focus on re-creating, analyzing, discussing, and interpreting past experiences and on working through defenses and resistances that operate at the unconscious level."

Adlerian: "This group will be a place to experience belonging and connection and to receive encouragement toward desired change, to increase self-esteem and self-acceptance, and to work on social relationships. We will explore your perceptions of your childhood family, recognize assumptions you live by now that may relate to those perceptions, and explore alternative perceptions and choices."

Psychodrama: "This group will assist you in examining choices you've made about how you are living. In this group I'll be encouraging you to enact—not just talk about—your conflicts and the problems you'd like to explore. By releasing your feelings about a particular reenactment of an event in your life, you are likely to come to a different understanding of that event. You will be encouraged to experiment with different ways of behaving that may help to increase your creativity and spontaneity."

Existential: "This is a group for people who want to become truthful with themselves and clarify what gives meaning to their present and future. It is a context in which to look at oneself, decide the degree to which one is a fully functioning person as opposed to reflecting what others expect, and consider what choices might be more authentically one's own. Members can openly share their fears related to living in unfulfilling ways and come to see how they have compromised their integrity. The group offers many opportunities for tackling life's challenges. Members can gradually discover ways in which they have lost their direction and can begin to be more true to themselves."

Person-centered: "We will determine together what kind of group this will be. My role is to create a climate that facilitates growth more than that of the expert that structures and decides things or uses techniques to make growth happen. I strongly believe that, within a safe setting, your own sense of what you need will guide you to make the desired changes in your life."

Gestalt: "We will pay particular attention to the here-and-now and deal with whatever prevents you from maintaining a present-centered awareness. The focus will be on the *what* and *how*, rather than the *why* of behavior. One of my functions is to assist you in identifying your unfinished business from the past, bringing it into the present, and achieving more understanding of how your past may be impeding your present experiencing. I may at times suggest various exercises and experiments to group members that could help increase awareness."

Transactional analysis (TA): "This is a structured, psychoeducational group focused on teaching you to identify early childhood decisions leading to your chosen life script, current behavior patterns that reinforce that life script, and methods for making new decisions to facilitate desired change. We will learn about the different ego states that individuals manifest and find ways to operate from the one most appropriate to the reality of the given situation. We will also work a lot with interactions we have with others, including any 'games' that we may play that prevent intimacy with others."

Cognitive behavioral: "My main goal in this group is to assist you in determining whether your current behavior meets your needs adequately. If you discover that it doesn't and if you decide to change, we will work collaboratively to identify specific goals, to gather baseline data on the current level of relevant behaviors, and to formulate a plan of action designed to promote change. The group will offer you a place to practice this plan for change."

Rational emotive behavior therapy: "Our thinking patterns and behavior strongly influence our emotions. In this group we will explore an educational model that will help group members reduce troubling emotions through paying attention to and changing unhelpful self-talk. Group members will be expected to engage in the process of change through active participation in group meetings and through the completion of homework."

Reality therapy: "All of our behavior is our best attempt to control the world around us in order to satisfy certain basic needs. In this group, my role is to help members make self-evaluations and to formulate and carry out plans to change behavior. Essentially, this group focuses on solving current problems through changes in thinking and behavior, and will provide a supportive environment of accountability for group members to contract and complete desired change."

Solution-focused brief therapy: "In this group, we will focus on solutions instead of problems. There is a strong emphasis on identifying goals and emphasizing your competencies. As a group leader, I will ask questions that will encourage you to focus on the language that you use, the prior solutions that you have used in other situations, and the *exceptions* (examples of times in which you have *not* had the identified problem)."

Role and Functions of the Group Leader: Various Perspectives

As a group leader, what is your role: facilitator, therapist, teacher, catalyst, coach, consultant, generator of solutions, problem solver, guide, fellow explorer, technician, director, tour guide, mentor, or evaluator? How you answer this question will depend in part on your theoretical perspective, but ultimately your answer will be based on your own definition of the leader's role and on your evaluation of what the most significant functions of the leader are. Certain criteria also cut across all the theoretical approaches: for example, the type of group and its goals, the setting, the nature of the participants, and the demands of your job.

Before discussing the various perspectives on the group leader's role and functions, let's briefly review some of the tasks that are essential to successful group leadership:

1. Group leaders initiate and promote interaction by the way they structure the group and model behaviors. They demonstrate how to share, take risks, relate honestly, and involve others in interactions.

2. Group leaders orient members to the group process, teaching them how to get the most from their group and helping them become aware of the group dynamics.

3. Group leaders must be capable of sensitive, active listening. Only by paying full attention to the members' verbal and nonverbal communication can they help participants move toward a deeper level of self-exploration and self-understanding.

4. Group leaders are responsible for creating a safe and supportive climate conducive to exploring personally significant issues.

5. Group leaders have the tasks of setting limits, establishing group rules, informing members of their rights and responsibilities, and protecting members.

As we have seen, each therapeutic approach stresses different roles and functions for the group leader. For example, the person-centered approach emphasizes the role of facilitator. In this model the group is seen as having the resources to direct itself, and the leader is supposed to facilitate rather than direct group process. In solution-focused brief therapy, the group leader disavows the role of expert, preferring a more collaborative stance. The leader-as-expert is replaced by the group member-as-expert. Other approaches view the leader as a teacher; rational emotive behavior therapy, reality therapy, cognitive behavior therapy, and transactional analysis are all based on the assumption that group counseling is largely an educational and learning process. In these models the leader's key function is teaching skills and providing a cognitive framework that will lead to reeducation and behavioral changes.

Other models, such as the psychoanalytic approach, focus on the role of the group leader as a technical expert who interprets intrapsychic and interpersonal processes as they manifest themselves in a group. Still other models, such as psychodrama and the existential, person-centered, and Gestalt approaches, stress the leader's role in helping members gain an experiential awareness of their conflicts through meaningful relationships with the leader and others in the group. As we have seen, your roles and functions as a group leader are many; which of them you choose to emphasize is partly determined by your theoretical orientation. As groups move through the various developmental stages, the needs of group members will change, and your role will change as well as you accommodate the needs of the group. As you review the different perspectives summarized in Table 17.2 (p. 472), consider what elements you want to incorporate from each of them in defining your own role as group leader.

Degree of Structuring and Division of Responsibility: Various Perspectives

Group leaders are often concerned with the question of what constitutes the optimum degree of structure in a group. It should be clear that all groups have a structure. Even the least directive group leaders, who avoid imposing a format on the group, do make the choice of having an open structure and letting the participants determine the course of the group.

Group structuring exists on a continuum, from extremely nondirective to highly directive. On the nondirective end of the continuum are psychoanalytic groups, person-centered groups, and some existential groups. In these groups the leader tends to assume a less directive stance and encourages group members to assume much of the responsibility for the direction the group takes.

At the opposite end of the continuum are those leaders who provide a high degree of structure for the group. Some of these leaders tend to use structured exercises to open the group sessions; also, they often employ techniques to focus members on specific themes or problem areas. Many cognitive behavior therapy groups are characterized by a very active, structured, and directive group leadership. This is also true of reality therapy groups, REBT groups, TA groups, and solution-focused groups. Typically, there is a progression from session to session, the meetings are organized in accordance with a predetermined agenda, and certain procedures are used to direct the group toward exploration and resolution of specific problem areas or attainment of members' goals.

Like structuring, division of responsibility can be conceptualized in terms of a continuum. At one end are those group leaders who see themselves as experts and who believe they should actively intervene to keep the group moving in productive ways. These leaders believe the group's outcomes are largely dependent on their expertise and skills. Because therapy is considered an educative process, the group leader is seen as a teacher in charge of the reeducation of group members. For effective results, group leaders use a methodology aimed at cognitive restructuring and behavioral change. Practitioners who embrace this perspective include those with orientations such as cognitive behavior therapy, rational emotive behavior therapy, transactional analysis, reality therapy, and solution-focused brief therapy. However, despite the active and directive role assigned to the leader, these approaches also place a considerable share of responsibility for directing the group on the members, who are expected to be active in the sessions and practice between group sessions.

At the other end of the continuum are group leaders who inform participants at the beginning of a group that the members are responsible to define the direction the group takes. This type of leadership is characteristic of the person-centered leader, who sees the participants as knowing what is best for them. Rather than assuming the role of directing the course a group takes, the therapist functions as a facilitator by creating a trusting climate wherein members can safely explore significant personal issues and search for the necessary resources within themselves.

Somewhat in the middle of the continuum are Gestalt group leaders. They are typically active, in that they make interventions that provide the group with structure, but they also expect members to participate in the creation of experiments that will heighten their awareness. Group leaders are responsible for being aware of their own experience throughout the group process and for suggesting appropriate experiments to intensify group work. Members are responsible for bringing up personal concerns that they want to investigate in the group and for making their own interpretations. Solution-focused group leaders are active, yet they strive to create a collaborative therapeutic partnership with the members. Facilitators of a solution-focused group do their best to show members how they can use the strengths and resources already available to them to construct solutions to their concerns. Table 17.3 (p. 473) gives you an idea of the variety of theoretical positions on structuring and division of responsibility.

From my perspective, group leaders need to achieve a balance between assuming too much responsibility for the direction of the group and assuming too little. If leaders believe group members do not have the capacity to take care of themselves, members soon begin to live up to this expectation. Besides undermining members' independence, leaders who assume an inordinate amount of responsibility burden themselves greatly. They tend to blame themselves for whatever failures or setbacks the group suffers. If members do little productive work, these leaders view this as a reflection of their lack of skill. This style of leadership is draining, and the leaders who use it may soon lose the energy required to lead groups.

In contrast, leaders who place all the responsibility for the direction and outcomes of a group on the participants may be minimizing their own role in the outcomes of their groups. When a group seems to flounder and is not engaged in productive work, these leaders ignore their role in the group process.

The Use of Techniques: Various Perspectives

Techniques are quite useful both as catalysts for group action and as devices to keep the group moving. But techniques are just tools, and like all tools they can be used effectively or ineffectively. When leaders fall into a pattern of employing methods mechanically, they become technicians and are not responding to the needs of the particular group they are leading. Also, indiscriminate use of techniques can increase the resistance level of the group instead of facilitating deeper communication and exploration. Some leaders, overly eager to use new methods, rely too much on techniques to bring energy to the group and provide it with a direction. Others, out of anxiety over not knowing how to deal with certain problems that arise in a group, may employ techniques without understanding their purpose. Group leaders should have a sound rationale for using particular methods of intervention. Techniques need to be an extension of who the leader is as a person, and group leaders should not force themselves to use methods that don't suit their personality and their unique leadership style.

My basic assumption is that techniques ought to facilitate group process, not artificially create action in a group. I also assume that group techniques are most effective when the group leader learns how to pay attention to the obvious. They can deepen feelings that are already present, and they should grow out of what is occurring in the group at the time. There is always something going on in a group, and this seems like a good area of focus. I like the notion of leaders and members collaboratively creating experiments that grow out of what is happening presently within a group, which is a perspective shared by Gestalt therapists. Although I tend to use techniques to introduce material at the initial stage of a group and often use them to integrate what members have learned at the final stage, I generally do not have a preset agenda. I take my cues from what is occurring within the group and flow with that, rather than attempting to direct the group to pursue a specific theme. For example, if I notice that there is little energy in the room and that few members appear willing to be engaged in significant work, I do not introduce an exercise designed to elicit feelings or promote interaction. Instead, I tend to let the group know what I am thinking or feeling, and I try to get an assessment of what each person is experiencing.

In choosing techniques to facilitate group process, you need to consider several factors. Your theory, of course, will influence what methods you employ. If your theory of choice focuses on cognitive dimensions, your techniques are likely to encourage members to look for the connection between their thought patterns and their actions. If you have an experiential orientation, your techniques will tend to promote an awareness of present feelings and an intensification of these feelings. If you adhere to a solution-focused orientation, you will be asking members to talk about exceptions to their problems and encouraging them to generate possibilities. If you are behaviorally oriented, many of your techniques will be geared to getting members to monitor their actions and experiment with specific behaviors. If you are cognitively oriented, your techniques are likely to be aimed at assisting members to identify their beliefs and self-talk and to create functional beliefs. Your style of leadership also has much to do with what methods you will use. Finally, the population with whom you are working, the purpose of your group, and the stage of development of the group are all factors to consider in the selection of techniques. Regardless of your theory, you need to understand the relationship between techniques and theoretical concepts and be fully aware of why you are using certain methods. Of course, it is important to continually assess the effects of these techniques.

As illustrated by Table 17.4 (p. 475), the various group models offer a variety of strategies for initiating and maintaining group interaction. As a group leader, there is no reason for you to restrict yourself to the techniques of a single approach simply because that's the approach you favor. If you have an existential orientation, you can draw on techniques from the cognitive behavioral approaches or from the solution-focused model. In summary, you can use your imagination to discover ways of adapting techniques from various theoretical models to the specific type of group you lead and of modifying them to suit your leadership style and the needs of your group members.

Group Work in a Multicultural Context: Various Perspectives

Each of the theories presented in this book has been briefly examined for its relevance to culturally diverse populations. As can be seen in Table 17.5 (p. 476), each perspective has certain concepts or techniques that can contribute to effective multicultural group counseling. Yet they all have some limitations, and caution is needed in using certain techniques that flow from a given theory (see Table 17.6, p. 478). Technical eclecticism seems especially necessary in working with a diverse range of cultural backgrounds. Harm can come to group participants who are expected to fit all the specifications of a given theory, whether or not the values espoused by the theory are consistent with their own cultural values. Rather than stretching the group members to fit the dimensions of a single theory, your challenge is to adapt your practices to fit the unique needs of the members of your groups. This requirement implies that you possess knowledge of various cultures, awareness of your own cultural heritage, and skills to assist diverse clients in meeting their needs within the realities of their culture.

It is essential for you to be able to assess the special needs of the members of your groups. Depending on the group member's ethnicity and culture and also on the individual concerns that bring a member to a group, you need to show flexibility in utilizing diverse therapeutic strategies. At times, some members will need more direction. Others will be very hesitant in talking about themselves in personal ways, especially during the early phase of a group. Be patient and avoid quickly pushing members to "open up and be real." Furthermore, you need to recognize that what may appear to be resistance is very likely to be the client's response to years of cultural conditioning and respect for certain values and traditions. It is useful for you to be familiar with a variety of theoretical approaches and to be able to employ and adapt your techniques to fit the person-in-the-environment. It is not enough to merely assist members in gaining insight, expressing suppressed emotions, or making certain behavioral changes. Your task is to find practical strategies for adapting the techniques you have developed to enable group members to question the impact their culture continues to have on their life and to make decisions about what facets of their life they want to change. Being an effective group leader involves reflecting on how your own culture influences you and your interventions in the group. This awareness will be a critical factor in your becoming more sensitive to the cultural backgrounds of the members in your groups.

Applications of an Integrative Model

The term *integrative model* refers to a perspective based on concepts and techniques from the various theoretical approaches. It is the model I use in my own practice of group work. In this section I describe how I apply my synthesis at each stage of a group's development. This model is designed to address the three factors of thinking, feeling, and doing. As you've seen, some of the 11 theories discussed in Part Two focus on cognition, others on experiencing feelings, and others on behavior. My goal is to blend the unique contributions of these theories so that all three dimensions of human experiencing are given attention at each phase of a group. At the same time, it is important to avoid the trap of emerging with a hodgepodge of unamalgamated theories hastily thrown together. Your goal should be to develop a consistent conceptual framework that you can use as a basis for selecting from the multiple techniques that you have studied. I want to emphasize that developing your own integrative approach is a long-term venture, and doing this soon after graduation is probably an unrealistic goal. It takes considerable study of many different theories to form a basis for making intelligent choices of what to use from these various approaches.

THEORIES APPLIED TO THE PREGROUP STAGE

The preparatory period in the formation of a group may be the most critical of all. If the group's foundation is weak, the group may never get out of the starting gate. Effective groups do not simply "happen." The hard work and careful organization that go into planning a group are bound to have payoffs once the group gets under way. At this point it would be a good idea for you to review the major considerations in forming groups, found in Chapter 4.

The cognitive behavioral theories are particularly relevant at the pregroup stage; they emphasize assessing both the need for a particular kind of group and the participant's readiness and appropriateness for a group. As a group leader, you must have clear expectations, a rationale for why and how a group is an effective approach, and a sense of how to design a specific group tailored to the unique needs and interests of the members. If you are clear about how a group can benefit prospective members, you'll be better able to help them decide whether or not to join. If members know what they are getting into, the chances are increased that they will become active and committed participants.

In this regard, the therapeutic approaches that structure a group on a contractual basis have much to offer. A contract can help demystify the group process, can increase the members' sense of responsibility to become active agents in their own change, and can structure the course a group takes. Contracts set forth the division of responsibility between the members and the leader, and they provide the leader with some therapeutic leverage. As you will remember, the cognitively and behaviorally oriented therapies stress contracts as a way of beginning the process. TA groups, and, sometimes, cognitive behavioral groups, rational emotive behavior therapy groups, and reality therapy groups operate on a contractual basis. Whatever your theoretical orientation, open-ended and flexible contracts can be drawn up before the group actually meets as a whole.

THEORIES APPLIED TO THE INITIAL STAGE

Basic Characteristics The early phase of a group is a time for orientation and exploration. Some of the distinguishing characteristics at this time are these:

- Members are attempting to find a place in the group.
- They are trying to get acquainted and learn what a group is all about.
- They are gradually learning the norms and expectations.

At this time, there is a certain tentativeness within the group. Perhaps the most basic issue pertains to creating and maintaining trust. The attitudes and behaviors of the group leader are directly related to the creation of a level of trust that will promote significant interaction.

Drawing on Theories The relationship-oriented approaches (especially person-centered therapy, existential therapy, Gestalt therapy, and psychodrama) provide an excellent foundation for building a community characterized by trust and the willingness to take the risks that are necessary for change. The leader's modeling is especially important, as members learn more from what the leader does than from what he or she says. Here is where enthusiasm about groups can be communicated to the members by a dedicated, competent, and caring group leader. A basic sense of respect for what the members are experiencing as they approach a new group can best be demonstrated by a leader's willingness to allow members to express what they are thinking and feeling in the here-and-now. Typically, members do have some initial anxieties. They may fear an unfamiliar situation, rejection, or closeness. Some may fear opening up more than they will be able to manage, disrupting their life outside the group, or incurring the disapproval of others in the group. A genuine interest in listening to these feelings sets the tone for caring, attentiveness, and compassion and goes a long way toward creating a climate in which members can be free to share what they feel and think.

Defining Personal Goals It is during the initial stage that the *cognitive behavioral* approaches have special relevance. I like the cognitive behavioral emphasis on helping members identify concrete aspects of their behavior that they most want to change. From there the leader may do some teaching to show members how involvement in the group can be instrumental in attaining their goals. I see it as counterproductive for leaders to impose on members specific goals that they should work toward, for unless the members really want to change, there is little hope that change can be forced on them. For this reason I value the Adlerian concept of goal alignment. Adlerians make special efforts to negotiate a congruence of goals between the client and the therapist. TA groups are also characterized by mutually agreed-upon therapeutic goals. In a reality therapy group the members are asked to evaluate their wants and to determine whether their needs are realistic. Reality therapy also invites members to look at their behavior and decide whether it is working for them. If members make the evaluation that their current behavior is not working, the process of making specific behavioral changes can begin. Solution-focused group facilitators assist members to identify their goals by asking them the miracle question: "If a miracle were to occur and your problem were solved, what would be different in your life?" The group leader works with members in developing well-formed goals as soon as possible. Questions that lead to goal setting include "What will be different in your life when your problems are solved?" and "What will be going on in the future that will tell you and the rest of us in the group that things are better for you?"

If members are not aided in making an evaluation of their wants, needs, and current behavior, they find it very difficult to know where to begin. Careful consideration of this personal evaluation is a way to engage the group members and to motivate them to do something different. Of course, the skill in facilitating a group involves showing members how a group can help them get what they say they want. I cannot overstress the importance of challenging members to decide if they really want to change some of their thoughts, feelings, and behaviors.

Although I am sympathetic toward the existential goal of learning how to live more creatively by accepting freedom and responsibility, I think such broad goals need to be narrowed down so that members have a clear idea of what thoughts, feelings, and actions they are willing to change and how to bring this change about. A way to help members specify their goals is to ask them to write them down.

THEORIES APPLIED TO THE TRANSITION STAGE

Learning to Deal With Conflict and Resistance One of the most challenging and often frustrating periods in the life of a group is the transition phase. Before a group can progress to the working stage, it typically must learn to recognize and deal with anxiety, defensiveness, reluctance, conflict, the struggle for control, challenges to the leader, and various other problematic behaviors. Some groups reach the transitional period only to remain stuck there. This impasse can be traced either to an earlier failure to establish norms or to ineffectual handling of resistance and conflict within the group. It is essential that conflict be both recognized and then dealt with therapeutically if the group is to move forward. One way to recognize potential resistance is to regularly assess the group members' level of satisfaction with their participation in the group. This can be done in a brief written evaluation, which can then be tabulated and brought back to the group. It is useful to get members accustomed to regular assessments, for in this way problems within the group can be detected and then worked on in the sessions. Specific questions can be asked about each member's level of investment, satisfaction with the sessions, trust level, and willingness to take risks. Refer to the *Student Manual* of this text for ideas about inventories that can be used to assess group process. Of course, this type of assessment is consistent with behavioral approaches that stress specificity of behavior, outcomes, and regular feedback about the process as a way to determine whether the group interventions are effective.

Again, the role of leader modeling is critical when it comes to accepting and dealing with avoidance or resistance. At times, leaders create defensive behavior on the part of members by what they do or don't do. If leaders take too personally problems that occur within the group, they burden themselves and tend to become defensive. It is essential to give members some room to maneuver; to avoid responding sharply or defensively; and, most certainly, to avoid sarcasm. The manner in which the group leader deals with the inevitable reluctance that manifests itself in various avoidances and defensive behaviors will determine how well the group meets the developmental tasks at the transition phase. It is useful for you to view resistance as a normal and healthy sign of a group's movement toward autonomy. Rather than viewing member hesitation or any form of resistance as a nuisance to be gotten around, you can help members understand and deal with the sources of their behavior in a therapeutic way.

Ways of Conceptualizing Resistance Several theoretical perspectives shed some light on the dynamics of resistance and suggest methods of dealing with it constructively. From a psychoanalytic perspective, resistance is seen as anything that prevents members from dealing with unconscious material. It is the unconscious attempt to defend oneself from the anxiety that would arise if the unconscious were uncovered. It helps me to remember that members have to struggle with intrapsychic conflicts as well as interpersonal conflicts. A leader who is sensitive to the ambivalence that members experience—both wanting to be a part of the process of self-discovery and fearing self-knowledge—can help participants begin to look at their fears and defenses.

I see ways of combining the psychoanalytic and Adlerian views of resistance. Members typically reexperience some of the old feelings they had in their original family. Sibling rivalry, position in the group, acceptance/rejection feelings, strivings for attention and success, authority issues, managing feelings, and childhood traumas all surface in the group experience. People are often stuck in a developmental sense because of these unexplored situations that now intrude on their ability to function effectively. In many ways the group can resemble one's family of origin. By working with their projections, transferences, attractions, and feelings toward others in the group, the members can experiment with new ways of thinking about themselves and others.

A Thinking, Feeling, Behaving Perspective When a group is in transition, I appreciate the freedom given by the person-centered approach to express any feelings and have this expression accepted. My hope is that members will allow themselves to *feel* the ways in which they are resisting and to intensify those feelings. Here is where I draw on some of the action-oriented techniques of Gestalt therapy and psychodrama so that clients will have a way to experience as fully as possible whatever they feel. It is important to assess what members need, however, and to work within the framework of their cultural background. Some members, because of their cultural injunctions, would have a difficult time getting involved in the emotional aspects of Gestalt experiments or emotionally intense psychodramas. It is certainly not therapeutically productive to push individuals to experience emotions, but it could be helpful to explore with them their beliefs associated with expressing emotions.

At some point I would also want to work with the belief systems and self-talk of the members. Here is where I find transactional analysis, rational emotive behavior therapy, and the cognitive behavioral therapies of value. For example, a member might participate very little in a group because she is following parental injunctions such as these: "Don't show what you feel." "Don't talk in public about your family and personal problems." "Don't trust others." "Be strong, and don't give in to feelings of self-pity." I think TA provides a useful framework within which members can gain awareness of these parental messages and their early decisions. Although a group experience can help these clients eventually challenge the validity of certain messages, it is important to avoid confronting some of these values too quickly. Patience and respect are extremely important at this time.

REBT and other cognitive behavior therapies are also of value in helping members challenge some of the self-defeating beliefs that lead to an entrenchment of their defensiveness in the group. Some members may say very little because of their fear of disapproval or because they are convinced that they must say things "perfectly" if they hope to be understood. Once members allow themselves to experience their hesitations on a feeling level, they are better able to genuinely challenge their cognitions associated with defensive behavior. Here is where writing helps again. If members can be encouraged to keep a journal of their thoughts (and how these thoughts lead to some unwanted behaviors and feelings), they can then do some in-depth exploration of certain self-talk that is not productive. They can learn new and more functional cognitions, and they can practice them both in and out of group. Related to this is their willingness to begin to behave in different ways. I like the emphasis of both reality therapy and solution-focused brief therapy on paying attention to what one is *doing* and REBT's emphasis on *practicing* new behaviors as the basis for making lasting changes. Solution-focused therapy and reality therapy provide some particularly useful questions that can lead members to make plans for change. This planning can be one way for members to actually begin to act differently.

THEORIES APPLIED TO THE WORKING STAGE

During the working stage there is a commitment by members to explore the significant problems that they bring to the sessions and to express their reactions to what is taking place within the group. I find that this stage requires the least degree of structuring. In part this is because members bring up issues they want to work on, freely interact with one another, have the feeling of being a group rather than a bunch of strangers, and assume responsibility to keep the sessions moving.

Concepts and Techniques My preference is to let the members raise the issues they are willing to pursue seriously rather than taking the responsibility for calling on them, drawing them out, or telling them what they should talk about. I still find it helpful to ask members to create their own agenda for each meeting, and I like to begin a group session by asking each person to declare as clearly as possible what he or she wants for the session. This does not imply a passive stance, however, for during the working stage I am very willing to suggest experiments and to invite members to take part in a technique that is designed to heighten whatever it is that they are experiencing. Again, my concern is with the thinking, feeling, and doing dimensions, and the techniques I suggest reflect this type of integration. Once members declare that they do want to work and decide what it is they want to accomplish, I typically ask them if they are willing to participate in an experiment.

Generally, I start by helping members to pay attention to what they are experiencing or what they are aware of in the here-and-now. Gestalt experiments are most useful in focusing on present-centered awareness and bringing any unfinished business from the past to the surface. I favor the approach that asks members to bring any past issue into the present, as is true of both psychodrama and Gestalt. There is a lively quality to the work, and members rather quickly begin to experience what they feel rather than talking abstractly about feelings and thoughts. For example, if a woman becomes aware that she is afraid of growing up to be just like the mother she resents, a good place to begin is to ask her to "bring your mother into the group" symbolically. Again, Gestalt therapy and psychodrama offer a variety of techniques to help her get into focus and intensify her experience. She might assume her mother's identity and actually speak to others in the group "as her mother." Although I value the contact with feelings, I think it is of limited value to stop with catharsis or the mere expression of her feelings. I am likely to suggest that she identify some of the beliefs that she has picked up from her mother. Perhaps she has uncritically accepted some self-defeating beliefs and is keeping herself upset by not challenging these beliefs.

Coupled with her emotional work, some exploration of her cognitions is likely to reveal how her daily behavior is limiting her. Therefore, I see debates as productive in a group. Especially valuable are debates that members can learn to have among themselves. They can challenge untested assumptions, argue the pros and cons of a given issue, and think about how they sometimes set themselves up for defeat. Finally, working at a cognitive behavioral level is an excellent way to correct faulty thinking and emotional disturbances.

My particular emphasis during the working phase is to focus on what members are doing outside of the sessions. Therefore, I like to allow time toward the end of each session to ask every member to respond to questions such as these: "What did you learn about yourself in today's session?" "What kind of behaviors can you practice during the week?" "What is one specific homework assignment that you are willing to give yourself and carry out?" This approach reinforces in-group learning, and it helps members continually think about how to apply new ways of thinking and behaving in everyday situations.

THEORIES APPLIED TO THE FINAL STAGE

Review of Tasks The final stage of the group's evolution is critical. During this stage, members have an opportunity to clarify the meaning of their experiences in the group, to consolidate the gains they have made, and to revise their decisions about what newly acquired behaviors they want to transfer to their daily life. The major task facing members during this consolidation stage is to learn ways of maintaining these changed behaviors in the outside world. My focus is on getting the members to review the nature of any changes on a thinking, feeling, and behaving level. What resources and strengths did they discover in themselves? Have they learned the value of expressing their feelings rather than swallowing them? Have they learned that repressing their feelings results in some indirect expression of them? What cognitions have they modified? Have they let go of some dysfunctional cognitions that lead to emotional upsets? Have they critically evaluated their beliefs and values and made them their own? What concrete behavioral changes have they made that they value? How did they make these changes? How can they continue to behave in ways that are productive? What plan for action can they devise now that the group is coming to an end so that they can continue to make progress?

Theoretical Perspectives I tend to use the most structure during the beginning and ending phases of a group. I don't believe members will automatically transfer specific cognitive, emotional, and behavioral changes from the group to the outside world. Therefore, I provide a structure that I hope will promote this transfer of learning. I have mentioned that in ongoing groups I do whatever I can to promote action on the part of the members by getting them to create their own homework assignments and then to report on their progress at the next group meeting. This is a way of continually using the group as a place to learn how to be different and then of carrying this new behavior into life. The group is a means to an end and should never become an end in itself.

Whereas I tend to use experiential therapies and exploration of feelings during the working phase, during the final stage I lean toward the cognitive behavioral therapies and toward putting one's learning into some type of conceptual framework. From the cognitive behavioral therapies I draw techniques such as practice and rehearsal for leaving a group, self-monitoring procedures, building a support system beyond the group, and learning methods of self-reinforcement. I see therapy as a teaching/learning process, and I try to help members devise a conceptual framework that will ensure that they make sense of what they have experienced. Therefore, at the final stage I tend to frequently ask, "What did you learn in this group that you value, and how did you learn it?" I don't want members attributing their changes to the magic of the group but to the specific actions that they took to change. Cognitive behavior therapy, TA, REBT, reality therapy, and solution-focused brief therapy are relevant models at this point in a group's history because they stress the importance of developing specific plans for change, making a commitment to do what is needed to bring about change, and evaluating the outcomes of the therapeutic process.

Although members are urged to try out a plan of action during the working phase, it is during the final stage that such a plan assumes top priority. It is also important to help members find ways to continue to build on their newly acquired skills. Members can promote their change by deciding toward the end of the group on other paths for growth. They can make decisions about specific

activities that will keep challenging them. They can make contracts to behave in certain ways once the group ends.

I emphasize cognitive work and behavioral plans for action during the final stage, but I do not assume that feelings are unimportant at this time. It is critical that members deal with their feelings about separation and termination, that they express any fears or reservations they may have about making it in the world without the support of the group, and that they learn how to say good-bye. Also, the opportunity to complete any unfinished business is paramount at this time.

Toward the end of a group's history there is a place for the role of the leader as a teacher. Leaders can caution members and provide them with practical strategies for dealing with setbacks once they leave a group. Members need to learn that the path toward growth is bumpy and uneven. At this time they can be taught how to evaluate the impact of the group on themselves as well as assess the progress they have made as a group.

THEORIES APPLIED TO POSTGROUP ISSUES

After the group comes to an end, the members' main task is applying their in-group learning to an action program in their daily life so that they can function in self-directed ways. I value setting aside time for individual interviews with each member, if possible, along with arranging for a follow-up group session. Such procedures build in accountability, for both the members and the leader can more accurately assess the impact of the group. Again, the cognitive behavioral approaches stress this accountability and evaluation, which enable the leader to make modifications in future groups based on what seemed to work. Follow-up procedures also provide a safety valve. If members left the group with unresolved issues or negative reactions, they can at least discuss them with the group leader.

THE PROS AND CONS OF AN INTEGRATIVE MODEL

As I've said many times, I'm convinced that as a group practitioner you need to find a style that fits you as a person; the model I've described is the result of my own search for an approach to groups that fits me both professionally and personally. It reflects my view of groups as entities that express in an integrated fashion the thinking, feeling, and doing dimensions of individual members. It also combines the didactic with the experiential because I believe what we experience in a group needs to be supported by a conceptual framework. Without such a framework, it would be difficult for us to make sense of the experience and to understand its implications for our daily existence. My model brings together action-oriented, insight-oriented, and experientially oriented approaches—that is, the cognitive, affective, and behavioral dimensions—to pursue more effectively the basic goal of any therapeutic group: change.

I believe an integration of therapeutic perspectives provides the best way to develop your interventions in a group, but creating an integrative stance is an ongoing project that comes with experience and reflection. You cannot simply pick bits and pieces from theories in a random and fragmented manner. In forming an integrative perspective, it is important to ask yourself these questions: "Which theories provide a basis for understanding the cognitive dimensions? the feeling aspects? the behavioral dimension?" Most of the 11 therapeutic orientations I have presented focus on a primary dimension of human experience. Although the other dimensions are not necessarily ignored, they tend not to be emphasized.

As I mentioned earlier, developing an integrative perspective requires much reading, thinking, and actual counseling experience. Unless you have an accurate and in-depth knowledge of these theories, you cannot formulate a true synthesis. A central message of this book has been to encourage you to remain open to each theory, to do further reading, and to reflect on how the key concepts of each theory fit your personality. Building your personalized theory of counseling, based on what you consider to be the best features of several theories, is a long-term venture. Becoming an effective leader involves a process of defining and refining a personalized group theory that will guide you in your practice and allow you to make sense of what occurs in groups. Of course, the specific type of group that you are leading and the makeup of the people in your group are critical variables in deciding what strategies are most appropriate. Be open to modifying your techniques so that they fit the needs of the members of the group, including their social and cultural background.

Having said all that, I wish to add that there are potential drawbacks to encouraging the development of an integrative approach, as opposed to sticking primarily with one theory. At its worst, an integrative approach can be an excuse for sloppy practice—a practice that lacks a systematic rationale for what you actually do in your work. If you merely pick and choose according to whims, it is likely that your selections will just reflect your biases and preconceived ideas. At its best, however, integration can be a creative synthesis of the unique contributions of diverse approaches, dynamically integrating concepts and techniques that fit the uniqueness of your personality and style.

Summary and Review Tables

At this point it would be useful for you to reflect on the major insights you have gained through taking this course and reading this book. Most of all, think about what theories seemed to have the most practical application in helping you understand your present life situation. You might consider what changes you are interested in making and which approaches could provide you with strategies to modify specific thoughts, feelings, and behaviors. This is a good time to review what you may have learned about your ability to establish effective relationships with other people. Especially important is a review of any personal characteristics that could either help or hinder you in developing solid working relationships with the members in your groups.

After you make this review of significant personal learning, I suggest that you also review and reflect upon what you have learned about group process. It has been my experience that between the first and the last day of an introductory course in group counseling, students find that what seems at first to be an overwhelming mass of knowledge and a bewildering array of theories eventually becomes a manageable store of understanding about the basis of counseling. Moreover, I hope you will be patient enough to recognize that much of the theoretical foundation you have received in this book will take on new meanings when you gain more practical experience in leading various groups. The same is true for the many professional and ethical issues that were discussed in the book. I think it is essential that you reflect on these basic issues, that you begin to formulate your own position on them, and that you discuss them with fellow students and instructors. Even though experience will teach you many new lessons, you will be far better equipped to deal with these and related issues when you meet them if you reflect on them now.

As you review the tables (Tables 17.1 through 17.6) summarizing the 11 theories, consider which particular approaches you would be most inclined to draw from with respect to these dimensions: (1) goals of group counseling, (2) group leader's role and function, (3) degree of structuring and division of responsibility, (4) group techniques, and (5) adapting theories to the practice of multicultural group counseling.

AUTHOR LECTURES

Watch *Gerald Corey's Perspectives on Theory and Practice of Group Counseling* DVD or visit the *Theory and Practice of Group Counseling* CourseMate website at www. cengagebrain.com/shop/ISBN/0840033869 to watch videos of Dr. Gerald Corey presenting lectures for each chapter. Also available are unique eAudio lectures for each chapter and quiz questions for self-study.

TABLE 17.1 COMPARATIVE OVERVIEW OF GROUP GOALS

MODEL	GOALS
PSYCHOANALYTIC	To provide a climate that helps clients reexperience early family relationships. To uncover repressed feelings associated with past events that carry over into current behavior. To facilitate insight into the origins of faulty psychological development and stimulate a corrective emotional experience.
ADLERIAN	To create a therapeutic relationship that encourages participants to explore their basic life assumptions and to achieve a broader understanding of lifestyles. To help members recognize their strengths and their power to change. To encourage clients to acquire a sense of social interest and to find purpose in life.
PSYCHODRAMA	To facilitate the release of pent-up feelings, to provide insight, and to help clients develop new and more effective behaviors. To encourage clients to live in the present. To develop openness, honesty, and spontaneity. To open up unexplored possibilities for solving conflicts and for living more creatively.
EXISTENTIAL	To provide conditions that maximize self-awareness and reduce blocks to growth. To help members discover and use freedom of choice and assume responsibility for their own choices. To make it possible for members to encounter others in the here-and-now and to use the group as a place to overcome feelings of alienation.
PERSON-CENTERED	To provide a safe climate wherein members can explore the full range of their feelings and their experiencing. To help members become increasingly open to new experiences and develop confidence in themselves and their own judgments.
GESTALT	To enable members to pay close attention to their moment-to-moment experiencing so they can recognize and integrate disowned aspects of themselves.
TRANSACTIONAL ANALYSIS	To assist clients in becoming free of scripts and games in their interactions. To challenge members to reexamine early decisions and make new ones based on awareness.

(contd.)

TABLE 17.1 (contd.)

MODEL	GOALS
COGNITIVE BEHAVIOR THERAPY	To assist members in evaluating how their thinking influences how they are behaving. To help group members eliminate maladaptive behaviors and learn new and more effective behavioral patterns. (Broad goals are broken down into precise subgoals.)
RATIONAL EMOTIVE BEHAVIOR THERAPY	To assist group members in achieving both unconditional self-acceptance and unconditional other-acceptance. To eliminate the members' self-defeating outlook on life and replace it with a more tolerant and rational one.
REALITY THERAPY	To guide members toward learning realistic and responsible behavior. To assist group members in evaluating their behavior and in deciding on a plan of action for change.
SOLUTION-FOCUSED THERAPY	To help members adopt an attitudinal and language shift from talking about problems to talking about solutions. To encourage members to choose the goals they want to accomplish in the group. To assist members in identifying their competencies and strengths that will lead to new possibilities.

TABLE 17.2 COMPARATIVE OVERVIEW OF LEADER'S ROLE AND FUNCTIONS

MODEL	LEADER'S ROLES
PSYCHOANALYTIC	Facilitates group interaction by helping create an accepting and tolerant climate. Focuses on transferences and multiple transferences within the group. Signals indications of resistance and transference and interprets their meanings. Helps members become conscious of and work through unfinished business. Sets limits for the group by developing a therapeutic frame.
ADLERIAN	Assists members in gaining insight into their patterns through lifestyle assessment. Models attentive caring. Helps members accept and utilize their assets. Encourages members to develop the courage needed to translate what is learned in the group to behavior outside of the group.
PSYCHODRAMA	Has the job of warming up the group, helping set up a psychodrama, directing the enactment, and then processing the outcomes with the participants. Specific tasks include facilitating, observing, directing, and producing.
EXISTENTIAL	Has the central role of being fully present and available to individuals in the group and of grasping their subjective being-in-the-world. Functions by creating a person-to-person relationship, by disclosing him- or herself, and by confronting members in a caring way.

PERSON-CENTERED	Facilitates the group (as opposed to directing it)—deals with barriers to communication, establishes a climate of trust, and assists the group in functioning effectively. Central task is to be genuine in the sessions and demonstrate caring, respect, and understanding. Has the primary role of helping members follow their inner direction.
GESTALT	Suggests experiments designed to help participants intensify their experience and be alert to their body messages. Assists members in identifying and working through unfinished business from the past that interferes with current functioning. Focuses on whatever is in the foreground of the members' awareness.
TRANSACTIONAL ANALYSIS	Has a didactic role and assists members in identifying injunctions. Teaches members how to recognize the games they play to avoid intimacy, the ego state in which they are functioning in a given transaction, and the self-defeating aspects of early decisions and adopted life plans.
COGNITIVE BEHAVIOR THERAPY	Functions as an expert in modifying clients' thinking and behavior. The leader tends to be directive and often functions as teacher. Imparts information and teaches coping skills and methods of modifying behavior so that members can practice outside group sessions.
RATIONAL EMOTIVE BEHAVIOR THERAPY	Functions didactically: explains, teaches, and reeducates. Helps members see and rigorously confront their illogical thinking and identify its connection with self-defeating behavior. Teaches members to change their patterns of thinking and behaving.
REALITY THERAPY	Teaches members the basics of choice theory as a way to help them understand why they behave as they do. Encourages members to evaluate their current behavior and make more effective choices. Helps members to formulate and implement a plan for change.
SOLUTION-FOCUSED THERAPY	Facilitates the group by eliciting the perspectives, resources, and unique experiences of members. Creates opportunities for members to see themselves as competent and resourceful. Assists members in functioning as cofacilitators who support and encourage each other and keep the focus on exceptions rather than problems.

TABLE 17.3 COMPARATIVE OVERVIEW OF DEGREE OF STRUCTURING AND DIVISION OF RESPONSIBILITIES

MODEL	STRUCTURING AND RESPONSIBILITIES
PSYCHOANALYTIC	*Leader* shies away from directive leadership and allows the group to determine its own course; interprets the meaning of certain behavioral patterns. *Members* raise issues and produce material from the unconscious; assume increasing responsibility for interacting spontaneously, making interpretations, and sharing insights about others; become auxiliary therapists for one another.

(contd.)

TABLE 17.3 (contd.)

MODEL	STRUCTURING AND RESPONSIBILITIES
ADLERIAN	*Leader*, at the outset, works toward goal alignment; takes active steps to establish and maintain a therapeutic relationship, to explore and analyze the individual's dynamics, and to communicate a basic attitude of concern and hope. *Members* develop insight about themselves; assume responsibility for taking positive measures to make changes; and consider alternative beliefs, goals, and behaviors.
PSYCHODRAMA	*Director/leader* suggests specific techniques designed to intensify feelings, re-create past situations, and provide increased awareness of conflicts; makes sure that the protagonist is attended to and that other members of the group have a chance to share what they experienced during the psychodrama. *Members* produce the material for psychodramas and, when in the role of protagonist, direct their own psychodramas.
EXISTENTIAL	*Leader* may structure the group along the lines of certain existential themes such as freedom, responsibility, anxiety, and guilt; shares here-and-now feelings with the group. *Members* are responsible for deciding the issues they want to explore, thus determining the direction of the group.
PERSON-CENTERED	*Leader* provides very little structuring or direction and allows members to determine how time is spent in group. *Members* are seen as having the capacity to find a meaningful direction, of being able to help one another, and of moving toward constructive outcomes.
GESTALT	*Leader* is responsible for being aware of his or her present-centered experience and for using it in the context of the group; brings structure to the group by introducing appropriate experiments to intensify whatever the member is experiencing. *Members* must be active and make their own interpretations.
TRANSACTIONAL ANALYSIS	Because of the stress on an equal relationship between leader and members, responsibility is shared, as specified in a contract. *Members* and *leader* spell out in the contract what changes members want to make and what issues they want to explore in the group.
COGNITIVE BEHAVIOR THERAPY	*Leader* is responsible for active teaching and for having the group proceed according to a predetermined and structured agenda. *Members* are expected to be active, to evaluate their thinking, to apply what they learn to everyday life situations, and to practice new behaviors outside the group.
RATIONAL EMOTIVE BEHAVIOR THERAPY	*Leader* is responsible for confronting any signs of member behavior based on faulty thinking; structures the group experience so that members stay with the task of making constructive changes in thinking and behaving. *Members* are responsible for exploring their own self-defeating thinking; they are expected to continue this work outside the group.

REALITY THERAPY	*Leader* teaches members to assume responsibility for how they are living. Structures the group by assisting members to evaluate the degree to which what they are presently doing is getting them what they want. Helps members to assess the quality of their interpersonal relationships, both in daily life and in the group. *Members* decide on specific changes they want to make and design an action plan for implementing these changes.
SOLUTION-FOCUSED THERAPY	*Leader* moves the group from a problem focus to a solution focus; creates a collaborative partnership with members to show how they can use the strengths and resources they have to construct solutions. *Members* keep on a solution track instead of a problem track; pay attention to what is working in daily life and continue doing more of this; observe what they are doing when things are going better.

TABLE 17.4 COMPARATIVE OVERVIEW OF GROUP TECHNIQUES

MODEL	TECHNIQUES
PSYCHOANALYTIC	Interpretation, dream analysis, free association, analysis of resistance, and analysis of transference—all designed to make the unconscious conscious and bring about insight.
ADLERIAN	Analysis and assessment, exploration of family constellation, reporting of earliest recollections, confrontation, interpretation, cognitive restructuring, challenging of one's belief system, and exploration of social dynamics and of one's unique style of life.
PSYCHODRAMA	Self-presentation, presentation of the other, interview in the role of the other and interview in the role of the self, soliloquy, role reversal, double technique and auxiliary egos, mirroring, and future projection.
EXISTENTIAL	Since this approach stresses understanding first and techniques second, no specific set of methods is prescribed. However, leaders can borrow techniques from other therapies to better understand the world of clients and to deepen the level of therapeutic work, as long as the focus is on a subjective understanding of a member's world.
PERSON-CENTERED	The stress is on the facilitator's attitudes and behavior, and structured or planned techniques are generally not used. In place of techniques, attitudes include active listening, reflection of feelings, clarification, support, empathy, and "being there" for the client.
GESTALT	Many action-oriented techniques are available to the leader, all of which intensify immediate experiencing and awareness of current feelings. Techniques include empty chair, game of dialogue, fantasy approaches, rehearsal techniques, exaggerating a behavior, staying with feelings, dialogues with

(*contd.*)

TABLE 17.4 (contd.)

MODEL	TECHNIQUES
	self or significant others in the present, and dream work. Experiments are designed to enable participants to gain increased awareness. Experiments are best done in a collaborative way between the leader and a member.
TRANSACTIONAL ANALYSIS	Techniques include the use of a script-analysis checklist or questionnaire to detect early injunctions and decisions, games, and life positions; family modeling; role playing; and structural analysis.
COGNITIVE BEHAVIOR THERAPY	The main techniques, which are based on behavioral and learning principles and are aimed at behavioral changes and cognitive restructuring, include Socratic dialogue, self-monitoring, self-help techniques, reinforcement and supportive measures, behavior rehearsal, coaching, modeling, feedback, and procedures for evaluating and changing cognitions.
RATIONAL EMOTIVE BEHAVIOR THERAPY	Leaders use a wide range of cognitive, behavioral, and emotive interventions to bring about change. Leaders teach, model, probe, confront, challenge, and actively direct. Cognitive methods include disputation of faulty beliefs, use of coping self-statements, psychoeducational work, and cognitive homework. Behavioral methods include role playing, behavior rehearsal, homework assignments, and skills training.
REALITY THERAPY	A wide range of techniques is used, such as role playing, modeling, use of humor, contracts, using the WDEP model, and designing specific plans for action.
SOLUTION-FOCUSED THERAPY	Main techniques include raising questions, asking clients to look for exceptions to a problem, the miracle question, scaling questions, focusing on strengths, use of metaphors, and carrying out homework assignments.

TABLE 17.5 COMPARATIVE OVERVIEW OF CONTRIBUTIONS TO MULTICULTURAL COUNSELING

MODEL	CONTRIBUTIONS
PSYCHOANALYTIC	Focus on family dynamics is appropriate for working with many minority groups. Therapist formality appeals to those clients who expect professional distance. Notion of defense is helpful in understanding inner dynamics and dealing with environmental stresses.
ADLERIAN	Culture is viewed as a perspective and background from which meaning in life can be derived. Each individual will make a different meaning out of his or her personal cultural experience.

PSYCHODRAMA	For reserved clients, this approach invites self-expression in the present. Director can create scenes that are culturally sensitive and assist members in understanding the impact of their culture on them. Through enactment, nonverbal clients have other means of communication. Opportunities arise for developing spontaneity and creativity within the framework of one's culture.
EXISTENTIAL	A core value is the emphasis on understanding the member's phenomenological world, including cultural background. This approach leads to empowerment. It can help members examine their options for change within the context of their cultural realities.
PERSON-CENTERED	Main strengths are respect for client's values, active listening, welcoming of differences, nonjudgmental attitude, understanding, willingness to allow clients to determine what will be explored in sessions, and prizing cultural pluralism.
GESTALT	Focus on expressing oneself nonverbally is congruent with those cultures that look beyond words for messages. Approach provides many ways of working with group members who have cultural injunctions against freely expressing feelings.
TRANSACTIONAL ANALYSIS	Contractual method acts as a safeguard against therapist imposition of values that may not be congruent with a client's culture. This approach offers a basis for understanding the impact of cultural and familial injunctions. It provides a structure that many group participants will value.
COGNITIVE BEHAVIOR THERAPY	Focus on thinking and behavior, rather than on feelings, is compatible with many cultures. Strengths include preparation of members by teaching them purposes of group; assisting members in learning practical skills; educational focus of groups; and stress on self-management strategies. Expertise of leader, structure of group, and practical slant are viewed positively by many participants.
RATIONAL EMOTIVE BEHAVIOR THERAPY	This approach provides ways of questioning one's beliefs and identifying values that may no longer be functional. Its focus on thinking and rationality (as opposed to expressing feelings) is likely to be acceptable to many participants. Emphasis on teaching/learning process tends to avoid the stigma of mental illness. Many members may value the leader directiveness, structured approach, and stress on homework.
REALITY THERAPY	Focus is on members making their own evaluation of behavior (including how they respond to their culture). Through personal assessment they can determine the degree to which their needs and wants are being satisfied; they can find a balance between retaining their own ethnic identity and integrating some of the values and practices of the dominant society.
SOLUTION-FOCUSED THERAPY	This approach works best with individuals and cultures with preferences for engaging in direct behavior change rather than approaches that deal mainly with feelings. The emphasis on the experience of clients rather than on working from the therapist's framework is an advantage. This model appeals to people who want a practical approach to making things better as soon as possible.

TABLE 17.6 COMPARATIVE OVERVIEW OF LIMITATIONS IN MULTICULTURAL COUNSELING

MODEL	LIMITATIONS
PSYCHOANALYTIC	Focus on insight, intrapsychic dynamics, and long-term treatment is often not valued by clients who prefer to learn coping skills in dealing with pressing environmental concerns. Internal focus can conflict with cultural values that stress an interpersonal and environmental focus.
ADLERIAN	This approach's detailed interview about one's family background can conflict with cultures that have injunctions against disclosing family matters. Leader needs to make certain that the goals of members are respected and that these goals are congruent with the goals of a given group.
PSYCHODRAMA	Emphasis on experiencing and expressing feelings, on catharsis, and on enacting past problems in the present can be highly threatening for some clients. Caution is needed in encouraging clients to display their intense emotions in the presence of others.
EXISTENTIAL	Its values of individuality, freedom, autonomy, and self-realization often conflict with cultural values of collectivism, respect for tradition, deference to authority, and interdependence. Some may be deterred by absence of specific techniques. Others will expect more focus on surviving in their world.
PERSON-CENTERED	Some of the core values of this approach may not be congruent with the group member's culture. Lack of leader direction and structure are unacceptable for many clients who are seeking direction, help, and solutions from a knowledgeable leader.
GESTALT	Members who have been culturally conditioned to be emotionally reserved may not embrace Gestalt techniques. Some may not see how "being aware of present experiencing" will lead to solving their problems.
TRANSACTIONAL ANALYSIS	Terminology of TA may distract clients from some cultures with a different perspective. Leader must establish clear contract of what the group member wants before challenging the person's life scripts, cultural and familial injunctions, and decisions. Caution required in probing into family patterns.
COGNITIVE BEHAVIOR THERAPY	Leaders need to help members assess the possible consequences of making behavioral changes. Family members may not value clients' newly acquired assertive style, so individuals must be taught how to cope with resistance by others.
RATIONAL EMOTIVE BEHAVIOR THERAPY	If leader has a forceful and directive leadership style, members may retreat. It is necessary to understand client's world before forcefully confronting beliefs perceived as irrational by leader.
REALITY THERAPY	Approach stresses taking charge of one's own life, yet some members hope to change their external environment. Leader needs to appreciate the role of discrimination and racism and help members deal with social and political realities.
SOLUTION-FOCUSED THERAPY	The "not-knowing stance" of the group leader, along with the expectations of the "client-as-expert," may not be welcomed by group participants who are looking for directions and solutions from the expert leader.

CHAPTER EIGHTEEN

The Evolution of a Group: An Integrative Perspective

COAUTHORED BY MARIANNE SCHNEIDER COREY AND GERALD COREY

Introduction

To give you a better picture of the practical application of the various approaches discussed in Part Two, this chapter provides glimpses of an actual group. This 3-day residential group, cofacilitated by Marianne and Jerry Corey, was convened for the purpose of making an educational video, *Evolution of a Group*, which is now part of a new DVD titled *Groups in Action: Evolution and Challenges— DVD and Workbook.** The first program, *Evolution of a Group*, is designed to bring to life the unfolding of a group from the initial to the final stage.

In this chapter we feature an integrative perspective, demonstrating how theory can be applied to practice. We pay special attention to working with individual members, and we attempt to link members with common personal issues. Many of the themes that emerged in this weekend workshop are described to show a variety of ways of exploring personal issues at the various stages of a group. However, not all of the themes discussed grew out of the actual group proceedings. Some material is expanded and modified for teaching purposes. We present each theme and then illustrate ways we draw from various theoretical perspectives. This chapter reflects our own personal integration. Our hope is that this illustration will encourage you to reflect on how you might draw from several orientations to develop your own personal style of group practice.

ABOUT THE GROUP

The participants in this group are not actors. They were not following a script, nor were they merely role-playing fictitious cases. They were willing to be themselves and explore some of their real concerns.

---

* Corey, G., Corey, M., & Haynes, R. (2006). *Groups in action: Evolution and challenges. DVD and workbook*. Belmont, CA: Brooks/Cole, Cengage Learning.

The group we describe in this chapter is a closed and time-limited intensive group that met for about 20 working hours. It consists of eight members (five women and three men) and two coleaders. Although this particular group was a residential workshop, the process we describe (both in the DVD and in this chapter) does not necessarily differ a great deal from the process of a group that meets weekly. Certainly, the techniques we demonstrate can be used in groups that meet weekly. Many of the concerns raised by these group members are no different from personal concerns that are typically explored in many counseling groups.

THE EMERGING THEMES

We have selected the following themes to discuss in this chapter from among the many that typically emerge during the life of a group:

- Clarifying personal goals
- Creating and maintaining trust
- Bringing interactions into the here-and-now
- Dealing with fears and resistances
- Making internal dialogue explicit
- Exploring feelings of isolation
- Dealing with parents
- Dealing with feelings of separation and loss

These themes are developed by describing how they apply to various members of our group. We demonstrate the use of interventions drawn from the various theoretical approaches as they apply to the individual members and the group as a whole.

We are not suggesting that we would make all of the interventions we have included here. However, for teaching purposes, in this chapter we describe many different ways of pursuing group themes with one individual. Sometimes we draw on relationship-oriented approaches or experiential therapies. At other times we rely on psychoanalytic or Adlerian perspectives when employing interventions. And at other times we utilize cognitive behavioral techniques with an individual's work. The chapter concludes with a description of how we would use concepts and techniques from these various approaches to deal with some issues characteristic of the ending stages of a group.

Formation of the Group

THE PREGROUP MEETING

All the participants in this group had some prior group experience. Before making the decision to be a part of this group, the members participated in a pregroup meeting in which they met each other and both coleaders. At this time they had the opportunity to get acquainted with one another and to determine whether they wanted to participate in this type of special group experience.

Of course, all the participants knew in advance that the purpose of this workshop was to produce an educational video. We also discussed at length the special circumstances associated with participating in a group that is being videotaped, such as informed consent, confidentiality, and revealing sensitive personal information. We wanted members to be themselves by sharing their real concerns, yet we emphasized it was for them to decide what specific personal subjects they would be willing to introduce. Furthermore, we reassured them that they had control over what would or would not be included in the final video. Throughout the weekend workshop, and for some time later, group members had opportunities to tell us if they wanted to omit any portion of their actual work. Furthermore, all of the group members had a chance to review this chapter and to suggest changes.

IMPORTANCE OF PRELIMINARY PREPARATION

It is ideal to arrange for a pregroup meeting after members have been screened and selected. This meeting is an orientation session where leaders can provide further information regarding the group to help the members decide if this group is suitable for them. If a pregroup meeting is impractical, then the first group meeting can be used to orient and prepare members for a successful group experience.

Many groups that get stuck at some point do so because the foundations were poorly laid at the outset. What is labeled as "resistance" on the part of group members is often the result of the leader's failure to provide adequate orientation. This preparation can begin at the individual screening and can be continued during the initial session. Although building pregroup preparation into the design of a group takes considerable effort, the time involved pays dividends as the group evolves. Many potential barriers to a group's progress can be avoided by careful planning and preparation.

Initial Stage

The initial stage of a group is a period for members to get to know one another (see Chapter 4). It is difficult to build a climate of safety if members do not have a sense of one another. At the first meeting we try to heighten members' awareness of the atmosphere in the room rather than explore deep personal issues. This is a time for getting acquainted, learning how the group functions, developing the norms that will govern the group, exploring fears and expectations pertaining to the group, identifying personal goals, and determining if this group is a safe place. As coleaders we are aware that the manner in which we deal with members during the initial sessions determines the degree of trust that can be established later in the group. (Refer to Chapter 17 for a summary of the characteristics of the early phase of a group and how I draw from a range of theories in addressing the key tasks of the initial stage.)

In these early sessions we are shaping specific group norms—working in the here-and-now, talking directly to one another, expressing persistent reactions, dealing with expectations and fears, establishing personal goals, and so on. As coleaders, our main attention is on establishing a foundation of trust. We do this by getting members to talk about afterthoughts, by teaching them how to pay attention to what they are experiencing in the here-and-now, by noticing their reactions to others in the group, and by verbalizing these reactions. We do considerable teaching about how the participants can most productively involve themselves in the ongoing group process.

In most groups the initial sessions are devoted to exploring group goals and clarifying the members' personal goals. We also ask members to identify what might get in their way of accomplishing those goals.

We usually begin a group by having the members state their goals as clearly and concretely as possible. Our aim is to help the members formulate specific contracts for their own work, which will provide a direction for the group. We are also interested in assisting members in evaluating their current behavior to determine the degree to which their behavior is getting them what they want (drawing from reality therapy). Here are some of the questions we are likely to pose to the members to stimulate this self-evaluation:

- What do you have in your life now that you most value?
- What is at least one thing that is missing in your life?
- If you had what you wanted now, how would your life be different?
- What can you begin to do today to get what you say you want?
- How can you best use this group to get what you want?

The aim of this line of questioning is to get members to realize that if what they are thinking, feeling, and doing is not satisfactory to them, they have the power to change and choose better behaviors.

Our attempt during the early stage of this group is to work cooperatively and collaboratively on the goals that will govern the direction the group takes (which is characteristic of the Adlerian perspective). For example, one of us might say something like this: "Since this is your group, I'd like to hear from each of you what you expect from this group. After each of you has a chance to state your expectations, perhaps we can spend some time formulating group norms that will help us accomplish these goals." Cooperation on a common therapeutic task is essential if change is to occur. Resistance is to be expected if group leaders impose an agenda on the group rather than helping the members create their own agenda.

Each individual may experience overlapping goals or a combination of goals. Here is a summary of what each member of this group hoped to get from participating:

Jacqueline (late 40s) sometimes does not feel a part of various groups in which she is involved. She refers to herself as an African American woman who, at times, finds it difficult to relate to others and states that she often feels "marginalized." One of her goals is to explore ways she seeks approval from others.

SusAnne (age 27), of Hispanic background, would like to explore relationships in her life. At times she feels that she has put a wall around herself to prevent herself from getting hurt. She wants to explore the price she is paying for staying safe and not taking the risks of pursuing the relationships she wants.

Jyl (age 39), a Euro-American, is willing to deal with struggles pertaining to perfectionism. She also wants to explore the impact of significant losses in her life. Jyl experiences difficulty in asking others for what she wants or in letting others care for her.

James (age 35) describes himself as an educated Latino who has to "prove himself." Because of his cultural background, he often feels oppressed. He also is considering working on significant relationships (mother, brother).

Andrew (age 35), a Euro-American, is struggling with issues of trust and with deciding how close he wants to get to people, especially women in an intimate relationship. Having been betrayed in marriage, he is very protective of his feelings, which keeps him safe, but somewhat lonely.

Darren (age 27), of Hispanic background, sometimes worries about how he expresses himself and is concerned about the impression he makes. He realizes he rehearses before he talks so that he will sound intelligent. He is willing to work on "talking out loud" more often in the group. Many times he feels like an outsider, and he wants to belong.

Casey (age 23) refers to herself as a Vietnamese American. She struggles with messages she received as a child that now get in her way. She worries about others' judging her, and she sometimes keeps herself separate in social situations. She would like to challenge her fears of feeling judged, which she feels keep her back at times.

Jackie (age 43), a Euro-American, puts a lot of pressure on herself to be perfect, to get everyone to like her, and to keep everyone happy. She sometimes feels that she is not enough, no matter what she accomplishes.

THEME: CREATING AND MAINTAINING TRUST

As a group gets under way, members will often question their ability to trust the group leaders, the other members, and even themselves. To create a climate of trust, we typically ask members to share what they are thinking and feeling at this first meeting, especially as it pertains to what they are aware of in this group. They are also asked to share their expectations pertaining to the group experience.

We also mention to members that it does not make sense to open up too quickly without a foundation of trust. A good way to create trust is to get members to verbalize their fears, concerns, and here-and-now reactions during the early sessions. We emphasize that it is up to each member to decide what to talk about and how far to pursue a topic. During the early phase of a group, we are not likely to make interventions that lead to in-depth exploration of what members are saying. Rather than focusing immediately on the first member who speaks, we make sure that all members have a chance to briefly introduce themselves.

The following excerpts are typical of what members are sometimes thinking during the first or second group meeting. Our goal is to assist members in talking more openly about what might get in the way of their ability to trust themselves and others in this particular group.

Jackie: My expectation is to go through this group without making anyone mad at me or without crying. I want feedback that I am okay, and I want to be liked and valued.

Jacqueline: I'm afraid I won't say things well. I tend to beat up on myself after a group, telling myself that I didn't say what I wanted to say clearly enough.

SusAnne: I am not sure that I trust that people in here will care about me if I let my pain and hurt show, so I censor what I say.

James: In a group I sometimes feel on the outside. You won't know this, because most of the time I won't let you know.

Andrew: I also sometimes feel like an outsider. I'm concerned I will censor my emotions and isolate myself from the group if I feel I'm being judged while talking about the pains of my past.

Darren: I feel young and invisible. I don't know how to get in with you guys.

Jyl: It's scary when I think of opening up. I'm afraid I'll lose control and start crying and not stop.

Casey: When I'm in a group, I observe a lot. I rehearse in my head before I speak. I'm afraid I can't articulate myself and that you won't understand me. I want to sound intelligent.

Typically, during their early stages, groups deal with matters of trust such as those illustrated by these examples. If members are to drop their defenses and reveal themselves—as indeed they must if the group is to be effective—they need assurance that the group is a safe place to do this. Members can learn that by being open and taking risks they have the potential to live fully.

We know that confidentiality is essential if members are to feel a sense of safety in a group. We introduce the topic of confidentiality in all the groups we colead, even if group members do not raise their own concerns. We typically caution members of our groups about how confidentiality can be broken and provide guidelines for maintaining the confidential nature of the exchanges. Specifically, we emphasize how easy it might be to break confidentiality without intending to do so. We ask members to refrain from talking about what others are doing in the group. We ask members about any concerns they may have about confidentiality, and we provide information about how best to maintain it. We talk about the limitations of confidentiality. We emphasize to members that it is their responsibility to make the room safe by continuing to address their concerns regarding how their disclosures will be treated. If they do not feel trusting because they are afraid that others will talk, this doubt will certainly hamper their ability to fully participate.

For this particular group, confidentiality took on special significance. Because they were being videotaped and being written about in a textbook and a workbook, group members had an opportunity to eliminate any portions of their work they did not want to make public.

Helping to build trust in the group is a vital task at the early stages of a group, and as coleaders, we realize that the way in which we approach the group is of crucial importance. Our main aim is to give members opportunities to express their reactions about the level of trust in the group and to talk about ways that they can feel safe so that they can move into personally meaningful work. To illustrate some of the messages we want to get across early on in this group, here are some sample comments from various theoretical orientations that we might use to open a group:

Psychoanalytic therapy: "In this group I'll be paying a lot of attention to what is going on in the here-and-now, with particular attention on your reactions to one another. I'll look for patterns in the way you relate, and my job is to help you see how your earlier experiences often influence the way you perceive others and react to them."

Existential therapy and psychodrama: "This group will assist you in examining choices you've made about how you are living. I'll be encouraging you to enact—not just talk about—your conflicts and the problems you'd like to explore. By releasing your feelings about a particular reenactment of an event in your life, you are likely to come to a different understanding of that event. You will be encouraged to experiment with different ways of behaving."

Gestalt therapy: "We will pay particular attention to the here-and-now and deal with whatever prevents you from maintaining a present-centered awareness. The emphasis will be on the *what* and *how* rather than the *why* of behavior. One of my functions is to assist you in identifying your unfinished business from the past, bringing it into the present, and achieving greater awareness of how your past may be impeding your present experiencing."

Transactional analysis (TA) and cognitive behavior therapy: "Each of you is my colleague in your own therapy. I don't presume the right to special knowledge about you; rather, I assume that you will decide on the course of your work in here, largely by developing clear contracts that will specify what you want to change and how you want to do it. The group will offer a context for this learning and give you the support you need to reinforce any changes you make so that they become an integral part of you."

Reality therapy and cognitive behavior therapy: "My main goal in this group is to assist you in determining whether your current behavior meets your needs adequately. If you discover that it doesn't and if you decide to change, we will work collaboratively to formulate a plan of action designed to promote change. The group will offer you a place to practice this plan for change."

Solution-focused therapy: "My role is to be your tour guide. I will attempt to facilitate your interactions in this group to create opportunities for each of you to see yourself as the expert on your own life. The focus of our conversations will be on discovering problem-free times, which I hope will motivate you to identify exceptions to your problems and to search for solutions."

THEME: BRINGING INTERACTIONS INTO THE HERE-AND-NOW

During the initial stage of a group, we pay attention to here-and-now reactions and teach members the importance of sharing these reactions with one another. In this particular group some important racial and cultural issues emerged, which would need to be addressed as a prerequisite for building a safe and accepting environment. We ask members what they were thinking since we first met as a group at the preliminary orientation session, or pregroup meeting, and what they were aware of as they were driving to this residential workshop.

James: I often feel that I have to prove myself, especially since I am an educated Chicano. I've experienced discrimination in a number of places, so I wonder about how I'll fit into a group.

We suggest that James pay attention to ways that he might feel that he has to prove himself in this group.

Coleader: James, how do you feel in this group? Will you let people know how you are experiencing them in this group? Are you willing to let us know when you do not feel a part of this group?

As James talks about his awareness of being different from some others in this group, Jacqueline brings herself into the discussion.

Jacqueline: As an African American woman, there are times when I feel marginalized. And because of this I feel that I am not taken seriously. As I look at some of you, I feel different from you.

Jyl brings herself into the interactions, for she has reactions to what both James and Jacqueline are saying. She feels that she is not being given a chance to be herself with them.

Jyl: Being with you [Jacqueline] is not safe. I am going to have to protect myself, for I am aware of feeling judged by you. [and to James] You know, I don't know what it is like to be an educated Chicano. But I do know what it's like to be an educated White woman who is sometimes treated like a piece of fluff.

Jyl goes on to talk about some of the ways that she can identify with the feelings of both James and Jacqueline.

Dealing with diversity issues can bring the group together. However, if members do not talk about the ways they may feel different from others in this group, a hidden agenda is likely to develop. When members are willing to express their here-and-now thoughts and feelings as they pertain to the group, the energy level increases. Once members are willing to deal with the present, there is plenty to explore. Even if participants have problems in their past, it is still useful to try to get them to relate these concerns to how these past issues might influence how they are in this present group.

Here are some comments group members made relatively early in the life of this group:

- I have a tendency to think that what others have to say is more important than what is on my mind.
- When I look around the room, I wonder if I will fit in this group.
- I'm afraid of what people in here will think if I show my emotions.
- It's hard for me to ask for time in group.
- When others are talking, it's difficult for me to bring myself into the group.

We consistently ask members to pay attention to their present reactions and perceptions about one another. For a group to achieve a genuine level of trust, it is essential that members express persistent reactions that pertain to what is going on in the context of the group. We underscore the importance of members saying what is on their mind, even if they fear that what they have to say might be interruptive. When members keep their reservations to themselves, the group cannot deal with their concerns. When participants share certain reactions that could get in their way of participating fully in the group, we have a basis to do some productive work.

We are interested in both a here-and-now focus and a there-and-then focus. However, we find that members usually are not ready to take the risk of dealing with significant personal issues outside the group until they first deal with their reactions to one another in the room. When members bring up either a present or past problem situation outside of the group, we explore how this might be played out in the context of the present group. For example, James says that he often feels that he has to prove himself at work. Both Jacqueline and Jackie inform us that they often seek approval. Andrew talks about feeling isolated. All these members are asked to take note of when they experience these feelings or thoughts in the group.

Although we emphasize here-and-now reactions, we also ask members to explore how their present reactions in the group may reflect how they feel away from the group. Jackie expresses her concern that she will not live up to our expectations, nor will she get our approval. Eventually, as the group becomes more established, we hope she will also increase her awareness of how her struggles operate in her everyday life.

Developing a here-and-now orientation in a group is consistent with person-centered therapy, existential therapy, Gestalt therapy, psychodrama, and solution-focused therapy. Dealing with here-and-now concerns does not exclude exploring the past. As you recall, both Gestalt therapy and psychodrama are present-centered approaches in that they require members to bring either past or future concerns into the present tense. We frequently remind participants that if they become aware of something or someone in the group it is best to talk about it. When it comes to expressing reactions pertaining to what is going on in the group, we prefer for members to say too much rather than too little.

Transition Stage

THE CHALLENGES OF THE TRANSITION PHASE

Before groups progress to a working stage, they typically go through a transition phase, which is characterized by anxiety, defensiveness, resistance, the struggle for control, and intermember conflicts. During the transition phase, it is the members' task to monitor their thoughts, feelings, and actions and to learn to express them verbally. Leaders can help members come to recognize and accept their reluctance and at the same time encourage members to challenge their tendencies toward avoidance. For members to progress to a deeper level of exploration, they must talk about any anxiety and defensiveness they may be experiencing. Some fears members may have during the early or transition stages of a group include the fear of rejection, losing control, being inappropriate, being involved in a conflict, or looking foolish. These fears may be manifested as resistance, and it is important that group leaders understand there is a purpose for this resistance. Above all, members' struggles need to be respected, understood, and explored.

We do not think it is helpful for us to directly attack resistance, but it is a mistake to bypass or ignore problematic or defensive behaviors exhibited by members. Some groups remain stuck at the transition stage because reluctant behavior is unnoticed, ignored, or poorly dealt with by the group leader. Teaching members how to challenge themselves is a basic task at this time, yet it is also essential that members learn how to respectfully confront others in a caring and constructive fashion. We teach members the importance of talking more about themselves and how they are affected by the behaviors of a member they are confronting rather than telling a member how he or she is, or judging that person.

In our role as coleaders, we model how to remain open and nondefensive in receiving feedback from others. If conflicts arise, it is essential that members recognize these conflicts and develop the skills to resolve them. Again, what we model when addressing conflict in a firm and respectful manner is every bit as important as what we tell members about conflict resolution. If conflict is not addressed, it then becomes a hidden agenda, which blocks open group interaction. How we intervene with the members is crucial to building trust.

During the initial stage, members generally address their fears or reservations about participating in the group. However, during the transition stage, there is a more extensive and more specific discussion of how these fears are manifested within the group. Doing this enables members to feel the support and safety that is required for the intense work they are getting ready to do.

THEME: DEALING WITH FEARS AND AMBIVALENCE

As a group moves into a transition stage, members typically express fears about getting involved and are reluctant to delve into personal concerns. Some members keep their fears about becoming involved in the group to themselves, whereas others seem eager to express their fears and put them to rest so that they can begin to work. Whether the fears are expressed or not, they tend to give rise to some ambivalence—the desire to reveal oneself is balanced by a reluctance to expose oneself. Here are some typical expressions of ambivalence:

- I tend to isolate at times. Part of me wants to let others know me in here, yet another part of me wants to pull back and check things out quietly.
- I'm afraid to get involved because I may make a fool of myself, and then people will judge me negatively.
- I'm afraid that if I say what I really think and feel people in here will not accept or like me.
- If I see myself as I really am, I may not like what I find.
- Right now my life is rather comfortable; if I become too involved in the group, I may open up more than I can handle.
- I'm somewhat afraid of disclosing myself to others, not only because of what they may think but also because of what I might find out about myself.
- I want to protect myself by not letting myself care. If I get too close to people in the group, I'll feel a real loss when it ends.

We encourage members to express their concerns and fears by talking directly to each other. When members talk to us (as leaders) about an individual in the group, we instruct them to look at and talk directly to that person.

Coleader: I'd like each of you to share some of your fears about being in this group. As you do so, look at different members in the group. Share any fears you may be experiencing with the group members.

This strategy is borrowed from the experiential approaches and is aimed at building group cohesion. Depending on what emerges in individuals within the group, we may work on a feeling level or we may focus on members' thoughts, or both. Using a Gestalt orientation, we deal with ambivalence of members by inviting them to rehearse their fears out loud.

SusAnne: I'm not sure I trust that people in here will care if I share some hurtful experiences. What I generally do is keep most of my hurt to myself.

Coleader: What do you usually do when you feel uncertain about others?

SusAnne: My first instinct is to disappear. But I really would like to be able to trust people more fully.

Operating within the spirit of reality therapy, we offer a challenge to SusAnne:

Coleader: What would happen if during this weekend you try something different? Instead of withdrawing, you could experiment with opening up. If what you typically do doesn't work too well, are you willing to make some changes and see what that would be like?

Here the leader is helping the member make a general idea more concrete so that she can operationalize it into a personal goal.

SusAnne: I'm willing to push myself a bit and give voice to some of the fears that I typically keep to myself. I feel lighter and I'm not quite as afraid. It helps to verbalize my thoughts.

Note that it is SusAnne who makes the evaluation of what she is currently doing and what she may want to change. It is not our function, as group leaders, to make these decisions for SusAnne.

Casey brings herself into the group by saying that she is having reactions to SusAnne. We invite Casey to tell SusAnne directly how she is being affected by SusAnne.

Casey: I feel afraid that if you know certain things about me you will judge me, that you won't want anything to do with me, and that you'll not like me.

Through this kind of dialogue, we want to provide Casey with the opportunity to identify and challenge ways that she often stops herself from being herself because she fears judgment from others, especially SusAnne. Both SusAnne and Casey are actually making the room safer for themselves by expressing the fears and reservations that they typically keep to themselves. This process allows them to check out the reality of some of their assumptions about each other, as well as others in the group.

Darren holds back because of his fear of being rejected by the group. We ask him to talk to each group member and complete this sentence: "You could reject me by _____." By completing the sentence in a different way with each member, Darren can express the full spectrum of the fears of rejection he normally keeps inside of himself. Doing this exercise gives Darren an insight that many of his fears of rejection lie within him rather than coming from others in the group (Gestalt therapy).

Another way to begin with Darren would be to pursue cognitive work. Drawing from a rational emotive behavioral orientation, we might challenge Darren with questions such as "What would be so terrible if everyone in here did reject you?" or "What is the worst thing that you can imagine if you were to be rejected?" The attempt here is to show Darren that he has uncritically bought the self-defeating idea that he would find rejection devastating. With this new insight, Darren may be able to challenge the notion that everyone will reject him. After working with Darren on his fears of rejection, we invite other members to express similar fears and then proceed to teach the group members how they contribute to their problems by subscribing to beliefs that they have accepted without questioning the validity of such beliefs.

Our orientation emphasizes giving members an opportunity to express their feelings and thoughts, and to explore them. We do not think it is useful to provide quick answers. When a member raises self-doubts, fears, or struggles, we block other members from offering reassurance too quickly. This allows the individual an opportunity to explore his or her concern. For instance, when Jyl is crying as she is talking to James, we do not facilitate members giving her reassurance or telling her that she has no reason to feel embarrassed. Instead, when Jyl says she feels exposed, our intervention leads her to say more about what it is like for her to feel exposed and with whom. Although quick reassuring feedback from members may make Jyl feel good for a brief moment, it is doubtful that this feeling will be long lasting. This is based on the assumption that Jyl's critic lies within her and not primarily with others.

THEME: MAKING INTERNAL DIALOGUE EXPLICIT

In many groups it is what members won't say that will bog the group down—not what they do say. We encourage members to identify what they might be silently saying to themselves, both before they come to a session and during the group meeting. If members decide to make their internal dialogue explicit, others often are able to relate to what is being voiced. We want to teach members the value of verbalizing their thoughts and feelings, especially if they have a tendency to observe a great deal and think about how they will present themselves.

A good example of a member who engaged in a great deal of internal dialogue is Casey. At different times in the group, Casey indicates that she carefully thinks about what she wants to say before she speaks. Because of wanting to appear articulate, she censors many of her thoughts. Noticing that Casey is looking down as she speaks, we ask her what she is feeling. She indicates that she is scared of being judged by others. Our work with Casey consists of asking her to select those members whom she fears are judging her and then tell them about the judgment she fears they are making about her. Once she deals with her concerns about who might judge her, she realizes her fears of judgments are imagined more than rooted in reality. This illustrates what the Gestalt therapists refer to as owning one's projections. This exercise creates the safety that is crucial for Casey's deeply personal work later on.

If members experience the group as being a safe place, they will be inclined to move into the unknown and challenge themselves. In our role as coleaders, we assume that it is useful to provide members with a general understanding of the techniques and methods we may employ in our work with them. To increase the chances that members will benefit from Gestalt methods, we think group leaders need to communicate the general purpose of these interventions and to create an experimental climate. "Let's try this experiment" conveys this inventive attitude on the part of the leader. It is not our intention to prove a point; rather, our aim is to encourage the members to experiment with novel ways of thinking and acting, and then to determine for themselves how they might expand their behavioral repertoire.

In this section we have given examples of some ways to assist members in exploring their concerns about group participation. For a more complete discussion of group process issues at the transition stage, review Chapter 4. You may also find it useful to review the section in Chapter 17 that deals with how I apply various theories to the key tasks of the transition phase.

Working Stage

MOVING TOWARD A DEEPER LEVEL OF INTERACTION

There are no arbitrary dividing lines between the phases of a group. In actual practice these phases merge with each other. This is especially true of the movement from the transition stage to the working stage. The line is somewhat thin between expressing anxieties and ways of avoiding, which is so characteristic of the transition stage, and doing what is required to move the group into a more advanced stage of development. If a group does move into the working stage, it can be expected that earlier themes of trust, conflict, and reluctance to participate will surface from time to time. As a group takes on new challenges, deeper levels of trust have to be achieved. A group can be compared to an intimate relationship. Neither is static; both are dynamic. Perfection is never achieved in a group; commitment is necessary to do the difficult work of moving forward and facing future challenges.

Once a group enters the working stage, it is unlikely that all members will be functioning at the same level of intensity. Some members may be on the periphery, others may still be holding back, and still others may be more resistant or less willing to take risks. Indeed, there are individual differences among members at all stages of a group. Some members may be very willing to engage in intense emotional exploration, and this can have the effect of drawing more hesitant members into active participation. (For a more detailed discussion of the working stage, review Chapter 5. Also review the section in Chapter 17 that describes how I integrate concepts and techniques and apply them to the working stage.)

THEME: EXPLORING FEELINGS OF ISOLATION

Andrew has mentioned several times that he has a tendency to isolate himself. He refers to being locked up emotionally, yet he realizes that he has the key to open himself to others. Andrew also talks about a wall that surrounds him, which has the effect of keeping him safe, yet isolated. Andrew asks himself why his marriage did not work out: "Am I to blame for what happened? Will I be able to trust anyone again? Will I be able to get over the hurt of the divorce?"

There are a number of ways to work with Andrew. Using a person-centered perspective, we could invite Andrew to tell his story. While he does so, we pay full attention not only to what he is saying but also to his nonverbal expressions of pain over his loss. This attention and the support of the group will allow him to fully experience and share the intensity of his feelings. By letting us in on some of his painful experiences, he is decreasing his feelings of isolation. As Andrew stays connected to others in the group, he becomes aware of their compassion for him, which encourages him to share more of himself.

An alternative approach to dealing with this theme involves drawing on psychodrama techniques. In doing this, Marianne (coleader) might ask Andrew where he feels most stuck in regard to his divorce. Andrew replies, "There are a lot of things that have gone unsaid—things that I feel stuck with, things that I'm afraid I won't ever say." Marianne asks Andrew to reveal one of the things he might not ever say. Andrew is then asked to select a member to play his ex-wife's role. He picks Jyl and begins by expressing his hurt. Jyl (as his symbolic wife) at first just listens and may later respond. She could respond as if she were his wife or as she imagines his ex-wife might respond. Andrew could provide a few lines of what his wife is likely to say as a way to coach Jyl in playing this role.

In doing the role play, Andrew expresses feelings of being hurt and betrayed and of being slow to trust again. As he is talking to his symbolic wife, Andrew repeats that he is not good enough to keep a relationship together. At this point Darren, who identifies with Andrew's feelings, is selected as Andrew's double and steps next to Andrew, saying a few of the things that Andrew is not verbalizing. By having someone speak on his behalf, Andrew may eventually find his own words and release some of his deeper feelings.

After engaging in this role play, Marianne asks Andrew to imagine the kind of intimate relationship he would like 5 years from now. He says that he would like to see himself as feeling trusting enough to form meaningful relationships. In working with Andrew we have attempted to understand his subjective world (existential) and have drawn on the support of the members to further Andrew's work. The use of psychodrama results in intensification of emotions. By expressing his emotions, Andrew will experience some relief from keeping certain feelings bottled up inside. Not only will this emotional release result in his feeling better, but Andrew can decide that he does not have to be isolated and that he can share his pain with caring people in his life. He may learn that he can trust selectively and that everyone will not let him down.

In psychodrama the participants enact conflicts as if they are occurring in the present moment rather than narrating past events. Leaders with a psychodrama orientation frequently say to members, "Don't tell us, show us." A basic tenet of psychodrama is that reliving and reexperiencing a scene from the past gives the participants both the opportunity to examine how that event affected them at the time it occurred and a chance to deal differently with the event *now.* By replaying a past event in the present, Andrew is able to assign new meaning to it. Through this process he can work through unfinished business and put a new and different ending to that earlier situation.

Still another level for working with Andrew is to engage him cognitively. From a cognitive behavioral perspective, Andrew can talk about his beliefs and some conclusions he has reached about intimacy and allowing others to hurt him emotionally. In doing this cognitive work, Andrew discovers that he has been avoiding making contacts with other women because he has convinced himself that women may not want to become involved with him, and if they did, they would certainly hurt him. Jerry (coleader) challenges Andrew's perceptions about the catastrophic consequences of becoming intimate. Even though he has been deeply wounded, it does not stand to reason that he will necessarily be hurt in every close relationship. The future does not have to be a repeat of the past. The aim is to have Andrew put himself in situations where he has to critically appraise the validity of his beliefs regarding emotional closeness.

With encouragement and direction, Andrew begins to challenge his self-defeating notions. Jerry (coleader) suggests that he role-play initiating a conversation with a woman in the group. The purpose of this exercise is to enable Andrew to more freely engage in dialogue with a woman. Andrew discusses his fears of getting involved again, which we then explore further during this session.

There are other ways that we could work with Andrew's ambivalence over wanting to get close to others and also wanting to keep others at a distance. Drawing on concepts from transactional analysis, a productive strategy might be to focus on exposing and working with an early decision that Andrew made, for example: "If you open yourself to being loved by others, or if you let yourself care about others, you are bound to be hurt. It's best to seal off your feelings and become emotionally numb so you won't feel the pain." We engage his thinking processes by asking Andrew to consider when and why he decided to keep his emotions in check as a way to protect himself. He is also asked to think about how that decision most likely gets in the way of current relationships, and if he might like to redecide. Finally, some of his injunctions may be the focal point of further exploration: "Don't get close." "Don't let people know what you are feeling." "Be careful who you trust." "Protect yourself."

Certain ideas from TA and Gestalt therapy experiments often work well together. We could follow up his work on his early decisions with some Gestalt exploration. Andrew states that he wants to work on his mixed feelings about intimacy with women. First, Marianne (coleader) asks him to face each woman in the group and state his worst fear about getting close to her. As he does this, he becomes keenly aware of his here-and-now fears toward the women in the group, especially Jyl and SusAnne. Marianne suggests that Andrew look at Jyl and SusAnne, allowing each of them to be the focus of a conflicting side of himself. As he looks at Jyl, he expresses the side of himself that wants to care and get involved.

Andrew: It feels so lonely and cold behind the walls that I build around myself. I work so hard to keep people out. I want to get out of these walls, but I'm afraid of what is out there. Acting this way is really bottling me up because it isn't representative of my true nature. This isn't who I am.

Coleader: Andrew, look at SusAnne and let yourself be the side of you that wants to remain behind those walls.

Andrew: Stay behind those walls that you've worked so hard to build. You're isolated, but at least you're safe. You know what happens whenever you let yourself really care: you get burned, and that pain isn't worth the effort of getting involved.

This dialogue helps Andrew become more aware of the polarities within himself, without forcing him to choose between his two sides. By exaggerating and staying longer with each side, he may be better able to make a decision about which way he wants to live.

In working with Andrew's struggle between wanting to be involved in relationships and wanting to keep himself safe, we have illustrated a variety of therapeutic strategies: person-centered, existential, psychodrama, Gestalt, transactional analysis, and cognitive behavior therapy. Of course, we are not suggesting that we would make all of these interventions with Andrew. Instead, these illustrations are intended to show how, drawing from different theories, one could work in a variety of ways. It is important to pay attention to the client and what he is willing to do in this particular situation. Certainly we could involve Andrew as a collaborator in designing experiments he could carry out in this group.

THEME: DEALING WITH PARENTS

Jyl lets it be known that she is ready to work on feelings about her father. Jyl says that it is so sad that it took her dad so long to tell her what she wanted to hear. As Jyl continues to talk, she expresses her pain over not hearing her father tell her that she could have made it as a musician. Jyl so much wanted her father to believe in her, yet it wasn't until he was dying that he told her that she could have been successful in a music career.

We ask Jyl to pick a person in the group whom she could look at and talk to as her father. The fact that he died recently does not diminish the intensity or meaningfulness of Jyl's talking to her father. The purpose of this psychodrama technique is to provide Jyl with an avenue to give verbal and nonverbal expressions to many of the things she may be keeping inside. If there is unfinished business with Dad, engaging in this dialogue is an effective way to address it.

Once Jyl has done this role play, the work could take any number of directions. We might simply ask: "Jyl, having said what you did, what has this been like for you? What would you like to do next?" Taking our clue from Jyl would be the best way to proceed. As a follow-up experiment, we are likely to ask Jyl to write a letter to her father, even though he is no longer alive. In this letter Jyl could say what she most wanted from her dad, what she misses about him, and what she wishes she might have said. The rationale for writing a letter is to give Jyl an opportunity to release feelings over not getting what she wanted from her father. Perhaps then she will be able to give herself increased affirmation, and she may be more open to receiving support from others. It seems that Jyl is extremely hard on herself for what she has done or failed to do. Writing the letter may be a way for her to come to appreciate her talents and what she has accomplished.

Jackie is drawn into Jyl's work with parents. One of Jackie's struggles is allowing herself to feel "good enough" as a person, regardless of her performances or accomplishments. It is as though Jackie is operating on the premise that if she were perfect, she would receive universal approval and feel adequate as a person.

Jackie: My mom left when I was 7 years old. I always felt responsible. I felt that if I was funnier, more desirable, prettier, then she might have wanted to stay. In my head, I know I wasn't responsible for her leaving, but there are times that I feel that if I were more, then she would have stayed. I wanted to be the center of her world.

Marianne (coleader) works with Jackie on her intense feelings about her mother, reflecting Jackie's possible belief that if she were more perfect her mother would not have left.

Even if we do not work with Jackie by using psychoanalytic techniques, the psychoanalytic perspective can provide a context for understanding Jackie's problem. Looking at Jackie's dynamics, we might speculate that in some ways she is looking at others to feed her and nourish her as a person. She has not given up the fantasy of being the type of young girl that her parents wanted; this frustration of her need to be seen as the "ideal daughter" by her parents may bring about feelings of insecurity, disillusionment, and anxiety. We might interpret her behavior as seeking the parents she has always wanted. Jackie may now be treating others in the group as she treated her parents.

Because of the transference at the working stage, Jackie may reexperience some old and familiar patterns, which will be seen as material to be worked through in the group. How she behaves in the group sessions provides some clues to the historical determinants of her present behavior. It may be useful to make timely interpretations so that some of Jackie's past can be brought to the surface. Another focus will be guiding her in working through her transferences with the coleaders. In the group situation it is probable that she has re-created her original family; this transference interferes with her accurate appraisal of reality, because she is now projecting onto others in the group feelings she had for her parents. Furthermore, Jackie may be searching for the approval she sought from her mother in many of us in this group.

An Adlerian interpretation would be quite different from this psychoanalytic interpretation. We would not devote time to exploring the possible causes of her struggle to win her parents' approval. Instead, we would pay attention to the here-and-now behavior Jackie displays and on ways in which she can begin to explore her thinking and thus make changes in her behavior. Working within an Adlerian model, Jackie is invited to consider our perceptions, or our interpretation, of her striving for parental approval. She explores her style of life to see how searching for approval may be a theme. The interpretation deals with her goals, purposes, and intentions, as well as her private logic and how it works. As she gains insight, through referring to her basic premises and to the ways these beliefs are mistaken, she can begin the process of modifying these cognitions and thus find ways of leading a more satisfying life.

If we were to utilize an action-oriented approach to Jackie's theme, we would employ psychodrama techniques to make the material come alive. We want to know whether Jackie remembers any time as a child when she wanted parental approval and love and didn't receive it. Let's say that Jackie recalls the time (at age 7) when she found out that her mother was leaving. Marianne (coleader) assists Jackie in reenacting this childhood scene with the help of two group members who play her parents. Here are a few possibilities for a psychodrama format:

- Playing herself as a child, Jackie says all the things now that she thought and felt but never said when her mother left.

- She asks her parents (still as the child) to love her and to stay together.

- The symbolic parents play their roles either as rejecting parents or as accepting parents.

- Other group members stand in for Jackie and say things that she finds difficult to express.

- Jackie projects a scene with her parents in the present that incorporates an interaction with them as she would wish it to be. In this case she coaches others to be the parents she would have wanted at age 7.

Following the psychodrama there is an effort to connect Jackie's present struggles with the feelings she had as a child. The ways in which she seeks approval of others, especially her wanting to be liked and valued by authority figures, could be much like her dynamics as a child. By participating in this psychodrama, she is likely to discover how striving toward perfect performances and winning the approval of everyone has become increasingly problematic. Jackie recognizes that nobody can ever give her the kind of approval she desperately wanted from her mother as a child.

As is the case with a group that has reached the working stage, a number of members can work on common themes. James has been affected by the talk of mothers. He says that he was thinking of his mom as Jackie was talking about her mother. Marianne (coleader) intervenes at this point, suggesting that he talk to Jackie as his mother (since he seems to have been triggered by her exploration). James lets Marianne know that he would like to use both Jackie and Marianne as his mother, since there are things he wants to say to both women. (This shows the importance of asking the client who can be most helpful to him or her in setting up a role-play situation. There is no need to restrict the dialogue to one person, and two or more symbolic mothers can add to the breadth of the work.)

James: If my mom were here, I'd say (hesitatingly and with emotion) that I love you. I haven't told you that recently, and I know that you are really a strong woman. You do a lot of good things for a lot of people. I wish you'd do these things for yourself and believe in yourself. You don't know how special you are.

After James says a few of the things he loves about Mom to Jackie, Marianne asks Jackie how it was for her to hear what James said.

Jackie: When you first started sharing, it felt real good, and those were the things I'd like to hear from my son. But all of a sudden I wanted more from you, and it felt like there was more that you wanted to tell me.

With that James continues talking to Jackie, telling her all the ways she is special.

Whether or not James tells his mother some of what he communicated in the role-playing situation is up to him. He needs to decide how not telling her what is in his heart might be getting in his way in having the relationship he would like with her. If he decides he would like a better relationship, this might be a good time to incorporate some aspects of reality therapy and behavior therapy into his dealings with his mother.

In reality therapy, James is asked: "If nothing changes between you and your mother, how would that be?" In solution-focused therapy, we could ask: "If you had with your mother what you wanted with her, how would your relationship be different? What would you be doing differently?" If he decides to actually talk to his mother, we could set up a behavioral rehearsal in which he tells her what is most important for him to express. He doesn't need to overwhelm himself or his mother by communicating everything in one encounter with her. Using reality therapy, we would draw on specific methods of making an action plan. His plan would need to be clear, specific, attainable, and realistic. At this juncture, we collaboratively design a plan that will enable him to meet with his mother and tell her some of what he would most like her to hear. His plan might include carrying out a homework assignment, such as scheduling a dinner date with his mother and engaging in the kind of dialogue with her that he would like.

Darren identifies in some ways with James. Darren lets us know that he feels it is hard for him to feel like an adult around his mother. Furthermore, Darren realizes that his relationship with his parents is getting in his way with people in this group. He tells James that he envies what he has with his mother. He finds it difficult to assert himself with us in an adult way, and he adds, "It's like a hole in my soul." Marianne (coleader) observes his powerful imagery and reflects his phrase "a hole in my soul." She says to Darren: "How about looking at a few people and saying again, I have a hole in my soul." As Darren repeats "I have a hole in my soul" to a few people, he begins to cry, expressing his feelings of loneliness as a child. "Growing up I didn't feel I could talk to my parents. I just wanted to be understood. I felt so lonely." Darren continues to express intense feelings about his relationships with his parents and how he wasn't sure of where he fit. Later he acknowledges that he is not blaming his parents, since he knows they did the best they could with what they had. However, after staying with his feelings he begins to see how today he often struggles with fitting in and feeling a sense of belongingness. He makes the connection between his way of being with his family and how this is played out with others in a way that is not fulfilling to him.

As Darren continues exploring how his relationship with his parents influences the person he is today, he might well decide that he wants to initiate a discussion with his parents in real life. Drawing on a behavioral rehearsal technique, he could be asked to pick a mom or dad and practice what he most wants to communicate to his parents. We would certainly caution him not to rush out after an intense emotional experience in the group to confront his parents with what they didn't do for him when he was a child. After rehearsal opportunities, Darren may be ready to establish a contract that would involve some form of homework assignment, which he gives to himself. The use of contracts and homework is a part of several modalities, such as transactional analysis, cognitive behavior therapy, and reality therapy. These action methods can assist James and Darren in translating their insights into concrete behavioral changes.

All of these themes have emerged from the group interactions or from an individual's explorations. The group provides the encouragement for members to begin listening to themselves and paying attention to their subjective experience. By openly sharing and exploring universal personal concerns, members develop a sense of mutuality. The close ties that they feel with one another give them many opportunities for using the group culture differently from other aspects of their culture. The group becomes a place where people can be together in deeply meaningful ways. Through the process of self-disclosure, the participants grasp the universality of basic human concerns that unite them, in spite of their differences. When they entered the group, some of the members likely felt that they would have a difficult time feeling connected with others. But as members make themselves known to each other, they build alliances. Members come to understand the existential reality that we all experience and share pain, even though the particulars of our stories are different.

Final Stage

To assist you in thinking about ways to integrate these different group models into your personal style, in this section we describe how we would use concepts and techniques from the various approaches in dealing with some typical issues that we observe during the last few sessions of most groups. As a group evolves toward termination, a number of tasks remain: dealing with feelings of separation, saying good-bye, dealing with unfinished business, reviewing the group experience, consolidating learnings, practicing for behavioral change, giving and receiving feedback, talking about ways to carry learnings outside of group, making contracts of what to do after a group ends, and talking about a follow-up meeting. We remind members again about the importance of maintaining confidentiality. We also ask members to talk about what they might do to discount what they actually did during the group, how they might recover from setbacks and how to create support systems. (For more discussion on the characteristics and tasks of the final stage, review Chapter 5; for ways that various theories can be integrated and applied to the tasks of the final stage, see Chapter 17.)

THEME: DEALING WITH FEELINGS OF SEPARATION AND LOSS

The final stage of a group is a difficult time. The members are aware that their community is about to dissolve, and they are beginning to mourn their impending separation. Some of them are pulling back; they are becoming less intense and are no longer contributing much new material to work on. Others wonder whether they'll be able to maintain the openness they have learned in the group once they can't count any longer on the group's encouragement and support. They fear that in their everyday life they won't find people to give them the kind of support they need to keep experimenting with change and, as a consequence, that they may regress to old ways.

In facilitating any group, members need to be given an opportunity to fully express their feelings about the termination of the group, in this case, an intensive weekend workshop. The person-centered approach, which stresses listening actively and giving permission to explore whatever feelings are present, offers a useful model for this phase of group work. The members do not need a great deal of direction; rather, they need to be encouraged to face the reality that after sharing in an intense experience they will soon be going their separate ways. In this particular group, it is necessary to allow members to talk about any unfinished business they may have concerning any work they initiated or any interactions that occurred during the entire weekend. If participants can fully express their feelings about separation, the transition period between leaving the group and carrying what they've learned in the group into their day-to-day life will be made easier.

We have often observed the concern on the part of many group participants that they won't be able to create in their everyday lives that which they have experienced within the group. It seems crucial that we help members come to understand what *they* did to make this group meaningful. If they see their part in creating a group that allowed them to be expressive, there is hope that they can bring this into everyday living. Our goal is to help participants see that their group has been a place where they could learn how to form meaningful interpersonal relationships, a process that is not restricted to the group but that can be applied in any setting.

In this regard there is some value in helping participants understand any connections that might exist between their past and their family, on the one side, and the relationships they have developed within the group, on the other. For that purpose the psychoanalytic approach is useful. In some ways the group represents a new family for its members, and by relating their behaviors in the group "family" to their behaviors in their actual families, members can learn much about themselves. To assist participants in their process of making connections among behaviors, we ask them to reflect on these questions:

- To whom was I drawn in this group, and what did I learn from that?
- With whom did I have the most conflict, and what did I learn from that about me?
- In what ways did my feelings and actions in this group resemble the ways in which I felt and acted as a child in my family?
- Were my reactions to the group leaders in any way similar to my reactions to my parents or others who are significant in my life?
- Did I experience feelings of competitiveness or jealousy within the group, and what insights did that provide?

LOOKING AHEAD

Another tool we use as the group is drawing to a close is the development of a plan of action. We find that too often group members don't allow themselves to imagine creatively how they would like to experience their life. To assist them in their endeavor, we ask members to picture themselves and their lives in some ideal future circumstance, a technique that is used by both the Gestalt and the psychodrama approaches. Applying the fantasy technique to this group, we might suggest these scenarios to members:

- Imagine that you are attending a reunion of the group 5 years from now and that we are meeting to discuss how our lives have changed. What do you most want to be able to say to us at this reunion?
- Let yourself imagine all the ways in which you want to be different in your everyday life once you leave this group. Close your eyes and carry on a silent dialogue between yourself and the people who are most special in your life. What are you telling them? What are they replying? Imagine that a year has passed since we ended the group. Let yourself consider that nothing has changed in your life—that you have continued the way you have always been. What would that be like for you?

We have found that some members and the group in general might benefit by sharing their hopes of how they want to be different in special relationships. To accomplish this, role-playing exercises are helpful. For example, we sometimes ask participants to select a member of the group to role-play a significant other. The role play begins by having the participant briefly tell the person selected what it is that he or she would like to change in their relationship and how he or she intends to make those changes.

During the final stages of the group, we also ask the members to review what they have learned about their early decisions as a result of participating in this group (an approach characteristic of existential therapy and transactional analysis). To stimulate this review, we typically ask these questions:

- Do you want to revise any of these early decisions?
- Are these decisions still appropriate for you now?
- What new decisions do you want to make?

In addition, we ask members to identify, even write down, the self-defeating statements they sometimes tell themselves, to share them, and to offer one another feedback concerning the validity of these self-statements, as well as suggestions on how to combat negative thinking.

During the final stages of the group, we rely heavily on the cognitive and action-oriented approaches characteristic of the cognitive behavior therapies, reality therapy, rational emotive behavior therapy, transactional analysis, and also solution-focused therapy. We see the group as a learning laboratory in which the members have identified the specific changes they are willing to make and have experimented with new behaviors. Assuming that this has indeed occurred, it becomes extremely important that the members carry out their own action-oriented programs outside the group.

Toward the end of the group we have members formulate a specific contract—a brief statement of the plans they have concerning behavioral changes once the group ends. The aim is to have members clearly define what they now want to do and how they specifically intend to do it.

Our experience has taught us that members tend to forget some of what they learned and to discount the actual value of what they did in the group. To help prevent this from occurring and to help members retain whatever they have learned—about others, about human struggling, about life, and about themselves—we ask them at the final session to review specific insights they had throughout the course of the group. It is our contention that unless one articulates and shares with others the specifics of what one has learned in the group, the group experience may soon become an indistinct blur.

Here, again, we find the principles of the behavioral approaches useful during the final session—specifically, application of feedback principles to help members strengthen the perceptions they gained during the course of the group. For example, we often ask members to complete feedback sentences such as these for every member in the group:

- "One of the things I like best about you is _____."
- "One way I see you blocking your strengths is _____."
- "My hope for you is _____."
- "My greatest concern or fear for you is _____."
- "The way I'll remember you in this group is _____."
- "A few things that I hope you'll remember are _____."

Focused feedback, whether verbal or written, can give the participants a good sense of the impact they had on others in the group and how they are viewed by others.

As the final session draws to a close, we give members a message to take with them—a message grounded in the existential approach:

Coleaders: We hope you have become aware of your role in bringing about change in your life. You can assume power by focusing on changing yourself rather than trying to get others to be different. Many of you have become aware of the choices that are open to you; thus, you can now reflect on the decisions you will make. Even if you decide to remain largely as you are, you now are aware that you can choose, that you don't need to have others design your life for you. Although choosing for yourself can provoke anxiety, it does give you a sense that your life is yours and that you have the power to shape your own future.

The cognitive behavioral approaches and solution-focused therapy stress developing clear goals, working on these goals during the sessions, and then evaluating the degree to which these goals are met. What members do after the group ends is as important as the group sessions. Therefore, we tend to devote ample time to suggesting ways in which members might consolidate their learning and carry it into daily living. Specifically, we encourage members to develop the habit of keeping a journal—writing down the problems they are encountering, describing how they feel about themselves in specific situations, and listing their successes and difficulties in following through with their contracts. New ideas can be a powerful catalyst in helping people make the changes they want to make, and we encourage members to select and read books on topics of interest to them as a way of continuing to work on themselves and to grow.

Finally, we schedule a follow-up session—several months after the termination of the group—for the purpose of allowing members to discuss what the group meant to each of them as well as to report on the extent to which they have fulfilled their contracts. We strongly encourage members to attend the follow-up meeting, even if they did not complete some or all of their contracts. The follow-up session provides rich opportunities for evaluation of the process and outcomes of a group. This allows members to evaluate what they learned about themselves, as well as to reflect on the degree to which they are applying what they learned in the group to everyday living. As coleaders, we continue to find that a follow-up session is one of the best ways to evaluate the effectiveness of a group. Over the years that we have been leading groups, our practice has been influenced by this feedback from members.

Develop Your Own Style of Leadership

In this chapter we have given examples of how we might draw from the various approaches with respect to the themes that have emerged in the illustrative group. Although it is valuable to practice working within the framework of each theory as you learn about it, there is no need to limit yourself to practicing any one model exclusively. Instead, you can integrate various components from all these models and begin to develop your own leadership style—a style that suits your personality and the kind of groups you may lead. The single most important element in effective group leadership is your way of being in a group.

We have described a variety of techniques in dealing with the themes that members introduced, but we use these techniques as means to further the agenda presented to us—not as ends in themselves. Techniques are no better than the person using them, and they are not useful if they are not sensitively adapted to the particular client and context. A leader's competence and confidence in using a technique are key to a successful outcome. Success is also affected by the climate of the group and by the relationship between the leader and the members. Techniques are merely tools to amplify emerging material that is present and to encourage exploration of issues that have personal relevance to the members.

More important than the techniques we use are the attitudes we have toward members, which are manifested by who we are and what we do in the group. When we are fully present and ourselves, we are able to teach by our modeling. We can be catalysts for members to engage in introspection, relevant self-disclosure, and risk-taking. We believe that our primary function as coleaders is to support members in their journey of making decisions regarding how they want to live. We work with people who are often struggling, who may be lost, or who are in a lot of psychological pain. The group experience affords members avenues for finding themselves and enables them to live more peacefully with themselves and others. We can be part of their journey as they increasingly discover themselves at their best.

AUTHOR LECTURES

Watch *Gerald Corey's Perspectives on Theory and Practice of Group Counseling* DVD or visit the *Theory and Practice of Group Counseling* CourseMate website at www.cengagebrain.com/shop/ISBN/0840033869 to watch videos of Dr. Gerald Corey present lectures for each chapter. Also available are unique eAudio lectures for each chapter and quiz questions for self-study.